CALEDONIAN RAILWAY CARRIAGES

Frontispiece
This location south of Stirling was a favourite spot for the official photographer – see, for example, page 262 in *Caledonian Railway Livery*. This view is from the NRM collection, ref: SRX243. Rebuilt Class '66' 4-4-0 No. 75 is posed at the head of a rake of six brand new 'Grampian' carriages on what may have been a running-in turn sometime in 1907. A view from the rear of the train was also taken (SRX309), which enables all the carriages to be identified. From the front, a Diagram 97A 7-compartment Brake Third is followed by a Diagram 94 Composite. Three 9-compartment Thirds to Diagram 96 are next, with another Diagram 97A Brake Third 1347 at the end. This is shown in Plate 9.13. The carriages are described and illustrated in Chapter 9.1. Most of the 'Grampian' stock built in 1907 was fitted with dual brakes, including one Diagram 94 Composite, number 130. The dual brake provision explains the presence of 4-4-0 No. 75 at the head of the train.

Caledonian Railway Carriages

Mike Williams

Lightmoor Press & the Caledonian Railway Association

CONTENTS

CHAPTER 1: INTRODUCTION AND SOURCES OF INFORMATION
  1.1: Introduction 7
  1.2: Sources of Information – The Caledonian Railway 9
  1.3: Sources of Information – Constituent and Associated Railway Companies 15
  1.4: Sources of Information – Contractors' Records 17
  1.5: Sources of Information – Books and the Press 19

CHAPTER 2: THE DEVELOPMENT OF THE CARRIAGE FLEET – SAFETY AND OPERATIONAL EFFICIENCY
  2.1: Brakes 21
  2.2: Communication Between Driver and Guard 33
  2.3: Passenger Alarm Systems 35
  2.4: Aspects of Carriage Construction 41
  2.5: Slip Carriages 48
  2.6: Infrastructure and Deployment 51

CHAPTER 3: THE DEVELOPMENT OF THE CARRIAGE FLEET – RISING STANDARDS OF COMFORT AND CONVENIENCE
  3.1: Classes of Travel 57
  3.2: Workmen's Trains and Residential Expresses 61
  3.3: Sleeping Cars 65
  3.4: Heating, Ventilation and Smoking 67
  3.5: Lighting 77
  3.6: Lavatories and Corridors 83

CHAPTER 4: LIVERY, IDENTIFICATION AND FURNISHING
  4.1: Livery, Crests and Insignia 87
  4.2: Letters, Numbers and Numbering 93
  4.3: Internal Decor 95

CHAPTER 5: GENERAL SERVICE STOCK FROM OPENING TO 1867
  5.1: Stock for the Opening of the Line 101
  5.2: Stock Added and Replaced in the 1850s 105
  5.3: Stock Built and Acquired 1860-1867 108
  5.4: Stock Absorbed from Northern Scottish Railways 111

CHAPTER 6: GENERAL SERVICE STOCK 1867-1882
  6.1: Carriages of the Late 1860s 119
  6.2: Stock Built and Acquired 1870-1874 125
  6.3: Stock Built 1875-1882 137

CHAPTER 7: GENERAL SERVICE STOCK 1882-1895
  7.1: Four-Wheeled Carriages 143
  7.2: Six-Wheeled Designs 149
  7.3: The 49-Foot Bogie Carriages 153
  7.4: The 45-Foot Bogie Carriages 157
  7.5: Drummond's Immediate Successors 159
  7.6: Carriages from West Coast Joint Stock 169

CHAPTER 8: THE MCINTOSH ERA – EVOLUTION TO 1905
  8.1: 45-Foot Carriages 171
  8.2: 48-Foot Carriages 177
  8.3: Conversions and 50-Foot Designs 185
  8.4: Carriages from West Coast Joint Stock 191

CHAPTER 9: THE McINTOSH ERA – REVOLUTION IN 1905
    9.1: The 'Grampian' Stock 195
    9.2: Carriages Associated with the 'Grampian' Stock 209
    9.3: The Caledonian Railway Dining Cars 215
    9.4: Rebuilding, Conversions and Reclassifications 219
    9.5: The 57-Foot Designs 221

CHAPTER 10: PULLMAN CARS
    10.1: Pullman Services 1914-1916 229
    10.2: The Pre-War Pullman Cars 234
    10.3: Post-War Pullman Cars and Services 241
    10.4: The LM&SR Takes Over 249

CHAPTER 11: GENERAL SERVICE STOCK 1914-1923
    11.1: Construction Authorised up to 1917 251
    11.2: The 1919 Coaching Stock Crisis 254
    11.3: Post-War Bogie Carriages and Brake Vans 256
    11.4: New Stock for the Balerno Branch 267

CHAPTER 12: AMBULANCE AND OTHER WAR SERVICE TRAINS 273

CHAPTER 13: SALOONS, FAMILY AND INVALID CARRIAGES
    13.1: Early Saloons and Family Carriages 277
    13.2: Saloons Built in the 1870s 281
    13.3: Drummond and Lambie Saloons and Family Carriages 288
    13.4: McIntosh Period Saloons 297
    13.5: Officers' and Inspection Saloons 303

CHAPTER 14: ROYAL MAIL VEHICLES
    14.1: Legislation and Infrastructure 307
    14.2: Early Mail Services on the Caledonian 310
    14.3: Early CR Post Office Vehicles 312
    14.4: The Growth in Anglo-Scottish Traffic 317
    14.5: Later CR Vehicles and Services 319

CHAPTER 15: SPECIAL PURPOSE VEHICLES
    15.1: Dummy Vans, the Corpse Box and the Prison Car 321
    15.2: The Inchture Horse Bus 323
    15.3: The Connel Ferry Rail Motor 325

CHAPTER 16: SOME UNIMPLEMENTED DESIGN PROPOSALS
    16.1: The Steam Motor Carriage 329
    16.2: Spacious Suburban Carriages and Corridor Stock 331

APPENDICES
    I: Numbers of Carriages in Traffic 333
    II: Diagram Book Numbers 341
    III: St. Rollox Carriage Order Numbers 343
    IV: Known Orders Placed with Contractors 349
    V: St. Rollox and Contractors' Drawings 351

INDEX 357

Published by LIGHTMOOR PRESS in conjunction with the CALEDONIAN RAILWAY ASSOCIATION
© Mike Williams, Lightmoor Press and the Caledonian Railway Association 2015
Designed by Nigel Nicholson.

British Library Cataloguing-in-Publication Data. A catalogue record for this book is available from the British Library
ISBN 9781 911038 00 9

LIGHTMOOR PRESS
Unit 144B, Lydney Trading Estate, Harbour Road, Lydney, Gloucestershire GL15 5EJ
www.lightmoor.co.uk
Lightmoor Press is an imprint of Black Dwarf Lightmoor Publications Ltd.
Printed in Poland; www.lfbookservices.co.uk

Private.   (18)

CALEDONIAN RAILWAY.
No. 25.

MARSHALLING of MAIN LINE TRAINS.

OCTOBER, 1912,
And until further notice.

EXPLANATION OF REFERENCES.

X Corridor Vehicle with end Gangway.
† Brake-end leading.
✲ Brake-end trailing.
‡ Six-Wheeled Vehicles.
L—Lavatories in First Class only.

L L—Lavatories in both classes.
C—Cupboard Carriage.
Lu.—Luggage.
P—Parcels.
L.P.—Luggage and Parcels.

Unless a special remark is made to the contrary all the Vehicles shewn herein are Bogie Vehicles.

Outside Cleaning,	(1)	Working Side and Trailing-end Cleaning,	(5)
Inside Cleaning,	(2)	Complete Cleaning,	(6)
Inside Cleaning, M O, W O, and F O,	(3)	Complete Cleaning, M O, W O, and F O,	(7)
Inside Cleaning, T O, Th. O, and S O,	(4)	See Local Roster,	(8)

The figures shewn above the description of Vehicles indicate that each of these Vehicles must be cleaned as defined before the commencement of the journey. In addition, all Vehicles must be swept and dusted at the end of each run.

The Vehicles working on the Through West Coast Trains between Scotland and England must be cleaned at the starting point prior to the commencement of each Journey.

ENGINE HOME STATIONS.

Ab.—**Aberdeen.**	Cle.—**Carlisle.**	Fr.—**Forfar.**
Pth.—**Perth.**	Stg.—**Stirling.**	Cs.—**Carstairs.**
Pol.—**Polmadie.**	Dde.—**Dundee.**	Ob.—**Oban.**
Ed.—**Edinburgh.**	S.R.—**St. Rollox.**	Gk.—**Greenock.**

Other references as per Working Time Table.

The composition of the different Trains, as herein laid down, is calculated to meet the average requirements; but the fluctuations in the Traffic must be carefully watched in order that additional accommodation may be provided when required, and also that unnecessary Vehicles may be discontinued.

By all Express Trains on which a Brake Van is not shewn to be marshalled next the Engine two leading Compartments must be locked up, except in cases where a Brake Compartment, or a Vehicle not containing Passengers is next to the Engine.

Through Vehicles for Foreign Lines.—Care must be taken that such Vehicles are fitted with the Vacuum Brake or Pipe. In the case of the N. B., G. N. of S., and N.-E. Lines the Vehicles do not require to have the Vacuum Brake or Pipe if they are to work to these Railways direct.

The Carriages and Vans shown herein as working to and from London (Euston), Birmingham, Liverpool, Manchester, and other places South of Carlisle, are all Corridor West Coast Joint Stock, unless where otherwise specified.

Luggage and Parcels must be so placed on the Platforms as will enable them to be loaded without incurring delay to Trains.

Station Masters and other persons in charge will be held responsible for seeing that those placed under them are fully conversant with, and adhere to, these arrangements.

When Traffic necessitates extra Vehicles will be added and Trains may be run in duplicate, therefore, the attached loading instructions and the position of Vehicles may be altered, but as far as possible they must be strictly adhered to.

Labelling of Carriages.—Carriages and Brake Vans running on all Trains must have destination labels exhibited on both sides.

The Steps or Waist-panel Slates (where provided) of all Cupboards and Luggage Vans to be plainly chalked, to show for what traffic they are to be used.

Station Masters, Platform Inspectors, Foremen, and Porters, before the arrival of the Trains, must take care to have the Luggage and the Parcels placed in such positions on the Platform as will admit of their being loaded for the different destinations without delay to Trains.

Marshalling of Excursion Trains.—Unless when otherwise instructed regarding the Composition of Special Trains for Manchester and Liverpool, the Vehicles must be so marshalled that the Train will arrive at Carlisle with the Manchester portion in front.

A separate Circular is issued showing the working of Vehicles between England and Scotland only, particulars of which are also shown in this Circular.

MCCORQUODALE & CO. LIMITED, GLASGOW AND LONDON.

CHAPTER 1
INTRODUCTION AND SOURCES OF INFORMATION

1.1: INTRODUCTION

This book was commissioned by the Caledonian Railway Association (CRA), which is registered in Scotland as an educational charity. It is a companion to *Caledonian Railway Wagons and Non-Passenger Coaching Stock*.[1]

STRUCTURE OF THE BOOK

Chapter one deals with the sources of information which provided material for the book. It has three purposes. Firstly, it serves as a bibliography. Secondly, it gives the reader an insight into the rich material that is available concerning a railway that ceased to exist three generations ago. Last, it may encourage students of rolling stock to delve still further and add to the information presented in this book.

Chapters 2 and 3 give an overview of the Caledonian Railway's reaction to technological developments in railway passenger transport and the increasing attention paid to passenger comfort and convenience. Chapter 4 builds on a chapter in *Caledonian Railway Livery*.[2] It covers livery, lettering, running numbers and internal fittings. Information has been discovered which sheds a new light on the evolution of CR carriage livery.

Chapters 5-9 deal with general service stock from the line's opening in 1847 to the end of McIntosh's tenure as Superintendent, which more or less coincided with the outbreak of World War I. Pullman cars come next, followed in Chapter 11 by the Pickersgill regime which lasted until the end of the CR's existence. The CR Ambulance Train and other vehicles in war-time service are in Chapter 12.

The remaining chapters deal with vehicles which were not part of general service stock. Each covers the whole period of the Caley's (to use the familiar name for the CR) existence. Saloons and Invalid carriages are described in Chapter 13, and Travelling Post Offices in Chapter 14. Special purpose vehicles such as the Prison Car, the Inchture horse bus and the Connel Ferry rail motor are in Chapter 15. The final chapter deals with some proposed designs of carriages that never saw service. Appendices give information about the number of carriages in the fleet, carriage orders and building dates and list the available works drawings of carriages, with their location.

ACKNOWLEDGEMENTS

Books like this cannot be written without material help and just as importantly encouragement, constructive criticism and counsel. Archive staff at the following locations have kindly given access to material over a number of years:

- National Records of Scotland, formerly National Archives of Scotland
- National Railway Museum
- Birmingham City Archives
- The Historical Model Railway Society
- The National Archives at Kew
- The Post Office Archive
- The Glasgow University Business Archive

The NRM has generously given permission to use photographs from its collections to illustrate this book in return for the cataloguing work undertaken at York by a group of CRA members. At the time of writing, The Ballast Trust was working on the CRA's drawing collection and was also cataloguing a large number of St. Rollox drawings from the National Records of Scotland archive which had not been accessible. The freedom to browse has led to many insights, especially about early rolling stock development.

This book has had a long gestation. In response to a member's letter, a short note appeared in the Caledonian Railway Association's magazine *The True Line* in 1992 saying that '*a group of members have been working on a definitive history of Caledonian Railway coaching stock for some years.*' The writers went on to say that they were well on their way to completing the task, but that there was still a long way to go. They were right. One hopes that the present book is worth the wait.

The material which had been assembled over the years by Niall Ferguson and edited by Keith Fenwick was generously handed over to the present author. It has been used as research notes, and has undoubtedly saved time in writing the book by directing the writer to original sources.

Caledonian Railway Association members have contributed from their collections of photographs, drawings and information. Jim Smellie and John Boyle offered all their drawings, which supplement copies of originals from St. Rollox Works and contractors. Ronnie Cockburn deserves a special mention for his work in transcribing the *Coaching Plant Stock Book*.

Grateful thanks go to Neil Parkhouse of the Lightmoor Press and designer Nigel Nicholson – to Neil for taking another book on, and to Nigel for once again turning a collection of text files, captions and illustrations into a classy product.

FACTS AND INTERPRETATIONS

Statements of fact are based on documentary evidence. Full documentation does not exist for a railway that was born over 160 years ago and merged into the LM&SR over 90 years from the time of writing. To present as complete a picture as possible therefore requires reasonable supposition. Where deductions and interpretations are made, they are identified as such and supporting reasons are given. This is especially true of Chapter 5, where many of the suggestions are speculative because very little documentary evidence has survived.

ERRORS AND OMISSIONS

There are sure to be errors and misinterpretations when dealing with the wealth of material and the complex history of 120 years of carriage stock development. There are several places in the text which leave loose ends, especially in the years up to 1882. No doubt, too, there is information that has not yet come to light. Fresh eyes could provide new insights. This was the case for *Caledonian Railway Wagons*, as the forthcoming supplement will show. Anyone with additional material, factual evidence or an alternative point of view that will add to the story of Caledonian carriages is encouraged to get in touch via the CRA's website.

REFERENCES
1. By Mike Williams, Lightmoor Press, 2012
2. By Jim MacIntosh, Lightmoor Press, 2008

Caledonian Railway Company
General Manager's Office
302 Buchanan Street Glasgow
Septr. 3: 1890.

H. Smellie Esq
Locomotive Supt.,

Dear Sir,

The Board at their meeting yesterday authorised the building of 50 third class Carriages.

The question to be considered is, how many of these are to have Lavatory accommodation and to what extent, and how many of them are to have Brake Compartments.

I have asked Mr. Kempt to confer with you and our Plant Superintendent so as to have these points settled, and when once you are all agreed I should like you to favour me with a tracing shewing what is proposed, for my consideration and approval.

Of course the Carriages are to be of our standard size.—

I am
Yours faithfully
James Thompson

Plate 1.1
Relatively few extracts from Committee minutes as passed to the Locomotive Department are addressed to Hugh Smellie. As recounted in Chapter 7.5, fifty Third class carriages were authorised for construction, but this memo shows that the number to be built with lavatories had not been decided – no doubt because this was the first carriage design to provide lavatory accommodation for Third class. The final decision was to build fifteen with lavatories. Note also the reference to *'our standard size.'* As will be seen in Plate 1.3, deviation from standard practice or adoption of a new design was only permitted with Board approval.

BELOW: Plate 1.2
The Board of Trade return for the half year ending 31st January 1878. Over 10% of passenger carrying vehicles were out of service, awaiting or undergoing repair.

[No. 6.]

RETURN OF WORKING STOCK.

	Locomotive.		Coaching.										Merchandise and Mineral.										
	Engines.	Tenders.	First Class.	Second and Third Class.	Composites & Saloons.	Post Office Vans.	Horse Boxes.	Carriage Trucks.	Fish and Milk Trucks.	Stores Vans.	Luggage Vans.	Total.	Goods Wagons.	Covered Goods Wagons.	Cattle and Sheep Trucks.	Brake Vans.	Swivel Wagons.	Mineral Wagons.	Gunpowder Vans.	Tank Wagons.	Crane Wagons.	Ballast Wagons.	Total.
Plant at 31st July, 1877,............	663	615	209	712	179	11	116	89	91	2	160	1,519	8,546	1,290	862	357	750	26520	2	2	9	248	38,586
Worn out—Half-year ending 31st Jan., 1878,	13	11	2	9	2	...	...	...	...	...	...	13	161	9	16	5	23	473	...	...	...	1	688
	650	604	207	703	177	11	116	89	91	2	160	1,506	8,385	1,281	846	352	727	26047	2	2	9	247	37,898
Renewals on account of Plant worn out to 31st January, 1878,	12	11	...	19	...	...	...	...	...	...	2	21	161	2	...	5	22	473	...	...	...	1	664
	662	615	207	722	177	11	116	89	91	2	162	1,527	8,546	1,283	846	357	749	26520	2	2	9	248	38,562
Added at Expense of Capital, Half-year ending 31st January, 1878,	15	15	...	27	...	...	...	...	...	...	14	41	25	...	...	...	...	2031	...	...	...	...	2,056
Total Stock of Working Plant at 31st January, 1878,............	677	630	207	749	177	11	116	89	91	2	176	1,568	8,571	1,283	846	357	749	28551	2	2	9	248	40,618
Portion of above Stock under or waiting repairs at 31st Jan., 1878,	100	92	23	89	23	1	7	6	8	...	9	111	135	19	12	9	6	802	...	...	...	4	987

RENEWAL ACCOUNT.

	Locomotive.		Coaching.										Merchandise and Mineral.											Amount.		
	Engines.	Tenders.	First Class.	Second and Third Class.	Composites & Saloons.	Post Office Vans.	Horse Boxes.	Carriage Trucks.	Fish and Milk Trucks.	Stores Vans.	Luggage Vans.	Total.	Goods Wagons.	Covered Goods Wagons.	Cattle and Sheep Trucks.	Brake Vans.	Swivel Wagons.	Mineral Wagons.	Gunpowder Vans.	Tank Wagons.	Crane Wagons.	Ballast Wagons.	Total.	£	s.	d.
Plant remaining unconstructed at 31st July, 1877, ...	2	...	7	10	4	...	...	2	...	...	2	25	...	...	13	...	3	...	...	...	...	6	22	15,286	4	0
Plant worn out—Half-year to 31st January, 1878, ...	13	11	2	9	2	...	...	...	...	...	...	13	161	9	16	5	23	473	...	...	...	1	688	46,464	19	10
	15	11	9	19	6	...	...	2	...	...	2	38	161	9	29	5	26	473	...	...	...	7	710	61,751	3	10
Less replaced or rebuilt—Half-year ending 31st January, 1878, ...	12	11	...	19	...	...	...	...	...	...	2	21	161	2	...	5	22	473	...	...	...	1	664	46,168	3	10
Plant not yet renewed, ...	3	...	9	...	6	...	...	2	...	...	...	17	...	7	29	...	4	...	...	...	...	6	46	*15,583	0	0

* At Credit of "Rolling Stock Renewal Fund" for Value of Plant not Replaced at 31st January, 1878.

1.2: SOURCES OF INFORMATION – THE CALEDONIAN RAILWAY

This section sets out the sources of information from the Caledonian Railway which were used in compiling the book. It is not a complete list of the information that is available, which can be accessed from the National Records of Scotland website. Some items can also be consulted in the Caledonian Railway Association archive, The National Archives at Kew and the National Railway Museum.

BOARD AND COMMITTEE MINUTES

A full set of *'Minutes of Meetings of Directors and Committees,'* starting in 1844 and continuing to 1923, is in the National Records of Scotland archive.[1] The volumes include decisions concerning the Locomotive & Stores and Traffic committees which dealt with rolling stock, either as renewals (paid for out of revenue) or capital expenditure.

The amount and detail of information in the existing minutes is uneven. In the early years reports on new rolling stock requirements are recorded as *'read and approved.'* Details are sketchy, and refer mainly to tenders let to outside contractors. The renewal of rolling stock was put on a formal basis in September 1887, when a Board Minute recorded that *'At the end of each half year the Locomotive Superintendent to prepare statement of renewals of working stock and cost estimate.'*[2]

From about 1890 onwards, the minutes are detailed enough to relate to specific orders for rolling stock, built either by St. Rollox or contractors. The half year ending 31st January 1893 was the first time that proposed rolling stock renewals were set out in detailed form. The situation becomes less clear again from 1918 to the 1923 Grouping, where totals of stock, but not the types, are mentioned.

There was a delay between authorisation and construction. In the early years of Drummond's tenure, the six-monthly programme was agreed just before the start of the period. By 1895, the go-ahead was given earlier, typically two months in advance. By 1900, the decision was taken earlier still. For instance, the programme for the half year which began on 1st August 1901 was agreed on 23rd March. This typical timetable continued up to the end of the Caledonian's existence.

In Appendices III and IV which record post-1885 St. Rollox and contractors' orders, the authorisation date is given where known. The date that an order of carriages was actually put into service could be anything between nine and fifteen months later. Plant built to the capital account was added to the balance sheet on the final day of the accounting period, which further extended the elapsed time from authorisation.

The minutes also record events such as the fitting of dual brakes and steam heat pipes. All these are grist to the mill of the rolling stock historian.

Indices to each volume show entries by subject matter. Jim MacIntosh extracted most of the relevant information some years ago, *'to develop a comprehensive record of the Goods and Mineral Wagons built by the Company over the period 1845 to 1923,'* but he also included entries relating to carriages and non-passenger coaching stock. The extracts can be downloaded from the Caledonian Railway Association archive catalogue.[3] The entries cited have been cross checked against the company minutes and in many cases additions have been made.

EXTRACTS OF MINUTES

A series of five volumes lists extracts from various Board of Directors and Committee minutes from 1872 to 1922.[4] They were collected for the Locomotive Department. Many of the copies merely repeat the Board and Committee minutes, but there is also correspondence at senior officer level which amplifies and in some cases alters the official record. An example of such a document is shown in Plate 1.1. The extracts are the sole source of information about the rolling stock crisis after World War I and the steps taken to overcome it, which are described in Chapter 11.

OFFICERS' MINUTES

An equivalent set of Officers' minutes is not known to have survived. Many of the decisions taken about modifications to rolling stock would have been taken at this level. Some of the loose ends left in this book, where there is no minuted record, would no doubt be tied up if the volumes ever became accessible. One volume of Locomotive Committee minutes from 1865 is in private hands and has been seen by the author. By great good fortune, it includes a minute that throws a completely new light on carriage livery in the 1860s. This minute and its implications are discussed in Chapter 4.

THE BOARD OF TRADE AND ACTS OF PARLIAMENT

The Board of Trade, through its Railway Department, was the regulatory body of the railway industry during the Caledonian's existence. As well as requiring statistical information about each railway (see Rolling Stock Returns below) it was actively concerned in improving safety for passengers and railway employees through enforcing Acts of Parliament.

The Caledonian's responses to these Acts and directives are discussed in Chapter 2. Other Acts' requirements to offer cheap travel are covered in Chapter 3.

The Railway Department also investigated and reported on accidents and resolved disputes between the public and the railway companies. An example of the former is discussed in Chapter 14 and the latter in Chapter 15.

ROLLING STOCK RETURNS

Information about rolling stock changes was provided at six monthly intervals for the Board of Trade. Copies are held at the National Records of Scotland and The National Archive at Kew.[5] For many years, as well as listing the absolute numbers of each type of carriage owned on a given date, the returns also gave details of how many carriages of each type were withdrawn, renewed, or added to stock.

Because the companies tended to combine their returns with a report to the shareholders, there was often additional information to be found with the figures. At various times through the company's existence it re-ordered the way in which it classified its stock so that, for example, in 1857 the Second and Third class carriages, which had previously been listed separately, were consolidated under a single heading. Saloons and Family/Invalid carriages were assimilated into the Composite carriage heading from January 1878. A typical example is shown in Plate 1.2.

Statistics from these returns have been tabulated by Jim MacIntosh. They have been used to estimate the number of carriages built, particularly in the early days, when minute entries are scanty. The returns have also been used to confirm whether carriages were charged to the capital or revenue account.

In 1913, when the Railway Companies (Accounts and Returns), 1911 Act came into force, the classifications were simplified into carriages of uniform class, that is, Firsts or Thirds, and Composites. Additions and lists of withdrawals were discontinued, thus making the returns practically useless for the purposes of this book.

RECORDS OF CAPITAL EXPENDITURE

Replacement vehicles were charged to the revenue account. Carriages that were added to the fleet were charged to capital. This included surplus vehicles that were taken over from West Coast Joint Stock.

All capital expenditure was recorded in reports to the Board. Ledgers record each addition to the Capital Stock within days of its delivery with separate tabulations for Engines, Carriages and Wagons under the heading *Working Stock.* Those recording transactions from 1861 to the Grouping have survived in two sets, which overlap each other for the period ending 31st July 1869.[6] The first set are yearly accounts, the second are half yearly summaries. For the Caledonian and most other companies the dates were 31st January and 31st July of each year. Again, these returns have been tabulated by Jim MacIntosh.

VALUATIONS AND CENSUSES

Caledonian rolling stock was counted at various times outwith the half yearly changes mentioned above. A list is shown below. Full details of the findings form Appendix I.

DATE	DETAILS
1849	Valuation
1855	Internal review
1867	Census
1874	Independent valuation

COACHING STOCK LISTS

At the beginning of each year, the CR apparently published a list of coaching and non-passenger coaching stock in general service. The January 1921 list has lain undiscovered up to now, bound into one of the service timetable books at NRS.[7] The lists for other years are not known to have survived. The 1921 list is reproduced in its entirety in Appendix I. It did not include carriages that were used on workmen's trains, or those stored out of service for excursion traffic.

COACHING STOCK DIAGRAM BOOKS

Two sorts of railway company rolling stock Diagram Book usually exist: a 'Pocket Diagram Book', which was used on an everyday basis to marshal trains based on the size and capacity of the various types of vehicle available, and a 'Large Diagram Book,' which was used for reference purposes.

Pocket Diagram Books usually contain a sketch of each type of vehicle with a note of its length, tare weight and the number of each class of passenger it could seat. The Large Diagram Books contain detailed plans of each class of carriage and, in the case of some railway companies including the Caledonian, a list of the numbers carried by the carriages of that type.

The original decision to produce diagrams of stock was taken on 20th September 1887, when *'the General Manager [was] to have Diagrams prepared of all the Standard Rolling Stock in use on the line.'*[8] The full instruction is shown in Plate 1.3.

Both CR diagram books, along with the corresponding small goods wagon book, were updated as new designs appeared. A copy of the small book which probably dates from 1898 is in the NRS Archive[9] and there is a reprint available from the CRA.[10] An example page is shown in Plate 1.4.

In the Large Diagram Book carriage plans were arranged one to a page in a numerical sequence, starting with the shortest carriages and ending with the longest. A particular design of carriage occupied its own individual page. This page number was used as an identifier by railway staff.

If a design was modified to any great extent, or a new type of carriage of similar length and class was built or acquired from the West Coast Joint Stock, it was given a new page. In order to

Plate 1.3
The hand-written copy of the Board minute requiring the establishment of diagram books in 1887. The same minute initiated the formal submission for Committee approval of the rolling stock renewal requirements for the ensuing six months, plus cost estimate.

That the General Manager have Diagrams prepared of all the Standard Rolling Stock in use on the line; and when approved of, that no alteration or departure therefrom be made without first having obtained the approval of the Board. —

D. Drummond Esq.
Locomotive Superintendent
St Rollox.

keep carriages of the same length together, and to avoid having to renumber pages, the new page was inserted in the appropriate place with a suffix letter.

Hence there were two pages with 57-foot Corridor Brake Composite carriages, both with two First and four Third class compartments. Those on Page 111 were built before World War I and were 8 feet 8 inches wide on 10-foot wheelbase bogies. Those on the next page, 111A, which were not built until 1923, were 9 feet wide and ran on 8-foot wheelbase bogies.

A composite version of the Large Diagram Book, based on various surviving records, has been published in facsimile by the Caledonian Railway Association and is referred to throughout this work.[11] Some of the diagrams are used to illustrate the internal layout of carriages.

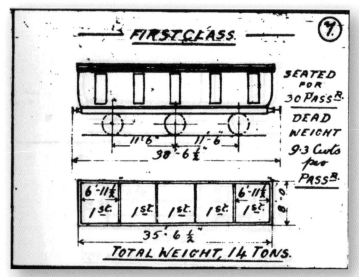

ABOVE: Plate 1.4
This is an example of a page from the Small Carriage Diagram Book, which was compiled in about 1898 and updated with a new page when a new carriage design appeared. The sketch gives the details needed for day-to-day operations – external body dimensions and wheelbase, compartment size, carrying capacity and tare weight per passenger. The page number in the corner became the 'Diagram Number.'

The sequence of diagram numbers in the large and small books differs. Carriages acquired from West Coast Joint Stock are not included in the Small Book. The correlation between the two books forms Appendix II.

DIAGRAMS OF SALOONS, FAMILY AND INVALID CARRIAGES

Jim Summers discovered this 'Saloon Diagram Book' on the Scottish Railway Preservation Society's premises at Bo'ness and photographed the pages to inform this book. Dated 10th June 1896, it shows diagrams of twenty-one types of carriage with their running numbers, in the same style as the Large Diagram Book. While a few of the vehicles appear in the latter book, the Saloon Book provides details of the carriages that were withdrawn in the first decade of the twentieth century. It also gives some dimensions which are omitted from the Coaching Plant Stock Book, which is described in the next section. Its front cover and index are shown in Plates 1.5 and 1.6.

THE COACHING PLANT STOCK BOOK

The other principal source of detailed information on the later carriages of the company is contained in this large volume. The original is in the Caledonian Railway Association archive.[12] The book is divided by class of carriage. An entry gives each individual carriage a number, length, width, the number of compartments of each class, lavatories if any, plus Brake and luggage compartments, method of lighting, upholstery (described as 'trimmed'), type of brake and date of construction (to be accurate, the half year in which it was built). It also includes details of non-passenger coaching stock. A sample spread of part of two pages is shown in Plate 1.7.

The register was compiled after World War I and maintained until early in World War II. It therefore does not contain information about stock scrapped before 1914. Amendments written in a different hand give the LM&SR numbers together with details of any Caledonian period down-rating and renumbering, as well as a final withdrawal date, if that happened before 1940. The numbers of LM&SR carriages built in 1925 and allocated to the Northern Division are included separately, as are details of the Pullman cars that ran on the Caledonian and in LM&SR days.

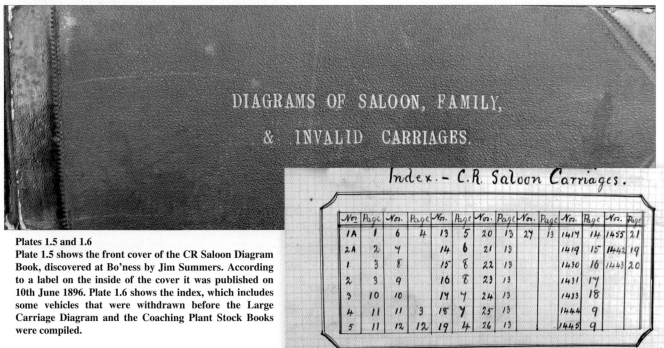

Plates 1.5 and 1.6
Plate 1.5 shows the front cover of the CR Saloon Diagram Book, discovered at Bo'ness by Jim Summers. According to a label on the inside of the cover it was published on 10th June 1896. Plate 1.6 shows the index, which includes some vehicles that were withdrawn before the Large Carriage Diagram and the Coaching Plant Stock Books were compiled.

Plate 1.7

A part of the Coaching Plant Stock Book which, like all the entries, runs across two pages. Five West Coast Joint Stock 6-wheeled Luggage Tri-Composites originally built in 1877 were renumbered 260-264 on acquisition by the CR, and a handbrake was added. Number 260 was withdrawn in 1912. Its replacement was a Diagram 111 Brake Composite – one of the first 57-foot carriages built by the Caledonian. Numbers 262 and 263 were withdrawn in 1906/7 to be replaced by 'Grampian' stock. The remaining two lasted until 1925/26. Number 261 was not replaced, but LM&SR standard carriage 15850 was deemed for accountancy purposes to have replaced 264. Carriages 265-9 were Diagram 26 Composites built under Lambie to order H108.

THE COACHING PLANT STOCK BOOK TRANSCRIPTION

A typed version of the Stock Book is available from the Caledonian Railway Association.[13] The transcript is by CRA member Ronnie Cockburn. It covers the CR-built carriages, West Coast Joint Stock acquisitions and non-passenger coaching stock.

It adds a considerable amount of information to the original. The organising principle is the diagram numbers in the Small Carriage Diagram Book, which are tabulated as the first item. This is followed by the H-series carriage order list (see below), cross-referenced to the diagram numbers. Each order also has the number of carriages built and the number traced through analysis of the carriage details in the original book.

The body of the work takes each type of carriage in turn and groups them by diagram number. Carriages acquired from West Coast Joint Stock, and those built before the introduction of the Diagram Book, are included at the end of each section. There are a very small number of errors in the transcription, mostly attributable to information that was not available when the transcription was published in 2001. The corrections are detailed in various chapters against specific types of carriage.

COACHING STOCK ORDERS

From 1885 an order number code was established for rolling stock built at St. Rollox. Carriage orders were given numbers prefixed by the letter H. The original list was transcribed by the late Duncan Burton. The list of carriages built to H orders, cross-referenced by the author to Large Diagram Book pages and to the Small Diagram Book where applicable, forms Appendix III.

Orders placed with contractors are in Appendix IV. These orders were not normally included in the H series, except for some post-war orders that were contracted out because St. Rollox lacked capacity. The list is based on minutes which recorded the tendering process

for orders placed with outside contractors. As such, it is probably incomplete as, especially in the early days of the company's existence, the information in minutes is sketchy, or non-existent.

THE ST. ROLLOX DRAWINGS REGISTERS

Six notebooks containing lists of drawings of rolling stock, machinery and other items survive in the NRS archive.[14] Entries usually show the date of the drawing, the job number, a brief description, and the name of the draughtsman. In later registers the drawer number (its location in the drawing office filing system) is included. This number appears on each drawing in the stencilled form of an extended letter D with a number written inside it. A St. Rollox Works order number is sometimes included on drawings and in the register description.

The scope of the registers is shown in the following table. Register 5 is a rewrite of Register 1 and part of 2. It does not always record the full detail of the entries in Register 1, so both must be read together. In Register 1, the early drawings are the product of the Greenock Works, which were leased by the CR. Drawings 399-420 contain many references to the fitting out of St. Rollox Shed and Works, where construction was concentrated after 1856. And yes, drawing 3509 is not in Register 1 or 2; it can only to be found in Register 5. A sample page from Register 2 forms Plate 1.8.

	DATES COVERED	JOB NUMBERS
Register 1	1847-1883	1-3508
Register 2	1883-1892	3510-7134
Register 3	1892-1899	7135-9622
Register 4	1899-1907	9623-14327
Register 5	1847-1888	1-5621
Register 6	1907-1939	14328-27342

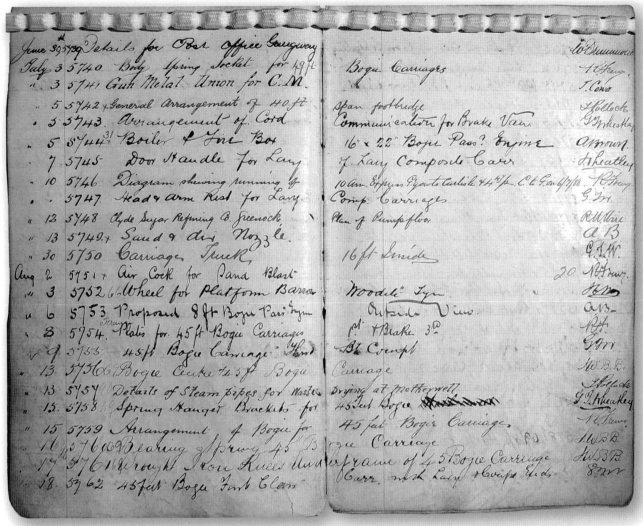

Plate 1.8
This sample spread from St. Rollox Drawing Register 2 dates from 1888. At the top of the page, drawing 5743 refers to the Harrison cord alarm system. Towards the bottom of the page it records the first drawings for the new 45 foot long bogie carriages. Two of these carriages and one Coupé First (drawing 5762) were marshalled into rakes for the Callander & Oban line. As recounted in Chapter 7, Drummond was required to submit the drawings to the Board of Directors. Drawing 5755 is shown in Chapter 7, Figure 7.14.

In Register 6, the last drawing number in the Caledonian's existence was 22253. An annotation in one of the books indicates that entries scored through with crayon were destroyed in a fire at Derby on 17th July 1939. Although we know how many drawings were produced and brief details of the subjects, the final number of surviving drawings is still to be determined. The surviving St. Rollox drawings are discussed in the next sub-section.

SURVIVING ST. ROLLOX DRAWINGS

St. Rollox drawings are located in three archives. The National Railway Museum (NRM) has microfiche copies of all the railway drawings which were catalogued by the BR/Oxford Publishing Co. Joint Venture Group in the 1970s. The drawings were originally stored at Clapham Museum and transferred to York when the NRM was opened. The known St. Rollox drawings are now lodged in Edinburgh, following a decision to store all Scottish material in what was then the National Archives of Scotland (NAS).

The NRS catalogue lists these drawings in the Register House Plan (RHP) series. Requests for viewing are made to the Historical Search Room at General Register House in Edinburgh. Most of the plans are not digitally imaged, but the originals can be consulted at Thomas Thomson House on the Sighthill Industrial Estate near Edinburgh Park railway station. Viewing is currently (2015) limited to Wednesdays. Drawings can be photographed for private research purposes.

A large number of these drawings are with the Ballast Trust awaiting cataloguing. RHP numbers were not allocated at the time of publication. 'RHP' followed by a blank in the references and in Appendix V denotes a drawing awaiting cataloguing.

The third source of a limited number of drawings is the Caledonian Railway Association Archive. The carriage drawings currently available are listed in the archive catalogue.[15]

CONTRACTORS' DRAWINGS

A number of contractors' drawings survive from the companies that came together to form the Metropolitan Amalgamated Railway Carriage & Wagon Company Ltd. These drawings are discussed in Chapter 1.3.

In the chapters on carriage types, St. Rollox and contractors' drawing numbers are quoted. Appendix V cross-references the St. Rollox numbers to the Edinburgh and York archives as RHP and NRM respectively. The Appendix also lists the contractors' drawings, with the Birmingham City Archive reference and the CRA archive reference where applicable.

OFFICIAL PHOTOGRAPHS

No attempt was made to create an official photographic record of Caledonian carriages in the way that albums of its locomotives and wagons were produced. The NRM's St. Rollox collection contains a number of carriage photographs, of both interiors and exteriors, which have been used throughout this book.

OTHER PUBLIC PHOTOGRAPHIC COLLECTIONS

Selective enlargements of photographs containing carriages have also proved a fruitful source. Some have been taken from the A.B. McLeod, Locomotive & General Railway Publishing and Locomotive Club of Great Britain collections at the NRM. Others have come from the CRA Archive which includes the Alsop collection of CR postcards.

GRAEME MILLER

Miller started work with the Caledonian as a premium apprentice in 1911, and was appointed as a draughtsman in 1916. After war service he was re-engaged in 1919.[16] He was instrumental in preserving and perhaps contributing to a short hand-written technical history of CR carriages that is now in the National Railway Museum.[17] The history was compiled shortly after 1923. It outlines the main developments from 1872 to the Grouping. Neither this, nor the companion wagon document, covers non-passenger coaching stock.

PUBLIC AND WORKING TIMETABLES

A set of bound service timetables from 1853 to the Grouping is in the NRS under the generic heading BR/TT/S/54. Originally one timetable served for the whole system; latterly the Caledonian issued timetables in two parts – one for the Southern, Eastern and Western Sections, and another for lines north of Greenhill or Glenboig.

WORKING TIMETABLE APPENDICES

These volumes appeared periodically. They cover a wide range of operational matters, as well as 'instructions supplementary to those contained in the Book of Rules and Regulations.' Appendices were issued in April 1890, May 1891, November 1892, January 1894 and 1895, May 1896 and 1902, October 1906 and May 1915. They are all bound into the timetable sets referred to above. The May 1915 Appendix is also in the CRA Archive and a reprint can be purchased.[18]

The 'supplementary instructions' mentioned above contain many items concerning the working and maintenance of carriages. These are referred to in the following chapters. Page numbers refer to the 1915 Appendix.

TOPIC	CHAPTER
Carriage cleaning pp. 79-80	2.6
Heating pp. 83-84	3.4
Lighting pp. 81-83	3.5
Catering p. 97	10
Corridor trains pp. 80-81	3.6
Passengers' luggage and bicycles pp. 105-7	3.1
Dogs p. 104	3.1
Slip carriages pp. 55-59	2.5
Empty carriage stock and trial running p. 89	2.6

CARRIAGE WORKING AND MARSHALLING CIRCULARS

These documents provide information about the regular working patterns of passenger and non-passenger coaching stock such as milk vans. Some give details about carriage gassing points and the allocation of the Travelling Gas Tanks. A selection of these documents is also in the CRA Archive.[19] Details have been used in Chapter 2 to make general statements about stock deployment and in various chapters to explain the working of specific items of carriage stock.

STATION TRAFFIC BOOKS

These books were compiled annually for each station on the Caledonian, giving information on the number of passengers booked and receipts, as well as an analysis of goods traffic in and out under various categories. A set covering the period from 1883 until the Grouping is in the NRS.[20] Two returns are available on disc at the CRA Archive.[21] While the books are of limited value to the carriage historian, the information has proved useful in fleshing out the story of the Connel Ferry rail motor service discussed in Chapter 15.

POSTERS AND PUBLICITY MATERIAL

The Caledonian was very aware of the power of advertising and what we now call 'building a brand.' A register of posters from 1911 to 1922 is in the NRS.[22] Some of the posters detail service developments such as the residential express services of 1911, the introduction of Pullman cars and the restoration of the service after World War I.

CARRIAGE TRIMMERS' NOTEBOOKS

Two hand-written pocket notebooks in the NRS date from 1925 and 1926/27 respectively. One details the prices for interior cleaning and repairing upholstery in various types of carriage at St. Rollox Works.[23] A double page is reproduced in Chapter 2 as Plate 2.23. The second records details of carriages awaiting repair at St. Rollox in 1926/27 and gives an insight into the renumbering of carriages in the first few years after the Grouping – see Plates 4.15 and 4.16 in Chapter 4.[24]

REFERENCES
1. NRS BR/CAL/1/7-82
2. NRS BR/CAL/1/31 entry 1131
3. CRA Archive ref: 2/3/1/9, 10
4. NRS BR/CAL 5/4, 5, 11-13
5. TNA RAIL 1110/48
   NRS GD344/11/1
6. NRS BR/CAL/23/1-14, 15-18
7. BR/TT/S/54/61
8. NRS BR/CAL/5/9
9. NRS BR/CAL/5/11 entry 33
10. CRA Archive ref: 3/4/1/5
11. CRA Archive ref: 3/4/1/1
12. CRA Archive ref: 3/4/1/14
13. CRA Archive ref: 1/6/40
14. NRS BR/CAL/5/56, 113-117
15. CRA Archive ref: 6/1/1/1
16. Information taken from the List of Special Apprentices, NRS BR/CAL/15/13
17. NRM C&W/CR/1 (C&W 109)
18. CRA Archive ref: 3/1/4/2
19. In CRA Archive, section ref: 3/3/2
20. NRS BR/CAL/4/86-100
21. CRA Archive ref: 3/8/6 has BR/CAL/4/87, 88, 90
22. NRS BR/CAL/4/156-161
23. NRS BR/CAL/5/61
24. NRS BR/CAL/5/62

1.3: SOURCES OF INFORMATION –
CONSTITUENT AND ASSOCIATED RAILWAY COMPANIES

The Caledonian grew by amalgamation in two stages. In the first five years of its existence it took over a number of railway companies around Glasgow that had been formed before the Caledonian was founded. In the mid-1860s, two amalgamations with northern Scottish companies extended its reach to Aberdeen. In both waves of amalgamation the CR inherited rolling stock. This section deals with the information available concerning these companies.

A number of other railways were nominally independent, but operated by the Caledonian. Most were treated as integral parts of the CR system in Board and Committee minutes. The CR built special rolling stock for the Callander & Oban Railway, hence its separate reference in this section.

Joint working arrangements existed for Anglo-Scottish traffic. The Caledonian was a major partner in the West Coast Conference. West Coast Joint Stock ran on the Caledonian and the design conventions imposed by the L&NWR affected CR practice, especially in the matter of continuous brakes and alarm systems. The Post Office was also concerned with Anglo-Scottish traffic.

The final company to be associated with the Caledonian was the Pullman Car Company, which operated catering vehicles over CR metals from 1914 onwards and made stipulations concerning rolling stock. The Caledonian, the Scottish Central Railway and the L&NWR built specialised vehicles. Most of the stock was handed over to the newly-constituted West Coast Joint Stock fleet in 1879.

THE GARNKIRK & GLASGOW RAILWAY

Built to a gauge of 4 feet 6 inches, the Garnkirk & Glasgow Railway was the first railway to connect the Airdrie and Monklands coalfields with the centre of Glasgow. It opened officially on 26th September 1831 and was absorbed by the Caledonian in 1849. The surviving records in the NRS are under the generic heading BR/GGC.

THE WISHAW & COLTNESS RAILWAY

The Wishaw & Coltness was incorporated by an Act of Parliament of 1st of June 1829 and ran from a junction with the Monkland & Kirkintilloch Railway at Whifflet to what would become a junction with the CR near Overtown, with intermediate branches to Woodhall, Cleland and Morningside, as well as to a number of collieries.

Initially a horse-powered mineral line with a gauge of 4 feet 6 inches, it adopted locomotive power in the summer of 1840 and was absorbed by the Caledonian on 2nd February 1849 after conversion to standard gauge. The Board and Committee minutes are under the reference BR/WIC at NRS.

THE GLASGOW, PAISLEY & GREENOCK RAILWAY

The GP&G was incorporated on 15th July 1837 and ran from Glasgow to Greenock via Paisley, Bishopton, and Port Glasgow. The first seven miles of track to Paisley was owned jointly with the Glasgow, Paisley, Kilmarnock & Ayr Railway (the first reference to a joint line anywhere) which, after reaching Paisley, continued to

Ayr via Irvine, Troon, and Prestwick. The GPK&A merged with the Glasgow, Dumfries & Carlisle Railway to form the Glasgow & South Western Railway in 1850 while the Glasgow, Paisley & Greenock merged with the Caledonian in 1851. Surviving records are in the NRS under BR/GPG.

THE PORT PATRICK RAILWAY

Not strictly a constituent of the Caledonian, but the CR inherited some carriages and wagons from it in 1864, as a result of an agreement to operate the line for twenty-one years until October 1885. The railway also saw the only Sleeping carriage built by the Caledonian, described in Chapter 13. The records are in NRS under BR/POR.

THE SCOTTISH CENTRAL RAILWAY

The SCR ran from a junction with the Caledonian Railway at Castlecary through Stirling to Perth. Also included was a section of line from Stirling to a junction with the Edinburgh & Glasgow Railway at Greenhill Upper Junction.

The company was incorporated by Act of Parliament on 31st July 1845. The first section to Greenhill Upper Junction opened on 1st March 1848 with opening through to Perth on 22nd May.

Eventually the Scottish Central constructed other branches to South Alloa, Crieff, Denny, and Tillicoultry. In 1863 it absorbed the Dundee, Perth & Aberdeen Junction Railway. The SCR was taken over by the Caledonian in July 1865, just after completion of the Dunblane, Doune & Callander Railway, which later connected the Callander & Oban Railway to the Caledonian system. The surviving records of its independent existence are in the NRS, reference BR/SCC.

EARLY CONSTITUENTS OF THE SCR

The Dundee & Newtyle Railway (NRS reference BR/DNR) was incorporated by Act of Parliament in 1826, but did not open for another five years. In 1845 it was leased by the Dundee & Perth Railway before the latter line opened for business. The D&PR later became the Dundee, Perth & Aberdeen Junction Railway (NRS BR/DPA).

THE SCOTTISH NORTH EASTERN RAILWAY

In 1856 the SNER was formed by the amalgamation of the Scottish Midland Junction and the Aberdeen railways, which were themselves the product of earlier amalgamations, as outlined below. When it was absorbed by the Caledonian in 1867, the CR's aim of reaching Aberdeen was completed. The surviving records are in NRS under reference BR/SNE.

EARLY CONSTITUENTS OF THE SNER

The Dundee & Arbroath Railway (NRS BR/DAR) was completed in 1840. The Arbroath & Forfar Railway (NRS BR/AFR) was incorporated in 1836. In May 1845 a conference was held in London between representatives of the Dundee & Arbroath, the Dundee & Perth and the Arbroath & Forfar railways to agree the provision of through traffic over the three railways, which required adoption of standard gauge throughout.

The Scottish Midland Junction Railway (NRS BR/SCM) was incorporated on 31st July 1845. The company's main line ran from Perth to Forfar via Coupar Angus, and opened for passenger traffic on 2nd August 1848. Two branch lines to Blairgowrie and Kirriemuir were constructed some years later.

The Aberdeen Railway (NRS BR/ABN) was incorporated on the same date as the Scottish Midland Junction Railway and ran from Guthrie, on the Arbroath & Forfar Railway, to Aberdeen, with branches to Montrose and Brechin. Its main line and the branch to Brechin opened on 1st February 1848. In the same year the Aberdeen Railway took over the lease of the Arbroath & Forfar Railway, although that railway continued as a separate company.

THE CALLANDER & OBAN RAILWAY

Starting in 1870, the C&O was built in stages from an end-on connection with the Caledonian's Dunblane, Doune & Callander Branch, finally reaching Oban in 1880. It and the independent Killin Railway were operated by the Caledonian, but it had its own Board of Directors with CR representation.

Its scenic nature and difficult working conditions required some specially designed rolling stock. The 45-foot carriages of 1889 are described and illustrated in Chapter 7.4; the 50-foot semi-corridor carriages of 1909/10 are described and illustrated in Chapter 9.2. The later branch to Ballachulish saw a specially adapted motor charabanc which provided a primitive motor-rail service across the Connel Bridge. This is described in Chapter 15. The material in NRS is filed under BR/COB.

POST OFFICE RECORDS

Although not strictly a railway company, the carriage of mail was the subject of detailed agreements between railway companies and the Post Master General which required specialised vehicles. The Post Office Archive at Mount Pleasant in north London has agreements with the Caledonian (1857, 1867 and 1873), the Dundee & Perth, Scottish North Eastern and the Dundee & Aberdeen railways (all 1862).[1] There is also a limited amount of information on Travelling Post Office vehicles and lineside apparatus.[2] This material has been used in Chapter 14.

THE WEST COAST CONFERENCE

A quarterly meeting was established in 1848, at which senior managers of the railways making up the route between London Euston and Aberdeen discussed matters of common interest. Minutes of their deliberations and decisions are available at Kew and Edinburgh.[3]

When the vehicles of one company travelled over the lines of another the owning company built up credit with the company owning the track. The west coast companies transferred the credits to a suspense account at the Railway Clearing House. In 1862 the West Coast Conference decided to cut reciprocal working and its associated administration by establishing a joint stock of carriages. The East Coast Conference had done this a year earlier.

The West Coast Joint Stock pool of vehicles started operation on 1st March 1863. It was originally funded by the L&NWR, CR, SCR and SNER in proportion to their route mileage. After the absorption of the latter two, the Caledonian was responsible for 36.54% of the cost of vehicles.

WCJS vehicles were designed by the L&NWR and built at Wolverton. In the late Victorian and Edwardian years, carriage design and amenities for long-distance travel evolved rapidly, driven by competition between the East and West Coast routes and the

Midland/Glasgow & South Western service to Glasgow. As a result, carriages with only ten to fifteen years' service were superseded by more modern designs.

Surplus carriages in the West Coast Joint Stock fleet were first divided between the two partner companies in the half year ending July 1871. The normal ratio was 2:1 in favour of the L&NWR, with a cash adjustment as necessary. This was based on the proportion of the original expenditure borne by the two companies.

All the transfers should have been recorded in the capital expenditure returns, where the exact proportional cost to the CR was treated as a credit. On a few occasions no entry was made. A separate entry was made in the half-yearly rolling stock returns for WCJS transfers. This did not always appear or reconcile with the information in the corresponding capital expenditure returns.

THE EAST COAST CONFERENCE

A similar arrangement to the West Coast agreement existed among the railways that made up the East Coast route from London to Scotland. The Caledonian inherited an interest in its affairs through its amalgamation with the Scottish Central Railway and the Scottish North Eastern. East Coast Conference traffic from Inverness to the south passed over Scottish Central tracks; Aberdeen traffic travelled over both railways.

Minutes from 1905 to 1922 are in NRS[4] and the full set of minutes are in The National Archives.[5] There is very limited reference to the Caledonian. In 1872 there was correspondence with George Oakely, the General Manager of the GNR, concerning the provision of eight additional vehicles.[6] The Traffic Committee agreed to this, but there is no record of any financial transaction. In February 1878, the Traffic Committee:

'Read Mr Oakley's letter of 4th inst. intimating the East Coast Companies' intention to withdraw about 50 Carriages of the present stock and to replace them by vehicles of a more modern description and asking the Caledonian Company's consent.'[7]

The Committee ordered James Smithells *'to arrange.'* It is possible that three of the surplus carriages were disposed of to the Caledonian,[8] but there is no record in the capital expenditure or rolling stock returns.

THE PULLMAN CAR COMPANY

The Pullman Car Company designed and built carriages for use on the Caledonian. It commissioned the construction of the vehicles at its own expense and retained ownership of them. A number of cars ran on the CR before and after World War I. Further cars supplied to the LM&SR also ran on Caley metals.

Most of the company records are believed to have been destroyed by enemy action in World War II. The agreements between the Pullman Car Co. and the CR are in Edinburgh, Kew and the CRA Archive (later agreements only).[9] The agreements and the cars are discussed in Chapter 10.

REFERENCES
1. POST 11/2, 8 and 96
2. POST 18/1
3. NRS BR/WCC/1/4-8
   TNA RAIL 727/1-3
4. NRS BR/NBR/1/367-372
5. TNA RAIL 172
6. NRS BR/CAL/1/19 entry 1663
7. NRS BR/CAL/1/24 entry 411
8. *An Illustrated History of East Coast Joint Stock*, p. 113
9. NRS BR/CAL/3/86-89
   TNA 1204/9, 21, 24, 48, 53
   CRA Archive ref: 2/2/1/4/1-4

1.4: Sources of Information – Contractors' Records

Until the arrival of Dugald Drummond, the Caley relied heavily on contractors, because St. Rollox Works lacked the capacity to build new vehicles to meet the demands of rapidly expanding traffic while keeping the existing stock in running order. The problem was particularly acute in the 1870s and early '80s. This deficiency is discussed in more detail in *Caledonian Railway Wagons*.[1]

After Drummond expanded and reorganised the company's works, most carriages and wagons were built in-house. While work on wagons was again let to contractors during the large-scale wagon replacement programme that was launched in 1903, very few carriages were built outside St. Rollox until after World War I. A list of carriage orders built by contractors forms Appendix IV. From 1885 they are cross-referenced to the diagram book numbers, where known.

This section describes the surviving information from contractors who provided carriages and components for the Caledonian, and who have left significant archive material.

Hurst, Nelson

Hurst, Nelson established a wagon and carriage works at Motherwell in 1880. It built about 3,500 wagons and some carriages for the CR up to the Grouping. The firm took publicity photographs of their output. The complete collection is held at the Motherwell Heritage Centre. Copies of some photographs also form part of the collections of the Historical Model Railway Society (HMRS) and the Caledonian Railway Association.[2] 'An example is shown overleaf, and an electrically-lit carriage is shown in Plate 8.1, p. 171.

Leeds Forge Co. Ltd

The Leeds Forge Co. Ltd was formed in 1873 to take over the existing tool making business of Samson and William Fox, and to erect a works for the manufacture of iron and steel. The manufacture of rolling stock and components of patented pressed steel construction commenced in 1887.

This new technology was used extensively by the Caledonian. The firm produced heavy and lightweight standard bogies for Caledonian carriages and a steel underframe for 6-wheeled Passenger Brake Vans and non-passenger coaching stock. These are discussed and illustrated in Chapter 2.4.

The Leeds works closed after amalgamation with Metropolitan Cammell in 1923 and the business was transferred to Saltley. Drawings of carriages, pressed steel underframes and bogies for the CR are in the Metropolitan Cammell collection – the reference is in the next sub-section.

Metropolitan Cammell

The Metropolitan Railway Carriage and Wagon Company Ltd came into existence in 1862. It grew out of the firm of Joseph Wright who founded a carriage and wagon works in Saltley, Birmingham in

1845. In 1902 the Metropolitan Amalgamated Railway Carriage & Wagon Company Ltd was formed to take over the business of the Metropolitan Company and to amalgamate with the following rolling stock manufacturers:

– The Ashbury Railway Carriage & Iron Co. Ltd (founded as a public company in 1862)
– Brown, Marshall & Co. Ltd (founded 1853)
– The Lancaster Railway Carriage & Wagon Co. Ltd (1863)
– The Oldbury Railway Carriage & Wagon Co. Ltd (1859)

These companies were major suppliers of carriages to the Caledonian and its constituents up to 1882. Various drawings of carriages built for the Caledonian and the Scottish Central Railway have survived. They form part of the Metropolitan Cammell collection. The originals are presumably in store at the headquarters of the HMRS, but are not currently available. Many of the drawings are also in the CRA Archive.[3] The drawings are listed in Appendix V.

The surviving drawings can be viewed on microfiche in the Wolfson Research Centre in the new Birmingham City Library.[4] The paper catalogue has not yet been digitised. A4 size reference prints can be made. Birmingham and CRA archive references are given in the end notes to chapters. The microfiche drawings are generally in poor condition and not all are suitable for reproduction. Where necessary, they have been redrawn by John Boyle to illustrate the text.

Construction resumed in 1921, and some publicity photographs are shown in Plate 11.5 (p. 258) and Plates 11.10 and 11.11 (p. 266).

R.Y. Pickering

In 1864, John Pickering, who originated from Yorkshire, chose Wishaw as the site for his wagon works. His son, Robert Young Pickering took over the business in 1878. Activities included wheel building, wagon repair and hire, but Pickering became increasingly involved in the building of new carriages and wagons. A number of carriage orders from the Caledonian were secured in the late 19th and 20th centuries and some were photographed – see, for example, a Mansell carriage wheel set (Plate 2.13, p. 45) and two early electrically lit carriages (Plates 8.3 and 8.4, p. 180). There are further examples in Chapter 11, including 4-wheeled carriages for the Balerno Branch, along with a detailed cost breakdown of a carriage built in December 1922.

The Glasgow University Business Archive holds the original enquiry books from 1896 and order books from 1888.[5] There is also some information about painting and lettering. Some Pickering drawings and photographs are in the HMRS and CRA collections.

References

1. *Caledonian Railway Wagons*, p. 33
2. CRA Archive ref: 7/1/2
3. CRA Archive ref: 6/1/1/2
4. Birmingham City Archive ref: MS99
5. The generic reference for the Pickering collection is UGD12/. A complete list is available on application to Glasgow University Archive Services

Plate 1.9
The Hurst, Nelson records have not survived, but some of the CR publicity photographs are used in this book. The firm's immaculate Andrew Barclay works shunter heads a rake of five Diagram 118 9-compartment Thirds. Ten of these carriages were to be built by St. Rollox to order H351, but were sub-contracted to the Motherwell-based company for construction in the half year ending December 1921. Their numbers were 1410-1419. A further eleven were built by Metropolitan, one of which is illustrated in Plate 11.10. It's good to see that the shunter echoes the Caley practice of resting the front coupling link back against the buffer beam.

1.5: Sources of Information – Books and the Press

This final section deals with publications, magazines and historical works that provided general railway information and opinion or items specific to the Caledonian, during the CR's existence. It does not deal with the general railway history books and albums that have been published in a steady stream, with the exception of the books quoted below.

Economic History

Two academic books have been consulted to explain the high level of Third class travel in Scotland compared with the rest of the UK. This topic is discussed in Chapter 3. *The Origins of the Scottish Railway System 1722-1844*[1] provides information on the amount of traffic carried by the pioneering railways and quotes from depositions to the Board of Trade. *The Rise and Fall of Scottish Industry*[2] gives information about the distribution of labour and the economic development of Scottish industry.

Francis Whishaw

In 1840 *The Railways of Great Britain* was published. Whishaw toured Britain's emerging network of railways and reported on what he saw. Although his tour pre-dated the opening of the Caledonian, he visited a number of railways which later formed part of the CR system and described their carriages, some of which may have entered service on the Caledonian.

The L&NWR Perspective

The senior partner in the West Coast Conference and designer of the West Coast Joint Stock had a significant influence over CR affairs. It is fair to say that the 19th-century L&NWR was a conservative organisation with a strong aversion to spending money to the detriment of shareholders' dividends. It was also run by extremely dominant personalities, even by the standards of an age when running a railway was not for shrinking violets.

The biography of Richard Moon describes one man's rise to be chairman of the L&NWR.[3] It shows how his attitude and beliefs dictated the company's policy and explains the reasoning behind many of the decisions taken over a period of thirty years from 1861, when pressure to adopt continuous brakes and alarm systems forced the railways to make technical advances.

The second book provides insights and information from an operational perspective.[4] G.P. Neele entered railway service in 1847 and became Passenger Superintendent at Birmingham on the L&NWR in 1861. He subsequently rose to become Superintendent of the Line. He retired from the L&NWR in 1895. His views on brakes and alarm systems are often contrary to those expressed by the L&NWR Chairman, and paint a picture of the operational difficulties they caused.

West Coast Joint Stock

The prime source of secondary information is the Historical Model Railway Society's publication *West Coast Joint Stock*. The information is based on the original West Coast Conference minutes – see Chapter 1.3. Quotations taken from the book have been checked against the original minute books referred to in Chapter 1.3 and referenced accordingly.

David Jenkinson's book on L&NWR carriages overlaps the subject matter in *West Coast Joint Stock*. From the modeller's point of view it scores over the latter book because it provides side elevation drawings of carriages. Its drawback is that it only deals in detail with stock built after 1890.

The Historical Model Railway Society's *LNWR Liveries* provides useful information on the evolution of carriage livery which has informed the description of the changes in CR carriage livery described in Chapter 4.

Pullman Cars

The first two books in the *Pullman Profile* series cover the 12- and 8-wheeled cars that ran on the Caledonian. The descriptions of the interior fittings have been quoted at length in Chapter 10.

The North British Railway

Bill Sewell's privately published *NBR Coaches: A Design Review* provided information about Drummond's designs before he moved to the Caledonian, which are included in Chapter 7. There is also useful background material on carriage construction.

Sidney Stone

Stone held management positions with the Great Central, the Great Eastern and the South Western railways. He was also at one time Assistant General Manager of the Metropolitan Carriage & Wagon Company. Between 1892 and 1897 he published a series of articles on the general principles of carriage and wagon design and construction in *The Railway Engineer*. These were collated for publication in 1903. There are some direct references to, and drawings of, CR carriages and components used by the company. Information from these publications has been used in Chapters 2 and 3.

Technical Periodicals

Three technical journals published regular articles on general railway developments and occasionally on developments on the Caledonian Railway. Two journals appeared weekly – *The Engineer*, which started in 1866, and *Engineering*, which started ten years later. Many of these volumes and their indexes are available for download or viewing through the Grace's Guide to British Industrial History website.[5] They have been particularly useful in charting developments in continuous brakes and alarm systems that appear in Chapter 2.

The Railway Engineer was a monthly publication which first appeared in 1880. Some St. Rollox drawings that have not survived were reproduced in articles and have been used in the text. All three journals are available for consultation at the NRM.

The Railway Enthusiasts' Press

One of the Caledonian Railway Association's projects is to create a definitive list of published material about the company and to make it available to the researcher. The current catalogue is contained under the archive reference CRA9/2: Historical Publications Extracts. This section is confined to sources which have contributed material to this book.

The Railway Magazine published a full account of the launch of the 'Grampian' service in 1905, which has been used in Chapters 4 and 9. A Diamond Jubilee edition on the Caledonian was published in 1907. It also published details of the 1914 Pullman services which have misled later commentators. This material is discussed in Chapter 10.

As to livery, *The Locomotive Magazine* described carriage and non-passenger coaching stock liveries of railway companies, including the Caledonian, as they were in 1897. The Stephenson Locomotive Society published a book celebrating the centenary of the CR's formation in 1947, but confined its description of all its rolling stock to three pages. It repeated the description of 1897.

The Caledonian Railway Association and its predecessor the Caledonian Railway Consortium of Modellers have helped to address the deficiency in information about coaching stock. Articles on carriages and passenger traffic have been published in the CRA journal *The True Line*. These are acknowledged in the reference sections. *Caledonian Railway Livery* contains a chapter on carriages and non-passenger coaching stock. This material has been used as the basis for Chapter 4.

Histories of the Caledonian

In 1961 O.S. Nock produced a concise history of the Caledonian.[6] Like many of his works, there was an emphasis on locomotive construction and performance. It did, however, contain drawings of a 45-foot Coupé Luggage Composite, a 50-foot Corridor Brake Composite and two examples of 'Grampian' stock.

David Ross' history is a much more substantial work and concentrates on the development of the company as a business.[7] It places rolling stock development in the context of economic factors, competition for traffic and expansion into new territories.

James McEwan planned to write a history of the Caledonian, but he died in 1991 before the work was complete. The material is in the William Patrick Library in Kirkintilloch.[8] A paper catalogue is available. It consists of chapters and notes on episodes in CR history and its constituents which are mostly unsupported by references to sources. This makes it difficult to separate fact from anecdote.

196 ENGINEERING. [Feb. 21, 1890.

curled horsehair, and covered with blue cloth of the best quality, trimmed with rich blue and crimson lace, Greek key pattern. The door squabs, arm and elbow rests, are similarly stuffed and covered with buffalo hide of best quality, of a colour to match the cloth.

The smoking compartment in the first-class carriage is finished and upholstered in a similar manner to the others, with the exception that "buffalo hide" is substituted for blue cloth.

The floors are covered with blue and gold Brussels carpet with horsehair rugs of a colour and design to harmonise. The floors of the lavatories are covered with the usual Caledonian Railway standard pattern of oilcloth. The lavatory compartments are finished with polished mahogany panels and facings. All the metallic fittings in this and the other compartments are of arquzoid.

Each coupé is fitted with a large mirror and a table, and the glazing throughout is of special quality.

The cushions and backs of the third-class carriages are stuffed with best curled hair, and the backs are upholstered for a height of 3 ft., and covered with carpet. The third-class carriage, illustrated in Fig. 3, is not the one which took part in the trial trip noticed before, but is a still later pattern containing eight compartments.

The carriages are painted crimson lake, picked out in gold, and fine-lined in red.

The underframing throughout is of the best American white oak, as is also the body framing, with the exception of the pillars and rails, which are of the best Moulmein teak. The side soles (Fig. 5) are plated with mild steel bars $\frac{1}{2}$ in. thick. The headstocks are of oak plated with mild steel $\frac{5}{8}$ in. thick, and the intermediate cross-stays are of oak planks with mild steel sandwiched between them. The main bogie frames (Figs. 14 to 17) are of mild steel $\frac{3}{4}$ in. thick, and have four Timmiss' and four laminated steel springs. The pivot of the bogie is placed 2 in. nearer one axle than the other, to the end that one pair of wheels may become the guiding medium, and thus do away with the sinuous movement incidental to ordinary bogies. The wheels are of the ordinary Caledonian type, 3 ft. 9 in. over the tread, with Bessemer steel tyres and Mansel fastenings. The centres (Fig. 17) are of teak with segments carried into pockets cast on the wheel boss. The axles are of the best Siemens mild steel, and the wheels are forced on to them by an hydraulic pressure of 50 tons.

The axle-boxes (Figs. 18 to 21) are fitted with Macnee's dust excluder and metallic lubricators (Fig. 20).

Figs. 7 and 8 show the Westinghouse brake arrangement on the first-class carriage, and Figs. 9 and 10 that on the third-class carriage. Figs. 11 to 13 show the brake levers on the trucks.

AXLE-BOX FOR CARRIAGES; CALEDONIAN RAILWAY.

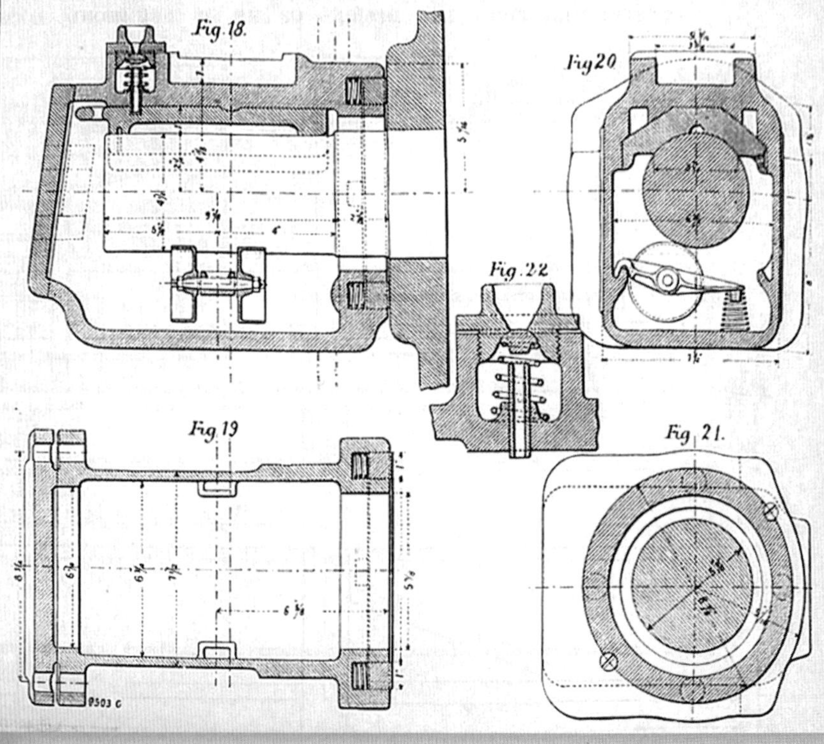

Plate 1.10

The technical press often carried detailed descriptions of innovative rolling stock designs and components. In 1890, Drummond built sets of carriages for the Callander & Oban and Gourock services. They were the subject of a long illustrated article in *Engineering*. The drawing of the bogie is shown in Figure 2.15, and the full description of the interior, part of which is visible on this page, is quoted in Chapter 4.3. This extract shows the construction of the standard CR carriage axlebox and describes the materials used for the underframe.

References

1. By C.J.A. Robertson, Lecturer in Economic and Social History, University of St. Andrews, John Donald Publishers Ltd, 1983
2. By R.H. Campbell, Professor of Economic History, University of Stirling, John Donald Publishers Ltd, 1980
3. *The Railway Moon*, by Peter Braine, pmb publishing, 2010
4. *Railway Reminiscences*, McCorquodale, 1904
5. http://www.gracesguide.co.uk/
6. *The Caledonian Railway*, Ian Allan Ltd, 1963
7. *The Caledonian, Scotland's Imperial Railway*, Stenlake Publishing Ltd, 2013
8. East Dunbartonshire Archive ref: T25/1

CHAPTER 2
THE DEVELOPMENT OF THE CARRIAGE FLEET – SAFETY AND OPERATIONAL EFFICIENCY

2.1: BRAKES

In the 1840s, passenger trains were stopped in an emergency by putting the locomotive into reverse and applying hand-operated brakes (usually spelt break at that time) which were distributed in carriages along the train. The Railway Department of the Board of Trade developed a formula concerning brake power. The last carriage in a train and every fourth carriage had to be equipped with brakes capable of being applied in an emergency.[1] The average CR passenger train in 1852 had seven carriages,[2] necessitating two brake fitted vehicles.

The brakes were not controlled by a guard in a separate compartment. Ordinary carriages were fitted with brakes which were controlled by a 'travelling breaksman.' He sat on the roof of

the carriage, from where he could observe the train and, by turning a wheel attached to a spindle which ran down the end of the vehicle, applied the brakes through a worm and pinion linkage under the carriage. The driver used the engine whistle to request a brake application. A typical carriage with brake, dating from 1845, is shown in Figure 2.1.

EARLY BRAKES ON THE CALEDONIAN SYSTEM

The earliest drawing of a brake arrangement in the St. Rollox register was Greenock 67, which was for 'part of carriage with brakesman's seat.' The number pre-dates that of the Saloon carriage that entered service in 1847, which is described in Chapter 13.1, so it must have applied to the carriages ordered for the northern end of the system. An example of the seat is shown in Plate 2.1. There is a similar arrangement in Figure 2.1.

The first mention of 'breaks' in CR company minutes was in January 1857, when four Composite and four Third class carriages were to have 'Guard's seats and breaks' fitted at a cost of £22 above the price for the rest of the order.[3]

Being a breaksman was a risky job. A number were killed or seriously injured by receiving blows to the head from overbridges. As a result, the simple coachman's seat was changed into something resembling a sentry box within the loading gauge, although still open to the elements. Later, a door provided protection against the weather. One of the later arrangements can be seen on the leading coach of the train in Plate 2.2, which dates from circa 1860. Figure 5.3 is a drawing derived from this photograph.

CLASSES OF BREAKSMEN

In 1866, a petition was received from breaksmen for an addition of 2s per week to their wages 'which are at present 1st Class 22s

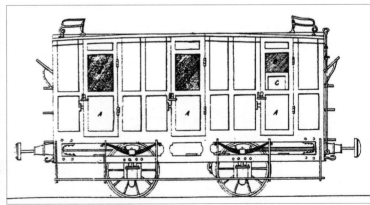

Figure 2.1 and Plate 2.1
This drawing of an Arbroath & Forfar Railway Third shows two breaksman's seats and a brake mechanism at the right-hand end. Turning the vertical rod operated a shaft underneath the carriage floor through a worm and pinion to apply the brake. One brake block sufficed. The photograph shows how vulnerable the breaksman was to obstructions such as overbridges.

per week, 2nd Class 19s per week and 3rd Class 16s per week.' The different classes probably reflected the relative importance of trains, rather than the class of traveller. The Caledonian's General Manager recommended the concession, which was agreed by the Board.[4]

The Need for a Continuous Brake

Train lengths and speeds increased during the 1850s. The 1840 formula required more carriages with brakes and therefore more breaksmen, which increased operating costs. Despite the increase in carriages fitted with brakes, BoT inspectors frequently cited

inadequate braking power in accident reports. In addition, the 1862 edition of the Statutory Requirements for Railways recommended a means of communication between guard and driver. The 1840 formula was repeated and continuous brakes were mentioned for the first time, but only as a means of reducing costs. The *Precautions Recommended in the Working of Railways* section stated:

1. *There should be a break-vehicle with a guard in it at the tail of every train; this vehicle should be provided with a raised roof and extended sides, glazed to the front and back; and it should be the duty of the guard to keep a constant look-out from it along his train.*
2. *There should be a means of communication between a guard at the tail of every passenger train and the engine driver.*
3. *There should be at least one break-vehicle to every three or four carriages in a passenger train, a proportion of which may be economically provided by the use of continuous breaks.*[5]

The evolution of systems for communication between the rear-most guard and the driver is discussed in Chapter 2.2.

The CR's First Involvement with Continuous Brakes

In the 1870s the Caledonian became involved with three continuous braking systems. It favoured an air brake system, and evaluated the Westinghouse and Steel-McInnes designs. It was also compelled to work with the Clark-Webb chain brake through its West Coast Joint Stock arrangement with the L&NWR.

First Experiment with the Westinghouse Brake

In 1871 George Westinghouse arrived in the UK to demonstrate the braking system he had developed in the USA two years earlier.

Above: Plate 2.2
Breaksmen were eventually given protection from the weather as shown in this photograph, which is believed to date from the 1860s. Access to the 'sentry hut' was through the adjacent compartment.
Right: Figure 2.2
The first, non-automatic, Westinghouse brake as fitted to the carriages in the 1872 trial on the CR. The triple valve that operated the brake was on the locomotive.
Below: Figure 2.3
The automatic version of the brake had a triple valve (F) under each carriage. The drawing also shows clasp brakes, with two blocks operating on each wheel. This reduced strain on the axle journals, by equalising the pressure on the wheel tread when braking.

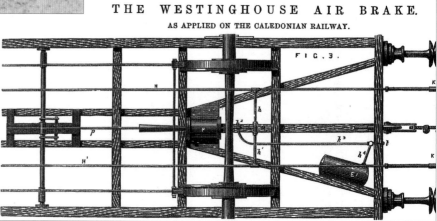

THE WESTINGHOUSE AIR BRAKE.
AS APPLIED ON THE CALEDONIAN RAILWAY.
FIG.3.

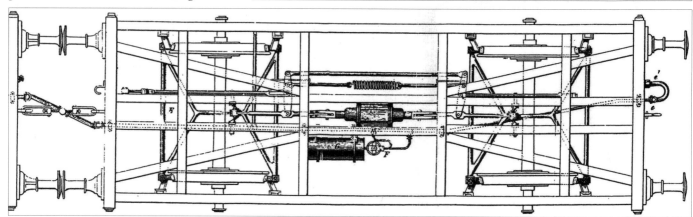

In Scotland the only railway company to show any interest was the Caledonian, which conducted trials on the Wemyss Bay line in early 1872. St. Rollox drawing register entries 1261 and 1262 refer briefly to the brake. Neither drawing has survived.

The technical press gave a full, illustrated, report of the trial and the satisfactory performance of the brake.[6] The arrangement of the brake on the leading carriage is shown in Figure 2.2. The locomotive depicted in one set of illustrations was Conner Class '98' 2-4-0 number 101. McEwan stated the locomotive was number 92, the first of the '98' class.[7] *The Engineer* reported that '*for some months past the brake has been in use on two passenger trains,*' so the illustration and McEwan were probably both correct.

'A special train consisting of twelve passenger carriages and two vans, fitted up throughout with the new brake, left Bridge Street station, Glasgow, at eleven o'clock on Thursday morning, March 28th … The experiments included five stoppages between Glasgow and Wemyss Bay.'

The first stop at Houston station was on the level. The next at Bishopton was on an up gradient. The other three were on falling grades at Langbank, the Ravenscraig Incline and near Inverkip station – the latter at a gradient of 1 in 68. The stops were all reported as being '*wonderfully prompt.*'

Although not mentioned by G.P. Neele in his *Railway Reminiscences*, the L&NWR tested the Westinghouse brake at the same time as the Caledonian. The press report on the CR trial recorded that the L&NWR trial on the main line between Stafford and Crewe produced equally impressive results. The train comprised six carriages, plus brakes on the locomotive's tender. It was not sufficient to convince the L&NWR to adopt the brake; it chose to adopt a cheaper, simpler (and therefore more reliable and easier to maintain) arrangement.

THE WESTINGHOUSE AUTOMATIC BRAKE

Originally, the brake was non-automatic, but in late 1872 Westinghouse developed an automatic version. Each carriage was fitted with an air cylinder and triple valve. Equal air pressure

was maintained in the auxiliary reservoirs and in the train pipe at all times when the brakes were 'off.' The valve's functions were to charge the auxiliary reservoir and to apply and release the brake. The new system also enabled the guard to apply the brake. There is a full description and drawings in *The Engineer*.[8] A drawing of the arrangement on a Brake Van is shown in Figure 2.3.

To apply the brakes to all of the carriages at about the same time, pressure was released from the train pipe, causing the triple valve on each carriage to put the brakes 'on.' A malfunction in the pipework such as a leak or a train division would apply the brake. To release the brakes on each carriage, pressure was increased in the train pipe until it exceeded that in each auxiliary cylinder. This threw the triple valve, closing the inlet to the brake cylinder and opening the inlet to the auxiliary reservoir from the train pipe, allowing the two pressures to be equalised.

THE STEEL-McINNES BRAKE

Westinghouse's system was not the only continuous brake tried out by the Caledonian. James Steel, a Glasgow engineer, and John McInnes, who had joined the Garnkirk & Glasgow Railway in 1844 and was by then the CR Brakes Inspector, developed a continuous brake which was first tested on the CR in 1875. It was fully described and illustrated in *The Engineer*.[9]

The brake, later to be known as the Steel-McInnes Pneumatic Reaction Brake but at first called Steel's Disruption Brake, was similar in principle to the Westinghouse system, in that air pressure released the brakes and held them 'off.' A compressor fitted to the locomotive could be operated either indirectly off its motion or directly by a donkey engine. The compressor filled a reservoir which provided the air to operate the brake.

At the end of each carriage a cylinder operated a piston which applied the brakes through a linkage. The carriages were connected by flexible pipes, but the through pipes ran over the roof of the carriage rather than through the underframe. The compressor filled the various cylinders with air at 75psi. This is illustrated in Figure 2.4.

The actuating cylinders were divided into two parts separated by a piston. Pressure in the lower part of the cylinders remained constant

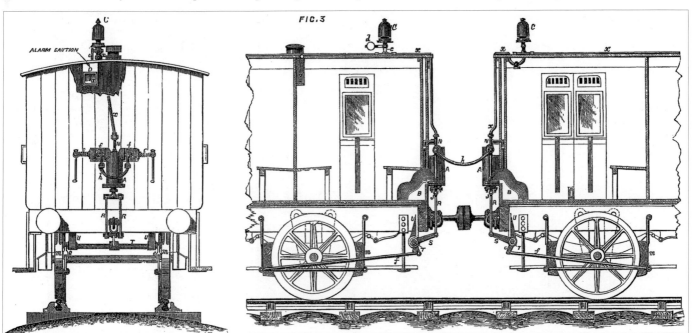

Figure 2.4
The Steel-McInnes brake as used by the Caledonian at the Newark trials in 1875. It incorporates a passenger alarm system, which sounded a whistle when the internal lever was pulled. It also had a tell-tale arrangement to indicate which carriage was the source of the problem.

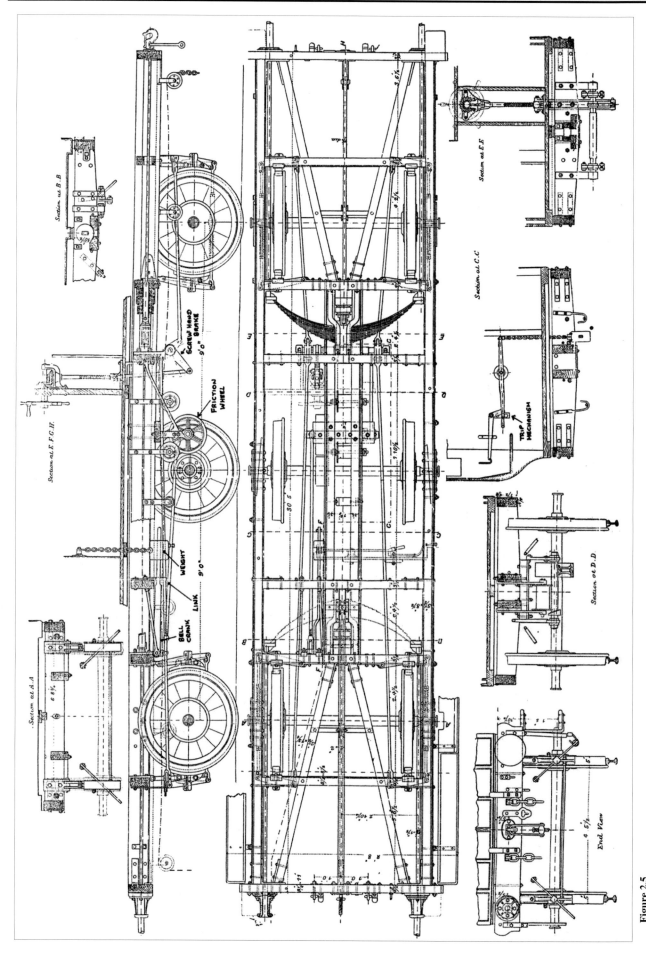

Figure 2.5
The Clark-Webb chain brake as adopted by the L&NWR and therefore applied to the West Coast Joint Stock. A small number of Caledonian carriages engaged in through running onto the L&NWR were fitted with the brake.

and, when the brakes were off, the pressure in the upper portion was equal to that in the lower, placing the piston centrally in the cylinder. The lower parts of the cylinders were each fed via a cut-off valve intended to maintain the pressure in that part of the cylinder should a break in the system be caused by the train breaking apart or similar. The upper portions of all the cylinders were connected to a three-way cock.

To apply the brake, air was bled from the upper part of the cylinders. The piston was forced upwards by the higher pressure in the lower part, thus applying the brakes. To release them the position of the cock was altered so that air was reintroduced into the upper portion of the cylinder, forcing the piston downwards towards the centre.

FIRST TRIAL OF THE STEEL-McINNES BRAKE

This took place on 28th January 1875. A report appeared in the *Leeds Mercury* of 6th February. At 11.00am the train, carrying a collection of such worthies as James Napier, the famous engineer, Steel himself, and Benjamin Conner, left Buchanan Street. The train, hauled by a 7-foot 2-4-0, consisted of two First and three Third class carriages, each having a Brake compartment.

The first test of any importance took place when the train reached Garnkirk where, on a level line, the train was brought to a halt from a speed of 40 m.p.h. in fifteen seconds and a distance of only 200 yards.

The next test involved a demonstration of the brake's automatic action. While passing Omoa on the Cleland & Mid-Calder Branch and ascending an incline of 1 in 80 at 36 m.p.h., the locomotive was deliberately uncoupled from the train. This resulted in a division of the two air pipes connecting the upper and lower sets of cylinders and an immediate application of the carriage brakes, bringing the carriages to a halt in only 74 yards and within five seconds. The locomotive then reversed to the train but was unable to move the carriages even on the downward slope. The carriages were then left on the gradient for nearly an hour, held only by the automatic brake, while lunch was served.

A further impressive example of automatic action was given on a downhill gradient of 1 in 65 on the Morningside Branch when the locomotive was again detached at a speed approaching 50 m.p.h. The carriages were halted in less than 100 yards but the locomotive took over half a mile to pull up. A final test near Holytown was also satisfactory.

THE CLARK-WEBB CHAIN BRAKE

As the CR's Anglo-Scottish traffic partner and builder of West Coast Joint Stock carriages, the L&NWR dictated its braking arrangements. It preferred the Wilkin and Clark chain brake, later the Clark-Webb patent, which extended the primitive braking arrangement from one carriage to three or four. A drawing from *Engineering* with an explanatory caption from the same source was reproduced in *West Coast Joint Stock*.[10] It is shown in Figure 2.5.

It consisted of a wheel which the guard turned to wind a chain around a drum attached to the axle of the carriage. It was then connected to a similar chain on the adjoining carriage and so on. In order to brake the adjoining carriage the chain had to slide over the drum of the first. To apply the brake to the next carriage it had to slide over two and so on. Eventually frictional forces meant that no further carriages could be braked.

The brake was under control of the guard, but was only to be used in an emergency. Normal stops were made with the handbrake. In later years the driver could also apply it in an emergency by means of a cord. Successive Superintendents of the L&NWR maintained the view that the guard was in charge of the train. Neele tried to convince John Ramsbottom otherwise:

'The attempt to force responsibility on to the guards, I told him, was like expecting the bus conductors to pull up the horses of an omnibus; but all in vain, the idea permeated the Locomotive Superintendents' view for years. The driver's whistle was to be the means by which the guards should be warned to act and apply the brake; forgetful of the fact, that oftentimes the brake whistle failed amid the jar and rattle of the travelling train to be heard by the guard.'[11]

Marshalling trains was a complicated business, because the chains and communication cord had to be disconnected, reconnected and adjusted. Carriage inspectors were appointed to instruct station staff on connecting the brake and specially trained men were deployed at stations throughout the L&NWR to maintain the brakes and rectify defects. A full list of the thirty-one stations can be found in *West Coast Joint Stock*.[12]

In 1870 the L&NWR opened negotiations with Wilkin and Clark with a view to fitting the brake to L&NWR carriages and by extension to the WCJS.[13] The decision was made to fit the brake to WCJS vehicles in 1874.[14] Initially sufficient carriages were fitted for the two Limited Mails and the 10.00am departures from London and Glasgow. The decision to fit the brake to CR Saloons which regularly travelled south of the border was made later in the year.[15] Two thirds of WCJS carriages had been fitted with the brake by early 1876.[16]

THE NEWARK BRAKE TRIALS

In June 1875 the Board of Trade staged brake trials on the Midland Railway line between Newark and Nottingham. The trials were part of the fact-finding phase of the Royal Commission on Railway Accidents, which had been launched the previous year. Public opinion had put pressure on the government to act. In the early 1870s there had been a number of very serious accidents. These included Kirtlebridge on the Caledonian, in which eleven people were killed and fifteen injured, but not as the result of poor brakes.

Eight brake systems were tested, as shown in the table:

BRAKE TYPE	RAILWAY
Clark-Webb chain	L&NWR
Barker hydraulic	MR
Clark hydraulic	MR
Westinghouse vacuum	LB&SCR
Smith vacuum	GNR
Westinghouse air	MR
Steel-McInnes air	CR
Fay hand operated (improved)	L&YR

The CR Board had been sufficiently encouraged by five months' experience to authorise the fitting of the Steel-McInnes brakes to *'a number of the CR Carriages for the purpose of being tested by the Railway Commission on Accidents'*, but with the caveat: *'Allow the trial on getting sufficient guarantee against infringement of the patent.'*[17]

The trials were comprehensively reported in *The Engineer* and *Engineering*.[18] *The Engineer* described the Caledonian's entry as follows:

'The Caledonian train was drawn by a fine outside-cylinder engine. ... The engine has no brake. The tender has the ordinary hand brake with wood blocks. The train was apparently made up from the first stock which came to hand, and did not compare very favourably with that of other companies and the carriages did not run smoothly'

FIRST REACTIONS TO THE RESULTS OF THE TRIALS

The L&NWR's G.P. Neele, who was present at the trials, wrote nearly thirty years after the event that the chain brake stopped the train quickly, but not as quickly as the Westinghouse-fitted Midland Railway train and went on to say that:

'The weather, the weight of the train, the state of the rails, were all the subject of comment, if not dispute, among the experts; and each of the patentees went away from the refreshment tent at Rolleston Junction, self-satisfied that their own system was the best.'[19]

The Engineer's reporter did not share Neele's view:

'It is indisputable that, regarded as a train stopper, the Westinghouse Automatic brake was by far the most efficient … it actually stopped a train in less time and in a shorter distance than any other train on the ground moving at the same speed … due to the admirable promptitude with which every block in the train was brought into operation.

The great feature of the automatic brake is that the carriages are practically independent of the engine; that is to say, each carriage conveys, stored up beneath it, the power required to apply the brake.'[20]

As for the Caledonian train's performance, the reporter observed that, although the Steel-McInnes brake performed reasonably well in stopping the train, it,

'is complex in appearance and was noisy in operation. A good deal of leakage appears to be at present inseparable from the system, the pump running constantly at 60 to 70 double strokes per minute to maintain the pressure.'[21]

ANALYSIS OF THE TRIALS IN THE TECHNICAL PRESS

A week after the report of the trials, the full test results were published.[22] A week later The Engineer urged readers not to draw false conclusions from the results. 'There are not only certain problems which the competition could not solve, but there are questions which it appeared to answer and did not.'[23] While not decrying the useful information that was gained, the reporter put the event into perspective by stating:

'Instead of being a refined and exhaustive investigation into the resistance of trains, and the efficiency of various systems of brake, it [the trial] was nothing more than a comparatively rough-and-ready inquiry into the various powers possessed by continuous brakes generally.

… a little reflection will show that a very large number of questions connected with the practical working of continuous brakes in regular work on railways was not touched at all by the trial. For example, nothing was learned about the relative durability of the different systems. … As to the relative cost of working each system, apart from repairs and maintenance, nothing could be learned that was trustworthy.'

The last remark is pertinent to the L&NWR's later lack of enthusiasm for the Westinghouse brake and its adoption of the simple vacuum system. It was undoubtedly more complex, more expensive in first cost and more difficult, and therefore more costly, to maintain. This is borne out by Neele, who quoted statistics from the Board of Trade returns for 1880-85 set out in the following table.[24]

BRAKE	FAILURES	MILES PER FAILURE
Simple vacuum	555	118,102
Automatic vacuum	519	80,714
Westinghouse	3,944	18,096

The author of The Engineer article drew two other lessons from the trials. The first was the importance of a simultaneous brake application throughout the train. The chain brake, which was applied by the guard, had actually snapped a carriage drawhook during the first trail run because the brakes were operated from the rear vehicle and then progressively to those in front of it. Applying the brake to the front carriages before the rear was equally dangerous as it risked derailing the rear carriages, especially on a curve.

The second lesson mentioned was that an emergency stop with an efficient brake like the Westinghouse caused the water in the locomotive boiler to surge to the front, exposing the fusible plug in the firebox. This had occurred during the trial, when 'it was estimated that the water fell as much as a foot below the firebox crown sheet.' It was therefore vital that a brake should be powerful, but that it could be applied gradually.

DRUMMOND'S TRIAL ON THE NORTH BRITISH RAILWAY

The NBR did not participate in the Newark trials. In December 1876 Drummond organised a competitive trial between the Smith simple vacuum and the Westinghouse automatic systems, supervised by a neutral panel of four locomotive engineers. The data collected was more comprehensive than that at Newark. It took place on the Edinburgh–Glasgow line. James Smithells and George Brittain from the Caledonian were among the large number of observers.

John Thomas describes the trial in his history of the NBR. The narrative was based on a report in The Engineer.[25]

'The weather was damp and misty and the rails were greasy. The train (with the Westinghouse brake) was put through a programme of routine and emergency stops. At 60 m.p.h. it was brought to a stand in 29½ seconds "and that without the slightest feeling of shock on the part of those occupying the carriages." … In all cases the brake began to act between a quarter and three quarters of a second after application.'[26]

Thomas published a table comparing the performance of the two brakes, the data for which was extracted from The Engineer article. The Westinghouse system exhibited the same superiority in train-stopping described in the Newark trial report.

SPEED (M.P.H.)	WESTINGHOUSE		SMITH'S VACUUM	
	DISTANCE (YARDS)	TIME (SECONDS)	DISTANCE (YARDS)	TIME (SECONDS)
40	550	16	800	23
49½	798	19	1,170	27½
54	952	21	1,310	28
55	910	21	1,375	28

Within three weeks of the trial the NBR Board, on Drummond's advice, resolved that the Westinghouse brake should be adopted for passenger trains and coaching stock. The decision was acclaimed in Engineering:

'We confess that, having in view the extreme sluggishness that characterises the managements of railways in this country we were unprepared for such prompt action on the part of the North British.'[27]

The article deplored a report in the *Times* that the Great Northern Railway had decided to adopt the simple vacuum brake:

'If this be true the managers of that line are incurring a grave responsibility in selecting a notoriously imperfect means of controlling their fast trains, when other means, proved beyond all doubt to be thoroughly efficient, are available.'

The *Engineering* article went on to say:

'It remains now to be seen what action, if any, other large railway companies will take in this matter of continuous brakes, whether they will follow the example thus set by the North British, or adopt other and inferior means of controlling their trains, or continue in a state of indifference until forced into action by the pressure of public opinion, which is far more powerful – when fairly exerted – than the strongest prejudice or indifference of individuals.'

EARLY MISTRUST OF AUTOMATIC BRAKES

The views of the article's author were not shared by everyone. The automatic brake, especially when coupled with the powerful braking force of the Westinghouse system, was held to be dangerous. Richard Moon, the L&NWR chairman, told his shareholders in 1879:

'He did not believe that any man in his senses would say that they ought to trust their trains to the self-acting brake. It might sometimes act when they required it, but it was more likely to involve them in a new class of accidents, of which they had no experience.'[28]

Colonel Yolland of the BoT Railway Inspectorate expressed similar misgivings about the Westinghouse brake. Apart from its complication,

'The liability to apply itself when it is not required and when there is no accident, and to fail to act or go on when absolutely required by the engine driver, constitute two grave defects in its present construction.'[29]

FURTHER TRIALS ON THE CALEDONIAN

The Newark trials had shown that the air brakes were superior to other brakes in terms of stopping power and the trials on the NBR demonstrated the superior braking power and speed of application of the Westinghouse system compared with the simple vacuum. Immediately after the NBR trial, the Caledonian Board noted in early January 1877:

'The competition trials of Breaks recently made on the NBR were referred to and Mr Smithells stated that he has the subject in hand and will report as soon as possible.'[30]

In the previous September the CR Board had recorded that *'The question of the application of a continuous break apparatus to the Passenger Trains generally was remitted to Mr Smithells to report upon.'*[31]

The Caledonian set its face against the vacuum brake, but as yet made no firm decision in favour of either of the air brake systems. In February a Board minute stated:

'the question of Continuous Breaks was again discussed, and remit was made to the Manager to report to the next Board Meeting upon the cost and merit of the Westinghouse and the Steel-McInnes Breaks.'[32]

Meanwhile, Drummond was gathering data about *'cost and merit.'* Rather than immediately implement the NBR Board's decision to adopt the Westinghouse system, he ran an extended trial of the two brakes. Ten locomotives and trains were fitted with each type of brake and tested in normal service for six months. The cost of materials and labour was £493 17s 9d for the Westinghouse fitted trains and £433 8s for the simple vacuum – approximately 14% less.[33]

In the middle of 1877 *The Engineer* reported on *'The Progress of Continuous Brakes.'*[34] The source was a parliamentary paper published under the auspices of the Board of Trade. The BoT had circulated a questionnaire to the railway companies to ascertain what they were doing about continuous brakes. The Caledonian's reply was as follows:

'We are fitting up two trains of the Westinghouse automatic brake and we propose to fit up a train with Clark and Webb's automatic chain brake, and to test them carefully in daily use, till we can speak confidently as to their merits.
Two engines and twenty carriages have been fitted with the Westinghouse ordinary brake; two engines and thirteen carriages have been fitted with the Steel-McInnes' brake; and eleven carriages have had the chain connection for Clark and Webb's brake applied to them; 108 West Coast Joint carriages have been fitted with Clark and Webb's brake complete, and six carriages have been fitted with the chain connection only.
They are in use on passenger trains as follows, viz.: Westinghouse on the Wemyss Bay line; Steel-McInnes on the Edinburgh and Glasgow line; Clark and Webb on the through trains between England and Scotland by West Coast Route.'

In February 1878 Brittain suggested to the Traffic Committee that *'the 4.05 p.m. train (summer) between Glasgow and Callander be fitted up'* with the Steel-McInnes brake.[35] Approval was not forthcoming for the summer season because in August the CR Board authorised the trial of an improved version.[36] This was fitted to carriages for use on the Callander & Oban.[37] St. Rollox drawings 2450, 2453, 2457 and 2466-2468 dating from late 1878 refer to the brake as applied to C&O carriages, including *'Composites and Saloons.'*

CR No. 9, a Neilson-built Class '1' 2-4-0, was modified at the same time. Most of the St. Rollox drawings between 2460 and 2510 were for modifications to the locomotive and tender. They were issued in January/February 1879. None of the drawings quoted has survived. More than one locomotive was involved, as the capital expenditure return for the half year ending January 1880 records a charge of £326 9s 5d for fitting the brake to *'engines'* and £695 12s 7d for *'carriages'.*[38]

This was the last record of capital expenditure on the brake, but St. Rollox drawing 2908, which dates from the first half of 1881 was for a *'Pipe Arrangement Steel McInnes Air Brake, Engine 163.'* The drawing has not survived. No. 163 was one of the 2-4-2 radial tank engines that ran for a short time, unsuccessfully, on the Callander & Oban, which probably took over from CR No. 9.

The experiment on the C&O ended in 1882 with the introduction of the Class '179' 4-4-0s, which were the first CR locomotives to be built with the Westinghouse brake.

THE RAILWAY RETURNS (CONTINUOUS BRAKES) ACT

The Royal Commission on Railway Accidents published its report in 1877. In 1878 an Act of Parliament was passed which required railway companies to submit a six-monthly return detailing the type of brakes in use.[39] Although continuous brakes were not yet a statutory requirement, the Act was designed to put pressure on companies to adopt some form of automatic continuous brake. Five questions had to be answered:

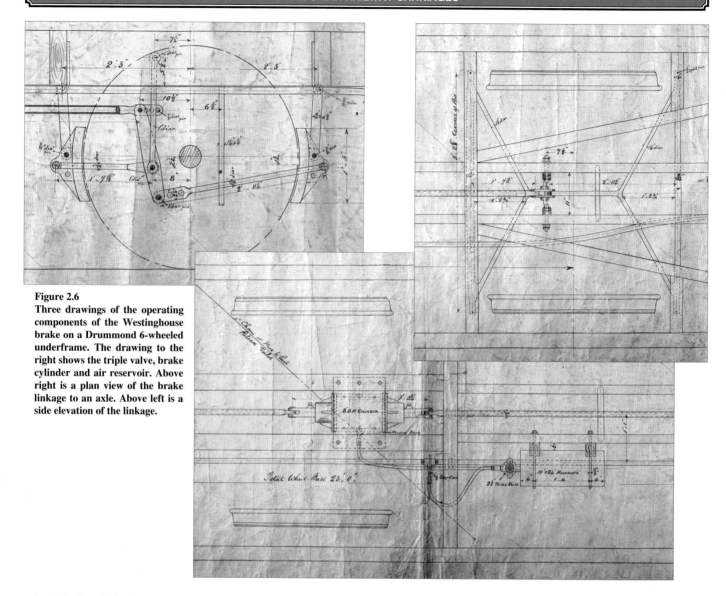

Figure 2.6
Three drawings of the operating components of the Westinghouse brake on a Drummond 6-wheeled underframe. The drawing to the right shows the triple valve, brake cylinder and air reservoir. Above right is a plan view of the brake linkage to an axle. Above left is a side elevation of the linkage.

1. Whether the brakes are instantaneous in action and capable of being applied by engine driver and guards.
2. Whether self-acting.
3. Whether capable of being applied to every vehicle of a train.
4. Whether in regular use in daily working.
5. Whether the materials employed are of a durable character, easily maintained and kept in order.

Details also were requested of *'all cases in which Continuous Brakes have, from any cause, failed to act when required to be brought into action.'*

The Caledonian was still undecided about which system to adopt. James Smithells tried to persuade the Board to adopt the Westinghouse system. In July 1879 he reported a proposal from Westinghouse *'as to the application of this brake to the Company's plant.'*[40] The proposal was declined.

FINAL ADOPTION OF A CONTINUOUS BRAKE

The delay in settling on a braking system was probably caused in part by Brittain's poor health. A resolution to the CR's dilemma began to emerge in 1880. In the previous July, *The Engineer* had published details provided by Drummond of the cost of repairs to Westinghouse brake-fitted stock over the period October 1878 to June 1879.[41]

'The tables have been extracted for us by Mr. D. Drummond from the books of his Company. Every penny that has been expended during nine months in maintaining the automatic brake in perfect order on 333 vehicles, and over 35 engines in regular service on the North British Railway. We may add that the outlay on repairs as compared with the first cost of the apparatus, is as nearly as possible one penny per annum per pound sterling of first cost.'

The list detailed the type and the labour plus materials cost of ninety-seven repairs to twenty-three of the locomotives and 184 repairs to 119 carriages and non-passenger coaching stock.

It should be remembered that *The Engineer* strongly supported the Westinghouse brake and fiercely opposed the simple vacuum system. While it was indeed *'impossible to take exception'* to the data about the repairs, the report presented a very narrow view of the cost to the railway of maintaining the brake. Drummond did not provide information about the length of time that stock spent out of service while under repair and *The Engineer* made no comment. Neither was anything said about the frequency of repairs compared with other braking systems.

A CR Board Meeting in September *'resolved that the Trains of this Company shall as soon as possible be fitted with Continuous Brakes'* and a committee of four Directors was set up to oversee the process.[42]

THE STEEL-MCINNES BRAKE FALLS OUT OF FAVOUR

Although the Board minute did not specify the type of brake to be adopted, the Steel-McInnes system was falling out of favour. In January 1880 five First class carriages were under construction by Brown, Marshall & Co. The Traffic Committee '*Read Mr Brittain's letter asking authority to fit these carriages with Westinghouse brakes. Work to be done at lowest practical cost.*'[43]

On 21st September the Traffic Committee '*read Mr Steel's letter of 26 ultimo. asking a Certificate in regard to the working of his brake upon the Caledonian line.*' The Committee declined to provide the certificate.[44]

At the time of the Newark brake trials, *Engineering* described the Steel-McInnes system as:

'*one which we cannot help regarding as more perfect in theory than practice. The idea of carrying a store of compressed air in each carriage and applying the brakes by relieving the pressure in the connecting pipes is undoubtedly good, but the means … appear to be faulty. The arrangements are especially such as to lead to great – and we fear unavoidable leakage – while they also fail in giving that promptness of action which is so essential to the efficiency of a continuous brake.*'[45]

A technical treatise on continuous brakes published in 1882 amplified the latter problem:

'*A second objection is the enormous amount of air used at each application of the brake. To apply the brake with full power, all the cylinders, with the brake-pipe, have to be emptied.*

A third objection is the unavoidably slow action resulting from the fact that, at the engine, an enormous volume of air has to be discharged through a pipe of comparatively small diameter before the brakes are applied.'[46]

FINAL ADOPTION OF THE WESTINGHOUSE SYSTEM

By November 1880 Mr Sharp (one of the four Directors on the CR committee) '*reported his communications with the Westinghouse Company representative.*' The Board authorised him and Smithells '*to bring up an agreement with the Westinghouse Company for supplying this Company with their Brake.*'[47]

A fortnight later it was agreed to fit 500 carriages and fifty locomotives with the Westinghouse brake. There was clearly an on-going dispute with Steel, because the Board resolved in the same minute '*to accept the arrangement with Steel & McInnes and the Westinghouse Co. suggested by Mr Sharp (on the terms contained in Mr Mackenzie's letter of 23rd inst.).*'[48]

In mid-1881 it was formally recognised that non-passenger coaching stock needed through pipe fittings. The Loco & Stores Committee authorised Brittain to '*get 100 sets for Vans from Westinghouse Co. at contract price.*'[49] A month later the Traffic Committee '*read Mr Brittain's letter of the 24th ulto. reporting that we have about 250 Vehicles to which the connecting pipes without Brakes should be applied. The cost will be £5 each vehicle.*'[50]

By January 1882 the initial order for carriage and locomotive brakes was still not complete and the Board minutes recorded '*The question of extension to all the stock was delayed till the Brakes ordered are completed.*'[51] Two months later the Traffic Committee agreed that sixty new carriages which were under construction should also be Westinghouse fitted.[52]

PROGRESS IN FITTING THE WESTINGHOUSE BRAKE

In May the Traffic Committee reported that 754 vehicles had been fitted with Westinghouse brakes at a cost of £17,700 '*leaving to complete the Company's stock 824 vehicles*' and approved the '*suggestion to put in pipe connectors on Horse Boxes, Carriage Trucks and Fish & Game Trucks.*'[53] The estimated cost for completing the work was £12,000.

In June 1882 Irving Kempt informed the West Coast Conference that:

'*the Caledonian Co. had decided to adopt the Westinghouse's break on their own coaching stock, a portion of which had been already fitted up with it, and that his Directors desired that meantime new West Coast coaching stock be constructed with Westinghouse break appliances.*'[54]

Drummond assumed responsibility for the completion of the continuous brake programme. In November 1882 the Loco & Stores Committee recorded a letter,

'*from Mr Drummond reporting that the Rolling Stock ordered to be fitted with Westinghouse Brake has been completed. He estimates the cost of fitting the remaining plant at £30,000 and recommends that £5,000 be spent for this purpose each half year until the whole are completed.*

Mr Drummond authorised to fit, with as much despatch as possible, plant to the amount of £5,000.'[55]

The capital expenditure returns up to and including the half year ending January 1889 record sums averaging between £4,000 and £5,000 on existing locomotives, carriages and non-passenger coaching stock. Parts of a drawing which shows a Westinghouse installation on a Drummond 6-wheeled carriage underframe are shown in Figure 2.6. Some years later, the Westinghouse Company used a St. Rollox official photograph in its advertising material – see Plate 2.3.

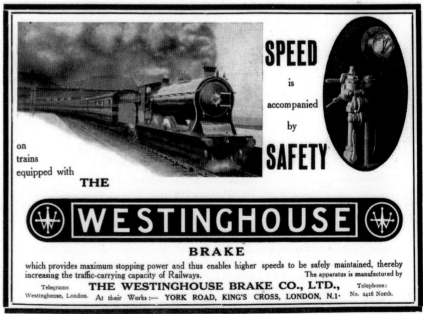

Plate 2.3
The Westinghouse Company heavily retouched an official CR photograph to use in its advertising material. The original photograph of *Sir James King* standing at the head of a train at Gourock is shown in Plate 9.12.

The End of the Chain Brake

Although the Caledonian phased out the Clark-Webb system on its own carriages, it was still to be found on WCJS trains. In 1880 the brake was modified so that it could be applied to carriages behind a Brake Van as well as to those in front. The improved system was fitted to WCJS carriages at £38 each.[56]

Even with this modification the brake's weaknesses were definitively exposed in an accident at Lockerbie on 14th May 1883, when the 9.15pm WCJS express from Glasgow could not stop in time to avoid hitting two wagons from a goods train that had been thrown foul of the Up main line by a previous minor collision.[57] The 14-carriage passenger train, travelling at 50 m.p.h., was so long that the brake could only act on half of them, three vehicles from the locomotive and four from the rear Brake Van. With brakes acting on only 126 tons out of a total weight of 270 tons it was impossible to pull up before the obstruction. Seven people, including the crew of the passenger train's leading locomotive, were killed.

In his comments Major Marindin, the Inspecting Officer, said:

'If he [the WCJS driver] had had at his command a quick-acting continuous brake throughout the whole train he might have done much to reduce speed before the collision took place … The Caledonian Company have adopted the Westinghouse continuous brake and are rapidly bringing it into use on their system. If the two West Coast Companies cannot agree on the same continuous brake, it is not too much to ask that the whole of the stock comprising these important trains should be so fitted.'[58]

Another collision in July 1883 at Perth involving a WCJS tourist train fitted with the chain brake was the last straw, according to Neele.[59] The Caledonian insisted that all WCJS vehicles should have continuous brakes.

Neele's final words on the chain brake episode and the L&NWR's choice of continuous brake were as follows:

'The Chain Brake had indeed proved itself so great a discomfort to travellers, had ceased to be used by any other Companies than the North London and the North-Western, had been condemned again and again by the Government Inspectors, that at last steps were taken by the Directors to adopt in some form a vacuum brake; unfortunately they determined to fit the stock with the Simple Vacuum, instead of the Automatic, and further trouble was in store in consequence.'[60]

The L&NWR did not adopt the Westinghouse air system, but opted initially for a vacuum brake. The real motivation behind the L&NWR's decision seems to have been ease of conversion and conformity with English companies with which it interchanged services.[61] The latter factor was not a consideration for Anglo-Scottish traffic, which ran straight through to its destination.

In consequence traffic travelling onto the Caledonian still required dual braking systems, with the added complication and expense in both fitting and maintenance. The dual system also increased the weight of the carriage. On newly built WCJS carriages, the common part of the brake gear was a joint expense, with the two companies paying for their particular brake components and the cost of fitting.

Drummond, of course, had tested the simple vacuum brake over a six-month period in 1877 and proved that the Westinghouse brake was far superior. The simple vacuum's shortcomings are described in more detail in the following paragraphs.

The Simple Vacuum Brake

In this system a vacuum was created in the train pipe by an ejector on the locomotive. The vacuum collapsed flexible cylinders under each carriage, which applied the brakes. It was not 'fail safe;' in the event of a leak or blockage in the pipe, the brakes could not be applied. To quote one of the reports of the Newark trials:

'it would be possible in five or six minutes to ruin a Smith [simple vacuum] brake from end to end of a train with no more lethal weapon than a pen knife.'[62]

Other major drawbacks to the system were highlighted as follows. Exhausting the train pipe used a great volume of steam; in a long train, there was a time lag before the brakes were applied to the rear carriages and the guard could not apply the brake unless an exhauster was fitted to the Brake Van, working through an axle-driven pump.

The Simple Vacuum Brake Fitted to WCJS

Agreement was reached in July 1883 to fit the simple vacuum brake to the WCJS fleet, but the demands of the summer season prevented the removal of carriages from traffic to make the modification. According to Neele,

'The two required separate fittings, but by a clever arrangement, Mr. Webb was able to make the brake block on the vehicles subservient to both systems, and to either separately.

On 10th March [1884] the 10.00 a.m. express train made its first journey from Euston fitted with the two brakes, the North-Western engines only capable of actuating the vacuum brake, and the Caledonian engines from Carlisle only being capable of applying the Westinghouse. Irrespective of the question of divergence of system, the brake, when applied to the 42 feet (radial) stock, was only serviceable on the two centre pairs of wheels, one half of the wheels running free.'[63]

The CR fitted the simple vacuum brake to a small number of carriages. In late 1884 a Traffic Committee minute authorised its fitting to *'three family carriages, five composites and ten brake vans'* at a cost of about £450.[64] All were types that were used in trains travelling over other railway systems. The work was completed in the first half of 1885, when the capital expenditure return contains an entry for *'vacuum brakes'* at £475 19s 11d.[65]

The simple vacuum brake did not last long on the L&NWR. At Carlisle in December 1886,

'One of our down expresses ran through the Citadel Station and struck a Midland engine standing 300 yards to the north. The vacuum was fitted to all fourteen vehicles on the train. A plug of ice was found about one foot on each side of the junction of the vacuum pipes, water having collected in the droop of the pipes.'[66]

The blockage had rendered the brakes inoperative. If a plug of ice had formed in the pipe of a train fitted with the Westinghouse brake or the automatic vacuum, the brakes on the carriages could not have been released.

Adoption of the Automatic Vacuum Brake

A month before the accident the L&NWR Directors had agreed to adopt an arrangement *'by which the vacuum brake could be worked either as automatic or non-automatic, with the understanding that as the automatic brake became general then the non-automatic could be dispensed with.'*[67]

The automatic brake acted in exactly the opposite way to the simple vacuum. The brakes were normally 'on' and were released by creating a vacuum in the train pipe. It was therefore fail-safe. The brakes were applied by admitting air to the pipe which rapidly filled the vacuum. Unlike the simple vacuum system the guard could apply the brake as easily as the driver, without the need for exhauster equipment in the Brake Van. A drawing of the final dual arrangement is shown in Figure 2.7.

THE REGULATION OF RAILWAYS ACT 1889

This far-reaching Act[68] signalled the end for the simple vacuum brake. It was enacted as a result of the Armagh disaster, in which a long excursion train was deliberately divided on a gradient after the locomotive had stalled. The rear of the train, which had the simple vacuum brake, ran away down the incline and collided with another train. Eighty lives were lost. The Act empowered the Board of Trade to require any railway company to adopt the block system of signalling, provide for the interlocking of points and signals and, echoing the wording of the 1878 Act,

'provide for and use on all passenger trains continuous brakes; the brakes must be instantaneous in action; self-applying in the event of any failure in continuity; capable of being applied to every vehicle of the train; and in regular use in daily working.'

At the time the Act became law, the L&NWR still had 790 vehicles fitted with the chain brake, 1,825 with simple vacuum and 1,096 with the automatic version. By June 1892 only fifteen chain-braked vehicles remained, and 6,587 vehicles had the automatic brake.[69]

The 1889 Act involved the Caledonian in further expenditure. An extract from the minutes in September 1890 informed Hugh Smellie of the decision to fit continuous brakes to CR stock to comply with the Act at an estimated cost of £21,854[70] – see Plate 2.4. The capital expenditure returns from the half years ending January 1891 to January 1893 record expenditure on *'Westinghouse Brake Fittings, Fitting up Old CR stock with, in compliance with Railway Regulation Act 1889.'*[71] The recorded expenditure also included fitting the brake to locomotives, non-passenger coaching stock and the usual CR contribution for West Coast Joint Stock expenditure.

Special drawings were issued. The register entry for drawing 6749, dated 19th May 1891, was for *'General Arrangement of W'house Brake on old CR carriages at present fitted with slide brake arrangement.'*[72] This is reproduced as Figure 2.8. Other drawings issued at the same time were numbers 6752 and 6760. These have not survived.

IDENTIFICATION OF PIPED-ONLY VEHICLES

Commencing in January 1905, the end pipes of the piped-only vehicles were painted red to distinguish them from braked vehicles, whose pipes were black. The practice applied to Westinghouse and vacuum braked stock alike.[73]

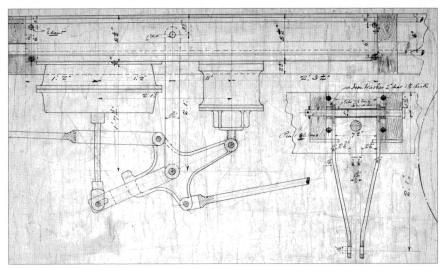

Figure 2.7
This is the dual Westinghouse/automatic vacuum brake fitting. It was applied to all the WCJS carriages and to Caledonian stock which was used for through traffic off the CR system. A large number of CR non-passenger coaching stock was also fitted with the device.

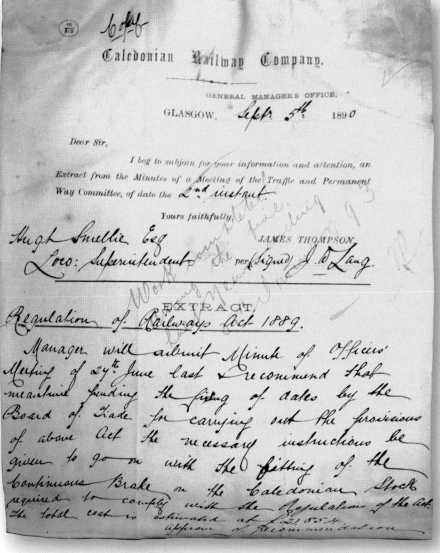

Plate 2.4
A copy of the memo authorising the conversion programme at a total cost of £21,854. The diagonal annotation, originally in red ink, reads *'work completed during the five half years ending 31st January 1893.'*

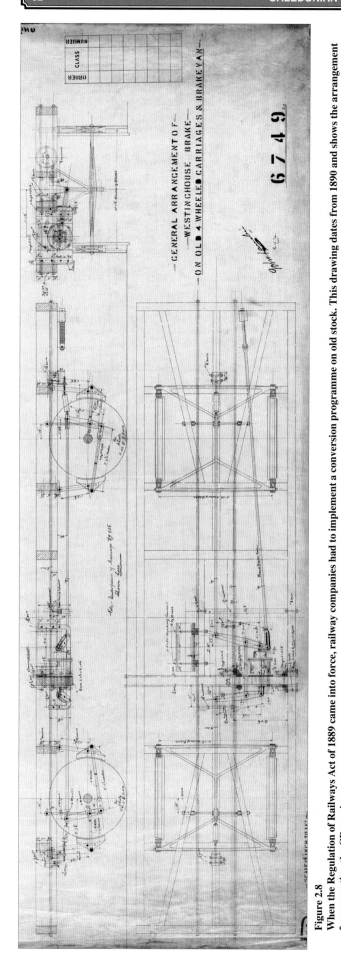

Figure 2.8
When the Regulation of Railways Act of 1889 came into force, railway companies had to implement a conversion programme on old stock. This drawing dates from 1890 and shows the arrangement for converting the CR carriages.

REFERENCES

1. *Government and the Railways in the Nineteenth Century*, p. 170
2. NRS BR/CAL/1/1 p. 590
3. NRS BR/CAL/1/11 entry 551
4. NRS BR/CAL/1/14 entry 1982
5. Copied from the Statutory Requirements publication sent to the Caledonian in 1867 concerning the working of the Crieff & Methven Railway, in NRS BR/CAL/4/27
6. *The Engineer*, 24th May 1872, pp. 360-61
   Engineering, 24th May, pp. 344-47
7. *Locomotive Magazine*, volume 51 (1945), p. 7
8. *The Engineer*, 18th June 1875, pp. 418-19
9. *The Engineer*, 18th June 1875, p. 427
10. *West Coast Joint Stock*, p. 304
11. *Railway Reminiscences*, p. 169
12. *West Coast Joint Stock*, p. 307
13. NRS BR/WCC/1/6 minute 925
14. NRS BR/WCC/1/7 minute 1313
15. NRS BR/WCC/1/7 minute 1394
16. NRS BR/WCC/1/7 minute 1406
17. NRS BR/CAL/1/22 entry 820
18. *The Engineer*, 18th June 1875, pp. 415-16
    Engineering, 18th June, pp. 511-16
19. *Railway Reminiscences*, p. 206
20. *The Engineer*, 25th June 1875, p. 434
21. *The Engineer*, 18th June 1875, p. 415
22. *The Engineer*, 25th June 1875, pp. 433-34
    Engineering, 25th June, pp. 524-30
23. *The Engineer*, 2nd July 1875, p. 1
24. *Railway Reminiscences*, p. 320
25. *The Engineer*, 5th January 1877, pp. 2-4, 6, 10
26. *The North British Railway*, Volume 1, pp. 190-92
27. *Engineering*, 19th January 1877, p. 53
28. *The Railway Moon*, p. 376
29. *The Railway Moon*, p. 376
30. NRS BR/CAL/1/23 entry 841
31. NRS BR/CAL/1/23 entry 407
32. NRS BR/CAL/1/23 entry 1023
33. *Engineering*, 15th November 1878, p. 401
34. *The Engineer*, 15th June 1877, p. 410
35. NRS BR/CAL/1/24 entry 410
36. NRS BR/CAL/1/24 entry 1047
37. NRS BR/CAL/1/24 entry 1223
38. NRS BR/CAL./23/4 (37)
39. 41 Vict. Cap. 20
40. NRS BR/CAL/1/25 entry 227
41. *The Engineer*, 18th July 1879, pp. 46-47
42. NRS BR/CAL/1/25 entry 1636
43. NRS BR/CAL/1/25 entry 823
44. NRS BR/CAL/1/25 entry 1670
45. *Engineering*, 25th June 1875, p. 530
46. *Continuous Railway Brakes*, p. 70
47. NRS BR/CAL/1/26 entry 42
48. NRS BR/CAL/1/26 entry 130
49. NRS BR/CAL/1/26 entry 1180
50. NRS BR/CAL/1/26 entry 1348
51. NRS BR/CAL/1/27 entry 300
52. NRS BR/CAL/1/27 entry 448
53. NRS BR/CAL/1/27 entry 816
54. NRS BR/WCC/1/8 minute 1947
55. NRS BR/CAL/1/27 entry 1441
56. NRS BR/WCC/1/7 minute 1772
57. Described in *West Coast Joint Stock*, pp. 286-87
58. TNA RAIL 1053/72/23, pp. 32-46
59. *Railway Reminiscences*, p. 300
60. *Railway Reminiscences*, p. 277
61. *The Railway Moon*, pp. 377-78
62. *The Engineer*, 18th June 1875, p. 415
63. *Railway Reminiscences*, p. 300
64. NRS BR/CAL/5/11, p. 19
65. NRS BR/CAL/23/5 (32)
66. *Railway Reminiscences*, p. 319
67. *Railway Reminiscences*, p. 320
68. 52 & 53 Vict. Cap. 57
69. *Railway Reminiscences*, p. 398
70. NRS BR/CAL/5/11 p. 65
71. NRS BR/CAL/23/7 (34), (37), (32), (29) and (31)
72. RHP 68569
73. Special instructions, *July 1906 Working Timetable*, p. 151

2.2: COMMUNICATION BETWEEN DRIVER AND GUARD

Communication between driver and guard was an early concern of the Board of Trade and the railway companies. One-way communication was originally by means of the engine whistle, but trains became longer, speed increased and the breaksman who was exposed to the elements gave way to a guard within a carriage. There was now no effective means of communication between front and rear of the train. As mentioned in the previous section, this was addressed in 1862, when the Statutory Requirements for Railways included the statement *'There should be a means of communication between a guard at the tail of every passenger train and the engine driver.'*

In 1865, Captain Tyler of the Railway Inspectorate was asked to write a report for the Secretary of the Board of Trade *'on the subject of inter-communication in railway trains.'* It was requested to inform the deliberations of a Railway Clearing House committee. The report, which contained a potted history of the subject, was published in *The Engineer*.[1] The salient points are described below.

The main danger that exercised railway management was when *'carriages were dragged along, sometimes for miles, in a disabled condition, or on fire, unknown to the engine driver.'* The first solution was for an *'under guard'* to act as a lookout facing backwards to supplement the breaksmen of the time, whose duty was to look forward along the train. The *'under guard'* was adopted by the GWR and L&NWR and was publicised by the Commissioners of Railways in 1847. The L&NWR proposed in addition to enable the lookout to *'have the power of sounding the whistle on the engine.'* The arrangement for doing this was not specified, but must have been some sort of cord system.

CONTINUOUS CARRIAGE FOOTBOARDS

In 1851 a second circular was issued suggesting that *'the power of travelling along trains while in motion should be given to the guards'* and urging the more general adoption of rear-facing guard's seats. The idea of a guard clambering along the outside of carriages while the train was in motion sounds odd to the modern reader, but it was common practice in Belgium at the time. It avoided the need to stop the train to attend to an emergency signal.

At the time, carriages were fitted with individual steps under each door, like their stage coach predecessors. Several English railway companies were willing to entertain the idea of lengthening the footboards, with the result that a Railway Clearing House sub-committee was set up to consider the proposal in detail. A list of questions was drawn up and circulated to every UK railway company. Only thirty-five replies were received.

The Caledonian was one of the non-respondents. The Board minute was entitled *'Hand Rails along Carriages,'* but obviously referred to the RCH questionnaire.

'Read circular by Railway Commissioners recommending the adoption of hand rails along carriages, as a means of enabling persons to pass along trains in motion.

Resolved to decline to adopt the suggestion but no answer to be sent.'[2]

Most of the comments that were received were negative. Among the objections to the idea were those concerning operational problems such as inadequate clearance at bridges and the encouragement of crime – all but five of the replies thought that passengers would defraud the company by moving into a superior class compartment and all but one thought that robberies and assaults would occur.

Four companies had tried the idea, mainly for ticket collection purposes. One had discontinued it after an accident and one in anticipation that an accident would happen. All four thought that the drawbacks outweighed the benefits.

The sub-committee summarised the replies as follows:

'That there are several railways the dimensions of whose permanent structures would prevent the plan from being generally adopted, without which it would be inoperative; that the expense of the alteration [which the sub-committee estimated at £165,855] would be out of all proportion to the benefits that would be derived from it; that it would expose the public to great danger and to robbery, and the companies to fraud; and that, therefore, it is not desirable to adopt it.'

Continuous footboards were introduced eventually, but not to allow access by the guard. In late 1878 the Caledonian Board was informed of the Board of Trade's *'suggestion'* about continuous carriage footboards and an increase in platform height. The Board agreed that they should *'be altered gradually.'*[3]

GOVERNMENT PRESSURE FOR A COMMUNICATION SYSTEM

There the matter rested until 1853, when another serious accident occurred on 3rd January on the L&NWR. Three people were killed in a head-on collision between two trains on single track near Oxford.[4] This led to an investigation into good practice in Britain and on the Continent. An elaborate report was drawn up which identified three systems in current use.

An electrical system on the Orleans Railway did not work very well. A mirror on another French railway, placed so that the guard could see back down the train was *'admitted to have many defects.'* Finally, *'a rope attached to a bell on the tender, or to the steam whistle, carried along the tops of the carriages, supported on brackets, and placed within reach of the guards and brakesmen,'* was used on the Dutch, Prussian, Hanoverian, and other German railways.

Members of the select committee of the House of Commons on Railway and Canal Bills reported to the House the resolution,

'That provision should be made for enforcing the means of constant communication between all the servants to whom the safety of the passengers in any train is entrusted.'

SLOW ADOPTION OF COMMUNICATION SYSTEMS

Further circulars were issued in 1854 and 1857, but there was little progress. By 1858, the House of Commons Select Committee was losing patience. Having already said in one circular that *'it should be imperative on every railway company to establish means of communication between guard and engine driver,'* a second, more strongly worded, circular in September said:

'My lords regret that the railway companies have as yet made so little progress in adopting a means of communication between the engine driver and guards of trains, by means of a cord or otherwise, which shall be certain of attracting the immediate attention of either the guard or driver, and not be liable to be misunderstood; and my lords trust they will no longer delay to provide an efficient means of communication as well as a sufficiency of brake power for stopping the trains.'

The Scottish North Eastern, at least, was quick to comply. In the Locomotive Superintendent's report to shareholders in 1859, Thomas Yarrow stated that *'Communication between Guard and Engine Driver has been in full operation since September last and is working well.'*[5]

The arrangement used is not recorded, but one assumes that it was a cord system of some description.

FIRST USE OF AN ALARM SYSTEM ON THE CALEDONIAN

In September 1857 a CR Director had raised the subject of communication between guard and engine driver. The matter was remitted to the Loco & Stores Committee.[6] Later in the year a letter from the Board of Trade and a report by Colonel Yolland of the Railway Inspectorate was remitted to the Board for action.[7]

The Caledonian first experimented with a communication system in 1858, when two separate minutes record first the Board of Trade letter on the lack of progress and the resolve to try a system on the Greenock line,[8] and second in November the agreement to a trial.[9] There is no record of the trial's outcome or the type of communication system used.

THE CORD ALARM SYSTEM

The Board of Trade approved the cord alarm system in 1859 for communication between guard and driver.[10] The system used in the UK was developed by Thomas Harrison, the North Eastern Railway's Chief Engineer. In his report on the Penrith accident of 1871, by which time it had also been adopted as a passenger alarm, Capt. Tyler described it as follows:

'Individual cords are fitted to both sides of every vehicle, each cord running the length of the vehicle through rings or pulleys generally mounted at the cornice or at the roof edge at an average of 3 feet apart, so that the cord is accessible to passengers.

Only the cords on the off-side of the train (i.e. right hand side in direction of travel) are coupled up to form the means of communication. It is clearly desirable, as long as the cord communication is employed, that the passengers should find it always on one particular side of a train; and as the carriages may run either end first, it has for that reason been considered necessary to provide cords on both sides of them.

The unused cord on the near-side of the train is a fixture, its ends being fastened down to the ends of the carriage with hooks and eyes.'[11]

The cord's termination was a spring clip similar to that used to attach a dog's lead to its collar. An enlargement of a photograph (Plate 2.5) shows the arrangement.

THE CALEDONIAN ADOPTS THE CORD ALARM

In December 1860 the Caledonian's General Committee read and remitted to the West Coast Conference,

'a letter from Mr Cawkwell intimating that the L&NW Co. have resolved to establish communication between Guard and Driver by means of a rope and bell and asking the Company, in common with others with whom they interchange traffic, to furnish them plant with the necessary apparatus.'[12]

Although there is no minute of a Board decision, there is no reason to doubt that the Caledonian followed the trend of the railways north of the Thames and adopted the Harrison cord shortly after the L&NWR's decision. St. Rollox drawing 547 was for a *'cord pulley for communication between Driver and Guard.'* Its date cannot be ascertained, but it was before 1864.

ALERTING THE DRIVER

Communicating with the driver on a noisy footplate was problematic. The L&NWR used an auxiliary whistle, which the cord operated by means of a lever. This was the last item in Neele's lengthy catalogue of the cord system's shortcomings:

'the testing prior to starting from stations, when the guard had to satisfy himself that all was complete by awaiting the sound of the responding whistle – the startling scream of this whistle suddenly bursting out, to the dismay and almost terror of the bystanders, all added to the annoyances with which the scheme was burdened.'[13]

The Caledonian originally used a gong attached to the offside of the tender towards the front. It was sounded by a hammer driven by clockwork. No reference to a drawing has been found in the St. Rollox register. There are examples of the arrangement in the Album of CR Locomotives which was produced in 1897. The arrangement with its connecting cord is shown in Plate 2.6.

Later, the CR followed its West Coast partner in using a cord connected to the whistle. This change probably took place in 1883, when it was combined with the passenger alarm system. St. Rollox drawing 3342 dated November 1882 refers to a *'Passenger Communication Apparatus'* and drawing 3434 of January 1883 was for *'Cord Communication to Whistle.'*[14] The drawing, which shows the component parts, is in poor condition and not suitable for reproduction. The arrangement was probably first fitted to the two exhibition locomotives 123 and 124. Figure 2.9 shows the arrangement.[15]

The system was adapted for passenger communication and probably remained in use until the adoption of the internal 'communication cord' system in 1900 – its successful activation was quoted in the accident involving Miss Pirie in 1889, which is described in Chapter 14. His attempt to rectify a twist in the cord connection to the locomotive whistle caused the fatal accident to David Fenwick, the driver of the Royal Train in 1898.

REFERENCES

1. *The Engineer*, 7th July 1865, pp. 1-3, and 14th July 1865, p. 18
2. NRS BR/CAL/1/10 entry 548
3. NRS BR/CAL/1/24 entry 1346
4. TNA RAIL 1053/51/66
5. NRS BR/SNE/1 p. 7
6. NRS BR/CAL/1/11 entry 1101
7. NRS BR/CAL/1/11 entry 1295
8. NRS BR/CAL/1/11 entry 1348
9. NRS BR/CAL/1/11 entry 2011
10. TNA MT7/29 under 'Communication'
11. TNA RAIL 1053/60/57
12. NRS BR/CAL/1/12 entry 1229
13. *Railway Reminiscences*, p. 168
14. RHP 67881
15. *The Engineer*, 31st May 1895, supplement

2.3: PASSENGER ALARM SYSTEMS

The Railway Clearing House committee report of 1853 which was quoted in the previous section had this to say about providing a means of communication between passengers and the train crew. Again, the quotation is from Captain Tyler's report of 1865.

'Without overlooking the possibility of such an arrangement being occasionally of service, the committee have been unable to persuade themselves that it would not lead to greater disasters than it could, on any view of the matter, prevent. Unless the guards and engine-drivers had orders to stop the train whenever a passenger made a signal the privilege would be useless to the latter. It, however, requires little acquaintance with railway travelling to be convinced that its dangers would be greatly increased if the train were to be stopped whenever and wherever a passenger, under the influence of fear or levity, chose to make a signal.

The committee is not, therefore, prepared, in the first instance, to recommend any arrangement or regulation which would put it in the power of the timid or reckless to control the discretion of the guard or engine driver, and to put the safety of the whole train in peril. ... Should it, however, appear that the advantage of providing passengers with such means of communication countervails its dangers, the committee see no mechanical difficulty in the way.

But it is of the opinion that no such concession should be made until the legislature has specially guarded against the abuse of the privilege by making it penal.'[1]

PUBLIC OPINION FORCES CHANGE

Nuisance and crime of a petty and more serious nature were rife in the confines of British and Continental railway carriage compartments from the start of railway travel. An article in *The True Line* describes the activities of cardsharps around Glasgow in the 1850s.[2] Passengers in America, where carriages were open from end to end with a conductor circulating throughout the train, were much less vulnerable.

A typical expression of the groundswell of opinion was contained in a letter written by Vaughan Pendred, the editor of *The Mechanic's Magazine*, who later took over the editorial chair of *The Engineer*. By the time he composed his letter, a man had been murdered in the compartment of a French train. Ironically, the assassin had gained access to the compartment by using the continuous footboards; he escaped the same way.

Pendred echoed the RCH committee's statement that there was no mechanical difficulty in providing a passenger alarm system.

'A cord run along the roofs of the carriages is all that is necessary to establish a certain, simple, and effectual means of communication between the guard and engine-driver·, and thus far the plan has been adopted with good results on a few lines. It is at least a step in the right direction; but this is not enough.

The guard may indeed see what takes place outside his train, but he is of course totally unaware of what takes place within. He cannot know that in one compartment the garrotter

ABOVE LEFT: Plate 2.5
This enlargement shows the termination of the Harrison cord. It was a metal spring clip that was connected to an eye on the cord of the adjacent carriage.

ABOVE RIGHT: Plate 2.6
This enlargement from NRM St. Rollox collection ref: SRX 198 shows the tender attached to Conner 2-4-0 number 34. The Harrison cord runs from an eyelet towards the rear of the tender to the actuating mechanism of the gong.

RIGHT: Figure 2.9
This drawing from *The Engineer* shows the arrangement for attaching the Harrison cord to the whistle, which was a more effective warning device than the gong. The locomotive is the Lambie Class '13' 4-4-0.

is throttling his victim, or rendering him insensible with a handkerchief steeped in chloroform. He never dreams that the madman in another place, endued with that more than human strength which usually follows the loss of reason, meditates foul murder on the helpless individual sitting opposite him. He cannot be aware of the brutal assault which may take place in the very next carriage to him. He knows nothing of it till he reaches the next station, perhaps thirty miles off; he hears no cries for help, though uttered by a soul in their last extremity.

We find that an express train presents us with the strange spectacle of four or five hundred people divided into isolated communities for hours together, without laws, without police, who may at any moment be placed in the most extreme danger, without the power to extend a finger to save themselves, or those dearer to them than life itself, from agony and death.'[3]

The language and style may seem melodramatic and over-wrought to the modern reader, but it no doubt accurately reflected the feelings and mood of the time.

More than a decade after the committee's pronouncements, and two years after Pendred's letter to *The Engineer*, the first murder of a passenger in Britain occurred, when the banker Thomas Briggs was killed at night on a North London Railway train.[4] The public outcry and the demand for a communication system between passengers and the driver and guard could no longer be ignored. *The Engineer* described it as follows:

'the influence of the great pressure at last brought to bear by a public incensed by the indifference with which railway men regarded a series of calamities which might have been avoided by proper precaution.'[5]

THE INVESTIGATION OF 1864

As a direct result of the public's reaction to Briggs' murder, a sub-committee of railway general managers was set up under the auspices of the Railway Clearing House. There were no Scottish representatives. Its task was to examine best practice in Britain and on the Continent and to evaluate new designs for passenger communication.

THE SUB-COMMITTEE'S REPORT

The report's findings were trailed in *The Engineer*, and subsequently covered in full. The preliminary article gave some idea of the sub-committee's thinking:

'a means of communicating between passenger and guard is certainly not required on metropolitan or suburban lines which have stoppages of the trains at short and frequent intervals. The principle of communicating by electricity is considered to be the best, provided it can be carried out free from various practical objections which have been urged against the system.'[6]

Two different system requirements were emerging. Passengers were supposed to communicate with the guard, while the guard communicated with the driver.

Having excluded the need for a passenger alarm from trains on the North London Railway where the murder took place, the full report appeared in the technical press in April.[7] It was informed by Captain Tyler's report, and leant heavily on his summary of the 1853 findings.

'Then, as now, a great variety of optical signals, and signals by sound and electricity were suggested, which experiments, so far as they have gone, have proved to be too inefficient

and uncertain in their operation to make them admissible in practice.'

A major factor in the sub-committee's deliberations was the *'frequent re-arrangement and subdivision of trains at the principal towns and junctions,'* which dictated that any arrangement had to be simple, robust and in universal use.

Whatever system was to be adopted, the difficulty of gaining quick access to the distressed passenger remained. The idea of using outside footboards was again proposed and rejected. The sub-committee could not *'doubt that the amount of risk of life and limb involved in this practice is such as to render its introduction in England utterly unjustifiable, even if possible.'*

With regard to the adoption of the American practice of *'internal communication from one part of the train to the other, by means of a central passage'*:

'the sub-committee is satisfied that the habits of English travellers would not tolerate any such system. Apart from the enormous outlay which would be involved in the reconstruction of the stock of the different companies to secure a doubtful advantage, the delays which would arise in the loading and unloading of trains, particularly in the metropolis and at other great centres of population, would be productive of very serious evils.'

The sub-committee made no firm recommendation for a communication system, having examined *'the very many plans brought before it.'*

'the members are satisfied that no one of these plans in its present shape presents in itself the means of effecting the communication with that degree of certainty which would make it practically efficient and to be depended upon, and which would justify them in recommending its adoption. The sub-committee believes that the value of the most promising of such inventions can only be established by their being put into use for a reasonable period of time, and being subjected to and tested by all the fluctuating and disturbing circumstances which are involved in the passage of trains made up of many component parts over a complicated system of railway.'

Having rejected all the available solutions, the sub-committee concluded that:

'it is desirable, if practicable, to give passengers by express, or other trains running for a considerable distance without stopping, the means, in case of emergency, of attracting the attention of the guard, and of enabling him to stop the train at the next station or under the protection of the next fixed signals, and they recommend that no effort should be spared on the part of the railway companies to attain this object, it being borne in mind that, in order to give the public the full advantage of the communication upon the long through trains, many of which traverse several lines of railways, it is absolutely necessary that all the companies should adopt the same plan.'

EXPERIMENTS ON THE CALEDONIAN

In April 1866, the CR Board noted that a Bill was going through parliament *'to compel communication between passengers and guards.'[8]* The Caledonian saw the way the wind was blowing. In 1867 the General Committee authorised the trial of one system *'on a Third Class carriage'* and considered another.[9] There are no details of the systems and no records of any outcome.

THE 1868 ACT OF PARLIAMENT

A new Regulation of Railways Act was passed in 1868.[10] It followed the sub-committee's recommendation that an alarm system was only needed on long-distance trains. Its Provisions for Safety of Passengers (Section 22) required that:

'After the First Day of April One thousand eight hundred and sixty-nine every Company shall provide, and maintain in good Working Order, in every Train worked by it which carries Passengers, and travels more than Twenty Miles without stopping, such efficient Means of Communication between the Passengers and the Servants of the Company in charge of the Train as the Board of Trade may approve.'

A railway company contravening the regulation would be liable to a fine 'not exceeding Ten Pounds for each case of default.' The railway companies were granted their wish to penalise passengers for improper use.

'Any Passenger who makes use of the said Means of Communication without reasonable and sufficient Cause shall be liable for each Offence to a Penalty not exceeding Five Pounds.'

THE RAILWAY MANAGERS' PROPOSALS

Having been obliged by the Act to provide a passenger communication system, but armed only with the opinion that an effective system did not yet exist, the sub-committee reconvened to present the views of the railway managers to the Board of Trade. The technical press reported that:

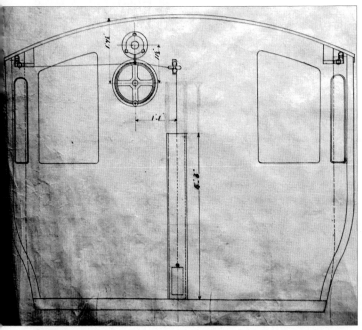

Figure 2.10
Part of St. Rollox drawing 3454 of 1883, which shows the weight that tensioned the Harrison cord. Also visible is the device for sounding the alarm bell in the guard's compartment. To quote a description in *The Engineer*: 'The cord in the van is passed around a wheel having a diameter of about 15 inches furnished with a groove round its circumference. An adjustable cam is screwed onto its circumference so that, when the wheel is turned by the cord on its being pulled, the cam strikes and pushes over a lever projecting from a bell, and the bell then rings on continuously for about seven minutes, unless purposely stopped and put out of action by the guard.'

'A deputation of railway managers lately attended at the railway department of the Board of Trade, in order to lay before the officials, for their approval, a system of train communication. Since this interview, in which the managers of most of the principal railways declared themselves in favour of one particular system, another on an entirely different principle has been tried, and with such favourable results that they have postponed their decision as to the choice of a universal system; this ultimate decision to be communicated in due time to the Board. We are not in a position at present to publish more information, but we may add, to correct a mistaken impression, that the selection of the system to be adopted will rest, not with the Board of Trade, but with the railway companies, subject to the veto of the Board.'[11]

THE APPROVED ALARM SYSTEMS

The Board of Trade approved the cord system again, this time as meeting the requirement for passenger communication in the 1868 Act. Two electrical systems, which had been developed by the South Eastern and the London, Brighton & South Coast railways were approved at the same time.[12]

The system adopted by the London & South Western Railway was patented by Preece, the L&SWR's Telegraph Superintendent. It was described by Capt. Tyler in his report as 'the most promising apparatus that I have yet seen.' It required the passenger to break a glass, which allowed a heavy iron semaphore arm to drop. This completed the electrical circuit and actuated a trembler bell. The position of the semaphore arm indicated the compartment where the alarm was raised.

THE WEST COAST CONFERENCE ADOPTS THE CORD SYSTEM

Two months after the 1868 Act became law a pair of WCJS Composite carriages was fitted up with the cord system for inspection. The system was approved and it was decided that all WCJS carriages should be so fitted.[13] A joint CR/L&NWR notice to passengers, which used the standard wording produced by the Railway Clearing House with a minor alteration, was agreed at the same time. According to Neele, 'an undertaking was given to bring it in general use [on the L&NWR] on 1st August, 1869.'[14]

The cord was to be sited on the edge of the carriage roof 'supported by pullies.' At the previous West Coast Conference Meeting, the CR's Benjamin Conner and Richard Bore of the L&NWR had 'explained the difficulty in placing the cord under the carriage roof, there not being room between the top of the door and the cornice of the carriage.'[15] A later section of the same minute stated that the cord would be 'attached to a bell or whistle on the engine.'

ADOPTION OF THE CORD SYSTEM BY THE CALEDONIAN

Although there is no clear-cut evidence in Board or Committee minutes, it is reasonable to assume that the CR adopted the cord system at the same time as the L&NWR, although the first drawing to appear in the St. Rollox register is number 1470, dated May 1873. This was for a 'bell for passenger brake van signal apparatus.' They were probably the six vans that were built to the capital account in the period ending July 1873. The vans are described in Chapter 6.2. Other drawings (2231, 2232, 2240 dating from 1877) describe a cord bell signalling apparatus. The drawings have not survived.

Drawing 3454[16] which dates from 1883 shows the system's other essential component. A counterweight in the Brake Van held the cord in tension – see Figure 2.10. When pulled the cord released a cam which caused a bell to ring for several minutes. The bell's mechanism was driven by clockwork and was wound up by the guard before the start of each journey.

DEFICIENCIES OF THE CORD ALARM

Various accident reports highlighted the system's drawbacks after Board of Trade approval. They were summed up in the report on the 1871 accident at Penrith, in which Captain Tyler produced a general report on the cord system, based on his own experience when travelling on L&NWR trains.[17]

He summarised the failings as follows:

'There are too many adjustments to be attended to whenever a train is made up, and before it is started, … such that this very simple system depends for success upon a complication of adjustments which must be difficult to invariably enforce; and which are the more liable to be neglected by railway servants, after a long period during which the system has been proved to be not required. The cord system is, no doubt, capable of some improvement. … But I do not myself think that the cord-system will ever be a satisfactory system.'

THE BoT WITHDRAWS APPROVAL OF THE HARRISON CORD

A little over two years after approving Harrison's cord system as meeting the requirements of the 1868 Act and its general adoption by the railway companies, the Board of Trade wrote to James Allport on 15th July 1872 intimating that, on account of the inefficiency of the system, and in some cases its total failure, approval would be formally withdrawn within three months.[18] Companies were requested to submit some other means of communication for approval. On representation from Allport the time for the withdrawal of approval was extended to the 1st August 1873.[19] A letter dated 30th July 1873 was sent by the Board to 123 railway companies notifying the withdrawal.[20]

A SENIOR RAILWAYMAN MAKES EXCUSES

In the 1874 Shipton-on-Cherwell accident on the GWR, about 100 passengers were either killed or injured. The accident was caused by a broken tyre, but passengers had tried and failed to raise the alarm by pulling the cord. The ineffectiveness of the cord alarm system was again highlighted in the Inspecting Officer's report.[21] James Grierson, the General Manager of the GWR, no doubt spoke for many of his counterparts in a long appendix to the report, which included the following statement:

'If therefore the Board of Trade or their officers were and are acquainted with a more reliable system [than the Harrison cord], it is not the fault of the railway companies that it has not been adopted, as notwithstanding their repeated applications, they have never been told what it is.'

This was pure bluster and an attempt to cover up the railway companies' lack of initiative. Grierson sat on the managers' sub-committee, and must have known that, as quoted at the end of the article written five years previously,[22] the BoT's powers were:

'limited to the _approval_ of the means of communication which any company may wish to employ and they have no authority to prescribe any particular system for general adoption.'[23]

THE CALEDONIAN'S USE OF AN ELECTRICAL ALARM SYSTEM

Six new sets of carriages were drafted onto the Callander & Oban in summer 1889, and an unspecified number of similar vehicles were assigned to the new Gourock service which opened on 1st June. As reported in the technical press, the carriages for the C&O were fitted with a 'system of electrical communication between passengers, guard and driver.'[24] Drawings had been issued in October the previous year. Number 5825 was for 'whistle for Electric Communication with Brake Van' and 5833 was for the apparatus 'between Compartments and Brake Van on Passenger Train.' It was operated by:

'pulling a small knob, placed over one of the side windows in each compartment. This completes an electric circuit and a detent engaging into a small wheel on the alarm apparatus in guard's or brake compartment is disengaged by an electro-magnet. The detent wheel is fitted on the end of a cock communicating with the brake pipe and whistle, and by means of a spring coil … sounding the whistle and applying the brake.'

It is not known how many more carriages were fitted with this apparatus. There is no reference to its use in new construction after Drummond's departure from the Caledonian in 1890.

THE RAILWAY COMPANIES CONDEMN THE CORD SYSTEM

Despite the withdrawal of Board of Trade approval, the cord system lingered on in default of anything better. Harry Pollitt, who was soon to become the Locomotive Engineer of the Manchester, Sheffield & Lincolnshire Railway summed up the cord alarm's deficiencies yet again in a paper read to the 1892 International Congress on Railways in St. Petersburg. Part of his speech was lifted almost verbatim from Tyler's 1865 report without acknowledgement, which says something about the speed of technological progress in this area. He also listed 'the practical requirements of a capable, simple and economical system.'

Early in 1898 the Board of Trade made a determined attempt to make the railway companies reach a final, acceptable solution. The President appointed a committee which met at Liverpool Street station to 'report upon the best means of communication between passengers and guards in railway trains.'[25] The committee included Major General Hutchinson of the Railway Inspectorate. Special trains fitted with different alarm systems were provided by the Great Eastern, the London, Brighton & South Coast and the Great Central.

In July The Engineer reported the committee's findings.[26] The first of its three observations was that:

'the outside cord system should be condemned as inefficient, while the systems in which the cord or wire is inside the carriages cannot be regarded as satisfactory; the principal electrical systems and the communication by means of the brake may, however, be held to be efficient.'

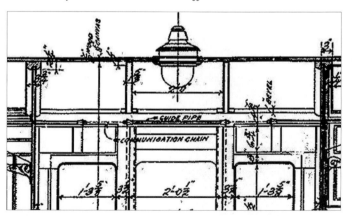

Figure 2.11
One of the first examples on the Caledonian of the familiar 'communication cord,' which the Caledonian, in common with other railways, adopted in 1900.

The committee then qualified the statement by saying that no electrical system could be definitively recommended.

Passenger and Train Crew Communication Combined

The committee's third observation led to the adoption of a system that allowed communication between everybody on every train. It suggested that the scope of the 1868 Act,

'should be extended so as to require the provision on all trains of an efficient means of communication between passengers and the servants in charge of the trains, which should also be used as a means of communication between the guards and the driver.'

Characteristics of a Suitable System

Finally, the committee set down six 'conditions which ... a method of communication should fulfil.' Most reiterated previous findings, such as universal adoption, but the fifth was new:

'it should not entail the use of additional couplings to those already existing-namely, the screw coupling, the side chains, the automatic brake and the heating apparatus – where in use.'

This left the way clear for a system that operated on the train brake, given the incompatibility of the various electrical systems. Ironically, Westinghouse and Steel-McInnes had offered this facility over twenty years previously.

Westinghouse's brake in the Caledonian trial in 1872 included a means of communication with the footplate crew. Each carriage had a cord which, when pulled, actuated a small semaphore on the end of the carriage. A spring-loaded valve allowed an escape of air in the train pipe, making a partial application of the brake. The pump was connected to the locomotive's whistle. A full description was given in the press.[27] Westinghouse brought out a modified arrangement in 1898[28] but it was not adopted by the CR.

In the Steel-McInnes system, whistles were connected to the pipes running along the carriage roofs, actuated by a cord running through each compartment. Pulling the cord sounded the whistle to alert the engine crew and guard and partially applied the brakes by releasing pressure from the upper part of the brake cylinder.[29] It can be seen in Figure 2.4.

The Final Universal Communication System

Parliament maintained the pressure to implement a universal, effective system which met the committee's recommendations. In February 1899 The Engineer reported:

Plate 2.7
This photograph shows how the operating spindle on the carriage end was cranked to clear the corridor connection.

'In reply to a question asked in the House of Commons as to which railway companies had taken steps to provide efficient means of communication on all passenger trains, as recommended by the report issued last June by the Departmental Committee appointed to inquire into the subject, Mr. Ritchie said the London, Brighton, and South Coast Railway, the South-Eastern, the Great Central, and the Furness Railway companies use approved means of communication. The question generally, he said, was being considered by a committee of general managers, and the Board will continue to press for a decision.'[30]

Six months later the following answer to a parliamentary question appeared in the technical press:

'Asked whether the railway general managers of this country had yet decided on the most suitable communication appliance to be fixed in passenger trains, the President of the Board of Trade said there was a preponderance of opinion in favour of what is known as the "brake system" of communication, and that most of the larger companies are taking steps to apply it.'[31]

The Caledonian Adopts the New System

In early 1900 the CR adopted the system that survived for the next sixty years. It was a sophisticated version of the Harrison cord, which removed the latter's major drawback by making each carriage self-contained. It put the system inside the carriage and was permanently operational on both sides and above each quarter-light, making four application points per compartment – see Figure 2.11. Compartments of corridor carriages had only two application points.

Each carriage was fitted with a control box attached to one end at about cantrail height. In the case of Brake Vans it was always at the end away from the Brake compartment. The control box contained a valve which was connected to the brake pipe. The air in the valve body was therefore under positive pressure from the Westinghouse reservoir. For dual-braked vehicles, the control box was connected to both brake systems.

The valve could be opened by rotating a spindle which ran across the end. The spindle was cranked through four 90 degree turns to clear the corridor connection, if fitted – see Plate 2.7. The spindle was connected at each end via cranks to the 'communication cord' in each compartment. This was a continuous chain that ran from one end of the carriage to the other. The cross spindle included a tell-tale device at each end which rotated to show a red face if the cord had been pulled.

Opening the valve bled air from a Westinghouse system, partially applying the brake. Air was admitted on vacuum-braked carriages with the same effect. The guard communicated with the driver in an emergency by making a brake application from his van. The partial brake application was sufficient to alert the driver of an emergency. The train remained within his control, as he could overcome the loss of pressure by pumping more air into the system, or exhausting it if the train was vacuum-braked. He then ran the train to a location where it could be stopped under the protection of signals.

The Transition Period

There are no Board minutes approving the adoption of the new communication system, or a published programme for the conversion of existing stock. One might have expected that the cost of conversion would have been charged to the capital account, but this was not the case.

The first drawing to depict the system as part of new carriage construction was St. Rollox 10150,[32] issued in early 1900. This was a Diagram 46 First to order H183. The end elevation of a Diagram

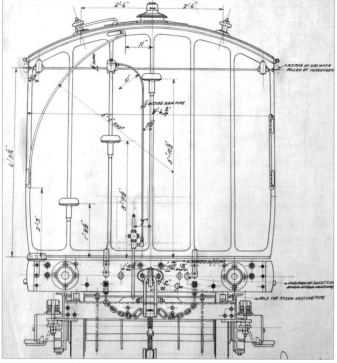

46 carriage with the system installed is shown in Figure 2.12. The Diagram 44 Composite drawing (St. Rollox 10562)[33] was also fitted.

Drawings for converting old stock were issued in February 1900. St. Rollox 10104 was entitled '*details for passenger communication apparatus*' and 10119 was an '*arrangement for passenger communication on carriages.*' Two months later drawing 10200 depicted the '*valve box and details.*' None of these drawings has survived.

The conversion programme took time to complete. Every railway was converting at the same time, so the demand on component manufacturers was huge. In the interim the Caledonian built new stock with cord rings to allow the use of old and new systems – see Plate 2.8. The last carriages to be fitted with cord rings on photographic evidence were the 50-foot Brake Composites to order H219, authorised in the half year ending January 1904 – see Plate 8.11. The last Pickering-built Diagram 47 Third of 1904 did not carry the rings, as shown in Plate 8.4.

Pending conversion of stock to the new system the Caledonian modified the working of the Harrison cord. Drawing 10084 dating from December 1899 shows it fitted to work directly on the brake valve in the guard's van. A better quality drawing of the same carriage design, but with an order number dating from December 1903, is shown in Figure 2.13. This indicates that the conversion process was still not complete.

CONVERSION COMPLETE

The CR Rule Book was a generic volume, common to all companies that were parties to the Railway Clearing House system, with alterations and additions to suit each railway. Appendix XII concerned the '*Regulations for Working Communication Cords between Passenger, Guard, and Engine Driver.*' The 1906 Rule Book stated that this Appendix was '*Not Applicable to Caledonian Line.*'[34]

ABOVE: Figure 2.12
The end elevation of Diagram 46 First fitted with the new passenger alarm system. The connection to the valve box was made from the Westinghouse brake standard upstand.

LEFT: Plate 2.8
A carriage from the transitional period before all stock was converted to the new alarm system which was fitted with Harrison cord rings to work with carriages that were not yet converted. It also gives a good view of the standard corridor connection.

RIGHT: Figure 2.13
The drawing dates from 1903. It shows the interim arrangement with the alarm bell removed and the Harrison cord rigged to apply the brake in the guard's van.

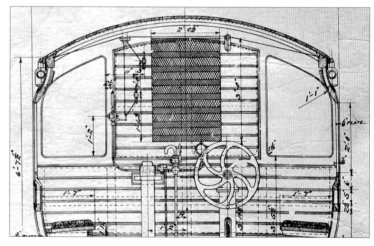

REFERENCES
1. *The Engineer*, 7th July 1865, p. 2
2. *The True Line*, issue 84, pp. 6-8
3. *The Engineer*, 22nd August 1862, p. 114
4. http://www.btp.police.uk/about_us/our_history/crime_history/the_first_railway_murder.aspx
5. *The Engineer*, 28th April 1865, p. 257
6. *The Engineer*, 3rd March 1865, p. 137
7. *The Engineer*, 28th April 1865, p. 257
8. NRS BR/CAL/1/14 entry 1957
9. NRS BR/CAL/1/15 entries 1018 and 1237
10. 31 & 32 Vict., Cap.119
11. *The Engineer*, 15th January 1869, p. 52
12. TNA MT7/47 under 'Communication'
13. NRS BR/WCC/1/8 minute 601
14. *Railway Reminiscences*, p. 168
15. NRS BR/WCC/1/8 minute 562
16. RHP 69656 and 68659
17. TNA RAIL 1053/60/57
18. TNA MT7/57 under 'Communication'
19. TNA MT7/57 under 'Communication'
20. TNA MT7/60 under 'Communication'
21. TNA RAIL 1057/2950/2
22. *The Engineer*, 15th January 1869, p. 52
23. TNA MT12/16 letter 1762
24. *Engineering*, 21st February 1890, p. 195
25. *The Engineer*, 25th February 1898, p. 185
26. *The Engineer*, 1st July 1898, p. 11
27. *Engineering*, 18th June 1872, p. 512
28. *The Engineer*, 22nd July 1898, p. 90
29. *The Engineer*, 18th June 1875, p. 427
30. *The Engineer*, 24th February 1899, p. 187
31. *The Engineer*, 27th October 1899, p. 424
32. NRM 7445/C RHP 70138
33. NRM 8002/C RHP 69165
34. CRA Archive ref: 3/3/1/8

2.4: ASPECTS OF CARRIAGE CONSTRUCTION

Almost all the carriages built by and for the Caledonian until 1869 ran on four wheels. The longest carriage was about 28 feet, supported on axles set a maximum of 14 feet 6 inches apart. If carriage length was to increase, additional support for the underframe was necessary. The British style of carriage body with multiple door openings was inherently weak and very little body distortion could be tolerated because doors would jam. The solution was to add a centre axle.

As described and illustrated in Chapter 6, some of the early 6-wheeled carriages were little, if any, longer than the earlier 4-wheeled stock. By the mid-1870s, however, carriage length had settled at 31 or 32 feet, on a wheelbase of 18 feet. This allowed an extra compartment in Third class carriages and more spacious accommodation and/or luggage space in superior class vehicles. This was an acceptable trade-off for the increased weight and cost of the new size carriages.

FLEXIBLE WHEELBASES

As carriages increased in length, their rigid wheelbase also increased. While this was not a problem on the wide radius curves of the original Caledonian main line, difficulties arose north of Perth. After the Caledonian established through services to Aberdeen following the takeover of the Scottish North Eastern Railway, it was noted that 15 feet 6 inches was *'the greatest distance between bearings of any carriage on the Caledonian system'* because of the *'sharp curves at Forfar on the Northern Section.'*[1] This effectively precluded rigid 6-wheeled carriages from travelling north of Perth. It also probably explains the continued construction of 4-wheeled carriages into the 1870s, after the establishment of the new standard carriage length of 31 feet on a 6-wheeled underframe. All these designs are discussed in Chapters 6. 2 and 6.3.

By the mid-1870s, if longer carriages were required, some solution to allow a longer wheelbase on existing track was needed. One of the major drawbacks of a long rigid wheelbase was that wheels skidded on curves, as the outer wheel travelled a greater distance than the inner. This led to increased wear on track and wheel, greater friction which required more tractive power, and a less comfortable ride for passengers. If the axles could be maintained at 90 degrees to the rail, as on straight track, skidding would cease.

The solution was a flexible wheelbase. This could be achieved by bogies, but they created other problems:

'The bogie car being supported only at or near the ends, its motion is little better than an ordinary short carriage, while the distance between the supports involves the use of very strong and heavy framing, and the bogies of themselves are of such weight that the paying proportion of the load, instead of increasing with the increased length, has in most instances decreased.'[2]

Other ideas centred on 6-wheeled carriages with a mechanism that steered all the axles. The theoretical advantages of such a system, which included the relative ease of applying it to existing stock, were described in the same article:

'The facts that the carriage is so thoroughly supported throughout its breadth and length, and that the existing frames, springs, hornplates, &c., are all applicable, as well as the general simplicity of the arrangement, very strongly recommend it.'

Two flexible wheelbase systems appeared in the 1870s. The Grover system appeared in 1870[3] and the better-known Cleminson system had been in use on the London, Chatham & Dover Railway since 1877. In the press description of the Cleminson system, it was suggested that extreme carriage lengths of 80 feet might be carried on an 8-wheel underframe.[4] A contemporary drawing of the Cleminson system is shown in Figure 2.14.

The Caledonian decided to try both systems in June 1881. The Glasgow Committee resolved that:

'the Order as given in London to Mr. Cleminson be proceeded with and the General Manager to ascertain from Mr. Grover to whom the Carriage to which his apparatus is to be attached is to be sent and the probable cost of the work.'[5]

This decision was taken because the Board had issued a minute two days previously that *'action should be taken without delay.'*[6] Drawing 3809 was issued in late September for the application of *'Grover's flexible frame for 6-wheeled Composite Carriages.'* In the event, the trial did not take place, probably because of Brittain's poor health and the demands of implementing the Westinghouse brake programme.

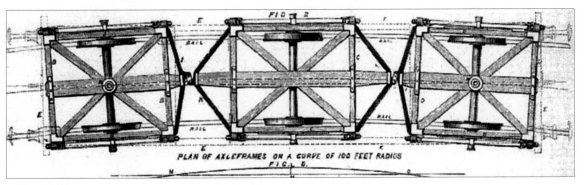

Figure 2.14
A drawing from *The Engineer* which shows an underframe with the Cleminson flexible wheelbase negotiating a 100-foot radius curve. All the axles are at right angles to the rails, which eliminated skidding wheels.

In March 1882 the Traffic Committee *'Read Mr Kempt's letter as to taking into traffic the two new carriages with Radial Axles, which have been standing at Buchanan Street Station for some time'*[7] and delegated Kempt with the power to take action. By now, Brittain was on sick leave and negotiations were also under way concerning the fitting of gas lighting to the carriage fleet. In June, Drummond was appointed as Locomotive Superintendent, which signalled the end of the Caledonian's interest.

According to Sewell, Drummond had visited the LC&DR to investigate the Cleminson underframe while he was on the North British.[8] He was clearly unimpressed, as on his return he designed a flexible chassis with the outer axles mounted on trucks which pivoted around a point half way between the outer and centre axle. The centre axle was rigid. It was fitted to two NBR First class Saloons, but was not repeated for passenger stock. The system reappeared on the first CR 15-ton rail wagons.[9]

SIDE PLAY ON CARRIAGE CENTRE AXLES

Along with most railways the Caledonian adopted a modification to the spring hangers of the centre axle of the 6-wheeled underframe to allow increased side play. This was achieved by suspending springs from J-hangers via three links. It was not possible to fit brake gear to the centre axle because of the side play, but the extreme wheelbase could now be extended to 23 feet, and the underframe lengthened to the new Drummond standard of 35 feet 6 inches. The arrangement can be seen in Figure 7.11. The problem of skidding wheels remained.

BOGIE CARRIAGES

Bogies were an American innovation. There, the majority of journeys were long-distance, often over permanent way that was sub-standard by British norms. Carriages were entered from the ends only, and tended to be massively constructed with the body and underframe as one unit. The bogie was the best form of suspension in these circumstances.

As stated earlier, the preferred method of supporting the British carriage design with multiple doors was the 6-wheeled underframe, if body length was to exceed 30 feet. The Cleminson flexible system was superficially attractive and could be applied to longer vehicles, but lost favour because it was difficult to maintain and friction in the connectors between the trucks caused undesirable noise and shuddering.

THE FIRST CR CARRIAGE BOGIE

Bogies first appeared on British railways with the Pullman cars imported from the USA by the Midland Railway in 1873. The Caledonian first contemplated bogie carriages in early 1876, when drawings 1952-1954 were issued for a proposed bogie carriage, Saloon and Officers' Saloon respectively. The proposals did not come to fruition and the drawings have not survived. In the same year the Caledonian proposed several bogie Sleeping carriage designs to the L&NWR, which were rejected, as described in Chapter 3.7. A trolly wagon with inside bearing bogies also made its appearance on the Caledonian in 1876.[10]

Drummond considered bogie carriages in 1884, but first built them for his pioneer 49-foot carriages in 1887. These 10-foot wheelbase bogies were of unique construction and are described in Chapter 7.3. They were replaced when the underframes of the carriages were rebuilt in 1898.

THE 8-FOOT BOGIE DESIGNS

The first 45-foot carriages appeared in 1888 and are described in Chapter 7.4. They were set on 8-foot wheelbase bogies which were to remain the standard for most of future CR carriage construction. The first bogies had metal side plates and wooden framing – see Figure 2.15.

The first mention of the Fox pressed steel bogie was drawing 9892.[11] It was applied to order H182, which was for seventy 48-foot Third class carriages. The initial part of the order was authorised for the period ending January 1900. A drawing from *The Railway Engineer* is shown in Figure 2.16 and a photograph in Plate 2.9.

After a period in the McIntosh era when 10-foot wheelbase bogies were used (see below), Pickersgill reverted to the 8-foot dimension. Increased carriage weight demanded a heavier version of the Fox bogie – see Figure 2.17.

OFFSET BOGIE CENTRES

As explained in Chapter 7, the bogies for the 49-foot carriages had pivots offset 3 inches to the rear of centre. When the 8-foot wheelbase bogies were adopted for the 45-foot stock, the offset was reduced to 1 inch. The offset was towards the centre of the carriage. Its purpose, to quote an article in *Engineering* describing the new carriages for the Callander & Oban line, was so that *'one pair of wheels may become the guiding medium, and thus do away with the sinuous movement incidental to ordinary bogies.'*[12]

The practice continued for all 45-foot carriage construction. It was also applied to the first 48-foot carriages built to standard underframe drawing 8914, but with the offset reversed, as described in Chapter 8.2. It was abandoned in 1900 with the advent of the 8 foot 6 inch wide stock, built on the underframe drawn in St. Rollox 9888, as shown in Chapter 8.2, Figure 8.12.

10-FOOT BOGIES

McIntosh fitted a 10-foot wheelbase bogie to his 57-foot carriages which were introduced in 1911. It too was a Fox pressed steel production. The drawing was 15917.[13] A close-up of the bogie is shown in Plate 2.10.

6-WHEELED BOGIES

The weight of the 'Grampian' stock dictated bogies with six wheels each. Again they were a Fox design. The first drawing issued was 12787 on 1st October 1904,[14] followed by 12812 on the 19th of the same month.[15] This showed some minor alterations. A side elevation of the bogie taken from a GA drawing appears in Figure 9.1 and a photograph is reproduced here as Plate 2.11.

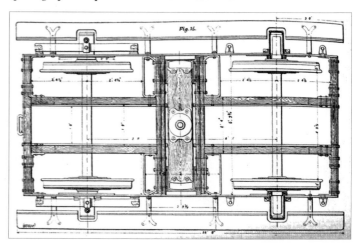

Figure 2.15
This is Drummond's original 8-foot wheelbase bogie as applied to his 45-foot carriages. It had steel side members, but the rest of the frame was wood. The drawing dates from 1889.

EARLY CARRIAGE WHEELS

Poor lubrication with grease of varying quality in early carriage axle boxes caused a problem at passenger train speeds. As a short-term solution the wheel diameter was increased to reduce the rotational speed of the axle. The maximum reached was 4 feet.

Spokes were made of wrought iron. Early drawings (for example, Figures 5.1 and 5.2) show 3-foot 6-inch diameter wheels with nine spokes. The two luxury Saloons which were built at Greenock shortly after the Caledonian opened merited 4-foot diameter wheels with twelve spokes – see Plate 2.12.

By the late 1890s the CR was using olive oil to lubricate carriage axles. For example, in 1899 the Loco & Stores Committee accepted an offer to supply 20 tons of the oil *'for delivery as required during the next six months.'*[16]

THE MANSELL PATENT WHEEL

Robert Mansell of the South Eastern Railway took out a patent in 1862 for a wheel which provided some resilience between track and underframe, thus improving the ride and reducing the noise transmitted to passengers. Its construction is shown in Figure 2.18. This is a later drawing which shows improved support for the wheel tyre which allowed it to be turned down when worn.[17] Each wheelset was balanced to run smoothly at 60 mph.

The CR was an early user. In 1862 Ashbury successfully tendered to supply seven Composites and two Passenger Brake Vans, with the option of Mansell or Low Moor Iron wheels. The General Manager and Benjamin Conner both recommended Mansell wheels at a premium of £20 per carriage.[18]

The Caledonian adopted the wheel for its carriage stock, both

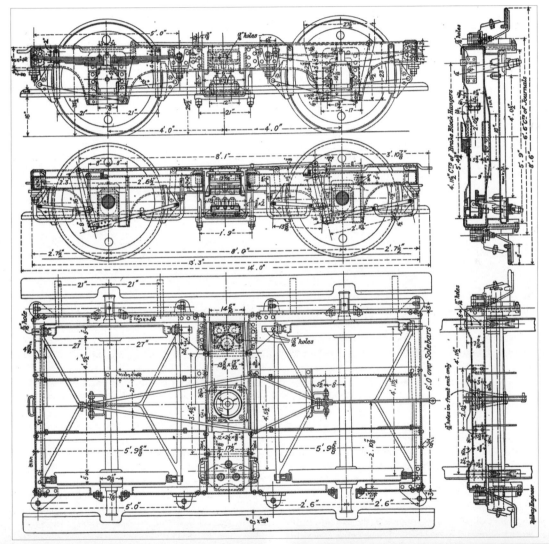

ABOVE: Figure 2.16 and Plate 2.9
The 8-foot wheelbase Fox bogie, made from pressed steel sections which were riveted together. This replaced the Drummond bogie in 1900.

Plate 2.10
The 10-foot wheelbase bogie, also made from Fox components.

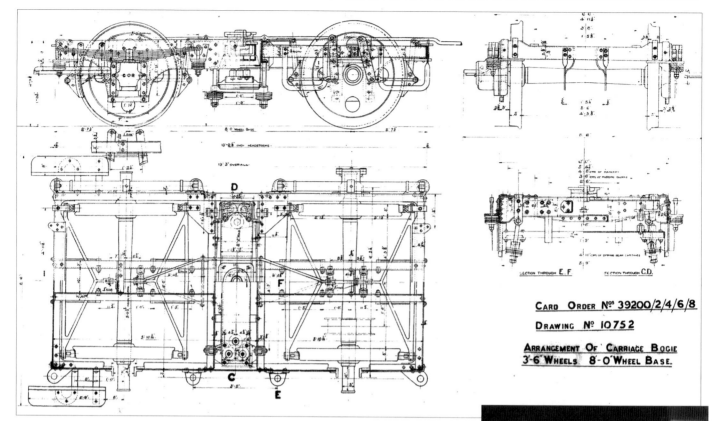

CARD ORDER Nº 39200/2/4/6/8

DRAWING Nº 10752

ARRANGEMENT OF CARRIAGE BOGIE
3'-6" WHEELS 8'-0" WHEEL BASE.

Figure 2.17
Increased carriage weight required a stronger bogie when Pickersgill reverted to the
8-foot wheelbase. This example is fitted with 4-hole disc wheels.

ABOVE: Plate 2.11
The six-wheeled bogie as used on the 'Grampian'
stock underframes.

ABOVE RIGHT: Plate 2.12
An example of an early carriage wheel which survived under Saloon 2A until it was photographed
around 1900. It has twelve wrought iron spokes and the diameter is 4 feet.

home-built and contracted. Wheels were made under license from
approved suppliers, with Mansell receiving a royalty for each set
supplied. Pickering was one of the suppliers to the CR, as shown in
Plate 2.13. Mansell's patent ran out in November 1878. In December
1876 he offered to sell the rights to the CR for £700. The Loco &
Stores Committee refused the offer.[19]

The wheel was superseded for new construction in 1906 for
reasons described below. The wheel remained in use on older
carriages, where it was perfectly serviceable. When track circuiting
was introduced, carriages with Mansell wheels could not be detected
because the wooden centre insulated the tyre from the axle. St.
Rollox drawing 14598[20] of the modification is shown in Figure 2.19.
This dates from 1908.

In January 1910 the Traffic Committee authorised the bonding of
wheels 'by the provision of two galvanised iron strips,' and noted that
the L&NWR proposed to bond all its carriage wheels, including West
Coast Joint Stock, at 1s 5d per set.[21] In 1914 the Traffic Committee
noted that 4,870 pairs of wheels required bonding, at a cost of 'about
£236'[22] – slightly less than 1s per set. This means that at least 1,500
CR carriages still ran on Mansell wheels. This represented about
three-quarters of the total coaching stock.

THE 'GRAMPIAN' STOCK DICTATES A CHANGE OF WHEEL

The inaugural set of 'Grampian' carriages built in the half year
ending January 1905 was fitted with Mansell wheels as seen in
Plate 9.3. When brake pressure is applied to a wheel the energy
dissipated by the reduction in the wheel's momentum is translated
into heat. Momentum is the product of mass and velocity. As carriage
weight (mass) and train speed (velocity) increased, greater braking
power was needed and more heat was generated in the process.

Operating experience must have quickly shown that the teak
centres of the wheels were deteriorating through heat damage where
the metal securing bolts passed through the wood segments. In August
and November 1905 three St. Rollox drawings (13181, 13358 and
13362) refer to 'carriage wheel with steel centre.' None has survived,
but St. Rollox drawing 15713[23] from 1911 is shown in Figure 2.20.

The second Aberdeen set and the inaugural Glasgow–Edinburgh
stock also ran on Mansell wheels. Plate 9.11 shows one of the first
non-corridor carriages on this service. Plate 9.4 shows a carriage
for the second Aberdeen train. This was built in the half year ending
July 1905, presumably with Mansell wheels, but was fitted with disc
wheels before it was posed for its official photograph.

RIGHT: Figure 2.18
This is a drawing of the Mansell patent wheel, first used by the Caledonian in 1862 and adopted as standard for all in-house construction until the early 1900s. *'The tyre is steel, and the portion of the wheel between the tyre and the boss is composed of 16 radiating sections of teak wood 3½ inches thick, and 14¼ inches in length. These sections are tightly packed, and secured to the tyre by two circular wrought iron rings, one inside and one outside, hooked into notches on the tyre, and bolted by 16 three-quarter inch bolts passing through the plates and the woodwork, with nuts on the inner side. At the centre the woodwork is secured to a circular casting, forming part of the boss, by eight one-inch wrought iron bolts which pass through the casting, the woodwork, and a cast-iron ring on the inside of the wheel, the nuts being on the inside.'* From the report on the Dunphail accident on the Highland Railway, 27th April 1894. The points of contact between the various metal components and the wood segments proved to be a weakness when carriage weights and train speeds increased in the early 1900s.

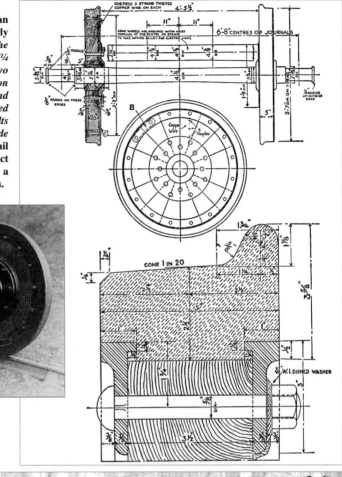

RIGHT: Plate 2.13
The R.Y. Pickering publicity photograph of a Mansell wheelset shows a balancing weight at 5 o'clock on the far wheel. These were applied to make the wheelset run true at 60 mph.

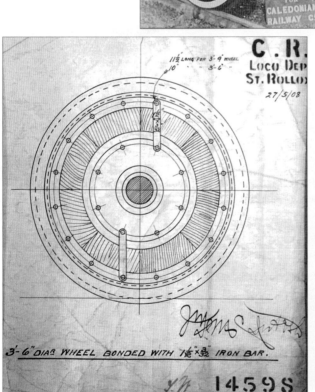

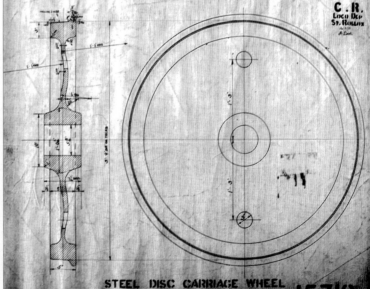

Figure 2.19
On wooden-centred Mansell wheels metal bonding between the axle and the wheel tyre was necessary for track circuit detection.

Figure 2.20
A St. Rollox drawing of the two-hole disc wheel that replaced the Mansell wheel for new construction after 1906.

ADOPTION OF THE STEEL DISC WHEEL

The 'Grampian' stock and other carriages built in the half year ending July 1906 and subsequently were fitted with the steel disc wheels from new – see Plate 9.5, which was a carriage built in 1907. Plate 9.7 shows one of the original low roof carriages at a later date, fitted with disc wheels.

FOUR-HOLE DISC WHEELS

In January 1914, St. Rollox issued drawing 17272 for the new design of 50-foot Passenger Brake Van. As can be seen in Figure 9.33 it ran on 10-foot bogies and the wheels had four large lightening holes. Photographs of carriages in their original state that were built when construction recommenced in 1919 also show these wheels – see for instance Plates 11.5 and 11.11. Plate 2.14 shows some of these wheelsets in St. Rollox carriage shop.

Older carriages which were originally fitted with Mansell wheels also showed these wheels when photographed in LM&SR livery (Plates 8.2 and 8.8). This evidence suggest that the four-hole disc wheel was adopted as standard by the Caledonian both for new builds and replacement.

UNDERFRAME CONSTRUCTION

Underframes up to the McIntosh era were made of wood. They followed wagon construction conventions, but the members were lighter in cross section, because the load was distributed over a longer body and humans with their luggage were not as dense as minerals or merchandise. The side member of a Drummond 6-wheeled underframe was 10 inches by 4 inches; the equivalent wagon sole bar was 12 inches by 5 inches. This lighter construction explains why milk trucks and other goods vehicles built on old carriage underframes were only rated to carry a 3 ton load.

As underframe lengths increased, it became common practice to 'flitch' the side members to increase their rigidity, rather than increase the cross section. This was done by screwing a ¼ inch mild steel plate to the outside. It is not clear whether contractor-built carriages of the 1870s were thus reinforced. Drummond's 4- and 6-wheeled designs were – see Chapters 7.1 and 7.2.

WOODEN BOGIE CARRIAGE UNDERFRAMES

After Drummond's unsuccessful experiment with an integrated body and underframe on his 49-foot carriages which is described in Chapter 7.3, bogie carriage underframe design reverted to 6-wheeled carriage conventions. In the first 45-foot design the side and main cross members were increased in thickness by ½ inch and 'flitched.' Because the underframe was only supported towards either end, truss rods were added. These were tensioned against queen posts which caused the side members to arc upwards towards the centre; the body's weight restored the horizontal level when the two components were united.

COMPOSITE STEEL AND WOOD UNDERFRAMES

One of the bogie carriage's shortcomings compared with 6-wheeled stock was an increase in underframe weight which was not matched by the greater seating capacity. The CR Small Diagram Book records the dead weight per passenger of a 60-seat 6-wheeled

Third as 4.3 cwt. The equivalent for an 80-seat 45-foot carriage was 5 cwt – a 16% increase.

The use of iron side members to reduce weight had been known for a long time. In 1881 the West Coast Committee noted that this could amount to half a ton per vehicle.[24] The Caledonian had experience of iron underframes almost from the start – Greenock drawing 351 was for a '24ft carriage – iron frame' and the 1868 Board of Trade report described in Chapter 6.2 concerned the poor riding of iron-framed carriages.[25]

While the L&NWR produced WCJS carriages with metal solebars from the early 1880s, the CR persisted with wood frames until February 1897, when drawing 8315 for a 'Standard Underframe for Bogie Carriages with Channel Steel Sole Bar' appeared. As implied, only the side members were steel. The rest of the components remained wood. The drawing seems to have been issued in connection with the renewal programme for the half year ending in July 1897. Carriages were still 8 feet wide at this point.

ALL-STEEL UNDERFRAMES

In 1900 the standard carriage width was increased to 8 feet 6 inches. The extract from the Board minute authorising the carriages' construction mentions the increase in width and the use of steel frames 'to be taken from the Leeds firm.'[26] Drawing 9888[27] was issued for an underframe which used pressed steel components from Fox. The underframe drawing is reproduced in Figure 8.12. The Small Diagram Book records that the Diagram 46 8 feet 6 inches wide Third was 1 ton 13 cwt lighter than its Diagram 40 8 feet wide predecessor.

STEEL UNDERFRAMES FOR NON-BOGIE STOCK

All-steel underframes for 6-wheeled Passenger Brake Vans and non-passenger coaching stock appeared in 1907. A design was first used for the Diagram 18 Passenger Brake Vans to order H264 which are described in Chapter 9.2. An example is shown in Plate 9.19. The underframe drawing was St. Rollox 14087.[28] Later underframes were built from Fox components, initially to drawing 14145.[29]

The replacement Balerno Branch carriage underframes were originally the subject of drawing 18985 of 1917.[30] The shorter First class underframe was re-issued in 1920 as drawing 20677.[31] The underframe was of similar construction to the contemporary 9 feet wide 57-foot stock, with which the 4-wheelers shared the body profile and internal fittings.

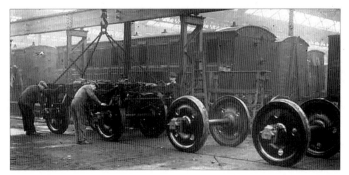

Plate 2.14
Lowering a bogie onto the wheelsets in St. Rollox carriage shop. The axle boxes on the wheelsets are being guided into the cut-outs in the bogie side frames. The later style of four-hole disc wheel is shown in the foreground.

RIGHT: **Plate 2.15**
These two photographs show the 'farm waggon' style of construction applied to a mineral 'bogie' (*left*) and an early carriage (*right*).

BODY CONSTRUCTION

The first railway carriage builders used existing design conventions – those of road vehicles. One was based on farm waggons, the other on the stagecoach. Indeed, some of the earliest companies to cater for railway customers in Scotland, such as Croall of Edinburgh, were established builders to the road carriage trade.

THE FARM WAGGON STYLE

This style was characterised by relatively heavy outside framing, with horizontal planks behind. The body was integral with the underframe. Its resemblance to the early mineral wagon called a 'bogie' in Scotland is obvious – see Plate 2.15. Joseph Wright was a leading exponent of this style. There is only one recorded instance of a successful tender to the Caledonian for carriages, but the company built many vehicles for the northern Scottish railways that were absorbed by the Caledonian in the 1860s. The carriages are described and illustrated in Chapter 5.2 (Caledonian) and 5.4 (absorbed railways). This style was eventually superseded in the mid-1860s by the style described below.

THE STAGE COACH STYLE

The body was built up from the floor and was united with a separately-built underframe. The sides had inner and outer skins, built around a wooden framework. Each compartment of a railway carriage was the equivalent of a stage coach body. An early Greenock drawing referred to a Third class carriage with 'five bodies.' Stage coach terminology also transferred to the railways. A stage coach body consisted of a floor, two ends, two doors and four 'quarters' (the body panels on either side of the doors), hence the term 'quarter-light' for their windows.

Stage coach ancestry could be often be seen in the shape of quarter-lights and carriage body detailing. An early example is shown in Figure 2.21. A residual form of the detailing at the ends of

the body sides lasted until the early 1870s – see Plate 6.8 and Figure 6.14 which depict carriages built in 1871. There are other examples in Chapter 6.

THE PRE-DRUMMOND STYLE

By 1877, the body style shown in Figure 2.22 was adopted. This was a slight variation of the 1874 design, with vertical beading at the lower body panel ends. It was probably initiated by Brittain, who, as described in Chapter 6.2, began to issue drawings for contractors instead of relying on their designs. The body style lasted until the arrival of Dugald Drummond in 1882.

THE DRUMMOND STYLE

As recounted and illustrated in Chapter 7.1, Drummond brought the three-layer style of panelling with him from the North British Railway. While it is often thought of as characteristic of the Caledonian, it was only applied in numbers to 4- and 6-wheeled carriages built between 1882 and 1891. Nearly all the 45- and 48-foot carriages were built in the simplified 2-layer panelling style described below.

THE FINAL PANELLED STYLE

John Lambie introduced the panelling style that continued until the end of the CR's existence. In one respect, it was a reversion to the pre-Drummond style, with beading enclosing the lower body as one panel. The body was a single layer, with the beading on top. Dimensions of the panelling elements for both classes of carriage are shown in Figures 8.1 and 8.4.

USE OF STEEL IN BODY CONSTRUCTION

As can be seen in Figure 9.3 the 'Grampian' stock continued the Lambie panelling style, but steel sheathing was used for the outer body panels over a wood frame.

The 57-foot carriages to Diagrams 113-119 dispensed with panelling, except for a small amount of beading between the windows. These designs are described and illustrated in Chapter 9.5. The Lambie/McIntosh panelled style returned after World War I with Diagram 121 and the post-war variants of the flush-bodied stock, but the panelling effect above the windows was painted, rather than in relief. The details are described and shown in drawings in Chapter 4.1.

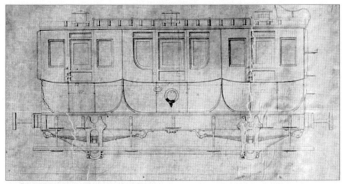

Figure 2.21
This Joseph Wright drawing of an Arbroath & Forfar Railway Composite dates from before 1845, when the firm moved to Birmingham. They are not mentioned in Francis Whishaw's account of his visit to the line in 1842. It is reproduced here as an example of the stage coach styling. It has three very obvious 'bodies' and the larger First class compartment windows echo the curves in the beading.

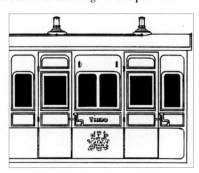

Figure 2.22
This enlargement shows the style of panelling adopted by the CR in the late 1870s. An example of a carriage in this style is shown in Plate 2.22 and there are others in Chapter 6. It was superseded by the Drummond three-layer panelling in 1882.

REFERENCES

1. Officers' Minute Book, January 1868, minute 6
2. *The Engineer*, 15th February 1878, p. 111
3. *The Engineer*, 24th March 1871, p. 194
4. *The Engineer*, 15th February 1878, p. 111
5. NRS BR/CAL/1/26 entry 980
6. NRS BR/CAL/1/26 entry 959
7. NRS BR/CAL/1/27 entry 449
8. *North British Coaches*, pp. 8-9
9. *Caledonian Railway Wagons*, pp. 125-28
10. *Caledonian Railway Wagons*, pp. 209-10
11. RHP 69629
12. *Engineering*, 21st February 1890, p. 196
13. NRM 11206/C
14. RHP 67558
15. RHP 67555
16. NRS BR/CAL/1/42 entry 1613
17. *The Engineer*, 21st August 1866, p. 132
18. NRS BR/CAL/1/12 entry 2199
19. NRS BR/CAL/1/23 entry 831
20. RHP 68615
21. NRS BR/CAL/5/12 entry 32/223
22. NRS BR/CAL/5/13 entry 36/64
23. RHP 69663
24. NRS BR/WCC/1/7 minute 1869
25. TNA MT29/29, report 504
26. NRS BR/CAL/5/11 entry 398
27. RHP 68810
28. RHP 68760
29. RHP 69136
30. NRM 7529/C
31. NRM 7528/C

2.5: SLIP CARRIAGES

Slip carriages enabled connections to branch line or intermediate stations without the need to stop an express train. The arrangement was first used by the LB&SCR in 1858, when a carriage for Lewes was detached from a Brighton-bound train at Haywards Heath.[1] The GWR was another early adopter and became the leading exponent of the practice. The L&NWR built a number of slip carriages for services in England but the facility was not provided on West Coast Joint Stock trains.

Drummond seems to have actively considered slip carriages in 1886, when drawing 4783[2] was issued for a type of slip carriage coupling. McIntosh issued almost identical drawing 6759 in 1891.[3] No slip carriages were built as a result of these initiatives. Strangely, Pickersgill re-issued the McIntosh drawing using the original number in 1922.[4]

SLIP SERVICES ON THE CALEDONIAN

In November 1903 the Traffic Committee approved a *'Proposal to fit up two brake composite carriages with slipping apparatus, estimated cost £20 per vehicle.'*[5] Drawings 12268, 12342, 12345 and 12352[6] dated October/November 1903 detailed the coupling equipment for the first carriages.

Services started in 1904 with two slips for Lockerbie and developed as shown in the following table. The entries, which have been verified in the CR Working Timetables, differ slightly from the tabulation in Fryer's book. The additional slip carriage to Lockerbie gave the station the unique distinction on the CR of receiving slip carriages from both Up and Down trains.

SLIP STATION	1906	1908	1910	1914
Carluke	1	1	1	1
Cleghorn			1	1
Coupar Angus	1	2	2	1
Falkirk Grahamston		1	1	1
Crieff Junct/Gleneagles		2	2	2
Guthrie		2	2	2
Larbert	1		1	
Lockerbie	2	2	3	3

The destinations of the slip carriages in 1914 were:

SLIP STATION	FINAL DESTINATION
Carluke/Cleghorn	Lanark
Coupar Angus	Blairgowrie
Falkirk Grahamston	Grangemouth
Crieff Junction/Gleneagles	St. Fillans
Guthrie	Arbroath
Lockerbie	Lockerbie/Whithorn

EXTRA CARRIAGES IN SLIP PORTIONS

Normally, one slip carriage sufficed. Provision was, however, made for extra stock. This involved special dispensation to

THE MAXIMUM NUMBER OF VEHICLES TO BE SLIPPED AT THE UNDERNOTED STATIONS WILL BE AS UNDER:—

When the weight of the Slip Portion exceeds that given below, the Train must be stopped at the Station at which the Slip Portion is usually detached, that Station being also advised by Telegraph or Telephone that the Train will stop.

SLIPPING STATION.	UP OR DOWN TRAINS.	MAXIMUM NUMBER OF VEHICLES TO BE SLIPPED.		GRADIENT APPROACHING SLIPPING STATION.
		With 8-wheeled 50-feet Slip Carriage, and only 4 Wheels of same operated upon by Hand Brake.	With 12-wheeled 65-feet Slip Carriage, and all the Wheels of same operated upon by Hand Brake.	
Guthrie	Up	3 equal to 4½ Vehicles	3 equal to 4½ Vehicles	1 in 382, and 1 in 232 rising.
Coupar-Angus	Down	3 equal to 4½ Vehicles	3 equal to 4½ Vehicles	1 in 850 rising.
Gleneagles	Down	1 equal to 1½ Vehicles (Slip Carriage only)	3 equal to 4½ Vehicles	1 in 101 falling.
Grahamston	Down	1 equal to 1½ Vehicles (Slip Carriage only)	3 equal to 4½ Vehicles	1 in 100 falling.
Carluke	Up	3 equal to 4½ Vehicles	3 equal to 4½ Vehicles	1 in 100 rising.
Cleghorn	Up	2 equal to 3 Vehicles	3 equal to 4½ Vehicles	1 in 204 falling.
Lockerbie	Up	2 equal to 3 Vehicles	3 equal to 4½ Vehicles	1 in 528 rising.
Lockerbie	Down	2 equal to 3 Vehicles	3 equal to 4½ Vehicles	1 in 528 falling.

T. W. PETTIGREW,
Superintendent of the Line.

Plate 2.16
The list of permitted extra carriages in slip portions is taken from the 1914 Working Timetable

attach a vehicle behind the slip carriage, which itself pushed the normal rule to the limit, as the Brake compartment was not at the preferred extreme end of the train. If the supplementary vehicles had side chains, they were to be coupled up as a safety measure.

Two extra carriages was the absolute limit, but at the slipping stations of Falkirk Grahamston and Gleneagles, where there was a falling gradient of 1 in 100, the shorter slip carriages, which only had braking power on eight wheels, were not allowed extra vehicles. As the list published in the Working Timetables shows (Plate 2.16),

(d) On approaching the Stations at which the Slip Carriages have to be left, the Slip Guard must look out for the Distant and Home Signals, and if the Distant Signal is at "All Right," and the train is running at the usual speed, he must first release the Westinghouse Brake Coupling and then apply his Hand-brake, so that the blocks may press slightly upon the wheels. He must then, and not before, uncouple the Slip portion, and immediately afterwards apply the Hand-brake a little more forcibly, so as to allow the train to get some distance from him, and must give the Engine-driver and the Guard or Guards of the train an "All Right" Hand Signal by exhibiting a Green Flag by day or a Green Light by night, waved slowly up and down. He may then, if necessary, release his Hand-brake to allow the Slip portion to run to the platform. The Carriages must not be uncoupled if the Engine-driver is slackening speed. When the Driver of the train finds, on approaching the Station at which the Carriage should be slipped, that the Distant Signal is at Danger, he must immediately reduce the speed of his train, and must come to a stand at the Platform for the Slip Carriage to be detached, notwithstanding that the Home and Starting Signals may be lowered before the train arrives at them.

ABOVE: Plate 2.17
The procedure followed by guards when making the slip.

if the slip portion exceeded the upper limit for the station, the train was stopped to detach it.

THE FIRST CR SLIP CARRIAGES

Ten non-corridor vehicles formed the initial slip carriage fleet. Six were ex-West Coast Joint Stock 45-foot Lavatory Luggage Composites which the CR converted to Brake Composites. The Caledonian acquired sixteen of these carriages in 1903. They were used on the Lanark and Lockerbie services, where they matched the WCJS carriages of the rest of the train. The carriages are described and illustrated in Chapter 8.4.

The other four carriages were built specifically as slips. They were Coupé Lavatory Brake Composites on the then-standard 48-feet by 8 foot 6 inches underframe. They were originally used for the Guthrie and Falkirk slips. This design is described and illustrated in Chapter 8.2.

65-FOOT SLIP CARRIAGES

With the introduction of the 'Grampian' stock, the 48-foot carriages, although less than two years old, were no longer deemed suitable for prestige services and were cascaded to slip duties where they did not look out of place with the rest of the train. They were replaced by four 65-foot non-corridor Brake Composites in the first half of 1906. In a retrograde step, there was no lavatory accommodation in the new design. These carriages are discussed in Chapter 9.1.

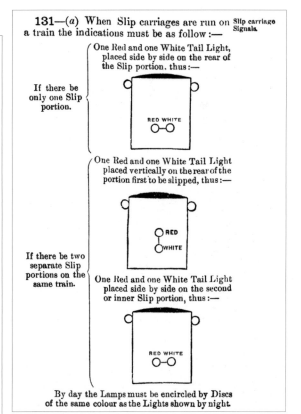

131—(a) When Slip carriages are run on a train the indications must be as follow:—

If there be only one Slip portion.
One Red and one White Tail Light, placed side by side on the rear of the Slip portion, thus:—
RED WHITE

If there be two separate Slip portions on the same train.
One Red and one White Tail Light placed vertically on the rear of the portion first to be slipped, thus:—
RED WHITE

One Red and one White Tail Light placed side by side on the second or inner Slip portion, thus:—
RED WHITE

By day the Lamps must be encircled by Discs of the same colour as the Lights shown by night.

LEFT: Plate 2.18
Diagram of the specialised equipment involved in releasing a slip carriage with a folding slip draw-hook.

ABOVE: Plate 2.19
The CR lamp codes as published in Working Timetable Appendices reversed the 1897 Railway Clearing House guidelines as published in Fryer's book, which stated that lamps on the first slip were one above each other.

EXPLANATION OF LETTERING ON SLIP CARRIAGE DIAGRAM.

A—Westinghouse intermediate pipe.
B—Cock on Westinghouse intermediate pipe.
C—Safety clip between Westinghouse intermediate pipe and train pipe.
D—Westinghouse coupling inside brake compartment of Slip Carriage.
E—Cock on stand pipe in brake compartment of Slip Carriage.
F—Westinghouse ordinary brake cock.
G—Lever for releasing lock of slip hook.
H—Slip hook.
J—Chains for hanging intermediate pipe to end of rear vehicle of corridor train.
K—Chains for hanging intermediate pipe to cross chain on end of rear vehicle of non-corridor train.
L—Cross chain on end of rear vehicle of train if non-corridor.
M—End cock on Westinghouse pipe of rear vehicle of main train.
N—Handle to assist in uncoupling Westinghouse pipe in Slip Carriage.
O—Pin for fixing lever G to quadrant in brake compartment.

A further two 65-foot slip carriages were built in 1909. This may have been prompted by the withdrawal of one of the ex-WCJS Slips in 1908, presumably as the result of an accident. St. Rollox issued drawings 14704, 14705 and 14709 for the slip apparatus.[7]

SLIPPING PROCEDURE

Slipping was only permitted when signals allowed the train to run through the slipping station at speed. If this was not the case, the train was stopped and the slip carriage detached. The full slipping procedure is shown in Plate 2.17.

SPECIALISED EQUIPMENT

The equipment for separating the slip carriage from the train is shown and described in Plate 2.18. The drawing was published in each issue of the Working Timetable Appendix. The major components were a means of shutting off the Westinghouse brake pipe, the hinged coupling hook, and its operating lever.

Some companies fitted an auxiliary air reservoir to the slip carriage in order to apply braking power to all the vehicles in the slip portion. The Caledonian relied purely on the handbrake, the Westinghouse brake having been immobilised in the 'off' position as part of the slipping process. In case the brake did not 'come off' properly, a release valve similar to that fitted under each carriage for shunting purposes was fitted inside the Brake compartment.

LAMP CODES AND SAFETY

Special lamp codes were used to designate the slip portion. They are shown in Plate 2.19. A guard was not allowed to operate under slip regulations until 'he had been properly instructed in his duties and been passed as competent for the work.'

The safety of company servants working on the line was also catered for. After slipping the carriage travelled silently, and could

catch a platelayer unawares. A gong was provided as an audible warning, to be used if the Slip guard spotted people working on the line. It was also sounded at level crossings and the approach to the destination station. The gong was not installed at the beginning of the slip service, as attested by the date of the drawing discussed below, and an entry in the July 1907 Working Timetable which stated that the gongs were 'being provided.'[8]

On the GWR and most other railways, the gong was fitted on the end of the carriage. The CR's arrangement was more discreet. It was attached to the underframe and was sounded by a detachable foot pedal which operated a lever passing through the floor of the van. This was placed adjacent to the handbrake, 'so that both may readily be used at one and the same time when necessary.' The arrangement is shown in Figure 2.23, which is reproduced from St. Rollox drawing 14109 dated April 1907.[9] This was for a vehicle with a wood underframe, so must refer to the earlier carriages. The associated procedure is shown in Plate 2.20.

WORKING HOME

After arrival at its final destination, the slip carriage had to be returned to base for the next day's working. The carriages were marshalled into trains where they served as ordinary Composite carriages. Some of the workings were quite convoluted, as described in an article by the late Charles Underhill.[10] A photograph of a slip carriage in the process of working home is shown in Plate 8.6.

POST-WAR SLIP CARRIAGE WORKING

It is not absolutely certain whether slip carriage working was reinstated after the Armistice, but it seems highly unlikely. There is no mention of slip carriages in the Southern, Eastern and Western timetables book of 1919, but the Northern Section of the book carries the 'S' for Slip Carriage abbreviation on the front page. There is, however, no record of a slip working in the timetables themselves.

REFERENCES
1. *A History of Slipping and Slip Carriages*, C.E.J. Fryer, p. 6
2. RHP 68455
3. RHP 68599
4. RHP 68802
5. NRS BR/CAL/1/48 entry 768
6. RHP 68809/5/7/8 respectively
7. RHP 68804, 68801 and 68798 respectively
8. 1907 Working Timetable, p. 138
9. RHP 68797
10. *The True Line*, issue 36, pp. 11-13

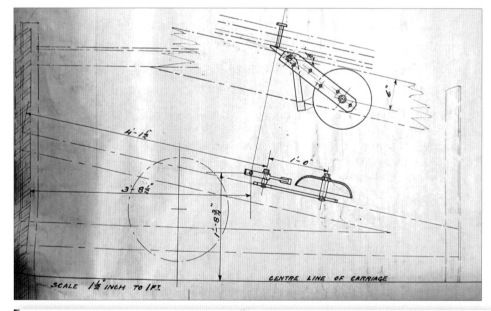

Figure 2.23 and Plate 2.20
The slip gong was introduced in 1907 to warn personnel on the line about a slip carriage's approach. The associated procedure is taken from the *'Extra Instructions for Slip Carriages'* in the Working Timetable appendices.

Gongs.—A Gong is provided on each Slip Carriage in order that the Slip Guard may be able to give audible notice of the approach of the Slip Portion after the same has been detached from the Main Train.

Whenever, after slipping, Slip Guards find it necessary to give warning to Platelayers and others of the approach of the Slip Vehicles, they must sound the Gong vigorously several times. This must always be done before passing Level Crossings or entering Stations.

The pedal for operating the Gong is placed on the floor of the Brake Compartment near to the Hand Brake, so that both may be readily used at one and the same time when necessary. To avoid the sounding of the Gong when not required for the purpose above stated, the pedal must be lifted by the Slip Guard from its position after use, and must, in accordance with arrangements made in each case, be returned to the Station at which the Slip Coupling is attached. The Slip Guard on each journey must see that the pedal is replaced in position before starting.

2.6: INFRASTRUCTURE AND DEPLOYMENT

At a rough count, about 1,500 passenger carriages and guard's Brake Vans were needed to provide the basic service on the Caledonian as set out in the July 1913 Carriage Marshalling Circular. The Circular contains the following statement on the front page. Other circulars have similar or identical wording.

'The composition of the different Trains, as herein laid down, is calculated to meet the average requirements, but the fluctuations in the Traffic must be carefully watched, in order that additional accommodation may be provided when required, and also that unnecessary Vehicles may be discontinued.'

West Coast Joint Stock vehicles are not included in the number above. According to the 1913 Report to Directors, the CR owned about 2,400 passenger carriages and Brake Vans.[1] The number is approximate, as Luggage Vans which were non-passenger coaching stock formed part of the total.

A percentage of the stock was out of service at any one time for refurbishment or repair. The arrangements are discussed later in this section. The remaining vehicles were kept in reserve to strengthen trains, replace vehicles that had developed faults, or serve on excursion traffic. Some stock was only required during the summer tourist season, particularly First class carriages and Family Saloons. Alexander Allan of the Scottish Central identified the problem associated with seasonal traffic in 1860, when he told the Board that he was:

'reluctant to recommend the purchase of more First Class Carriages until coverings are provided at some of the stations to protect them in winter when not in use.'[2]

Sheds and sidings were needed for two purposes – to store the spare carriages in the medium term and to park general service stock overnight, where it was cleaned and gassed if necessary.

The first mention of a dedicated shed appears in October 1870, when a *'Spare Carriage shed to hold 100 carriages'* was required.

The Traffic Committee was asked for a report on the cost.[3] There is no record of an outcome or of its proposed location.

STEPS ROAD SHED AND BUCHANAN STREET SIDINGS

The next attempt to provide covered accommodation took place in April 1878. Plans were submitted for a carriage shed and the Traffic Committee approved a *'plan for an iron shed … erect one in the meantime on ground bought for the purpose at Steps Road.'*[4] More information was also requested. There is no reference to the original plan in the St. Rollox register.

In August it was recorded that a shed would not be erected. Instead the Traffic Committee asked for a *'report as to the cost of sidings to be laid with old rails for standing room for carriages awaiting repairs.'*[5]

This seems to have sufficed until late 1879/early 1880 when the Traffic Committee agreed to *'the construction of carriage sheds after receiving reports on suitable locations.'*[6] A tender was accepted for £3,276 2s 11d. The shed was to have a wooden roof.

As part of Drummond's programme to improve the operational efficiency of the CR, drawing 5609 was produced in February 1888 for a *'carriage shed with zinc roof,'* followed in June by 5713, which was for a *'carriage shed to store 400.'* Neither drawing has survived. In November the Stores Committee agreed to:

'authorise Mr. Drummond to proceed immediately with the erection of carriage shed as per plan submitted to contain 276 carriages at a cost not exceeding £9,750 which is for wooden lattice girders, zinc covered roof, all rails and approaches and heating pipes etc. etc.'[7]

This was the final outcome of the plan to build a shed at Steps Road, as proved by the register entry for drawing 5861. This and two other drawings (5882 for roof girders and 5913 for the boiler house) have not survived. A drawing of the shed's location and layout is shown in Figure 2.24. Its purpose was to accommodate stock on services from Buchanan Street and to store carriages awaiting repairs at St. Rollox.

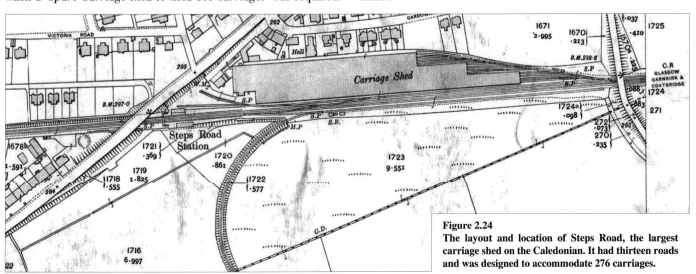

Figure 2.24
The layout and location of Steps Road, the largest carriage shed on the Caledonian. It had thirteen roads and was designed to accommodate 276 carriages.

Buchanan Street itself had a ladder of carriage sidings to the north of the station as shown in Figure 2.25. Cleaning and gassing of Coatbridge, Hamilton and Motherwell stock was undertaken there.

EGLINTON STREET CARRIAGE SHED

In January 1884 the Loco & Stores Committee agreed to close Eglinton Street running shed and remove the locomotives to Polmadie. The shed had only been open for six years to provide a quicker way to service engines from Glasgow Central than travelling out to Polmadie.[8] The Committee minute gave its approval to 'convert the shed into a storing shed for carriages to and from Central station.'[9] One pilot engine would be made surplus at a saving

of £2,000-£3,000 per annum. According to *LMS Engine Sheds*, it was gradually brought back into use as a stabling point for locomotives from 1902. Two inspection pits were installed in 1914.

GUSHETFAULDS CARRIAGE SHED

This seems to have been the successor to Eglinton Street, and became for a while the centre for maintaining the most modern carriages. In 1905, anticipating the introduction of the 'Grampian' stock, the Traffic Committee approved expenditure of £435 *'plus £10 per annum power'* on:

'siding, Examination Pit, Workshop, Bogie Tramway including Turntable and Motor Generator required for the examination and repair of Carriages fitted with Electric Light.'[10]

By 1912, the facility had become inadequate. The increase in electrically-lit carriages from 70 to 250 justified construction of a dedicated workshop at St. Rollox.[11] The estimated cost was £640.

SOME OTHER SHEDS AND SIDINGS AROUND GLASGOW

Overnight storage, cleaning and gassing of Cathcart Circle stock was divided between Larkfield (Figure 2.26) and Smithy Lye (Figure 2.27). Larkfield serviced stock on the Lanark/Muirkirk and Hamilton/Strathaven lines. It also shared part of the Balloch line stock with Rutherglen

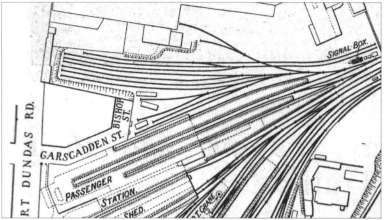

ABOVE: Figure 2.25
The carriage sidings associated with Steps Road were to the north of Buchanan Street platforms.

RIGHT: Figure 2.26
The carriage shed at Larkfield in 1910.

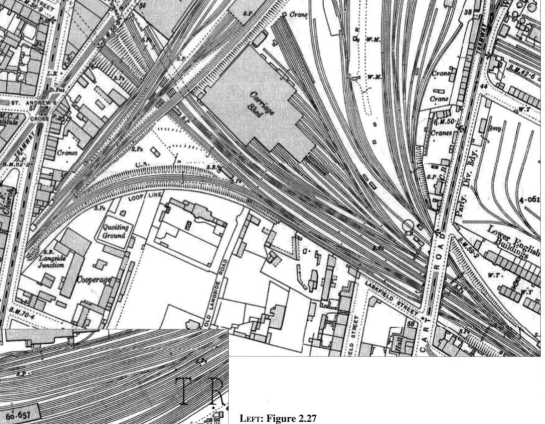

LEFT: Figure 2.27
The carriage shed at Smithy Lye in 1910.

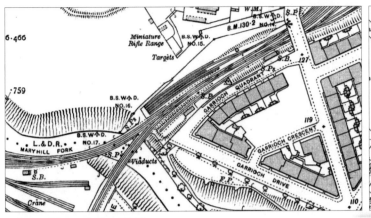

ABOVE: Figures 2.28 and 2.29
Maryhill sidings (*left*) and Law Junction carriage shed (*right*).

RIGHT: Plate 2.21
This shows the different levels of cleaning applied before World War I. It is taken from the front page of the *1912 Carriage Marshalling Circular*.

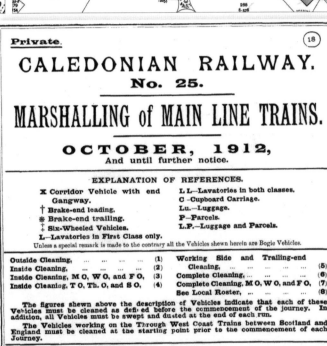

and the Edinburgh/Glasgow stock with Edinburgh. The latter shed also looked after most of the Gourock and Wemyss Bay, Kilmarnock/Ardrossan, Hamilton/Coalburn and East Kilbride stock. It also looked after some Maryhill/Airdrie carriages, the rest being serviced at Maryhill where there were two carriage sidings adjacent to the station platforms – see Figure 2.28. Carriages to strengthen trains on this route were also stored there.

Law Junction (Figure 2.29) was strategically situated near the divergence of the line to Wishaw Central and main line south to Carlisle. It serviced some of the stock on the Lanark/Muirkirk and Wishaw lines, and was the destination of a daily stock train from Larkfield.

EMPTY CARRIAGE STOCK WORKING

Reports to Directors included statistics about the annual mileage of empty carriage workings and carriage shunting miles. For example, the mileages in the years immediately before and after World War I are shown in the following table.[12]

COACHING MILES	1913	1920
Total	10,561,177	8,878,471
Loaded	10,185,622	8,590,436
Empty	375,555	288,035
Shunting	957,733	895,727

Empty carriage trains were not to exceed thirty vehicles. An 8-wheeled carriage was equal to 1½ vehicles and 12-wheeled carriages were counted as two.[13]

GAS SUPPLY FOR CARRIAGES

This was fully discussed in *Caledonian Railway Wagons*;[14] a summary is provided here. Carriages were gassed at fixed points and a fleet of travelling gas tank wagons worked from the fixed points to outposts of the system. The original gas works was at Dawsholm. A plant at Glasgow Cook Street catered for the gassing points at the nearby Larkfield and Smithy Lye carriage sheds. The gassing point for the Northern section was Perth. The gas works there was approved in 1887.[15] Plans for the Edinburgh Works at Lothian Road were submitted and agreed in December 1891.[16]

TRAVELLING GAS TANKS

Company minutes first refer to a '*gas travelling store*' in September 1883, when the Loco & Stores Committee considered a '*Letter offering to supply a Travelling Store holder, tank and all fittings complete for £320.*'[17] The Coaching Plant Stock Book includes seventeen Travelling Gas Tanks, but the list is far from complete. A fuller list and a description of the vehicles are provided in *Caledonian Railway Wagons*.

CLEANING MAIN LINE CARRIAGES

Before World War I an elaborate system for main line carriage cleaning was in force, as shown in Plate 2.21. Instructions were not given for every train in the Carriage Marshalling Circulars, but, as might be expected, the express trains from Glasgow and Edinburgh to places such as Aberdeen, Oban and residential areas such as Peebles and Callander were category 6 – completely cleaned inside and out after every journey. The detailed instructions about internal and external cleaning routines occupied one page in the Working Timetable appendices.[18] Particular attention was to be given to white painted carriages on main line trains and those working on the '*Underground Line.*'

Problems arose with cleaning the 'Grampian' stock shortly after its introduction. The 1907 Working Timetable special instructions stated:

Plate 2.22
The carriage cleaner has attempted to frustrate historians by interposing himself between the running number and the camera, but this is a down-rated Brown, Marshall & Co. Tri-Composite of 1879. The right-hand compartment was originally Second Class. The only white-painted, oil-lit example in the Coaching Plant Stock Book was Number 189. The photograph was taken before June 1922, when it was down-rated again to Third class and renumbered 562. The carriages are described and further illustrated in Chapter 6.3. The partially-visible Passenger Brake Van is a steel-bodied vehicle built in the second half of 1921. The location is possibly Bridge Street carriage sidings.

'Several of these Carriages have had to be sent … for repainting and considerable unnecessary expense has been incurred owing to the surface having been damaged by Carbolascene. … This liquid must not be used for such a purpose and any irregular use of this kind in the future will be severely dealt with.'

The notice only appeared in the section for the line north of Glenboig,[19] which suggests that the culprits were the cleaners at Aberdeen or Dundee.

LOCAL AND BRANCH LINE CARRIAGE CLEANING

These carriages did not receive the same attention as those on main line services. This was partly a matter of time constraint. Main line trains usually made one return trip per day and there was ample time to clean the carriages between trips. Carriages on lesser duties were cleaned at junction stations or in carriage sidings, and:

'must be swept and dusted at the end of each journey, unless the Carriages are not standing for sufficient time at the Station to permit of this being done.'

Even so, these carriages had to be rubbed with cleaning waste every day and *'lightly oiled not less than twice a week.'* A picture of a carriage cleaner going about his work is shown in Plate 2.22. An example of the rates for cleaning carriages at St. Rollox is shown in Plate 2.23.

REPAIRS AND MAINTENANCE

Reports to the Board included information about the number of vehicles repaired, and a snapshot of those undergoing or awaiting repair at the end of each half year period. For instance, in the period ending 31st January 1868, it was reported that forty-four carriages had received *'thorough,'* 117 *'ordinary'* and 619 *'light*

Plate 2.23
These are some of the piecework rates for cleaning carriages at St. Rollox in 1925.

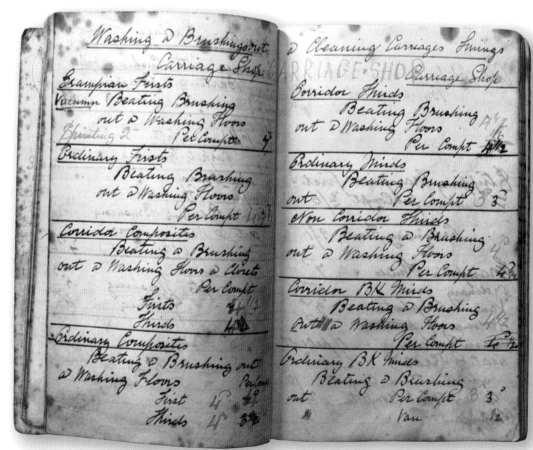

repairs.' There were 908 carriages in the fleet. Ten years later, 111 carriages were under or awaiting repair at the year-end out of a fleet of 1,144 – almost exactly 10%.[20] In 1926, a notebook showed that 260 carriages had received repairs at St. Rollox in the previous year.[21] Some carriages were only out of a service for two or three days, but many stayed for a week to ten days.

St. Rollox was the main repair shop for rolling stock, although some was undertaken at Perth. Light repairs were also undertaken at carriage sidings. An article in 1913 reported that the St. Rollox carriage shop accommodated *'90 carriages on 6 lines of rail.'* A separate paint and trimming shop *'had 5 lines of rails for carriages and 2 for locomotives.'*[22] Plate 2.24 is a photograph of the carriage shop and 2.25 is of the trimming and paint shop.

Examination of carriages and wagons when in traffic was the responsibility of train examiners. Aside from testing wheels, springs and the like in stations, the *Regulations for Train Examiners and Greasers* instructed them to pay particular attention to 'the bosses, bolts and bonding strips' of Mansell wheels *'and if any sign of looseness appears, the vehicles must be stopped for repairs.'*[23]

RUNNING-IN

New carriages, or carriages that had had repairs or replacements to their axle boxes and bearings, needed a running-in period to check that the bearings were running cool before entering traffic. They were usually marshalled in local trains out of Buchanan Street until they were deemed fit to resume normal duties. A label was affixed to the carriage to denote this – see Plate 2.26, which is reproduced from the Working Timetable Appendix.

If there were sufficient carriages, a special train was run between 10.00am and noon from St. Rollox to either Denny West Junction or Stirling. The locomotive carried the route indicator shown in Plate 2.27. The train was to be *'signalled as Express Passenger Train rather than Empty Coaching Stock.'*[24]

DAMAGE AND REFURBISHMENT

Vandalism on railway trains was not a late twentieth century phenomenon. The Caledonian published a tariff of charges for breakages which was published in Working Timetable appendices and updated as carriage design evolved – see Plate 2.28.

A notebook with the piecework rates for repair to every item of carriage furnishing has survived;[25] it dates from 1925/26. An example of damage to a First class Compartment door is shown in Plate 2.29 and the associated rate for repairing the damage in Plate 2.30.

REFERENCES
1. NRM 68D82/6/5/b/1-68D82/6/6/c/17 (Eshton Hall Collection)
2. NRS BR/SCC/1, p. 14
3. NRS BR/CAL/1/18 entry 1353
4. NRS BR/CAL/1/24 entry 558
5. NRS BR/CAL/1/24 entry 1061
6. NRS BR/CAL/1/25 entry 718
7. NRS BR/CAL/5/11 entry 42
8. *LMS Engine Sheds*, Volume 5, p. 152

Plate 2.24
The interior of St. Rollox carriage shop in early LM&SR days. One of the pre-war 12-wheeled Pullman cars is on the left. Two ex-Caledonian Passenger Brake Vans stand behind the Composite carriage.

Plate 2.25
In the St. Rollox trimming and paint shop, making Third class seat bottoms. A stack of the finished articles is in the foreground.

COACHING STOCK—HOT AXLES.

When Vehicles with newly fitted Bearings are turned out of St. Rollox Workshops to be put into traffic, a Label printed as under will be affixed to them :—

CALEDONIAN RAILWAY.

This Vehicle, No..

is to be kept on Local Trains until this Label is withdrawn.

..................................Station ....

Locomotive Foreman.

..................................191

Vehicles so labelled must only be worked between Buchanan Street, Stirling, Dunblane, Callander, and Perth on Local Trains until the Locomotive Carriage Inspector at Buchanan Street decides to have the Label removed. When occasion arises to fix these Labels on Vehicles at other outside Stations on the Line, Locomotive Department will advise the Coaching Plant Superintendent so that arrangements may be made to keep these Vehicles on a Local Run until it is in order for the Label to be removed.

Vehicles bearing " Slow Run " Labels must not be run on other than Local Trains.

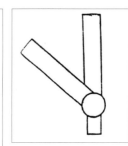

Plates 2.26 and 2.27
The procedure for running in carriages after attention to their bearings (*left*) and the route indicator for a special trial train of carriages (*above*).

BREAKAGE OF CARRIAGE WINDOWS.

The List of Charges shown at page 79 of General Appendix has been revised as under:—

	s.	d.				s.	d.	
Door Window Glass, ...	11	10	each.	Guard's End Window Glass, ...		20	9	each.
Side Light, First Class, ...	14	4	„	„ Screen Window Glass, ...		13	2	„
„ „ Third Class, ...	13	2	„	Lavatory Mirror, ...		19	0	„
„ „ 5 feet long, ...	45	3	„	Compartment Mirror, ...		8	3	„
„ „ 4½ feet long, ...	38	4	„	Photo Glass		6	0	„
Lavatory Window Glass, ...	60	0	„	First Class Window Strap, ...		6	9	„
Corridor Dropping Window Glass, ...	11	10	„	Third Class Window Strap, ...		3	9	„
„ Door to Compartment Glass, ...	16	3	„	Lavatory Window Strap, ...		2	11	„
Gangway Door Glass, ...	20	7	„					

ABOVE: **Plate 2.28**
The published tariff for glass breakage dates from 1915. Today's equivalent sum for breaking a lavatory window, which had the lion rampant engraved on the obscured glass, would be over £350.

9. NRS BR/CAL/5/11 entry 19
10. NRS BR/CAL/5/12 entry 162
11. NRS BR/CAL/5/13 entry 32/692
12. NRM 68D82/6/5/b/1-68D82/6/6/c/17 (Eshton Hall Collection)
13. *1915 Working Timetable Appendix*, p. 89
14. *Caledonian Railway Wagons*, pp. 270-72
15. NRS BR/CAL/5/11 entry 34
16. NRS BR/CAL/5/11 entry 92
17. NRS BR/CAL/1/28 entry 855
18. *1915 Working Timetable Appendix*, pp. 79-80
19. *1907 Working Timetable*, Northern Section, p. 75
20. NRM 68D82/6/5/b/1-68D82/6/6/c/17 (Eshton Hall Collection)
21. NRS BR/CAL/5/61
22. *The Railway Magazine*, March 1913, pp. 230-37
23. CRA Archive ref: 3/3/1/12
24. *1915 Working Timetable Appendix*, p. 89
25. NRS BR/CAL/5/61

Plates 2.29 and 2.30
The external damage to 'Grampian' Corridor Composite 137 is shown in Plate 9.1. This photograph (*right*) shows the torn buffalo hide padding on the inside of the damaged door. The original is in the NRM St. Rollox collection, ref: SRX 325. As can be seen in Plate 2.30 (*below*), the piece work rate for repairing the damage was 2s 9d.

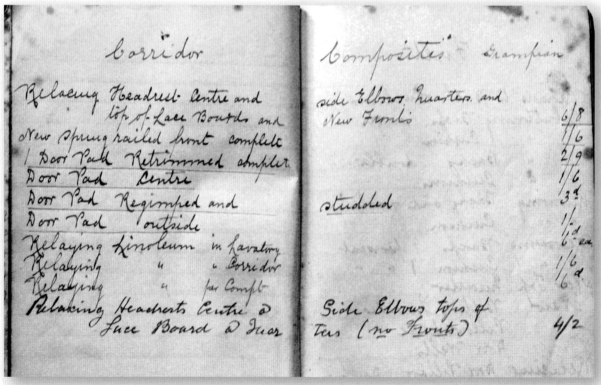

CHAPTER 3
THE DEVELOPMENT OF THE CARRIAGE FLEET –
RISING STANDARDS OF COMFORT AND CONVENIENCE

3.1: CLASSES OF TRAVEL

Social class was a very important aspect of nineteenth and early twentieth century life. Social mobility as we understand it in the twenty-first century was to all intents and purposes unknown. Class distinctions were rigid and everyone was expected to 'know their place.' The classes of passenger accommodation on the railways were equally distinct, but there was a certain amount of downward mobility, especially, as we shall see, on the Greenock Railway.

THIRD CLASS TRAVEL IN SCOTLAND

It had been thought initially that railway travel would be restricted to the upper and middle classes, as they were the only people who had previously travelled distances in any numbers. This was certainly the case in England, but for Scottish railway companies there was a large market for railway travel among the working classes. Captain Huish, the General Manager of the L&NWR, highlighted the difference between the two nations in evidence to the Standing Committee on Railway Communication in 1840:

> 'In England the principle revenue of the railways is derived from the better class of passengers; in Scotland it is derived almost entirely from the poorer class of passengers.'[1]

Many of the fast trains in England were for exclusive use of First, and perhaps Second, class. This was not the case in Scotland.

As confirmation of the difference between Scottish and English travel patterns, it was reported in 1842 that the two Arbroath lines carried twice as many Third class passengers as the London & Birmingham, the Grand Junction and the Great Western combined.[2]

As an example of the difference in attitude between English and Scottish railways, the Lancaster & Carlisle Railway objected in 1851 to a proposal for a Third class carriage to be run on the 9.05pm Up Mail and the Down Mail train leaving Liverpool at 10.00pm. The reaction from the Caledonian was unequivocal:

> 'The Board is strongly convinced of the importance of encouraging 3rd Class traffic and is particularly desirous of attaching (this carriage).'[3]

By 1859, the only provision of Second class travel on the Caledonian was on trains to Carlisle and the south. Travel on trains that ran exclusively in Scotland were for First and Third class passengers only. The only exceptions were mail trains, which also conveyed Second class. In his CR jubilee interview,[4] Sir James Thompson remarked that the Caledonian was the first railway to book 'third class passengers by all trains between stations over which we have entire control.' CR Public Timetables always advertised that Third class travel was available on all trains.

THE PARLIAMENTARY TRAINS

Before the Caledonian came into existence, the Regulation of Railways Act had been passed in 1844. It required railways to put on one train with provision for carrying Third class passengers on every line, every day, in each direction, stopping at every station. This Act was mainly aimed at railways in England, which had not provided services to meet government's aspirations concerning mobility of labour. A Select Committee in 1840 stated:

> 'To convey the labourer cheaply and rapidly to that spot where his labour might be most highly remunerated, was frequently stated to be one great benefit which would be derived from opening these new channels of intercourse.'[5]

On the so-called 'Parliamentary Trains',

– The fare should be one penny per mile.
– Its average speed should not be less than 12 miles per hour.
– Third class passengers should be protected from the weather and be provided with seats.

Of these, the last provision had the greatest impact for the very early Scottish railways, because their Third class fares were almost always already less than one penny per mile.

PARLIAMENTARY TRAINS ON THE CALEDONIAN

On the main line in 1859, the timetable shows that one train in the morning and one in the evening ran each way from Glasgow and Edinburgh to Carlisle. The trains conveyed First as well as Third class passengers. Stopping at all stations as the Act stipulated, the journey took about five hours. An express train took about three hours.

Between Glasgow and Edinburgh every train except one mail train was classed as Parliamentary and conveyed First class passengers as well as Third. Stopping at all stations, the 60 mile trip via Carstairs took about 3½ hours.

On the Glasgow and Hamilton line there were no parliamentary trains, and only one each way on the Greenock line. In both cases the standard Third class fare was below 1d per mile, so all the trains met the Act's conditions.

VARYING STANDARDS OF COMFORT

Different Second class standards were a source of conflict in the early days. In December 1848 the General Manager of the L&NWR requested that the Caledonian abolish cushions in Second class compartments, as the provision of such luxuries reflected badly on L&NWR carriages when Caledonian vehicles ran south of Carlisle on through trains.[6] Through working continued at least until the inauguration of the Joint Stock fleet. For example, in 1860 the West Coast Conference noted that the Caley was running single Composite carriages to Manchester by the two routes through Parkside and Bolton.[7]

The Caledonian decided to continue to provide cushions but Captain Huish did not let the matter rest as, approximately one year later, the Railway Clearing House, at his behest, contacted the Caledonian in an attempt to get the standard of Second class carriages on different railways to conform with each other.[8] Differences were resolved shortly afterwards. An 1850 CR minute concerning Second class reported the forthcoming production of a 'Standard to be agreed across all Companies by the Railway Clearing House.'[9]

A similar conflict arose in the early years of the Scottish Central Railway. In 1850 the SCR,

'agreed to let the Aberdeen Railway run their Second Class carriage without cushions on the Central Line and agreed not to renew the cushions on the Central line Second Class carriage when they are worn out.'[10]

Ten years later the position on the Caledonian had reversed. The General Committee noted that 'Attention was called to the uncomfortable state of the Second Class carriages' and it 'ordered that the Second Class Carriages attached to trains on the Main Line and Edinburgh Branch be fitted with Cushions.'[11]

General standards of comfort also varied between railways. The carriages inherited from the Greenock Railway differed dramatically from those of the Caledonian, which took over the former in 1850. The Greenock stock was a matter of public derision. A press article had this to say:

'A Greenock first class ... is certainly the best class on the line, but this is all that can be said of it. And you must not speak of its grandeur, or its luxury, or even its comfort, if you would not drag it into unwished for observation and so do it a great unkindness. The Greenock seconds ... are literally so many ale-house benches! Of course there is nothing but the hard deal boards to sit upon, and the cold bare walls all around are just in keeping with the rest of the fittings. Of light there is little, and of cleanliness (not to say comfort) there is none. Currents of air and clouds of dust find their way freely through a thousand crevices in walls and floors and the little pigeon holes on either side, called windows, make the whole compartment more like a prison cell than a railway carriage.'[12]

The Third class carriages, of course, were even worse:

'the Greenock thirds:- of course the latter are regular stand-ups – no seats of any kind; then each of them is subdivided into four spaces or pens, exactly like bughts [stalls] in a cattle market. "Are ye gaun in the bughts the day, Jock?" is quite a common phrase among the common people on the line; and although roofed over above, these carriages are quite open at both sides, so that the wind and rain drift freely through them; and from the quickness of motion, the train never starts but it blows a gale.'

It was not just the 'common people' who patronised Third class on the Greenock line. Class boundaries crumbled because there was an opportunity to save money. Travel in an unseated carriage was half the price of a seat. The national press reported that:

'The most wealthy and influential merchants of Glasgow are daily to be seen crowding into the third-class carriages; indeed, it is nothing uncommon to see them drive up to the station in their own carriages and then step into a 'stand-up', as they are called, at 6d for Greenock.'[13]

Therein lies the reason for the atrocious conditions suffered by the Greenock line's Third class passengers. The Chairman of the company, in response to a magazine article which said that the well-to-do crowded out the poor who should be the beneficiaries of cheap travel, said that there were no seats in Third class because:

'were they otherwise, those who took the second class, would crowd into them, and without the higher charges of the first and second class, the Company could not afford to keep the third class on the line.'[14]

Standards did not improve greatly after the Caledonian take-over. Chapter 5 discusses a petition to the Board of Trade in the mid-1860s, although the passengers' grievances were about the riding of carriages, not their furnishing. 'Stand up' carriages were still in use on the line up to 1875, as described in Chapter 6, and a Fourth class was available for those prepared to travel in a carriage attached to a goods train.

THE BEGINNING OF THE END FOR SECOND CLASS

In 1872 the Midland Railway decided to run Third class carriages by all trains. The decision benefitted the company as well as the travelling public. According to MR General Manager James Allport's obituary:

'The result was a remarkable improvement in the receipts and in the number of passengers carried, and it was found that, as duplicate trains were no longer needed, the expenditure was actually diminished, instead of increased, as the opponents of the change had predicted. Another result, however, soon became apparent that the second-class traffic was largely diminished, while the third-class traffic enormously increased.

In 1873 it was found that the revenue from first-class passengers was about 8d. per mile, that from second-class 7d., while that from third-class was no less than 2s. 8d., or more than twice as much as the two higher classes together. It was clear, therefore, that the trains must be carrying a large and increasing proportion of dead weight in the form of empty second-class carriages, and hence Mr. Allport was induced to consider whether it would not be better to abolish that class entirely. In order that the second-class passenger should not suffer, he reduced the first-class fare to the second class scale. Judging from past experience he anticipated that this change would result in no loss of revenue but in economy of working, lightening of trains and greater punctuality.'[15]

The matter was discussed among other railway companies in 1872. The CR's General Manager had been remitted by the Traffic Committee to 'consult with other companies and report' about the 'discontinuance of Second Class carriages.'[16] Apart from the Midland, there was no mood at the time for abolition.

To match the Midland's initiative, Third class travel was extended to all WCJS trains from 1st April 'including the Limited Mail.'[17] Previously, this train had been available to First and Second class passengers only. As a consequence of the decision, thirty WCJS carriages under construction were made as Tri-Composites.[18]

In fact this was the peak time for Second class travel on the Caledonian, as the following table recording the number of passengers carried shows. The figures are taken from Directors' reports.[19]

	1867	1873	1879
First class	1,042,714	1,107,102	1,241,424
Second class	529,346	1,168,505	1,068,236
Third class	7,177,702	10,087,587	10,709,198

In 1876 the Midland Railway took its first steps towards the abolition of Second class, although this was not its stated aim at the time. It and the G&SWR gave notice of their intention to withdraw from a joint agreement made in 1874 which specified 'padded seats, hat-cords, and racks, each compartment being separated by a division carried to the roof' for Third class accommodation. The West Coast Conference resolved:

'that the 3rd Class compartments in the new West Coast Stock be improved, and that the Managers adopt such other arrangements as may be necessary by the action of the Midland Company.'[20]

The major improvement was padding on the backs of Third class compartments in carriages built in 1877. The decision was reached *'having ascertained that the Glasgow and South Western Railway Company are fitting their new carriages with paddings.'*[21]

ABOLITION OF SECOND CLASS ON THE MIDLAND RAILWAY

In January 1878 the MR abolished Second class and further upgraded its Third class accommodation in readiness for the opening of the Settle & Carlisle route and Anglo-Scottish services from St. Pancras in collaboration with the Glasgow & South Western.

In 1879, Third class compartments on West Coast Joint Stock had to be upgraded again, this time because the East Coast route had acted first to compete with the Midland. Compartments were *'to be fitted up with window blinds and high stuffed backs.'*[22]

The L&NWR was strongly in favour of Second class travel, but the improved Third class facilities had a serious impact on First class as well as Second class bookings. Downward mobility was evidently not a quirk of Greenock residents. Neele recalled that:

'It was at the half-yearly meeting in August, 1884, that the Chairman (Richard Moon) called pointed attention to the striking change these 3rd Class facilities were making in the traffic, the half-year's return shewed a reduction of 50,000 1st Class passengers, and an increase of 500,000 on the 3rd Class, and waxing wroth with "those gentlemen of first position" who availed themselves of the 3rd Class accommodation intended only for the working classes, he added, "all I hope is that they will have sweeps or navvies riding with them!"'[23]

THE CALEDONIAN WITHDRAWS SECOND CLASS FACILITIES

Early in 1886, Irving Kempt wrote two letters to the CR Board which recommended *'the gradual withdrawal of all the local Second Class bookings, with the exception of those upon the Glasgow and Greenock and Wemyss Bay section.'* His proposal was approved in March.[24]

The Scottish railways were determined to act as one but they took their time. At a meeting on 28th December 1888, by which time some Second class local travel still survived on the Caledonian,

'Mr Thompson (Cal) said he was prepared to concur in the withdrawal of all these (services) with the exception of Wemyss Bay. Mr Thompson referred to Gourock and Mr Walker (NB) said that Gourock and Helensburgh should be the same – 1st and 3rd. Mr Walker instructed Mr Cathles to write to Mr Morton of the South Western Company to ascertain what he was prepared to do.'[25]

The following table shows the decline in Second class passenger numbers and the switch to Third class as the Caledonian gradually withdrew the facility.

	1885	1891
First class	1,245,472	1,208,063
Second class	753,727	417,670
Third class	14,700,415	21,912,318

The drop in revenue from the Second class passengers was even more significant than the fall in numbers; from £49,982 in 1885 it fell to £16,527 in 1891.

SECOND CLASS CEASES ON ANGLO-SCOTTISH SERVICES

In 1892 the Caledonian Board gave notice to the L&NWR about the accommodation in the new corridor trains that were to be introduced for the 1893 summer season. The CR would *'Approve the building of Corridor Trains as proposed provided they are composed of First and Third Class only.'*[26]

This signalled the end of Second class on Anglo-Scottish trains. The West Coast Conference noted that the abolition of Second class was a joint decision made by the East and West Coast conferences and that *'Mr Park has been instructed to alter the lettering of Second Class carriages to Third Class.'*[27]

The L&NWR persisted with Second class on services in England and Wales until 1912. The CR's early abolition was still a source of grievance to at least one shareholder who wrote to the Board from England in 1911. His complaint was that the standard of Third class carriages was now far too high, which caused First and Second class carriages to run empty. This reduced profits and therefore dividends to shareholders. He further complained that the Thirds were now so comfortable that it was not worth paying double to go First class.[28]

LUGGAGE

Long-distance passengers tended to travel with a great deal of luggage, especially on the Anglo-Scottish services, as G.P. Neele recalled:

'Much of this luggage … was roofed on the carriages and strapped down under heavy tarpaulins. … Mishaps were not infrequent owing to striking bridges through careless loading, luggage overhanging and falling off through getting out of position by oscillation while travelling, fire arose from engine sparks, and frequent annoyance was experienced through the carriage roof lamps going out, their supply of air being cut off by close packing of luggage. I had the satisfaction of seeing this roofing of luggage, a relic of old coaching days, gradually but entirely dispensed with, the manager agreeing to my recommendation to adopt the plan of a separate luggage compartment in the centre of the passenger carriages, similar in style to those I had observed in Birmingham on the North Eastern Railway stock. Among the first vehicles to be so furnished were the new Composite Carriages of what were called the West Coast Joint Stock.'[29]

The carriages referred to by Neele were introduced in 1871.[30] Many Caledonian carriages were fitted with railings on the roof to contain luggage until the 1870s, but the company also had Luggage Vans from the beginning. As will be seen in Chapter 5.1, ten vans were built for the Northern section of the line in 1846 and by 1853 eighteen were in service. This sufficed until 1862. Over the next three years the number doubled, and a large number of vans were inherited in the two amalgamations of 1865 and 1867. By the end of the McIntosh era, there were 160 Passenger Brake Vans and a further sixty-three vans numbered in the Luggage Van series, which were also used to convey perishable produce.

The 'Grampian' style carriages to Diagram 101A were modified in 1915 *'to provide more accommodation for luggage and parcels traffic.'* The details are in Chapter 11.1.

First class passengers were allowed to carry 120 lbs of luggage free of charge on services within Scotland, and Third class passengers half that. This rose to 150 lbs and 100 lbs on Anglo-Scottish services. Every article of luggage had to be properly labelled and addressed.

The luggage racks above the seats were:

'provided for light articles only … other heavy items … must be placed under the seats … or otherwise loaded in the Guard's

vans or in the proper luggage compartments of the trains. Any infringement of this instruction is attended by the risk of injury to passengers.[31]

During the Drummond and Lambie era provision of racks above the seats for light items of luggage seems to have been confined to vehicles that were used as through carriages. Examples are shown in Chapter 7, Figures 7.17 and 7.23. Around 1900, McIntosh seems to have extended the facility and adopted a new style of net cord support which continued in use until the outbreak of war. This is illustrated in Chapter 4, Plate 4.19.

TRANSFER AND DELIVERY OF LUGGAGE

For a fee of 6d per item, luggage could be transferred between any two of the four Glasgow terminal stations *'by the Railway Companies' Carts.'*

A passenger who lived within *'one mile the North Side of the Clyde from the Royal Exchange'* could deposit luggage at the left luggage offices at Central of Buchanan Street and have it delivered to their home at the rate of 4d up to 28 lbs and 6d up to 112 lbs. Passengers living on the south side of the Clyde were granted this facility if they lived within 1¼ miles of the Exchange.[32] In Edinburgh the parcel delivery system was used for the same fee.

BICYCLES

In 1902, the Caledonian began to fit bicycle racks into 48-foot Third class carriages with an enlarged Brake section. There is a drawing of the arrangement in Chapter 8.2, Figure 8.17. There was a similar fitting in some Passenger Brake Vans. The Brake Vans of 'Grampian' stock were also fitted with the racks. Card tickets were issued from all stations *'for Bicycles accompanied by their owners.'*

It was also possible, when *'Van accommodation on the train is limited,'* to convey bicycles in carriage compartments. A supply of special straps was kept at strategic stations. The strap was used to hang upto three bicycles per side from the luggage rack brackets.[33]

DOGS

Dogs were not allowed to travel in the compartment with their owners for the first thirty years of the Caledonian's existence. A by-law in the 1853 Public Timetable stated:

'Dogs will not be suffered to accompany Passengers, in the Carriages, but will be conveyed separately and charged for.'

They were put into 'dog boxes' which were separated from the passenger accommodation. The boxes can be identified by their louvred ventilators near the floor of carriage and Brake Van bodies. The company would only take responsibility for the animals if *'delivered to them properly addressed and secured with collar and chain.'* It would not be liable for loss or damage to any dog above the value of 20s, unless the value had been declared when the animal's ticket was issued.[34]

The boxes were only fitted to Second and Third class carriages and Passenger Brake Vans. The last carriages to be fitted with them seem to have been the Metropolitan-built Thirds of 1874.

Later, the by-law was supplemented by a regulation which allowed dogs in compartments, but only if they were fitted with:

'a wire cage muzzle so constructed as to render it impossible for such Dog while wearing the same to bite any person or animal, but not so as to prevent such Dog from breathing freely and lapping water.'

Shepherds' dogs and *'Dogs accompanying Passengers'* were included in the regulation. The only animals exempt were packs of hounds used for sporting purposes and dogs travelling to shows.[35] The usual way for dogs to travel was in a container in the Brake Van, although in some later vans they could be tethered to dog rings. The centre elevation in Figure 11.14 shows dog rings at the inner end of the Brake compartment.

REFERENCES

1. *The Origins of the Scottish Railway System*, p. 239
2. Second Report to the Board of Trade, quoted in *The Origins of the Scottish Railway System*, p. 237
3. NRS BR/CAL/1/10 entry 263
4. *The Railway Magazine*, October 1897, pp. 289-301
5. *The Origins of the Scottish Railway System*, p. 240
6. NRS BR/CAL/1/8 14th December 1848
7. NRS BR/WCC/1/6 minute 128
8. NRS BR/CAL/1/9 entry 175
9. NRS BR/CAL/1/9 21st February 1850
10. NRS BR/SCC/1/16 p. 47
11. NRS BR/CAL/1/12 entry 516
12. *The North British Railway and Shipping Journal*, 29th April, 1848
13. *The Railway Times*, 22nd October 1842
14. *The Origins of the Scottish Railway System*, p. 243
15. *The Engineer*, 29th April 1892, p. 365
16. NRS BR/CAL/1/20 entry 229
17. NRS BR/WCC/1/6 minute 1140
18. NRS BR/WCC/1/6 minute 1127
19. NRM 68D82/6/5/b1-68D82/6/6/c/17 (Eshton Hall Collection)
20. NRS BR/WCC/1/7 minute 1483
21. NRS BR/WCC/1/7 minute 1563
22. NRS BR/WCC/1/7 minute 1692
23. *Railway Reminiscences*, p. 295
24. NRS BR/CAL/1/30 entry 907
25. NRS BR/CAL/4/28
26. NRS BR/CAL/1/35 entry 1440
27. NRS BR/WCC/1/4 minute 2550
28. NRS BR/CAL/4/75/14 CRA Archive ref: 2/3/2/1
29. *Railway Reminiscences*, pp. 105-6
30. *West Coast Joint Stock*, p. 58
31. *1906 Rule Book*, paragraph 199
32. *1915 Working Timetable Appendix*, p. 106
33. *1915 Working Timetable Appendix*, p. 104
34. *Public Timetable 1859*, CRA Archive ref: 3/1/1/6
35. *1915 Working Timetable Appendix*, p. 106

3.2: WORKMEN'S TRAINS AND RESIDENTIAL EXPRESSES

In the Victorian era the major UK cities suffered from severe overcrowding, none more so than Glasgow, where the population density increased by 4½ times between 1850 and 1900. Overcrowding became a major political issue in the 1880s and one solution was to encourage working people to move to new housing outside the cities.

This had been a government aspiration since the early days of the railways. In 1840 a Select Committee had seen one of a railways' benefits as follows:

'the health and enjoyment of the mechanics, artizans, and poor inhabitants of the large towns would be promoted, by the facility with which they would be enabled to remove themselves or their families into healthier districts and less crowded habitations.'[1]

The introduction of the 'Parliamentary' trains in 1844 had not achieved this aim. They were not frequent enough, or convenient for people on shift work. The government brought in the Cheap Trains Act which came into force in October 1883.[2] All trains charging one penny per mile or less were exempted from Railway Passenger Duty. Journeys charged above one penny per mile attracted Duty at 2%.

The Board of Trade could decide whether a company's services were adequate and reasonably priced. If the BoT felt otherwise, it could remove the company's exemption from Duty on all its services. The Act applied to:

'workmen going to and returning from their work at such fares and at such times between six o'clock in the evening and eight o'clock in morning.'

To qualify under the Act, railway companies had to apply for specific stations to be approved. The main criterion for approval was that the stations were:

'within an area which has a continuous urban as distinguished from a rural or suburban character and contains a Population of not less than one hundred thousand inhabitants.'

Although not specified in the Act, workmen could carry 60 lbs weight of tools essential to their job free of charge.[3]

THE FIRST STATIONS TO BE APPROVED

In September 1883 the Caledonian submitted the following list of stations[4] *'for the purposes of the Act, situated within one Urban District, viz:-'*

1st	Glasgow Central, Bridge Street, Eglinton Street, Pollokshields, Rutherglen, Bridgeton, London Road, Saint Rollox and Buchanan Street
2nd	Edinburgh Princes Street, Merchiston, Murrayfield, Craigleith, Granton Road, Newhaven and Leith
3rd	Dundee, Magdalen Green and Lochee

The Glasgow and Edinburgh stations were approved, but Lochee was removed from the Dundee list as *'it is separated from Magdalen Green by a long rural district.'*

In 1886, with the opening of the Cathcart Railway, the stations between Mount Florida and Cathcart Road were approved. Major Marindin, the inspecting officer, noted that:

'there are other stations on the Caledonian Railway in the neighbourhood of Glasgow area which are probably entitled to a certificate and the Officers of the Company are to consider the question and forward a revised application.'

Further applications were duly made. As a result Strathbungo, which was already certified for the G&SWR, was approved for Caledonian services. Cathcart was rejected because between the stations (Cathcart and Mount Florida) *'there is no continuous line of houses, but often fields under cultivation.'*

APPLICATIONS IN 1899

The next expansion of workmen's services occurred when the Lanarkshire & Dumbartonshire Railway opened. This was an independent line worked by the CR. Approval was also sought for stations on the completed Cathcart Circle, the Glasgow Central Railway and the Tollcross and Carmyle line.

Approval was given in early 1900 for all the stations which merited inspection except three. Instead of immediately sending an inspector, the BoT asked the Caledonian to investigate the population density around the stations in question. The reply from the CR General Manager's office claimed:

'the line of houses between them and the stations already certified nearest them respectively, is practically continuous, but that the population is not so dense in the direction of Tollcross, Cathcart and Maxwell Park as at the stations nearer the centre of the city of Glasgow and ... the Company will not in the meantime press the application in respect of the three stations referred to.'

In connection with this expansion of services, twelve Third class carriages were converted to Brake Thirds, probably becoming Diagram 16A. There are more details in Chapter 8.3 and a drawing of the internal layout in Figure 8.22.

FURTHER EXPANSION IN 1906

In 1906/7, urban expansion stimulated a fresh application. By now, too, the municipal tramways were making serious inroads into railway traffic. The BoT wrote to the Caledonian that it would be prepared to approve the following additional stations in the three districts. Some of the stations had been voluntarily excluded from previous applications or rejected by the Board of Trade.

Glasgow	Maxwell Park, Shawlands, Pollokshaws East, Langside & Newlands, Cathcart, Ibrox, Tollcross, Carmyle, Mount Vernon, Cambuslang, Kirkhill, Burnside, Yoker, Clydebank, Kilbowie Road and Dalmuir
Edinburgh	Dalry Road
Dundee	Lochee West and Lochee

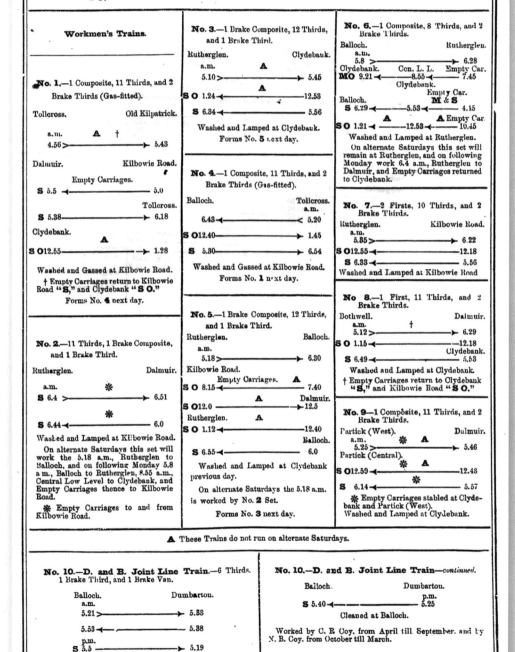

11

HAMILTON, MOTHERWELL, RUTHERGLEN, MARYHILL, DAWSHOLM, AND BALLOCH SECTIONS—Continued.

Notes.—These Trains are made up of Bogie Vehicles, consisting of 1 First, 1 Third, and 2 Brake Thirds, with the exception of those shewn to be strengthened, and are Cleaned at **Rutherglen** (with the exception of Nos. **14, 15,** and **17** sets which are cleaned at **Larkfield**), and Gassed at **Larkfield, Dawsholm, Maryhill,** and **Rutherglen.**

Maryhill will gas the 10.20 p.m. Train.

Rutherglen to strengthen Trains as required on Saturdays. Maryhill to strengthen No. **10** set at 7.9 a.m. **"W O"** and **"S O."**

Workmen's Trains.

No. 1.—1 Composite, 11 Thirds, and 2 Brake Thirds (Gas-fitted).
Tollcross. / Old Kilpatrick.
a.m.   A   †
4.56 > → 5.43
Dalmuir. / Kilbowie Road.
Empty Carriages.
S 5.5 ← 5.0
Tollcross.
S 5.38 → 6.18
Clydebank.   A
S O12.55 ← → 1.28
Washed and Gassed at Kilbowie Road.
† Empty Carriages return to Kilbowie Road "S," and Clydebank "S O."
Forms No. 4 next day.

No. 2.—11 Thirds, 1 Brake Composite, and 1 Brake Third.
Rutherglen. / Dalmuir.
a.m. ※
S 6.4 > → 6.51
※
S 6.44 ← 6.0
Washed and Lamped at Kilbowie Road.
On alternate Saturdays this set will work the 5.18 a.m., Rutherglen to Balloch, and on following Monday 5.8 a.m., Balloch to Rutherglen, 8.55 a.m., Central Low Level to Clydebank, and Empty Carriages thence to Kilbowie Road.
※ Empty Carriages to and from Kilbowie Road.

No. 3.—1 Brake Composite, 12 Thirds, and 1 Brake Third.
Rutherglen. / Clydebank.
a.m.   A
5.10 > → 5.45
A
S O 1.24 ← 12.53
S 6.34 ← 5.56
Washed and Lamped at Clydebank.
Forms No. 5 next day.

No. 4.—1 Composite, 11 Thirds, and 2 Brake Thirds (Gas-fitted).
Balloch. / Tollcross.
a.m.
6.43 ← 5.20
S O12.40 → 1.45
S 5.30 → 6.54
Washed and Gassed at Kilbowie Road.
Forms No. 1 next day.

No. 5.—1 Brake Composite, 12 Thirds, and 1 Brake Third.
Rutherglen. / Balloch.
a.m.
5.18 > → 6.30
Kilbowie Road.
Empty Carriages.   A
S O 8.15 ← 7.40
Dalmuir.
S O12.0 → 12.5
Rutherglen.   A
S O 1.12 → 12.40
Balloch.
S 6.55 ← 6.0
Washed and Lamped at Clydebank previous day.
On alternate Saturdays the 5.18 a.m. is worked by No. 2 Set.
Forms No. 3 next day.

No. 6.—1 Composite, 8 Thirds, and 2 Brake Thirds.
Balloch. / Rutherglen.
a.m.
5.8 > → 6.28
Clydebank. Con. L. L. Empty Car.
MO 9.21 ← 8.55 → 7.45
Clydebank.
Empty Car.
Balloch.   M & S
S 6.29 ← 5.53 → 4.15
A   Empty Car.
S O 1.21 ← 12.53 ← 10.45
Washed and Lamped at Rutherglen.
On alternate Saturdays this set will remain at Rutherglen, and on following Monday work 6.4 a.m., Rutherglen to Dalmuir, and Empty Carriages returned to Clydebank.

No. 7.—2 Firsts, 10 Thirds, and 2 Brake Thirds.
Rutherglen. / Kilbowie Road.
a.m.
5.35 > → 6.22
S O12.55 ← 12.18
S 6.33 ← 5.56
Washed and Lamped at Kilbowie Road.

No 8.—1 First, 11 Thirds, and 2 Brake Thirds.
Bothwell. / Dalmuir.
a.m.   †
5.12 > → 6.29
S O 1.15 ← 12.18
Clydebank.
S 6.49 ← 5.53
Washed and Lamped at Clydebank.
† Empty Carriages return to Clydebank "S," and Kilbowie Road "S O."

No. 9.—1 Composite, 11 Thirds, and 2 Brake Thirds.
Partick (West). / Dalmuir.
a.m. ※ A
5.25 > → 5.46
Partick (Central).
※ A
S O12.59 ← 12.43
※
S 6.14 ← 5.57
※ Empty Carriages stabled at Clydebank and Partick (West).
Washed and Lamped at Clydebank.

A These Trains do not run on alternate Saturdays.

No. 10.—D. and B. Joint Line Train.—6 Thirds, 1 Brake Third, and 1 Brake Van.
Balloch. / Dumbarton.
a.m.
5.21 > → 5.33
5.53 ← 5.38
p.m.
S 5.5 → 5.19

No. 10.—D. and B. Joint Line Train—continued.
Balloch. / Dumbarton.
p.m.
S 5.40 ← 5.25
Cleaned at Balloch.
Worked by C. R. Coy. from April till September, and by N. B. Coy. from October till March.

Plate 3.1
The Clydebank workmen's trains timetable from 1906. The notes at the top of the page do not apply. The carriages that were 'lamped' were oil-lit. It was normal practice to work on Saturday morning in addition to Monday-Friday.

If the Caledonian wished to press for a certificate for Cardonald, Muirend and Robroyston in the Glasgow district, Slateford in Edinburgh and Baldovan and Barnhill in the Dundee district, an inspection would be necessary. The CR replied that it would not press for these stations to be certified, with the exception of Muirend, which *'is simply an extension of Cathcart with which it has a continuous tenement connection.'* Colonel Yorke duly inspected and recommended its inclusion in the certificate because *'Muirend is practically a continuation of Cathcart and the tramways from Glasgow run into Muirend.'*

WORKMEN'S SERVICES IN 1906

The bulk of the workmen's trains ran to the factories and docks on the north bank of the Clyde. In 1906 nine sets of carriages were involved. Another train, which ran between Dumbarton and Balloch, was worked jointly by the Caledonian and the North British for six months each per year. The composition of these trains is shown in Plate 3.1.

On the Lanarkshire & Dumbartonshire line, the 1907 Timetable stated that all Up (towards Glasgow) trains after 10.00am were to have the front compartments of the leading Third class carriage labelled 'Workmen' to accommodate holders of 'stamped' tickets. Companies issued workmen's tickets stamped 'Ordinary Train' to employees who were laid off work for whatever reason. The compartments were also to be used by *'Workmen paying full Ordinary Fare, but whose clothes are soiled by their work, and who must not be allowed to mix with other Passengers.'*[5]

One set of carriages comprising a First, a Composite and two Brake Thirds were provided for the Port Glasgow and Gourock workmen's train. No special provision was made for workmen on the Cathcart Circle. One set of carriages conveyed Caledonian Railway servants from Buchanan Street to St. Rollox. In Edinburgh, an extra Third and Brake Third reserved for workmen were attached to normal service trains on the Leith Branch.

Four sets of carriages were also used for workmen in the Coalburn and Muirkirk area, but these services were outwith the Cheap Trains Act agreement.

CLYDEBANK WORKMEN'S SERVICES IN 1913

By this time only two sets of carriages were oil-lit. The increased demand for gas prompted the Traffic Committee to authorise the construction of a triple-tank gas wagon for 'Gassing Workmen's Trains on Lanarkshire & Dumbartonshire line running between Rutherglen and Alexandria.'[6] It was built to drawing 18752,[7] allocated number 27 and based at Rutherglen.

CLYDEBANK WORKMEN'S SERVICES IN 1921

The same level of service as in 1913 was maintained on Clydebank, but the carriages were now all Third class. Twenty-six Brake Thirds and 139 Thirds were involved. Two sets were still oil-lit. One of these trains was formed of twelve Third class and two Brake Thirds. The other was a short train of one Third and two Brake Thirds.

THE BEATTOCK SERVICE

Beattock village was an isolated railway settlement, with additional railway servants' dwellings scattered from the foot of the bank to the summit ten miles away. Although it did not qualify under the Act, one outward and return train ran each Wednesday and Saturday 'for the convenience of the Company's Servants and their Families employed between Summit and Auchencastle when requiring to travel for marketing purposes.'[8]

The trains were worked by a single Brake Third carriage and one of the banking locomotives. Although it was not specified in the 1907 Working Timetable, the 1913 and 1921 Local Working of Carriages Circulars state that the carriage was 6-wheeled.

OTHER WORKMEN'S SERVICES IN SOUTH WEST SCOTLAND

A set of two Brake Third carriages running between Carlisle Yard and Kingmoor is shown in the 1921 Local Working of Carriages circular. Although not stated, they were probably 6-wheeled. The service did not appear in 1906 or 1913, so one must assume that it was a war-time innovation. It made a return trip before 6.00am and a similar one in the evening. An extra return trip was made at lunch time on Saturday.

A similar service ran between Dumfries and the Arrol-Johnston motor car factory at Heath Hall. Although the factory built cars before World War I, the service only figures in the 1921 circular. The service was probably put on when the factory re-opened in 1918. This was a large train, composed of eight Thirds and two Brake Thirds. It ran in the morning, lunchtime and evening Monday to Friday. Work finished at lunchtime on Saturday. There is no mention of empty carriage working, so the train must have been stabled at Heath Hall during the daytime.

VOLUME OF WORKMEN'S TRAIN TRAFFIC

Directors' reports to shareholders[9] itemised workmen's transportation separately and highlighted the vital role it played in Scotland's industry – see the following table which shows the number of passengers conveyed.

	1913	1920	1921
Third class	34,442,595	31,676,655	26,094,681
Workmen	10,720,225	14,222,994	7,274,538

The 50% drop in journeys from 1920 to 1921 can be explained in part by a reduction in employment in heavy industry that occurred throughout the UK, and additionally by the switch to alternative forms of transport.

RESIDENTIAL EXPRESSES

At the other end of the social spectrum from workmen's trains, the Caley worked hard to attract professionals who were wealthy enough to live in the country during the summer and travel to Glasgow or Edinburgh by train. This reached its peak with the summer timetable of 1911, as reported in the press.[10]

'The outstanding feature of the early summer train arrangements announced by the Caledonian Railway Company ... is the institution of a large number of new and improved long-distance residential express services.

The rapid growth of such places as Bridge of Allan, Dunblane, Doune, Callander and Crieff is entirely due to the admirable service of residential trains provided ... from and to Glasgow and Edinburgh.'

The article then went on to detail the new services in the various districts, including Strathearn, Auchterarder, Dundee and the north. Part of a pocket timetable for the services in the Dundee area is shown in Plate 3.2. The article concluded:

'On the southern sections of the line, the principal changes ... are in connection with the residential services between Glasgow and Edinburgh and the districts of the Upper Ward of Lanarkshire and the Vale of Tweed.'

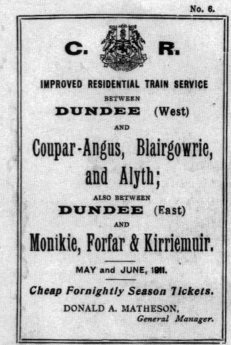

Plate 3.2
The cover and inside of the Residential pocket timetable for trains from the two Dundee stations. The time tables were just under 4 inches by 3 inches when folded.

ADVERTISING AND NAMED TRAINS

A series of posters was issued to publicise the services.[11] The first, see Plate 3.3, set out most, but not all, of the towns benefitting from the new services. The remainder (Plates 3.4-3.8) were for specific places or areas.

Part of the promotion was the naming of certain of the express trains. This practice had originated with the 'Grampian Express' and its return working the 'Granite City' express in 1905. In the 1912 Public Timetable the 'Tinto Express' ran from Moffat to Glasgow Central. From Buchanan Street, the 'Strathearn Express' ran from St. Fillans via Crieff, partnered by the 'Stirling & Ben Ledi Express' which went through to Callander. On Fridays only (northbound) and Mondays only (southbound) during the summer holiday season the 'C&O Hotel Express' ran between Buchanan Street and Oban.

STOCK USED ON THE RESIDENTIAL EXPRESSES

By the time the services were launched, the Caledonian had completed construction of the 'Grampian' stock and twenty-four matching semi-corridor 50-foot carriages. The carriages are described in Chapter 9. As an example of formations, in 1913 the 'Tinto Express' consisted of two Brake Composites from Moffat and two more plus a Composite from Peebles. All the carriages were 'Grampian' stock. There is a photograph of the Moffat portion of the express in 1921 in *Caledonian Cavalcade*.[12]

REFERENCES
1. *The Origins of the Scottish Railway System*, p. 240
2. 46 & 47 Vict. Cap. 34
3. *1915 Working Timetable Appendix*, p. 106
4. References for station approvals are from TNA MT6/1559/9
5. 1907 Working Timetable, p. 129
6. NRS BR/CAL/1/67 entry 631
7. RHP 67529
8. 1907 Working Timetable, p. 129
9. NRM 68D82/6/5/b/1-68D82/6/6/c/17 (Eshton Hall Collection)
10. *The Railway Gazette*, 31st March 1911, pp. 319-20
11. NRS BR/CAL/4/156
12. *Caledonian Cavalcade*, p. 44

TOP LEFT: Plate 3.3
This poster shows thirty towns served by residential services. It does not include all the towns served by the residential expresses – Moffat and Peebles are omitted for instance.

ABOVE AND FACING PAGE: Plates 3.4-3.8
Examples of the posters advertising the new residential expresses when the services were launched in 1911.

3.3: SLEEPING CARS

It could be argued that a Saloon built at Greenock in 1847 was one of the first carriages intended to offer sleeping accommodation on a British railway, although it was for private hire only. This vehicle is described in Chapter 13.1. Nearly twenty years later, James Ashbury had a design with which he approached railway companies. G.P. Neele described it as a:

'vehicle in which three beds in each compartment were provided by pulling down the apparent back of each seat, an operation which resulted in three coffin-like beds appearing side by side, the access to all being extremely difficult, and the centre one of the three the most inconvenient of the lot.'[1]

Ashbury tried to sell his concept to the Caledonian in 1865. He submitted a design, but nothing came of it.[2]

EARLY EXPERIMENTS BY THE WEST COAST COMPANIES

In 1871, St. Rollox produced drawing 1119 for a *'proposed sleeping carriage.'* Nothing came of the design, which was not formally discussed at the West Coast Conference. The drawing has not survived.

At the time, the L&NWR was experimenting with *'sleeping apparatus'* in ordinary First class carriages.[3] The improved arrangement consisted of the current 'apparatus' for two opposing seats in a compartment and the removal of armrests from the remaining seats to *'afford sleeping accommodation … for 3 persons in each compartment.'[4]* This arrangement offered *'sleeping facilities for twelve passengers as against the Ashbury of six – four places for ladies, eight for gentlemen.'[5]*

A later minute recorded that this included *'the provision of stretchers between the two seats opposite each other.* The minute went on to say that *'The Conference did not concur in the proposal to build special sleeping carriages.'[6]* Instead, the arrangement described was applied in 1872 to the two First class compartments in twenty-two new Tri-Composite carriages.[7] This was in response

to the intelligence that the East Coast Companies were considering *'the question of providing sleeping carriages on their through night trains,'* which was first reported in November 1871.[8]

Eventually the North British Railway pioneered dedicated Sleeping carriages in the UK on a scheduled service. An Ashbury-built Saloon was put on the Edinburgh–London route as part of the East Coast Joint Stock in 1873.[9]

THE FIRST WCJS CARS

The East Coast initiative galvanised the West Coast Conference officials. They reversed their decision not to build dedicated Sleeping carriages. In 1873 Colonel Mann submitted a design to the L&NWR which was later adopted on the Continent. The L&NWR decided to go its own way. In March it was considered that *'sleeping carriages should be adopted without delay. … A specimen carriage built by … the LNWR was inspected but the internal arrangements were not considered suitable.'[10]* Neele described it as follows.

'The four day seats in each compartment, the same as the four window seats in an ordinary first-class, by a mechanical appliance, could be formed into two beds, while "hammock" beds brought down from the roof by a riser on each side, provided the third and fourth bed in each compartment.'[11]

The original intention was to build *'a minimum number of eight sleeping carriages for the West Coast Traffic.'[12]* In summer, one was to run to Perth by the Limited Mail, returning by the 7.30pm Up train. Two carriages were to serve Perth and Glasgow. The Perth carriage would return by the Limited Mail and the other on the 9.10pm from Glasgow.

In the event, the West Coast Conference introduced one Sleeping car as an experiment on the Limited Mail between Euston and Glasgow, going north one night and south the next. There were ninety-seven passengers in October, fifty-three of them travelling to Scotland. This encouraged the Conference to commission another Saloon to travel

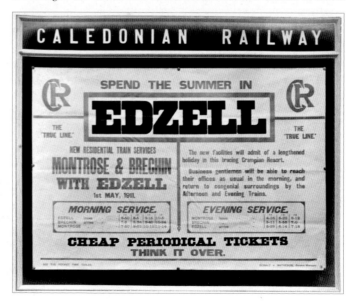

on the Mail.[13] A daily each-way service was established in 1874 using some of the four L&NWR-designed Sleeping carriages numbered 101-104.[14] Passenger numbers rose to 237 in the first full month.[15] The supplementary fare was ten shillings.[16]

The Caledonian suggested that the southbound carriage should be put on the 9.10pm departure from Glasgow[17] but the proposal seems to have been rejected by the L&NWR.

A Caledonian Prototype

The CR then began to investigate an alternative form of Sleeping carriage which reached the prototype stage and got no further. It ran for perhaps ten years between Stranraer and London before it was converted to a Third class Saloon. This was CR Sleeping Saloon number 12, which is fully described in Chapter 13.1.

More Caledonian Proposals

A Pullman Sleeping car service was introduced in 1876 on the joint MR/G&SWR overnight express from St. Pancras to Glasgow via the newly opened Settle & Carlisle line. As well as Sleeping cars, the ordinary carriages in the train were bogie stock, Second class was abolished and Third class upgraded in comfort.

No doubt spurred by the rival companies' introduction of bogie coaches and a Pullman Sleeping car on a train terminating in Glasgow, the Caledonian took the initiative within the West Coast Joint Committee, whose services were still exclusively composed of 6-wheeled stock. In January 1876[18] the Traffic Committee proposed the construction of a Sleeping Saloon,

'47 feet long (on bogie wheels), with accommodation convertible from day into night use, and lavatories; and also with ordinary compartments at each end.'[19]

The carriage was probably the subject of drawing 1953, which has not survived. The proposal was remitted to the West Coast Conference but the concept was not acceptable to the L&NWR, which remained wedded to 6-wheeled stock until 1882. Even then, the first 8-wheeled carriages were only 42 feet long and mounted on radial trucks. Instead of adopting the CR suggestion, the West Coast Conference minute quoted above continued:

'after careful consideration it was finally decided that Mr. Bore (London and North Western Company) be instructed to prepare plan and estimate, in duplicate, of the saloon of the length now in use and on the principle shown in the Caledonian Co.'s plan, omitting the ordinary compartments at each end.'

Wolverton put into service four 6-wheeled Sleeping carriages in October 1876, by which time the charge for travelling in earlier WCJS Sleeping Saloons had been reduced to eight shillings to compete directly with the Midland Railway.[20]

A Pullman Proposal

The Caledonian was not satisfied with the L&NWR's solution. In December 1880, its Board of Directors instructed the Secretary to communicate the following minute to his opposite number,

'viz: Resolved that the Board of the Caledonian Coy. Consider that in the interest of the WC route the time has arrived when it is absolutely necessary to adopt the Pullman Sleeping Car, and they suggest, as an experiment, that one carriage be run

each way, leaving Glasgow and London by the existing trains about 9pm.'[21]

The reply arrived within a week, and the Board noted the L&NWR Directors' 'unfavourable views in relation to these cars.'[22] Pullman cars were long and mounted on bogies, which remained a sticking point for the L&NWR. The fact that the Pullman Car Co. retained ownership of the carriages would also be anathema to a company that operated on totalitarian lines. Early in 1881 the exchange of correspondence was referred by the CR Board to the West Coast Conference.[23] There is no record of an outcome.

Wolverton Assumes Responsibility

In January 1882, a CR Traffic Committee minute[24] under the heading 'Sleeping Saloons' recorded:

'Read a memo recommending that two of these vehicles be taken over from LNWR and added to WC Joint Stock.
Remit for report on the whole question of English & Scotch passenger traffic, especially as regards Edinburgh.'

The final outcome was the Conference's decision to build two pairs of permanently coupled Sleeping Saloons, connected by a vestibule. The standard of accommodation was roughly equivalent to a Pullman car, including the provision of lavatories and heating, but the riding quality was said to be very poor.[25] The addition of radial trucks did not improve matters sufficiently and the cars were taken out of Anglo-Scottish service in 1886.

At this point the Caley tried again to influence L&NWR policy. In rapid succession during March 1886 St. Rollox produced drawings for 42-foot,[26] 44-foot[27] and 45-foot Sleeping Saloons.[28] The drawings have not survived.

None of the proposals was accepted by the L&NWR. Instead of using a Caledonian design or Pullman cars, it built increasingly luxurious carriages at Wolverton Works for day, night and dining services between England and Scotland.

References

1. *Railway Reminiscences*, p. 191
2. NRS BR/CAL/1/14 entries 310, 355 and 381
3. NRS BR/WCC/1/6 minute 925(2)
4. NRS BR/WCC/1/6 minute 971(2)
5. *Railway Reminiscences*, p. 191
6. NRS BR/WCC/1/6 minute 992(2 & 3)
7. NRS BR/WCC/1/6 minute 1127
8. NRS BR/WCC/1/6 minute 1088
9. Described in *NBR Coaches, a Design Review*, p. 59
10. NRS BR/WCC/1/7 minute 1214
11. *Railway Reminiscences*, p. 191
12. NRS BR/WCC/1/7, August 1873 meeting Appendix A, p. 7
13. NRS BR/WCC/1/7 minute 1275
14. *West Coast Joint Stock*, pp. 64-66
15. NRS BR/WCC/1/7 minute 1292
16. NRS BR/WCC/1/7 minute 1259
17. NRS BR/CAL/1/21 entry 1329
18. NRS BR/CAL/1/22 entry 1769
19. NRS BR/WCC/1/7 minute 1406
20. *West Coast Joint Stock*, p. 69
21. NRS BR/CAL/1/26 entry 251
22. NRS BR/CAL/1/26 entry 291
23. NRS BR/CAL/1/26 entry 352
24. NRS BR/CAL/1/27 entry 179
25. *West Coast Joint Stock*, p. 68
26. Drawing 4820
27. Drawing 4824
28. Drawings 4819 and 4844

3.4: HEATING, VENTILATION AND SMOKING

It is almost certain that the earliest carriages built by the company were unheated. In fact, for some of the small companies taken over by the Caledonian, the inferior classes of accommodation (Third, Fourth if present, and sometimes even Second class) had no glass in the carriage windows. For these railways it was more important to protect passengers from the wind and rain than to keep them warm. The first measure to provide heat for passengers was the foot warmer.

FOOT WARMERS

At first these devices were only provided for the highest class of traveller. The facility was extended in 1870 when the Loco & Stores Committee reported that 300 extra foot warmers had been ordered at 9s 6d each. The Committee approved their use for Second class passengers *'but recommend that they only be used for long journeys.'*[1]

The foot warmers were reminiscent of galvanised metal hot water bottles. They were filled with water, heated at strategic stations on the system and then placed under the seats, dissipating their heat fairly rapidly There are numerous examples of drawings for foot warmer tanks in the St. Rollox registers.

In 1879 Francis Webb of the L&NWR,

'introduced to the Directors' notice, a novel application for heating and re-heating the existing foot warmers, by the substitution of acetate of soda for the water; he shewed in experimental operations, a small portion of the crystal powdered, falling into the block in a flask, and in a very short space of time the contents of the flask changed from a cold solid block to a very hot fluid. The principle was adopted for our foot warmers.'[2]

St. Rollox drawing 7783 of a Caledonian foot warmer dating from 1895 is shown in Figure 3.1.[3] In 1896, the Traffic Committee agreed to a proposal to *'utilize the hot water discharged from Condensing Engines for heating Carriage Warming Pans'* at Maryhill.[4]

Many CR carriages never received any form of steam heating,

so foot warmers continued in use. It is not clear whether they were regularly available in Third class compartments. McEwan claimed that the usual provision was two for a First class compartment and one for a Third *'if supplies permitted.'*[5]

The 1915 Working Timetable Appendix gave instructions for their use and care, including the statement that they must be kept perfectly full of water, because they became *'oxidised at the level that the water stands in them and as a consequence get worn out much sooner than they otherwise would do.'* There is no mention about the use or application of acetate of soda.[6] This suggests that the L&NWR's innovation was not taken up by the Caledonian.

HEATING BY STOVE

In 1883 the L&NWR fitted the WCJS 42-foot Sleeping Saloons with a form of heating known as King's Patent. This used a coke-fired central heating stove located in a cupboard. The system is described by Sidney Stone in *Railway Carriages & Wagons*, Part 2.

Similar systems were widespread in America, but they caused frequent fires which destroyed wooden carriages. This prompted the invention of a carriage made of iron, which is discussed in Chapter 6.3. The stove system was only effective in saloon-style carriages; British compartment stock needed something different.

HEATING BY EXHAUST STEAM

In February 1880 the Board decided to investigate better methods of carriage heating and remitted the matter to James Smithells to report.[7] There is no formal record of the report's recommendations, or of its reception by the Board.

With the arrival of Dugald Drummond in 1882 a major advance was made. He developed a system using the exhaust from the locomotive's Westinghouse pump and, when the pump was not running or it was generating insufficient steam, the blastpipe. A pipe from these two sources passed under the firebox and heat was controlled from the foot plate. It was a pressure system, with no heat storage facility.

The Board approved a trial of the system at a meeting in May 1883. An Edinburgh–Greenock train was selected for the purpose with the

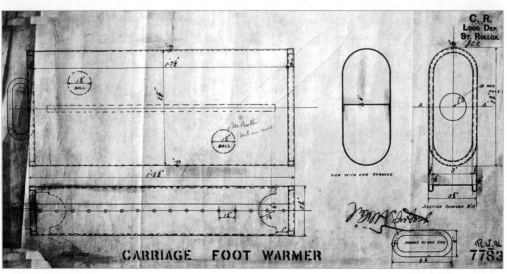

Figure 3.1
An 1895 drawing of the standard carriage foot warmer. Many CR carriages never received steam-heating apparatus, so foot warmers were still in use up to, and perhaps beyond, the Grouping.

expense charged to revenue.[8] The trial was sufficiently encouraging for the Board to request in April 1884 that:

'Mr Thompson to communicate with LNWR Coy. and endeavour to arrange for the apparatus being tried on the WCJS also to fit up one on the Edinburgh and one on the North Districts.'[9]

In the period between January 1885 and January 1887, more locomotives and sets of carriages were fitted with the apparatus. The only surviving CR drawing of the arrangement is reproduced as Figure 3.2, which is taken from St. Rollox drawing 4225, dated 15th November 1884.[10]

This time the cost was charged to capital, which suggests that the system had been approved for general use, although there is no minute confirming this. The total cost was £581 14s 4d.[11]

In 1889 *The Engineer* reported on the system[12] with the preamble that *'The foot-warmer system, as now in use, is just one degree better than nothing.'* The description of the system forms the caption to Figures 3.3 and 3.4, which are reproduced from the magazine.[13] The article concluded:

'A maximum temperature of 62 deg. Fah. can be maintained during the most severe weather experienced in the North on the Caledonian Railway system. The net cost of fitting an engine and tender and carriages is £4 9s for the former, and £1 16s per compartment for the latter. Twelve trains, heated on this system, have been running for three winters, and have given so much satisfaction that the directors have ordered all trains to be similarly fitted. The proportion of heating surface to cubic capacity of space has given entire satisfaction, and the passengers, without receiving any instructions as to the working of this arrangement have, of their own accord, regulated the temperature of the compartment by means of the ventilator over the door. Is it too much to hope that the excellent example set by Mr. Drummond will be followed on other lines before 1889 has passed away?'

THE LOCOMOTIVES INVOLVED

It is not possible to identify positively the first locomotive to be modified, but the register entry for drawing 3644, which dates from September 1883, was for *'Details for Steam heater 119 E.'* The drawing has not survived. It could refer to a Neilson-built example of the 7 foot 2 inch 2-4-0s of Class '98', which were built in 1868. This class would have been appropriate for the Edinburgh–Greenock service and it was among those listed as having the Westinghouse brake apparatus fitted retrospectively.[14]

Drawing 4225 shows the steam heating pipe as fitted to a Class '125' 4-4-0. It is dated 15th November 1884. The addition probably took place at the same time as the class was given new boilers in

1885. As described in the caption to Figure 3.2, the drawing differs in certain respects from the locomotive as rebuilt, but the 7 foot 2 inch driving wheels in the drawing were only fitted to that class. It was probably the class of locomotive used for the train in the *'North District'* mentioned in the Board minute of 1884. By this time the locomotives, which were poor steamers, had been relegated to secondary duties around Dundee.

As further evidence, a St. Rollox photograph (reproduced as Plate 3.9) shows the pipework fitted to number 127. Another photograph shows number 126 similarly fitted.[15] In 1887, drawing 5234 was for a *'Three-way Cock for Steam Heating Arrangement Class 125–9.'*

Drawing 5006 is dated 8th October 1886. It refers to an *'Arrangement for heating pipes 16in. by 22in. Bogie Passenger Engine.'* It has not survived. This was the Class '171' 0-4-4T which was used at that time on the Cathcart Circle. Two more drawings of details (numbers 5031 and 5184) were also made. The associated drawings for the carriages are described in the next section. Two subsequent drawings (St. Rollox 5286 dated 19th April, and 5522 dated 11th November 1887) were also for this class.

Drawing 5298 showed the steam apparatus fitted to *'6ft 6in Bogie Passenger Engine class 67-75.'* It was dated 30th April 1887. These locomotives were part of the Class '60' 4-4-0s. Finally, drawing 5405 (22nd August 1887) showed the arrangement of *'injector, brake & heating pipes 5 ft. 9in. Bogie Passenger Engine.'* This was the Class '80' 4-4-0, known as *'Coast Bogies'* for their work on the Gourock line.

CARRIAGES FITTED EXPERIMENTALLY WITH STEAM HEATING

Unfortunately, a carriage marshalling circular from the 1880s which might have detailed the trains fitted with heating has not survived in the public domain. The apparatus could have been fitted to carriages already in existence, or to carriages that were built as replacements, with the extra cost of the heating charged to capital.

The Coaching Plant Stock Book lists some carriages with heat from the right era, but omits others which are definitely identified as heated in the following paragraphs. Some insights are given from the St. Rollox drawing registers, but none of the drawings has survived.

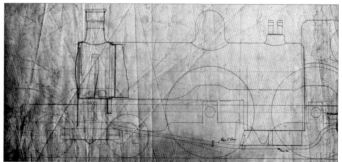

Figure 3.2
St. Rollox drawing 4225 shows the exhaust steam heating apparatus fitted to a Class '125' 4-4-0.

Plate 3.9
The official St. Rollox photograph (NRM St. Rollox ref: 225) shows Class '125' 4-4-0 No. 127 fitted with the exhaust steam heating apparatus.

In November 1883 drawings were produced for the Edinburgh–Greenock train. St. Rollox 3745 was for *'pipes for steam heating carriages,'* followed by 3747-49 for Third class, First class and Brake Third carriages respectively.

In May 1884 (in time for the Edinburgh and Northern District trains) drawing 3993 was for *'Steam Heating Apparatus for 1st Class Carriage,'* but there are no corresponding drawings for the other classes. It is possible that the First class carriage differed from that covered in drawing 3748 while the previous drawings were used for the other classes.

In March 1885 two drawings (St. Rollox 4344, 4348) were for unspecified carriages. In October, drawing 4671 was for the apparatus as fitted to *'Brake Third No. 618.'* This carriage cannot be identified from the Coaching Plant Stock Book, where number 618 was a 31-foot Third, not a Brake Third, which was renumbered to make way for a 'Grampian' carriage in 1905.

In October 1886 drawings 4969-71 were for the apparatus as applied to close-coupled carriages of Third, First and Brake Third respectively. Drawing 4972 was for the apparatus as fitted to *'Coatbridge and Cathcart trains.'* Drawing 4973 is a mystery, entitled *'Single Compt. Brake Third & Third Buss.'* The carriages were for use with the Class '171' 0-4-4T locomotive of drawing 5006 mentioned above, and they and the locomotive are depicted in *The Engineer* drawing of 1889 shown in Figure 3.3. None of these carriages are recorded as heated in the Coaching Plant Stock Book, so one must assume that the apparatus was removed at some point after Drummond's departure from the Caledonian.

The final carriages to be fitted were the 49-foot bogie stock built in 1887. Drawing 5231 was a *'General Arrangement of Steam Heating for 49ft Carr.'* These trains could well have been hauled by the Class '98' locomotives that were fitted with heating apparatus in 1883. When the use of exhaust steam was abandoned, these particular carriages do not seem to have received heating under the new system, as all but one were recorded as unheated in the Coaching Plant Stock Book.

ABANDONMENT OF THE DRUMMOND SYSTEM

The article in *The Engineer* opened by stating that *'The heating of carriages by exhaust steam on the Caledonian system is being rapidly extended to its stock, adding much to the comfort of the travelling public,'* but this does not seem to have been the case. Drummond resigned in 1890 and the company committed much of its capital expenditure immediately afterwards to fitting the

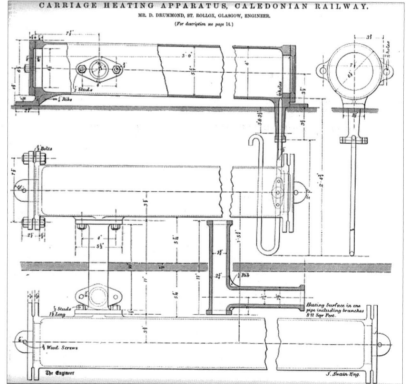

CARRIAGE HEATING APPARATUS, CALEDONIAN RAILWAY.
MR. D. DRUMMOND, ST. ROLLOX, GLASGOW, ENGINEER.
(For description see page 14.)

Figures 3.3 and 3.4
Figure 3.3 *(top)* shows the exhaust steam heating apparatus fitted to a Class '171' 0-4-4T and accompanying Cathcart Circle carriage. Figure 3.4 shows the heater in detail. The accompanying description is from *'The Engineer'* article:

'The steam used for heating the carriages is taken exclusively from the Westinghouse brake exhaust, which is found to be sufficient. When this source is not available, the engine exhaust is used. In both cases an auxiliary supply pipe from the boiler is connected to the heating main, and is used as supplementary, if necessary, to the Westinghouse exhaust; and entirely with the engine exhaust for heating trains at terminal stations before starting, or when running without steam on falling gradients.

The steam is conducted from the engine through a wrought iron pipe of 1in. internal diameter, fixed to the under-frame of each vehicle. The continuity between the vehicles is effected by flexible india-rubber piping with gun-metal couplings, similar in design to those of the Westinghouse pressure brake, but with metallic faces. As the couplings occupy the lowest points in the main pipe, a hole 1in. in diameter is provided to keep the depression free from water of condensation. The main steam pipe under the carriages is covered with felt, with an outside covering of canvas to hold it together. Each carriage compartment has a thin cast iron cylindrical reservoir, with an external surface of 8.25 square feet, placed transversely, and under one of the seats. The reservoirs are arranged in pairs, so that one branch from the main pipe supplies steam to two compartments.'

Westinghouse brake to old carriages as dictated by the Regulation of Railways Act of 1889. Carriage heating was not a priority.

Dr Bell's Heating System

In 1893 it was reported that a new system was on trial by the Caledonian, invented by a Glasgow physician.[16] The drawing is reproduced as Figure 3.5. St. Rollox drawing 7138 of December 1892 depicted its application 'as on Carr 48 1st Class.' This was a Diagram 8 6-wheeled carriage. Drawing 7178 was for the air box fitting inside the compartments. Neither drawing has survived.

The system worked on the forced air principle. Air was collected at carriage roof level and passed down a vertical pipe on the end of the carriage. Beneath the underframe, the pipe came into contact with another pipe carrying steam from the locomotive, thus heating the air. The heated air was diffused through branch pipes into each compartment. There is no information about how the steam was supplied from the locomotive. The article identified two advantages for the system:

'It would be easy to give the passengers some control of the warming of the carriages ... owing to the air in the carriage constantly being changed, an efficient system of ventilation is provided.'

The system was also tested by the North British, in the presence of Robert Urie, the CR's Chief Draughtsman. The article quoted data from both trials. Once again, the Caledonian trial took place on the Wemyss Bay line. The outside temperature was 48 degrees Fahrenheit.

'On leaving the Central (presumably far enough away for air to be admitted to the system and heated) the heat in the third compartment registered 62° at the apertures on the floor, at 8 in. from the floor it registered 52° while at the seat it was 53° and at the rack 51°. On arrival at Wemyss Bay (31 miles) the heat at the apertures on the floor was 120°, at 8in from the floor 70°, at the seats 68° and at the rack 65°.'

Intermediate readings were taken at Paisley and Port Glasgow. The tests seem to have been satisfactory, and continued for an extended period. Drawing 7194 dating from January 1894 was for an 'Air Diffuser for Bell's Heating Apparatus.' In November 1894 drawing 7639 was for an alteration to the air intake cowl. Despite the extended trial, there is no further mention of the system in the CR records.

Trouble with Hoses and Couplings

One factor which inhibited the general adoption of steam heating was the short life of the hose pipes which connected the carriages. In 1900 The Engineer devoted two of its columns to the problem, which it described as follows:[17]

'continuous exposure to steam heat produces in a greater or less time the state of over-vulcanisation, whereby the rubber loses to a great extent its pliability, develops a tendency to crack on the surface, and ultimately becomes hard and useless. This effect of heat, it should be said, is largely influenced by the actual temperature to which the rubber is exposed and to a lesser degree by the time of exposure.'

One problem was the continuous application of heat in systems such as Dr Bell's. Storage heat systems such as the Consolidated and Laycock's worked by the application of steam for a period before starting, which was turned off when the desired temperature had been reached.

Accurate and consistent heat regulation seemed to be difficult to achieve. Steam from the boiler was passed through a reducing valve to lower the pressure. At 40 lbs pressure 'there is plenty of evidence to show that rubber piping is capable of giving satisfaction for the length of time during which it can reasonably be expected to last – that is for two or three years.' A number of examples were quoted of poor regulation, with steam at 100 lbs.

The Caledonian was clearly aware of the problem caused by excessive steam pressure, as the 1915 Working Timetable Appendix instructed drivers to begin heating the train at 25 lbs pressure, unless the train was very long, in which case 40 lbs could be used to speed up the process. When the heaters were fully charged the driver would notice a rise in pressure as the drip valve and tail cock were closed. He was then to reduce the steam pressure until 25 lbs was maintained.[18]

Twisting of the hose when coupling up led to surface cracking of the rubber. The article quoted a railway official who stated that his hoses 'suffered much more injury in the coupling-up than they did by the action of the steam.'

This bad practice was a concern on the Caledonian. In 1908 the Locomotive Superintendent complained that:

'Steam Heating Coupling Pipes are not being hung up when disconnected, and that, in consequence, the Fittings are continually knocking against the Coupling Ball and sustaining damage.'[19]

To return to the article in The Engineer, the final factor that shortened the life of hoses was storage in incorrect atmospheric conditions, a practice which may have implications for modellers.

'In talking of the life of these rubber pipes we must not forget that they are only in use for a portion of the year; during the summer months they are detached from the coaches and put in store.'

The Consolidated Heating System

In 1894 the West Coast Conference agreed to test the Consolidated carriage heating system on the 2.00pm 'Corridor,' which had entered service the previous year.[20] The Consolidated Car Heating Company was founded in America in 1889. The supplier in the UK was G.D. Peters, the rolling stock components company that designed the Havock ventilator used by the Caledonian. A drawing of the system is shown in Figure 3.6. It was a development of the foot warmer system in the sense that it was a heat storage arrangement using acetate of soda.

In September the Caledonian prepared to run its own trial. Drawings 7592A and B refer to the company's apparatus fitted to '45-foot bogie Brake Third; First; Composite.' Drawing 7612 was for the couplings between the carriages, annotated 'drawing L&NW' and 7628 was for the heating pipes 'for 18in x 26in x 6ft 6in Bogie Passenger Engine' – presumably a Class '60' 4-4-0.

On Boxing Day afternoon 1894 the Caledonian conducted the trial on a return trip from Glasgow to Edinburgh. The results were recorded in graph form on St. Rollox drawing 7665.[21] Part of this is shown in Figure 3.7. On the outward journey to Edinburgh, steam was put through the system for half an hour, eleven minutes of which was while the train was waiting to depart. On the return trip the carriages were heated for an hour before the journey commenced and then steam was shut off. Both procedures charged the heating reservoirs to 180 degrees Fahrenheit.

Temperature readings were taken at the front, middle and rear of the train at seat and luggage rack levels as well as in the reservoirs at the three points. The number of carriages involved was not stated. A mean temperature of about 60 degrees was maintained throughout

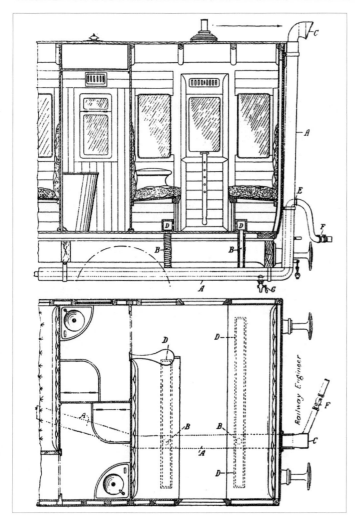

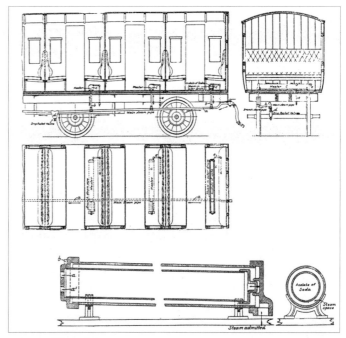

LEFT: Figure 3.5
This drawing of Dr Bell's heating apparatus appeared in *The Railway Engineer*. Air was scooped in through the intake and passed over a heated pipe. Its chief advantage was the continuous circulation of fresh air in the compartment.

ABOVE: Figure 3.6
The Consolidated heating system was introduced on the stock that formed the Anglo-Scottish 'Corridor' express. It was first tried on the Caledonian on Boxing Day 1894.

BELOW: Figure 3.7
Part of the graph indicating the heating system's performance on the first run between Glasgow and Edinburgh. Steam was applied to the system for half an hour, eleven minutes of which was prior to departure. The top line shows the temperature of the reservoir at the front of the train and the second is of the reservoir at the centre. They both peak when the application of steam ceased. They then discharge heat steadily. The lower lines indicate temperature in the compartments at seat and luggage rack levels. Readings were taken at the front, centre and back of the train. They are all similar except for that in the front compartment, where the temperature rose to over 75 degrees Fahrenheit. The heat is maintained at a steady temperature via the discharge of the heat in the reservoirs. The bottom line is the atmospheric temperature.

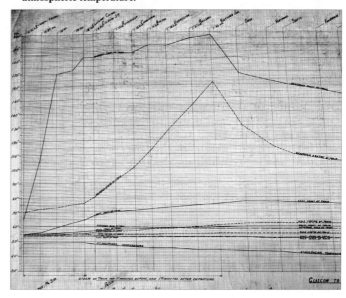

both journeys. The temperature outside the train was about 45 degrees for most of the outward journey and below 40 degrees on the return.

EARLY APPLICATIONS OF STEAM HEATING

According to *West Coast Joint Stock*, the Consolidated system was adopted for newly constructed L&NWR suburban carriages in 1900. WCJS carriages were fitted with the system as they came into works from March of that year.[22] There had been a similar delay in adopting carriage heating on the Caledonian. In the half years from July 1895 to July 1900, 370 carriages had been built and only a few were heated. The exceptions were the Saloons and the Coupé Composite designs. Not even First class travellers on ordinary trains were given the comfort.

One type of Brake Third did receive heating, however. This was the Diagram 43 Lavatory Third, eighteen of which were built to orders H187 and H192. The side elevation drawing which shows the heating apparatus under the seats is reproduced as Figure 8.14. There is an enlargement of the heating arrangement in Figure 3.8. These carriages were probably used for through traffic, which would justify the provision of heating.

Carriages were built with steam heating from 1901, but, apart from Diagram 43, Thirds were not usually fitted up. One exception to the rule was in the rolling stock renewal programme for the half year ending January 1901, when, having approved the programme in August, the Traffic Committee authorised the retrospective '*Fitting up of the following carriages with steam heating. 4 Bogie Brake Composites, 2 Bogie Composites, 5 Bogie Thirds, 6 Bogie Lavatory*

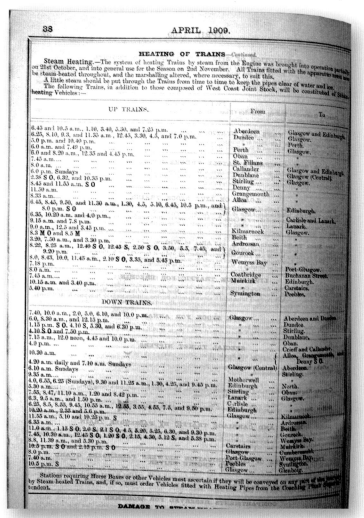

38   APRIL 1909.

HEATING OF TRAINS—*Continued.*

Steam Heating.—The system of heating Trains by steam from the Engine was brought into operation partially on 21st October, and into general use for the Season on 2nd November. All Trains fitted with the apparatus must be steam-heated throughout, and the marshalling altered, where necessary, to suit this.

A little steam should be put through the Trains from time to time to keep the pipes clear of water and ice.

The following Trains, in addition to those composed of West Coast Joint Stock, will be constituted of Steam-heating Vehicles:—

ABOVE: Plate 3.10
This page is extracted from the 1909 Working Timetable. It details all the CR trains fitted with steam heating *'brought into use on 2nd November.'*

Figure 3.8
The Diagram 43 Lavatory Thirds were doubly interesting. They were the only early Third class carriage to be fitted with heating and they were one of the first to be fitted with the new passenger communication system, as shown in the right-hand compartment.

Thirds. Estimated cost £654.'[23] The last of the list was the H192 order mentioned in the previous paragraph.

PRE-HEATING OF TRAINS

At Glasgow Central and Edinburgh Princes Street the station hotel boilers were used to heat trains prior to departure. This was introduced at Central in 1904, according to drawing 12610. The corresponding reference to a drawing for Princes Street has not been discovered. The 1915 Working Timetable Appendix stated:

'Steam Pipes are provided at the end of Docks, 1 to 13 at Glasgow (Central) Station and Docks, 1–5, at Edinburgh (Princes Street) Station, by means of which Trains can be heated from the rear, before departure, by Steam from the Boilers underneath the Station.'[24]

The section went on to explain the procedure, which was under the control of the Inspector in charge of the platform. The locomotive would normally only put steam through the system after departure, unless the train was very long. In these cases the locomotive would supplement the pre-heating under instruction from the Inspector. At other locations one assumes that the train locomotive was attached sufficiently early to raise the temperature – or perhaps the station pilot, if one was available, was employed.

HEATING BECOMES STANDARD FOR NEW CARRIAGES

Steam heating on the Caledonian only became standard when the 'Grampian' stock was introduced. These carriages used the Consolidated system. This led to the retrospective fitting of heating to existing stock, but only that employed on main line express work. In February 1906 the Traffic Committee agreed to:

'Fit 137 vehicles 100 engines with steam heating appliance. 137 vehicles £5,000, 100 engines £2,400 to be spread over 2 years.'[25]

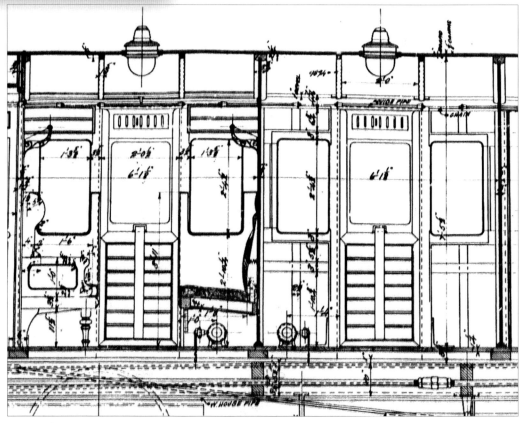

This probably included all the First and Composite carriages built in the late 1890s that are marked as steam heated in the Coaching Plant Stock Book. By 1909 the number of heated trains had increased to the extent shown in Plate 3.10.

NON-PASSENGER COACHING STOCK

Passenger carriages were not the only consideration. Non-passenger coaching stock, which was routinely marshalled immediately behind the locomotive, had to be *'fitted with pipes only to maintain the continuity of the steam heating throughout trains.'*[26]

The first minute recording this in March 1901 concerned five Horse Boxes that were part of the renewal programme for the period ending January 1902. These were steam heated, but in June the same year the Traffic Committee authorised pipes to be fitted to twenty Horse Boxes, ten Covered Carriage Trucks and sixty Fish Vans at a cost of *'about £810.'*[27] The number of Fish Vans was subsequently reduced to forty.[28]

POST-WAR EXPANSION OF CARRIAGE HEATING

A review of the state of the Caledonian's rolling stock was undertaken in 1919.[29] The situation concerning the number and condition of the carriage fleet is discussed in greater detail in Chapter 11.2.

The review also reported that only 585 of the total stock of 2,087 carriages were fitted with steam heating. Ninety-three carriages had been so fitted since 1911, but sixteen had been lost when the CR Ambulance Train was requisitioned in 1916. Robert Killin recommended that 628 bogie carriages should be fitted with steam heat at the rate of about 200 per annum, comprising:

104 Firsts
57 Composites
30 Brake Composites
267 Thirds
170 Brake Thirds.

The cost of fitting the carriages was estimated at £56,930 – an annual commitment of about £20,000. This compared with a pre-war price of £27,154. There was a debate about whether the cost should be charged to capital or revenue.

'If the charge in respect of steam heating could be properly described as a charge to capital there would appear to be no great objection to the work being authorized provided the Government agrees to it. On the other hand, however, if the charge has to be debited to the Revenue Account arrears of maintenance would be affected.'

The sub-committee agreed to the proposal and treated the work as capital expenditure. The increase in heated trains required more non-passenger coaching stock to be fitted with through pipes. In January 1920 the Traffic Committee agreed that:

'The following 123 vehicles should be fitted with Steam Heating connections:
61, Horse Boxes
19, 6-wheel Fish Vans
11, 4-wheel Fish Vans
7, 4-wheel Covered Carriage Trucks
5, 4-wheel Open Caravan Trucks
2, 6-wheel Open Trucks
2, 4-wheel Open Trucks
16, Gas Tanks'[30]

PROGRESS IN IMPLEMENTING THE PROGRAMME

Progress was made in 1920, but not at the rate of two hundred per annum. The number of general service carriages fitted with heating is shown in the table below. The individual vehicles fitted with heating are shown in Appendix V. The number of carriages in the second column is taken from the Coaching Plant Stock Book.

CARRIAGE TYPE	HEATED	
	1921	1923
First	64	118
Composite	101	134
Brake Composite	136	169
Third	240	406
Brake Third	170	200
TOTALS	721	1,027

If one assumes that the three-year programme should have been completed by the end of 1922, Killin's target of over 1,200 heated carriages was not achieved. The diminishing purchasing power of the available budget may well have been a factor, with fewer carriages than planned absorbing a fixed budget.

VENTILATION

In the earliest carriages, ventilation was only available by lowering the window in the compartment door. Very soon afterwards holes were pierced in the top of the door and covered on the outside by a hood – see Plate 3.11. By the 1860s the arrangement was more sophisticated, with a sliding shutter on the inside of the door to give passengers some control over the admission of air.

The contractors who built most of the CR's carriages in the 1860s and '70s applied their own style of external hood. The standard CR pattern seems to have emerged late in the Brittain era – see Plate 6.19. It remained in use until the introduction of the 'Grampian' stock in 1905, when ventilators over the doors were abandoned.

The slide ventilator was not effective in changing the air in a compartment, because foul air accumulated in the arc of the roof – a particular problem in smoking compartments. Various designs of ventilator were developed which extracted air from compartments. Three types used by the Caledonian are described in the following paragraphs.

THE HAVOCK VENTILATOR

The Caledonian's preferred ventilator model was the Havock Air Extractor, designed by component suppliers G.D. Peters. The motion of the train sucked air out of the carriage, drawing in fresh air at the same time. A drawing showing the principles of operation is shown in Figure 3.9. A CR drawing showing the dimensions of the two sizes of ventilator in use is Figure 3.10.

Their first use was to ventilate lavatories. This was the smaller size. Plate 7.7 shows a Smellie-designed Lavatory Third with them. The purpose of the larger size, which seems to have been initiated by McIntosh, was to draw the fug out of smoking compartments. With the introduction of the 'Grampian' stock, ventilators were fitted over each compartment as well. This became standard practice, so ventilators with hoods over the carriage doors were no longer needed.

THE ANDERSON PATENT VENTILATOR

The Caledonian used this device in lavatories and smoking compartments. It was invented by John Anderson, the Secretary of the Callander & Oban Railway. It was a development of the simple

LEFT: Plate 3.11
An ornamental version of the piercing for the ventilator over the carriage door, taken from the photograph of the early carriage used as a bothy at St. Rollox.

BELOW: Figures 3.9 and 3.10
The top drawing shows the principle of the Havock Air Extractor. The forward motion of the train creates a vortex which draws air out of the compartment. The bottom drawings shows the two sizes of ventilator used on the CR.

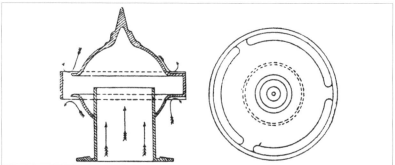

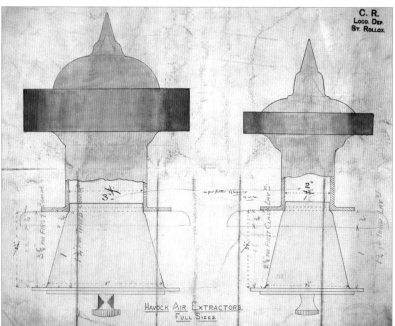

HAVOCK AIR EXTRACTORS.
FULL SIZES.

door ventilator with an air intake and exhaust arrangement behind the hood on the carriage exterior. The forward motion of the train drew air in and created a partial vacuum to the rear which drew out foul air. A drawing of the arrangement is shown in Figure 3.11.

The first recorded application of the ventilator was on the rakes of carriages built for the Callander & Oban and Gourock services in 1889.[31] The device was fitted to the Smellie Lavatory Thirds (see Plate 7.7 and Figure 7.28) and its use continued through the Lambie era.

THE LAYCOCK TORPEDO VENTILATOR

In 1917, the Laycock torpedo ventilator replaced the Havock design as a standard fitting. St. Rollox drawing 19201[32] was issued in August 1917. As discussed in Chapter 11.1, carriage construction was about to cease until after the war, so it can be described fairly as a post-war innovation.

In fact the ventilator first appeared in 1885 on the Diagram 50 Saloons – see Plate 13.3. It was next fitted to the Diagram 29 Coupé Lavatory Composites which were built in 1893 – see Plate 7.13, but its use seems to have been limited to these carriages. Contemporary St. Rollox drawings 7323 and 7364 were for this ventilator, the latter for the 2½ inch size, which was fitted over lavatories.

SMOKING

Discomfort for some, an amenity for others. Originally, the Caledonian, like other railways, was a non-smoking organisation. For example, the 1853 Public Timetable[33] quotes the following by-law, along with a similar edict on *'intoxication or committing a nuisance.'* The penalty in each case was *'not exceeding 40 shillings.'*

Smoking is strictly prohibited, both in the carriages and the Company's Stations. ... After being warned to desist (anyone who continues to do so) will be ejected immediately or if travelling at the first opportunity.'

The prohibition of smoking ended as a result of the Regulation of Railways Act 1868,[34] in which clause 20 stated:

'All Railway Companies, except the Metropolitan Railway Company, shall, from and after the First Day of October next, in every Passenger Train where there are more Carriages than One of each Class, provide Smoking Compartments for each Class of Passengers, unless exempted by the Board of Trade.'

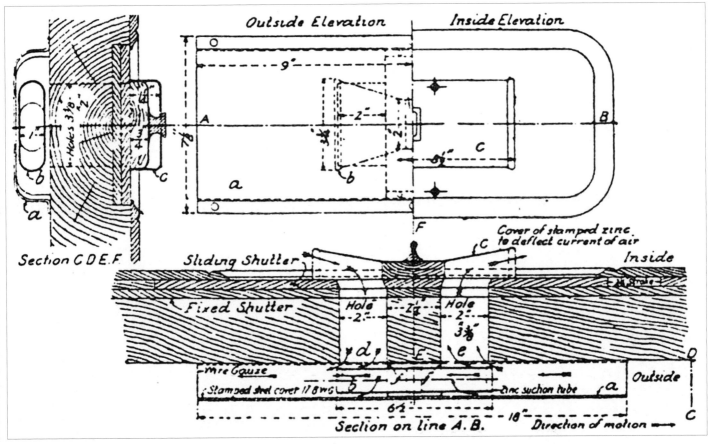

Figure 3.11
John Anderson, the Secretary of the Callander & Oban Railway, patented this type of ventilator, which was first used on CR carriages in 1889, appropriately for new stock on the C&O. It was fitted over the carriage doors and in lavatory compartments. The forward motion of the train created a partial vacuum which drew air out of the compartment.

The CR by-law was altered to impose the penalty on people smoking in any compartment that was not designated for the purpose.

Not everybody wished to smoke and many passengers wished to avoid those who did, so a way to identify smoking compartments was necessary. The method used by the Caledonian immediately after the Act came into force was a wooden notice, permanently fixed. This proved impractical because a designated smoking carriage might be marshalled in a train as the only one of its class, thus putting it outside the Act. In November it was recommended that:

'holders be provided above the carriage doors, into which the boards may be placed as they may happen to be required.'[35]

A month previously, the Committee had decided to use coconut matting in First class smoking compartments instead of carpets.[36]

Identification by boards did not last long. Caledonian smoking compartments were usually at the end of the carriage and were identified with a blue SMOKING sign on the right-hand window of the compartment – see Plate 3.12, which shows two variations. The CR called the sign a *'transparent label.'* In 1919 the same sign, without the roundel enclosing it, was sand-blasted onto the window. Drawing 20223[37] is reproduced as Figure 3.12.

A Havock ventilator was installed for the compartment as a supplementary means of clearing the tobacco smoke. These devices have been discussed previously in this section.

The 9-compartment non-corridor Third class 'Grampian' style carriages were provided with four smoking compartments, two at one end, one in the middle and one at the other end. This was the subject of a special entry in the Working Timetable Appendix for 1908, about two years after the carriages entered service.[38]

Ashtrays were an essential adjunct. They were not present on GA drawings, and St. Rollox drawing 13600, dated April 1906, has not survived. Thanks to Jim Summers, a photograph of an ashtray on one of the preserved carriages at the SRPS is shown in Plate 3.13. The brass casting was hinged to its frame at the bottom.

Restrictions on smoking were included in the CR Rule Book, where it was stated to be *'strictly forbidden'* except *'in the compartments specially set apart for the purpose.'* Guards had to make sure that trains had a *'sufficient number of compartments reserved for smokers and be careful not to place ladies in the compartments so reserved.'* Clearly, no respectable member of the fair sex would be seen smoking in public.[39]

REFERENCES
1. NRS BR/CAL/1/18 entry 1435
2. *Railway Reminiscences*, p. 241
3. RHP 70093
4. NRS BR/CAL/5/11 entry 293
5. *Appendix to the Working Timetable*, May 1915, p. 85 of General Instructions
6. McEwan Archive ref: T25/1/30
7. NRS BR/CAL/1/25 entry 968
8. NRS BR/CAL/1/28 entry 295
9. NRS BR/CAL/1/28 entry 1749
10. RHP 67501
11. NRS BR/CAL/23/5 (39), BR/CAL/23/6 (33), (24) and (22)
12. *The Engineer*, 4th January 1889, p. 14
13. *The Engineer*, 4th January 1889, pp. 3 and 5
14. *Caledonian Railway Livery*, p. 320
15. *Caledonian Railway Livery*, p. 210
16. *The Railway Engineer*, April 1893, pp. 117-18
17. *The Engineer*, 3rd August 1900, pp. 103-4

Figure 3.12 and Plate 3.12
The main photograph shows the designation of a smoking compartment used for most of the CR's existence. Lettering is blue on a white background. Occasionally the sign was reversed, as seen inset. This was taken from a Hurst, Nelson publicity photograph of 48-foot Third 605, built in 1900. The drawing dates from 1919 and shows the practice in the last years of the Caley.

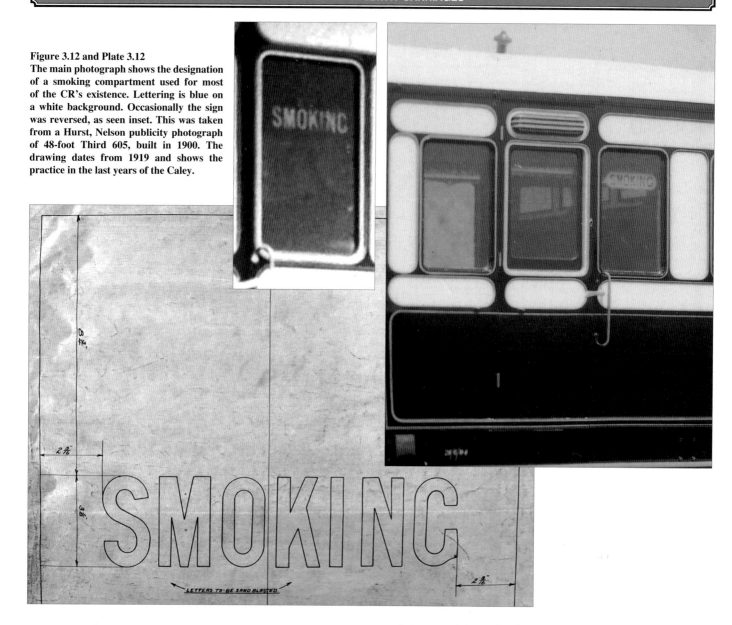

18. *Appendix to the Working Timetable*, May 1915, p. 84 of General Instructions
19. *Appendix to the Working Timetable*, April 1908, p. 40 of General Instructions
20. NRS BR/WCC/1/4 entry 2607
21. RHP 70091
22. *West Coast Joint Stock*, p. 38
23. NRS BR/CAL/1/44 entry 283
24. *Appendix to the Working Timetable*, May 1915, p. 84 of General Instructions
25. NRS BR/CAL/1/52 entry 876
26. NRS BR/CAL/1/44 entry 859
27. NRS BR/CAL/1/44 entry 1380
28. NRS BR/CAL/5/12 entry 23
29. NRS BR/CAL/5/6
30. NRS BR/CAL/1/74 entry 317
31. *Engineering*, 3rd May 1889, p. 514
32. RHP 68490
33. CRA Archive ref: 3/1/2/1
34. 31 & 32 Vict. Cap. 119
35. Officers' Minute Book entry 153
36. Officers' Minute Book entry 140
37. RHP 68417
38. *Appendix to the Working Timetable February 1908*, p. 25
39. *1906 Rule Book*, paragraph 195

Plate 3.13
An ashtray in one of the preserved carriages at the SRPS.

3.5: LIGHTING

Lighting was not considered necessary in the earliest railway carriages, probably because none had been provided in the stagecoaches from which they developed. Stagecoaches had not needed internal lighting as it was unusual for them to travel at night. Long-distance travellers stopped at coaching inns before or soon after darkness fell.

When passenger trains started running during the hours of darkness some form of internal illumination was needed. Caledonian carriages, as with most other railway companies, were initially illuminated by means of lamps, usually burning rape oil, which were lit on the platform before being lowered through a hole in the carriage roof; the hole being filled with a wooden plug when the lamp was not in use.

As there were either no or only half-height partitions in many carriages a lamp for each compartment was not needed. Lamp sockets were either placed over the partitions so that the light from one lamp was shared between two compartments or, particularly in Thirds, a single lamp sufficed for the whole carriage. With the introduction of full-height partitions it became necessary to have one lamp per compartment, but the level of illumination was still low. A drawing of a late CR oil lamp is shown in Figure 3.13, and carriages with typical early fittings are shown in Plate 3.14.

LIGHTING BY GAS

Alexander Allan installed the first example of gas lighting on a train in Scotland on the Scottish Central Railway. It used a system patented by Newall. On 8th December 1862, the evening Edinburgh train left for Perth on the system's inaugural run. It was fitted to a fixed set of First and Second class carriages:

'being brilliantly lighted by means of pipes (with expanding couplings carried from roof to roof) communicating with the

reservoir placed in a specially constructed compartment of the guard's break-van.

Throughout the journey the lights remained perfectly steady and clear, and the passengers were much gratified with the successful introduction of this vastly superior method of illumination.'[1]

On the Caledonian, Conner first broached the subject of gas lighting in 1870, when the Traffic Committee read his letter *'reporting the cost of introducing Gas into carriages.'* The Committee decided to *'delay for further consideration.'*[2] There is no information about the type of gas to be used, or the method of storage. The L&NWR was experimenting with gas lighting at the same time, but a gas holder exploded and destroyed the carriage.[3] This may explain the Caledonian's reluctance to proceed.

Oil lamps remained the method of lighting until the late 1870s when a number of companies developed systems to light carriages with compressed oil or coal gas supplied from storage cylinders, typically mounted on the carriage underframe. The major advantage of oil gas was that it retained most of its illuminating power when compressed; coal gas lost most of its power. Another factor in favour of oil gas for Scottish railways was the availability of large deposits of oil-bearing shale in West Lothian. The Lightmoor Press publication *The Scottish Shale Oil Industry & Mineral Railway Lines* has full details.[4]

Nothing further was recorded in CR minutes about a change from oil lighting until 1877, when the Traffic Committee delegated James Smithells, the General Manager, to consider the information in a letter from Pintsch & Pischon & Coy concerning *'a new method of fitting up and lighting carriages with gas'* and make a report.[5] By then the Metropolitan and Great Eastern railways had adopted the Pintsch system.[6]

No immediate action was taken. The first record of the Pintsch

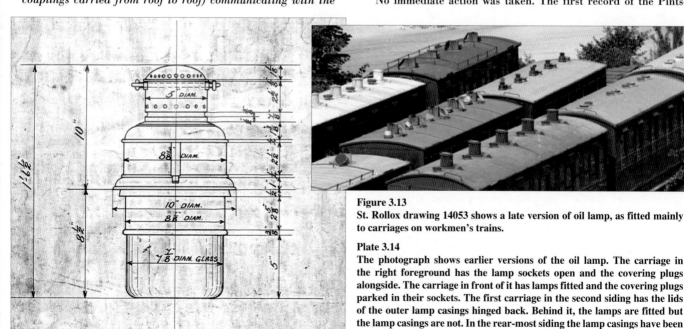

Figure 3.13
St. Rollox drawing 14053 shows a late version of oil lamp, as fitted mainly to carriages on workmen's trains.

Plate 3.14
The photograph shows earlier versions of the oil lamp. The carriage in the right foreground has the lamp sockets open and the covering plugs alongside. The carriage in front of it has lamps fitted and the covering plugs parked in their sockets. The first carriage in the second siding has the lids of the outer lamp casings hinged back. Behind it, the lamps are fitted but the lamp casings are not. In the rear-most siding the lamp casings have been painted white to match the carriage roof.

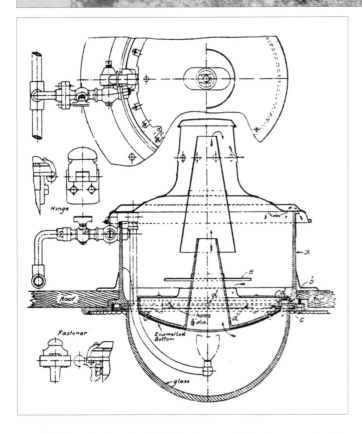

Plate 3.15
The photograph is of the accident in June 1886 on the Callander & Oban at Succoth, near Dalmally, when an excursion train was derailed. The end carriage shows the control rod for the Pope's gas lighting system on the end and the connecting pipe to the gas lamps.
Figure 3.14
The two rival gas lighting systems. That of Pope (*below left*), and the Pintsch original system (*below*). Both used a flat flame burner.

system being used on the CR is in August 1881 when a tender for fitting the system to existing stock was accepted.[7] The tender offered to fit gas lighting at a cost of £30 per carriage for four lights, £35 for five, and £40 for six.

A few months later Pope, the other main supplier of gas lighting, wrote to the Caledonian offering to fit their system, but they were informed by the Traffic Committee that it was '*not proposed at present to introduce Pope's gas lighting.*'[8] Almost immediately the Loco & Stores Committee countermanded the decision. Having received a further letter from Pope, it gave a '*Remit to the Glasgow Committee to have a trial of Pope's and Pintsch's systems at the expense of the patentees.*'[9]

In March the same Committee:

'*Submitted costs of Pope's and Pintsch's systems. Gas Works of Pintsch's System to supply 500 Carriages will cost £2650 and each Carriage £39 10s.*

The Committee are of the opinion that we should adopt Pintsch's System and fit up the Gas Works but only fit up 100 Carriages.'[10]

Pintsch immediately went ahead with a formal tender for the works as instructed. The Loco & Stores Committee delegated powers '*to see and approve the site of the works and carry out the erection as early as possible.*'[11]

Despite the apparent ascendancy of the Pintsch system, that was not the last of Pope's system on the Caledonian. G.D. Peters, the agents for Pope, approached the CR with an offer to supply lamps and fittings. The Loco & Stores Committee sensed an opportunity to use competition to the CR's advantage and agreed to accept,

'*subject to the conditions as to quality of fittings being as good as Pintsch's but only to the extent of 50 Carriages, prices 5% below Pintsch's.*'[12]

3.5: LIGHTING 79

A rake of carriages fitted with Pope's apparatus is shown in Plate 3.15. To accommodate the different filling arrangement, the Loco & Stores Committee accepted Pintsch's offer:

'to supply six double necked filling hose heads and eighteen couplings, free of charge, to enable Pope's Coaches to be gassed at Pintsch's filling posts and vice versa.'[13]

In 1883 a tender was accepted to supply gas lighting for twenty First class carriages which were being built by the Midland Carriage & Wagon Co. At the same time the Caledonian arranged for Pintsch's system to be installed on twenty Thirds and another twenty Brake Thirds which were also under construction at the Midland's works.[14] Pintsch charged £43 9s per Third (six lights) and £31 6s for a Brake Third (four lights). Pope equipped the 5-compartment Firsts for £37 7s 6d each.

In 1886 another supplier was added to the list. The Loco & Stores Committee sought tenders from 'three makers' to provide fittings for fifty-eight carriages.[15] Pintsch secured an order for twenty-eight, with the remainder going to Laidlaw.[16] Laidlaw had previously tendered unsuccessfully in 1885.[17] Laidlaw's system seems to have been almost identical to that of Pintsch, as the operating instructions were almost identical. Laidlaw secured a further order in 1890 when four First, eight Third and four Brake Third carriages were fitted.[18] These were the 45-foot carriages built to orders H47-H49.

THE ORIGINAL PINTSCH LAMP

A drawing of the original style lamp is shown in Figure 3.14, with the Pope design for comparison. The Pintsch lamps were lit from outside by hinging back the chimney assembly, which was fitted with a conical copper baffle to prohibit any down-draught of air which might extinguish the flame.

Because the early lamps were frequently damaged, and the carriage's gas supply could run out, the lights were made of an identical diameter to the earlier oil lamps. In an emergency the gas light reflectors could be removed and oil lamps inserted in the roof holes.

CONTROL OF THE GAS SUPPLY

For the Pintsch and Laidlaw systems each carriage was provided with a main stopcock, by which all of its lamps were turned on and off. A special key was needed to operate this. The supply of gas to the lamps was controlled by an on/off valve located at the end of the carriage. A regulator between the valve and the gas tanks beneath the underframe controlled the pressure of the gas supply.

In the Pope system a rod ran horizontally across the end of the carriage, with a handle at each end, to enable the gas in all its lamps to be turned on, lowered, or shut off. No special key was needed to operate the system except in the case of WCJS carriages, to which it was also fitted.

CHARGING CARRIAGES WITH GAS

In all systems the gas was carried in cylindrical tanks which the CR called 'gas recipients' or 'receivers' fitted beneath the carriage underframe. The 1915 Working Timetable Appendix stated that gas cylinders were 'considered to be fully charged when the Gauge on the Carriage indicates a pressure of six atmospheres, or 90 lbs to the square inch.'[19] The infrastructure to supply gas for carriage lighting is discussed in Chapter 2.6.

THE INCANDESCENT BURNER

Early Pintsch and other companies' lamps had open flame burners which produced about seven candlepower. Carriages fitted with open flame burners can be identified in photographs by the taller lamp chimney. The incandescent mantle was developed in 1892 but, in common with other British railways, was not immediately adopted by the Caledonian.

The original incandescent burner was fragile. It gave a better and more economical light, but was very susceptible to vibration. In 1905 it was reported that a more robust mantle had been successfully tried on the LB&SCR, 'The mantles are sufficiently tough to easily give a life of from one to two months.'[20] The article outlined the economic and passenger benefits of the new mantle:

'The illuminating power [compared with the original mantle] is increased 300% on little more than half the consumption of gas. The effect of adopting this system would, therefore, be to practically double the lighting capacity of all the oil-gas works without altering them in the least.'

In two later articles the magazine quoted a paper on trials held on the GWR, involving a 'large corridor coach.'

'This carriage is still running, and the latest figures show that in 14 weeks of continuous working, running 15,624 miles, only seven mantles had to be renewed in the nine lamps.'[21]

The other article recorded a trip in a Pullman car on the LB&SCR at the invitation of the Pintsch Company.

'The mantles which are specially made for railway carriage lighting of a much tougher material than formerly, stand the strain well for about two months, and are commonly run for as long as four months without being destroyed. They also have the advantage of slightly increasing in illuminating intensity after having been in use for a short time.'[22]

No doubt reassured by these successful reports, in late 1905, just as electric lighting was adopted for new construction, the Caledonian tested the incandescent burner on an Airdrie and Maryhill train. The cost was £1 5s per compartment, £36 5s in total.[23] The light output was about three-quarters that of the four-bulb 'electroliers' that were fitted to the Third class compartments of the 'Grampian' stock described in Chapter 9.

Starting in 1908, the Traffic Committee agreed to spend £1,600 from the revenue budget each year 'to equip all the gas fitted carriages at the rate of 400 to 500 lamps per half year' with incandescent burners.[24]

St. Rollox drawing 14063[25] dated 19th July 1907 shows the standard gas lamp fitting with the addition of an 'inverted incandescent burner.' The arrangement is shown in Figure 3.15. The Coaching Plant Stock Book distinguishes between ordinary and incandescent burners. Only a small number remained unconverted by the time the book was compiled. They were mostly ex-WCJS carriages.

LIGHTING AND CLEANING THE LAMPS

The original Pintsch flat flame burners were lit from the carriage roof. Incandescent burners were lit from inside the carriage. In the latter case:

'Only a Methylated Spirit Torch must be used … and great care must be taken to keep the flame of the Torch away from the roof of the Carriage, in order to avoid the blackening of the paint.'[26]

Detailed instructions were also provided for cleaning the globes and reflectors. This was also undertaken from the roof or inside the carriage, according to the type of burner. Seat cushions had to be turned over to avoid soiling when men stood on the seats to reach the lamps. '*Saloons 32, 36 and 37 are provided with stools ... which must be used by men attending to the Lamps. The saloon Furniture must not be used for this purpose.*'

OIL-LIT SURVIVALS

Analysis of the Coaching Plant Stock Book suggests some carriages that were originally oil-lit were converted to gas lighting at some point. Others, however, remained oil-lit to the end. Most were 31- or 32-foot carriages of both classes built in the 1870s. There does not seem to be any reason why some were converted to gas and others not – age was not a factor.

Many of these carriages were marshalled into rakes for the workmen's trains on Clydebank which are described in section 2 of this chapter. In 1906, seven out of nine trains were oil-lit, comprising three Firsts, two Composites, seventy-five Thirds, three Brake Composites and sixteen Brake Thirds.

By 1913, only two sets were oil-lit, involving one First, one Composite, twenty-two Thirds and four Brake Thirds. The same two sets were rostered in 1921. The other carriages were not withdrawn; presumably they were stored as spares and used on excursion traffic. Most survived, like their gas-lit companions, until just after the Grouping.

Other oil-lit survivors were the unique Diagram 11 Brake Composite on the Killin Branch (see Chapter 7.5), one Diagram 17 and twelve Diagram 4 Passenger Brake Vans and a number of Saloons that were built in the late 1860s and the 1870s. The Saloons are described in Chapter 13.

EXPERIMENTS WITH ELECTRIC LIGHT

According to Sidney Stone, who was writing between 1892 and 1897, the LB&SCR was the first large-scale user of carriages

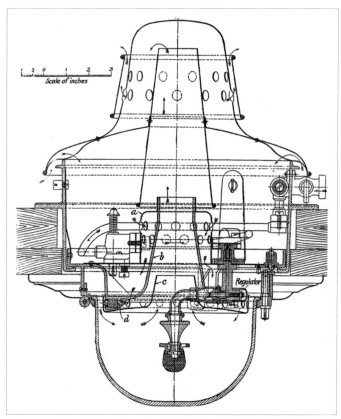

Figure 3.15
This drawing depicts the incandescent mantle with inverted burner which was adopted by the Caledonian in 1908.

lit by electricity generated by a dynamo with the energy stored in accumulators. Four hundred carriages were so fitted. A book from the Locomotive Publishing Company in 1914, *Train Heating by Electricity*, covers the early experiments and the systems that were developed for widespread use in more detail.

The Stone's system used a patented double battery arrangement, which was developed in 1896 from an earlier single battery system.[27] The Highland Railway had fitted eight carriages with the Stone's system in 1895 when it decided to abandon oil lamps, but then adopted gas lighting using the Pintsch system and the CR gassing facilities at Perth.[28]

The Caledonian was an early experimenter with electric light. In April 1896 the Loco & Stores Committee accepted a proposal for:

'*the fitting up of a train of six wheeled vehicles @ £50 per vehicle with Stone's Electric Light system for trial for three months and if not satisfactory to be removed at the end of the period at their expense.*'[29]

The trial on the Caledonian was sufficiently successful for the Loco & Stores Committee in March 1897 to approve '*Lighting of Five Bogie Carriages by Electricity, accept offer for one Train, ... delivered in London, J Stone & Coy.*'[30]

The minute tallies with the Coaching Plant Stock Book, which records that five 45-foot carriages were built with electric light in the period ending January 1898. They were First 277 to order H155, Brake Thirds 1037, 1038 (order H157), Composite 104 (order H159) and Third 438 to order H161, which would indeed form a representative train. Further corroboration is given by the capital expenditure return which shows one First class carriage at a cost of £852 while nineteen others cost £803, and two Brake Thirds costing £579, while the rest of the order cost £521 or £530 10s.[31]

Other First class carriages built with electric light during this period were eight 48-foot Diagram 38s in 1899 to order H176 plus one built by Pickering. The St. Rollox carriages were the major part of a tender from Stones & Co. '*for the fitting up of 1 Bogie Family Carriage 48 feet long and 8 Bogie First Class carriages 48 feet long with Electric Lighting apparatus.*'[32] The next meeting of the Loco & Stores Committee reported that the offer had been accepted at '*£95 per carriage.*'[33] Stone fitted out another of the Family carriages at £184 10s.[34]

After the initial trial train, Hurst, Nelson built an electrically-lit 48-foot Third (number 650) at the same time as St. Rollox built thirty gas-lit examples to order H182 in the period ending January 1900. West Coast Joint Stock carriages were electrically lit from 1900 onwards.[35]

At this point sufficient experience had been gained for McIntosh to make a formal report to the Loco & Stores Committee '*on electric lighting of carriages, especially as regards the comparative cost of electricity and gas.*'[36] The report was submitted and read by the Board in May.[37]

FURTHER CONSTRUCTION OF ELECTRICALLY-LIT CARRIAGES

Electrification was not confined to carriages. The 1899 minute book records the installation of electric light at Ross and other marshalling yards, and in the offices and waiting rooms at Central Low Level station.[38] For the next few years, however, new gas-lit carriages were still in the majority. Only fifty carriages out of 270 put into service between 1898 and 1904 were electrically-lit. Presumably the significant extra first cost (about £50 per carriage) was a deterrent at a time when there was heavy demand on finance to build new and replacement rolling stock.

Six Diagram 46 Firsts were built with electric light in 1902 to order H206. By this time the width of carriages had increased to 8 feet 6 inches. Pickering added a further example in 1905.

Four Coupé Brake Composites built in the period ending January 1903 to order H209, and four more built in the subsequent half year to order H214 were fitted with electric light. Their numbers were 56, 169, 172 and 249 (H209) and 113-116 (H214). Two of these carriages are illustrated in Plate 8.5.

St. Rollox built six 8 feet 6 inches wide Thirds to order H211, also in the half year ending January 1903. Their numbers were 19, 22, 126, 657, 1074 and 1123. Pickering built a further example (number 1291) in 1904. This carriage is shown in Plate 8.4.

St. Rollox built five electrically-lit Brake Thirds in 1903 to order H215. Their numbers were 29, 63, 297, 510 and 604. The last numbered carriage was originally gas-fitted according to the Coaching Stock Register, but *'later converted to electric light.'* Two of the eight carriages built to order H220 were electrically-lit (numbers 610 and 654). Orders H222 and H229, which were the last carriages built in 1904 before the 'Grampian' stock, were also lit by electricity. Their numbers were 335, 610-612 and 988 (H222), and 614-616 plus 1075 (H229).

Adoption of Electric Light as Standard

The 'Grampian' stock of 1905 with its elaborate 'electroliers' marked the end of new gas-fitted vehicles and, with the exception of some 6-wheeled Brake Vans, all subsequent passenger vehicles were electrically-lit. By 1912, 250 carriages were so fitted – about one-eighth of the passenger-carrying stock.

Electric Light Connections

Each carriage had its own dynamo and accumulator box, but the train lighting was controlled by the guard. This entailed connections between the carriages. An example of the connections is shown in Plate 3.16. The internal arrangement in the guard's compartment is shown in Figure 3.16. Lights were to be switched *'half on 20 minutes and full on 10 minutes before the time of departure'* when a train was scheduled to leave a terminal station after sunset.[39]

Electrically-Lit Tail Lamps

Carriages with Brake compartments were fitted with lamps, which, like signal lamps, were originally illuminated by oil. Fixed lamps were fitted at the top of the lookouts in the Brake compartment, and a hand lamp was hung on a bracket at the rear. This was to comply with the Board of Trade requirement that the last vehicle in every train displayed a lamp so that the signalman could be satisfied that the train was complete as it passed his box.

Plate 3.16
A photograph of the electric light connectors on the end of Diagram 115 Semi-corridor Composite number 440 in LM&SR days. The corridor side of the carriage is shown in Plate 9.27.

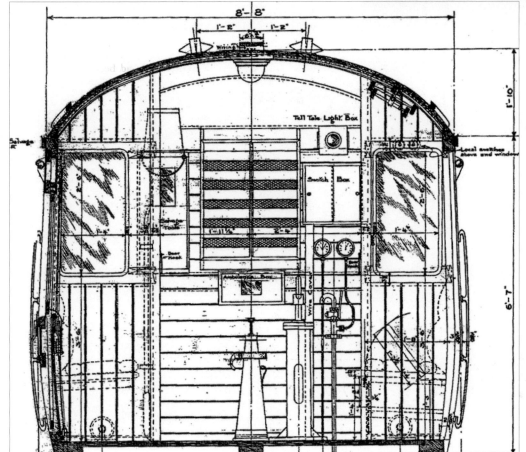

Figure 3.16
This shows the interior of a guard's compartment with the electric light switchgear adjacent to the right-hand window. It is taken from St. Rollox drawing 21779 of the Diagram 119B Brake Third.

With the arrival of electricity, oil illumination for the side lights was dispensed with. The 'Grampian' stock and subsequent carriages had electrically-lit fixed lights, but the oil-lit hand lamp remained in use during the hours of daylight. Non-corridor Brake carriages were also fitted with an electric central light.

GAS-LIT SURVIVORS

In 1913 the Traffic Committee noted the Board of Trade's recommendation that *'electricity should be substituted for gas as an illuminant for railway carriages running on main lines.'*[40] This followed the accident at Ditton Junction on the L&NWR. Despite this, nearly all Caledonian carriages built before 1900 were still gas-lit into the 1930s when they were withdrawn, whether *'running on main lines'* or not. The incandescent gas burner provided adequate light and the capital cost of large-scale conversion to electricity could not be justified on stock that was already partly life-expired.

REFERENCES

1. *The Engineer,* 12th December 1862, p. 343
2. NRS BR/CAL/1/18 entry 460
3. *West Coast Joint Stock,* p. 38
4. By Harry Knox, Lightmoor Press, 2013
5. NRS BR/CAL/1/23 entry 1002
6. *Railway Carriages & Wagons, Their Design and Construction,* part 2
7. NRS BR/CAL/1/26 entry 1285
8. NRS BR/CAL/1/27 entry 113
9. NRS BR/CAL/1/27 entry 202
10. NRS BR/CAL/1/27 entry 465
11. NRS BR/CAL/1/27 entry 645
12. NRS BR/CAL/1/27 entry 742
13. NRS BR/CAL/1/27 entry 1261
14. NRS BR/CAL/1/28 entry 716
15. NRS BR/CAL/1/30 entry 926
16. NRS BR/CAL/1/30 entry 961
17. NRS BR/CAL/1/30 entry 245
18. NRS BR/CAL/1/33 entry 1171
19. General Instructions, p. 82
20. *The Railway Engineer,* March 1905 pp. 69-70
21. *The Railway Engineer,* July 1905, pp. 186-87
22. *The Railway Engineer,* August 1905 p. 216
23. NRS BR/CAL/1/51 entry 1361
24. NRS BR/CAL/1/55 entry 1332
25. RHP 68491
26. *1915 Working Timetable Appendix,* p. 82
27. *Train Heating by Electricity,* p. 3
28. *Highland Railway Carriages and Wagons,* pp. 23-24
29. NRS BR/CAL/1/39 entry 780
30. NRS BR/CAL/1/40 entry 792
31. NRS BR/CAL/23/9 (31)
32. NRS BR/CAL/1/42 entry 554
33. NRS BR/CAL/1/42 entry 649
34. NRS BR/CAL/1/42 entry 1501
35. *West Coast Joint Stock,* p. 40
36. NRS BR/CAL/1/43 entry 1516
37. NRS BR/CAL/1/43 entry 1745
38. NRS BR/CAL/1/42 index under *'electric light'*
39. *1915 Working Timetable Appendix,* p. 82
40. NRS BR/CAL/5/13 entry 34/185

3.6: LAVATORIES AND CORRIDORS

Provision of lavatories in early railway carriages was not a consideration. Like their predecessors in a stage coach, passengers had to wait for a station stop to attend to a 'call of nature.' While the lack of facilities was not too inconvenient on the relatively short internal Scottish services, long-distance travel on Anglo-Scottish services was a different matter.

The first lavatories on the West Coast Joint Stock were fitted in the pioneer Sleeping Saloons of 1874.[1] Writing at the turn of the century, G.P. Neele was less than complimentary:

> 'Mr. Bore's efforts at Wolverton at introducing sleeping berths and lavatory accommodation were not very successful at first, indeed, his 'prentice attempt at the latter was of such a primitive character that even a Dutch Boer would have felt astonished.'[2]

Sleeping Saloons continued to be the only WCJS carriages that benefitted from lavatories until 1877, when a number of Lavatory Composites were built. The exception was the Caledonian's only Sleeping Saloon, which was built in 1877 without a lavatory and ran between Stranraer and Euston. The facility was fitted in 1879. The carriage is fully described in Chapter 13.2.

EARLY CALEDONIAN CARRIAGES WITH LAVATORIES

Drummond built the first CR carriages with lavatories in 1888. They were 6-wheeled Composites, but the lavatory was only accessible to First class travellers. One lot was built for through traffic to the Highland Railway. They are described in Chapter 7.2. In 1889, the CR acquired some surplus WCJS Composites and fitted lavatories to them. They are described in Chapter 7.6. Again, only First class passengers had access. The only other Drummond-built carriages with lavatory access were the 45-foot Diagram 24 Coupé Firsts, described in Chapter 7.4.

The first Third class carriages with lavatory facilities were designed by Smellie in 1890, but built after his death. Lambie built two *coupé* designs with lavatories to Diagrams 29 and 30. Diagram 29 had First class-only lavatories; Diagram 30 provided limited access for Third class passengers. All these designs are described in Chapter 7.5.

The Drummond and Lambie *coupé* carriages had seats in front of the lavatory doors which had lift-off cushions. A drawing and photograph are shown in Figure 3.17 and Plate 3.17. The arrangement was a feature of two WCJS Composite designs in the

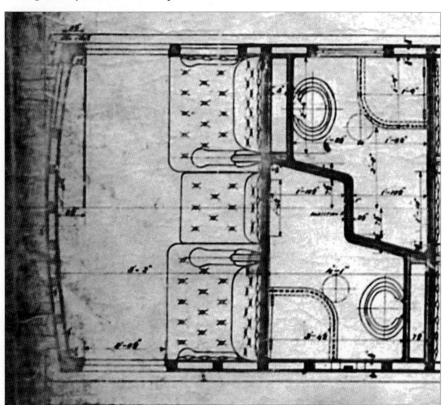

Figure 3.17 and Plate 3.17
The early 45-foot lavatory carriages had lift-up seats which gave access to the lavatory. The drawing, part of St. Rollox 7546, shows the access from the *coupé* compartment of a Diagram 30 Lavatory Luggage Composite. The photograph of Diagram 29 Lavatory Composite number 39 shows the seat moved out of the way and the lavatory door open. The arrangement continued until 1910.

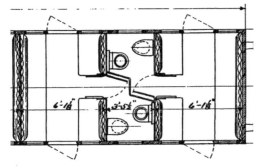
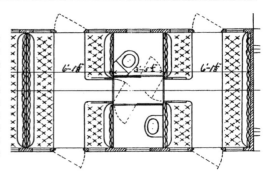

Figure 3.18
The Diagram 37 carriage (*left*) is only 8 feet wide. Two cramped lavatory and washbasin compartments were placed between compartments. When the carriages were widened by 6 inches a short central corridor linked the compartments (*right*). Although the intervening section remained the same size, there was now a lavatory on one side and a washbasin on the other, as shown in the Diagram 43 design.

early 1880s.[3] It was not very convenient, but lasted on the CR until the second decade of the next century.

'The Caledonian Railway has an economical type of lavatory coach. It is usual for a seat to be sacrificed to provide an entrance for the lavatory. Some of the older carriages … however, seat the full complement of passengers, the back of one of the seats forming the door by which the lavatory is entered, the cushion of the seat lifts off, and the frame is a hinged flap. A man can step over the seat, but a lady would probably have to remove the cushion and turn up the seat. If the seat that gives entrance to the lavatory is occupied, and any other passenger desires to enter, or come out of, the lavatory, a rather inconvenient state of affairs is introduced. This has been recognized by the Caledonian Railway, and the arrangement is being altered when coaches of this type are in the shops for thorough overhauling.'[4]

CORRIDOR ACCESS TO LAVATORIES

The increased width of the 48-foot stock from 1900 allowed better access to lavatories than previously. Rather than providing extra seats in Third class compartments, an internal corridor simplified access to more spacious lavatory facilities. The two drawings in Figure 3.18 show the difference. The carriages affected are described in Chapter 8.2.

LATER CARRIAGES WITH LAVATORIES

From the start of the McIntosh era up to the period ending July 1901, 456 carriages were built. Those intended for services exclusively within Scotland did not receive lavatories. Only sixty carriages were so fitted, comprising twenty-eight Coupé Saloons, twenty-four Thirds, three Saloons and five Brake Composites. All the designs were intended for through (that is, long-distance) traffic, as evidenced by their dual brake systems. These carriages are described in Chapters 8.1 and 8.2.

PROBLEMS WITH LAVATORIES AND THEIR USERS

Fittings and the equipment in lavatories posed a temptation to passengers. Instructions were issued drawing attention to,

'the serious loss sustained by the Company in replacing the equipment in Lavatories, and especially in towels, owing to the large quantity continually going missing from the Lavatories.'

Guards were required to *'examine Trains before starting … and again on arrival at destination … with the view of finding out, if possible, where the leakage takes place.'[5]*

WINTER OPERATION

Water cans were provided in winter for carriages that were not steam heated. The water tanks were drained to prevent burst pipes. Comprehensive instructions were given for carriages that were not required during the winter timetable – see Plate 3.18.

LAVATORIES FOR GUARDS

Company servants had needs as well as passengers. Drawing a discreet veil over the likely actions of the early breaksmen on their exposed (and cold) perches, the first Brake Vans had no lavatory facilities.

Plate 3.19
The Edinburgh portion of the afternoon 'Corridor' express at Princes Street. Apart from the corridor connections, one of the 45-foot 12-wheeled Dining Saloons which was later acquired by the Caledonian is seen in the train.

INSTRUCTIONS REGARDING SLEEPING SALOONS, SLEEPING COMPOSITES, DINING CARS, SALOONS, CORRIDOR CARRIAGES, AND ORDINARY LAVATORY CARRIAGES DURING FROSTY WEATHER.

During Frosty Weather, Sleeping Saloons, Sleeping Composites, Dining Cars, Saloons, Corridor Carriages, and Ordinary Lavatory Carriages fitted with the Steam-Heating Apparatus, which are not engaged in daily Traffic, must, on arrival at Carriage Depots, be dealt with as follows in order to prevent the Lavatory Tanks and Steam-Heating Apparatus becoming frozen, viz.:—

(1) All Lavatory Tanks and Flush Cisterns to be emptied, including the Auxiliary Flushing Tanks in the W.C's. To ensure this being done in a number of the West Coast Sleeping Saloons it is necessary to turn the Cock over Tank to "Off" position and pull Handle.

(2) Steam-Heating Regulators in Compartments to be put to the "Off" position.

(3) The Steam Trap Chains to be pulled in the case of West Coast and L. & N.-W Stock, and the Steam Trap Levers raised in the case of Caledonian Stock to ensure that all Water is liberated from the Steam-Heating Apparatus. In the case of Sleeping Saloons and Sleeping Composites the small Square Taps in the Pantry to be turned by means of a Special Key supplied to Stations for the purpose.

(4) All Flexible Steam-Heating Pipes to be uncoupled.

(5) Lavatory Tanks and Flush Cisterns must only be refilled when the Vehicles are being put into order for traffic.

(6) When Vehicles have been emptied of water a label must be affixed in the Lavatories and Pantries indicating that such has been done, in order to avoid Vehicles being put into traffic before they have again been supplied with water.

These instructions supersede the instructions at page 83 of the General Portion of the Appendix to the Working Time Table under heading "Heating Stoves in Carriages, Dining Saloons, Sleeping Saloons, &c."

In the case of Lavatory Carriages not fitted with Steam-Heating Apparatus, all Lavatory Tanks must be kept Empty during Winter, as shown in the instructions (22) page 80, of the General Portion of Appendix to Working Time Table.

The first design known for certain to have a lavatory in the guard's compartment was the Diagram 31 Coupé Lavatory Brake Composite of 1898. The pedestal was concealed beneath one of the seats built into the lookouts – see Figure 3.19. This amenity was a standard fitting from then on.

CORRIDOR ACCESS THROUGHOUT THE TRAIN

The Caledonian's first involvement with corridors throughout a train was with the West Coast Joint Stock. In July 1893 new trains were introduced on the 2.00pm departures from Glasgow and Euston. In August a portion for Edinburgh was added. This is shown in Plate 3.19. G.P. Neele described the train as follows:

'The vehicles formed what the Americans would call a solid train, though the connections between the various vehicles were at first of the accordion, and not of the "vestibule" order. A complete thoroughfare existed from one end of the train to the other, down the sides of the carriages, except in the dining saloons, where its course followed the American system of a central passage.

ABOVE: Plate 3.18
The instructions for preventing damage to lavatory and steam heated carriages that were not in regular service during the winter.

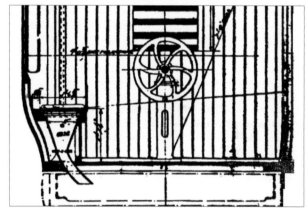

Figure 3.19
Lavatory facilities for guards first appeared in 1898 in the compartment of the Diagram 31 Coupé Lavatory Brake Composite. These carriages were used on long-distance through workings, hence the amenity under the seat. The drawing is St. Rollox 8861.

The July Time Tables came out with some striking red and blue announcements of the train as having first and third refreshment and dining cars attached. A folding sketch accompanied the bills showing the elevation and the constitution of the ten vehicles. No such train had ever previously run on any English line giving an end to end communication.[6]

As an aside, this type of train at last enabled a guard to attend immediately to a passenger in distress who had activated the communication cord without the necessity of stopping the train.

EARLY CALEDONIAN CARRIAGES WITH CORRIDORS

All subsequent WCJS carriages were fitted with corridor connections, but the CR did not build such carriages for its own use until the second half of 1901. These early 50-foot carriages are described and illustrated in Chapter 8.3.

The Corridor Thirds to Diagram 91 had a centre aisle. They were one of the first general service carriages in Britain with an open plan seating arrangement. The design was not perpetuated by the CR. The acceptable combination of privacy and accessibility was the side corridor configuration with separate compartments. It will be remembered from Chapter 2.3 that *The Engineer* considered that the open plan arrangement was:

'so opposed to the social habits of the English, and would interfere so much with the privacy and comfort which they now enjoy, that these considerations … would forbid its adoption in this country.'[7]

It was also no doubt for reasons of privacy that Saloons were not fitted with corridor connections. The open plan was acceptable when confined to the household or private party, but the general public had to be excluded. The only exception to the rule on the Caledonian was the Diagram 99 design, which was lettered as a *'corridor saloon'* and was intended to be coupled to 'Grampian' stock trains which had restaurant facilities.

TROUBLE CAUSED BY CORRIDORS

Corridor carriages became more widely available on the Caledonian with the introduction of the 'Grampian' stock. Dining facilities were provided for both classes of traveller, which caused unwelcome social mobility. In the Glasgow portion of the train, some Third class passengers had to pass through the First class section to reach the Dining car – see the marshalling diagram in Chapter 9, Figure 9.4. Free movement throughout a train was forbidden. The General Instructions were explicit:

*'dividing doors between the First and Third class Corridors must be kept locked throughout the entire journey **excepting when Passengers are being conducted to and from the Dining Saloon by the Attendants**; and it must be distinctly*

understood by the men in charge of the Train that the object of the corridor system is not to give passengers the opportunity for promenading the whole length of the train, but to afford ease of access to the Dining Saloons, and give each Passenger the use of a Lavatory.'*[8]

These instructions were not always conscientiously carried out. To quote from the special instructions in the Northern section of the 1907 Working Timetable:

'Complaint is made that the Third Class Passengers are frequenting the First Class corridor … owing to the doors in the Corridors … being left open or not locked. The Corridor doors must be kept locked, and the Third Class Passengers must not be allowed to go through the First Class Corridor unless proceeding to and from the Dining Car. Guards must give this order their careful attention and see that there is no cause for further complaint.'[9]

SEMI-CORRIDOR CARRIAGES

The logical development of the notion that corridors were not for *'promenading the whole length of the train'* was the semi-corridor carriage. This style became possible when carriage widths were increased to 8 feet 8 inches or 9 feet, which gave room for a corridor just under 2 feet wide without sacrificing seating capacity. The corridor allowed movement between each compartment and the lavatory facilities, but not movement between carriages, as no corridor connections were fitted. In addition, movement between classes within the carriage was discouraged. Each class had its own lavatory and a door in the corridor divided the two sets of accommodation.

The Caledonian started to build semi-corridor carriages in 1900 and continued construction until 1922. In total there were fifty-five Composites and forty-five Thirds. The carriages are described in Chapters 8, 9 and 11.

The semi-corridor concept led to an anomaly on the Callander & Oban when the Observation Car *Maid of Morven* was introduced. This car was fitted with a corridor connection that was redundant, because the rest of the train was composed of semi-corridor carriages. It became in effect a self-contained saloon, with catering facilities for the exclusive use of the passengers riding in it.

REFERENCES

1. *West Coast Joint Stock*, pp. 64-66
2. *Railway Reminiscences*, p. 106
3. *West Coast Joint Stock*, pp. 81-83
4. *Railway & Travel Monthly*, May 1910
5. *July–September 1907 Working Timetable*, p. 124
6. *Railway Reminiscences*, pp. 409-10
7. *The Engineer*, 15th January, 1869, p. 52
8. *October 1906 Working Timetable*, pp. 68-69
9. *October 1907 Working Timetable*, p. 74

CHAPTER 4
LIVERY, IDENTIFICATION AND FURNISHING
4.1: LIVERY, CRESTS AND INSIGNIA

Carriage livery was covered fully in Jim MacIntosh's book, to which the reader is referred.[1] This chapter does not repeat the detail in Jim's book but summarises the evolution of the livery and adds new information. The second section deals with numbering conventions and the final section covers internal décor in detail.

LIVERY DEVELOPMENT

Carriage livery changed several times over the years, until it stabilised in the 1890s. Even then, two styles existed side by side until the Grouping, with the lower body and ends of all carriages a common colour. Most carriages had white upper panels, but a limited number did not.

The progression from the earliest days to this situation is still not entirely clear. To repeat the information from newspaper reports in Chapter 5.1, the carriages for the southern section of the new line in 1847 were painted *'blue'* (First class) *'russet brown up to window level'* – implying white above (Second class) and *'dull brown'* (Third class). Those of the northern end were painted *'lake.'* This may have been the same colour as the stock on the then still independent Glasgow, Paisley & Greenock Railway, a line also controlled by Errington and Locke, which was described as *'Grand Junction lake.'*

Already, therefore, livery was far from uniform. That said, the few early photographs that survive show a preponderance of carriages with white upper panels – see Plate 5.1 which dates from about 1860, and the photograph of old carriages at Buchanan Street (Plate 4.1). The exception seems to have been the Greenock line which was by now part of the Caledonian, where the sugar broker's Saloon of 1859:

'is distinguished from the others [carriages] by the upper part being painted white.'[2]

Presumably the rest of the carriage stock was still 'lake.' Five years later, *The Greenock Advertiser* reported that Greenock line carriage livery had changed to white upper panels:

'first class are painted in chocolate, white and gold, … the second and third class are painted green and white.'[3]

The first West Coast Joint Stock carriages which were put into service in 1863 also had white upper panels. The L&NWR carriage stock followed suit in 1869.[4] David Jenkinson repeated a suggestion that the WCJS livery was the stimulus for the Caledonian to introduce white upper panels[5] but on the available evidence he was clearly mistaken.

THE FIRST ATTEMPT AT UNIFORMITY

The 1860s culminated in the takeover of the Scottish Central and Scottish North Eastern Railways. The combined carriage fleet carried a variety of liveries – for instance, SCR carriages were green. In December 1867 there was clearly uncertainty about carriage livery. As described in Chapter 6.1, a large order for carriages had been placed with Metropolitan. The CR Board *'Read Mr Conner's letter for instructions as to painting the Carriages being built for the Company,'* and resolved *'Paint as previously ordered.'*[6]

There is no record of what that meant, but in 1869 a CR Officers' Meeting minute recorded the decision that:

'the painting of the upper part of the carriages white be discontinued, and that first class and composite carriages be uniformly painted lake and the second and third class carriages green.'[7]

White upper panels were therefore the norm at that time. It may be significant that 1869 was the year when patents were taken out

Plate 4.1
A well-known view of early carriage designs at Buchanan Street. Most have white upper panels. On the left, carriage number 10 has the designation **FIRST CLASS**, with slightly larger initial letters. This was L&NWR practice, but the configuration and number do not match a West Coast Joint Stock vehicle. Next is an old low-roofed carriage marked **THIRD CLASS**. To its right on the nearest track is a carriage bearing a destination board marked **GLASGOW**. To its right is a carriage with sliding shutters for windows.

for the synthetic production of alizarin crimson from coal tar, which made crimson paint cheaper and more easily available. Repainting in the new colours does not seem to have been pursued with vigour if the photograph of a train at Stewarton in 1873 (Plate 5.4) is representative of the whole railway.

This Officers' Meeting minute puts the next resolution recorded in *Caledonian Railway Livery* in an entirely new context. A Loco & Stores Committee Meeting minute in August 1873 recorded: '*Paint the Carriages a uniform colour.*'[8] This was not a change from white upper panels to lake as originally thought, but a livery change for Second and Third class to conform to the lake-painted superior class carriages.

Two months later the Traffic Committee read Conner's letter under the heading '*question as to colour*' and approved the content.[9] It is reasonable to assume that this reference in the singular confirms that Second and Third class carriages were to be repainted to match the Firsts and Composites. As further evidence, numerous photographs of the carriage sidings at Barnhill show rakes of carriages painted a uniform dark colour.

The Return of White Upper Panels

No definitive date has so far been discovered for the re-adoption of white upper panels. Jim MacIntosh suggested that it might have coincided with the introduction of the 'Boat Trains' to Gourock, Wemyss Bay and Ardrossan in 1890.[10]

The introduction of new sets of 45-foot carriages for the Callander & Oban was reported in the press in February 1890. The carriages were illustrated and described in detail, both inside and out. '*The carriages are painted crimson lake, picked out in gold, and fine-lined in red.*'[11] The article stated that similar carriages were to be introduced on the Gourock service, but made no mention of their livery.

In the summer of 1890 Drummond resigned, to be succeeded for a very short time by Hugh Smellie. John Lambie took over in April 1891 and it is hardly likely that carriage livery was a high priority during a period when senior management was in this state of flux.

An internal memorandum from the CR's General Manager James Thompson to Lambie dated 8th June 1892[12] confirms that '*the 45-foot bogie carriages being built are to be painted white*' – see Plate 4.2. This referred to the first set of 45-foot carriages to be constructed under the Lambie regime, which were built with a simplified two-layer panelling style. This development is described and illustrated in Chapter 7.5. Perhaps Lambie and James Thompson decided on white upper panels to coincide with this change in style.

The Final Livery Colours

When it began publication in 1897 *The Locomotive Magazine* ran a series of articles on railway companies' liveries. Its publisher was F. Moore, a pseudonym for two brothers called Bell who worked for the Great Eastern Railway. 'F. Moore' was well-known for coloured postcards and paintings of railway locomotives and trains. The description of the CR carriage livery was:

> '*The older passenger stock is painted a dark purple lake, with yellow striping, having a fine vermilion edge. The newer carriages are painted with the lower portion the same colour as the above, and the upper panels white, with lines in yellow and fine white edge; in each case the lettering is in gold, shaded with red and black, and the coat-of-arms is put on the lower panels.*'[13]

The '*older stock*' referred to carriages that were painted under the 'uniform colour' regime. The two liveries continued until the end of the Caledonian's independent existence.

Lake

As stated in *Caledonian Railway Livery*,[14] 'lake' on its own is not a colour, although the term is often used as such. Indeed, the Caledonian used the term when it supplied information to the *Railway Year Book*. Lake is a semi-transparent pigment which varies across the red end of the spectrum, depending on the raw material used to create it and its fixing agent. Its transparency means that the overall effect is influenced by the colour of its undercoat.

Apart from the 1897 statement, the only two references to the lower body colour used by the CR are the 1890 *Engineering* article and a Loco & Stores Committee minute of March 1890 which, under the heading 'Carriage Lakes,' refers to the supply of '*crimson lake required for the painting of carriages.*'[15]

'Crimson lake' and '*purple lake*' are not necessarily contradictory colours. The former could refer to the pigment used on top of a darker undercoat, which would give the visual effect described by the latter.

White

It has been generally accepted that the white panels of CR carriages had a faint bluish-green tint.[16] This assumes that, like the L&NWR, the Caledonian added ultramarine blue (about 1 part in 100) to the white lead pigment. This was done to avoid the colour appearing as cream under coats of varnish, which at that period had a yellow tint. The present author suggests that the CR did not follow this practice. The description of the L&NWR carriage livery in *The Locomotive Magazine* gives the colour as '*white tinged with blue.*'[17] The Caledonian upper panels in the foregoing quotation were simply described as '*white.*'

Paint Specifications

Detailed specifications for painting must have existed for CR internal use and for issuing to contractors. No such document for Caledonian carriages has come to light.

An L&NWR paint specification records the top coat as '*carmine lake*' laid on top of '*body brown*' over a first coat of '*lead colour.*' A

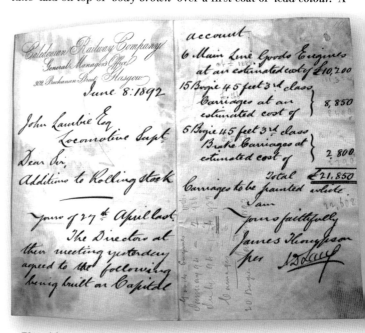

Plate 4.2
The internal memorandum which instructed John Lambie to paint his first 45-foot carriages with white upper panels. This was not mentioned in the original Board minute.

final coat of part carmine lake and part varnish was applied, before four further coats of clear varnish.[18]

The terms 'carmine' and 'crimson' lake were often used interchangeably, even though their sources and colours were different. Carmine is a stronger red than crimson, which tends slightly towards purple. According to Sidney Stone, it was expensive and not durable, its use being confined to interior decoration. This leads to the conclusion that crimson was used in both L&NWR and CR liveries.

The L&NWR 'body brown' was an equal mixture of black and indian red. It was presumably the colour of this coat that made the difference between the CR finish and that of the L&NWR. If the Caledonian used proportionately more red in the undercoat formula, the finish would have been lighter, as described in *Caledonian Railway Livery*.[19]

The correlation of the carriage colours with British Standard colour definitions was set out in *Caledonian Railway Livery*.[20] This was established by British Railways Scottish Region in 1957. In view of the discussion concerning the white shade above, it is likely that the definition of *'New Grey Mist'* (BS 9-093) is incorrect. There is no reason to doubt the other definition *('Sepia' BS 3-039)*.

BRAKE VAN ENDS

James McEwan seems to have been the first commentator to state that Brake Van ends were vermilion, presumably by analogy with those of CR Goods Brake Vans.[21] The feature was not mentioned in the Stephenson Locomotive Society's CR centenary publication of 1947.[22] McEwan wrote in his notes for a history of the Caledonian that *'brake ends were vermilion, except for 'Grampian' and gangway stock.'*[23] The statement seems to have taken root and attempts have been made to rationalise the practice to include the painting of the sides of lookouts in carriages with a centre guard's compartment.[24]

Returning to the 1897 livery description, its last sentence is *'The ends of passenger brake vans are vermilion.'* Passenger Brake Vans accommodated a guard, luggage and parcels only. They did not cater for passengers. The latter vehicles were called Brake Thirds or Brake Composites. It is not surprising that commentators have struggled to find evidence of light red ends on Brake Thirds and the like – the statement indicates that they did not exist on passenger-carrying vehicles with a Brake compartment.

Finding evidence of vermilion-painted Passenger Brake Van ends is not easy either, because photographs showing the vans are rare, and good quality photographs showing an end are even rarer. The 6-wheeled van in Plate 7.8 may be one example. Despite the lack of firm evidence, the contemporary description is unequivocal and should be trusted.

LINING

Lining was first mentioned in the 1864 press description of the Greenock line's First class carriages discussed earlier. It is not known whether this was standard practice throughout the CR system. The next firm evidence of lining comes from a Cravens Bros publicity photograph of 1880 – see Plate 4.3.

In the Drummond era panels were edged with a thin gold or yellow line, placed on the edge of the beading. On the outside edge of the whole carriage was another thin, red line; with a white vertical line at each end of the side and along the bottom of the coach side. There are illustrations in Chapter 6. This style of lining was applied to carriages until the Grouping.

VARIATIONS IN LIVERY WITHIN TYPES OF CARRIAGE

All bogie carriages were painted or repainted with white upper panels when the final livery was established, but 4- and

6-wheeled carriage livery varied. Details of individual carriages are recorded in the Coaching Plant Stock Book. The following paragraph summarises the position.

Pre-Drummond carriages retained their all-over brown livery. Drummond's 4-wheeled First and Third class carriages were also brown, but half of the Brake Thirds received upper panels. All his 6-wheeled Firsts and Composites were repainted white, and 140 out of the 174 Thirds. The majority of the 4- and 6-wheeled Brake Vans were white.

PICKERSGILL LIVERY

The later Pickersgill carriages were sheathed in steel over a wooden frame, removing the need for beading to cover panel joints above the waist. The panelled appearance was maintained by paint, but lining was not applied. An example of the instructions issued to contractors is shown in Figure 4.1, with illustrations in Plates 4.4 and 4.5. More examples are in Chapter 11.

BROWN AND WHITE CARRIAGES IN THE SAME TRAIN

There is another tradition that all-over brown carriages were not mixed with those with white upper panels. *Caledonian Railway Liveries* showed photographs disproving the statement, but did not offer an explanation.[25] One possibility is that a brown carriage, if available, was used as a 'leader' to avoid having to lock the front two compartments of the first carriage proper in the train as a collision precaution.

ROOFS AND UNDERFRAMES

Roofs were made of wood planks, covered with canvas. This was protected with several coats of white lead, which oxidised to grey. Rain strips seem to have appeared in the Lambie era.

L&NWR underframes were painted body colour and lined out until the 1890s.[26] There is insufficient photographic evidence to state whether early CR carriages were treated in the same way. Later carriages had black underframes and fittings. Footsteps on the end of carriages were black.

Plate 4.3
This is an enlargement from Plate 6.18 on p. 140. It shows that carriages in the uniform all over brown livery were lined in 1880.

CRESTS

An 1848 newspaper description of one of the Greenock-built Saloon carriages said that *'externally it is painted a rich lake colour, and on each side are emblazoned the Company's arms.'*[27] These two carriages, described in Chapter 13.1, were luxury vehicles that regularly travelled south of the border. They may have been the only carriages thus adorned. As mentioned in Chapter 3.1, ordinary CR carriages ran through to Liverpool and Manchester from an early date and may also have carried the crest. Presumably the crest was the version described below.

The first known emblem to appear on the carriages of the Caledonian Railway was a development of that used from the opening of the company – see Plate 4.6. According to George Dow who was an authority on railway heraldry, it was painted on some carriages from about 1860.[28] It appeared on the drawing of a Caledonian train recording the first Westinghouse brake trials on the line in 1872.[29]

By 1882 it was superseded by a crest based on the Scottish royal armorial device. The date is given by the photograph reproduced in Plate 6.20 of a carriage that was delivered between May and July in that year, according to the Coaching Plant Stock Book. A further development of the crest superseded it in 1899.[30] The final version is

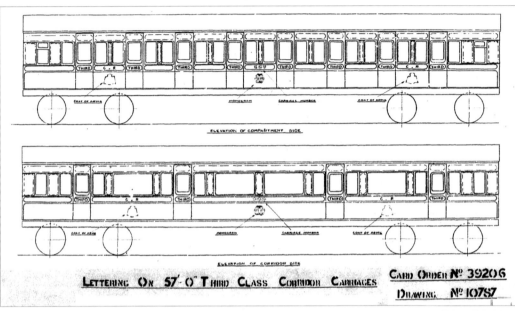

Figure 4.1
This drawing was issued to R.Y. Pickering. The chain-dotted lines set out the areas where paint was to be applied to simulate panelling above the waist line. The location of numbers, class lettering and CR insignia is also shown.

BELOW: Plate 4.4
The result on a Diagram 122A Corridor Brake Third, built at the very end of the Caledonian's independent existence.

shown in Plate 4.7. This also shows the lion rampant element of the original crest as a decoration in the obscured glass of the lavatory window. Clearer reproductions of all the crests are in *Caledonian Railway Livery*.[31]

MONOGRAMS

The first style of monogram (in modern parlance 'corporate logo') was introduced by McIntosh. For a symbol of ownership it was rather discreet, but in a style that was common at the time, with elaborately ornamented, intertwined letters. It is shown in Plate 4.8.

Pickersgill introduced a new monogram – see Plate 4.9. It was almost certainly used from his arrival in post, as the posters advertising the pre-war Pullman services carried it, as shown in Plates 10.1-10.4.

Plate 4.5
Taken inside the paint shop at R.Y. Pickering's works, with Diagram 115A Semi-corridor Brake Composites being readied for the road. The publicity photographs of a finished carriage are shown in Plate 11.9.

ABOVE: **Plate 4.6**
The first CR crest, applied to carriages from the 1860s. It may even have figured on the two Saloons built for Anglo-Scottish traffic in 1848.
RIGHT: **Plate 4.7**
This is the final design of CR crest, on a Diagram 99 Saloon. Above is the rampant lion heraldic device as part of the obscure glass on a lavatory window. The lion also appears on the First class compartment mat shown on the back cover.

BUILDER'S PLATE

Drummond-designed carriages had been built at St. Rollox from 1883 in tandem with those built by contractors. The carriages and their builders are discussed in Chapter 7.1. A cast iron plate was introduced to show that a carriage had been built 'in house.' Drawing 4014[32] was dated 2nd June 1884. This is reproduced in Figure 4.2 and a surviving example from the McIntosh era is shown in Plate 4.10. Drummond fitted a similar plate to wagons, replacing painted numbers.[33]

DESTINATION BOARDS

Most, but not all, carriages carried brackets for destination boards above the windows on the centre line of the vehicle, unless a door or lookout prevented it. The Caledonian called them 'label boards' in the instructions written in the Working Timetable Appendices.[34]

In common with the L&NWR and WCJS the boards were 2 feet 3 inches long.[35] Most were reversible, with, for example, ABERDEEN on one side and EDINBURGH PRINCES STREET on the other. There were two sizes. The most common was 3¼ inches high, as seen in Plate 4.11. The other was 6 inches high, but with ends reduced to fit the brackets – see Plate 4.12. The examples seen of the larger boards were not reversible.

ABOVE: Plate 4.8
The first style of monogram applied to a 'Grampian' carriage. The ornate lettering and numbering style used for this stock is also shown.

BELOW: Plates 4.9
The final design of monogram was introduced in 1914. The photograph also shows the standard block lettering and numerals.

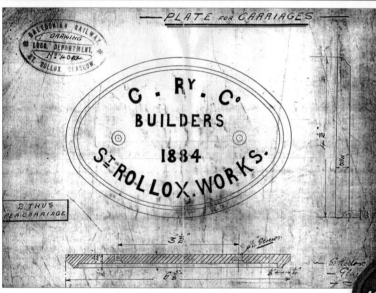

ABOVE: Figure 4.2
St. Rollox drawing 4014 depicts the builder's plate that was attached to the solebars of carriages built at the CR works.

RIGHT: Plate 4.10
The photograph of a later builder's plate comes courtesy of CRA member Michael Dunn.

Plates 4.11 and 4.12
Two examples of destination boards. Both fitted on brackets just below the carriage eaves. The narrower example was reversible.

REFERENCES
1. *Caledonian Railway Livery*, pp. 242-60
2. *Caledonian Railway Livery*, p. 244
3. *Caledonian Railway Livery*, p. 244
4. *LNWR Liveries*, p. 88
5. *An Illustrated History of LNWR Coaches*, p. 22
6. NRS BR/CAL/1/16 entry 245
7. Officers' Minute Book, March 1869, minute 201
8. NRS BR/CAL/1/20 entry 1782
9. NRS BR/CAL/1/21 entry 163
10. *Caledonian Railway Livery*, p. 246
11. *Engineering*, 21st February 1890, p. 196
12. NRS BR/CAL/5/11 p. 110
13. *The Locomotive Magazine*, October 1897, p. 138
14. *Caledonian Railway Livery*, p. 246
15. NRS BR/CAL/1/33 entry 1235
16. *Caledonian Railway Livery*, pp. 246-47
17. *The Locomotive Magazine*, January 1897, p. 130
18. *LNWR Liveries*, pp. 125-26
19. *Caledonian Railway Livery*, p. 246
20. *Caledonian Railway Livery*, p. 247
21. *Caledonian Railway Wagons*, p. 50
22. *Caledonian Railway Centenary*, pp. 57-58
23. McEwan Archive T25/1/30
24. *Caledonian Railway Livery*, p. 258, caption to Plate 33
25. *Caledonian Railway Livery*, pp. 154 and 157
26. *LNWR Liveries*, pp. 93-94
27. *North British Railway and Shipping Journal*, 19th December 1848
28. *Caledonian Railway Livery*, p. 59
29. *The Engineer*, 24th May 1872
30. Dow, quoted in *Caledonian Railway Livery*, p. 59
31. *Caledonian Railway Livery*, pp. 59 and 61
32. RHP 70021
33. *Caledonian Railway Wagons*, pp. 67-68
34. *1915 Working Timetable Appendix*, pp. 78-79
35. *LNWR Liveries*, p. 115

4.2: LETTERS, NUMBERS AND NUMBERING

The standard carriage letter and number styles are illustrated in colour in *Caledonian Railway Livery*. They were the same style as the numbers used on the rear of tenders and bunkers, but the shading and highlighting were slightly different.[1] A typical example of the standard style is shown in Plate 4.9.

Although evidence is very scanty, it seems that carriages were always lettered and numbered in block style – see Plate 4.1. The practice thus differed from the early locomotives, which used a serif style.[2]

THE 'GRAMPIAN' STOCK STYLE

The 'Grampian' style carriages and the associated Saloons merited special lettering and numbering. The characters were the same height as the standard style, but were much more ornate – see Plate 4.8. A larger version was used above the windows to advertise the routes of the initial services as shown, for example in Chapter 9, Plate 9.11.

Jim MacIntosh suggested that Family Saloons 14 and 15 were also lettered in this style, but this seems unlikely as the Saloons were built in 1899, six years before the introduction of the 'Grampian' stock.[3] Comparison between the word SALOON on the Family Saloon and that on the Diagram 99 Corridor Saloon built at the same time as the 'Grampian' stock shows that while the earlier lettering was similar, it was not identical – see Plates 4.13 and 4.14. This suggests that the lettering on the two Family Saloons, which were by some stretch the most luxurious design of carriage prior to the arrival of the 'Grampian' stock, served as a prototype for the later carriages.

NUMBERS INSIDE CARRIAGES

The carriage number and often its class was repeated inside the compartments. Lack of photographic evidence prevents the establishment of a starting date for this convention. The earliest known drawing showing class designations inside a carriage is for a Metropolitan Tri-Composite of 1877[4] – see Figure 6.20. The L&NWR also pursued this policy, but again no date is given.[5] Illustrations of CR practice will be found in Chapter 4.3.

CARRIAGE NUMBERING CONVENTIONS

Originally the CR divided its stock into five classes – Firsts, Seconds, Composites, Thirds and Saloons. This was reduced to four after the company abolished Second class in 1893. In common with many railways, each class was numbered in a separate sequence starting from 1.

Construction of rolling stock was charged either to revenue or to capital account. If a new vehicle was built as a replacement for another which was either scrapped or down-rated – for example, from a First to a Third – it was considered to be a 'renewal' and the new vehicle took the number vacated by the old one. If the vehicle was considered an 'addition' – that is, it increased the total stock of carriages of that class – its construction was charged to the capital account and it took a number which extended the series. Carriages acquired from the West Coast Joint Stock were similarly treated as additions to the fleet.

DOWN-RATING AND RECLASSIFICATION

Carriages were re-classified and converted in the McIntosh period. As discussed in Chapter 9.4, a number of First class carriages were turned into Composites as well as a smaller number of Thirds. During World War I a large number of the First class and Composite carriages that were built in the late 1870s were down-rated to Thirds.

When a carriage was down-rated it was renumbered into the new sequence, taking a vacant number rather than a new one. The transcription of the Coaching Plant Stock Book contains a record of the various renumberings.

RENUMBERING WITHIN A CLASS

Some carriages were renumbered within a class sequence. This happened to a number of Drummond's 6-wheeled carriages which were technically replacements, as discussed in Chapter 7.2. They were allocated numbers which extended the series as if they were treated as capital. This was a short-term measure until the old carriages that they replaced could be scrapped. They then took over the old carriage numbers. Sometimes carriages were re-allocated vacant numbers to make way for new construction.

DUPLICATE NUMBERS

When a carriage was considered to be totally depreciated in value from an accounting point of view, but still capable of further use, it was 'duplicated' and a replacement built. Two groups of carriages were affected. Thirds dating from the late 1860s and early 1870s were renumbered into a series starting at 3000. Seventeen survived to be included in the Coaching Plant Stock Book. A similar series from 1400 upwards served some old Saloons.

RIGHT: Plate 4.13
Picture of the lettering on Saloon number 15, which appeared in late 1899.

FAR RIGHT: Plate 4.14
The same word on a Diagram 99 Saloon for comparison. The latter carriage was lettered to match the 'Grampian' stock introduced in 1905. While the overall style is similar, the letter O is different.

THE GROUPING AND AFTER

The final CR carriage number series at the Grouping are shown in the following table.

CARRIAGE TYPE	NUMBER SERIES
Saloon	1-46
First	1-312
Composite and Brake Composite	1-447
Third and Brake Third	1-1459
Luggage and Passenger Brake Van	1-271

As can be imagined, rationalising and renumbering the newly-acquired fleets of several constituent railways took time. One of the carriage trimmer's notebooks[6] shows that most CR carriages still carried their original numbers in 1926 – see Plate 4.15. In early 1927 (Plate 4.16) LM&SR numbering was almost universal.

REFERENCES
1. *Caledonian Railway Livery*, p. 18 (carriages), p. 16 (locomotives)
2. *Caledonian Railway Livery*, Chapter 5
3. *Caledonian Railway Livery*, p. 249
4. Birmingham City Archive ref: MS99 2285
   CRA Archive ref: 6/1/1/2/7
5. *LNWR Liveries*, p. 123
6. NRS BR/CAL/5/61

Plates 4.15 and 4.16
Two pages of the entries in a carriage trimmer's notebook that record carriages in for repair at St. Rollox. The figures in the narrow columns indicate the number of First and Third class compartments. In 1926, CR numbers were in the majority; less than a year later there were hardly any. The LM&SR numbers were those with five digits.

4.3: INTERNAL DECOR

Only fragmentary written evidence exists of the early carriage interiors and photographs are of course nonexistent. The descriptions are set out in Chapter 5.1. The main distinctions between the classes were the cushioning or lack of it on seats, and the covering of the internal wood panelling with cloth for the superior class. As recounted in Chapter 3.1, the Caledonian originally provided padded seats in Second class. The practice was discontinued for a time following representations from the L&NWR.

INTERIORS IN THE 1860s AND 1870s

Examples of interior furnishing of Scottish Central Railway carriages are shown in Chapter 5. Contractors' drawings showing Caledonian carriage interiors of the late 1860s and 1870s appear in Chapter 6. First class carriages were well upholstered, with the material also used to line carriage sides and doors below the window. Arm rests and curtains were usually fitted. Second class seats and backs were upholstered and Third class passengers still made do with wooden seats and varnished wood interiors.

PRE-DRUMMOND PERIOD INTERIORS

The back of the photograph of Midland C&W Tri-Composite 205 in the CRA Archive[1] carries the following hand-written description of the interior furnishing – source unknown. It probably represents standard practice in the late Brittain period.

> *'1st blue cloth, sycamore veneer walnut bands, gilt moulding*
> *2nd repp sides etc., waxed cloth, gilt moulding*
> *3rd repp sides etc., painted and grained.'*

THE DRUMMOND PERIOD

The major development in the Drummond period was the improvement in Third class comfort. Most carriages now had upholstered seats and backs – see the interior plans taken from the Large Diagram Book in Chapter 7. Drawings of First and Third class compartment interiors are shown in Figures 4.3 and 4.4.

Inside the carriages built for the C&O in 1890:

> *'The interiors of the first class compartments … are finished with polished sycamore panels, and selected bird's eye maple facings, the angles being filled by gilt mouldings. The cushions, sides, backs and side quarters are well stuffed with best curled horsehair and covered with blue cloth of the best quality, trimmed with rich blue and crimson lace, Greek key pattern. The door squabs, arm and elbow rests, are similarly stuffed and covered with buffalo hide of best quality, of a colour to match the cloth.*

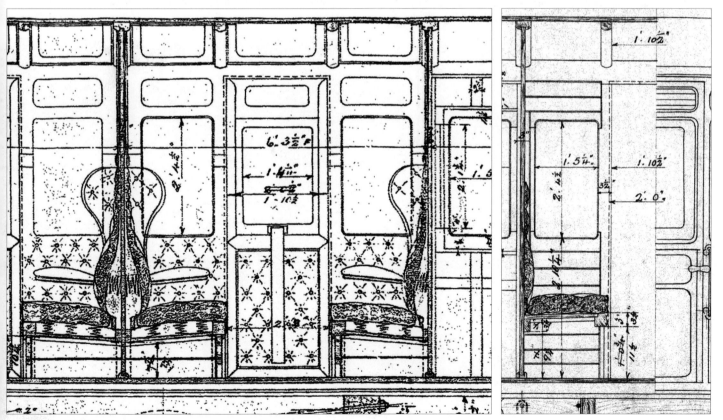

Figures 4.3 and 4.4
These two drawings show the interiors of Drummond 45-foot carriages.

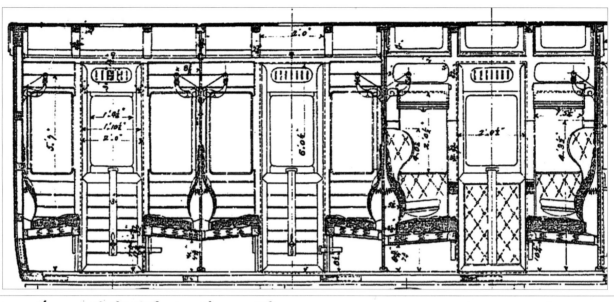

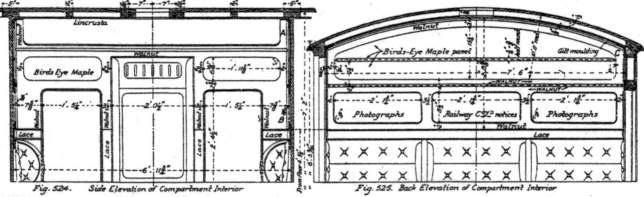

Fig. 524. Side Elevation of Compartment Interior

Fig. 525. Back Elevation of Compartment Interior

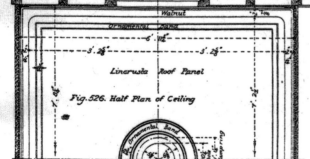

Fig. 526. Half Plan of Ceiling

Figs. 524 to 526. Interior of First Class Carriage, Caledonian Railway.

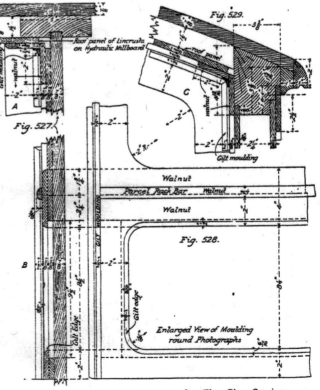

Figs. 527 to 529, Details of Corners, &c., First Class Carriage, Caledonian Railway.

TOP OF PAGE: Figure 4.5
The two classes of compartment in the Lambie era. The seats in Third class are now sprung instead of padded.

MAIN DRAWING: Figure 4.6
This drawing was originally published by Sidney Stone in *The Railway Engineer*. It shows the internal decoration of a Lambie First class compartment.

The cushions and backs of the third class carriages are stuffed with best curled hair, and the backs are upholstered for a height of 3 ft., and covered with carpet.'[2]

The colour of the Third class compartments was not mentioned, but it was presumably red. There was also a description of the *coupé* compartments and the lavatory accommodation.

Plates 4.17 and 4.18
These interiors date from the McIntosh regime. Plate 4.17 (*above*) shows electrically-lit 48-foot First number 305, built by R.Y. Pickering in 1905. The exterior is shown in Chapter 8, Plate 8.3. The window blinds are down. There is no carriage number on the inside of the door. Notice the lace decoration above the seats and along the seat base, with the same motif on the straps at the side of the door. The door is padded with leather. The alarm signal plate on the right-hand side was lettered yellow on a red background. It read *'To Stop the Train Pull down the Chain.'* The penalty for improper use was £5. The CR official notice on the left starts with an injunction to passengers not to lean out of the window.
Plate 4.18 (*below*) depicts the interior of one of the three Corridor Third class carriages built with a centre aisle in 1902. A drawing of the carriage is shown in Figure 8.25.

LAMBIE AND McINTOSH INTERIORS

Up to the end of the Drummond regime, Third class seats were made of material stuffed with horsehair. Lambie introduced sprung seats, as shown in Figure 4.5. The backs of the Third class seats were still padded, but those in First class had a small amount of springing. The decoration of the First class compartment of a Lambie carriage is shown in Figure 4.6. The interior of a McIntosh-designed First is shown in Plate 4.17 which closely resembles the description of the Drummond interior. The 50-foot centre aisle Corridor Third interior is shown in Plate 4.18. This design was built in 1902 and is described in Chapter 8.3.

THE 'GRAMPIAN' CORRIDOR STOCK

After the official launch of the train, an article described the carriages' construction and interior finish.[3] This was based on a company press release, as an almost identical account appeared in *The Railway Magazine.*[4]

First class compartments seated three each side and were finished in polished walnut relieved with gilt scrolls and much other gilt work. The upholstery was brown tapestry moquette trimmed with lace. Twelve dozen antimacassars were purchased *'at 1s 2¼d to 3s 9d according to size.'*[5] The electrolier (so called because it was in effect a chandelier with electric bulbs rather than candles) was gilded and rated at 40 candle power. The non-smoking compartments were given cashmere rugs over the floor linoleum. The doors were padded with embossed morocco leather.

Third class provided four-a-side seating with a central armrest. Careful attention was paid to the springing and upholstery of the seats which were covered in *'peacock blue French carpet having a black floral pattern with orange spots.'* The floors were covered with brightly patterned cork linoleum. The ceilings were covered in white enamelled lincrusta panelling and the walls were finished in mahogany. The four light bronzed electrolier was rated at 32 candle power. A patent device allowed the window blind to be fixed in any desired position and automatic draught excluders were incorporated.

The electroliers were obviously attractive items, as the following instruction from the January 1906 Working Timetable demonstrates.

'A large number of Lamps and Shades of the Electroliers, in the new 65-feet Carriages, are being broken and stolen, and it is suspected that Passengers are sometimes the guilty parties. Guards and others concerned must keep a sharp look-out to detect cases of the kind, and report fully.'[6]

In both classes the dividing wall panels were decorated with mirrors and railway notices, including the then newly prepared panoramic map of the Caledonian and *'a plan of Glasgow and the district.'* A drawing of the interior of both classes of compartment is shown in Figure 4.7. A photograph of the luggage rack support brackets that were used for the 'Grampian' stock is shown in Plate 4.19.

The lavatories were lined with zinc sheets coloured to imitate tiling and were reported to be the first in the UK with hot water, albeit only when the train heating

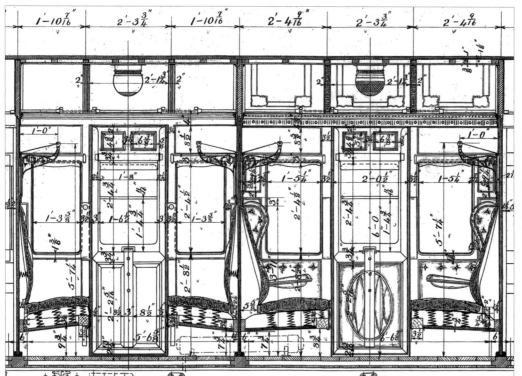

LEFT: Figure 4.7
First and Third class compartment interiors of a 'Grampian' Corridor Composite. Note the differences in ceiling decoration and the two types of 'electrolier.'

ABOVE AND BELOW: Plate 4.19
The two photographs are from Michael Dunn. They show the ornate 'net rod support' that was introduced by McIntosh, with the company initials stamped on the base. The original drawing was annotated with the requirement to increase the clearance holes by one sixteenth of an inch to take larger securing screws, with effect from November 1898. This information should have made it possible to fix the date of this particular example. Michael's relic has yet another size of hole.

Plates 4.20 and 4.21
These views were taken inside non-corridor 'Grampian' Composite number 362. The moulding on the lincrusta panel in the First class compartment (*above*) is picked out in gilt, while that in Third class (*right*) is left plain.

RIGHT: Plate 4.22
The advertisement for the products of G.D. Peters appeared in CR Public Timetables. As well as lincrusta, Peters also supplied the company with Consolidated Heating apparatus and Havock ventilators, as well as buffalo hides for door padding, laces and on occasions, the Peters Patent Seat.

BELOW: Figures 4.8 and 4.9
The composite half sections show the simplified interior décor of First and Third class compartments in the Pickersgill era. The side elevation is a Third class compartment.

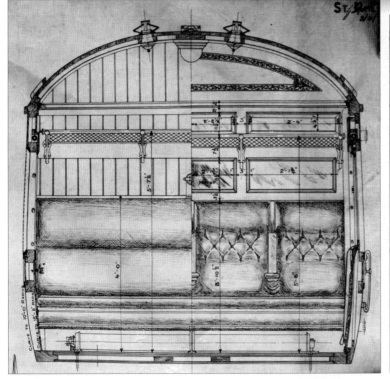

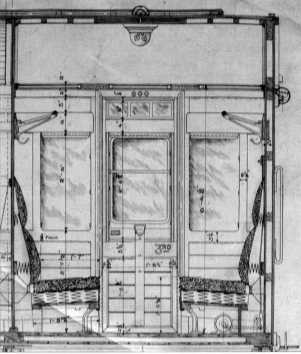

equipment was in use. This was not the case. In June 1900 the Traffic Committee *'acquiesced'* to the introduction of *'Hot Water into Lavatories of West Coast Corridor Carriages'* at a cost of *'about £15 per vehicle.'*[7] The guard's compartments were fitted with the brake equipment, controls for the train heating and lighting (half lighting could be selected) as well as a safe and bicycle racks.

GRAMPIAN NON-CORRIDOR CARRIAGES

Décor was essentially similar to the original corridor stock, but the wider compartments allowed four passengers per side in

First class and six in Third class without an arm rest. Photographs of both interiors are shown in Plates 4.20 and 4.21.

LINCRUSTA-WALTON

This trade-marked material superseded waxed cloth for lining compartments above the seats and carriage ceilings. G.D. Peters was the British supplier, as shown in Plate 4.22, which is the advertisement that was published in each CR Public Timetable. To quote from Sidney Stone's article which first appeared in *The Railway Engineer*:

'Lincrusta-Walton is a compressed composition moulded in floral and other designs, so that certain portions are in relief or embossed, which can be picked out in various colours, gilded, &c., when fixed in position.

The lincrusta is supplied mounted on stout mill board and cut out to templates so as to fit quarter-lights &c., the inside casing boards, partitions or roof boards must be finished with an even surface, the lincrusta is then fixed with panel pins and the edges of joints are covered with suitable mouldings.'

There are numerous examples of patterns for lincrusta panels in the St. Rollox drawing registers. The drawings were issued when a new carriage design appeared.

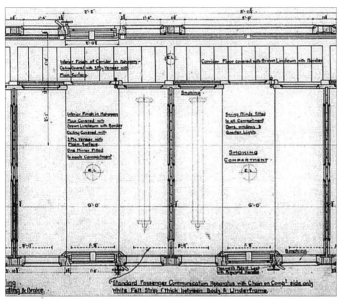

ABOVE: Figure 4.10
Part of a Metropolitan drawing for a Diagram 122 Corridor Brake Third.

BELOW: Figure 4.11
Saloons merited elaborate decoration. This is part of the interior drawing for a Lambie-built diagram 57 Family Saloon. The complete drawing is shown in Figure 13.21.

PICKERSGILL INTERIORS

In common with changing fashion, the post-war carriage interiors were simplified. A composite drawing of a First and Third class compartment forms Figure 4.8. A side elevation of a Third class interior is Figure 4.9. An example of a later Metropolitan Corridor Third interior is shown in Figure 4.10.

BALERNO STOCK

These carriages were based on the contemporary 8-wheeled stock, as discussed in Chapter 11.4. The Third class compartments were finished in mahogany with white-painted plywood ceilings while the First class compartments were in mahogany-stained walnut. The plywood ceilings had Lincrusta ornamental bordering. The partitions in the Third class were covered with Lincrusta decorated millboard. Brake compartments were finished in pitch pine.

Upholstery in Third class was repp; in the Firsts it was moquette and the doors were finished with leather. In all compartments the floors were covered in linoleum supplemented with velvet pile rugs in the First class compartments or horsehair rugs in the smoking compartments.

SALOONS

As might be expected, Saloons received special treatment. The very first examples, built shortly after the opening of the original Caledonian main line merited detailed descriptions in the press – see Chapter 13.1. According to the Coaching Plant Stock Book, the four Lambie First class Day Saloons were furnished in 'crimson velvet,' 'old gold crisp cloth' (one in each), and two in 'blue cloth.' The interior of his Diagram 57 Family carriage is shown in Figure 4.11. The interior of the Third class Saloons built to match the 'Grampian' stock is shown in Plate 13.12.

REFERENCES
1. CRA Archive ref: awaiting re-cataloguing
2. Engineering, 21st February 1890, pp. 195-96.
3. The Railway Engineer, September 1905, p. 224
4. The Railway Magazine, January to June 1905, p. 405
5. NRS BR/CAL/1/51 entry 229
6. NRS BR/TT/S/54/39, special instructions, p. 12
7. NRS BR/CAL/1/43 entry 1772

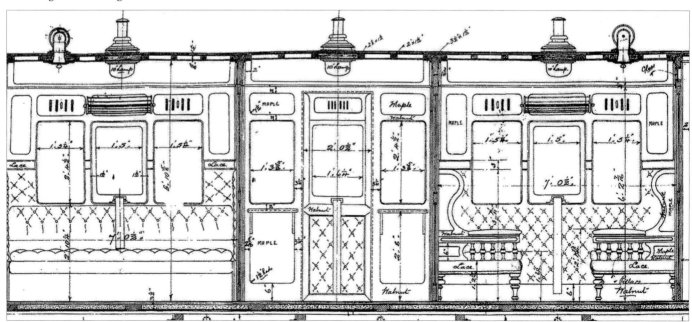

CHAPTER 5
GENERAL SERVICE STOCK FROM OPENING TO 1867

5.1: STOCK FOR THE OPENING OF THE LINE

Although the Caledonian's main line did not open until 1847, it was necessary to decide rolling stock requirements well before then as there was a heavy demand on manufacturers. At the meeting of the CR Board held on 7th August 1845 John Errington, the company's superintendent, was asked:

'*to report what number of Engines and Carriages will be required for the Railway and suggest the best method of obtaining them, of the best quality and on moderate terms.*'[1]

On the 29th of the month he wrote in reply:

'*I think it would be prudent for the Board to direct the engineers to furnish a specification of the Engines and Carriages and to obtain offers for 50 Engines; 100 First Class Carriages; 200 Second Class Carriages; 100 Third Class Carriages.*'[2]

Tenders were to be sought for consideration at the next meeting. It had become clear that the line would be built in two sections, and that it would be necessary to acquire separate sets of carriages. The southern portion from Carlisle to Beattock Bridge would almost certainly be the first section to open.

By July 1846 it was reported that carriages were under construction, '*fifteen Firsts, ten Seconds and ten Thirds and no more will be required at the Carlisle end.*'[3] The same minute authorised Errington to order the following carriages for the Glasgow portion of the line:

'*Five Firsts and five Composites from Mr. Wallace of Perth, at prices not exceeding those which he is supplying to the Scottish Central Railway*
Ten Seconds and ten Thirds from Croall of Edinburgh at prices to be arranged by the Engineer
Five Composites from Mr. Dunn of Lancaster at prices to be arranged.'

The Caledonian had close links with the Glasgow, Paisley & Greenock Railway through Joseph Locke and John Errington. The GP&GR's works at Greenock had sufficient capacity to build rolling stock for itself and the Caledonian rather than contract out the work. At the July 1846 meeting the Board also authorised construction of the following coaching stock from Greenock Works:[4]

'*20 First Class carriages*
15 Composite carriages
40 Second Class carriages
40 Third Class carriages
10 Luggage Vans'

The first 40 miles of line, from Carlisle to Beattock Bridge, opened on 9th September 1847. The sections from Glasgow to Beattock and from Carstairs to Edinburgh opened on 15th February 1848. Prior to that, passengers were conveyed by coach. Coach fares from Beattock Bridge to Glasgow and Edinburgh had been discussed and agreed in July 1847.[5]

Ten days after the line was fully opened from Carlisle to Glasgow and Edinburgh it was reported that '*35 engines and 50 carriages*

are at work and nearly as many more in hand in the Company's workshops.'[6] An engineer's report a short time later recorded the carriage stock as eighty.[7] The carriages for each end of the line were somewhat different in appearance. They are described below.

STOCK ON THE SOUTHERN SECTION

According to James McEwan's typescript notes for a history of the Caledonian,[8] Carlisle newspaper reports described the carriages as being similar to those on the Lancaster & Carlisle and Grand Junction railways, which were both familiar at Carlisle. The First class, resembling three stage coaches joined together '*on one body*' were about 17 feet long and were described as '*roomy internally.*' They accommodated six adults in each section, with their luggage carried on the roof.

They were about 5 feet 6 inches in height, upholstered in blue cloth (including the partitions and sides) and fitted with arm straps and armrests. Double cushions were provided for the seats. Blue cloth also covered the partitions and sides. The interior of the roof seems to have been covered in white oilcloth. Two lamps were provided per compartment. The reports stated that the '*coaches are painted blue and are heavily varnished.*'

The *Greenock Advertiser* reported that '*as an insulation against both cold and noise*' the carriages were constructed with a double-bottom stuffed with hair felt and that they were '*higher in the roof than normal, tall enough for passengers to stand.*' One of these carriages may have been photographed at Biggar – see Plate 5.1.

The Second class carriages were also said to be about 17 feet long and were described as '*similar in construction, but smaller, with the space between the walls reduced.*' This probably referred to their width. Each compartment probably seated eight and '*were also elaborately upholstered*' but in their case only to the height of the seat back, the remainder being either oilcloth or painted wood. Passengers were only provided with a single cushion and one lamp per compartment. The carriages were described as russet brown up to window level, implying that they were white or cream above.

There seem to have been at least two types of carriage, with a report that '*some are not so wide as others of a similar class.*' The last statement may reflect variation between builders but, as the only exclusively Second class carriages ordered for the opening of the line were reported to have been the ten ordered from Croall, and as the newspapers fail to mention any Composite carriages, it may be that the reporter confused Second class carriages with Composites.

The *Greenock Advertiser* reported[9] that the Seconds were lined inside with plain mahogany and had upholstered bottom seats and plate glass on the door and side lights, whilst the *North British Railway and Shipping Journal*, writing nearly a year later, said that the Seconds also had partially cushioned seat backs.[10]

The *Greenock Advertiser* described the Third class carriages as '*simply made*' and, again, similar to those on the Lancaster & Carlisle Railway. If that was the case they would have been slab-sided with sides made from tongued and grooved boarding with the joins running vertically.

They were longer than the other two classes, at about 19 feet, and were described as having four compartments each accommodating eight passengers on plain wooden seating with wooden backrests.

The interiors were varnished. Only two lamps per carriage were provided, implying that compartment partitions were not to full height. They were painted dull brown.

In a later issue, one Carlisle newspaper remarked that the level of lighting was so bad that it only accentuated the darkness and that some passengers resorted to carrying candles, creating a significant fire hazard. The *North British Railway and Shipping Journal* described them as:

'*barbarous … they have no glass windows, but a board to shut against the weather, and in shutting this a panel is opened, which makes things as bad as before.*'

All three classes ran on underframes having wheels with four spokes. The First and Second class vehicles were provided with long-spindle forged buffers whilst, according to James McEwan, the Third class had to be content with shorter buffers.[11]

All these carriages seem to have been designed by the contractors who supplied them. The only early carriage drawings in the CR register refer to those built at Greenock for the northern section of the line. These carriages are described below.

STOCK ON THE NORTHERN SECTION

The Directors' report to shareholders dated 31st August 1847 claimed that:

'*the Engines, carriages etc. are in a most forward state, and have been manufactured chiefly at the Company's extensive workshops in Greenock.*'[12]

Reporting the opening of the northern end of the line, the *Glasgow Herald* stated that all the carriages which were available for the opening of the line had been built at Greenock under the supervision of Robert Sinclair.[13] Apparently fifteen First and twenty-five Second class carriages from the order authorised in July 1846 were available by mid-February.

The article described the First and Second class carriages as '*handsome and commodious.*' They were reported to be 22 feet 9 inches overall and '*about 26 feet over the buffers*' with incurving ends. They were 8 feet wide and ran on 4-wheeled underframes with a wheelbase of 13 feet. Internally the carriages were 6 feet high with three compartments per carriage. The compartments were 7 feet wide between partitions. The discrepancy between the external and internal dimensions implies that the sides and ends were of substantial thickness.

As with the southern carriages, the Firsts were lined with blue cloth. The upper sides and ceilings were covered with cream oilcloth, and interior woodwork was varnished mahogany. The windows were glazed and above them were stained glass lights which opened outwards. The carriages were painted '*lake*' and varnished.

A glass plate of an official drawing for a Second class carriage annotated '*Greenock 6th August 1847 for Robert Sinclair*' has survived and is at some variance with the above description, which suggests that it should only refer to the First class carriages. It depicts a four compartment vehicle as shown in Plate 5.2 and redrawn as Figure 5.1.

The underframe had a wheelbase of 9 feet 9 inches, the body of the carriage being approximately 18 feet long and 7 feet wide. There was a door fitted with a droplight and two quarter-lights for each of the compartments, but the internal compartment partitions went only as high as the top of the seat backs. The seats were padded but the seat backs were planked with a single padded bolster 15 inches above the seat.

The principal difference between the carriage depicted in the drawing and that described by the *Glasgow Herald* was that the carriage in the drawing had only two oil lamps. In the absence of full height partitions, two lamps served the entire carriage.

Plate 5.1
The photograph of a train at Biggar dates from about 1860. The second carriage, a First with '*three bodies,*' may be one of the first carriages built for the northern portion of the main line in 1847. The front carriage is probably a Brake Second, with a guard's compartment – the development of the exposed seat on top of the carriage. There is a dog box in the centre compartment. There is a close-up of this carriage in Chapter 2, Plate 2.2. A drawing from this photograph is shown in Figure 5.3. The rear carriage is a 5-compartment Third.

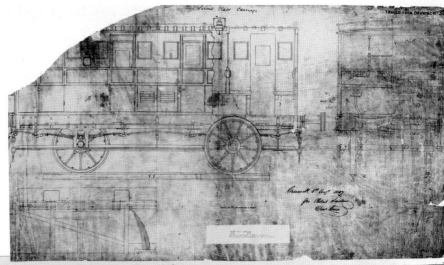

Plate 5.2 and Figure 5.1
A photograph of a damaged glass plate showing the only surviving drawing of the carriages built for the northern portion of the line in 1847. It is redrawn in Figure 5.1.

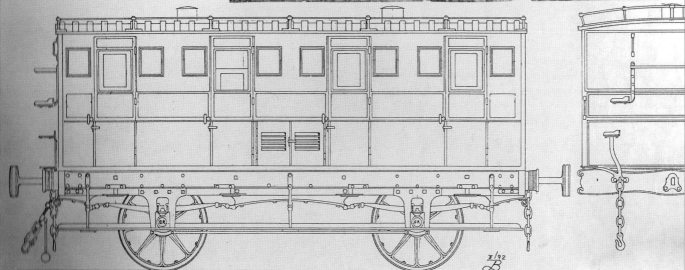

It would appear that the only means of increasing the ventilation in the compartments was by lowering the droplights as, although the drawing seems to show ventilators above the droplights, the internal view implies that there was no means of opening them.

There was a continuous lower footboard at axle box height with individual footsteps bolted below each door. There was a line of beaded panelling at the waist and a dog box was fitted between the middle compartments. Steps were fitted at one end to give access to the roof. A railed area was provided for luggage.

The Third class carriages, of which it would seem only a limited number were available, had four compartments, each holding eight passengers. Another newspaper description said that the half-height partitions were only 4 feet 6 inches apart – which would give an overall length of about 19 feet – and that they were high internally. Above their compartment doors there were three slots to provide ventilation, but it would seem that the only glazing was in the droplights in the compartment doors. The article recorded that forty passengers could be accommodated '*in four divisions*' and that there was '*a solitary roof light*' and an animal box in the centre of the vehicle. They were probably built to drawing 86, which was for a '*3rd Class carriage with seats.*'

Drawings of all the carriages built at Greenock, signed by Robert Sinclair, were brought from St. Rollox by Graeme Miller and put on display at the Caledonian Railway centenary celebrations at the Glasgow Central Station Hotel in 1947. Apart from the glass plate mentioned above they seem to have disappeared. However, the body of one type of carriage, a Composite with a central First class compartment flanked by two Second class, is shown in Plate 5.3, while it was in use as a bothy at St. Rollox in 1894.

These carriages were apparently identical to those built for the opening of the Scottish North Eastern Railway, and a drawing forms Figure 5.2. The First class compartment bore a marked resemblance to a contemporary horse-drawn carriage with curved quarter-lights (boarded over in the photograph) and false curvature to the beading at the waist and along the bottom of the carriage. The register entry for drawing 52 of a Composite carriage, which may apply to this vehicle, includes the description '*centre compartment 5ft 8 ins.*' The end compartments, on the other hand, were square except for the curved quarter-lights.

Above both the door and the quarter-lights of the centre compartment were small windows, but the end compartments had only louvred wooden ventilators in that position. This particular coach was equipped for a breaksman, and his seat on the roof, footrest, and steps can be seen at the right-hand end.

Six carriages, each weighing about six tons, together with a Brake vehicle of about four tons, made up a train. The Brake carriages were also about 19 feet long with four wheels and had a seat on the roof which was to be '*occupied by specially employed men when using the incline at Beattock.*' The first mention of such a vehicle in the drawing register is number 67, which was for '*part of carriage with brakesman's seat*' – note the modern spelling.

The Luggage Vans built at this time seem to have had sliding doors; drawings 145 and 335 are both described in this fashion in the drawing register.

STOCK FOR THE GARNKIRK AND WISHAW LINES

It was intended that the Caledonian would operate these lines as soon as the northern portion of its line was open and they had been re-gauged from 4 feet 6 inches. Locke and Errington's report to the Board for the period ending December 1846 stated:

> 'The extensive stock of Engines, Carriages wagons and other material required for the working of your line is all in hand, several of the Engines are far advanced, and a proportion of Engines, Carriages and wagons, sufficient for the working of the Garnkirk and Wishaw and Coltness Railways on the 4 feet 8½ inch gauge will be ready early in summer.'[14]

When the engineers reported at the end of December 1847 that the lines had been re-gauged, they also stated that eighty carriages were working the system 'sufficient for the present traffic. Arrangements are made for an increased number to meet the summer traffic.'[15]

THE CALEDONIAN FLEET IN 1849

At the company's March 1850 General Meeting the Board tabled a 'Valuation of Rolling Stock on the Caledonian Railway at 12th March 1849.'[16] The number of carriages is shown in the table. The full table with the valuations is in Appendix I. The Saloons are described in Chapter 13.1 and the Post Office vehicles in Chapter 14.3.

CARRIAGE TYPE	NUMBER
First class	35
Second class	43
Third class	48
Composite	15
Saloons, Greenock made	2
Post Office	4
Luggage Van	9
Total	158

REFERENCES

1. NRS BR/CAL/1/7 p. 192
2. NRS BR/CAL/1/7 p. 226
3. NRS BR/CAL/1/7 p. 359
4. NRS BR/CAL/1/7 p. 360
5. NRS BR/CAL/1/8 no entry number
6. NRS BR/CAL/1/7 p. 127
7. NRS BR/CAL/1/7 p. 133
8. McEwan Archive T/25/1/2
9. *Greenock Advertiser*, 28th March 1847
10. *North British Railway and Shipping Journal*, 19th February 1848
11. McEwan Archive T25/1/2
12. NRS BR/CAL/1/1 p. 107
13. *Glasgow Herald*, 18th February 1848
14. NRS BR/CAL/1/1 pp. 69-70
15. NRS BR/CAL/1/1 pp. 133-34
16. NRS BR/CAL/1/1 pp. 412-16

Plate 5.3 and Figure 5.2
The First/Second Composite dates from 1847 and survived as a bothy until the 1890s. Another photograph of the breaksman's seat is shown in Chapter 2, Plate 2.1.
Figure 5.2 is a sketch drawing based on the photograph.

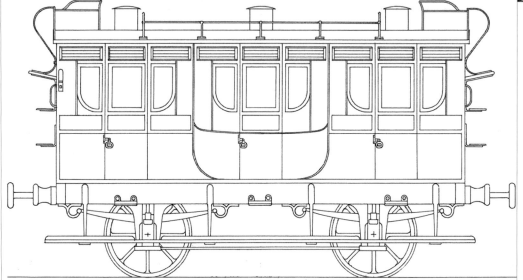

5.2: STOCK ADDED AND REPLACED IN THE 1850S

By 1850, the Caledonian had absorbed the plant of the Greenock, Wishaw & Coltness and Garnkirk & Glasgow railways, which included a total of 124 carriages and ten Luggage Vans. When the Caledonian took possession in August 1851 the carriages were found to be a dubious asset.

The stock was later described in a letter from Robert Sinclair to the CR Board as of:

'very little effective value for the purposes of traffic – a part of it being very ill adapted for anything but the service of a mineral railway in its most primitive state, and a very large proportion of it being completely worked out, and useless except to break up for the old material it contained.'[1]

The information in the following table was included in the letter, which rather contradicts Sinclair's sweeping statement, as more than half of the absorbed railways' passenger stock was still on the books five years later in 1855 when the letter was written. Five of the ten Luggage Vans that the CR inherited were also still in service.

	FIRST	SECOND	THIRD	COMP
Greenock Railway	20	35	29	2
Wishaw Railway	3	8		1
Garnkirk Railway	3	9	14	
TOTAL	26	52	43	3
Destroyed by 1855	19	14	24	2
LEFT	7	38	19	1

THE GREENOCK STOCK

Robert Sinclair, the Caledonian's Locomotive Superintendent, was previously employed by the Greenock Railway and had told the latter's Directors prior to the Caledonian's takeover that their rolling stock was quite unfit for service, and should be replaced. In fact, the Caledonian had operated a large proportion of the services over the Greenock line before the formal takeover. As Sinclair made clear in the same letter:

'had the Greenock company been obliged [to operate] at their own resources their line would have been stopped by the entire failure of their rolling stock.'

The fleet inherited by the Caledonian included 'stand-ups' which, as their name implies, had no seats. For example, drawing 290 was for a *'3rd. Class carriage 24ft. 0ins stand-up.'* Although they and the rest of the Greenock stock were much derided, as described in Chapter 3, the 'stand-ups' would run on the Greenock line for many years to come. The October 1856 Public Timetable for the Greenock section stated that *'The 9.00 a.m. Up and 4.00 p.m. Down are Express and do not carry Passengers Travelling 3rd Class without seats.'* At this time there were eleven trains each way. The fare was *'6d. single, 3d. without seats.'*[2] In the 1864 timetable, trains conveyed all classes of passenger and Third class carriages with seats were provided on only five trains out of the sixteen.

Some of the carriages were phased out in 1872, because two were converted into 'Dummy Vans' as described in Chapter 15. The final disappearance of the 'stand-ups' is discussed in Chapter 6.3.

THE GARNKIRK AND WISHAW STOCK

The stock on the Glasgow & Garnkirk was described by Francis Whishaw when he visited the line in 1839.[3] The larger carriages (it is not known whether they were First and/or Second class) were smaller than the CR equivalent at 13 feet 6 inches long, 6 feet wide and 5 feet 2 inches high. Their framing was of American oak with panelling of American pine.

The smaller carriages cost about £50 each, and again compared unfavourably with their CR counterparts. They were only 12 feet 6 inches long and 6 feet wide, but were 5 inches higher at the eaves than the larger carriages. The three compartments only had doors on one side, *'on account of the prevailing north wind.'* The compartments each had a small glass droplight on one side, and a single small square of glass on the other. Whishaw commented that the sides of some carriages were taken off in fine weather.

Carriage stock on the Wishaw and Coltness Railways was equally poor, as is borne out by an inventory of rolling stock in the autumn of 1849.[4] It valued the combined stock of the two railways as follows. The six First class carriages (three from each railway) were worth only £480 in total and seventeen Seconds were valued at £940 the lot (nine Garnkirk and eight Wishaw &Coltness). The Garnkirk Third class carriages were valued at £560, a mere £40 each. For comparison, the Third class carriages owned by the Caledonian Railway itself were valued at an average of nearly £250 each. It seems unlikely that any Wishaw & Coltness carriages, except possibly two First class ones built to be convertible to standard gauge, lasted much beyond 1855, if even until then.

CARRIAGES BUILT IN 1854

In the half year ending January 1855, twelve First class carriages and twenty-one Thirds were withdrawn and not immediately replaced. Second class carriage numbers increased by seventeen. They were probably built by the company as there is no record of a tender process. They may have been built to drawing 327, which was for a *'2nd Class carriage with brake attached.'* Drawing 328 was for the brake gear components (modern spelling in both cases). One of these carriages may be the leading vehicle in Plate 5.1. A sketch derived from the photographs is shown in Figure 5.3.

Sinclair referred to the cull of carriages in his report to the half-yearly General Meeting for the period ending January 1855. He wrote:

'a large part of the Rolling Stock of the leased lines was entirely worn out when it came into the possession of the Caledonian Railway Company, and so much as was in that condition has now been removed from the list of our Plant as it has hitherto only served to swell the roll without ever having been employed in earning any of the Revenue of the Company.'[5]

By 1855, when a review was made of all rolling stock, about half of the inherited carriages had been broken up. The details of the CR carriage stock at this point are shown in Appendix I.

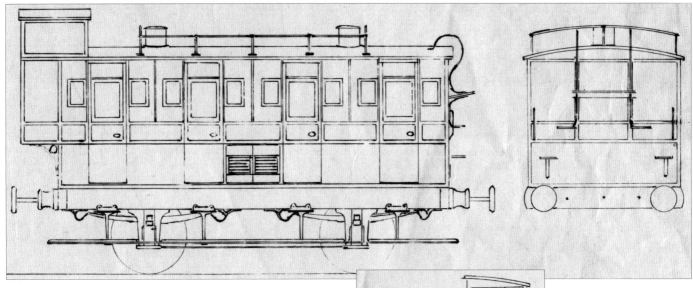

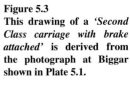

THE NEW STOCK FOR THE GREENOCK LINE

As evidence of the serious problem inherited with the Greenock line takeover, the CR Board agreed to take tenders for forty carriages as part of a wholesale improvement of rolling stock on the Greenock section, and to charge the cost to the capital account.[6] There is no record of an outcome to the tender process, which suggests that the carriages were actually built at Greenock Works.

Between August 1851 and January 1855 the Caledonian built ten First class carriages at an average cost of £450 each. They may have been to drawing 402, which was for a First class carriage which the register quotes as having '11 feet centres.' In the same period twelve Second class carriages with an average value of £350 each were also built. Drawing 401 states that they had five compartments.

Finally, eight Third class carriages had been built in the same period. Their average value was £300.[7] These carriages may have been built on iron frames. The iron underframe carriages were the subject of complaint to the Board of Trade in the 1860s, as described in Chapter 6.2. Colonel Hutchinson described them as '… *thirty feet long, supported on 6 wheels (the two centre wheels smaller than the end ones).*'[8] Drawings 496 and 502 may have been used. The latter drawing was for a '*3rd Class carriage with seats for the Greenock branch.*'

Iron underframes had been used previously, as drawing 351 was for a version 24 feet long, presumably on four wheels. Five years after Hutchinson's report the Loco & Stores Committee '*Submitted comparison of prices for twelve old Iron Frames from the Greenock Line*' and agreed to '*Accept P&W McLellan at £505 the lot.*'[9]

CONNER TAKES OVER

A year after Robert Sinclair's report to the Caledonian Board on the state of its rolling stock he resigned to become Locomotive Superintendent of the Eastern Counties Railway. Christopher Johnstone replaced him as General Manager. Benjamin Conner, Works Manager at the Hyde Park Works of Neilson and Co., was appointed to the newly-created post of '*Locomotive Superintendent and Manager of Locomotive Works*' with effect from the 1st October, 1856 at an annual salary of £400.[10] The division of responsibilities coincided with the opening of St. Rollox Works.

CARRIAGE BUILDING IN 1856

In the half year period ending January 1857 the number of Third class carriages more than doubled from ninety-two to 190. There is

Figure 5.3
This drawing of a '*Second Class carriage with brake attached*' is derived from the photograph at Biggar shown in Plate 5.1.

no record of a tender process, so one assumes that the carriages were built by the Caledonian.

It is possible that drawing 439 was used. This was for a '*3rd Class carriage (5 bodies) with one 2nd Class compartment*' – in other words, one of the compartments was better upholstered. Two photographs (Plates 5.1 and 5.4) show 5-compartment low-roof carriages.

CONTRACTOR-BUILT CARRIAGES

In January 1857 the General Committee placed contracts with Joseph Wright & Co. for ten First class carriages at £292 each.[11] One of these carriages appears in Plate 5.5. This St. Rollox official photograph appeared in *The Railway Magazine*, captioned '*built 1857.*'[12] Although it is designated as a Third in the photograph, the spacing of the quarter-lights between compartments mark it as originally of a superior class. Assuming the wheelbase was 13 feet, the body was 24 feet 6 inches long, giving a compartment about 6 feet between partitions, which was a common dimension for contemporary First class carriages. Their numbers cannot be identified in the 1874 Inventory.

At the same meeting Brown, Marshall & Co. secured an order for fourteen Third class carriages at £212 each, plus '*14 Third with Second Class compartments*' at £213 10s each. Four each of the Thirds and Composites were to be fitted with '*Guard's seats and breaks*' at an additional cost of £22 per carriage.

The rolling stock return for January 1857 explained that:

'*thirty eight new carriages for renewal are being delivered. The number stated in last half year [which had showed a corresponding increase in stock] included part of the stock*

Plate 5.4
Believed to have been taken at Stewarton in 1873, this photograph is included because the train contains four low-roofed 5-compartment Thirds, plus probably two higher-roofed 4-compartment Seconds and a First.

BELOW: **Plate 5.5**
Joseph Wright built ten First class carriages for the Caledonian in 1857. This St. Rollox official photograph (NRM St. Rollox collection ref: W78) was published in *The Railway Magazine*. The carriage has been down-rated to Third class. Wright built many similar carriages for the northern Scottish railways that were absorbed by the Caledonian in the latter half of the 1860s, as illustrated in Chapter 5.4.

taken over from Guaranteed Coys [the absorbed railways around Glasgow] which were old and small capacity.'

The ten Composite carriages were probably those numbered 106-115 in the 1874 Inventory. They had one Second and four Third class compartments, and were valued at £215 each. The Thirds cannot be traced in the Inventory. The four Brake Thirds were probably 116-119. They were valued at £235 each, which is almost exactly the price at which they were purchased. The four Brake Composite carriages were probably numbered 120-123, valued at the same price. They had one Second and three Third class compartments. The reduction of one compartment compared with the equivalent Composite suggests that the breaksman was accommodated inside the body of the carriage.

In August 1858 Brown, Marshall & Co. secured an order for six 'Passenger Vans.'[13] They appeared in the January 1859 rolling stock return. Four were replacements for vans that had been withdrawn in the previous period. The replacements were possibly the 4-wheeled vans numbered 62-67 in the 1874 Inventory.

A year later, two *'Third Class & Brake Combined at £225'* were ordered from Ashbury.[14] They cannot be traced in the Inventory.

REFERENCES
1. NRS BR/CAL/4/14/62, 17th January 1855
2. NRS BR/CAL/1/10 entry 890
3. NRS BR/TT/4/73/11
4. *The Railways of Great Britain and Ireland*, pp. 109-11
5. NRS BR/CAL/4/14/62
6. NRS BR/CAL/4/74
7. NRS BR/CAL/1/11 entry 199
8. TNA MT29/29, report 504
9. NRS BR/CAL/1/20 entry 440
10. NRS BR/CAL/1/11 entry 199
11. NRS BR/CAL/1/11 entry 551
12. NRM St. Rollox collection W78
    The Railway Magazine, October 1897 issue, p. 297
13. NRS BR/CAL/1/11 entry 1814
14. NRS BR/CAL/1/12 entry 218

5.3: STOCK BUILT AND ACQUIRED 1860-1867

In 1860 Brown, Marshall & Co. successfully tendered to supply ten double Composite carriages at £305 each.[1] According to the half-yearly report, four were replacements and six were new.[2] This suggests that they were the block of 4-wheeled carriages with two each First and Second class compartments with the random numbers 2, 14, 16, 17 (the replacements), and new carriages 50-55 in the 1874 Inventory.

CARRIAGES FOR THE LOCKERBIE LINE

A letter *'enumerating the new plant that will be required for working the Lockerby [sic] Line'* was considered in March 1862. The General Committee remitted it to the General Manager *'to arrange.'*[3]

The capital expenditure return shows that Ashbury supplied two Brake Vans, plus four Composites and eight Thirds which were charged to the Lockerbie account between March and May 1863.[4] The Composite carriages were the dearest at £360 each. The other carriages cost less than £300.

The Dumfries, Lochmaben & Lockerbie Railway opened in September 1863 and was absorbed by the Caledonian in July 1865. It is not possible to identify these carriages in the 1874 Inventory but, at the price paid, they were obviously small, 4-wheeled vehicles. Some of the carriages may appear in Plate 5.6, which depicts a train at Dumfries.

OTHER ASHBURY CARRIAGES

Two weeks after the Lockerbie plant was *'enumerated'* Ashbury successfully tendered to build:

> *'7 Composite Carriages at £265,*
> *2 Passenger Break Vans at £250, both with Mansell's Patent Wheels.'*

Ashbury had offered wheels made of Low Moor iron at £20 less per carriage, but the General Manager and Conner recommended the more expensive option of the Mansell wheel, which had just become available.[5] These carriages do not appear in the capital expenditure return.

STOCK FOR NEW BRANCH LINES

In March 1864 *'tenders for new carriages were submitted and opened.'* The General Committee awarded the contract to Ashbury for seventy-five carriages at a total cost of £26,667.[6] The lines concerned were probably those from Rutherglen to Coatbridge, and the Busby Railway, both of which opened in January 1866. Another possibility is that some of the stock was destined for the Methven–Crieff line which opened in May 1866.

The capital expenditure returns record a different set of transactions. From July 1864 to March 1865 Ashbury delivered a total of forty-two carriages, comprising six Passenger Brake Vans, five Firsts, twenty-two Thirds, two Brake Thirds and seven Composites. All were charged to *'Branch Line Capital.'*[7]

None of these carriages can be positively identified in the 1874 Inventory. The Passenger Brake Vans may be a block of six, some of which are described in the 1874 Inventory as *'small size'* or *'short van'* which bore numbers between 54 and 61.

Amazingly, two of the First class carriages seem to have survived until the Grouping. The Coaching Plant Stock Book's list of First class carriages records two vehicles dating from 1865 with four compartments. Their numbers were 1001 and 1002, and they had been down-rated to Third class in 1901 when they were fitted with bare wood seats. On down-rating they became numbers 3061 and 3039 respectively. The Stock Book does not give dimensions.

The Stock Book records a 6-wheeled brake Third with four compartments and a date of January 1864. This may refer to the original authorisation. It was withdrawn in 1924, having been allocated an LM&SR number. The total wheelbase was 23 feet; the width was stated to be 8 feet, but no length was given. Number 51, with the same dimensions, had a build date of January 1879. Both were gas-lit. Numbers 51 and 64 in the 1874 Inventory were small 4-wheeled Thirds with four compartments. The discrepancy between the two records cannot be explained.

Plate 5.6
These carriages may be some of those built for the Lockerbie Branch in 1863. From the front, there is a Brake Van, a 5-compartment Third, a 4-compartment Composite (the ventilator hoods are not evenly spaced, indicating compartments of differing widths), two more Thirds and another Composite. The final two carriages cannot be identified.

LEFT: Plate 5.7
An early train on the Leadhills Branch, which
was operated as a light railway. The extended
steps were needed to board the train from the
low platforms at the terminus. The carriage
behind the locomotive may be one of the two
4-compartment Firsts, 1001 and 1002, built
in 1865, that survived to be recorded in the
Coaching Plant Stock Book. The second carriage
is probably one of the eight Third class Saloons
numbered 20-27 – compare this photograph with
Plate 13.15 (p. 305). The saloons are described in
Chapter 13.2.

A Brake Composite, renumbered 1434, is also
recorded in the Stock Book as being built or
authorised in April 1864 and withdrawn in 1922.
There is a photograph of such a carriage bearing
this number in service on the Leadhills Branch
(see Plate 5.9).

The branch opened in 1901 and as a light
railway had no raised platforms. This necessitated
three levels of footsteps to access the carriages
from ground level. These were the subject of
St. Rollox drawing 10795 *'footstep hangers for
light railways.'* The stock itself was the subject
of drawing 10891 *'Diagrams of Carriages for
Leadhills and Wanlockhead Light Railway.'*
Neither has survived.

STOCK ACQUIRED FROM THE PORT PATRICK RAILWAY

The capital expenditure return for the half year
ending January 1865 records the acquisition
of the Port Patrick Railway rolling stock. In the
previous year the Caledonian had agreed to
operate the line for a period of twenty-one years
until October 1885. The carriage stock was valued
at £5,320.[8] This included six Horse Boxes and
three Carriage Trucks.

The rolling stock was separately identified in
the 1874 Inventory because it was dedicated to the
Port Patrick Line. For this reason, the carriages
and wagons had their own number series.

Seventeen 6-wheeled carriages were recorded.
There were no exclusively First class carriages.
Four Tri-Composites, numbered 2, 4, 5 and 6, had
two First and one each Second and Third class
compartments. The two Bi-Composites 1 and 3
had two First and two Second class compartments.
All the Composites were valued at £340 each.

There were four Third class carriages with four
compartments, numbered 7-10. They were valued
at £235 each. The seven Brake Thirds numbered
11-17 had three compartments. They were valued
at £225 each.

The stock recorded in the Inventory does not
exactly match the order for carriages placed by the
PPR with Joseph Wright in 1861. This consisted
of six Bi-Composite First and Second class, four

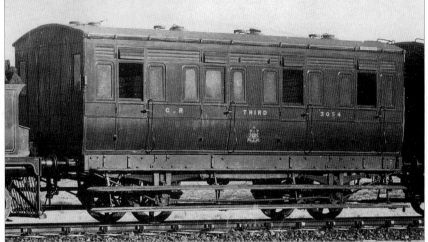

Plates 5.8 and 5.9
These two carriages were in use on the Leadhills Branch at a later date. They have extended
commode handles to aid access as well as an extra set of low footboards. It is possible
that they were built by Ashbury in 1864 or Oldbury in 1865. Plate 5.8 (*above*) is a Brake
Third and Plate 5.9 (*below*) is a Brake Composite. The Brake Third is not recorded in the
Coaching Plant Stock Book, but the Composite appears, with a date of April 1864 and the
note that it was down-rated to Third class at an unspecified date. Both retain the Harrison
cord, although the alarm system was out of use by the time that the line opened in 1901. The
carriages are oil-lit.

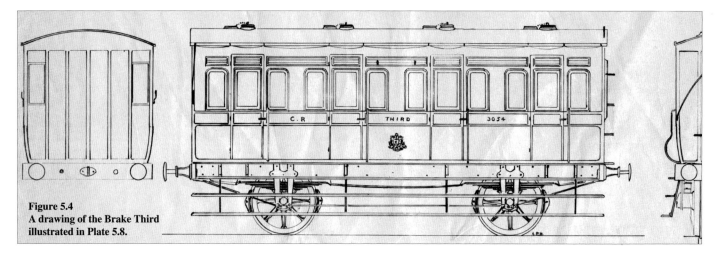

Figure 5.4
A drawing of the Brake Third
illustrated in Plate 5.8.

Second class and five Brake Thirds. It is likely that one of the Second class compartments in the Composites was down-rated to Third class in four of the carriages and that the Second class carriages, which according to the quotation were supplied *'without cushions,'* were down-rated to Third class.

On the face of it, the stock seems not to have lasted beyond the compilation of the Inventory, when a November 1874 Traffic Committee minute headed *'Port Patrick Rolling Stock'* recorded:

'read Mr Conner's letter of 23rd ultimo. Remit to Stores Committee with recommendation that the Plant be renewed as first constructed.'[9]

A fortnight later the Traffic Committee reported that:

'the Rolling Stock is the property of the Caledonian Co. and does not require to be handed over to the Portpatrick Co. at the expiry of the Working Agreement. Build new plant for this line on the Caledonian pattern.'[10]

There is, however, one carriage identified in the Coaching Plant Stock Book as 'ex-Portpatrick Railway' and built in June 1864. This purported to be a 4-compartment Brake Third, converted from a Third, renumbered 3045 from 1221. The carriage's original CR number was 150, according to the Stock Book.

CARRIAGES BUILT IN 1865-67

In April 1865 the General Committee accepted tenders and *'Mr. Conner's report'* for new carriages.[11] The number and type of carriage were not specified. The Committee was prepared to *'accept the Oldbury Carriage Company provided they engage to deliver within the period fixed viz. 1st August 1865.'* This was Oldbury's first successful tender, hence the stipulation.

The transaction seems to have been overtaken by events. In July the General Committee:

'Read Mr Ward's letter on the 15th inst. on the want of additional Carriages for passenger traffic. 50 Third Class Carriages, 5 with breaks required.'[12]

On 26th September the Board accepted a revised tender from Oldbury for *'Composites at £375, Third Class at £242, Break Vans at £247 and Third Class Break Vans at £263.'*[13] Again, the number of each type was not mentioned.

Lack of confidence in Oldbury's ability to deliver remained. Conner gave his opinion in writing to the General Committee. On 10th October the Committee took Conner's advice and decided that:

'Instead of giving the whole contract to the Oldbury Co. as per Minute of 26th inst. divide the order and give Brown, Marshall & Co. the order for 29 Third Class carriages and the Oldbury Co. the order for the remaining 30 vehicles.'[14]

The capital expenditure returns for 1866[15] and 1867[16] confirm the decision. The carriages were charged to the main line account.

Brown, Marshall & Co. built its quota of twenty-nine Thirds. Oldbury supplied the thirty Third class carriages as specified in the minute, plus six Brake Thirds, eight First/Second Composites and eight Passenger Brake Vans. A Brake Third and a Composite may have been allocated to the Leadhills Branch to replace the original stock, as shown in Plates 5.8 and 5.9 and Figure 5.4. These carriages were given additional footsteps, as described earlier.

It is not possible to identify the Third class carriages with certainty, but a block of fifty-three carriages in the 1874 Inventory is valued at £190 each, many of which have consecutive running numbers in the ranges 238-295 and 394-421. These carriages had four compartments.

The dimensions of this block of carriages is known through St. Rollox drawing 6749, produced in May 1891 for fitting the Westinghouse brake *'on old 4 wheel carriages and brake van,'* which specifically mentions carriage 238.

The drawing is reproduced as Figure 2.8 in Chapter 2.1, with an explanation of the circumstances surrounding its production. Although the underframe dimensions are not given, scaling them gives an expected wheelbase of 14 feet 6 inches, a length of 25 feet 1 inch and a width of 7 feet 6 inches.

The six Brake Thirds may have been numbered 116-119, 182 and 183. The Composites cannot be positively identified in the 1874 Inventory. The Passenger Brake Vans may have been the block with a common valuation of £200 numbered 15-20, 50 and 93.

REFERENCES
1. NRS BR/CAL/1/12 entry 600
2. In NRS BR/CAL/1/2, no page number
3. NRS BR/CAL/1/12 entry 2174
4. NRS BR/CAL/23/15
5. NRS BR/CAL/1/12 entry 2199
6. NRS BR/CAL/1/13 entry 1514
7. NRS BR/CAL/23/15
8. NRS BR/CAL/23/15
9. NRS BR/CAL/1/21 entry 1974
10. NRS BR/CAL/1/22 entry 41
11. NRS BR/CAL/1/14 entry 401
12. NRS BR/CAL/1/14 entry 581
13. NRS BR/CAL/1/14 entry 860
14. NRS BR/CAL/1/14 entry 921
15. NRS BR/CAL/23/16
16. NRS BR/CAL/23/17

5.4: STOCK ABSORBED FROM NORTHERN SCOTTISH RAILWAYS

In 1865 the Scottish Central Railway (SCR) became part of the Caledonian. This extended the CR main line from its junction with the SCR at Castlecary through Stirling to Perth. The CR reached Aberdeen in 1867 by absorbing the Scottish North Eastern Railway (SNER).

The two companies' stock was recorded as additions in the CR half-yearly rolling stock returns. The carriages are shown in the following table. The SNER Seconds and Thirds were aggregated.

Non-passenger coaching stock is not included in the table. These vehicles were discussed in *Caledonian Railway Wagons*[1] and more information will appear in the forthcoming supplement.

Carriage Type	SCR Jan 1866	SNER Jan 1867
First	60	48
Second	48	112
Third	110	
Composite	14	18
Post Office	2	
Family Carriage	1	1
Luggage Brake Van	31	17

The general service vehicles are described below. The two SCR Post Offices are described in Chapter 14, and the Family carriages inherited from the two railways are discussed in Chapter 13.

SCOTTISH CENTRAL FIRSTS

Many of the First class carriages in the 1874 Inventory can be identified as built for the CR by minutes authorising their purchase. Among those which cannot be identified are three blocks of carriages, total sixty vehicles, plus a Saloon. These carriages were probably from the Scottish Central.

There were at least three types of First class carriage. Some were converted from Composites. In 1858 Alexander Allan was asked *to 'report on the expediency of constructing some more of the composite carriages into saloons or First Class Carriages.'*[2] The alteration of a Composite into a Saloon at a cost of *'about £70'* had been approved in August 1857.[3]

Allan reported to the Directors that it would cost £500 to convert six and recommended that half of the twelve carriages requiring repair should be so treated.[4] Refurbishment to First class standard, although costing slightly more, would be a better investment than repair as Composites.

'The painting and lining on some of them is very much soiled so as to require £40 or £50 for use in their present shape and in this style they are really bad stock. They will accommodate four more passengers than your present First Class carriages.'

His proposal was approved, so it can reasonably be assumed that the six conversions were among the First class carriages handed over to the CR. The First class Saloons numbered 139, 144 and 145 in the 1874 Inventory may be survivors of these conversions. One of the original Firsts may have been photographed at Loch Tay – see Plate 5.10. A drawing derived from this photograph is shown in Figure 5.5.

The carriage was approximately 15 feet 6 inches long on a 10-foot wheelbase underframe, and the top of the low arc roof about 10 feet 6 inches above rail level – in other words, the body was about seven feet high to the apex of the roof.

There was a single window, which was wider than normal, between each of the compartment doors, but only a standard size quarter-light at each end. The compartment partitions only extended to the bottom of the windows, but each compartment still had a separate roof lamp. The body was horizontally planked, with vertical beading on either side of the doors and at the ends.

Two contractor's drawings for later First class SCR carriages exist, dating from 1862 and 1864. The earlier depicts a Coupé carriage built by Joseph Wright.[5] It had two full compartments flanked by a half compartment at each end – the equivalent of three compartments in the 1874 Inventory. The wheelbase was 13 feet 6 inches and the body length was 28 feet 6 inches. The two full compartments were 6 feet 10 inches between partitions. The width over beading was 8 feet 3 inches.

The drawing (see Figure 5.6) of the SCR carriage is identical to those built for the Highland Railway at the same time.[6] A photograph of one of the HR carriages is shown in Plate 5.11. There is another photograph in the National Railway Museum collection.[7] The SCR carriages were probably among the forty-five First class vehicles recorded in the 1862 Board of Trade return.

The third design was a conventional 3-compartment carriage built by Metropolitan in 1864, with the same body design as the Coupés.[8] They were smaller vehicles than the Coupés, which suggests that they were the block of carriages in the Inventory with the lower value. Figure 5.7 is a redrawing of the original, which is very poor quality. The carriage was 20 feet long, making the compartments slightly smaller than those in the Coupé on a 12-foot wheelbase. The interior width was 7 feet 6 inches. The original drawing shows the interior furnishings, which presumably were similar to the *coupé* version. Eighteen seats were available. Part of the original drawing is reproduced in Figure 5.8. These carriages may be those assigned CR numbers 40-43, 47-56 in the 1874 Inventory.

SCR SECONDS

The 1865 return shows forty-six carriages, while the number at handover was forty-eight. Two Joseph Wright drawings exist, both dated 1862.[9] The better quality version is shown in Figure 5.9. The annotation to the plan view of this drawing states that one compartment could be converted to carry luggage by *'letting the seats fall.'*

The carriage had four compartments, but the partitions were not full height, because only two oil lamps were provided. The compartments were very narrow compared with the Firsts – about 4 feet 10 inches between partitions. The body was 19 feet 6 inches long, but wide for the time at 8 feet. The wheel base was 10 feet 6 inches. The seating arrangement, taken from another drawing,[10] is shown in Figure 5.10.

The roof of one of these carriages may be visible in a photograph taken at Barnhill – see Plate 5.12. They cannot be identified from the 1874 Inventory, where there were seventy Second class carriages, but only fourteen with four compartments. There are very few exclusively Third class carriages with only three compartments, so it is unlikely

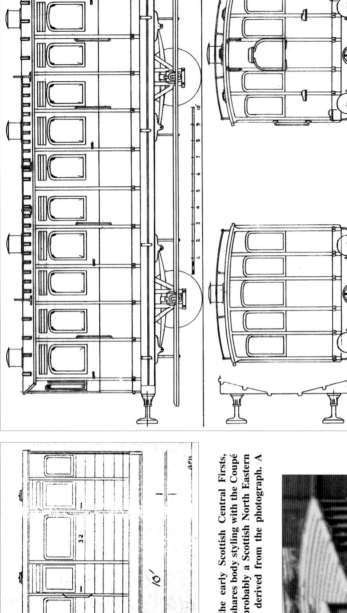

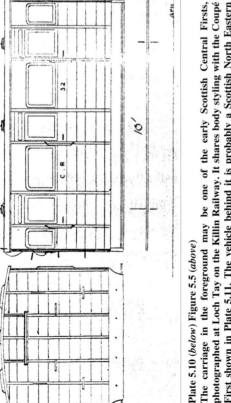

Figure 5.6 (*above*) and **Plate 5.11** (*below*)
The drawing depicts a Coupé First built for the Scottish Central in 1862 by Joseph Wright, just before the company became the Metropolitan Carriage & Wagon Works. It had two full compartments in the centre, flanked by two half *coupés*. Wright built the same type of carriage for the Highland Railway. One of these is shown on the Aberfeldy Branch train in Plate 5.11. It has been fitted with continuous brakes and the luggage rails have been removed from the roof. The photograph is from the NRM collection, reference LGRP7913.

Plate 5.10 (*below*) **Figure 5.5** (*above*)
The carriage in the foreground may be one of the early Scottish Central Firsts, photographed at Loch Tay on the Killin Railway. It shares body styling with the Coupé First shown in Plate 5.11. The vehicle behind it is probably a Scottish North Eastern Passenger Brake Van. The drawing of the First is derived from the photograph. A drawing of the Brake Van appears in Figure 5.16.

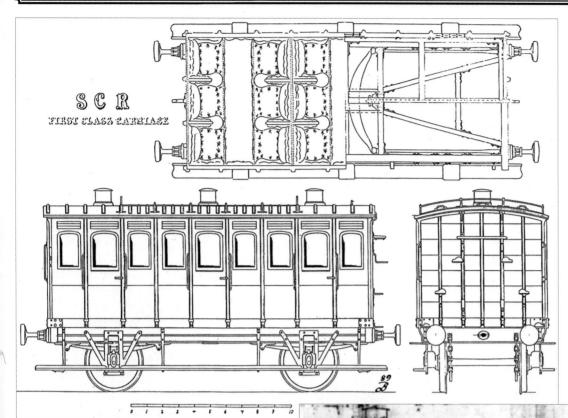

SCR
FIRST CLASS CARRIAGE

Figures 5.7 and 5.8
This more conventional 3-compartment First was built by Metropolitan for the SCR in 1864. It provided luxurious accommodation for eighteen passengers, as shown in Figure 5.8 (*below*).

that they were down-rated. It is more likely that they were taken out of service and then scrapped. Between the second half of 1868 and the end of 1871 eighty-four Second/Third class carriages were scrapped, according to the rolling stock returns.

SCR Composites and Thirds

Neither type of carriage can be identified in the 1874 Inventory. There must have been a significant number of Brake Thirds among the 110 carriages, but they were not separately listed at take-over. No drawings are known to exist of these carriages, although they were probably to the contemporary Joseph Wright design. It is possible that the two carriages in Plate 5.13 are examples of the Third class design. One of the Brake Thirds – which was simply adapted from a Third by the addition of windows in one end and, of course, brake gear – may appear in Plate 5.14.

Drawings survive for two Third class carriages built for the Dundee, Perth & Aberdeen Junction Railway, which was taken over by the Scottish Central in 1864.[11]

The first carriage (Figure 5.11) was open inside with seats for thirty-six passengers in the centre and along the sides and ends. This design was delivered for the opening of the line in 1847 and described in the local press.[12] Some may have survived to run on CR metals after 1865. A partial view of one of these carriages on the Montrose & Bervie line may appear in Plate 6.2.

Figure 5.12 shows a carriage similar in style to those built for the Scottish North Eastern Railway which are described below. It had four compartments, partitioned to the top of the seats. Forty passengers were accommodated.

SCR Brake Vans

A block of thirty-one 4-wheeled vans valued at the same price appears in the 1874 Inventory which probably refers to these

vehicles. The SCR Board of Trade return for the half year ending January 1865 records twenty-nine 'guards vans,' an increase of fourteen from the return of three years earlier. The Inventory includes a block of CR numbers from 111-132. The last two numbers in the block of thirty-one are 152 and 153, which are among the highest numbers given to CR Passenger Brake Vans at the time. It is possible that these two vans were built at the end of the SCR's independent existence, bringing the total up to thirty-one as recorded in the Inventory.

A redrawing of a '*passenger's luggage and brake van*' dating from 1861 is shown in Figure 5.13. It was built on an underframe of similar dimensions to the Second class carriage. Wheels with nine spokes are shown. A central raised lookout provided most of the illumination – the only window in the carriage body was in the door. The interior view of the van, which is taken from the original drawing,[13] is Figure 5.14.

Condition of the SNER Stock at Acquisition

Immediately after the SNER plant was acquired, the running department of the Caledonian had obvious doubts about its usefulness. The March 1867 Board Meeting reported that:

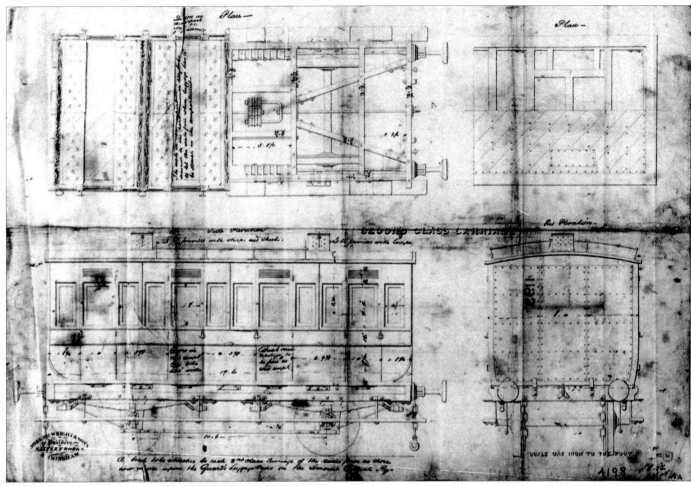

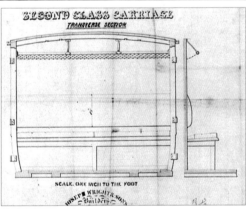

Figures 5.9 and 5.10, Plate 5.12
The drawing depicts a SCR four-compartment Second built in 1862. The interior cross section is taken from the original drawing. The enlargement from a photograph of Barnhill carriage sidings across the Tay from Perth shows a roof that was probably one of these carriages.

'the requirement for plant for that [the SNER] section must also be provided for. Expenditure is not immediately required, but will be charged, as incurred, during a series of years.'

After the November 1867 census, Conner asked for instructions as to whether the SNER stock should be included in future Board of Trade returns, which suggests that it was of limited use and would soon be withdrawn. The Finance Committee *'Resolved that the Rolling Stock of SNER as in existence on 31st July 1867 be adopted,'*[14] which echoes the Board's decision that it would be replaced piecemeal. It is not known how the statement applied to the SNER carriages.

Scottish North Eastern Firsts

Four of the carriages are known to have been built in 1860 by Joseph Wright at a cost of £349 each.[15] There is a block of

forty-eight 4-compartment Firsts in the 1874 Inventory that may refer to these carriages. The CR numbers were 67-89, 150-174. Number 71 was depicted in one of the drawings concerning the Newark brake trials. This carriage was identical to those built in 1867/68 by Metropolitan for the Cleland & Midcalder Railway. There is a drawing and description in Chapter 6.1.

SNER Seconds and Thirds

The Second and Third class carriages were aggregated in the capital expenditure return and cannot be identified in the 1874 Inventory. Positive identification is made even less likely because Brake Thirds were not separately listed among the carriages handed over.

Although no original drawings of these carriages are known to exist, a very similar, if not identical, example of a Third class carriage built

Plates 5.13 (*above*) and 5.14 (*right*)
These are possibly SCR 5-compartment Thirds. The number and position of the oil lamps suggests that two of the compartments were not divided to full height. Plate 5.14 may show the Brake variation of the SCR Thirds. It was taken at Loch Tay. The carriage behind it is possibly a Second or a First. At the rear is a clearly superior class carriage, of greater body height and arched windows. It seems to have a large guard's and luggage compartment.

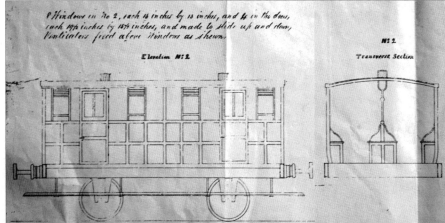

by Metropolitan for the Inverness & Aberdeen Junction Railway is shown in *Highland Railway Carriages*.[16] There are photographs of both types in CR service. A press article in 1903 shows Second, Third and First/Second Composite carriages.[17]

Both Second and Third class types had five compartments. The more spacious compartments of the Seconds dictated a longer body and wheelbase (26 feet and 14 feet respectively). This type is shown in Plate 5.15.

The Third class carriages are shown in Plates 5.16 and 5.17. They were also horizontally planked with vertical beading, about 23 feet 9 inches on a 13-foot wheelbase underframe. There were five compartments. As will be seen in Plate 5.17, the carriages were open above seat height.

As built, some of the Thirds were very gloomy. They may have been those inherited on amalgamation. In May 1859 the Locomotive Committee recorded that:

> '*In consequence of the numerous complaints made by passengers of the dark and uncomfortable condition of some of the company's 3rd class carriages … to have those complained of improved by the removal of some of the wood at the sides and the insertion of glass in its place.*'[18]

Twenty carriages were improved up to August 1860 '*by putting extra windows in them*' and the Locomotive Committee continued to renovate and improve the stock over the following years.[19] An example of a carriage fitting this description is shown in Plate 5.18, with a drawing in Figure 5.15. The single long light between each door and a quarter light at each end indicated that the partitions between the compartments did not

Figures 5.11 and 5.12
These are two drawings of Third class carriages from the Dundee, Perth and Aberdeen Junction Railway. The carriage in Figure 5.11 (*above*) was used at the opening of the railway in 1847. Assuming that the wheels were 3 feet in diameter, the wheelbase was 9 feet, the overall length 17 feet 2 inches and the width 7 feet 9 inches. The body was only 5 feet 5 high at the eaves. The end of one of these carriages may appear in Plate 6.2. The carriage in Figure 5.12 (*below*) was slightly shorter at 16 feet 10 inches, but the wheelbase was 9 feet 10 inches. It was 7 feet 6 inches wide and the body was more spacious at 6 feet 1½ inches to the eaves.

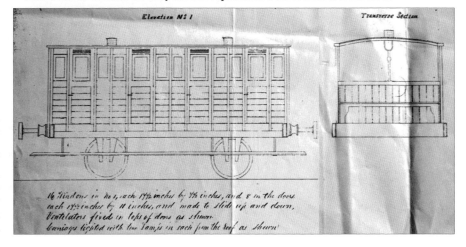

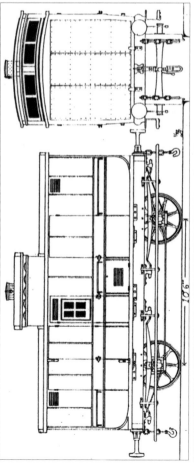

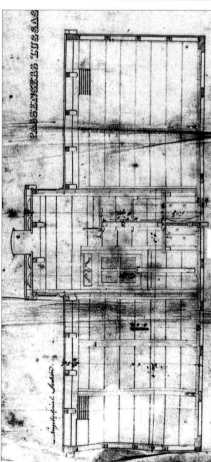

Figures 5.13 and 5.14
The SCR Passenger Brake Van had raised lookouts. This was part of the 1862 edition of the Statutory Requirements for Railways, although not all railway companies complied. This is discussed in Chapter 2.1. The interior view, taken from the original drawing, shows that the dog boxes also served as lookout platforms.

LEFT: Plate 5.15
The original St. Rollox photograph has not survived. This photograph appeared in *The Railway Magazine*, along with those in Plates 5.16 and 5.18. It shows an SNER 5-compartment Second, down-rated to CR Third 1327. It has been fitted with continuous brakes. It did not survive to be included in the Coaching Plant Stock Book.

ABOVE: Plates 5.16 and 5.17
Plate 5.16 shows the equivalent 5-compartment Third, now CR 1278. Plate 5.17 shows another Third after accident damage. It is included to show the partitioning that only went as high as the seat backs, and the wooden bench seating. The running number and the class designation are repeated on the inside of the doors.

reach full height, further confirmed by the presence of only three lamps.

According to the magazine article, the carriages were:

'withdrawn from traffic many years ago, but were made up into "block" trains, fitted with the Westinghouse brake and used ... for short distance cheap excursion traffic up to about three years ago'.

The article was written in 1903. There is a photograph of such a rake of carriages, taken at Barnhill in 1878, according to the catalogue entry. It is shown in Plate 5.19.

SNER COMPOSITES

It is not possible to identify the Composites in the Inventory because there is no block of carriages which corresponds to the configuration described below. It is known that two were built by Joseph Wright in 1860 as part of the tender for First class carriages mentioned above. They cost £298 10s each.

The *Locomotive Magazine* article shows a carriage with four compartments, the centre two being First class (see Plate 5.20). It diverged from the body design of the Second and Third class carriages by being of panelled construction. The article states that they were built in *'about 1862 [and] used on the mail trains.'* It goes on to say that they were the first SNER carriages to be fitted with Mansell wheels. This confirms the earliest possible building date for these carriages, as the Mansell wheel was patented in 1862 – see Chapter 2.4.

SNER BRAKE VANS

The 1874 Inventory records a block of thirteen vans at the same price, which probably refers to the bulk of the vans taken over by the Caledonian. The CR numbers were 45-47, 51, 70, 79-84, 150, 151. It is probable that one of the vans is shown at the rear of the excursion rake in Plate 5.19. There is a photograph of a similar van at Loch Tay in Plate 5.10 and a sketch based on this photograph in Figure 5.16.

Plate 5.18 and Figure 5.15 This shows another SNER Third, with larger windows between the doors. This was part of the train photographed at Loch Tay – see also Plate 5.10. The drawing derived from the photograph shows it as Second class, but the width between the compartment doors and the 13-foot wheelbase suggest Third.

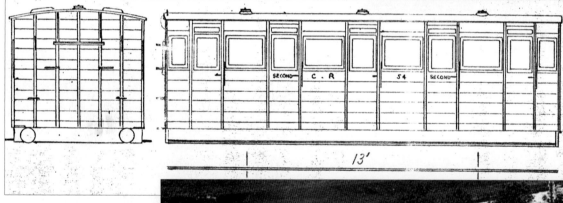

RIGHT: Plate 5.19
A rake of SNER carriages formed into an excursion set as described in *The Railway Magazine* article. At the end is an SNER Passenger Brake Van. The photograph shows clearly that the buffer casings and rams on these carriages were very short.

REFERENCES
1. *Caledonian Railway Wagons and Non-Passenger Coaching Stock*, pp. 173 and 193
2. NRS BR/SCC/1/26 p. 6
3. NRS BR/SCC/1/26 p. 14
4. Birmingham City Archive ref: MS99 8/92
5. *Highland Railway Carriages and Wagons*, pp. 33-34
6. LGRP 7914
7. Birmingham City Archive ref: MS99 4185
8. NRS BR/SCC/1/26 p. 14
   CRA Archive ref: 6/1/1/4/2
9. Birmingham City Archive refs: MS99 4198 and 4209
   CRA Archive refs: 6/1/1/4/3 and 6/1/1/4/4
10. Birmingham City Archive ref: MS99 4210
    CRA Archive ref: 6/1/1/4/5
11. CRA Archive refs: 6/1/1/3/1 and 2
12. *Stirling Advertiser and Journal*, 12th February 1847
13. Birmingham City Archive ref: MS99 4297
    CRA Archive ref: 6/1/1/4/6
14. NRS BR/CAL/1/16 entry 783
15. NRS SNE/1/1 p. 60
16. *Highland Railway Carriages and Wagons*, p. 30
17. *The Locomotive Magazine*, 17th October 1903, p. 235
18. NRS SNE/1/1, 5th July 1859
19. NRS SNE/1/1, 20th August 1860

Plate 5.20
The final illustration in *The Railway Magazine* article showed a Composite carriage built for the SNER in 1862. It originally had three First class and one Second class compartments.

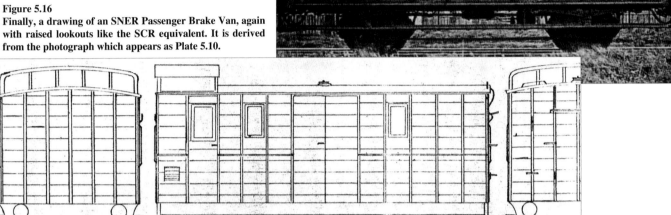

Figure 5.16
Finally, a drawing of an SNER Passenger Brake Van, again with raised lookouts like the SCR equivalent. It is derived from the photograph which appears as Plate 5.10.

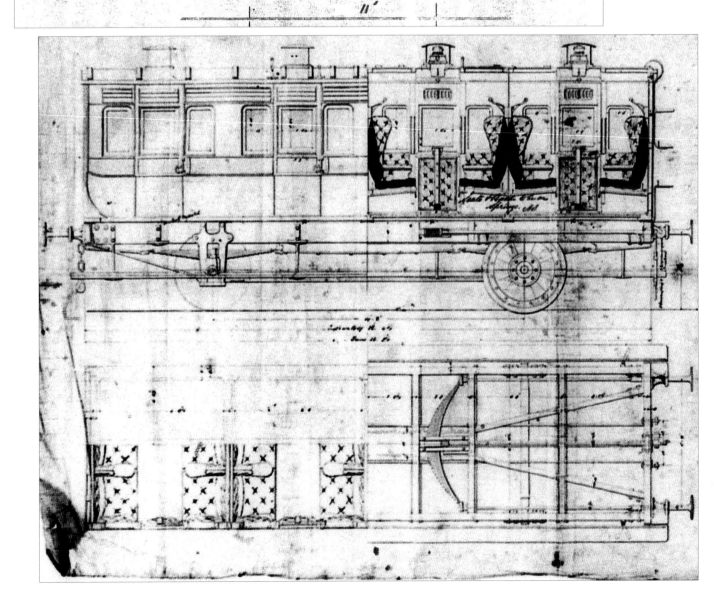

CHAPTER 6
GENERAL SERVICE STOCK 1867-1882

6.1: CARRIAGES OF THE LATE 1860S

In May 1867 the CR Board agreed *'the Coaching Stock requirements for the Cleland & Midcalder Railway, which should now be contracted for.'* The vehicles were to be delivered by 1st May 1868.[1] Metropolitan, Ashbury, and Brown, Marshall & Co. tendered for the order of fourteen First class carriages, fifteen Seconds, thirteen each Composites and Thirds, five Brake Thirds and twelve Brake Vans. The contract was awarded to Metropolitan for £20,795.[2] The carriages appeared in the accounting period ending 31st July 1868, so the delivery date was met. The line opened for passengers in July 1869.

The carriages were all built on 4-wheel underframes and Mansell wheels were fitted. Metropolitan's drawings for all except the Brake

Third are in the Birmingham City Archive. The carriages are described below.

FIRST CLASS CARRIAGES

The First class carriages[3] had four compartments, and were 26 feet 4¾ inches long and 7 feet wide on a wheelbase of 14 feet 6 inches. In order to fit the compartments into the body length, the two end compartments were just over 5 feet 9 inches between partitions, while the centre pair were 6 feet.

Stagecoach ancestry was still evident. Although there was a turn under of 1½ inches on the lower body sides, the carriage ends were flat. Despite this, the beading on the outer ends curved under in a similar manner to mail coaches, and the lower strip of waist panel beading curved up at the coach end – see Figure 6.1. This design feature also appeared on the Composites, but not on the Seconds, Thirds or Brake Vans.

The compartment doors were 2 feet 2 inches wide and fitted with a droplight, and there were two quarter-lights to each compartment. Above each door a ventilator could be opened or closed by passengers, and a line of dummy ventilators continued above the windows for the entire length of the carriage. Luggage was loaded onto the roof in an area enclosed by railings.

Compartments accommodated six passengers with the seats fully padded to head height and fitted with arm rests. The lower halves of the doors and the carriage sides below the quarter-lights were also padded. Netting racks supported by brackets were provided above the seats for small items and full height partitions dictated an oil lamp for each compartment.

A block of carriages numbered 198-211 appears in the 1874 Inventory valued at £390 which probably applies to these carriages. They were replaced in the early 1890s by 45-foot carriages to Diagram 21. Drawings of an identical carriage appeared in the technical press at the time of the first experiments with the Westinghouse brake on the Caledonian in 1872.[4] One of the drawings shows the carriage with the number 71.

SECOND CLASS CARRIAGES

Second class carriages, illustrated in Figure 6.2[5] and Plate 6.1, looked very different from the Firsts, and the Composites which are described below. The most striking difference was a panel edged with beading above each quarter-light, replacing the imitation ventilators of the Firsts and Composites. The sides and ends were completely flat, the body being 7 feet 8½ inches wide. The beading along the edges of the panels followed the body framing; no attempt being made to simulate a curved end. There were prominent ribs across the roof.

The 14-foot 6-inch wheelbase underframe carried a body 25 feet 5½ inches long with five compartments. Their dimensions varied. Those at the ends were 4 feet 9 inches between partitions, whilst the middle three were 5 feet. The doors were 1 foot 10 inches wide.

FACING PAGE AND BELOW: Figure 6.1
The original Metropolitan drawing for the First class carriages ordered for the Cleland & Midcalder Railway in 1867. The script writing in the side elevation reads *'seats and backs to be on springs.'*

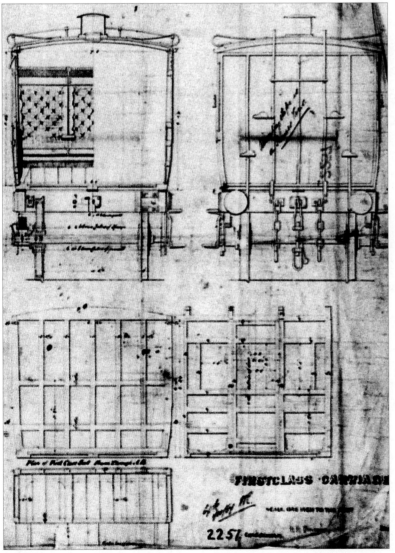

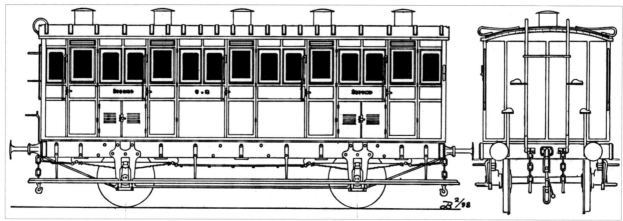

Figure 6.2 and Plate 6.1
The 5-compartment Second class design looked very different to the Firsts and Composites, with no curved panelling and a square body. Long commode handles are sited to the left of the doors, rather than the usual right.

Internally they were fitted out in an identical manner to the equivalent compartments in the Composites, with the seat backs padded to just below the level of the quarter-lights. Between the two outer compartments at each end was a dog box with double louvred doors. As there were no rails on the roof, these may have also been used for small items of luggage.

The 1874 Inventory records a block of carriages matching this description with the numbers 97-111, valued at £260 each. It is not possible to determine their withdrawal date, as they would have been renumbered when they were down-rated to Third class.

Composite Carriages

Externally, the Composites resembled the First class carriages. The line of the door ventilators continued over the entire length of the four compartments and the beading at the ends was curved in stagecoach style. Part of the original drawing[6] which shows the furnishing appears in Figure 6.3. The exterior is redrawn as Figure 6.4.

The wheelbase was the same as the other carriages, but the body was somewhat shorter at 24 feet 10¾ inches. There was a Second class compartment at one end, 4 feet 11¼ inches between partitions. The three First class compartments were slightly larger than those in the First class only carriages, at 6 feet 5¼ inches.

The First class compartments had fully padded seats with arm rests. Although the Second class seats had armrests, the padded

seat backs only extended to just above the bottom of the windows, and there was no padding on the inside of the doors or beneath the quarter-lights. They were probably the block of carriages numbered 37-49 in the 1874 Inventory. A carriage strongly resembling, if not identical to, this type is shown in Plate 6.2.

Third Class Carriages

The drawing of the Third class carriages[7] is shown in Figure 6.5 and photographed in Plate 6.3. A later, almost identical, design is shown in Figure 6.9. The later carriages are described in Chapter 6.2. Five compartments were fitted into a body 24 feet 1 inch long on a 14-foot 6-inch underframe. The compartments were 4 feet 8¼ inches between partitions.

Their internal construction resulted in a marked difference to their outward appearance compared with the other carriages in the order. There were no seats at the ends, making two half compartments. The partitions only reached to the top of the seat backs, just below window height. Two lamps lit the entire carriage. The seats were planked and opening ventilators were fitted above the doors.

The compartment doors were 1 foot 10 inches wide with a droplight. There was no window between the ends of the carriage and the first compartment door, and only a single one, placed centrally over the compartment partitions, between each pair of doors. Thus each carriage had five doors, but only four windows. There was a dog box at each end. The lower and waist panels were beaded, but there was no beading above the waist. Neither this design nor the Composites can be identified in the 1874 Inventory.

Brake Thirds

The exact appearance of the Brake Thirds is not known because no drawing or photographic evidence has been discovered. A very poor quality Metropolitan drawing[8] shows a modification to a CR carriage to transform one end into a Brake compartment. The drawing, annotated 'break compartment seat for 505' (presumably an order number) refers to a Second class carriage (or compartment), but it is reasonable to assume that a similar modification was carried out to provide Brake Thirds. The Brake compartment had a single door with a droplight, but no side windows. Two windows in the end provided further illumination.

This alteration to a carriage body to form a Brake carriage was common practice – see, for instance, Plate 5.8 and 5.14. Sewell

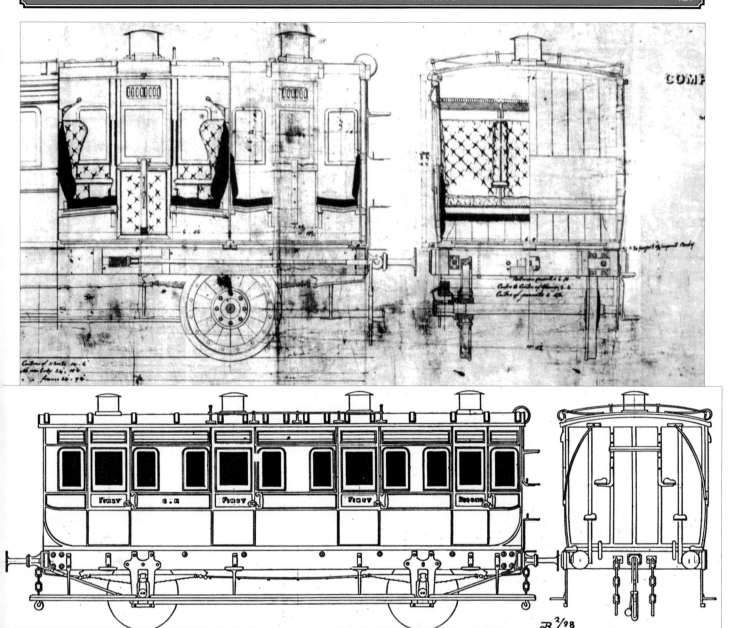

describes and illustrates a similar arrangement in a North British Railway 'contractor built' carriage for which a detailed drawing has survived.[9] This shows a brake stanchion fitted within a compartment that also includes seats.

PASSENGER BRAKE VANS

The twelve Brake Vans were built on a different underframe.[10] The van body was 21 feet long and 7 feet wide. The wheelbase was 12 feet. The lookouts projected 6¾ inches. Wooden brake blocks operated on both wheels on one side. They were probably the vans numbered between 96 and 155 in the 1874 Inventory, which were valued at £240 each. The original drawing is reproduced as Figure 6.6 and a similar, perhaps identical, van is shown in Plate 6.4.

ST. ROLLOX DESIGNS OF 1867

In the second half of 1867, just before drawings were made for two proposed Family and Invalid Saloons, the following set of drawings for 4-wheeled carriages was issued by St. Rollox, none of which has survived. The Saloons are described in Chapter 13.1.

Figures 6.3 and 6.4, Plate 6.2
The Composite carriage had one Second class compartment, seen here at the right-hand end. The original drawing is included to show the difference between the interior furnishing of the two classes. The photograph was taken on the Bervie Branch around 1875. Also partially visible is a carriage that matches the drawing in Chapter 5 (Figure 5.11) of a Dundee, Perth & Aberdeen Junction Railway Third.

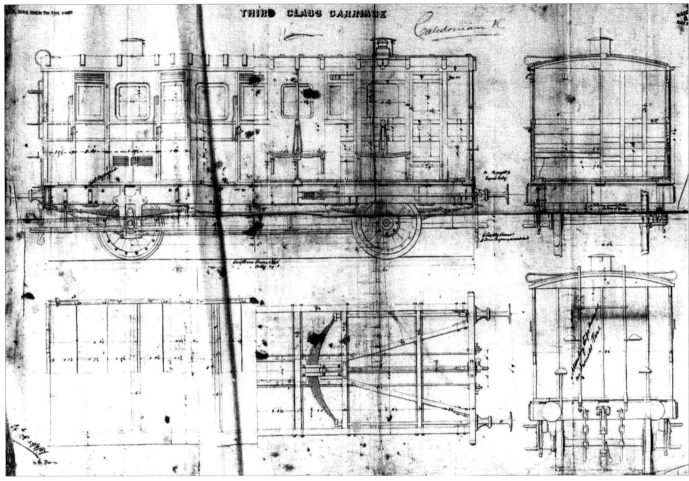

Figure 6.5 and Plate 6.3
The 5-compartment Thirds were similar in body style to the Seconds shown in Plate 6.1. The end compartments were half compartments and the partitions were on the centre lines of the windows. Three of the partitions only extended to the tops of the seats, while one was full height. Footboards under the doors are drawn, but marked *'not required'*, as can be seen in the photograph. A later variation is shown in Figure 6.9.

SRX No.	DESCRIPTION
761	Second class carriage 5 compts wheel centres 14ft 6in
784	First class carriage 4 compts wheel centres 13ft
785	Composite carriage 3 1st & 1 2nd 14ft 6in centres
786	Third class carriage coupled wheels 14ft 6in centres

This amounts to a full range of carriage types, if one accepts that the Brake Third was made by adapting the end compartment of a Third as outlined above. At the time, the stock of the Scottish Central and Scottish North Eastern was being assimilated, and, according to the rolling stock returns, very little carriage construction took place. As explained in the next section, contractors continued to supply carriages to the Caledonian. It is possible that carriages built to these drawings were not constructed until early 1870.

REPLACEMENT CARRIAGES ORDERED IN 1868-69

During the second half of 1868 and the whole of 1869, fifty-one Second/Third class carriages were withdrawn and twenty were constructed by Metropolitan – two Composites at £319 each, fourteen Thirds at £234 and four Brake Vans at £208.[11] The tender was accepted in late November 1868.

A drawing of a Composite carriage for the Caledonian dated 6th January 1869 survives – see Figure 6.7.[12] It shows a vehicle almost identical

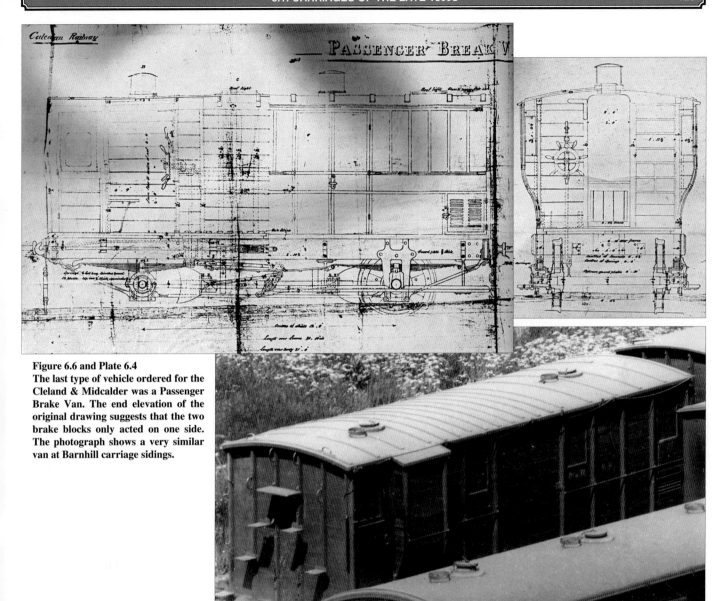

Figure 6.6 and Plate 6.4
The last type of vehicle ordered for the Cleland & Midcalder was a Passenger Brake Van. The end elevation of the original drawing suggests that the two brake blocks only acted on one side. The photograph shows a very similar van at Barnhill carriage sidings.

in outside appearance to those ordered in 1867. The Second class compartment – which was now 5 feet 6 inches between partitions, as compared with First class which had increased to 6 feet 6 inches – was at one end of the 24-foot 10-inch long body, which was again built on a 14-foot 6-inch wheelbase underframe. One of these carriages is probably shown in Plate 6.5.

It is not known which drawings were used for the Thirds and Brake Vans, but it is reasonable to assume that the designs were the same as for the Cleland & Midcalder stock. None of the carriages can be identified in the Inventory.

ADDITIONAL CARRIAGES IN 1869

In March 1869 the Permanent Way & Traffic Committee *'Read Mr Ward's application ... for four Composite carriages to run between Carlisle and Aberdeen'* and recommended that they should be built.[13] In late July a laconic Loco & Stores Committee minute headed *'Carriages and Wagons'* stated *'Accept Ashbury's offer as per letter of 10th July.'*[14]

It seems that only one of the carriages was charged to capital. The return for the period ending January 1870 included *'Composite carriages'* from Ashbury, but there is an erasure where the quantity

was entered and a value of £330 10s.[15] The rolling stock return recorded the renewal of three Composite carriages and the addition of one, which tallies with the minute and the capital expenditure price.

In June the Board authorised invitations to tender *'from a selection of suppliers'* for forty-five Third class carriages plus five Composites, which were to have three First and one Second class compartment each.[16] These carriages were originally part of an *'estimate for capital plant'* planned for construction in the half year ending January 1869, along with five Brake Thirds and *'ten guard's brake vans for the Scottish North Eastern Section.'*[17] It is not clear whether the SNER reference applied to the whole estimate or just the Brake Vans. The estimated prices were £365 for the Composites, £265 for the Thirds, £298 for the Brake Thirds and £250 for the Brake Vans.

The Brake Thirds and guards vans (described as *'luggage vans'*) were recorded as built by Metropolitan in the capital expenditure return for the period ending July 1869, at a unit price of £246 and £208 respectively.[18] They are also listed in the rolling stock return for the period.

There is no mention of a successful tenderer for the Thirds and Composites, which suggests that the carriages were built at St. Rollox. These carriages are discussed in the following section.

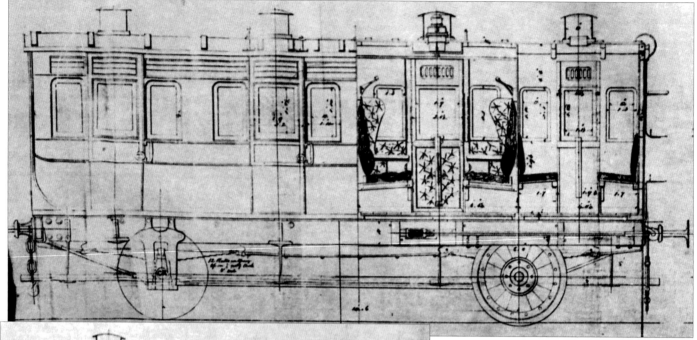

Figure 6.7 and Plate 6.5
The 1869 Composites were very similar to those built in 1867, but the compartment widths differed slightly. The poor quality photograph probably depicts number 103, which the 1874 Inventory valued at £390.

REFERENCES
1. NRS BR/CAL/1/15 entry 1480
2. NRS BR/CAL/1/15 entry 1611
3. Birmingham City Archive ref: MS99 2257
4. *The Engineer*, 24th May 1872, pp. 360-61
   Engineering, 24th May, pp. 344-47
5. Birmingham City Archive ref: MS99 2300
   CRA Archive ref: 6/1/1/2/11
6. Birmingham City Archive ref: MS99 2256
   CRA Archive ref: 6/1/1/2/3
7. Birmingham City Archive ref: MS99 2311
8. Birmingham City Archive ref: MS99 2258
9. *NBR Coaches*, p. 2 and drawing 2
10. Birmingham City Archive ref: MS99 2254
    CRA Archive ref: 6/1/1/2/1
11. NRS BR/CAL/1/17 entry 65
12. Birmingham City Archive ref: MS99 2294
    CRA Archive ref: 6/1/1/2/9
13. NRS BR/CAL/1/17 entry 554
14. NRS BR/CAL/1/17 entry 960
15. NRS BR/CAL/23/1 (39)
16. NRS BR/CAL/1/17 entry 884
17. Officers' Meetings Minute Book
18. NRS BR/CAL/23/1 (30)

6.2: STOCK BUILT AND ACQUIRED 1870-1874

The first half of the 1870s saw a high demand for new carriages. The first generation of rolling stock had reached the end of its design life. In any case, rising standards of comfort and technological advances had made it obsolescent. The carriage fleet also expanded in 1870/71, and again in 1874, as shown in the following table which is extracted from the half-yearly rolling stock returns.

CLASS		1870	1871	1872	1873	1874
First	Replace	7	6	0	7	7
	New	24	0	0	0	3
Second/Third	Replace	77	13	0	28	8
	New	56	21	0	0	39
Composite	Replace	0	2	6	10	5
	New	23	21	0	0	0
TOTALS	Replace	84	21	6	45	20
	New	103	42	0	0	42

STOCK FOR LANARKSHIRE AND THE SOLWAY JUNCTION

New carriages were required for the opening of the network of lines around Lesmahagow and Strathaven and for the Solway Junction Railway, which the Caledonian had effectively operated since its opening in 1869. In August 1869 the Loco & Stores Committee approved:

'For Strathaven Line
2 Double Composites of 2 Firsts, 2 Seconds,
3 Third Class, 1 of them with Break.
For Lesmahagow Line
3 Composites of 2 First and 2 Second class divisions each
6 Third Class, 2 with Breaks.
2 Guards vans
For Solway Junction Line
6 Double Composites of 2 First, 2 Second Class compartments each
10 Third Class, 2 of them with Brakes
2 Parcel Vans'[1]

Metropolitan won the contract, which was for one less Third and one extra Brake Third, making the actual order in total:

'11 Composite Carriages 6 wheel at £305 5s
13 Third Class, 5 compartment at £214
6 Third Class, 4 compartment & Breaks at £229
4 Luggage and Brake Vans at £194'[2]

Drawings exist for some of these carriages. The bodies of the Composites[3] were still only 23 feet 3¾ inches long, but the width had increased slightly to 7 feet 4½ inches. The short length explains the relatively low price compared with other Composites. The total wheelbase was only increased from the 4-wheeled standard of 14 feet 6 inches to 15 feet, which meant that adjoining springs shared a common hanger, as can be seen in Figure 6.8. The outer springs had twelve leaves and the central pair eleven.

The two inner First class compartments were 6 feet 5¼ inches between partitions, whilst the end compartments for Second class passengers were only 4 feet 8½ inches. First class compartments were fitted out internally as before, but the degree of comfort for Second class passengers had increased, as the seat backs were now padded to the same height as in the First class, although not as sumptuously, and they still lacked armrests. They did, however, have luggage racks above the seats.

Externally the carriages still had an imitation curve to the end bodywork and individual upper steps for each compartment, and in other stylistic respects they conformed to the appearance of the 1867 Firsts and Composites. Although comparatively few carriages matching their description were listed in

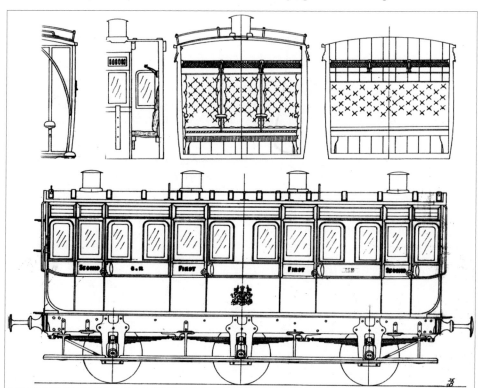

Figure 6.8
This short six-wheeled Bi-Composite was built for the new lines opened in 1869. Note the double hangers to support the centre springs on the short wheelbase underframe.

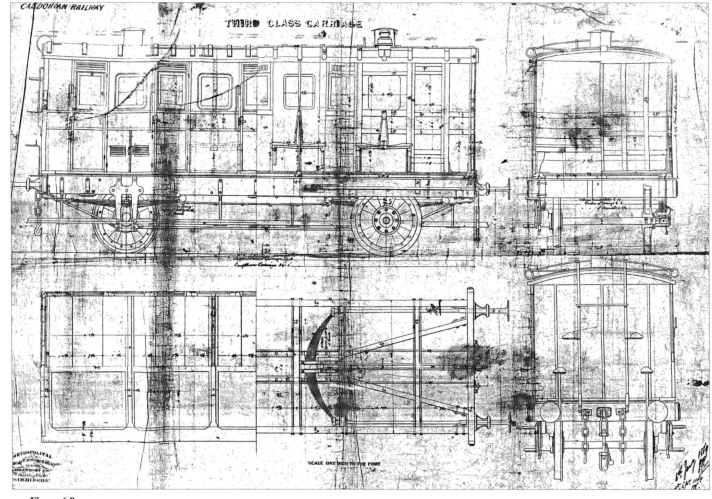

Figure 6.9
The drawing for the Third class carriages of 1869 was to the same body style and general internal arrangement as the carriage for the Cleland & Midcalder shown in Figure 6.5 and Plate 6.3. The seats now have some padding. A second full-height internal partition has been sketched in, which would imply three oil lamps.

the 1874 Inventory, they cannot be positively identified. Some may have been the carriages numbered 112-115 and 152-155, valued at £420 and £410 respectively.

The drawing for the Third class carriages[4] was identical externally to that used in 1867, with a full height partition separating one of the three full compartments from the other two. A further full height partition was sketched in, which would have required three lamps. It is not known whether this variation was implemented. Once again the end compartments only had seats against the inboard partition. Seats and backs now had a thin layer of padding. The original drawing is shown in Figure 6.9.

Presumably the Brake Thirds were to the same design with one end compartment fitted out with brake gear and with two windows cut in the end. The Third class carriages cannot be positively identified in the 1874 Inventory.

In late September the Loco & Stores Committee:

'Read Mr Smithell's letter asking instructions in regard to the conversion of 4 Composite Carriages from 2 First/2 Second Class compartments to 2 First/1 Second/2 Third Class compartments. Read also Mr Ward's letter of 28th inst.'[5]

The Committee agreed to the submission, which concerned part of the original order for eleven Bi-Composites, which in consequence was reduced to seven. The Metropolitan drawing[6] dated 6th October 1869 shows a 5-compartment Tri-Composite carriage with two

First class compartments, a single Second class and two Third class compartments with a hand-written note saying *'4 to this.'* The body was to the same style as the Bi-Composite and was just under 28 feet long, on a 6-wheel underframe with a total wheelbase of 18 feet 6 inches. The original drawing is reproduced as Figure 6.10, plus a redrawing of the end.

One example survived until 1917. The Coaching Plant Stock Book records number 1413 as a two First/three Third class Composite, built in October 1869. It had been down-rated to Third class in 1909. Its original number before allocation to the duplicate list was not recorded. They may have been the block of carriages numbered 104-107 in the 1874 Inventory, valued at £440 each.

The Passenger Brake Vans were built to the drawing issued in 1867, which carries notes of minor alterations to the internal partitioning for this order. This design was shown in Figure 6.6.

None of the carriages built to this order were specifically identified in the capital expenditure record. They must have been included among the 103 carriages charged to the 'Plant Account' in the period ending July 1870.[7] The four Passenger Brake Vans appeared as a separate item in the same entry.

THE ROBBINS PATENT CARRIAGE

In February 1870 the Caledonian, in common with other UK railways, was approached by the American inventor Edward Robbins. In late 1868 he had patented a fire-proof and crash-

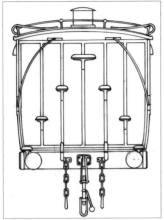

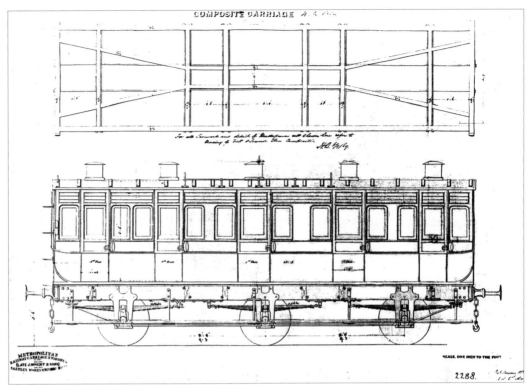

Figure 6.10
Part of the order for eleven Bi-Composites in 1869 was amended to four Tri-Composites. This is the amended drawing. Across the top is written '*4 to this.*' The annotation across the centre of the drawing reads '*For all ironwork and details of underframes not shown here refer to tracing of First and Second Class Composites 6/9/69.*'

resistant passenger carriage made of '*thin plates of wrought iron.*' A part drawing of the original design is shown in Figure 6.11. The practice of heating saloon-style wooden carriages by coal-fired stove in the USA had started numerous fires, some with fatal results, and had generated a great deal of adverse publicity.

Despite using the opportunity to exploit people's fears, he failed to gain any interest in his home country and modified the design for the UK market. No record of the modifications has come to light. His representative in the UK was William MacCartney of Glasgow.[8]

Two CR minutes refer to Robbins' proposition. The Chairman had received a letter on the 11th February and Conner was asked to report.[9] Just over a week later, Conner had done so, and the Board resolved to '*decline in the meantime.*'[10] Robbins ultimately spent twenty fruitless years trying to interest railway companies in the concept.[11]

COMPLAINTS AND IMPROVEMENTS ON THE GREENOCK LINE

In 1868 the public complained to the Board of Trade about the poor riding of stock on the Greenock line. Colonel Hutchinson of the Railway Department was sent to examine the situation. He identified:

> '*marks of considerable play between the naves [of the wheels] and the axle boxes, denoting most probably a wearing away of the brasses by the journals, giving rise no doubt to the oscillation complained of, especially when running round quick curves, some of which occur at the Greenock end of the line. In some cases washers have been put in to check the play, but I imagine no effective remedy can be applied except by renewing the brasses.*'[12]

In November 1868 the Permanent Way & Traffic Committee had '*Read a copy of Colonel Hutchinson's report to the Board of Trade on the condition of the large Greenock Carriages*' and recorded that '*the defects complained of are under correction.*'[13] The latter statement will sound familiar to readers of reports criticising the shortcomings of twenty-first-century public bodies.

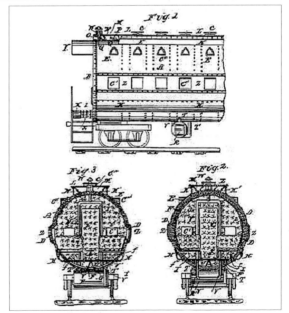

Figure 6.11
The Robbins patent fire-proof carriage was given short shrift by railways in America and Britain. These views are part of the original patent application. The interior was completely upholstered so it would have felt like travelling in a padded cell.

Almost exactly a year later, the Committee was asked for instructions concerning all the Greenock line carriages '*as to improving their condition, consequent on the opening of the Greenock & Ayrshire Line for passenger Traffic.*'[14] The matter was remitted to the Board, which passed it to the Glasgow Directors for a decision. They resolved in November 1869,

> '*that Mr Conner be instructed to alter the old First Class Carriages into Seconds and to turn the Seconds into Thirds and to report on the cost of lighting with gas.*'[15]

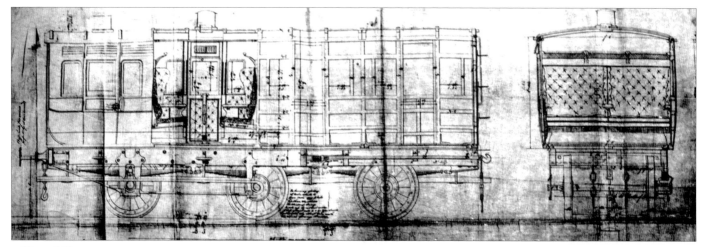

Figure 6.12
This short First class carriage was built for the Greenock line in 1870. The underframe is similar to that shown in Figure 6.8.

To release the old carriages for down-rating, tenders were taken up at the beginning of 1870 for thirty new First class carriages *'particularly for use on the Greenock line.'*[16] Once again, they were built by Metropolitan at £379 each.[17]

The new carriages had four compartments, the middle two being 6 feet between partitions, while the outer ones were only 5 feet 9 inches. The body was 26 feet 4 inches long and 7 feet 5 inches wide. The carriages ran on 6-wheeled underframes, this time with a wheelbase of 16 feet 6 inches.

The compartments were fully upholstered and fitted with a central arm rest, implying that the compartments seated four passengers per side. Part of the original drawing[18] is reproduced in Figure 6.12. The remainder is unsuitable for reproduction. They were probably allocated the block of numbers from 212-241 in the 1874 Inventory. They were valued at £460 each.

The Coaching Plant Stock Book records two 4-compartment First class carriages with a building date of May 1870. One was renumbered 1293 when it was down-rated to a Third at an unknown date. The original number was said to be 11, but the 1874 Inventory records this as a 4-wheeled carriage. It was replaced by a down-rated ex-WCJS Composite in September 1921.

The other had already received duplicate number 1034 before being down-rated to Third class with bare wood seats at an unknown date, so it cannot be positively reconciled with the original block of running numbers. Its number at withdrawal in June 1919 was 3145.

Although they were additions to the fleet, the carriages do not appear as such in the capital expenditure record. According to a note on the rolling stock return for the half year ending July 1870, that is, after the new carriages had been delivered, sixteen of the old First class carriages were converted into *'superior Second Class carriages.'* Presumably the superiority stemmed from their spacious compartments. There is no corresponding statement about the conversion of Seconds to Thirds, but twenty-nine Second/Thirds were recorded as replacements.

OTHER CONTRACTOR-BUILT CARRIAGES IN 1870

Metropolitan secured an order in December 1869 for five Composite carriages with five compartments at £348 10s each.[19] They were only charged to the capital account in the period ending July 1871, at £371 each.[20] Three carriages, numbered 118, 120 and 124 are recorded in the Coaching Plant Stock Book with build dates in early 1870 which may refer to them. They had all been down-rated to Third class, but were originally Tri-Composites according to the 1874 Inventory. Another carriage numbered 110 appears in the Stock Book with an 1870 date. This only had four compartments, as

confirmed by the Inventory, where it is listed with three First class compartments and one Second.

Eighteen 4-wheeled Thirds were ordered from Metropolitan at the same time at £222 each. The drawing[21] dated January 1870 is reproduced in Figure 6.13. It was another variation on the three full- and possibly two half-compartment theme, with the luggage rails omitted from the roof and two lamps. A photograph of one of these carriages appears as Plate 6.6. Number 37 was one of a block of sixteen carriages valued at £245 in the 1874 Inventory.

Two First and thirteen Second/Third class carriages were authorised in the middle of April as replacements during the period.[22] In May, Brown, Marshall & Co. secured an order for thirteen *'Third Class Carriages with breaks'* at £260 each.[23] There is no mention of the First class carriages, or any of the other inferior class vehicles that the rolling stock return records as replacements. One assumes that they were built at St. Rollox.

MANAGEMENT CHANGES AFFECTING WORKS CAPACITY

George Brittain, who would succeed Conner when he died suddenly in 1876, was put in charge of rolling stock for the whole line in April 1870,[24] having been Outdoor Inspector of Locomotives for the section north of Stirling since the amalgamations of 1866/67. The same minute effectively demoted Conner to *'Indoor Superintendent.'*

The expansion of Brittain's role at a salary of £500 was on the recommendation of an ad-hoc Chairman's Committee that an:

'Officer, independent of the Locomotive Superintendent, be appointed under the title of "Outdoor Locomotive Superintendent" to look after the Plant while working on the line, so that it may be duly sent in for repair and be generally properly utilized and attended to.'[25]

ST. ROLLOX-BUILT CARRIAGES OF 1870

One intended beneficial effect of the strengthened management team was that, for the first time for a long period, St. Rollox Works would have the capacity to build rolling stock as well as repair it.

In the period ending July 1870, the 103 new carriages in the summary table were charged to the 'Plant Account' at £29,711 9s.[26] This included the thirty carriages for the Lanarkshire and Solway Junction lines discussed earlier. The average price of about £288 10s implies that they were small 4-wheeled carriages, bearing in mind that just under one quarter of them were above-average cost First class vehicles.

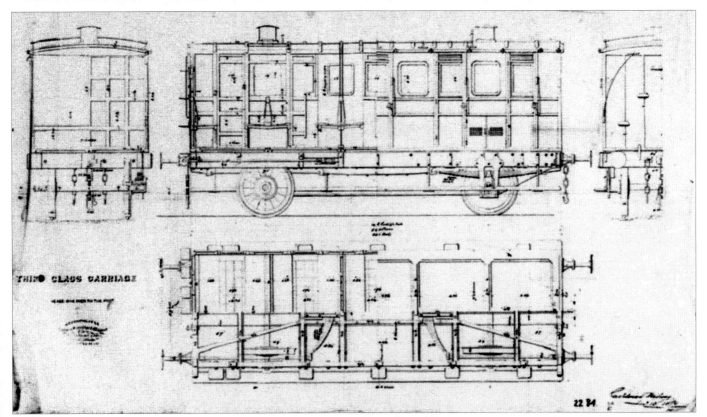

THIRD CLASS CARRIAGE

Figure 6.13 and Plate 6.6
Another variation of the designed depicted in Plate 6.3 and Figure 6.8. The end compartments had seats on both sides, but passengers on the seats at the end of the carriage did not have a window. Carriage number 37 was photographed on the Tay Bridge at Perth. It was valued at £245 in the 1874 Inventory. It probably lasted until 1890, when it was replaced by a 45-foot carriage.

There is no record of their authorisation. At this period of the Caledonian's history, Board and Committee minutes concerning rolling stock construction were confined to outside contractors, because a formal tender process was involved. This suggests that the remaining seventy-three carriages were built at St. Rollox.

The St. Rollox register in 1870 does not record any drawings for the carriages. It is possible that they were built to the 1867 drawings which were described in the previous section. Two of the Composite carriages may be the subject of Plate 6.7.

To confuse matters, only one 4-compartment Third (number 1345) and Brake Third 54, also with four compartments, appear with a build date of 1870 in the Coaching Plant Stock Book. They were both 6-wheeled vehicles. No dimensions were recorded for the Third; the Brake Third was 31 feet long and 8 feet wide. The overall wheelbase was 18 feet.

The carriages would have been replaced at the end of their design life in 1896/97 by 45-foot carriages, which means that, apart for the two exceptions quoted above, they did not appear in the Stock Book.

CARRIAGES ORDERED FROM ASHBURY IN 1871

In November 1870 the Loco & Stores Committee approved an order with Ashbury for three Tri-Composite carriages at £354 each to St. Rollox drawing 1085, twelve Bi-Composites with one Second and four Third class compartments at £242 each (drawing 1083), and six Third class carriages at £228 each (drawing 1084).[27] None of the drawings has survived.

Only two of the Tri-Composites were built according to the capital expenditure return for the period ending July 1871, where they were charged at £354 in agreement with the minute accepting the tender.[28] The Coaching Plant Stock Book records Composites 125 and 127 with a build date of May 1871. The first had an 18-foot total wheelbase, the second 20 feet. Number 127 is shown in Plate 6.8. Down-rated to Third class, the two carriages survived until the Grouping.

A Saloon was charged to the capital return for the next period.[29] This was a *'plain saloon'* for the Callander & Oban line for which tenders were requested in March 1871.[30] Although there is no mention of a successful tender, it was probably awarded to Ashbury as the third carriage of the original order. Further details about this carriage are in Chapter 13.2.

The Bi-Composites, which must have been small vehicles at the price quoted, do not appear in the capital expenditure or rolling stock returns. It seems the order was cancelled, because eight Composites were acquired from the West Coast Joint Stock instead. These carriages are described later in this section.

The cost of the Third class carriages implies that they had four wheels. Only five carriages were recorded in the July 1871 capital expenditure return at the agreed price, although six were recorded in the rolling stock return. One survived to be recorded in the Coaching Plant Stock Book. Number 608 was renumbered 3119 and withdrawn in 1923. It is recorded with a building date of October 1871; no dimensions are given. A block of four Thirds, valued at £226 each and numbered 603-605 and 608 in the Inventory, probably refers to these carriages. One may be illustrated in Plate 6.9. The carriage is equally likely to be one of eight ordered in January 1873, which are discussed later. The remaining two of the six, numbered 606, 607, were valued at the same price, but recorded with an extra luggage compartment.

METROPOLITAN-BUILT BI-COMPOSITES AND THIRDS

A week after placing the order with Ashbury, and presumably having cancelled most of it in the interim, the Loco & Stores Committee agreed to take tenders for twenty Bi-Composites, this time with two First and two Second class compartments plus a luggage cupboard to St. Rollox drawing 1087 and ten with two Second and three Third class compartments, but no luggage cupboard (drawing 1088).[31] Neither drawing has survived.

The minute quoted above asked Conner how many of the order could be built at St. Rollox. The answer was evidently *'none,'* as Metropolitan secured the contract to build all the carriages in January 1871.[32] The price was £371 each for the First/Seconds and £272 for the Second/Thirds.

A Metropolitan drawing for the carriages with luggage cupboards is reproduced as Figure 6.14.[33] The cupboard was centrally located with two compartments on either side. The two First class compartments immediately flanked the luggage cupboard. The wheelbase was 18 feet 6 inches and the overall length was 30 feet.

A problem arose about delivery, no doubt in part because of the short notice in placing the order. Only five of the First/Second Composites were charged to the capital expenditure return for the period. In early July it was noted that delivery was delayed[34] and the Loco & Stores Committee ordered *'Mr Gibson to write to the Company that we must decline to order from them in future.'* A letter of explanation sent by return of post was read a fortnight

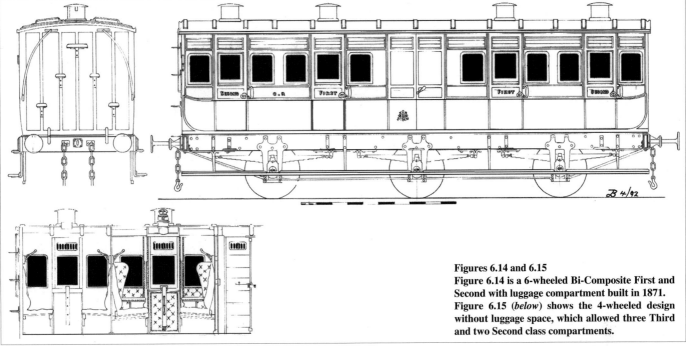

Figures 6.14 and 6.15
Figure 6.14 is a 6-wheeled Bi-Composite First and Second with luggage compartment built in 1871. Figure 6.15 (*below*) shows the 4-wheeled design without luggage space, which allowed three Third and two Second class compartments.

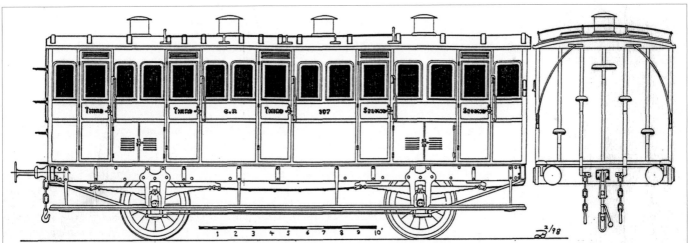

later[35] which seems to have been sufficient to repair relations, at least for the time being.

The delay seems to have given the CR an opportunity to revise the order. The remainder was recorded in the capital expenditure return for the period ending January 1872 – a slippage of six months. The return lists the ten Second/Third Composites, six extra Thirds at £291 each and fourteen First/Second Composites, making a total of nineteen out of the twenty ordered.[36]

Number 128 is the only First/Second Composite carriage with a luggage compartment in the 1874 Inventory, but the Coaching Plant Stock Book records four Brake Composites numbered 128, 139, 140 and 143, built during the latter half of 1871, which probably applies to these carriages. They were recorded with a 9-foot by 9-foot wheelbase – a variation from the drawing. They had been down-rated to Thirds, mostly in the first decade of the 1900s. Three lasted until the Grouping and were allocated, but did not carry, LM&SR numbers. They were oil-lit to the end.

The vehicles without luggage cupboards[37] were 27 feet 6 inches long on a 15-foot wheelbase, 4-wheeled underframe and are shown in Figure 6.15. The two Second class compartments at one end of the carriage were 5 feet 10½ inches between partitions. They were fitted with the usual padded seats. The end Third class compartment was

5 feet 4½ inches between partitions, but the other two were smaller at 5 feet 2¾ inches.

Internally the partitions were still only as high as the seat backs but the oil lamps were placed directly over the compartment partitions so that there were four in total. Externally there was no beading above the waist and the line of the door ventilators was not continued above the quarter-lights. The droplights were the same width for both the Second and Third class compartments, but the quarter-lights for the Second class, at 15½ inches, were 3 inches wider than those in Third class.

The 1874 Inventory records ten carriages of this configuration among the Third class carriages, numbered 593-602, valued at £260 each. They were replaced by a variety of carriages in the last two decades of the nineteenth century, when their numbers were assigned to the carriages that bear them in the Coaching Plant Stock Book.

CARRIAGES ACQUIRED FROM WCJS IN 1871

West Coast Conference minutes record the withdrawal in November 1870 of thirty-three '*inferior carriages*' comprising twenty-four Composites and nine Thirds.[38] This was the first time that surplus stock was disposed of to the two partner companies. It was necessary to calculate and agree the ratio of cost to be borne by each company.

This was based on the original contributions made to the cost of the carriages in 1862 – the CR's share being increased by that of the SNER and SCR. The division of costs had originally been calculated on the mileage over the various railways that the carriages would cover between Euston and their destination. The CR and L&NWR's mileage was always the same at 125 and 301 respectively. Carriages on the Perth service had an extra 45 added for the Scottish Central. Those for Aberdeen had a further 90 added for the journey over SNER metals.[39] It so happened that a large proportion of the carriages were designated for Perth or Aberdeen traffic, thus inflating the Scottish companies' contribution. The agreed ratio was L&NWR 63.46% and CR 36.54%.

The CR rolling stock return for the half year ending July 1871 records the acquisition of eight Composites and six Second/Third class. A hand-written annotation to a later West Coast minute[40] states that the Caledonian made a balancing payment – see Plate 6.10.

Nothing is known for certain about the WCJS carriages. The Composites may have been the 4-wheeled Tri-Composites numbered 160-167 in the 1874 Inventory. It is likely, however, given their inferior nature, that they did not survive for very long. There were enough carriages of both classes described as 'worn out' in the returns during the 1870s.

In November 1871[41] the West Coast Conference approved the withdrawal from service of twenty-two carriages because they lacked luggage accommodation, to be 'apportioned between the two Companies (in the same manner as the 33 vehicles above mentioned).' They were to be replaced 'in time for use next season' by 'a like number of carriages of an improved type having compartments for luggage.'[42]

Although the cost of the replacements was included in the capital expenditure return for the half year ending July 1872, the acquisition of a share of the old stock was not.[43] There is no mention of a transfer in the rolling stock return. Nothing can be ascertained about these carriages in CR service. It is possible, given the lack of records, that the Caledonian did not take up their option or that they were scrapped on transfer.

ADDITIONS AND REPLACEMENTS BETWEEN 1871 AND 1873

In July 1871 the Loco & Stores Committee authorised six new Passenger Brake Vans from contractors.[44] A fortnight previously, the Committee had considered the replacement programme for the next half year and decided 'Mr Conner to arrange,'[45] which suggests that this was to be undertaken at St. Rollox.

In August the Glasgow Committee accepted tenders from Ashbury for seven Brake Vans at £178 15s. Perhaps the extra van was a consequence of a lower than expected unit price. The 1874 Inventory contains a block of seven 4-wheeled vans numbered 89, 136-141 which probably refers to these vehicles. One of these vans may have figured in one of the photographs recording the opening through to Oban of the C&O – see Plate 6.11. A side elevation of a similar van with the number 138 was published in the technical press at the time of the first trials of the Westinghouse brake on the Caledonian in 1872. Another, better quality, version of the same drawing from the same week's edition of *Engineering* is shown in Figure 6.16.[46]

At the same meeting the Glasgow Directors accepted a tender for three First class carriages from Metropolitan at £410 each. They were based on the Greenock line design of 1870; the original drawing records alterations to be made in August 1871. They cannot be identified in the 1874 Inventory.

(3.) APPORTIONMENT OF 33 DISUSED VEHICLES (Min. 995/2). The following valuation by Mr. Bore and Mr. Conner was submitted:—

COMPOSITES.				£	s.	d.
8 at 220	14	0 each	...	1765	12	0
8 at 237	0	0 each	...	1896	0	0
6 at 257	0	0 each	...	1542	0	0
2 at 333	0	0 each	...	666	0	0
				£5869	12	0

THIRD CLASSES.				£	s.	d.
2 at 165	9	6 each	...	330	19	0
2 at 206	16	6 each	...	413	13	0
2 at 166	18	0 each	...	333	16	0
1 at 221	10	0	...	221	10	0
2 at 250	0	0 each	...	500	0	0
				£1799	18	0

x Value £7669 10 0

per minute 1077 the divisions are L&NW 63.46 Caledn 36.54 own to pay in addition £276.3.4

Plate 6.10
The West Coast Committee minute recording the first distribution of surplus carriages to the L&NWR and CR, and the percentage proportions used to calculate the liability. Although the CR had to pay a balancing sum of over £96, it did not appear in the capital expenditure return.

Later in the month the Loco & Stores Committee noted that six 'Third class carriages with break vans' were wanted and agreed to take tenders.[47] There is no record of an outcome to the tender process and no entry in the rolling stock returns. The request was made again in July 1872, 'to be supplied as early as possible,'[48] but again the lack of a record in the capital expenditure or rolling stock returns suggests that the order was not proceeded with.

In February 1872 Metropolitan secured an order for six Composite carriages[49] at £435 each which were recorded as replacements in the stock return for the period ending January 1873. The Coaching Plant Stock Book records three carriages numbered 170, 172, 175, built in December 1872/January 1873 which may refer to this order. If so, they had three First and two Third class compartments, and their total wheelbase was 18 feet. They were down-rated to Thirds in the early years of the twentieth century.

Also in 1872, six Passenger Brake Vans were requested.[50] The Traffic Committee agreed to the request and remitted it to Loco & Stores. Seven vans appear as replacements in the half-yearly return for July 1873. As described in Chapter 14, the original intention was to order a Travelling Post Office as well. In the event, this was built by the L&NWR, and the order was changed. The vans appear in the capital expenditure return at £380 each, built by Ashbury.[51] A group of 6-wheeled vans valued at £370 appear in the 1874 Inventory, numbered 76, 98, 108, 109, 146-148. One of these vans may have been photographed in 1933 as an LM&SR service vehicle – see Plate 6.12.

In January 1873 the Loco & Stores Committee accepted tenders for eight Thirds (Ashbury, £235 each) and seven more Composites (Metropolitan, £482 10s).[52] As previously stated, one of the Ashbury-built Thirds may appear in Plate 6.9.

All the carriages built in 1873 were replacements. It is not possible to identify these carriages in the 1874 Inventory. One of the Composites, numbered 57, is recorded in the Coaching Plant Stock Book as built by Metropolitan in January 1873. In August 1916 it was down-rated to a Third and renumbered 1332. It was finally withdrawn in 1925. A further carriage, number 175, was also recorded with the same build date. It was down-rated in 1900 to Third 463 and withdrawn in 1922.

NEW AND REPLACEMENT PLANT IN 1874

In August 1873 an application for 'fifty Third Class carriages, ten to be provided with brakes' was submitted to the Traffic Committee and agreed.[53] The Loco & Stores Committee sought and received tenders for fifty carriages of the following types:

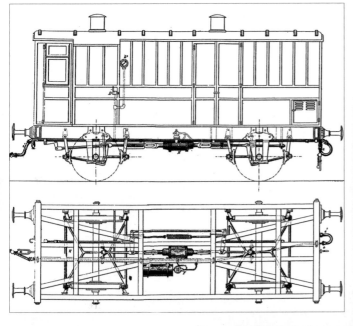

Plate 6.11 (*above*) and **Figure 6.16** (*above left*)
The photograph and drawing probably show one of the Passenger Brake Vans built by Ashbury in 1871. The photograph was taken at the opening of the Callander & Oban Railway in 1880. The drawing, which shows a van of similar construction but with the lookout in a different place, is from the technical press at the time of the CR's first trial of the Westinghouse brake in 1872.

LEFT: **Plate 6.12**
This may be the equivalent 6-wheeled design built by Ashbury in 1873. It has become a service vehicle in LM&SR livery and has been fitted with disc wheels. The dog box is just visible at the rear.

'*10 Third Class Carriages with Breaks*
7 Third Class Carriages, luggage compartments
10 Third Class Carriages, 6 compartments
20 Third Class Carriages, 5 compartments
3 Tri-composites'

At the same time tenders were opened for '*10 First Class Carriages and 2 Bi-composites.*'[54]

Caledonian management was still nervous about Metropolitan's reliability, because Conner was ordered to visit the potential manufacturers in Birmingham '*particularly as to time of delivery and to report.*'[55] After his visit, tenders were finally accepted in late November. Brown, Marshall & Co. received orders for the ten Brake Thirds at £613 10s each, ten 6-compartment Thirds at £520 10s, seven 4-compartment Thirds with luggage section at £489 10s each, the Tri-Composites for £594 10s and the Bi-Composites for £607 10s. To complete the numbers, Metropolitan was given orders for twenty 5-compartment Thirds with four wheels at £435 each and the ten Firsts at £762 10s each.[56]

St. Rollox drawings were issued for all the carriages, but they have not survived. Drawing 1535 was for the 6-compartment Third, 1536 was for the Brake Third, 1537 was the luggage Third, and the 5-compartment carriage was 1538. Finally, drawing 1539 was described as a '*pure 1st class carriage, 5 compartments.*' Drawing 1603 for the Tri-Composites was for '*2 1st, 2 2nd, 2 3rd.*' This was probably a transcription error for one Second class compartment. The Bi-Composite (drawing 1604) had two First and two Second class compartments, plus a luggage box.

Some of the First class carriages (see Figure 6.17) were recorded in the Coaching Plant Stock Book with a building date of December 1873. The original Metropolitan drawing[57] is not suitable for reproduction. Numbers 126, 133-135, 137 and 141 all had five compartments with a wheelbase of 18 feet. They were 8 feet wide and 31 feet long, according to the Stock Book. The compartments, 6 feet 0½ inches between partitions, seated four passengers per side with a central arm rest. Their external appearance was somewhat different from the 4-wheeled Thirds, as inset panels surrounded each quarter-light, but their appearance was otherwise broadly similar.

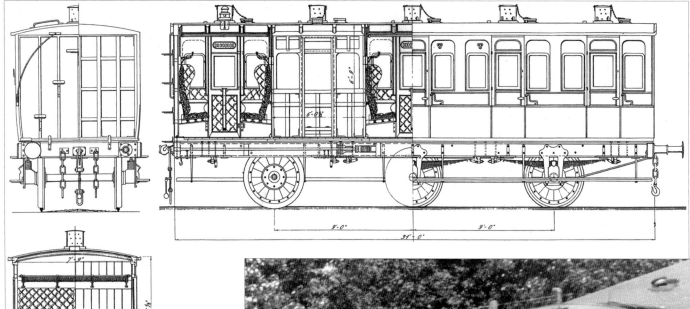

Figure 6.17
This is a redrawing of a Metropolitan original that is not suitable for reproduction. Ten of these carriages were built in 1874.

Plate 6.13
Seven Thirds with luggage compartment were built by Brown, Marshall & Co. in 1874.

Another carriage with the same dimensions but only four compartments, number 61, was also recorded in the Stock Book. The First class carriages were down-rated to Thirds in the second decade of the twentieth century. Most lasted until just after the Grouping.

A photograph of one of the 4-wheeled Luggage Thirds appears in Plate 6.13. They may have been the block of carriages numbered 69, 75, 494, 497, 499-501 in the 1874 Inventory.

Eight 4-compartment Brake Thirds were recorded in the Coaching Plant Stock Book in a block from 609-617 with a building date of December 1873. They were 31 feet long by 8 feet wide on an 18-foot wheelbase. They were renumbered into the 3xxx duplicate list in 1904. To confuse matters, a further five Brake Thirds to the same dimensions and with the same building date are also recorded. They were numbered 629, 630, 678-680. A photograph of a Brake Third is shown in Plate 6.14, along with one of the Bi-Composites described below. A Brake Third drawing, derived from another photograph, is shown in Figure 6.18.

The Coaching Plant Stock Book records three 5-compartment Composites numbered 85, 86 and 123 as built in December 1873.

These may have been the Bi-Composites. They had been down-rated to Thirds and lasted until the Grouping. A carriage matching this configuration and bearing a three-figure number is shown in Plate 6.14.

The Stock Book records 6-compartment Thirds numbered 620-627 as built in December 1873. They were 31 feet long, on a 9-foot by 9-foot wheelbase. They were allocated LM&SR numbers but did not carry them. A carriage of this type is partially visible in Plate 6.15.

The Metropolitan 5-compartment Thirds were probably built to a drawing dated 22nd February 1874[58] – a redrawn version is shown in Figure 6.19. They were 26 feet 6 inches in length and 7 feet 9 inches wide with a wheelbase of 15 feet. The compartments were 5 feet 1¾ inches between partitions. Externally they corresponded to the now established style of square cornered beading for the waist panels, and curved upper corners to the quarter-lights, upper panels and the upper corners of the ventilators.

The Coaching Plant Stock Book shows eleven survivors of a block of carriages numbered 681-700, built December 1873. These carriages did not correspond with the drawing. They had five compartments,

Plate 6.14 (*above*) and **Figure 6.18** (*below*)
The photograph was taken at Lochearnhead, soon after the opening of the line from Crieff round to Balquhidder in 1905. On the left is a Brake Third dating from 1874. The right-hand carriage may be one of three Bi-Composites built at the same time, perhaps number 123. The Brake Third drawing is derived from another photograph.

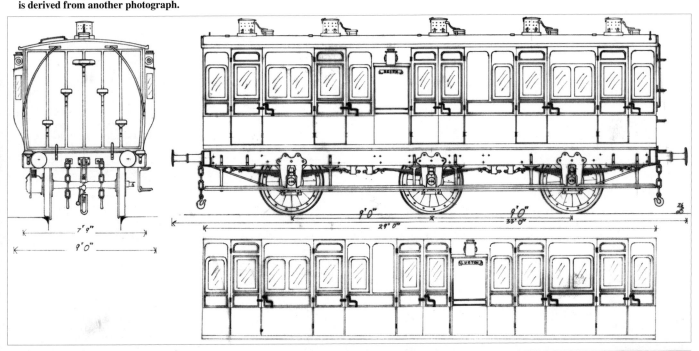

RIGHT: **Plate 6.15**
This is one of ten 6-compartment Thirds, also built by Brown, Marshall & Co. in 1873/74. Eight survived until the Grouping.

were 28 feet 6 inches long and 8 feet wide. The wheelbase was 16 feet. They lasted until just after the Grouping.

WCJS LUGGAGE VANS ACQUIRED IN 1874

In March 1873, the West Coast Conference had decided that twenty Brake Vans should be replaced by 6-wheeled vans '*with a view to better accommodation of salmon traffic.*'[59] The new 30-foot 6-wheeled '*double break vans*' entered WCJS service in April 1874. Seven vans were transferred to the CR. They appear in the rolling stock return for July 1874 with a note '*charge to capital*' but not in the capital expenditure record. The capital cost of constructing the replacement vans does appear, however.[60]

The old vans were among the earliest vehicles built for the Joint Stock and had been in service since the mid-1860s. Very little is known for certain about them. *West Coast Joint Stock*[61] plausibly suggests that they were similar to contemporary L&NWR vans, which were 21 feet long with a guard's section at one end, side lookouts and end windows. The wheelbase was 12 feet.

The vans should have appeared in the 1874 inventory, which was not completed until August. It is possible that they were the 4-wheeled vans numbered 89, 136-141, which were valued in a block at £245 each. As there is no capital expenditure return entry, this cannot be cross-checked.

There is no record of the vans in the Coaching Plant Stock Book, because they were withdrawn before it was compiled. The numbers suggested above were taken by Brake Vans built in the 1890s and early 1900s. This would imply that the original vans had a life of between thirty and forty years.

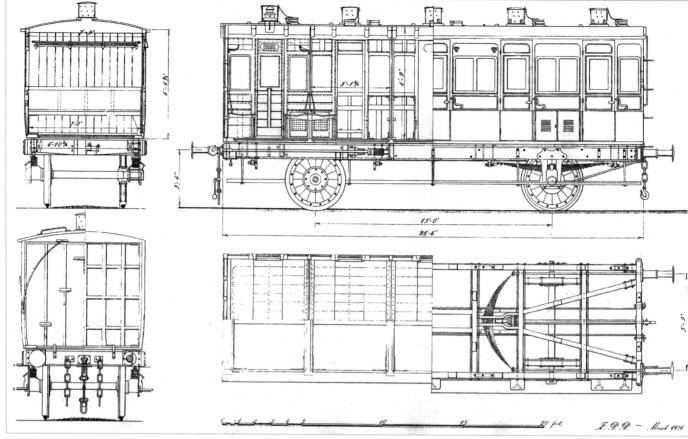

Figure 6.19
A drawing of the smaller Metropolitan 5-compartment Thirds, built in 1874.

REFERENCES

1. NRS BR/CAL/1/17 entry 1005
2. NRS BR/CAL/1/17 entry 1064
3. Birmingham City Archive ref: MS99 2301
   CRA Archive ref: 6/1/1/2/12
4. Birmingham City Archive ref: MS99 2310
5. NRS BR/CAL/1/17 entry 1179
6. Birmingham City Archive ref: MS99 2288
   CRA Archive ref: 6/1/1/2/8
7. NRS BR/CAL/23/1 (30)
8. As recorded in *The London Gazette*, 29th November 1872, p. 5887
9. NRS BR/CAL/1/18 entry 330
10. NRS BR/CAL/1/18 entry 351
11. http://midcontinent.org/rollingstock/builders/steel_carco1.htm
12. TNA MT29/29, report 504
13. NRS BR/CAL/1/17 entry 82
14. NRS BR/CAL/1/17 entry 1373
15. NRS BR/CAL/1/17 entry 1470
16. NRS BR/CAL/1/18 entry 71
17. NRS BR/CAL/1/18 entry 153
18. Birmingham City Archive ref: MS99 2314
    CRA Archive ref: 6/1/1/2/15
19. NRS BR/CAL/1/17 entry 1503
20. NRS BR/CAL/23/1 (30)
21. Birmingham City Archive ref: MS99 2284
22. NRS BR/CAL/1/18 entry 562
23. NRS BR/CAL/1/18 entry 753
24. NRS BR/CAL/1/18 entry 650
25. NRS BR/CAL/1/18 entry 535
26. NRS BR/CAL/23/1 (30)
27. NRS BR/CAL/1/18 entry 1487
28. NRS BR/CAL/23/1 (30)
29. NRS BR/CAL/23/1 (30)
30. NRS BR/CAL/1/19 entry 288
31. NRS BR/CAL/1/18 entry 1517
32. NRS BR/CAL/1/18 no entry number
33. Birmingham City Archive ref: MS99 2262
    CRA Archive ref: 6/1/1/2/4
34. NRS BR/CAL/1/19 entry 728
35. NRS BR/CAL/1/19 entry 795
36. NRS BR/CAL/23/1 (30)
37. Birmingham City Archive ref: MS99 2299
    CRA Archive ref: 6/1/1/2/
38. NRS BR/WCC/1/6 minute 995
39. NRS BR/WCC/1/6 minute 287, Appendix D
40. NRS BR/WCC/1/6 minute 1022
41. NRS BR/WCC/1/6 minute 1077
42. NRS BR/WCC/1/6 minute 1071
43. NRS BR/CAL/23/1 (29)
44. NRS BR/CAL/1/19 entry 794
45. NRS BR/CAL/1/19 entry 731
46. Supplement to *The Engineer*, 24th May 1872 and *Engineering*, 24th May, p. 344 respectively
47. NRS BR/CAL/1/19 entry 959
48. NRS BR/CAL/1/20 entry 158
49. NRS BR/CAL/1/19 entry 1562
50. NRS BR/CAL/1/20 entry 112
51. NRS BR/CAL/23/1 (29)
52. NRS BR/CAL/1/20 entry 935
53. NRS BR/CAL/1/20 entry 1696
54. NRS BR/CAL/1/21 entry 344
55. NRS BR/CAL/1/21 entry 422
56. NRS BR/CAL/1/21 entry 465
57. Birmingham City Archive ref: MS99 2277
58. Birmingham City Archive ref: MS99 2305
    CRA Archive ref: 6/1/1/2/14
59. NRS BR/WCC/1/7 minute 1223
60. NRS BR/CAL/23/2 (42)
61. *West Coast Joint Stock*, p. 54

6.3: STOCK BUILT 1875-1882

Between 1875 and 1877, not much change in rolling stock numbers occurred, according to the rolling stock returns. From 1880, a great deal of work and the available finance was devoted to fitting continuous brakes to existing stock as well as to new construction.

The rolling stock return records that six First and seventeen Second/Third class carriages were renewed in 1876. In 1877 forty-eight Second/Thirds were built, twenty-one as renewals. The lack of documentation concerning the renewals suggests that the work was done in-house.

There was more activity in the next five years, as shown in the following table. Apart from 1878, the emphasis was on the replacement of worn out plant. The figures take us up to the end of 1882. By this time, Dugald Drummond was in post, but the carriages built in that year had been authorised prior to his arrival.

CLASS		1878	1879	1880	1881	1882
First	Replace	16	4	6	20	10
	New	6	0	0	0	0
Second/Third	Replace	12	17	21	30	20
	New	30	0	0	0	0
Composite	Replace	9	9	15	4	21
	New	14	0	0	0	0
TOTALS	Replace	37	30	42	54	51
	New	50	0	0	0	0

THE END OF THE GREENOCK 'STAND-UP' CARRIAGES

At the end of 1875, Third class carriages with no seats were still to be found on the Greenock section. One Third, number 33, is identified in the 1874 Inventory as 'stand-up' with five compartments at a valuation of £130. The 'compartments' in this case were the divisions resembling cattle pens which are described in Chapter 3. There was another 5-compartment vehicle with the same number valued at £235, which suggests that the old carriages had been taken out of the official fleet.

In December 1875 the Loco & Stores Committee authorised Conner to 'take offers' for new Third class carriages for the line.[1] In January 1876 the Committee accepted a tender from Ashbury for six Thirds with six compartments at £485, and six with four compartments and a Brake at £535 'all to be delivered by 13th May next.'[2] This number of carriages would not have made much impact on the total stock required for the service.

The Coaching Plant Stock Book shows that all these carriages survived to the Grouping or just before. The Third class numbers were 556, 567, 560-563; the Brake Thirds were 565-568, 582 and 584. They were the standard 31 feet long by 8 feet wide on an 18-foot wheelbase.

In June the Traffic Committee postponed making a decision to discontinue Fourth class fares on the Greenock Section.[3] This class was originally designated for Third class carriages that were attached to goods trains. These seem to have been carriages with seats, because the January 1870 Public Timetable gives the Third class single fare of 1s between Greenock and Glasgow, Fourth class at 6d. and 'without seats' at 4d.

While there is no further reference to the matter in minutes, the January 1879 Working Timetable still showed Fourth class facilities on four passenger trains each way between Greenock and Glasgow in the early and mid-mornings, tea time and late evening.[4] The trains did not convey Fourth class passengers in the September 1879 timetable. In 1882 there was one workmen's train conveying Third class passengers only.[5]

OTHER CARRIAGES BUILT IN 1876

The Coaching Plant Stock Book records three Firsts numbered 23, 186, 188 and five Thirds numbered 570, 572, 577, 578, 583 with a build or authorisation date of September 1875. They seem to have been recorded in the period ending July 1876. The only contemporary drawing is number 1916 of November 1875, which was for 'Bearing and Buffing Springs for New Carriages,' which probably refers to these vehicles.

The Firsts were 5-compartment carriages 31 feet long. Three were down-rated to Third class, but one remained as a First until the end. The Thirds had six compartments. One Brake Composite, numbered 12, has a build date of February 1876 in the Coaching Plant Stock Book. It originally had two each First and Second class compartments and had been down-rated to a Brake Third.

The carriages were all withdrawn at the Grouping. The lack of references in minutes suggest that they were built at St. Rollox. The fact that no drawings were issued during the three years suggests that the carriages were established designs with improved suspension and buffer springing. There is no information on the remaining five Second/Third class carriages in the rolling stock return.

CARRIAGES BUILT IN THE FIRST HALF OF 1877

In February the Glasgow Committee was given authority by the Board to take tenders for:

> '12 Tri-composites
> 21 Third Class, 15 of which with Brakes, 6 lined as Seconds
> 6 Dummy Vans
> 10 Guards Brake Vans'[6]

The number of Third class carriages agreed with that of the replacements in the rolling stock return. In March the Loco & Stores Committee authorised Brittain to take tenders for carriages 'For replacement for half years ending 31st January, 31st July 1877 and 31st January 1878.'[7] The carriages comprised twenty-seven Thirds, six Seconds and three Composites.

The two sets of tenders were considered together. Brown, Marshall & Co. secured the order for the Brake Thirds at £388 each (to St. Rollox drawing 2140) and six Seconds at £429. It seems that the original tender wording meant that six carriages were to be built to a Third class design, but furnished to Second class standards. This is borne out by St. Rollox drawing 2146 issued on 19th March, which was for a '2nd class carriage, 6 compartments.' Craven Bros successfully bid £365 12s each for twenty-seven Thirds and £316 for the ten Passenger Brake Vans (drawing 2144). Metropolitan had to be content with the order for Dummy Vans at £110 10s. The Dummy Vans are discussed in Chapter 15. The Tri-Composites were not included in the list.

Fourteen of the Brake Thirds are recorded in the Coaching Plant Stock Book, numbered 736-739 and 741-750. They were withdrawn just before or just after Grouping.

The Second class carriages would have been down-rated to 6-compartment Thirds with the abolition of the Second class. Thirty-three Thirds are recorded in the Stock Book as built in April 1877. This was the original order for twenty-seven, plus the six carriages fitted out as Second class. Two blocks of numbers ran from 713-735 and 751-756, plus four random numbers. They too were withdrawn around the Grouping.

Two of the Passenger Brake Vans are identified in the Stock Book, numbered 158 and 165. They had six wheels and were withdrawn in 1923 and 1918 respectively. Other vans in the block of numbers from 156 to 165 have no details recorded, or were replaced by other vans. Most of the replacements date from World War I or afterwards, except 162, an 1897 van, and 164, built in 1910. These two were probably accident replacements.

In May the Loco & Stores Committee reiterated the need for the Tri-Composites and added twelve First class carriages. Brittain was authorised to take tenders.[8] Brown, Marshall & Co. secured the order for the Firsts at £562 and Metropolitan the Tri-Composites at £522 5s.[9] St. Rollox drawings were issued for a 4-compartment First (number 2166) and a Composite with two First, one Second and two Third class compartments (number 2165). Neither has survived, but a poor quality Metropolitan drawing for the Tri-Composite is shown in Figure 6.20.[10] A photograph of a carriage from a later order is shown in Plate 6.16.

Two Firsts, numbered 14 and 16, were recorded as built in 1877 by Brown, Marshall & Co. in the Coaching Plant Stock Book. They had four compartments with thirty-two seats. No dimensions were recorded. They were withdrawn at the Grouping. One may appear in Plate 6.17, but the two digit number cannot be distinguished.

The Tri-Composites were 32 feet long and 8 feet wide. The 6-wheeled underframe had a 20-foot wheelbase and ran on 4-foot diameter Mansell wheels. They were the first examples of a body style which lasted until Dugald Drummond's arrival. The two Third class compartments, 5 feet 6 inches between partitions, were at the ends of the carriage. They were fitted with padded seats, but still lacked padded backs.

Next to one of the Third class compartments was the Second class. It was 6 feet between partitions and had fully cushioned and padded seats with arm rests at each end, but none centrally, and simple wooden panelling. The two First class compartments were 7 feet between partitions and had fully padded seats, divided into three by padded arm rests, as well as padded compartment sides.

For the first time on a CR carriage of this class no attempt was made to imitate stagecoach styling. They retained beaded waist panels and the ends of the carriages were flat. The top corners of the quarter-lights were still curved, but the bottom corners were square. The width of the doors was increased to 2 feet 2 inches and the tops of the door ventilators were also given curved corners. This feature was repeated in the tops of the inset upper panels, which extended almost to the full height of the side.

All the Tri-Composites survived until the Grouping, with the Second class compartment down-rated in the 1890s. Half had been down-rated to all Thirds before World War I.

At the same meeting, Cravens' tender for two Brake Composites at £525 was accepted and also the Lancaster Carriage & Wagon Co.'s offer to supply six Second class carriages at £440. The four suppliers had to '*deliver by 15th April 1878 under penalty.*'

The Brake Composites were numbered 75 and 77 in the Stock Book. They had two First and two Third class compartments and survived until just after the Grouping. They had been built to St. Rollox drawing 2184. The Seconds were assimilated into Third class and cannot be identified.

In June, James Smithells reported to the Board on:

'*the proposed purchase from Ashbury Coy of Carriages constructed for the new Bothwell Railway, recommended by the Traffic Committee.*'

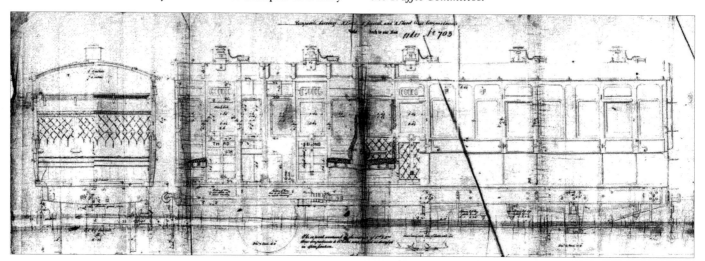

Figure 6.20
Metropolitan drawing 2285 is the contractor's version of St. Rollox drawing 2165, which has not survived. The title reads '*Composite Carriage two First, 1 Second 2 and 2 Third Class Compartments.*' The script below the underframe reads '*The exposed woodwork of 1st and 2nd class compartments to be lined and finished as defined in specification.*' In the two years between 1877 and 1879 thirty-four carriages were built to this design.

Plate 6.16
One of the last order for these Tri-Composites, built in 1879 by Brown, Marshall & Co. The destination board reads '*Glasgow and Motherwell.*' Another oil-lit example, painted white, is shown in Chapter 2, Plate 2.22.

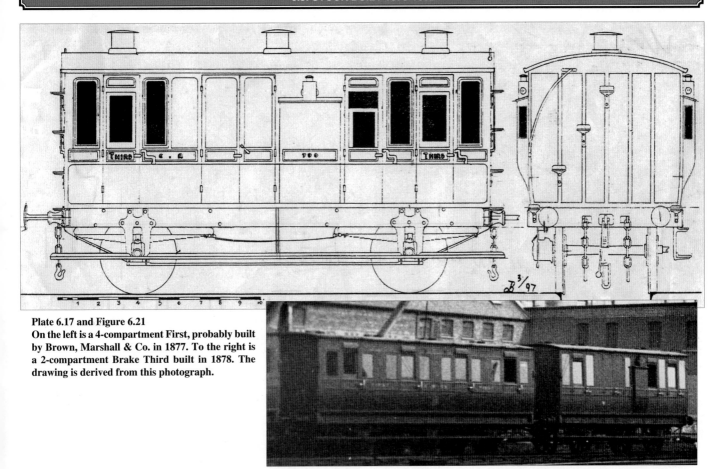

Plate 6.17 and Figure 6.21
On the left is a 4-compartment First, probably built by Brown, Marshall & Co. in 1877. To the right is a 2-compartment Brake Third built in 1878. The drawing is derived from this photograph.

The Board agreed to '*Offer £9,000 for the lot.*'[11] There is no capital expenditure entry that fits these carriages and no entry in the rolling stock returns which might refer to the relatively large number of vehicles that the sum of money implies. On the available evidence the transaction was not completed.

CARRIAGES BUILT IN THE SECOND HALF OF 1877

In early September the Loco & Stores Committee ordered the letting of tenders for thirty-six carriages, comprising:

'*10 First Class, 5 Compartment accommodate 40 people
8 Third Class, 6 Compartment accommodate 60 people
8 Third Class, 4 Compartment & Brake, 40 people
10 Second Class, 6 Compartment, 60 people*'[12]

St. Rollox issued drawings as part of the tender documentation described in the register as follows – '*2253 3rd with brake, 2256 3rd, 6 compt, 2258 2nd 6 compt and 2260 1st 5 compt.*' Brown, Marshall & Co. secured the contract at the following prices – £622 (Firsts), £399 (Seconds), £377 (Brake Thirds) and £362 (Thirds).[13]

The ten First class carriages survived until Grouping, all but two down-rated to Third class during World War I. Their original numbers were 21, 29, 31, 37, 128, 144, 149, 177, 184, 185.

The down-rated Second class carriages cannot be positively identified among the Thirds, but a block of ten carriages numbered 757-766 was dated 10/77 in the Coaching Plant Stock Book, along with eight others numbered 280, 420, 421, 432, 445, 447, 775 and 776. The Brake Thirds were numbered 767-774. They all lasted until the Grouping.

Also dated 10/77 was a block of 5-compartment Thirds numbered 777-782. There is no record of an order for these six carriages, so one can only assume that they were built at St. Rollox.

CARRIAGES BUILT IN 1878 AND 1879

The last carriages to be considered in 1877 for construction in the following year were intended for the Callander & Oban Railway, which was already under construction. The Caledonian was to operate the line for a percentage of the profits. The Traffic Committee reported:

'*The following rolling stock is required
2 Luggage Vans
8 First Class Carriages
7 Third Class Carriages
3 Third Class Carriages with Brakes. Estimated cost £7,775.
Ask for a drawing of proposed carriages.*'[14]

In January 1878 St. Rollox drawings 2319-2322 were issued for the C&O carriages and considered by the Traffic Committee at two meetings.[15] Drawing 2310 was also produced for a '*saloon carriage and Third Class carriage*' for the line.

In February the Committee decided to take tenders.[16] There was a change of plan from the original 1877 meeting, because it was unlikely that the line would be fully open for some time. In March the Lancaster Carriage & Wagon Co. successfully bid for:

'*7 Second and Third Class Composites at £319
3 Third Class Brake Carriages at £302
2 Passenger Brake Vans at £270
Delivery to be completed by end of June.*'[17]

The same meeting accepted Cravens' bid to supply '*8 First Class and saloon carriages at £391 each.*' They were to be delivered by 30th July.

The picture now becomes confused. The Coaching Plant Stock

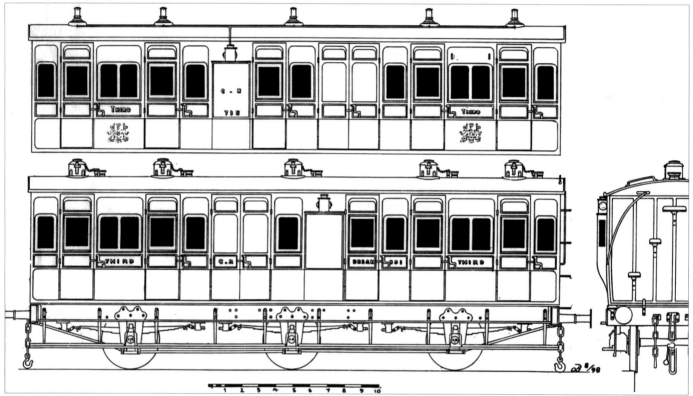

Plate 6.18 and Figure 6.22
Cravens of Sheffield built this carriage in 1880. Note the archaic spelling at this late date. It was not usual to identify the guard's compartment. The spoked wheels are 3 feet 6 inches diameter. Third class compartments now had padding up to head height. The lining on the underframe does not necessarily prove that all CR carriages were so treated. It may have been applied for the publicity photograph. The drawing shows both sides of the Brake Third. The top elevation is derived from Plate 6.14. The bottom is from the Cravens official photograph.

Book records nine carriages with a building or authorisation date of March 1878. They are all 4-wheeled Thirds, but no dimensions are given. Numbers 783-789 were 4-compartment Thirds, and 790, 791 were Brake Thirds with two compartments and a central guard's/luggage section. One of the Brake Thirds is shown in Plate 6.17 and a drawing derived from it is Figure 6.21. According to the Coaching Plant Stock Book, number 793 was upgraded to a Composite and renumbered 149 for use on the Leadhills Branch, which opened in 1901. The date of the conversion was not recorded.

Cravens delivered two Family and two Invalid carriages which are discussed in Chapter 13.2. There is no record of First class carriages in the capital expenditure or rolling stock returns.

In late July the whole of the C&O plant requirement was up for review. A Traffic Committee's minute recorded:

'Engines and other Rolling Stock required for the Callander & Oban Railway on its opening throughout in 1880.
Report recommendations to next meeting.'[18]

There is no record of the report and its recommendations in the minutes. In the event, the C&O had to make do with whatever passenger stock the Caledonian felt it could spare until the construction of new sets of carriages for the line in 1889. These designs are described in Chapter 7.4.

Returning to January 1879, Brown, Marshall & Co. secured an order for eight Composites at £459 and sixteen Brake Thirds at £356. The Loco & Stores Committee minute was headed *'Carriage Stock for Replacement.'*[19]

All the carriages survived until the Grouping. According to St. Rollox drawing 2447 the Composites originally had two First, one Second and two Third class compartments. They were 32 feet long and the wheelbase was 20 feet according to the Stock Book. The first two and the last were down-rated to Third class; the rest remained as First/Third Composites.

The Brake Thirds' numbers were 248, 277, 430, 433, 448, 450, 658, 704 and 793-799. They were built to drawing 2436 and were the standard 31 feet long.

Two other Brake Thirds, numbered 51 and 64, had 23-foot total wheelbases and were half a ton heavier. The length was not recorded. They too were withdrawn just after the Grouping. Nothing more is known about these two carriages.

In July 1879 Brittain had written to the CR Board *'in relation to the replacement of certain old Carriages by vehicles of modern construction.'* The Board agreed to take tenders.[20]

Plate 6.19 and Figure 6.23
Three Bi-Composites were originally built with central luggage lockers in 1881. They were converted to Brake Composites by the addition of a handbrake and lookouts. Number 80 was photographed in 1921, when it was spare carriage on the Peebles Branch.

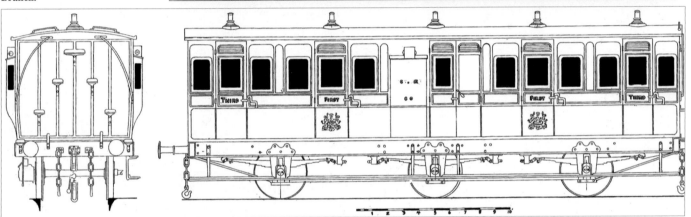

Brown, Marshall & Co. had clearly become preferred supplier of carriages at the expense of Metropolitan, as the company secured another order for replacement stock in September. This time the order was for fifteen Tri-Composites at £440 each, plus five Firsts at £545.[21] Presumably drawing 2447 was used again for the Tri-Composites.

Number 159 from this order can be seen in Plate 6.16. Another, number 189, is shown in Chapter 2, Plate 2.22. The fact that these carriages match drawing 2165 suggests that St. Rollox drawings 2447 and 2165 were identical. With this order, therefore, thirty-four of these Tri-Composites were built, as shown in the table below.

Date	Numbers	Total
05/1877	5, 21, 23, 55, 61, 177-180, 182, 183	11
01/1879	4, 36, 62, 79, 83, 84, 87, 156	8
09/1879	60, 78, 157-159, 184-193	15

Number 184 of the last order was withdrawn in 1917. The rest survived until Grouping, by which time nine had been down-rated to Thirds.

The Firsts were built to St. Rollox drawing 2606. They can be identified in the Coaching Plant Stock Book – numbers 24, 26, 30, 32 and 33. They remained as Firsts until withdrawal at the Grouping, except for numbers 30 and 32.

The Coaching Plant Stock Book also records the construction of nine Thirds and nine Brake Thirds for 10/79. The Thirds were numbered 564, 661, 705, 708, 712, 800-803. The Brakes were numbered 225, 229, 235, 239, 243, 284, 289, 430 and 450. Lack of any documentation suggests that they were built at St. Rollox.

CARRIAGES AUTHORISED FOR THE FIRST HALF OF 1881

In October 1880 the Traffic Committee reported that '*sixty vehicles are required for year ending 31st July 1881*' and agreed to take tenders.[22] This time, no St. Rollox drawings were issued. Cravens secured orders from the Glasgow Committee for fifteen each Thirds and Brake Thirds at £326 and £340 each respectively. Brown, Marshall & Co. contracted to build twenty Firsts at £520 and three Composites at £430. Oldbury was to build seven Passenger Brake Vans for £295 each.[23]

The entries for these carriages in the Coaching Plant Stock Book are all dated 11/80, which is when the tenders were accepted. Thirteen of the Thirds and twelve Brake Thirds can be identified. The Thirds were numbered 84, 88, 104, 110, 111, 190, 194, 198, 233, 247, 249, 256 and 263. The Brakes were numbered 271, 278, 286, 291, 394, 399, 400, 402, 404, 407, 411, 413. An official photograph of number 291 appears as Plate 6.18 and a drawing derived from it as Figure 6.22. Another example appears in Plate 6.14.

The Brown, Marshall & Co. five compartment Firsts were numbered 27, 28, 50, 51, 53, 56, 58, 60, 62, 66, 71, 140, 142, 190-195, 197. Only seven were down-rated to Third class after World War I.

The three Bi-Composites originally had luggage lockers flanked by two First class compartments with two Thirds at the ends. They were subsequently converted to Brake Composites. Apart from the addition of brake gear, they also received lookouts when converted. They were numbered 35, 80 and 194. A drawing and photograph of number 80 appear in Figure 6.23 and Plate 6.19.

The 4-wheeled Passenger Brake Vans cannot be identified. They must have been among the large number of vans at the end of the Coaching Plant Stock Book list that cannot be traced.

CARRIAGES BUILT IN 1882

A further large requirement for replacement carriages occurred in the first half of 1882. The Loco & Stores Committee noted Brittain's letter to James Smithells that *'60 vehicles are required'* and agreed to take tenders.[24] In November 1881 Brittain was ordered to *'prepare plans and ask for tenders,'*[25] but there is no register record of any such drawings. Perhaps existing drawings were re-used.

The Loco & Stores Committee:

'accepted as under
Midland Coy. 20 Composites
Birmingham Coy. 10 First Class
Birmingham Coy. 10 Third Class (6 Compartment)
Birmingham Coy. 10 Third (4 Compart.+ Luggage + Brake)
Railway Coy. Oldbury 10 Passenger Brake Vans.
All delivered by 1st May 1882'[26]

This time the Stock Book recorded the date of delivery for the order. Eighteen of the Composites were numbered in a block starting at 195 and ending at 213. Number 197 was missing, as was 214. They had two First and three Third class compartments, but they were originally Tri-Composites. Delivery dates ranged from May until July. Seven are recorded in the Stock Book with dual brakes, which were probably fitted retrospectively – it would most likely have been mentioned in the minute if they had been fitted when new. An official photograph of number 205 appears as Plate 6.20.

Nine First class carriages with five compartments were numbered 35, 57, 123, 131, 139 and 145-148. Four were down-rated after the war. Nine each of the Third class carriages can be identified. The 6-compartment Thirds were 12-15, 47, 79, 86, 90 and 97. The Brake Thirds were 415, 417, 418, 423, 428, 440, 441, 444 and 576. A photograph of First 147 and an unidentified Third or Brake Third is shown in Plate 6.21. There is no traceable record of the Passenger Brake Vans.

ABOVE: Plate 6.20
Tri-Composite 205 was one of twenty built by the Midland RC&W in early 1882, just before Drummond's arrival. All but two survived to be recorded in the Coaching Plant Stock Book.

LEFT: Plate 6.21
First 147, furthest away from the camera, was one of ten built by Birmingham RC&W in 1882. It is coupled to an unidentified gas-lit Third, which has spoked wheels. The picture was taken at Gourock.

REFERENCES

1. NRS BR/CAL/1/22 entry 1615
2. NRS BR/CAL/1/22 entry 1784
3. NRS BR/CAL/1/23 entry 132
4. NRS BR/TT/S/54/6
5. NRS BR/TT/S/54/9
6. NRS BR/CAL/1/23 entry 955
7. NRS BR/CAL/1/23 entry 1136
8. NRS BR/CAL/1/23 entry 1261
9. NRS BR/CAL/1/23 entry 1531
10. Birmingham City Archive ref: MS99 2285 CRA Archive ref: 6/1/1/2/7
11. NRS BR/CAL/1/23 entry 1464
12. NRS BR/CAL/1/23 entry 1727
13. NRS BR/CAL/1/23 entry 1961
14. NRS BR/CAL/1/24 entry 56
15. NRS BR/CAL/1/24 entries 197 and 253
16. NRS BR/CAL/1/24 entry 351
17. NRS BR/CAL/1/24 entry 456
18. NRS BR/CAL/1/25 entry 247
19. NRS BR/CAL/1/24 entry 1530
20. NRS BR/CAL/1/25 entry 228
21. NRS BR/CAL/1/25 entry 485
22. NRS BR/CAL/1/25 entry 1842
23. NRS BR/CAL/1/26 entry 45
24. NRS BR/CAL/1/26 entry 1658
25. NRS BR/CAL/1/26 entry 1677
26. NRS BR/CAL/1/27 entry 40

CHAPTER 7
GENERAL SERVICE STOCK 1882-1895

7.1: FOUR-WHEELED CARRIAGES

Like his predecessor Benjamin Conner, Brittain's last year in service was blighted by bad health. In April 1882 he wrote to the Board saying that he was *'confined to the house through illness.'*[1] His illness was serious enough for the Board to take immediate action. A fortnight later the Board received a Committee report,

> *'that in consequence of the readjustment of Mr Brittain's department from the increase of the work, they had to recommend the appointment of a Locomotive Superintendent. Mr Brittain's salary in the meantime to remain as at present and his duties for the future to be hereafter adjusted.'*[2]

In late June the Board reported:

> *'the engagement of Mr Dugald Drummond as Locomotive Superintendent of the Company at a salary at the rate of £1,700 a year.'*[3]

The salary was £1,000 more than that offered to Brittain at his appointment, proof of the Caledonian's determination to get their man. Probably, too, the likelihood that his departure would weaken the North British was a consideration. Brittain formally retired in November.

The arrival of Dugald Drummond at St. Rollox saw a radical change in the design of Caledonian carriages. He also brought from the North British Railway his experience of reducing costs and increasing operational efficiency through standardisation of designs and dimensions.

Although Drummond did not use the roof profile that he adopted on the NBR, he used other aspects of his designs. The Caledonian 4- and 6-wheeled carriages were directly copied from North British vehicles, including the three-layered panelling. Drummond's NBR designs, which first appeared in 1875, are described and drawn in *North British Coaches.*[4]

BUILDING AND WITHDRAWALS

The Drummond regime was characterised by modernising rather than expanding the carriage fleet, as the aggregated rolling stock returns for the periods ending January 1883 to July 1890 show. The only extra carriages were order H6 for ten Brake Thirds to Diagram 3.

Type	Worn Out	Replaced	Added
First	92	92	
Third	320	320	10
Composite/Saloon	14	14	
Total	426	426	10

PASSENGER STOCK

Drummond's 4-wheeled carriages had 28-foot 6-inch by 8 foot wide bodies on a wheelbase of 16 feet. The wood solebars were 'flitched' with a ¼-inch iron plate. There is no record of a tender process, which suggests that all the carriages were built at St. Rollox.

However, in the transcription of the Coaching Plant Stock Book, only six of the twenty-four Firsts built in 1886 and 1887 had an order number that could be traced, and there is a shortfall of ten in the Brake Third total.

The Diagram 1 First class carriages were built to drawing 3879[5] produced in January 1884. The eight-seat compartments were 6 feet 11½ inches wide and fitted with a central armrest – see Figure 7.1.

Comparing the running numbers with the 1874 inventory suggests that some of these carriages replaced Firsts which had come into the CR fleet from the Scottish North Eastern in 1867. The carriages built in 1886 were originally numbered 286-291 and 298-303. The first batch of numbers was taken by 45-foot carriages built in 1898, the second by 48-foot carriages built two years later.

The Third class carriages (Diagram 2) were built to drawing 3849[6] which was made earlier in January 1884. Compartments to seat ten people were 5 feet 6⅝ inches wide. With four exceptions, seats were upholstered on both squab and back as shown in the Diagram Book – see Figure 7.2. Some of those built in 1886 and 1887 were given numbers 914-917 and 920-929. They were renumbered when 45-foot carriages were built in 1894 and 1895.

For the Diagram 3 Brake Thirds, a guard's and luggage compartment replaced two passenger compartments at one end of the Third class

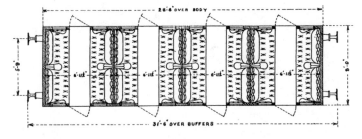

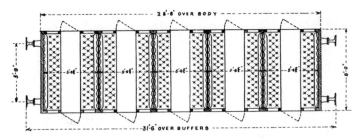

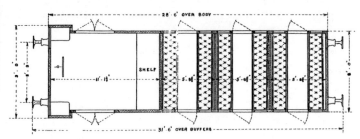

Figures 7.1-7.3
These plans, taken from the Large Carriage Diagram Book, pages 1-3, show the internal layout of the 28-foot 6-inch carriages – First, Third and Brake Third respectively.

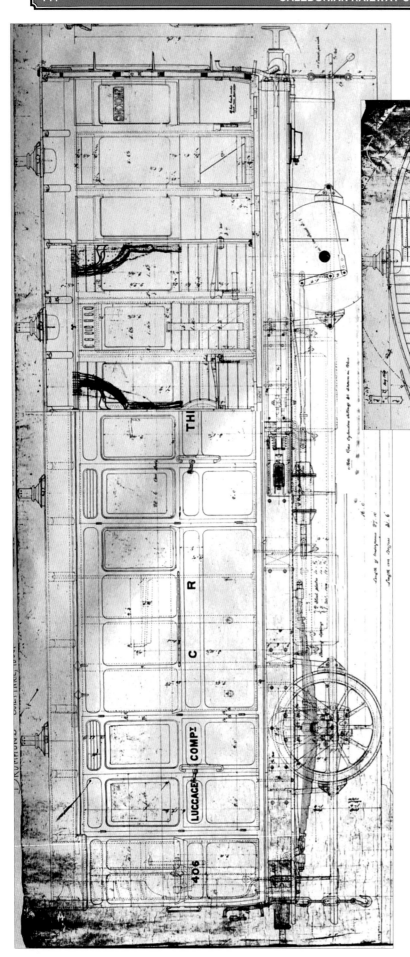

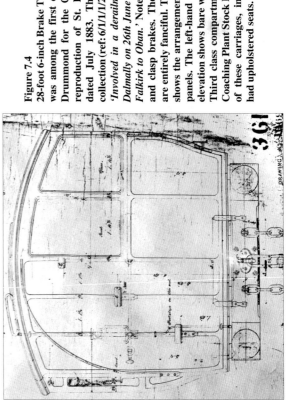

Figure 7.4

28-foot 6-inch Brake Third 406, built in 1884, was among the first carriages designed by Drummond for the Caledonian. This is a reproduction of St. Rollox drawing 3614, dated July 1883. The copy in the CRA collection (ref: 6/1/1/1/2A and 2B) is annotated '*Involved in a derailment at Succoth, near Dalmally on 26th June 1886 – excursion from Falkirk to Oban.*' Note the 12-spoked wheels and clasp brakes. The sketched-in curtains are entirely fanciful. The outer end elevation shows the arrangement of glass in the outer panels. The left-hand half of the inside end elevation shows bare wood furnishings in the Third class compartment. According to the Coaching Plant Stock Book the vast majority of these carriages, including number 406, had upholstered seats.

design – see Figure 7.3. Lookouts were fitted at the extreme end, with a pair of doors immediately inboard. This arrangement is shown in Figure 7.4, which is a reproduction of St. Rollox drawing 3614 dating from July 1883.[7] It depicts carriage number 406, which, according to the Coaching Plant Stock Book, was built in 1884.

The ten new carriages to order H6, authorised on the capital account in April 1885,[8] cost £250 each.[9] The nineteen carriages built to orders H10 and H15 in 1886/87 were originally given numbers in the range 886-913. The first six were renumbered to make way for 35-foot 6½ inch Thirds in 1891. The rest were renumbered to make way for 45-foot carriages in 1893-94.

Only a few of the Thirds and Brake Thirds took the numbers of carriages in the 1874 inventory, which suggests that they replaced vehicles that had been scrapped before 1874. The renumbered carriages also took numbers which did not appear in 1874.

The building dates of the carriages were as follows:

Year	First	Third	Brake Third
1884	8	4	21
1885	5	4	12
1886	12	10	29
1887	8	7	8
Total	33	25	70

The order list records that six more Thirds were built under Hugh Smellie's tenure in the half year ending January 1891, to order H56, making 134 carriages in total.

The carriages lasted until the early years of the Grouping. They were all gas-lit. The Firsts and Thirds are recorded in the Coaching Plant Stock Book as painted brown, but almost half (thirty-four out of seventy) of the Brake Thirds were painted in full passenger livery.

SEMI-PERMANENT COUPLINGS AND CENTRE BUFFERS

Although in both diagram books the carriages are fitted with conventional buffers, drawings 3849 (Third) and 3879 (First) show a centre buffer and semi-permanent coupling at both ends. The gap between carriages was 1 foot 6¾ inches between headstocks, compared with 3 feet in the diagrams – see Figure 7.5.

The drawing for the Brake Third (St. Rollox 3614, mentioned earlier) shows conventional buffers at both ends. To work with a rake with centre buffers, some Brake Thirds had centre buffers at the inner end as annotated on drawing 3879. Presumably those fitted with centre buffers were among the carriages that were painted all-over brown.

According to *The Cathcart Circle*,[10] three sets of close-coupled stock provided the service in 1893, composed of three Firsts and three Thirds, plus two Brake Thirds. This suggests that at least

Plate 7.1
Part of a rake of Cathcart Circle carriages sits in Glasgow Central. Nearest the camera is a Diagram 3 Brake Third, followed by two Diagram 2 Thirds.

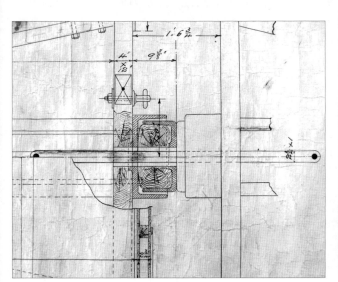

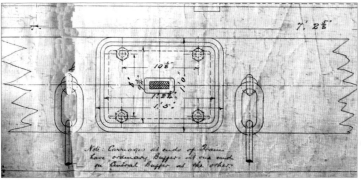

LEFT AND BELOW: Figure 7.5
The plan view (*left*), taken from drawing 3879, shows the centre buffer and close coupling arrangement. The connection between the carriages was a 2½ inch by 1 inch flat bar, pivoted at 4-foot 10¾-inch centres. The coupling was attached to a sprung drawbar on each carriage. The centre buffer consisted of two pieces of U-shaped iron, one fitting inside the other, with a wood block rubbing surface on the inner. The end elevation is shown below.

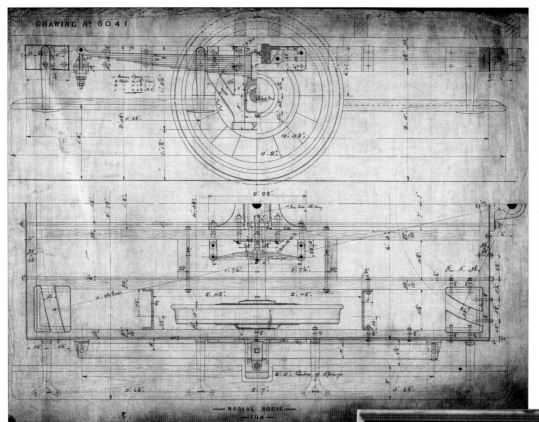

Figure 7.6
The last drawing for the 4-wheeled carriages shows the 'radial bogie' that was applied to one of the Cathcart Circle set trains. The original is a tinted drawing, with lines in coloured inks, hence the poor quality reproduction. The pivot for the bogie is at the right-hand end of the plan view. The bogie ran on two guides, as indicated by the radius measurements. The radial movement was dampened by the springs seen at the top of the view. This was a more complicated arrangement than the L&NWR version applied to contemporary West Coast Joint Stock carriages; these had two rigid inner axles which gave the necessary stability.

nine each First and Third, plus six Brakes, must have been semi-permanently coupled. Miller's brief history of CR carriages states that 'close coupled first, third and brake thirds, with centre buffer, [were] introduced on Cathcart circle' in 1884.

Some morning rush-hour trains were strengthened with spare carriages. The strengthening stock must also have had centre buffers, as they would have been marshalled inside the Brake Thirds. The Coaching Plant Stock Book does not record which carriages were fitted with centre couplings.

Radial Axles

It seems that the close-coupled Cathcart carriages as originally constructed gave trouble on curves. In May/June 1889 a series of drawings appeared[11] for 'bogie details for 4-wheeled carriage.' Of these, drawing 6041[12] has survived; part of it is reproduced here as Figure 7.6. Later drawings were for a 'radial casting and block for 4-wheel carriage,' 'Detail for 4-wheeled carriages with radial ends' and finally in November a 'General Arrangement of 4-wheel carriage with Radial Bogie.'[13] None of these drawings has survived.

The order list suggests that the modification was implemented on at least one train. Order H44 was probably executed in the half year ending July 1890, for eight unspecified vehicles. It was annotated 'Cathcart carriages converted into bogies.' There is no mention of the work in the minutes.

It is possible that all the carriages were modified. Such alterations were often undertaken without an order number. It is equally possible

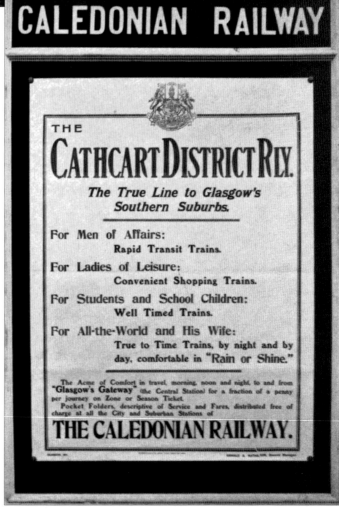

CALEDONIAN RAILWAY

THE
CATHCART DISTRICT RLY.
The True Line to Glasgow's
Southern Suburbs.

For Men of Affairs:
    Rapid Transit Trains.

For Ladies of Leisure:
    Convenient Shopping Trains.

For Students and School Children:
    Well Timed Trains.

For All-the-World and His Wife:
    True to Time Trains, by night and by
    day, comfortable in "Rain or Shine."

The Acme of Comfort in travel, morning, noon and night, to and from "Glasgow's Gateway" (the Central Station) for a fraction of a penny per journey on Zone or Season Ticket.
Pocket Folders, descriptive of Service and Fares, distributed free of charge at all the City and Suburban Stations of

THE CALEDONIAN RAILWAY.

RIGHT: Plate 7.2
A poster dating from 1914, extolling the Cathcart Circle service. The 'Acme of Comfort in Travel' was pushing it a bit unless you travelled First class. 'Comfortable in rain or shine' is a dig at the competition; Glasgow's trams at the time had an open upper deck.

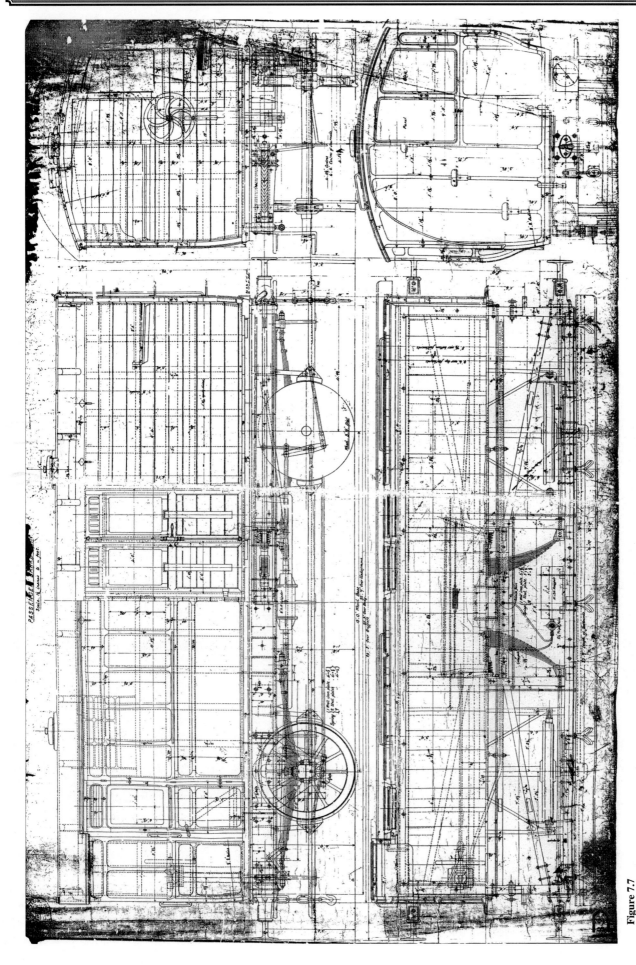

Figure 7.7
This shows the companion 4-wheeled Diagram 4 Passenger Brake Van, St. Rollox drawing 3392. Like the Brake Third, it is fitted with 12-spoked wheels. Most of these vans were oil-lit, like this example. The Brake end profile is the same as the Brake Third's. On the end elevation, the inner aperture is annotated 'panel', and the outer, 'glass'. The drawing is particularly useful for its depiction of the Westinghouse brake arrangement. The air reservoir and triple valve are located at the bottom centre of the drawing with the actuating cylinder on the longitudinal centre line.

that only one rake was modified or that the modified carriages were converted back to their original state. There is no mention of any modified carriages in the Coaching Plant Stock Book.

PASSENGER BRAKE VANS

The design of the Diagram 4 Brake Vans was also imported from the North British.[14] They were 23 feet 3 inches long by 8 feet wide on a 13-foot wheelbase, and were in fact the pioneers of the Drummond body design on the Caledonian. The guard's area and doors were at one end, plus double doors on each side. The lookouts projected 6 inches. They were built to St. Rollox drawing 3329[15] dated 24th November 1882 – see Figure 7.7.

Seventeen entered service in 1883 and 1884. They were intended to work with the 35-foot 6½-inch stock that was under construction at the same time, as very few 6-wheeled carriages with a Brake Van section were built before 1891. As further evidence, well over half the 28-foot passenger stock was built with guard's and luggage accommodation.

The Birmingham R&CW built the first five Brake Vans as part of a contract awarded in January 1883.[16] The Coaching Plant Stock Book records these as numbered 21, 48, 55, 60 and 61. The rest were presumably built at St. Rollox during the following year because there is no record of a tender process. The H order system was not established until 1885, making a definitive statement impossible. All the numbers allocated to these vans were carried by similar vans in the 1874 Inventory.

According to the drawing they had oil lamps, but the Stock Book records that the five contractor-built vans were gas-lit. They were all fitted with the Westinghouse brake only. Apart from numbers 49, 60 and 61 they were eventually repainted in full passenger livery. The vans were withdrawn between 1924 and 1927.

There is also an unnumbered diagram on page 4 of the Large Diagram Book for a 24-foot van, 8 feet 6 inches wide, with the same layout and sparred flooring. The design does not appear in the Small Diagram Book and no such vehicle is recorded in the Coaching Plant Stock Book.

REFERENCES

1. NRS BR/CAL/1/27 entry 530
2. NRS BR/CAL/1/27 entry 662
3. NRS BR/CAL/1/27 entry 858
4. *North British Coaches*, pp. 40-42 (4-wheeled) and pp. 43-44 (6-wheeled)
5. NRM 7482/C (on two sheets) RHP 70019
6. NRM 7483/C (on two sheets) RHP 70018
7. NRM 7479/C RHP 70002
8. NRS BR/CAL/1/29 entry 1207
9. NRS BR/CAL/1/29 entry 1212
10. *The Cathcart Circle*, Appendix 11
11. St. Rollox 6041, 6043, 6052, 6053 and 6061
12. RHP 68464
13. St. Rollox 6083, 6114 and 6142 respectively
14. *North British Coaches*, drawing 29
15. NRM 7474/C RHP 70005
16. NRS BR/CAL/1/27 entry 1473

Plate 7.3
A photograph taken in the aftermath of the Elliot Junction accident in December 1906, from Niall Ferguson's collection. He wrote an article on the accident in *British Railway Journal*, issue 44. It shows the remains of Third class carriage 125 or 350, with the underframe of Brake Third 343 behind it. The standard CR publicity photographs are visible, with that of the Central Hotel on the left. The official report on the accident enquiry is on the Railways Archive website: http://www.railwaysarchive.co.uk/documents/BoT_Elliot1906.pdf.

7.2: SIX-WHEELED DESIGNS

Drummond introduced several 6-wheeled designs with 35-foot underframes in parallel with the 4-wheelers described in the previous section. They were also 8 feet wide, and the wheelbase was 23 feet. Apart from the roof profile they were almost identical to the NBR design, but the latter had 4-foot diameter wheels; those on the Caledonian carriages were 3 feet 6 inches. Two Saloons to the same general design were also built, which are described and illustrated in Chapter 13.3.

FIRST CLASS CARRIAGES

The Diagram 8 5-compartment First had thirty seats according to the Diagram Book, which shows an arm rest between each seat (see Figure 7.8), as does the St. Rollox drawing. The Coaching Plant Stock Book records most with forty seats, which suggests that the arm rests were removed at some point. Thirty-five were built in 1883-84 to drawing 3268, dated 7th October 1882.[1]

With a few exceptions they took numbers which had been carried by 3- and 4-compartment carriages, according to the 1874 Inventory. Two were originally numbered 263 and 264. They were renumbered in 1897 to make way for two 45-foot carriages, which suggests that old carriages 79 and 80 whose numbers they eventually took survived until then.

Eight were down-rated to Diagram 9 Composites in 1910 and 1911 and are described in Chapter 9.4. The carriages were withdrawn 1924-29. By then, all except two had white upper panels.

THIRD CLASS CARRIAGES

The Diagram 14 6-compartment Thirds (Figure 7.9) seated sixty people. Two St. Rollox drawings were produced, in August 1882 (3203) and October (3285). The second drawing has survived.[2] A total of 194 of these carriages were built between 1883 and 1888. Lambie built a further fourteen in 1892.

Only a few of the numbers carried by these carriages correspond with stock in the 1874 Inventory which they might have replaced. Numbers 125 and 350 were 'completely destroyed' in the Elliot Junction accident on 28th December 1906 – see Plate 7.3. Three others involved in the accident were repaired. Six were upgraded to Brake Composites, Diagram 10A in 1910. The reclassification is described in Chapter 9.4.

CONTRACTOR-BUILT CARRIAGES

Some early orders for both the above designs were built by contractors. In late November 1882, the Loco & Stores Committee noted Drummond's recommendation:

'that certain numbers of Goods Engines, Passenger Engines, Carriages and Brake Vans be built by Contract to Revenue Account.'[3]

A week later, Drummond attended a Board Meeting 'with plans of proposed carriages.' He was authorised by a minute headed 'Carriages in Replacement' to seek tenders for:

'15 First Class, 35 feet 6 inches, 5 compartments, 6 wheel
40 Third Class, 35 feet 6 inches, 6 compartments, 6 wheel
5 Brake Vans, 4 wheel
All charged to Revenue'[4]

In the second week of January 1883, contracts were awarded to Brown, Marshall & Co. for the Third class carriages and to the Birmingham RC&W Co. for the remainder.[5] The carriages are not recorded as contractor-built in the Coaching Plant Stock Book.

Brown, Marshall & Co.'s drawing number 7871 for the Third class carriages, bearing the title 'built for the Caledonian Railway,' is in the NRM St. Rollox list and in the CRA collection.[6] It is dated 30th January 1884, so it must have been used as a supporting document in a subsequent tender for another railway – no carriages were built by contractors during the Drummond regime from 1884 onwards. St. Rollox drawing 3861 for a 'Birmingham Railway Carriage,' which probably refers to the second part of the order, is dated 29th January 1884. It has not survived.

Towards the end of May 1883 the Traffic Committee's authority was requested 'for sixty new Carriages to replace a similar number which will wear out during the half year ending 31st July 1884.' The request was referred to the Stores Committee 'to take tenders and to report to the Board as to the proportions of the various classes.'[7]

It was agreed that twenty each Firsts, Thirds and Brake Thirds should be ordered. In July specifications were sent to nine potential suppliers.[8] Ashbury was awarded the contract for the Thirds and Brake Thirds at £473 and £360 each respectively. One

Figures 7.8 and 7.9
The internal layouts of the Diagram 8 First (top) and Diagram 14 Third class 6-wheeled carriages. It seems that the two arm rests each side in the First class carriage were replaced by one that was centrally located. This allowed four people to sit each side rather than three.

Plate 7.4
Diagram 14 Third class carriage 137 was built in 1884, probably by Ashbury. The lettering elements were symmetrically disposed with 'THIRD' at either end and the company ownership and running number adjacent. This left a blank space in the centre waist panel with the Crest located below it.

of the Third class carriages is shown in Plate 7.4. Midland was to build fifteen First class carriages at £645 10s each and a further five for £3 more.[9] Again, the Coaching Plant Stock Book does not record these carriages as contractor-built.

The prices quoted did not include gas light fitting, which was charged to capital expenditure. According to the same minute Pintsch fitted the Third class carriages and Pope the Firsts, the work being undertaken on the carriage builders' premises. The price for fitting was not specified.

BRAKE AND LUGGAGE CARRIAGES

Very few of the early 6-wheeled carriages were built with guard's and luggage accommodation. Separate Passenger Brake Vans were used instead. Initially, the 4-wheeled vans described in Chapter 7.1 sufficed. Later, as the number of 6-wheeled carriages increased, more Brake Thirds and the 6-wheeled Passenger Brake design to Diagram 17 were built.

The Diagram 10 Brake Composites had central guard's and luggage accommodation with a First class compartment on each side and a Third at either end. The Diagram Book (reproduced as Figure 7.10) shows twelve First class seats with armrests between all seats while the Coaching Plant Stock Book shows sixteen seats, implying that only a central arm rest was provided. The Third class seated twenty.

Two were built in 1883 (numbers 215 and 216) followed by five in July 1888 to order H29 (numbers 1-3, 6 and 7) and four in July 1890 to H52 (numbered 31-34). A Traffic Committee minute in April 1890 referring to the last order stated:

'This is a serviceable vehicle and it is recommended that four be built, two of these to be used between Edinburgh and Stranraer. Estimated cost £500 each.'[10]

The capital expenditure return records the cost as £486 10s each.[11] The carriages were withdrawn between 1925 and 1929.

There is no record in the register of a drawing for these carriages, probably because standard dimensions were used for the two classes of compartment.

In October 1883 drawing 3702 was produced for a Brake Tri-Composite.[12] This was followed in April 1884 by drawing 3842 showing *'details for tri-composite carriage'* which has not survived. The 1883 drawing shows a Brake carriage with the same configuration as Diagram 10, but the right-hand compartment is upholstered to a lower standard than the adjacent First. This Second class compartment is the same dimension as the Third class accommodation, which has wooden seats. The drawing shows 3-foot 9-inch spoked wheels, but a note says that Mansell wheels should be fitted.

There is no record of a minute authorising construction of this design. The last order for a Tri-Composite carriage was sanctioned in September 1879.[13] During his time on the North British from 1875 to his arrival at St. Rollox, Drummond had only designed carriages with First and Third class accommodation.

CARRIAGES WITH LAVATORIES

Drummond modified a number of ex-West Coast Joint Stock carriages to accommodate lavatories. These are described in Chapter 7.6. Just before these conversions were made, he introduced a lavatory carriage on the standard 6-wheeled underframe. Diagram 13C was a Composite with lavatories for First class passengers only. It was built to drawing 5621[14] – see Figure 7.11. Seating capacity was twelve First and thirty Third. Eleven were put in service to orders H28 and H42 in 1888/89.

The carriages in the first order were numbered 8-11 and 13. The Coaching Plant Stock Book records that the carriages in the latter order, numbered 25-30, were dual fitted. This was necessary because they were built as *'Lavatory Carriages for Through Highland Traffic.'* On 21st May 1889 the Caledonian Board had accepted the General Manager's recommendation that they should be built instead of eight Thirds.[15]

Number 30 was not confined to services to the HR. It was involved in the accident at Carlisle on 4th March 1890, when it was marshalled into the 8.00pm 'Tourist Express' as a through carriage from Bristol to Glasgow.[16] Perhaps the other dual-fitted carriages also served on this duty. The opening of the Severn Tunnel in July 1888 had led to new services between Bristol and points north.[17] These services also required dual-fitted stock.

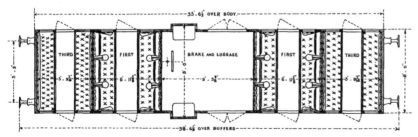

Figure 7.10
CR-designed 6-wheeled Brake Composites were rare beasts, although a number were converted later from West Coast Joint Stock. Standard compartment dimensions were used, leaving a Brake and luggage compartment in the centre.

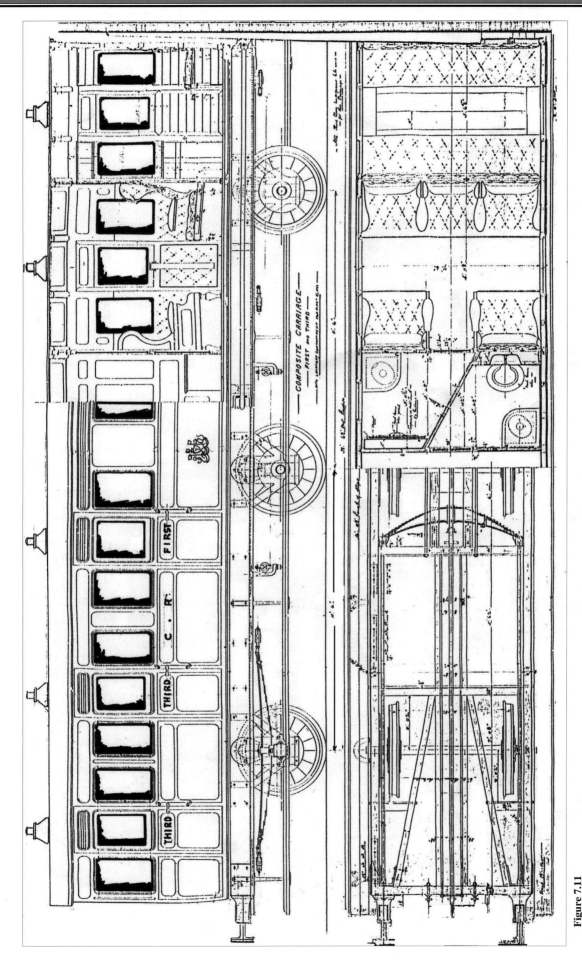

Figure 7.11
This is a drawing of the first CR carriage with lavatory accommodation, albeit only for First class passengers.

Plate 7.5
Here are three Drummond-style 6-wheeled carriages, two Diagram 14 Thirds with a Diagram 8 First between them. At the head of the train at Perth ticket platform is a Diagram 17 Passenger Brake Van with simplified panelling. Is the variation in tone between the end and the sides of the van evidence that the end was painted red? At the rear of the 6-wheelers is a Diagram 33 8-compartment Third, followed by another Diagram 17 Brake Van.

NUMBER OF CARRIAGES BUILT

By the time that Drummond left the Caledonian at the end of July 1890, he had constructed at St. Rollox, or had built by contractors, 251 6-wheeled carriages. The breakdown of the various designs is shown in the table below. All the carriages survived until just after the Grouping, except for the odd accident victim mentioned above.

DIAGRAM	TYPE	BUILT
8	5-compartment First	35
10	4-compartment Brake Composite	11
13C	5-compartment Lavatory Composite	11
14	6-compartment Third	194

6-WHEELED PASSENGER BRAKE VANS

The Diagram 17 vans were 30 feet long. They were described as *'double passenger van'* in the St. Rollox orders to distinguish them from the 4-wheeled vans with lookouts and the brake stanchion at one end. The latter were described as *'single end'* in the Coaching Plant Stock Book.

The Diagram 17 vans had centre lookouts. On drawings 4370[18] and 6501[19] the guard's door was to the left of the lookout viewed from the side; in the Diagram Book it was to the right. Perhaps the change was made when Lambie built the vans with simplified panelling. The luggage area was served by two pairs of doors. There is a reproduction of drawing 6501 in Chapter 7.5.

Forty-three were built between 1885 and 1894. The first orders were to drawing 4370. It shows spoked wheels and lookouts extended straight up to the roof with overhanging eaves, in the fashion of the Brake Vans described in Chapter 6. It is not known whether the first vans were built to this style, because the drawing is annotated for Mansell wheels and a line drawn freehand indicates that the top of the lookout should be faired into the body.

The first ten were reported to have cost £260 each,[20] which is confirmed in the capital expenditure return.[21] They were built to order H5 and numbered 172-181. In the Coaching Plant Stock Book number 173 is a 1921-built van, which suggests that the original van was the victim of an accident. This would explain why only nine vans were traced in the transcription of the Stock Book.

The order list states that ten more vans were built to order H7, which the transcription of the Stock Book suggests were authorised in 1888. This would place H7 out of number sequence. Only four vans have been traced. The Traffic Committee minutes for the half years ending January and July 1888 do not specify which vehicles were authorised. It may be that the ten vans were never built and that four vans were constructed to order H24, which was for four 6-wheeled Luggage Vans, which cannot be traced. Order H24 is within the sequence built in 1888.

REFERENCES
1. NRM 7465/C (on two sheets) RHP 70007
2. NRM 7480/C (on two sheets) RHP 70011
3. NRS BR/CAL/1/27 entry 1441
4. NRS BR/CAL/1/27 entry 1473
5. NRS BR/CAL/1/27 entry 1609
6. NRM 7461/C
7. CRA Archive ref: 6/1/1/1/3
8. NRS BR/CAL/1/28 entry 358
9. NRS BR/CAL/1/28 entry 639
10. NRS BR/CAL/1/28 entry 716
11. NRS BR/CAL/1/33 entry 1408
12. NRS BR/CAL/23/7 (32)
13. NRM 7481/C (on two sheets) RHP 70014
14. NRS BR/CAL/1/25 entry 485
15. NRM 7468/C (on two sheets) RHP 70035
16. NRS BR/CAL/1/33 entry 126
17. TNA RAIL 1053/79/9 pp. 1-26
18. *Railway Reminiscences*, p. 337
19. NRM 7510/C (on two sheets) RHP 70043
20. NRM 7478/C RHP 70059
21. NRS BR/CAL/1/29 entry 1212
22. NRS BR/CAL/23/5 (32)

7.3: THE 49-FOOT BOGIE CARRIAGES

Eight-wheeled carriages had been part of the West Coast Joint Stock since September 1883, when four Sleeping Saloons entered service. It was some years before the Caledonian Railway constructed its own 8-wheeled stock, although, as recounted in Chapter 3, from 1876 it designed and unsuccessfully advocated bogie Sleeping carriages of varying lengths for the West Coast Joint Stock.[1]

The existing 35 foot long underframe with a wheelbase of 23 feet represented the practical limit for a 6-wheeled carriage with the outer wheels rigidly mounted and the centre axle provided with limited side-play.

As stated in Chapter 2, the Cleminson and the Grover patent systems for 'radiating wheels' were investigated by the CR in 1881/82,[2] but, as no more was heard of the trial, the systems must have been rejected by Drummond. In any case, while the systems might have improved the ride quality, they would not allow significantly longer carriages, because of excessive end and centre throw when running on curved track.

Drummond had considered building bogie carriages on the Caledonian in June 1884. The register records three drawings concerning a 'Bogie Coupé Composite Carriage,' length unspecified.[3] Eight-wheeled carriages for ordinary WCJS service were first built in 1887. When the CR introduced bogie carriages in the same year, it adopted 4-wheeled bogies rather than the radial underframe used by their English partner, on which the inner pair of axles were fixed.

CHOICE OF LENGTH

Rather than the 42-foot body which was to be the standard for L&NWR and WCJS construction for some years to come, or 45 feet which would become Drummond's preference on the Caledonian, a length of 49 feet was adopted. This had already been used on the North British after Drummond's departure. In 1885 Holmes designed a Brake Composite on a 49-foot underframe with a body that was only 7 feet 6 inches wide. Only a few were built, but construction in quantity and in various configurations was resumed in 1902, with an 8-foot body width.[4]

The probable thinking behind the adoption of this length was that First class compartments in the 6-wheeled carriages were 6 feet 11½ inches between partitions. A 5-compartment First class carriage was therefore 35 feet long. One extra compartment gave the 42-foot length of the L&NWR and WCJS First class vehicles. Drummond presumably considered that one extra compartment did not justify the increased costs and complication of a bogie carriage and opted for seven compartments, giving a length of 49 feet. The St. Rollox drawing number was 5074.[5] It and the Brake Third drawing (number 5104[6]) were produced in December 1886. The latter is shown as Figure 7.12.

The 49-foot length also made sense for the Brake Thirds. A Third class compartment was 5 feet 6⅝ inches between partitions. Seven compartments would occupy approximately 39 feet, leaving over 9 feet for an adequate Brake and luggage compartment. Located at the end, it would remove the need for an extra vehicle as a 'collision buffer,' or the alternative, which was to lock the first two compartments of the leading carriage out of use. This practice was set out at the front of every carriage marshalling circular.

CONSTRUCTION DETAILS

Although the panelling style, the compartment sizes and the end profile marked the 49-foot carriages as a natural development of the 6-wheeled designs, very little about their construction was conventional. The body was designed to be robust and to offer a comfortable ride. This was meant to be the significant advantage of the design.

Unlike the NBR carriages where the body was attached to a conventional underframe, Drummond developed a variation of the integral body/underframe construction used by the Pullman Car Co. The bottom member of the sides formed the solebar, making the carriages immediately recognisable from a distance.

The underframe was massively constructed. The lower body member that formed the solebar was 12 inches by 5¼. The cross members on which the bogies pivoted were 12 inches by 9 and cross bracing was 12 inches by 3½ at 7-foot intervals.

The bogies and their mounting were also unconventional. Firstly, the wheelbase was longer than current practice at 9 feet 6 inches. The bogie pivot point was offset three inches backwards from the centre. As described in Chapter 2, this arrangement was quite common as a means of varying the load on each axle in the belief that it reduced bogie 'hunting' on straight track, but the offset was usually only one inch.

Vertical springing was more complex than normal, as the 4-foot axle-box springs were linked by compensating levers. The bogie frames had damper pads at their corners which bore on the underside of the body. Transverse springing of the bolsters further cushioned the ride.

SERVICE HISTORY

Six vehicles were constructed in 1887, two Diagram 19 First class carriages to order H19 and four Diagram 20 Brake Thirds to order H20. The carriages were marshalled into sets of a First between two Brake Thirds and when introduced were used on the prestigious Glasgow–Edinburgh services. They may have continued on this route until the introduction of the 'Grampian' stock in the latter half of 1905.

They were intended for steam heat[7] but only First 154 is recorded as being so fitted in the Coaching Plant Stock Book. As discussed in Chapter 3.3, Drummond was experimenting with heating from exhaust steam at the time of their construction, so the original fitting may have been short-lived. Steam heating was fitted to the First class carriages in 1920 to St. Rollox drawing 20866. The drawing has not survived. They were not recorded as steam heated in the 1921 Stock List, where they were included among the 48-foot carriages.

All six carriages lasted into the LM&SR era, the first to go being Brake Third 638, which was withdrawn in 1924 without receiving a post-Grouping number. Of the Brake Thirds only 642 survived long enough to carry LM&SR 16711, not being withdrawn until 1926, the same year as First class 155. The other First, 154, lasted until 1929 as 15459.

An annotation on the original drawing shows that in February 1898 it was decided to place the six carriages on conventional underframes, with the loss of their distinctive body profile. Drawing 8821, which has not survived, records the modification. The original

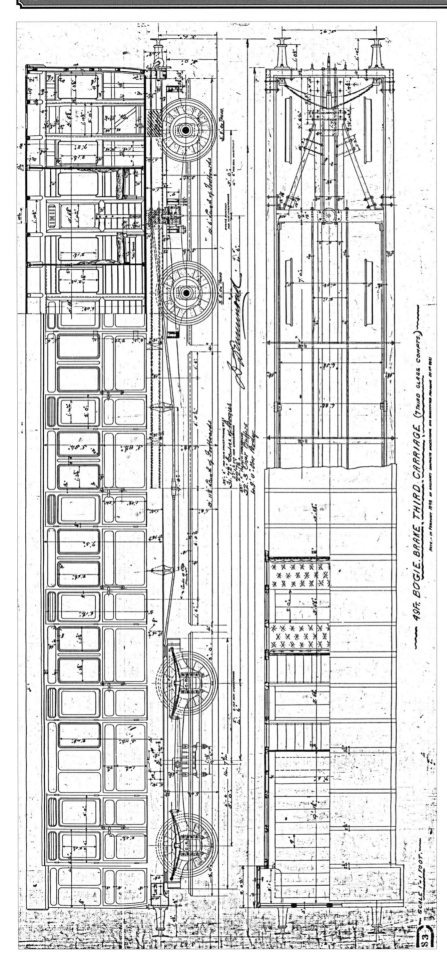

49ft. BOGIE BRAKE THIRD CARRIAGE (THIRD GLASS COMPTS)

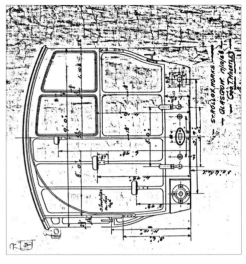

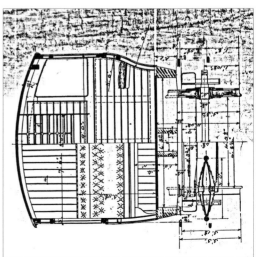

Figure 7.12
These drawings show the 49-foot Brake Third as originally constructed. In this guise the body was integral with the underframe, an American form of construction that was used on the all-wood Pullman cars. The panelling and compartment dimensions were the same as the 6-wheeled Drummond carriages. The annotation about rebuilding the carriages with *'an ordinary composite underframe'* is at the bottom of the drawing. The new dimensions following from the reorientation of the bogies are also visible. The riding lamp sketched in by the lookout in the end view was added later, as can be seen in the accompanying photograph.

Plate 7.6
Forty-nine-foot Brake Third number 645 at Glasgow Central after rebuilding with a conventional underframe. The original photograph shows a red carpet on the adjacent platform, which was laid for the visit of King George V in July 1914. By this time the carriage had been demoted to local passenger services. The prestige Edinburgh–Glasgow trains for which these carriages were originally designed were by then served by 'Grampian' stock.

drawing also states that the offset pivot point of the bogies was to be reversed at the same time. One of the Third class carriages after rebuilding is shown in Plate 7.6.

ABANDONMENT OF THE CONCEPT

According to a press article written shortly after their introduction, *'All express trains between Glasgow and Edinburgh are in future to be composed of these improved carriages.'*[8] The article went on to say that *'The Company ... are now in a position to put on these improved carriages to all express trains between the larger cities on the Caledonian system.'* The plans were not carried out.

As previously discussed, Drummond was required to present plans for his 6-wheeled carriages to the Board, in accordance with the 1883 directive described in Chapter 1, even though they were to a design which had been proven on the NBR. As described in the next section, he had to request formal approval for the 45-foot carriage designs. There are no official references to the 49-foot carriages apart from the drawings. One suspects that they were an experiment on Drummond's part, without consulting the Board.

In August 1888, a year after the 49-foot carriages were put into service, Drummond designed 45-foot carriages built conventionally with the body separate from the underframe. Some serious shortcoming must have presented itself soon after the 49-foot carriages entered service for Drummond to have reverted to what was

essentially a stretched version of his 6-wheeled designs, mounted on bogies.

The shortcoming was probably body distortion. As outlined in Chapter 2.4, one of the virtues of 6-wheeled stock was continuous support of the body. A bogie vehicle, on the other hand, was only supported towards each end, necessitating truss rods and queen posts to prevent distortion in the middle of the body. Drummond seems to have thought that an integral body/underframe would prevent the problem from occurring.

Even Pullman Cars with end entrances had truss rods, and, as can be seen in Figure 10.2, further reinforcement against distortion was provided within the body. This was of course impossible in carriages with door openings at regular intervals along the side of the body. Very small amounts of distortion would have caused the doors to jam.

REFERENCES
1. Chapter 3.4, p. 66
2. Chapter 2.4, p. 41
3. St. Rollox 4037, 4045, 4051 and 4063 – none of which has survived
4. *NBR Coaches*, pp. 46-47, drawings 38 and 39
5. NRM 7476 (on two sheets) RHP 70028
6. NRM 7460 (on two sheets) RHP 70029
7. Drawing 5231 dated 3rd March 1887 has not survived
8. *The Glasgow Herald*, 8th January 1887

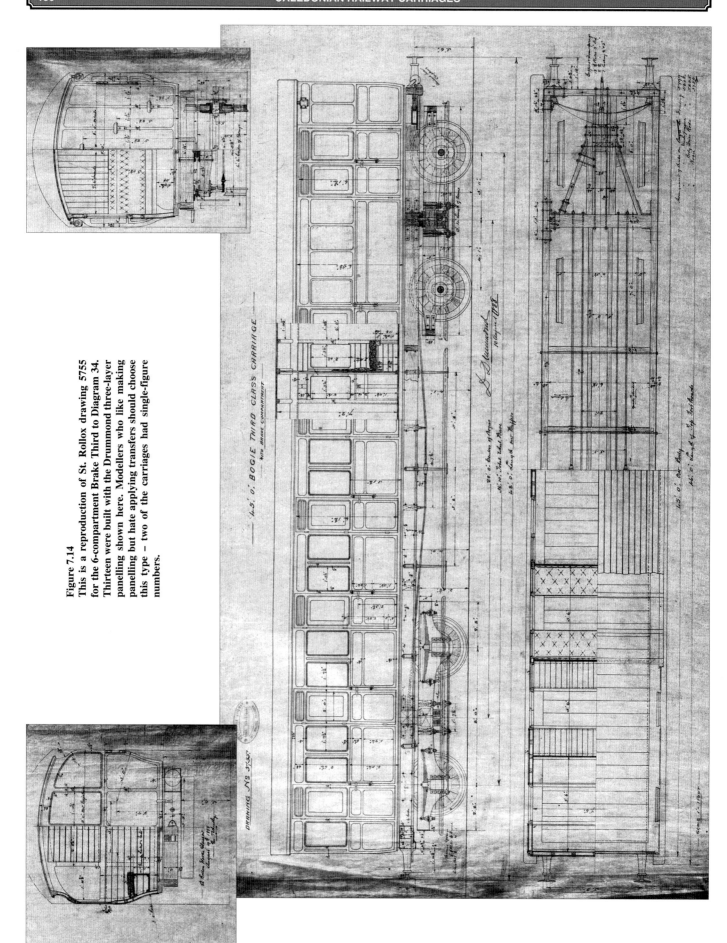

Figure 7.14
This is a reproduction of St. Rollox drawing 5755 for the 6-compartment Brake Third to Diagram 34. Thirteen were built with the Drummond three-layer panelling shown here. Modellers who like making panelling but hate applying transfers should choose this type – two of the carriages had single-figure numbers.

7.4: THE 45-FOOT BOGIE CARRIAGES

After the 49-foot vehicle experiment, carriages built on a 45-foot underframe became the standard. During the Drummond era the separate underframe continued to be made entirely of wood. The 45-foot type was first authorised in July 1888 when the Traffic Committee considered the rolling stock replacement programme for the half year ending 31st January 1889. Unlike the 49-foot carriages discussed in the previous section, these designs were put up for approval and officially sanctioned by the Board.

'The statement for approval together with diagrams of the First Class Bogie and Third Class Brake Carriages proposed to be built were submitted and approved.'[1]

The drawings for these pioneer carriages, which were made during August 1888, have survived. A variety of configurations was produced on a common underframe, initially to drawing 5808 and running on 8-foot wheelbase bogies to drawing 5799.[2] Some had *coupé* compartments at both ends, adding 6 inches to the body length, but with no modification to the underframe. They continued the three-layer panelling style of the 6-wheeled stock. The types built during the Drummond period are described below in order of appearance.

COUPÉ LAVATORY FIRST

These carriages were built to order H30 and drawing 5762,[3] which was dated 21st August 1888. They appeared on page 24 of the Diagram Book. There were four compartments and a *coupé* at each end. The two centre compartments had no access to a lavatory. They were designated as smoking compartments on the drawing. There were thirty-two seats: four per side with a single centre armrest, except in the compartments adjacent to the lavatories, which had two seats on each side and a central door – see Figure 7.13.

They were numbered 156-161. Number 160 appears in the Coaching Plant Stock Book as a 57-foot First built in 1916, which suggests that the Coupé carriage with that number may have been

an accident victim. These carriages were built for the Callander & Oban and Gourock lines, according to reports in the technical press.[4] Each one was marshalled in a set, flanked by two Diagram 34 Brake Thirds – see below. They and the Brake Thirds were fitted with the MacNee electric passenger alarm system. This, and its application to these carriages, is described in Chapter 2.3.

BRAKE THIRD

Five Brake Thirds were built to order H31 in the period ending January 1889 and a further seven to the same order number in July. Their numbers were 267, 303, 309, 311, 322, 324, 342, 354, 356, 521, 550 and 676. These twelve carriages formed the outer ends of the Callander & Oban and Gourock sets, flanking the First class Coupés described above.

Two more (numbers 27 and 33) were built to order H33 in the latter period. Before Drummond resigned, six more were built to orders H40 and H49 – numbers 4, 7, 425, 453, 464, 468. Only two of the running numbers were carried by Thirds of any description in the 1874 Inventory.

The St. Rollox drawing number was 5755.[5] They appeared on page 34 of the Diagram Book. Six compartments, which had over 3 inches less leg room than those in the 6-wheeled carriages, each seated ten passengers. The guard's lookouts were at the extreme end. The general arrangement and internal layout is shown in Figure 7.14.

THIRD CLASS

This design also appeared for the first time in the period ending July 1889, when six were built to order H39. The drawing number was 6000.[6] It was assigned to page 33 of the Diagram Book. The eight compartments were only 5 feet 6 inches wide, and seated eighty people. It was thus very effective as a high density load carrier – see Figure 7.15. Sixteen more were built to orders H48 and H55 before Drummond's resignation. Most were allocated numbers that were already vacant in the 1874 Inventory. Nineteen of the numbers were the lowest allocated to this diagram.

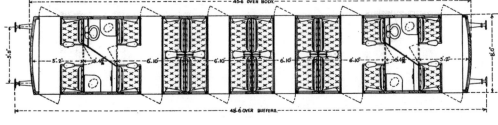

Figure 7.13
The Diagram 24 Coupé Lavatory First. As originally built, the washbasins folded down when not in use as shown in the lower of each pair of lavatories. They were altered to Diagram 24A after the Coaching Plant Stock Book was compiled.

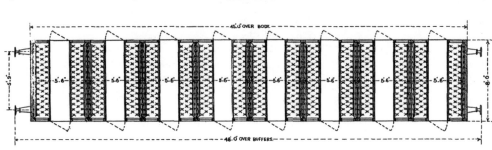

Figure 7.15
The internal layout of the 8-compartment all Third to Diagrams 33.

FIRST CLASS

St. Rollox drawing 5905[7] was dated 10th December 1888 – see Figure 7.16. Seven compartments with a central armrest accommodated fifty-six people. Nine carriages to Diagram 21 were authorised as renewals for the period ending January 1890. The details of the rolling stock for this period are not given in the minutes,[8] but, according to the rolling stock returns, nine First class carriages were withdrawn and replaced with a similar number. The order number was H34.

The carriages received numbers 162-166, 171-173 and 217. These numbers were carried by 4-compartment 4-wheeled carriages in the 1874 Inventory. According to the Coaching Plant Stock Book, seven of the nine were originally numbered in a block between 315 and 323 before they received their final numbers. This suggests that the old carriages were in the process of withdrawal at the time of their construction.

A further four to order H47 were built in the next period. Again the minute[9] does not give details, but the rolling stock return confirms. They were allocated numbers 167, 169, 170 and 198. All but one of these numbers was carried by ex-SNER carriages in the 1874 Inventory. Number 198 was the exception, which had been allocated to a Metropolitan-built carriage dating from 1868.

NUMBER OF BOGIE CARRIAGES WITH DRUMMOND PANELLING

A breakdown of the 45-foot carriages built with three-layer panelling is shown in the table below. As will be seen in the next section, Hugh Smellie, Drummond's immediate successor, did not build any bogie carriages. John Lambie continued and developed the concept, but simplified the panelling style.

DIAGRAM	TYPE	BUILT
21	7-compartment First	13
24	Coupé Lavatory First	6
33	8-compartment Third	22
34	6-compartment Brake Third	13

REFERENCES
1. NRS BR/CAL/1/32 entry 555
2. RHP 67559
3. NRM 7470/C RHP 70040
4. *Engineering*, 3rd May 1889, p. 514 and 21st February 1890, pp. 195-96
5. NRM 7472/C RHP 70039
6. NRM 7471/C RHP 70042
7. NRM 11230/C RHP 70041
8. NRS BR/CAL/5/11 entry 49
9. NRS BR/CAL/1/33 entry 1038

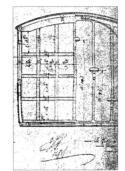

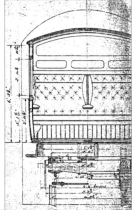

Figure 7.16
The final Drummond 45-foot design was the Diagram 21 First. This is a reproduction of St. Rollox drawing 5905.

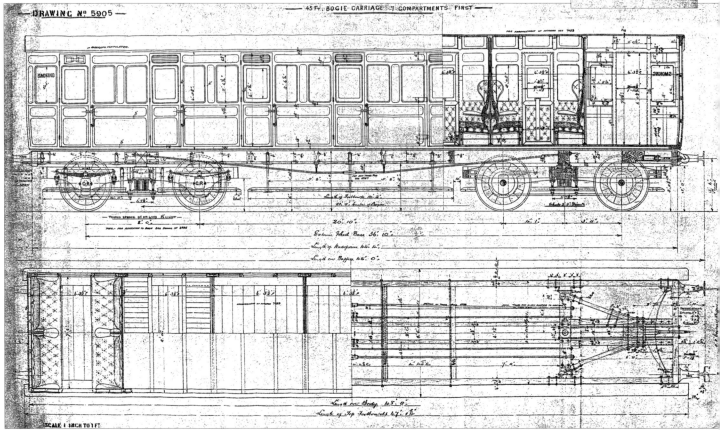

7.5: DRUMMOND'S IMMEDIATE SUCCESSORS

The five-year period between Drummond's departure and McIntosh's arrival saw both modernisation and expansion of the carriage fleet. Carriages were steadily replaced, and almost as many were added, as the table below shows. The total charged to the capital account in the period was nearly £87,000.

TYPE	WORN OUT	REPLACED	ADDED
First	18	18	10
Third	96	96	111
Composite/Saloon	32	32	15
TOTAL	146	146	136

HUGH SMELLIE'S TENURE

Smellie took over from Drummond in August 1890. Although his time in office was so soon cut short by his death that he could not make much impact on Caledonian Railway practice, he did design the first CR general service carriage with lavatory facilities for Third class passengers. It was proposed in September in drawing 6441, which was obviously approved because carriages were built to drawing 6536, dated 22nd October[1] – see Figure 7.17 for the interior layout, Figure 7.18 for the side elevation, and Plate 7.7.

The Diagram 15 Lavatory Thirds had a conventional centre Third class compartment flanked by two compartments, each with a pair of lavatories between them. One seat in each of the four compartments was sacrificed to allow access. The carriages seated forty-two passengers, thirty-two of whom could access a lavatory.

Fifty Third class carriages were authorised during Smellie's tenure, to be charged to the capital account.[2] Six of the fifteen Brake Thirds to order H65 were completed in the period ending January 1891, according to the capital expenditure return.[3] They cost £388 each and were allocated numbers 855-869.

The remainder were to be the Lavatory Thirds. These were built to order H62, but were not charged to the account until after Smellie's death. They were originally numbered 870-904. Carriages in the block 893-904 were allocated random low numbers in the period ending January 1893, when the 45-foot Thirds to orders H83 and H85 were built.

He also designed a new type of Brake carriage to Diagram 16 with a centre Brake and luggage compartment, and two Third class compartments on each side – see Figure 7.19. There were forty seats. The St. Rollox drawing is 6486,[4] dated 30th September 1890, which is annotated 'H63 15 off H65 15 off.' The drawing shows the carriages as oil-lit, but the Coaching Plant Stock Book records them as gas-fitted. It is not known whether the change was made when the carriages were built or at some later date.

Finally, a new Diagram 17 Passenger Brake Van drawing, St. Rollox 6501, was issued in October 1890.[5] It bore the lettering 'CR LUGGAGE' and shows Mansell wheels and a faired top to the lookout. It is reproduced as Figure 7.20. The drawing applied to the vans from order H58 onwards. The order list states that six vans were built to H58, but only five have been traced in the transcription. The vans were allocated random low numbers, replacing vans dating from the 1860s, according to the interpretation of the 1874 Inventory.

LAMBIE'S SIX-WHEELED CARRIAGES

Smellie had been seriously ill since the beginning of 1891 and died in April, when he was succeeded by John Lambie. Lambie completed the thirty-five Diagram 15 Lavatory Thirds to order H62 and the remaining nine Brake Thirds to order H65, which were charged to capital in the period ending July 1891.[6] The Lavatory Thirds cost £480 10s each. Three more Diagram 13C Lavatory Composites with

ABOVE: Plate 7.7
This shows a Smellie-designed Diagram 15 Lavatory Third in the carriage sidings at Barnhill, across the Tay from Perth. Note the different shape of the pressed steel Anderson ventilator covers above the lavatory windows.
RIGHT: Figure 7.17
Shows the internal layout of the first CR carriage that offered lavatory accommodation to Third class passengers.

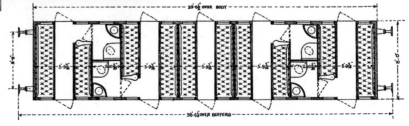

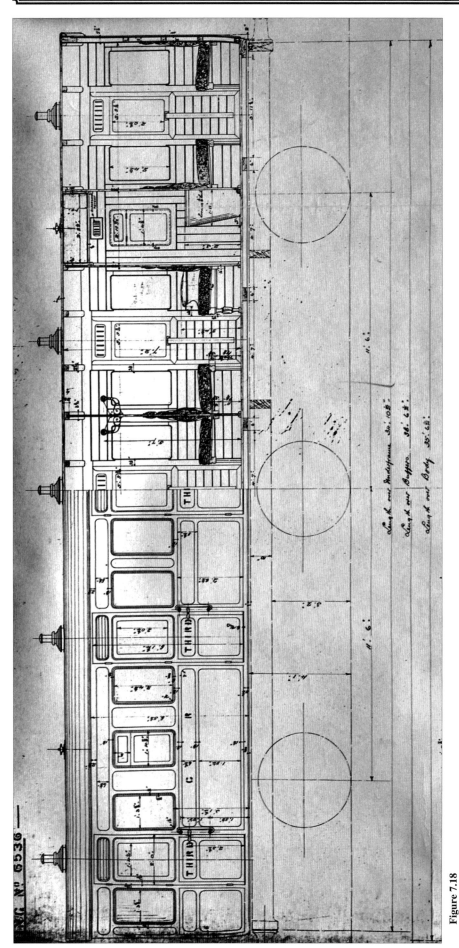

Figure 7.18
The reproduction from St. Rollox drawing 6536 shows the side elevation of the first CR carriage that offered lavatory accommodation to Third class passengers. The ventilator in the lavatory is annotated '*Anderson's Patent.*' The ventilator covers are not shown over the lavatory windows in the external elevation – compare with Plate 7.7.

Westinghouse brake only were also built in 1891 to order H64, numbered 40-42.

The Thirds were allocated a block of numbers from 855 to 869, followed by the Lavatory Thirds from 870 to 904. The Lavatory Thirds 893-904 were allocated low random numbers in 1893 to make way for the 45-foot carriages built to orders H83 and H85.

Lambie also built the Diagram 16 Brake Thirds to orders H63 and H65 respectively. One carriage from the first order was originally allocated number 528. It was fitted out as a Composite with Brake and luggage compartment. One inside compartment was converted to a First class compartment the standard 6 feet 11½ inches wide. The luggage section was correspondingly reduced. The window size and body side panelling were adjusted to match the new compartment width. There was seating for eight First and thirty Third class passengers. Figure 7.21 shows the internal layout.

The carriage was built to drawing 6609 dated 22nd December 1890.[7] This was a part elevation only, annotated with the omitted all-Third end '*to drawing 6486*' – see Figure 7.22. It was assigned to Diagram 11 and worked on the Killin Branch, carrying the number 50. Withdrawn in 1927, it remained oil-lit until the end, according to the Coaching Plant Stock Book and the 1921 Stock List. This made sense given its restricted sphere of operation. Gassing would have meant a special journey to Oban to use the travelling gas tank.

Another carriage from the first order is unaccounted for in the Coaching Plant Stock Book. It is possible that this was another example of Diagram 11, because the 1913 Carriage Marshalling Circular has the Killin Branch worked by two Brake Composites.[8] By 1921 a '*Brake Composite works all trains. Strengthened by 6-Wheeled Third when required.*'[9] Only carriage number 50 was recorded in the 1921 Stock List. This might account for the absence of the second carriage from the Register, although it is hard to imagine that a relatively new, low mileage vehicle would have been scrapped. It is much more likely to have been reclassified, but there is no evidence of this.

A further seven Lavatory Thirds built in the same period to order H66 were treated as replacements. In 1917, fourteen of these carriages were fitted with heating to form a military transport train. Details are in Chapter 12. The carriages to order H66 were the last Drummond-style 6-wheeled passenger vehicles to be built by the Caledonian.

RIGHT: Figure 7.19
The internal layout of the Diagram 16 Brake Thirds, designed by Smellie. A total of thirty-five were built by him and his successor Lambie.

BELOW: Figure 7.20
Drawing 6501 applied to Diagram 17 Passenger Brake Vans built by Smellie. It differed from the original Drummond drawing 4370 in having Mansell wheels and faired tops to the lookouts.

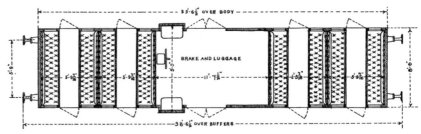

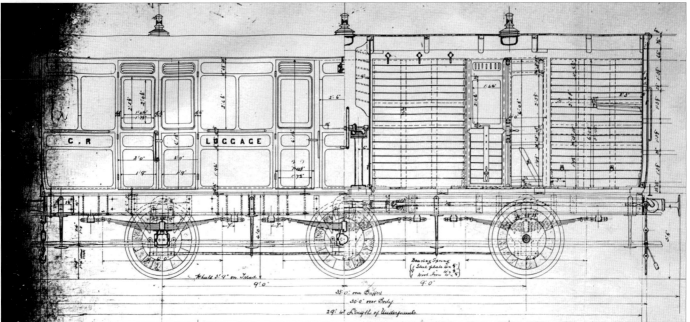

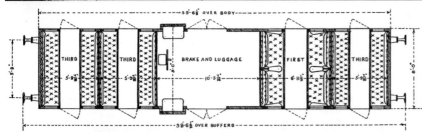

Figures 7.21 (*left*) **and 7.22** (*below*)
These drawings show the Diagram 11 Brake Composite carriage built for the Killin Branch. The carriage was originally part of an order for Diagram 16 Brake Thirds, but was modified to include a First class compartment. Unlike its companions it was oil-lit.

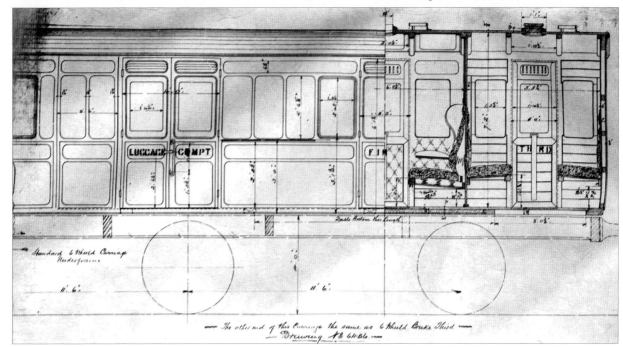

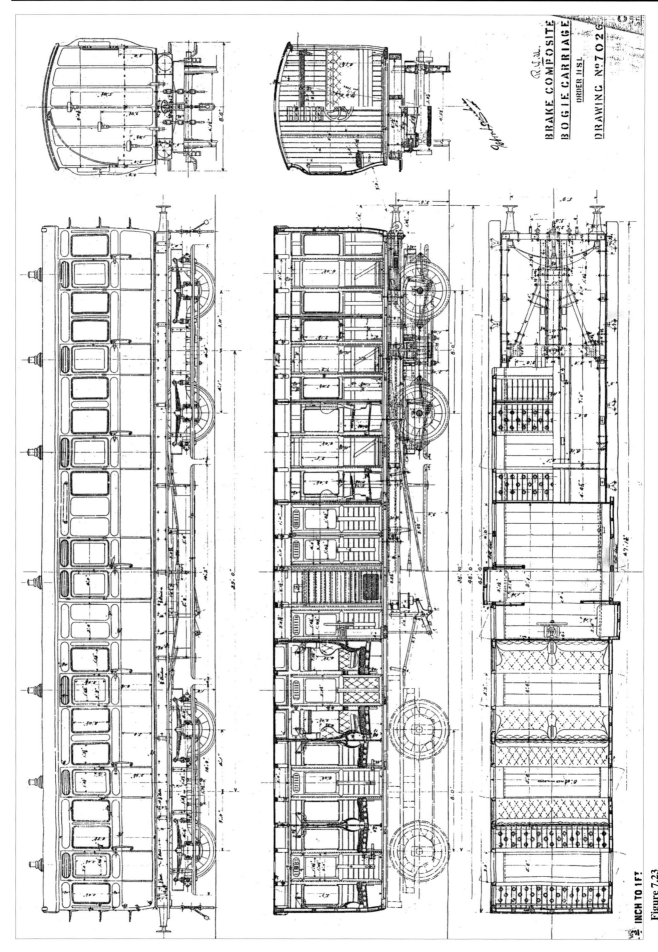

BRAKE COMPOSITE
BOGIE CARRIAGE
ORDER 11SL
DRAWING Nº 7026

INCH TO 1 FT

Figure 7.23
St. Rollox drawing 7026 shows Lambie's second design of Brake Composite to Diagram 23. It gives a clear view of the brake arrangement from the actuating cylinder and the connection to the handbrake in the guard's compartment.

ABOVE: Plate 7.8
This is an enlargement from Plate 7.5, showing a Diagram 17 Passenger Brake Van with the simplified panelling style. The guard's door is to the right of the lookout, as shown in the Diagram Book.

Lambie built ten Diagram 17 Passenger Brake Vans during 1892 to orders H79 and H87.[10] The panelling was simplified to match the bogie carriages described in the next section – see Plate 7.8. Number 56 of order H87 was fitted with a stove to run on trains between Oban and Dalmally. It was one of the few vans that were not dual brake fitted.

Ten more replacement vans were built in the first half years of 1893 (order H92) and 1894 (order H111), although only nine have been traced. Most of the vans built by Drummond and his immediate successors were repainted with white upper panels before the Coaching Plant Stock Book was compiled. The vans were all withdrawn between 1924 and 1928.

NEW BOGIE CARRIAGE STYLE AND COMPOSITE CARRIAGES

Lambie continued to build 45-foot carriages to Drummond's designs, but with single layer panelling over the body joints and a much simplified panelling arrangement below the waistline. This style is shown in the reproduction of drawing 7026 (Figure 7.23) and the Brake Third in Plate 7.9. He also introduced 45-foot Composite carriages. These are described in order of appearance.

The Diagram 22 Brake Composite had a central Brake and luggage compartment. The drawing was St. Rollox 6476,[11] which is annotated '3 off to H57.' There were two Third and one First class compartment on one side and a First and a Third on the other. There were sixteen First class seats and thirty Thirds. Three were built in 1891. A further five appeared during McIntosh's tenure. An example is shown in Plate 7.10.

ABOVE: Plate 7.9
The Diagram 34 45-foot Brake Third was originally designed by Drummond. Number 427 was authorised for construction in the half year ending January 1895 and shows the simplified lower panelling introduced by John Lambie.

RIGHT: Plate 7.10
This is an enlargement from a familiar photograph of a Crieff Branch train at Balquhidder. The first carriage is an ex-West Coast Joint Stock P15 Lavatory Composite. These carriages' career on the Caledonian is described in Chapter 8.4. More importantly for this chapter, the rear vehicle is a CR Diagram 22 Brake Composite, only eight of which were built. A drawing of the high roofed version appears in Figure 8.3 on p. 172.

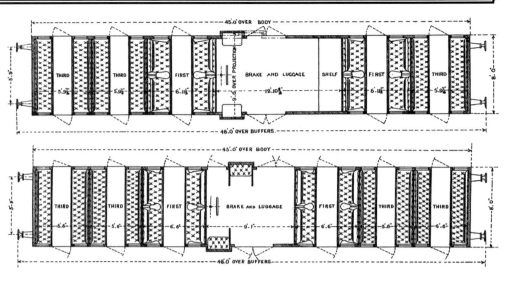

Figures 7.24 and 7.25
Lambie's two designs of Brake Composite are compared. Diagram 22 (*top*) was the first with five compartments. For Diagram 23 (*bottom*), an extra Third class compartment was included at the expense of reduced legroom and a smaller guards/luggage section.

Lambie was clearly not satisfied and introduced Diagram 23 in the period ending July 1892. This was the design to drawing 7026.[12] By reducing the compartment legroom and shortening the Brake compartment by 3 feet 9 inches, space was created for an extra Third class compartment and ten extra seats. The two internal layouts are compared in Figures 7.24 and 7.25. A photograph appears in Plate 7.11.

Eighteen were built during Lambie's regime to orders H81, H91, H98 and H118. The last two order numbers were charged to capital. H98 was approved in January 1893[13] and allocated numbers

250-254. H118 was approved in August 1894[14] and allocated numbers 270-274. Six were added in July 1896 to order H130.

The Diagram 26 Composites had three central First class compartments seating twenty-four, flanked by two Thirds on each side with seats for forty – see Figure 7.26 and Plate 7.12. Drawing 7140, dating from December 1892, depicted the *'Division of 45 ft. body into 3 1st and 4 3rd class.'* It has not survived. Ten carriages were built to orders H97 and H108 in 1893 and 1894.[15] They were allocated the blocks of numbers 255-259 and 265-269, and charged to the capital account.[16] A further twenty-two were built by McIntosh.

Plate 7.11
A Diagram 23 Brake Composite stands at the platform at Brocketsbrae. The carriage has been fitted with the modern train alarm system and the Harrison cord eyelets have been removed. The 1906 Local Working of Carriages Circular has a single Bogie Brake Composite working Circuit 13 on an afternoon return trip between Brocketsbrae and Lanark.

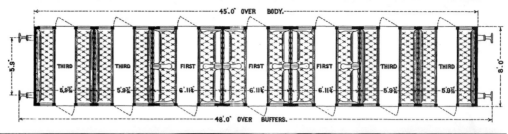

Figure 7.26
The drawing shows the internal layout of the Diagram 26 Composites, ten of which were built by Lambie.

ABOVE: Plate 7.12
This view taken at Edinburgh Princes Street gives a good impression of the neat outline of the Lambie style of panelling, compared with the Drummond style exhibited by the 49-foot carriage in Plate 7.4. Nearest the photographer are two Diagram 26 Composites and further away is a Diagram 33 8-compartment Third. The Composite nearest the camera has a number beginning with 25 or 26, which confirms it as one of the ten carriages built by Lambie. All the carriages have the earlier type of gas lamp with tall chimneys and all have rainstrips.

NEW AND EXISTING COUPÉ DESIGNS

The next designs to appear in the period ending July 1894 were two types of carriage with a single *coupé* end, rather than the double-ended version designed by Drummond.

In the Diagram 29 Lavatory Composite, four lavatories were accessed from all the First class compartments via seats with removable cushions and hinged frames. The two Third class compartments at the other end had no lavatory facilities. Six were built to order H110. They were authorised as renewals in 1894, at a cost of £800 each.[17] Drawing 7529, dated 19th May, has not survived. The internal layout is shown as Figure 7.27, and a photograph in Plate 7.13.

In the Diagram 30 Lavatory Luggage Composite design, all the passengers except those in the end Third class compartment had access to a lavatory via the same type of seat as that fitted to the Diagram 29 carriages. These seats in the First class were only to Third class standard, which made them marginally easier to negotiate when accessing the lavatory.

The Diagram 30 design was built to drawing 7546,[18] which was dated 19th June 1894 and annotated *'H109 for 6 off.'* The drawing is reproduced as Figure 7.28. A luggage compartment 6 feet 3 inches wide was located towards the centre of the body, accessed through double doors. There were nine First and thirty Third class seats. They were also authorised in the renewals programme for the half

year ending July 1894 at a cost of £700 each. Running numbers were 70, 91, 150, 161, 165 and 242.

Lambie also continued to build the Diagram 24 Coupé Lavatory Firsts designed by Drummond. The next order for these carriages was for four to H72. They were authorised as replacements for the period ending January 1892.[19] Their numbers were 4 and 203-205. The latter block of numbers had been carried by 4-wheeled carriages that had been put into service in 1868.

The final ten carriages to orders H119 and H125 were charged to the capital account for the period ending July 1895 at £941 each.[20] They were authorised as part of a capital programme of twenty-five carriages in August 1894.[21] The lavatories were again accessed via removable seats instead of gaps in the seating, which increased the capacity by four. This was the subject of drawing 7650. The new configuration was given Diagram 25 – see Figure 7.29. They were allocated a block of numbers between 239 and 248. The increased capacity is not shown in the Coaching Plant Stock Book, which suggests that they were the carriages modified in 1910, as reported in *Railway and Travel Monthly* and quoted in Chapter 3.5.

POST-GROUPING COUPÉ MODIFICATIONS

At some time after the compilation of the Coaching Plant Stock Book the fold-down wash stands were replaced by fixed basins. The toilets were also redesigned. The number of lavatories was

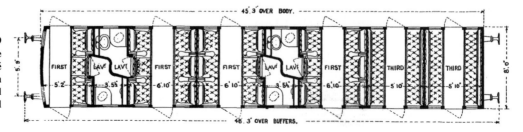

RIGHT: Figure 7.27
This is the layout of the Diagram 29 Coupé Lavatory Composite. These carriages and the Diagram 30 Coupé Lavatory Luggage Composite shown in Figure 7.28 had lavatories accessed via seats with removable cushions and hinged frames.

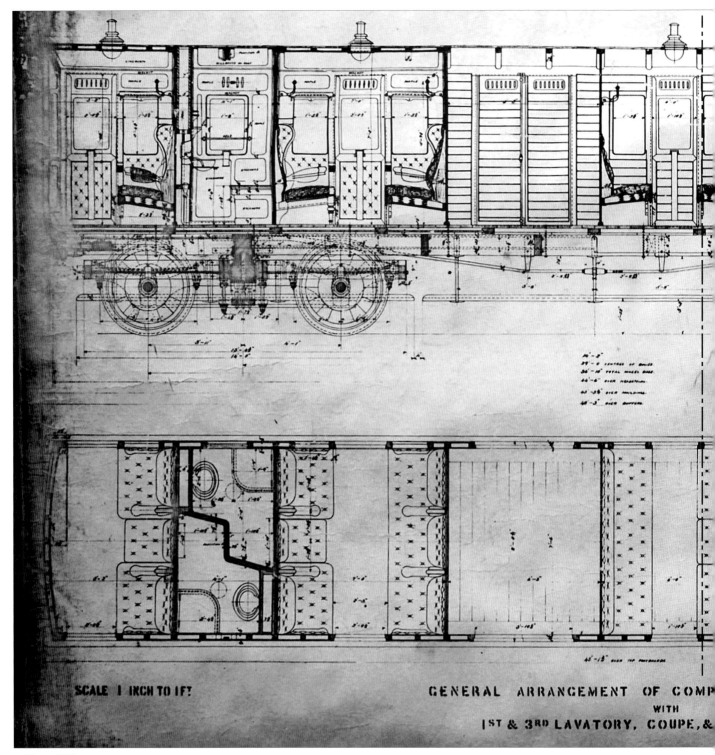

SCALE 1 INCH TO 1 FT

GENERAL ARRANGEMENT OF COMP
WITH
1ST & 3RD LAVATORY, COUPE, &

Figure 7.28
This is a reproduction of St. Rollox drawing 7546. It shows the version of
the Diagram 30 Coupé Composite design with a luggage compartment.
Note in the plan view that the seats in front of the lavatory doors in First
class were to the same dimensions as those in Third class. The lavatories
for First class have fold down washbasins, while Third class are fixed.

reduced from four to two to accommodate the new arrangement.
Access from the *coupés* and the adjacent First class compartments
was now by way of a short side corridor. This is shown in Diagram
24A – see Figure 7.30.

Most of the Coupés were withdrawn by the late 1920s but two
from Diagram 30 survived in original condition until 1933. After the
Grouping four had the lavatories removed and were down-rated to
Thirds. Longitudinal seats were fitted in the combined *coupé* and
original lavatory areas at either end of the carriage. In this guise they
appeared on page 25A of the Diagram Book – see Figure 7.31.

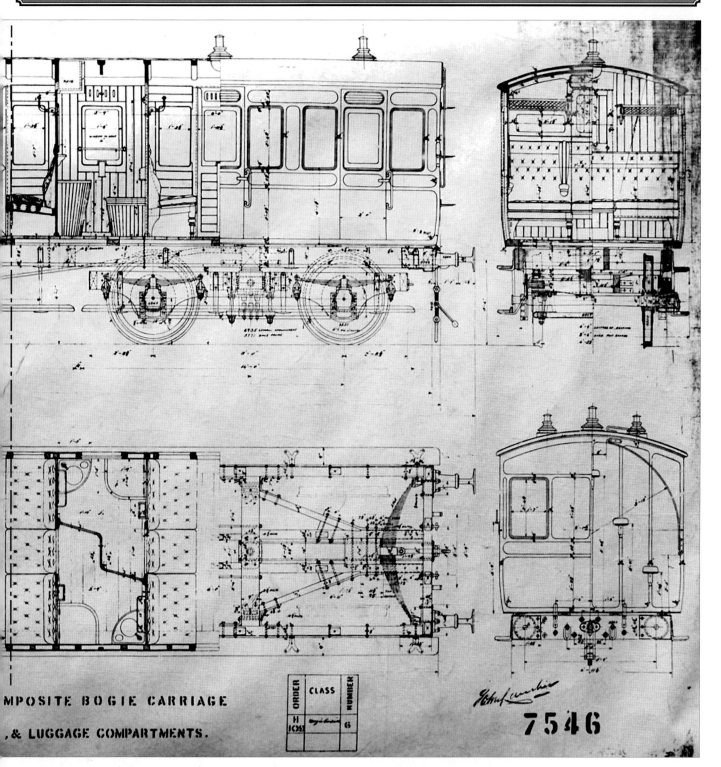

COMPOSITE BOGIE CARRIAGE

& LUGGAGE COMPARTMENTS.

ORDER	CLASS	NUMBER
H 1092	*composite*	6

7546

REFERENCES
1. NRM 7475/C RHP 70062
2. NRS BR/CAL/1/34 entry 125
3. NRS BR/CAL/23/7 (34)
4. NRM 7458/C RHP 70058
5. NRM 7478/C RHP 70059
6. NRS BR/CAL/23/7 (37)
7. NRM 7469/C RHP 70064
8. *Marshalling of Main Line Local and Branch Trains North of Greenhill*, 20, p. 8
9. *Local Working of Carriages North of Glenboig*, 37, p. 6
10. NRS BR/CAL/1/35 entries 263 and 827
11. NRM 7459/C RHP 70056
12. NRM 8001/C RHP 69133
13. NRS BR/CAL/1/36 entry 54
14. NRS BR/CAL/1/37 entry 1081
15. NRS BR/CAL/1/36 entry 54 and an unnumbered entry for 11th November
16. NRS BR/CAL/23/7 (33) and 23/8 (31) respectively
17. NRS BR/CAL/1/36 entry 1509
18. NRM 7453/C RHP 70087
19. NRS BR/CAL/23/8 (33)
20. NRS BR/CAL/1/34 entry 1217
21. NRS BR/CAL/1/37 entry 1081

Plate 7.13
NRM St. Rollox collection reference SRX442 is a fine
view of the First class end of Diagram 29 Coupé Lavatory
Composite number 39, which was built in 1894. The door
of the lavatory between the two nearest compartments
is open, but the seat cushion clearly extends across the
opening. The lavatory compartments and the smoking
compartment have Laycock torpedo ventilators. Note
also the running number repeated above the
window in the compartment doors, and
the eyelets for the Harrison cord
alarm system.

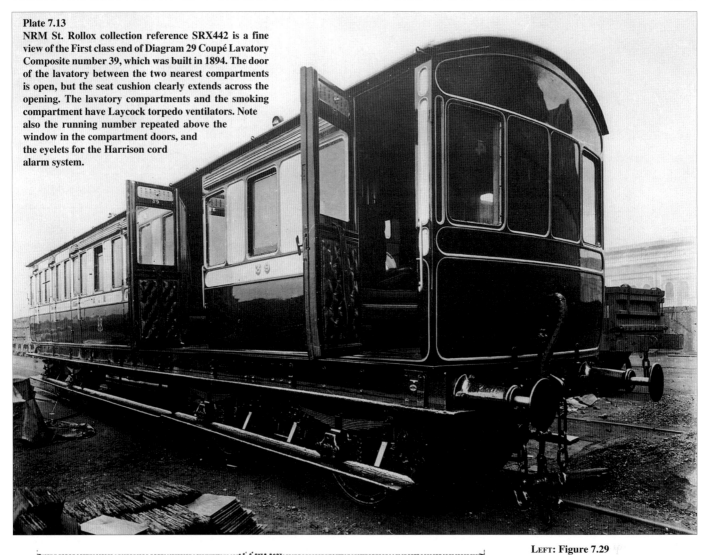

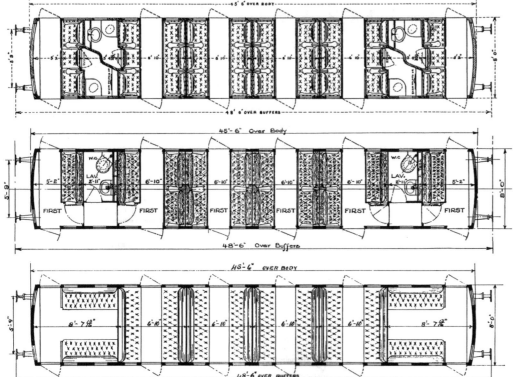

LEFT: Figure 7.29
The First class Lavatory Coupé to
Diagram 24 with a demountable
seat in front of the lavatory door.
According to *Railway & Travel
Monthly* the Caledonian began to
remove the seats from the middle
of 1910 – see the full quotation in
Chapter 3.5.

Figures 7.30 (*centre*) and **7.31** (*bottom*)
The modification in Figure 7.30 may
have been made by the LM&SR. The
pairs of lavatories in Diagram 24
Coupé First have been redesigned,
with access via a short side corridor.
It was now Diagram 24A.
Figure 7.31 definitely was a post-
Grouping modification. As part
of down-rating to Third class, the
lavatories were removed from
four Diagram 24 carriages and
longitudinal seats were fitted.
The carriages were re-assigned to
Diagram 25A.

7.6: CARRIAGES FROM WEST COAST JOINT STOCK

In December 1882 a West Coast Conference minute recorded that fourteen Third class carriages *'which have become unsuitable through long use'* should be replaced and divided between the two companies.[1] In *West Coast Joint Stock* they are identified as Type 5 27-foot 6-inch carriages numbered 62-75, which entered service in 1871.[2] Although the authors suggest that the Caledonian refused to take up its quota,[3] three carriages did in fact appear in the CR capital expenditure return for the period ending January 1883 at a cost of £904 1s 6d.[4] There is no record of these carriages in the Coaching Plant Stock Book, so they must have been withdrawn before its compilation.

SLEEPING SALOONS

Pioneer Sleeping carriages 101-104 became surplus in 1884. The two acquired by the Caledonian were probably renumbered 1 and 2 in the Saloon carriage series. There is no record of the transaction in the capital expenditure return or the half-yearly rolling stock return. Their CR career is described in Chapter 13.

TYPE 1 LUGGAGE TRI-COMPOSITES TRANSFERRED IN 1885-87

Twenty 6-wheeled Tri-Composites were withdrawn from WCJS service from *'want of lavatory accommodation.'*[5] The minute states that they had two First class compartments and one each Second and Third class. *West Coast Joint Stock* records that this was the original configuration retained by twelve carriages which were not altered when twenty-seven others were reclassified in 1885.[6] It is then further at variance with the minute by stating that all thirty-nine carriages were withdrawn between 1887 and 1891.

The Caledonian acquired eight of the twenty, one more than its allocation. This was because it did not take up its entitlement to one of the four Sleeping carriages 262-265 that were made surplus at the same time.[7] The Sleeping carriages had a reputation for bad riding which modification had not cured.[8] The transfer of the Tri-Composites appeared in the July 1885 rolling stock return but not in the capital expenditure record.

According to the capital expenditure and the rolling stock returns for the half year ending January 1888, eight more Tri-Composites were transferred to the CR at £325 each.[9] These would have been reconfigured to one each First and Second and two Third class compartments, plus luggage locker.

Although there is a blank entry in the Diagram Book index, these carriages were probably renumbered 230-237 and assigned to Diagram 12. The Coaching Plant Stock Book confirms the building date of 1871 and the configuration conforms to that shown in Diagram 12 – see Figure 7.32. Numbers 232 and 233 were withdrawn before the First World War.

Six of the original eight intake were probably numbered 218-223. The Coaching Plant Stock Book configuration matches, and records them a dual-braked, further supporting the theory that they were originally Joint Stock. The Diagram Book index places them in Diagram 13 (Figure 7.33). They were gas-lit and painted in full passenger livery. They were converted to order H43 in 1889, just after some of the Luggage Composites transferred in 1889. The first was withdrawn in 1925, the last in 1929.

SURPLUS LUGGAGE COMPOSITES

In 1888, the West Coast partner companies were again concerned about the lack of lavatory provision. The two General Managers wrote a letter to the Committee which stated:

'out of a total of 136 composite carriages 55 were not fitted with lavatories, and this accommodation could not be provided within the existing vehicles without curtailing the space for luggage and so lessening their suitability for the through English and Scotch traffic.

The Officers therefore recommend in lieu of altering the present non-lavatory composites that they be taken over gradually by the two Companies.'[10]

The letter then asked for instructions from the two Superintendents about how many vehicles should be replaced each year. In the event, the replacement process was spread over the five years from the period ending January 1889 to that ending January 1894. The CR acquired eighteen carriages, which are described below.

LUGGAGE COMPOSITES ENTERING CR SERVICE IN 1889

In the period ending January 1889, seven carriages were transferred to the CR at a cost of £2,758.[11] The winter was the quiet period for Anglo-Scottish travel, so they could be spared immediately. Their 42 foot long replacements entered service in May 1889, in time for the summer season.[12]

The CR allocated them numbers 14, 16-18, 20, 22, 24. They are erroneously described as having lavatories in *West Coast Joint Stock*,[13] contradicting the very reason for which they were deemed surplus to requirements. The wheelbase was 18 feet.

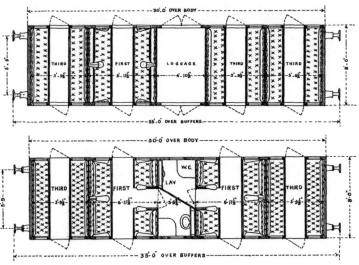

Figures 7.32 and 7.33
These figures show two modifications to West Coast Joint Stock Tri-Composites after acquisition by the Caledonian. Eight carriages were built to CR Diagram 12. The Diagram 13 carriages were more extensively modified, with the luggage compartment converted to a pair of lavatories.

In fact, the central luggage locker was converted under order H37 into a pair of lavatories as per drawing 6040 dated 27th May 1889. This was for 'alteration of 30' composite to Lavatory Comp.' A further drawing (number 6107 dated 11th November) was a 'General Arrangement of 3rd and 2nd lavatory carr.' Neither has survived.

Two First class compartments were arranged around a centrally placed pair of lavatories, accessed through a gap in the seating. The First class accommodation was flanked on each side by a Third class compartment.

They were also assigned to Diagram 13. In the diagram, the length is given as 30 feet, whereas the Coaching Plant Stock Book correctly gives the length as 30 feet 6 inches, as does the 1921 Stock List. Number 14 was withdrawn in 1918. The rest survived until or just after the Grouping. Number 18 was the only one to carry an LM&SR number.

LUGGAGE COMPOSITES TRANSFERRED IN 1892

Six more carriages were charged to the capital account in the half year ending July 1892 at £2,782 6s 7d.[14] According to *West Coast Joint Stock*,[15] the carriages renumbered 46-48 by the CR had two each First and Third class compartments and a small luggage locker. Numbers 49 and 52 had only one First class compartment and a larger luggage section. Number 51 had one First and three Third class compartments and a small luggage locker.

The *West Coast Joint Stock* description implies that the carriages were 30 feet 6 inches long. The 1921 Stock List gives this length to numbers 49 and 52 only. The other three were included with the Drummond Diagram 10 Brake Composites at 35 feet 6 inches long,

a dimension not used by the WCJS. There is no obvious explanation for this.

According to the Coaching Plant Stock Book all the carriages were converted by fitting a handbrake in the luggage locker or compartment. The Stock List confirms that they were Brake Composites. They did not appear in the Diagram Book. None carried an LM&SR number, although all but two lasted until after the Grouping.

LUGGAGE TRI-COMPOSITES ACQUIRED IN 1893

Five Type 9 32-foot carriages, built in 1877, were acquired by the CR and charged to the capital account in the period ending January 1894 at £2,135.[16] They were renumbered 260-264. The Third class compartment at one end, which had been upgraded to Second class while in WCJS service, reverted to Third class. There was a small 3-foot 10-inch luggage locker at the centre of the body. The double doors were consequently 3 feet 6 inches wide.

They did not appear in the Diagram Book, probably because only 261 and 264 survived beyond 1912. The numbers 262 and 263 were allocated to 'Grampian' Composites built in 1906. Number 260 was taken by a 57-foot Brake Composite in early 1912. The Coaching Plant Stock Book entry is shown as Plate 1.7.

The Coaching Plant Stock Book describes the two survivors as '*Brake Composites*,' which suggests that a handbrake was fitted in the luggage locker. If that was the case, a droplight would have been fitted in at least one of the double doors. The two survivors were allocated, but did not carry, LM&SR numbers. A photograph of one of these carriages is shown in Plate 7.14.

Plate 7.14
Five of these Luggage Tri-Composites were acquired in 1893 and only two survived beyond 1912. This example was photographed at Perth, date unknown. The Caledonian fitted the luggage compartment with brake gear, turning them into Brake Composites. A lookout appears to have been fitted to one of the doors, but there is no sign of glazing.

REFERENCES
1. NRS BR/WCC/1/8 minute 2002
2. *West Coast Joint Stock*, p. 58
3. *West Coast Joint Stock*, p. 62
4. NRS BR/CAL/23/5 (40)
5. NRS BR/WCC/1/8 minute 2242
6. *West Coast Joint Stock*, p. 60
7. NRS BR/WCC/1/8 minute 2318
8. *West Coast Joint Stock*, p. 68
9. NRS BR/CAL/23/6 (18)
10. NRS BR/WCC/1/8 minute 2390
11. NRS BR/CAL/23/6 (21)
12. *West Coast Joint Stock*, p. 97
13. *West Coast Joint Stock*, p. 62
14. NRS BR/CAL/23/7 (29)
15. *West Coast Joint Stock*, p. 62
16. NRS BR/CAL/23/8 (29)

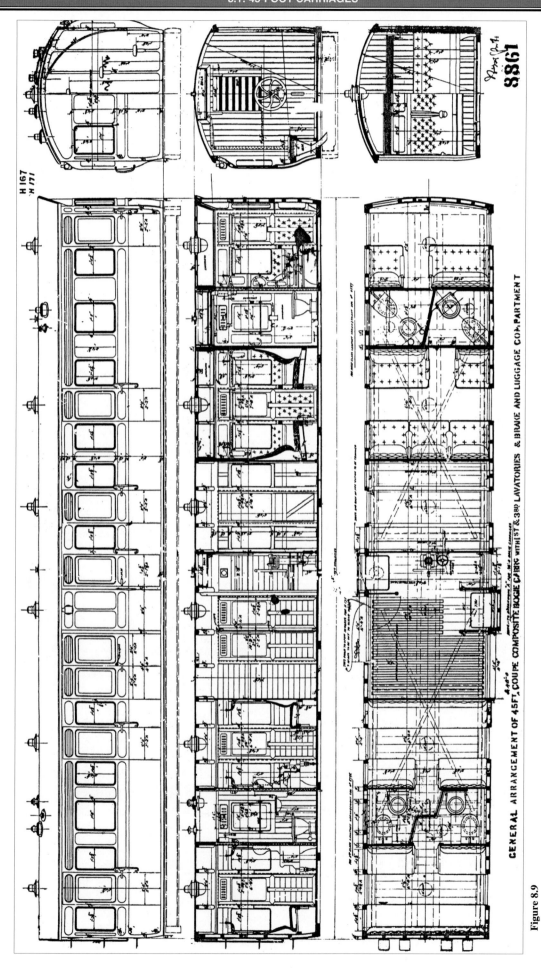

8861

H 167
H 171

GENERAL ARRANGEMENT OF 45FT. COUPE COMPOSITE BOGIE CARRG WITH 1ST & 3RD LAVATORIES & BRAKE AND LUGGAGE COMPARTMENT

Figure 8.9
Diagram 31 Coupé Luggage Composite was a new design built in the first half of 1898. The drawing also carries the dimensions for the 48-foot 3 inch version to Diagram 36. This design incorporated lavatory facilities for the guard as well as passengers, as can be seen in the centre cross section drawing. It is enlarged in Chapter 3, Figure 3.19.

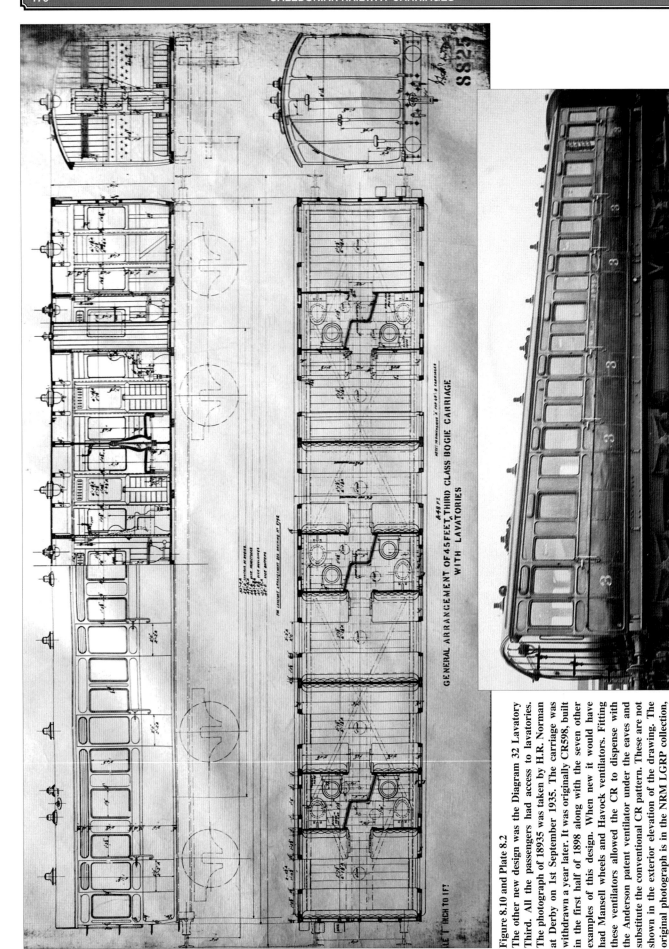

GENERAL ARRANGEMENT OF 45 FEET, THIRD CLASS BOGIE CARRIAGE
WITH LAVATORIES

Figure 8.10 and Plate 8.2
The other new design was the Diagram 32 Lavatory
Third. All the passengers had access to lavatories.
The photograph of 18935 was taken by H.R. Norman
at Derby on 1st September 1935. The carriage was
withdrawn a year later. It was originally CR598, built
in the first half of 1898 along with the seven other
examples of this design. When new it would have
had Mansell wheels and Havock ventilators. Fitting
these ventilators allowed the CR to dispense with
the Anderson patent ventilator under the eaves and
substitute the conventional CR pattern. These are not
shown in the exterior elevation of the drawing. The
original photograph is in the NRM LGRP collection,
ref: 6081.

8.2: 48-FOOT CARRIAGES

In April 1898 the lengthening of the standard 45-foot carriages was discussed. McIntosh submitted the inside measurements of the current 45-foot body, and dimensions for bodies of 48 and 49 feet.[1] On 13th April James Thompson wrote to McIntosh on behalf of Robert Millar:

'I have received from Mr Kempt copy of the Minute of Meeting of 31st ultimo recommending First and Third Class Bogie Carriages 48 feet in length over the body, and have written approving the recommendation.'[2]

McIntosh implemented the decision in the half year ending January 1899, starting with order H169. The change did not materially increase the leg room in compartments; instead, the seats in both classes were made deeper. As part of the development the doors reverted to 2 feet 2 inches wide. A new underframe drawing (St. Rollox 8914)[3] was produced. Compared with the 45-foot underframe, the bogie pivots were 3 feet 2 inches further apart. This seemingly odd variation is explained by the reversal of the one inch off-centre location of the bogie pivot. The original body drawings for the 45-foot stock were re-issued with the new dimensions added.

Construction of these carriages only lasted for eighteen months, after which the width was increased. The correlation between the diagram numbers assigned to the three types of carriage is shown in the table below. Only the 45-foot designs that were repeated at the increased length and/or width are shown.

TYPE	DIAGRAM		
	45 FEET	48 FEET	
		8 FEET	8½ FEET
7-compartment First	21	38	46
7-compartment Composite	26		44
Coupé Lavatory Composite	28		48
Coupé Lavatory Brake Composite	31	36	
6-compartment Lavatory Third	32	37	43
8-compartment Third	33	39	47
6-compartment Brake Third	34	40	45

Five Diagram 36 Coupé Brake Composites were built to order H171, authorised as renewals in the half year ending January 1899.[4] Numbers in the Large Diagram Book index and the 1921 Stock List were 240, 241, 244, 246, 248. They are erroneously assigned to Small Diagram Book 57 in the transcription of the Coaching Plant Stock Book.

Nine Diagram 37 Lavatory Thirds were authorised at the same time and built to order H169. The Coaching Stock Register only records eight carriages. These too were dual-fitted, no doubt for longer distance working on railways that employed the vacuum brake. The lavatories were removed from carriage 499 *'at a later date'* according to the Coaching Plant Stock Book, and assigned to Diagram 37A. It still had lavatories in the 1921 Stock List. In Diagram 37A, three compartments were converted into ordinary transverse seating, the other three replaced the lavatories with longitudinal seats – see Figure 8.11.

In the next accounting period[5] two more designs were built. Order H176 was for eight Diagram 38 7-compartment Firsts. A further example (number 304) was purchased from Hurst, Nelson in 1900. The carriages were electrically lit.

The 8-compartment Diagram 39 Thirds were built to order H182 and were gas-lit. An extra carriage (number 650) built by Hurst, Nelson at the same time was lit by electricity. These carriages were part of an authorisation for one hundred Third class carriages as capital expenditure.[6] The St. Rollox-built vehicles were allocated a block of numbers from 1185 to 1214.

As part of the renewals programme for the half years ending July 1899 and January 1900, fifteen Diagram 40 Brake Thirds with six compartments were built to orders H174 and H179.[7] They were gas-lit. One of the five carriages in the first order has not been recorded in the Coaching Plant Stock Book, which suggests that it was an accident victim.

WIDTH INCREASE

In 1900, after completion of thirty Third class carriages as part of order H182, the width of the body was increased by 6 inches. The officers' memorandum which authorised construction of the one hundred Third class carriages and ten each First class and Brake Vans records that Sir James Thompson (the Caledonian's General Manager) wanted to speak to McIntosh about the steel frames proposed to be taken from Leeds Forge and also about the proposal to make the carriages *'a little wider with a view of providing additional sitting accommodation.'*[8] A new standard underframe drawing was issued, St. Rollox 9888 – see Figure 8.12.[9] The extra width and the revised internal layouts warranted the new diagram numbers shown in the previous table.

IMPROVED LAVATORY ACCESS

In the new Lavatory Third design the increased width gave space for an internal corridor. The Diagram 43 carriages had six compartments with a centre corridor between each pair giving access to a lavatory on one side and a washbasin on the other. This was a

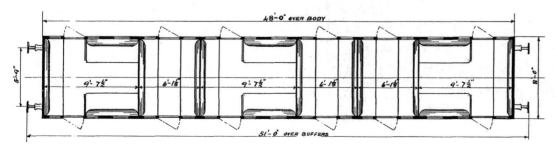

Figure 8.11
The modifications to 48-foot Lavatory Third 499, when it became Diagram 37A, may have taken place after the Grouping.

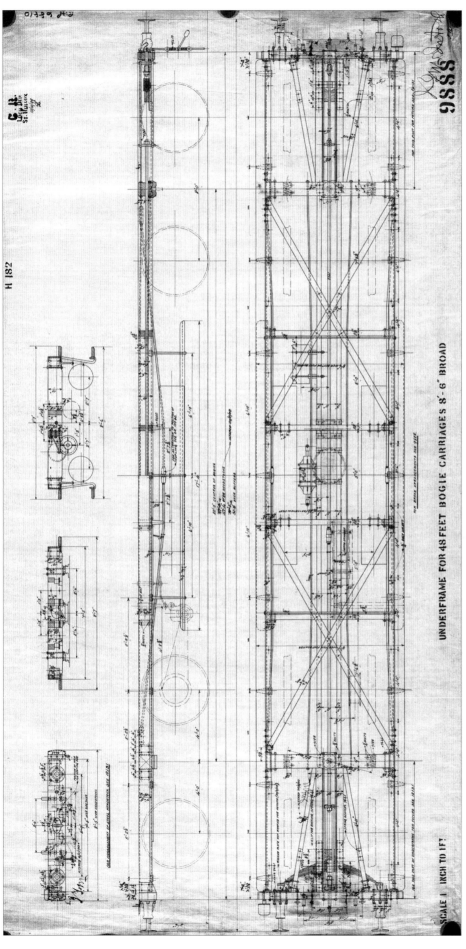

H 182

UNDERFRAME FOR 48 FEET BOGIE CARRIAGES 8'-6" BROAD

SCALE 1 INCH TO 1 FT

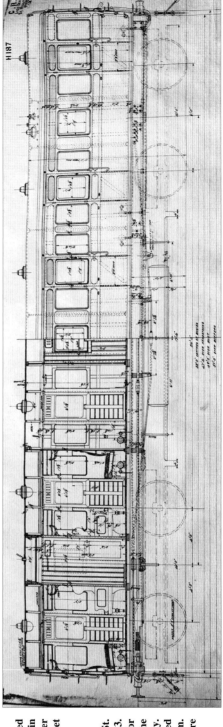

H 187

ABOVE: Figure 8.12
The 48-foot underframe was introduced in late 1898 and widened by 6 inches in 1900. This is drawing 9888 of the wider underframe. There is no longer an offset to the bogie pivots.

RIGHT: Figure 8.14
This side elevation of is taken from St. Rollox drawing 10511 for Diagram 43. It was produced for the second order for these carriages, but annotated for the first order built six months previously. The drawing shows the Consolidated Heating Co.'s carriage warming system. All eighteen carriages of this design were steam heated.

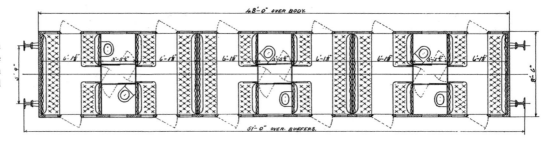

Figure 8.13
The extra 6 inches body width made lavatory access possible via short internal corridors in the Diagram 43 Lavatory Third design.

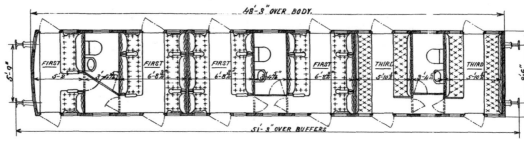

Figure 8.15
Diagram 48 Coupé Lavatory Composite was a modification of the 45-foot Diagram 28. The extra body width was used to improve access to lavatories by short side corridors.

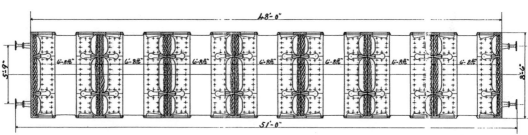

Figure 8.16
The rearrangement of arm rests in the Diagram 46 Firsts allowed four seats per side rather than three, to make the most of the 6-inch increase in body width.

much more spacious arrangement than in the narrower Diagram 37. It meant, however, that the number of lavatories was halved.

Twelve carriages to order H187 were authorised as renewals in the half year ending July 1900.[10] Presumably because they were a modification to Diagram 37, a full drawing was not issued immediately. Drawing 10029, dated 22nd December, showed the new lavatory arrangement, followed up by 10068 and 10069 in January 1900, none of which has survived. The internal layout is shown in Figure 8.13.

Six carriages were built to order H192, authorised for the next period.[11] This order was steam heated according to the minute. General arrangement drawing 10511 dated 2nd November 1900 was produced for order H192, but was annotated H187;[12] this is Figure 8.14. A drawing with the same St. Rollox number showed three cross sections of the carriage.[13] The earlier order was also steam heated according to the Coaching Plant Stock Book, which is corroborated by the drawing. The carriages had dual brakes, with through traffic off the CR system in mind.

Four Diagram 48 Coupé Lavatory Composites were authorised as replacements in the period ending January 1901.[14] The drawing number was 10694.[15] The lavatories were linked by side corridors to adjacent compartments – see Figure 8.15. They were dual brake fitted. Only three carriages were traced in the Coaching Plant Stock Book transcription and in the 1921 Stock List – numbers 129, 141 and 152. Number 141 was withdrawn in June 1921, to be replaced by a 57-foot Composite.

EXTRA SEATING

The Diagram 46 Firsts had two armrests per side with unequal spacing, which increased the seating capacity to eight per compartment, compared with six in the narrower carriages. The drawing number was 10150.[16] Another drawing with the same number showed the end elevations.[17] The revised internal layout is shown in Figure 8.16.

MORE SPACIOUS CARRIAGES

In most cases the increased width afforded extra space without an increase in seating. The Coaching Plant Stock Book records that ten Diagram 44 Composites were built to order H186, although there is no minute recording their authorisation. The drawing number was 10562.[18] They were numbered in a block from 311 to 320. Two (312 and 313) were dual brake fitted.

Twenty Diagram 45 Brake Thirds were built as part of the one hundred carriages authorised as capital expenditure. The drawing number was 10014.[19] Fifteen were built in the half year ending July 1901 to order H185. The remainder appeared in the next period to order H196. They were numbered 1255-1274.

Ten were authorised as capital expenditure for the period ending July 1900.[20] They were built to order H183 and given a block of numbers from 294 to 303. They cost £926 each.[21] Six more were authorised as replacements in July 1902[22] and built to order H206. A further example (number 305), built by Pickering in 1905,[23] was electrically lit. This carriage is shown in Plate 8.3. A photograph of its interior is shown in Plate 4.17.

Forty Diagram 47 Thirds were built as part of the hundred carriages to order H182. They entered service in the period ending July 1900, according to the Coaching Plant Stock Book, but only twenty-nine were charged at £677 according to the capital expenditure records.[24] Drawing 10344[25] confuses the issue, because it is annotated for orders H182 and H211, plus the running numbers for order H182 (1215-1254), but is dated 1st August 1900. A drawing with the same St. Rollox number[26] records the cross sections. This drawing does not carry any order number. Six more were built to order H211 during the period ending January 1903, plus one more by Pickering in 1904.[27] These last seven carriages were electrically lit. The Pickering carriage is shown in Plate 8.4.

Plates 8.3 (*above*) and 8.4 (*below*)
These are R.Y. Pickering publicity photographs of electrically-lit carriages. The Diagram 46 First number 305 was built in 1904. It has two Crests and a small Monogram. Diagram 47 Third number 1291 has one Crest only. This carriage was also built in 1904.

NEW DESIGNS

Two new designs were built. The Diagram 45A Brake Third had a larger guard's and luggage section than Diagram 45, which reduced the passenger accommodation to four compartments and forty seats. Drawing 11723, which showed the full carriage, has not survived. St. Rollox 11780 was for the extended Brake compartment,[28] which included a cycle rack. The revised brake end arrangement is shown in Figure 8.17.

Six were authorised as replacements in the period ending July 1903, to order H215.[29] Only five are recorded in the Coaching Plant Stock Book. They were electrically lit. Order H220 in the following period[30] was for eight carriages, two electrically lit, the rest gas. In the next half year[31] five were built to order H222. Finally, order H229[32] in the period ending January 1905 was for four electrically lit carriages. Although they were replacements, a block of numbers from 604 to 616 was allocated to these carriages, the remainder receiving random numbers. Numbers 610-616 were electrically lit.

The other new design was the Diagram 49 Coupé Semi-corridor Brake Composite. The four carriages to order H209 were authorised for the half year ending July 1902.[33] This contradicts the Coaching

Plant Stock Book which has the build date of January 1903. They seated nine First class passengers and twenty-eight Third, according to the Stock Book. They electrically lit and had dual brakes. They were numbered 56, 169, 172 and 249. Drawing 11302 was for the body only.[34] The internal layout is shown in Figure 8.18. A photograph of two carriages from this order is reproduced as Plate 8.5.

Diagram 49A was a variation of the H209 order, with the Brake and Third class compartments transposed. Windows were cut into the Brake end, improving the guard's view. The internal layout is shown in Figure 8.19 and a side elevation in Figure 8.20. The St. Rollox drawing was number 11978.[35] Four were built to order H214, authorised as renewals for the period ending July 1903.[36] They were numbered 113-116. A photograph is shown in Plate 8.6.

The Coaching Plant Stock Book records them as slip carriages, but there is no mention of this in the minute or on the drawing. The working of slip carriages is described in Chapter 2.5. The Stock Book states that number 116 was withdrawn in 1916, presumably as an accident victim. It was replaced by a 57-foot Composite carriage to Diagram 121A. This design is described in Chapter 11.1.

The number built of each type of 48-foot carriage is shown in the table opposite.

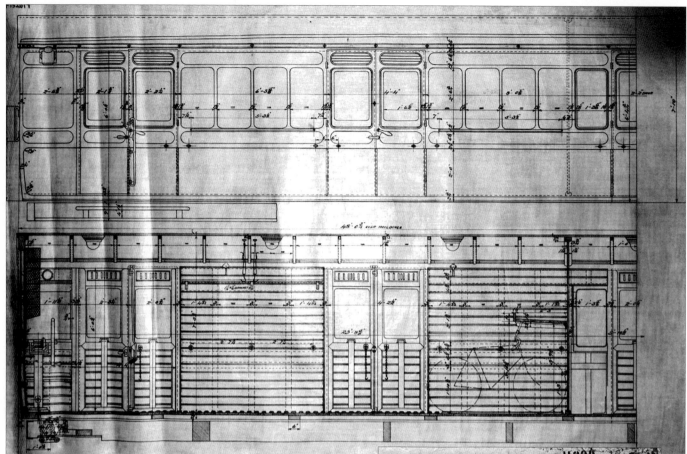

Figure 8.17
This is part of St. Rollox drawing 11780, showing the modification to the Diagram 45 Brake Third to produce Diagram 45A.

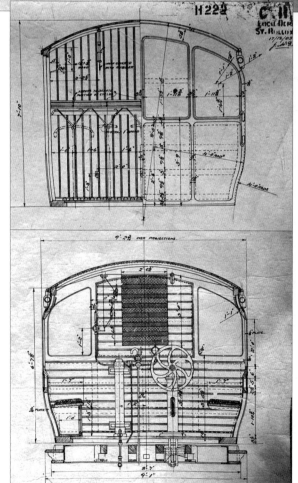

Type	8 Feet	8 Feet 6 Ins
7-compartment First	9	17
7-compartment Composite		10
Coupé Lavatory Composite		3
Coupé Lavatory Brake Composite	5	
6-compartment Lavatory Third	8	18
8-compartment Third	31	51
6-compartment Brake Third	14	20
Total	67	119

Bogie Brake Vans

The Brake Vans followed the same design evolution as the carriages. All three versions had a central guard's area with lookouts directly opposite each other and a single door alongside. There were two pairs of double doors on each side for luggage loading. The vans were gas-lit, dual-braked and fitted with steam heating pipes.

Diagram 35 was the 45-foot version. The St. Rollox drawing number was 8333 – see Figure 8.21.[37] Eleven were built to orders H147 and H160. They were treated as renewals and authorised for the half years ending July 1897 and January 1898.[38] Although it is not shown in the Diagram Book, all versions of the van, including Diagram 35, were fitted with a water closet under one of the guard's seats and a gas heater adjacent to the other. Drawings 8338 (*water tank and closet for Bogie Brake Vans H147*) and 8339 for the gas heater date from March 1897. They have not survived.

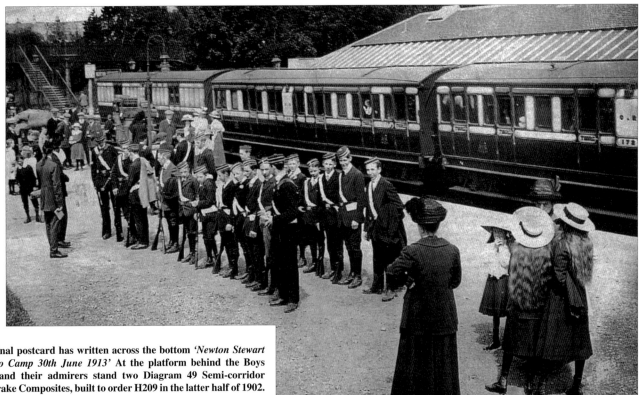

Plate 8.5
The original postcard has written across the bottom *'Newton Stewart B.B off to Camp 30th June 1913'* At the platform behind the Boys Brigade and their admirers stand two Diagram 49 Semi-corridor Coupé Brake Composites, built to order H209 in the latter half of 1902. Bringing up the rear is a Passenger Brake Van which looks to be the same width as the Composites. If that is the case it is a Diagram 42 van.

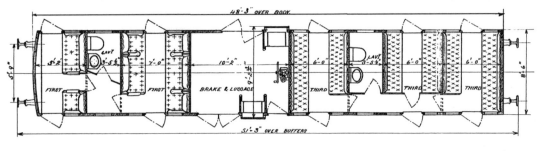

Figure 8.18
The Diagram 49 Semi-corridor *'composite with brake and luggage compartment'* built to order H198. Later orders had altered internal arrangements, as shown in Figures 8.19 and 8.20.

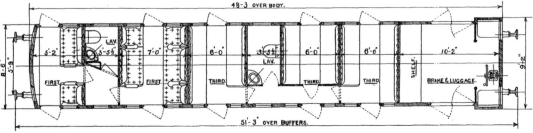

Figure 8.19
This version of Diagram 49 was assigned to Diagram 49A. The guard's and luggage compartment was moved from the centre of the body to the end to allow the carriages to be used as slip brakes.

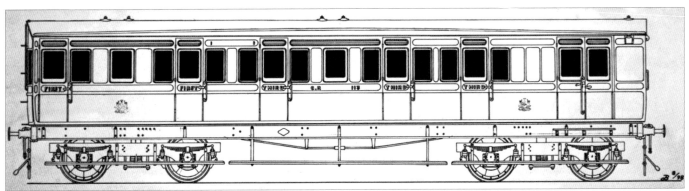

Figure 8.20
A side elevation of the revised Diagram 49A body, drawn by John Boyle from St. Rollox drawing 11978.

Diagram 41 was the first 48-foot development of Diagram 35, still 8 feet wide. The original drawing 8333 was re-issued with amended dimensions. Five were built to order H177, authorised in the renewal programme for the period ending July 1899,[39] and a further five to order H180 in the next half year.[40]

Diagram 42 was the same as Diagram 41, but 6 inches wider to conform to the contemporary carriage dimensions. Seventeen were built. The first ten were authorised in September 1899[41] and built to order H184. New drawings were issued, both with the St. Rollox number 10226: the general arrangement[42] was dated 4th May 1900, the other was for the end sections.[43]

They were not charged to the capital account until the period ending July 1902,[44] probably because there was pressure on the capital account from the absorption of old WCJS stock and the building of replacements. They received a block of numbers from 224 to 233. The Coaching Plant Stock Book records number 231 as a Bilsland's Bread Van.

Four more vans were built as renewals during the period ending in January 1901.[45] Only one is recorded in the Coaching Plant Stock Book. As discussed in *Caledonian Railway Wagons*,[46] it is possible that the others were converted into Diagram 42A Kitchen Vans for breakdown trains in 1917. The final order was for six vans to order H223. They were authorised as renewals in the period ending July 1904.[47]

Two each of the 45-foot and narrow 48-foot vans were withdrawn without receiving an LM&SR number, but most of the vans survived to receive a second LM&SR number. The 45-foot and narrow 48-foot vans were all withdrawn by World War II. Six of the wide 48-foot vans survived into the 1950s and one, number 5, was not withdrawn until October 1961. This van is shown in Plate 8.7.

Plate 8.6
This view from a postcard dated circa 1906 shows a Diagram 49A carriage at Airth station on the Alloa Branch from Larbert. According to the 1913 Marshalling of Trains Circular, all the services on the Alloa Branch except a return trip to Glasgow were worked by a *'Bogie Brake Composite, 4 Third and 2 First compartments.'* **Photograph © Falkirk Museums, licensor www.scran.ac.uk**

REFERENCES

1. NRS BR/CAL/5/11/315
2. NRS BR/CAL/5/11/316
3. RHP 68756
4. NRS BR/CAL/5/11 entry 323
5. NRS BR/CAL/1/42 entry 537
6. NRS BR/CAL/1/43 entry 141
7. NRS BR/CAL/1/42 entries 537 and 1033 respectively
8. NRS BR/CAL/5/11 page 399
9. RHP 68810
10. NRS BR/CAL/1/43 entry 449
11. NRS BR/CAL/1/43 entry 2075
12. NRM 7448/C RHP 70143
13. NRM 7489/C RHP 70144
14. NRS BR/CAL/1/43 entry 2075
15. NRM 7455/C RHP 70147
16. NRM 8002/C
17. NRM 7488/C RHP 70134
18. NRM 7445/C RHP 70138
19. NRM 8007/C
20. NRS BR/CAL/1/43 entry 141
21. NRS BR/CAL/23/9 (38)
22. NRS BR/CAL/1/45 entry 453
23. No record of card order number
24. NRS BR/CAL/23/9 (38)
25. NRM 7457/C RHP 70142
26. NRM 8006/C
27. No record of card order number
28. NRM 7450/C RHP to be assigned
29. NRS BR/CAL/1/46 entry 1363
30. NRS BR/CAL/1/47 entry 1127
31. NRS BR/CAL/1/48 entry 691
32. NRS BR/CAL/1/49 entry 769
33. NRS BR/CAL/1/44 entry 397
34. NRM 7449/C RHP to be assigned
35. NRM 7444/C RHP to be assigned
36. NRS BR/CAL/1/46 entry 1363
37. NRM 7515/C RHP 70099
38. NRS BR/CAL/1/40 entries 15 and 1484 respectively
39. NRS BR/CAL/1/46 entry 1363
40. NRS BR/CAL/1/42 entry 1033
41. NRS BR/CAL/1/43 entry 141
42. NRM 7514/C RHP 70140
43. NRM 7486/C RHP 70141
44. NRS BR/CAL/23/10 (28)
45. NRS BR/CAL/1/43 entry 2075
46. *Caledonian Railway Wagons*, p. 277
47. NRS BR/CAL/1/48 entry 691

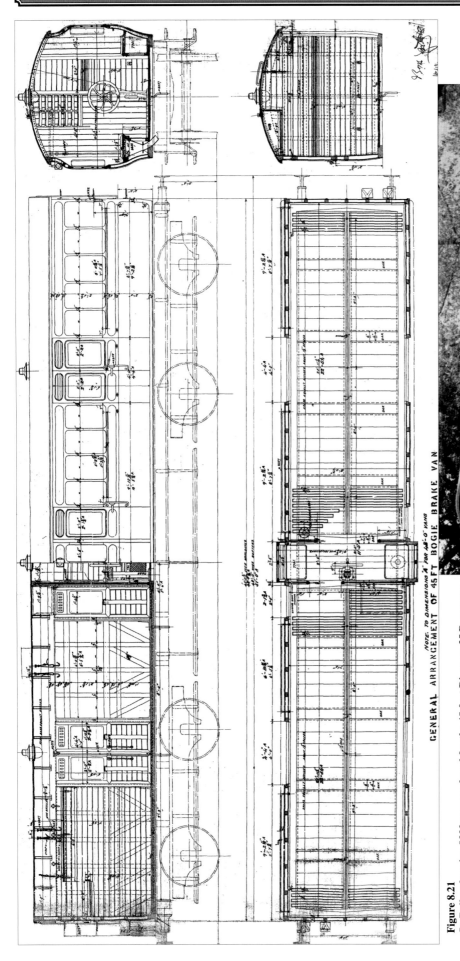

GENERAL ARRANGEMENT OF 45 FT BOGIE BRAKE VAN

NOTE: TO DIMENSIONS 'A' FOR 48'-0 VANS

Figure 8.21
St. Rollox drawing 8333 was produced for the 45-foot Diagram 35 Passenger Brake Vans in March 1897. It also carries dimensions for the narrow bodied 48-foot version to Diagram 41. A new drawing was issued for the wider vans.

Plate 8.7
The photograph, taken by A.B. McLeod (NRM ref: C127) records the last surviving CR Passenger Brake Van, withdrawn in 1961. Seen here in LM&SR livery as 33666, it was originally CR number 5, built in 1904 to order H223. It was 48 feet long and 8 feet 6 inches wide, to Diagram 42. Like many long-serving vehicles, the bottom beading has vanished, although the rest of the panelling is intact.

8.3: CONVERSIONS AND 50-FOOT DESIGNS

In 1897, ten Diagram 14 Thirds were rebuilt as Brake Thirds for the newly-opened Lanarkshire & Dunbartonshire line.[1] Neither Diagram Book records this configuration, so it is not possible to say whether a new carriage end with lookouts was provided, or if windows were formed in the existing end. The carriage numbers are not known, because the modification occurred before the Coaching Plant Stock Book was compiled.

Twelve more Thirds were converted for workmen's trains in 1899 when the Traffic Committee approved the conversion of '*12 of the oldest type of third class carriage into brake thirds. Cost £10 per carriage.*'[2] The carriages probably formed Diagram 16A. This shows a 31-foot Third with narrow compartments just over 5 feet between partitions. Originally there were six compartments, but the centre two had been gutted to form a Brake and Luggage section – see Figure 8.22. Wooden seats were fitted. The Coaching Plant Stock Book identifies ten carriages fitting this description. Their numbers were 239, 278, 433, 565, 582, 678-680, 795 and 3055.

In October 1901 the Traffic Committee authorised the conversion of '*20 six-wheel Third class carriages into Brake Thirds. Estimated cost £35 per vehicle.*'[3] In a minute in February 1904 the Committee agreed to '*alter 12 Old Composite Carriages into Brake Vehicles for use on Excursion Trains.*'[4] In October it was agreed that '*12, additional Old Composite Carriages to be converted into Brake Thirds*'[5] for the same purpose. It is not possible to identify these carriages from the Stock Book and they do not appear in the Large Diagram Book.

NEW FOUR-WHEELED CARRIAGE DESIGNS

As part of the renewals programme for the period ending July 1901 it was agreed that McIntosh would build nine 4-wheeled carriages comprising three Firsts, four Thirds and two Brake Thirds.[6] The development may have been prompted by the beginnings of the municipal tramway systems. Their use is not entirely certain, but the number and type of carriage authorised made up a standard Cathcart circle formation, as set out in the 1906 Local Working of Carriages Circular.

They were mounted on a common underframe which was the subject of drawing 10589.[7] This shows normal length buffers and a conventional coupling arrangement. Drawing 10654 depicts the First and Third class carriage bodies – see Figure 8.23.[8] They were shortened versions of the latest wide-bodied 48-foot designs, and thus an advance in comfort compared with the Drummond stock. There was no increase in seating capacity. The drawing refers to drawing

10014 for the Brake compartment arrangement, which was for the 48-foot Brake Thirds built to order H185 two years previously.

Although they were treated as renewals, they did not replace carriages of the previous Drummond design. They were built to orders H199 (First class, numbers 6, 92 and 189, Diagram 6), H200 (Third class, numbers 283, 593 and 636, 651, Diagram 7) and H201 (Brake Third, numbers 451 and 513, Diagram 7B). The Thirds had sparred wood seats.

All were gas-lit and painted brown, according to the Coaching Plant Stock Book. In the 1921 Stock List they were included with the earlier Drummond carriages, because the seating capacity was the same. They only lasted one or two years longer than the original Drummond designs. The last example was withdrawn in 1930.

CARRIAGE REBUILDING

Starting in the period ending January 1903,[9] the Traffic Committee authorised a programme to rebuild carriages as part of the renewals expenditure, rather than replace them. When rebuilding ceased in the period ending July 1905,[10] sixty carriages had been dealt with at a cost of £10,250. No details of the type of carriages were given. It is possible that they were 31-foot designs built in the 1870s which would be nearing the end of their design life.

CONVERSION OF DOUBLE-ENDED COUPÉ FIRSTS

Diagram 26B carries McIntosh's distinctive autograph. It shows a '*Bogie Composite converted from First Class.*' The drawing is annotated '*Present capacity 32 First. Altered as above 16 First and 36 Third Class Passrs.*'

The diagram must refer to the carriages in Diagrams 24 or 25, which were the only 45-foot 6-inch double Coupé Firsts that were 8 feet wide. There is no evidence that the conversion took place. The 1921 Stock Book records all the Diagram 24 and 25 carriages as Lavatory Firsts, as does the Coaching Plant Stock Book.

EARLY 50-FOOT DESIGNS

While retaining the same body style and end profile as the 48-foot stock, the carriage length was extended to 50 feet. Four designs were built on a common underframe (drawing 11262)[11] between 1901 and 1904, before the 'Grampian' stock described in the following section became the new standard. They were all dual brake fitted, steam heated and lit by electricity.

The renewals programme for the half year ending January 1902[12] authorised:

'*6, Bogie Third Class, end gangway, lavatory, steam heating, dual brakes*
4, Bogie Composite Corridor, end gangway, 2 first , 3 third and 1 luggage compartment, steam heating, dual brakes.'

The six Third class carriages appeared to two different designs, both to order H202. Diagram 90 was a side corridor carriage with lavatories at either end. Seven compartments seated fifty-six. It was built to drawing 10902, dated 4th July 1901. It has not survived. The internal layout is shown in Figure 8.24.

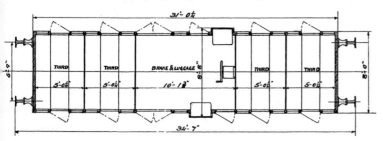

Figure 8.22
The Diagram 16A conversion of old Third class carriages to Brake Thirds by removing the centre two compartments.

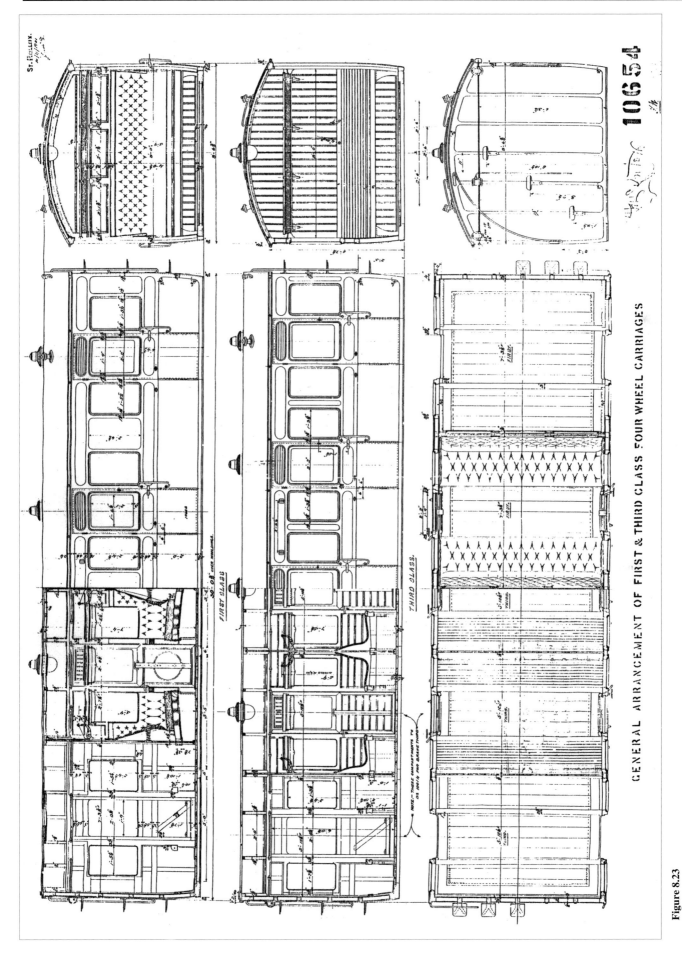

Figure 8.23

St. Rollox drawing 10654 depicts the bodies of the new four-wheel carriage designs authorised for construction in early 1901 to Diagrams 6 and 7. The guard's compartment in the Diagram 7B Brake Third was built to a drawing for a 48-foot vehicle.

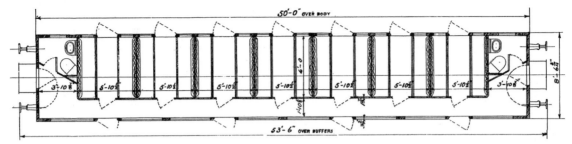

Figure 8.24 and Plate 8.8
The internal layout of the 50-foot side Corridor Third to Diagram 90, accompanied by one of the St. Rollox official photographs of number 982. The carriage is fitted with the modern train alarm system, but also has the Harrison cord system along the eaves. The dual arrangement is shown in Plate 2.8.

The three carriages were numbered 979, 980, 982. Three more carriages, numbered 983-985, were built in the half year ending January 1903 to order H207. They were modified to form part of the CR Ambulance Train described in Chapter 12. There are two photographs of 982 at the NRM and one of 984.[13] Number 982 is shown in Plate 8.8.

The second design was a centre aisle Third which was among the first of that layout in Britain to be built for ordinary use. Sixty seats were provided and two lavatories, centrally located. It was built to drawing 10837 dated 27th May 1901 and allocated Diagram 91. The drawing has not survived, but it was reproduced in *The Railway Engineer* – see Figure 8.25.[14] In the accompanying text the design was described as follows:

> *We know of only a few 'thirds' which could be ranked with the new Caledonian carriages, and of none that surpass them.*
>
> *Economy of space … has now become a factor of the highest importance, and in the plan of these carriages no space at all has been wasted.'*

Despite the fact that they seated four more passengers than the side corridor variation, the design was not perpetuated. Probably the British public expressed its reputed dislike for the lack of privacy of the open layout. The carriages were numbered 976-978. An official view of the interior of 978[15] appears in Chapter 4, Plate 4.18. In 1916 they were modified to form part of the CR Ambulance Train. When the Ambulance Train stock was replaced after the war, the design was not repeated.[16]

The Composites authorised in the same period were built to order H203. The GA drawing 10925, which has not survived, was issued in August 1901. The design appeared on page 92 of the Diagram Book. It had a side corridor with two First class compartments (twelve seats), four Third class (thirty-two seats), and a very small luggage

compartment in between. There were lavatories at either end of the carriage (Figure 8.26). They were numbered 86, 110, 171, 175.

The last design to appear was the Brake Composite to Diagram 93. Four carriages were authorised in the period ending July 1903 to order H219.[17] Their numbers were 81, 133, 144, 147. The design had originally been sketched in May 1903 (drawing 12044), but the GA drawing 12176[18] (Figure 8.27) was only completed in August. Three Third class compartments seated twenty-four and two Firsts seated twelve. The large Brake and luggage compartment had lookouts at the extreme end of the carriage. There was a single lavatory at the opposite end. A photograph of the compartment side of number 137 is shown in Plate 8.9 and the corridor side of an unidentified example in Plate 8.10. There is another photograph of one of these carriages at Oxenholme.[19]

REFERENCES
1. NRS BR/CAL/1/40 entry 208
2. NRS BR/CAL/1/42 entry 318
3. NRS BR/CAL/1/45 entry 424
4. NRS BR/CAL/1/49 entry 127
5. NRS BR/CAL/1/50 entry 297
6. NRS BR/CAL/1/44 entry 397
7. NRM 5730/C RHP 70145
8. NRM 7531/C RHP 70146
9. NRS BR/CAL/1/46 entry 508
10. NRS BR/CAL/1/50 entry 217
11. NRM 8084/C
12. NRS BR/CAL/1/44 entry 859
13. NRM St. Rollox collection ref: SRX307, 313 and 330
14. *The Railway Engineer*, July 1902, pp. 217-18
15. NRM St. Rollox collection ref: SRX316
16. NRS BR/CAL/1/67 entry 464
17. NRS BR/CAL/1/46 entry 1363
18. NRM 8003/C
19. *Caledonian Railway Livery*, p. 259

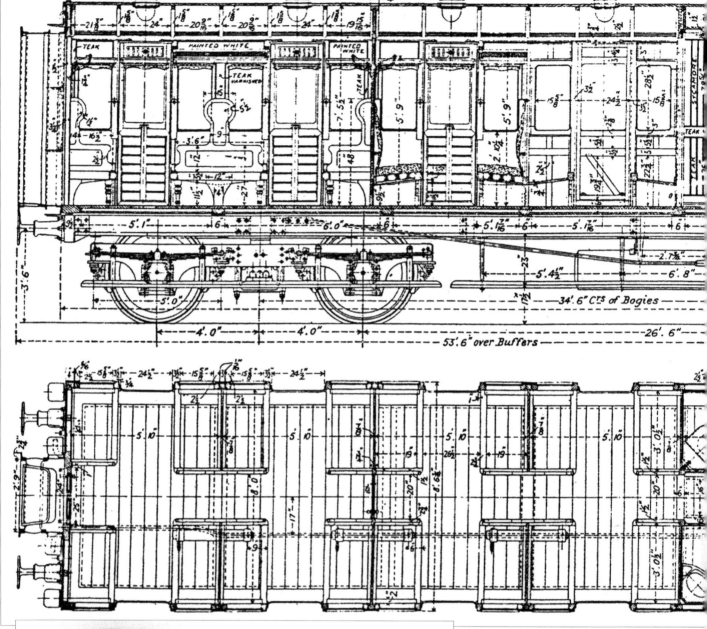

Plate 8.9
This shows the Brake end and the compartment
side of number 147, the last of the four Diagram 93
Brake Composites in order H219.

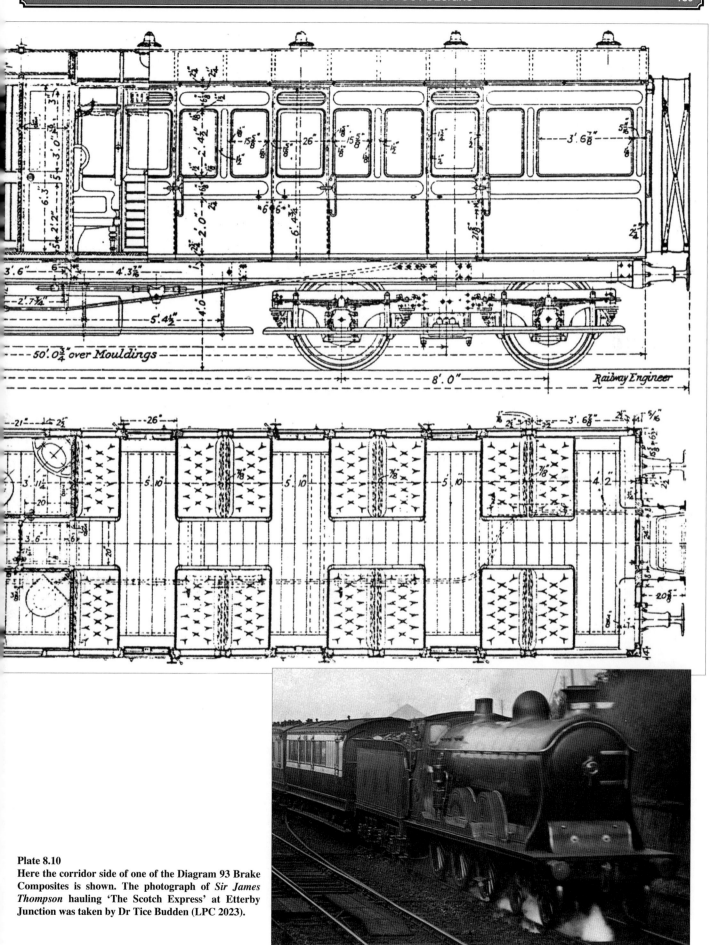

Plate 8.10
Here the corridor side of one of the Diagram 93 Brake Composites is shown. The photograph of *Sir James Thompson* hauling 'The Scotch Express' at Etterby Junction was taken by Dr Tice Budden (LPC 2023).

RIGHT: Figure 8.26
The Diagram 92 Corridor Composite had a small luggage compartment between the two classes of passenger accommodation. Each class had its own lavatory, and there was a door in the corridor which the guard would have kept locked to prevent fraternisation between the two classes.

BELOW: Figure 8.27
In the Diagram 93 Brake Composite carriage there was only one lavatory, at the Third class end. It was evidently socially acceptable for First class passengers to pass through the inferior class, while the Third class passengers had no need to trouble their superiors when attending to a call of nature. The figure is a reproduction of St. Rollox drawing 12176.

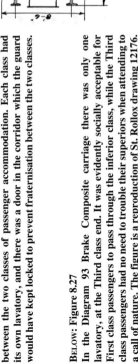

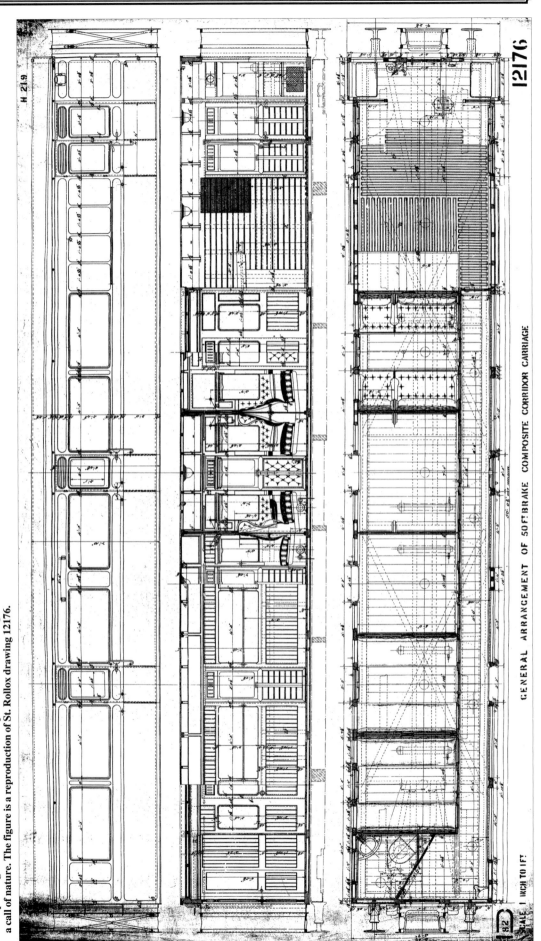

GENERAL ARRANGEMENT OF 50 FT. BRAKE COMPOSITE CORRIDOR CARRIAGE
SCALE 1 INCH TO 1 FT.

8.4: CARRIAGES FROM WEST COAST JOINT STOCK

The first half of the McIntosh era saw a large influx of WCJS carriages. The transfers came in three waves. The first was from 1895 to '98, when the CR acquired fifty-five vehicles as recorded in the Coaching Plant Stock Book, plus eight Brake Vans. In 1894 the West Coast Committee had decided to provide lavatories for both classes of traveller. It approved construction of ninety-nine corridor carriages, displacing 127 old vehicles.[1] A copy of the original minute is shown in Plate 8.11.

In 1901, thirteen 6-wheeled Brake Vans were transferred according to the Coaching Plant Stock Book, but only twelve were noted in the Capital Expenditure Record. The latter is the more likely figure, as the annual WCJS return for 1901 noted that thirty-five new 45-foot Brake Vans were added. Twelve would have been the expected proportion handed over to the CR. The half-yearly returns only record eight transfers.

During 1902/03, 124 more vehicles became surplus; the Caley received forty-five – its expected proportion. In this case the Stock Book and the capital expenditure returns agree. The capital account was duly credited on 31st July 1903 with £34,559 11s 4d.[2]

The carriages acquired by the Caledonian are described below in order of their acquisition. The diagram numbers and descriptions are those carried during WCJS service. The carriages were all

dual brake fitted. Nearly all were withdrawn in 1925/26 when the first standard LM&SR carriages were introduced. Exceptions are mentioned in the text. The ten ex-joint stock carriages that were used as Saloons by the Caledonian are included in Chapter 13.

Photographs of some of these carriages can be found in *West Coast Joint Stock*, as well as drawings of their internal layout. Drawings of altered internal arrangements in CR days are provided here, as well as a small number of photographs of the carriages in CR livery.

TYPE 6 AND DIAGRAM P32 BRAKE VANS

In April 1894 it was decided that the five Type 6 29-foot 6-inch Brake Vans and the twenty P32 30-foot vans should be replaced and divided between the companies.[3] The Type 6 vans had been built in 1871 and the P32s three years later.

Three of the earlier vans were transferred to the L&NWR.[4] By implication the other two (WCJS numbers 99 and 100) were acquired by the Caledonian. Seven of the P32 vans were transferred at the same time. Their WCJS numbers were 77-83. There is no information about any of these vans in CR service. Those taken over by the L&NWR were all scrapped by 1906. It is probable that the same happened on the Caledonian, which would account for their non-appearance in the Coaching Plant Stock Book.

P22 LAVATORY BRAKE TRI-COMPOSITE

These 42-foot carriages were built on radial underframes in 1889. Only the single First class compartment had lavatory access. There were three Third class compartments plus a half compartment for Second class, which allowed a reasonable size guard's and luggage section. They were transferred in February 1896. The half compartment was down-rated to Third class. They were allocated random numbers 66, 67, 105 and 224, and assigned to Diagram 22A.

The first two were down-rated to Brake Thirds in 1921 and 1923 and renumbered 1431 and 88 respectively. They then conformed to Diagram 34D. The lavatory was removed, and the space was combined with the adjacent First class compartment. This was down-rated to Third class with the usual bench seats, plus two single seats facing inwards – see Figure 8.28. There were now forty-five seats, according to the Coaching Plant Stock Book.

P29 BRAKE THIRD

These carriages were an early 42-foot design, built in 1887. According to *West Coast Joint Stock*,[5] they were the first Wolverton-designed carriage to incorporate a guard's compartment in a passenger-carrying vehicle.

ABOVE: Plate 8.11
West Coast Conference minute 2627 set in motion an influx onto the CR of over forty surplus West Coast Joint Stock carriages to make way for bogie stock with lavatory accommodation.
RIGHT: Figure 8.28
Diagram 34D was a late modification to two ex-WCJS Lavatory Brake Tri-Composites. The alterations took place in 1921-23.

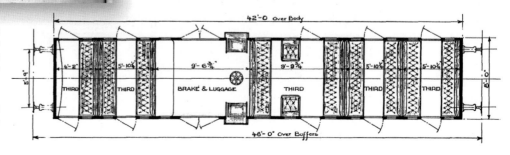

The Caledonian acquired four in February 1896 and renumbered them 953-956. They appeared on page 34A of the CR Diagram Book. The CR left them on their radial underframes and made only the minor alteration of relocating the handbrake stanchion.

P26 LUGGAGE THIRD

These 32-foot carriages were a 5-compartment Third with the centre compartment used as a luggage cupboard, accessed through a pair of small doors on each side. Two were handed over to the Caledonian in July 1896, renumbered 1078, 1079 and given Diagram 16B. A handbrake stanchion was fitted in the luggage compartment in 1907 as described in Chapter 9.4. They were originally oil-lit but are recorded as gas-lit in the Coaching Plant Stock Book and the 1921 Stock List.

P25 LUGGAGE THIRD

Five of these 34-foot carriages were transferred in 1896/97. The first three were renumbered 1123-1125 and the last two 959, 960. Five narrow compartments were separated by a 4-foot luggage locker accessed through double doors. A brake stanchion was fitted in the luggage locker in 1907.

They were given Diagram 16A, but the page in the Diagram Book is blank apart from the running numbers. Number 1123 was scrapped in 1903, presumably as an accident victim.

P21 LAVATORY COMPOSITE

These 32-foot carriages were the oldest general service vehicles to be acquired in the first wave, having been built in 1878. They did not have heating. Only the two First class compartments had access to lavatories. The CR numbered them 275-278 and assigned them to Diagram 13A. Number 276 was withdrawn in 1913.

P16 LAVATORY LUGGAGE COMPOSITE

Fourteen of these 42-foot carriages with radial underframes were acquired in 1897/98, and renumbered 279-292 by the Caledonian. A photograph of number 286 built new as number 25 for the WCJS is shown in West Coast Joint Stock, p. 96. The adjacent Third class compartment was incorporated into the luggage section and a brake stanchion was fitted. They were given Diagram 27B (Figure 8.29). In 1907, numbers 282-285 and 288 were set on bogies.

The remaining nine retained their radial underframe and small luggage compartment. In this guise they were assigned to Diagram 27A. As described in Chapter 9.4, they were altered to conform to Diagram 27B in 1907, but still with their radial underframe.

P17 LAVATORY LUGGAGE COMPOSITE

Five 34-foot carriages with one coupé end were taken over in the period ending July 1898 and allocated numbers 297-301. They were not allocated to a page in the Diagram Book. The lavatories were only accessible from the 1½ First class compartments, via 'turn up cushions' on the seats.

The luggage compartments in 300 and 301 were altered to 'small Bk. compt.' according to the Coaching Plant Stock Book. This presumably meant that a handbrake stanchion was added. The conversion took place in 1907, as described in Chapter 9.4.

P18 LAVATORY COMPOSITE

These were also 34-foot carriages with coupés at both ends. The First class/lavatory arrangement was the same as in P17. The rest of the accommodation consisted of two Third class and a half Second class compartment. The Caledonian was a two-class line by the time of acquisition, so the half compartment was treated as Third class.

The CR received four carriages and numbered them 293-296. Like the P17s, they were not entered in the Diagram Book. Number 293 was converted into Officers' Saloon number 1 to Diagram 52 in 1902. It is fully described in Chapter 13.5.

P19 LAVATORY COMPOSITE

A single coupé end 34-foot design, with a half First class compartment. Five carriages were taken over, renumbered 302-306 and assigned to Diagram 13B.

Two lavatories were accessed from the First class accommodation by way of 'turn up cushions.' The Caledonian removed this part of the seating to improve access, reducing the First class seating by two. This may not have happened when they were acquired. As discussed in Chapter 8.1 the CR provided the same type of lavatory access and the carriages were not modified until 1910. Probably as a consequence of this modification, the lavatory in the Diagram Book was 3 inches larger than shown in West Coast Joint Stock with a correspondingly smaller First class coupé compartment.

P20 SLEEPING COMPOSITE

Originally designed as Sleeping Tri-Composites in 1876, these carriages were modified while still in WCJS service to serve additionally as Day or Invalid Saloons. The CR acquired four in the period ending July 1898, renumbering them 307-310.

The First class sleeping compartment and adjoining lavatories were gutted to provide a 12-foot luggage and Brake section. The Second class compartment was redesignated as a narrow First. It is not known when the conversion took place. They were given Diagram 11A – see Figure 8.30.

P31 BRAKE VAN

Four 32-foot Brake Vans were taken over in September 1901. The Caledonian renumbered them 244-247. As built they had dog lockers at either end. Although not identified as such in Diagram 17B, they were retained by the CR. The four numbers are shown alongside the diagram, but the Coaching Plant Stock Book records 245 as withdrawn in June 1919. Withdrawal dates for the others are not shown, but they were not in the January 1921 Stock List. Numbers 244 and 247 were recorded as fitted with train heating pipes.

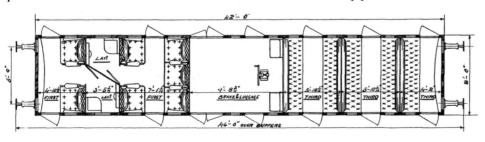

Figure 8.29
The Diagram 27B carriages retained their radial underframes after acquisition by the Caledonian. The original small luggage compartment was enlarged by incorporating the adjacent Third class compartment. Five were altered on acquisition in 1897; the remainder were altered ten years later.

P32 BRAKE VAN

According to the Coaching Plant Stock Book, nine vans were transferred in November 1901. They had very narrow flat sided 30-foot 6-inch bodies with overhanging eaves. A van in its WCJS days is shown in Plate 8.12.

Only four CR numbers are recorded – 240-243. The blank page 17A of the Diagram Book gives four more numbers (205, 206, 208, 209) plus 241, 243. The extra numbers on the page make the total number of both types of Brake Van transferred to twelve, as recorded in the Capital Expenditure Return.

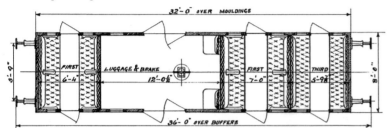

ABOVE: Figure 8.30
These carriages were originally WCJS Sleeping Saloons, subsequently adapted to serve as Invalid Saloons. In CR days as Diagram 11A, a Brake and luggage compartment was created out of the sleeping accommodation and adjoining lavatory.

A Diagram 98 Brake Van replaced number 242 in 1914. The index to the Diagram Book has no numbers under Diagram 17A, which suggests that they were taken out of revenue service at an early stage. They are not in the 1921 Stock List.

P15 LAVATORY LUGGAGE COMPOSITE

Seventeen 42-foot Composites built in 1890/91 were transferred during 1902/3. They had a single *coupé* First class half-compartment. By this time, pairs of lavatories were available to Third as well as First class passengers. Only the end Third class compartment lacked lavatory access. A small luggage locker with double doors separated the two classes.

They were renumbered 321-330 and 334-341, and assigned to Diagram 29A. The carriages in the range 328-341 had been built with radial underframes which were replaced by bogies before they were transferred.[6] A few lasted until 1930/31. A photograph of CR 330 is shown in Plate 8.13. An unidentified example is the first carriage in Plate 7.10, page 163.

ABOVE: Plate 8.12
This photograph is said to have been taken at Oban on the first day of the line's public opening to its western terminus on 1st July 1880. It shows the rear of a WCJS dual brake-fitted Passenger Brake Van with flat sides and a narrow body.

Plate 8.13
This was a WCJS Lavatory Luggage Composite, originally numbered 419 and renumbered 330 by the CR, to Diagram 29A. It has been fitted with the modern train alarm system.

P21A LAVATORY BRAKE COMPOSITE

In the period ending January 1903, three of these 42-foot carriages were transferred and renumbered 331-333. They had one First and three Third class compartments, all with lavatory access. The lavatories were too small to accommodate free-standing washbasins, so fold-down ones were fitted.

CR Diagram 36A only records one example. The Coaching Stock Plant Book records that numbers 332 and 333 were down-rated to Brake Thirds in 1907. They were renumbered 41 and 435. They then became Diagram 34B.

P21B LAVATORY LUGGAGE COMPOSITE

Sixteen 45-foot carriages were signed over from the West Coast Joint Stock in the first half of 1903. They had only been built seven years previously.[7] On acquisition, the carriages had a Third class compartment at one end with a small luggage compartment adjacent. The Caledonian allocated them numbers 338, 342-347 and 351-359.

As CR Diagram 29B, the luggage compartment was extended to the end of the carriage, a brake standard was fitted and windows cut into the end – see Figure 8.31 and Plate 8.14. The sides were unaltered except for the addition of a grab rail beside the guard's doors, which were the original Third class compartment entrances.

Carriages 338, 342, 356, 359 were fitted with slip coupling apparatus. Their use is described in Chapter 2.5. Number 355 was withdrawn in 1908, presumably as the result of an accident. The remainder lasted until the late 1920s/early 1930s. Two carried a second LM&SR number.

P21G LAVATORY BRAKE COMPOSITE

At the same time as the P21Bs were transferred, three 45-foot P21Gs were acquired and renumbered 348-350, filling the gap in the ex-P21B number series. Their configuration was identical to Diagram P21A, except that the guard's compartment was extended by 3 feet.

They appeared on page 36B of the Diagram Book. Only two carriages are recorded there. Number 348 was down-rated to Brake Third in 1908. It lasted until 1933, according to the Coaching Plant Stock Book; number 349 was withdrawn in 1936.

P48 45-FOOT LAVATORY BRAKE THIRD

In 1902, three of these 45-foot carriages were transferred and renumbered 1275-1277. They were given Diagram 34C. Two pairs of Third class compartments were separated by two lavatories, with a large central guard's and luggage section. Number 1277 lasted until 1932.

P24 42-FOOT LAVATORY LUGGAGE THIRD

Three examples were transferred in the period ending January 1903. They were renumbered 1278-1280. There were five compartments, one without lavatory access, and a small luggage section. Diagram 32A describes them as 'with lavatories and luggage compt.' The 1921 Stock List includes them among the ordinary Thirds. The Coaching Plant Stock Book transcription erroneously describes them as Brake Thirds. Number 1280 was not withdrawn until 1932. This carriage appears in a photograph at Perth in *West Coast Joint Stock*.[8]

REFERENCES
1. NRS BR/WCC/1/4 minute 2627
2. NRS BR/CAL/23/10
3. NRS BR/WCC/1/4 minute 2589
4. *West Coast Joint Stock*, pp. 62-63
5. *West Coast Joint Stock*, p. 93
6. *West Coast Joint Stock*, pp. 105-7, 114
7. *West Coast Joint Stock*, pp. 99-100
8. *West Coast Joint Stock*, p. 101

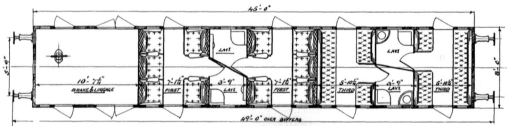

Figure 8.31 and Plate 8.14
Sixteen of these carriages were modified to CR Diagram 29B by incorporating the end Third class compartment into the luggage space. Windows were cut into the end. Four were fitted up as slip carriages. One of the carriages that was not fitted with slip couplings, probably number 351, was photographed at Perth. Behind it is a CR 8-compartment Third with an underframe in very poor condition.

CHAPTER 9
THE McINTOSH ERA – REVOLUTION IN 1905

9.1: THE 'GRAMPIAN' STOCK

By the middle of the first decade of the twentieth century, McIntosh's modernisation plan was well under way. High capacity mineral wagons had been built in quantity and a large-scale wagon replacement programme began to supersede primitive and inefficient mineral wagons and upgrade other designs.[1] The saturated 4-4-0 locomotive was developed to its design limit and a new breed of 4-6-0 would be introduced. Infrastructure was also being expanded, with new lines, docks on Clydebank and at Grangemouth, the extension and remodelling of Glasgow Central and the opening of the Caledonian Hotel in Edinburgh.

BUILDING AND WITHDRAWALS

The aggregate of the half-yearly returns from the period ending July 1905 to December 1912 is shown in the table below. After 1912 the report was not produced. The Third class additions nearly all took place from the start of the period up to the end of 1907.

Thirty-one of the additions to the Composite fleet were the result of converting First and Third class carriages, which started in the period ending July 1910 and continued until 1912. The returns show the reductions from the First and Third class fleet in a separate column. The carriages involved are described in Chapter 9.4.

TYPE	WORN OUT	REPLACED	ADDED
First	31	31	2
Third	173	173	71
Composite/Saloon	93	93	55
TOTAL	297	297	125

THE INTRODUCTION OF THE 'GRAMPIAN' STOCK

After nine years in office, McIntosh produced a set of carriages which placed the Caledonian in the forefront of British railway companies. The train between Glasgow and Aberdeen that was to become known as 'The Grampian Express' was unveiled in a carefully orchestrated publicity campaign.

McIntosh produced a set of corridor carriages that were 65 feet long and ran on 6-wheel bogies. The end and side throw coupled with their extreme width of 9 feet 3¾ inches concerned the North British, whose contemporary carriages were 9 feet wide at most. Four months after the trains started the service the CR Board reported correspondence[2] with the NBR and decided to:

'remit to Solicitor and Manager to consider whether the width of the handles and rails on the carriages could be reduced or failing that to grant an indemnity to the North British Railway so far as the extra width of the carriages is concerned.'

Modifications were made. St. Rollox drawings 13208–10 were for the door and commode handles, annotated *'for 9ft stock.'* The drawings have not survived. Nervousness about the generous dimensions was not confined to the North British. Caledonian Working Timetable appendices contained strict instructions about shunting the carriages and the need for care in sidings with structures close to the railway. Two St. Rollox photographs show the side of Composite 137 with damaged doors and commode handles – see Plate 9.1.

The stock formed the first set of carriages with corridor connections throughout that were designed for travel wholly within Scotland. The contemporary North British Railway's carriages on its service to Aberdeen were 49 feet long, gas-lit and semi-corridor.[3]

The Railway Engineer[4] was full of praise for the CR vehicles:

'They are fitted with every convenience, including hot and cold water in the lavatories, and form the finest trains ever built for purely Scottish traffic. The carriages are connected by gangways throughout. They are fitted for steam heating and electric light (Stone's system).'

To provide a smooth, quiet ride, the bogies were elaborately sprung and the coaches double-floored with the entire body insulated from the underframe by rubber blocks. A drawing of the bogie is shown in Figure 9.1. A layer of hair felt was inserted under the floor, in the side walls and along the roof to reduce noise. A description, drawing and photographs of the internal arrangements are given in Chapter 4.3. The salient dimensions of the 'Grampian' body style are shown in Figures 9.2 and 9.3.

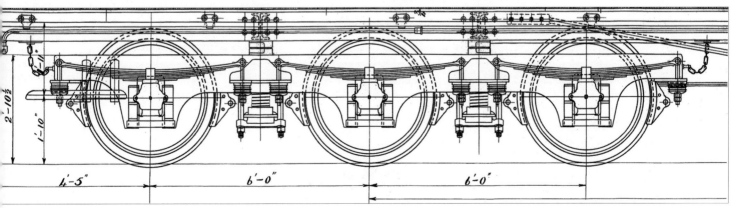

Figure 9.1
According to *The Railway Magazine*, the 'Grampian' bogie had three different varieties of springs. The secondary coil springs are prominent in this drawing.

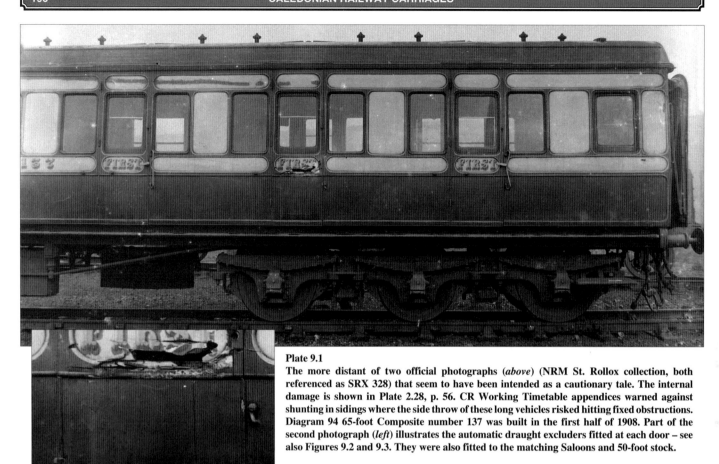

Plate 9.1
The more distant of two official photographs (*above*) (NRM St. Rollox collection, both referenced as SRX 328) that seem to have been intended as a cautionary tale. The internal damage is shown in Plate 2.28, p. 56. CR Working Timetable appendices warned against shunting in sidings where the side throw of these long vehicles risked hitting fixed obstructions. Diagram 94 65-foot Composite number 137 was built in the first half of 1908. Part of the second photograph (*left*) illustrates the automatic draught excluders fitted at each door – see also Figures 9.2 and 9.3. They were also fitted to the matching Saloons and 50-foot stock.

STOCK FOR THE ABERDEEN SERVICE

Until the arrival of the 'Grampian' stock, CR trains to Aberdeen were composed of 48-foot carriages, presumably with lavatories – the equivalent of the NBR carriages mentioned earlier. The marshalling diagram (St. Rollox drawing 12520)[5] of the new train is shown in Figure 9.4. The compartment measurements on this drawing (produced in late March 1904) were less spacious than those in the drawings of the carriages (produced mid-September) although the seating capacities remained the same. In the case of the Composite carriage the Third class compartments were increased in width by sacrificing 4 inches from the very generous First class compartment dimension. The revised measurements are shown in Figures 9.5 to 9.7.

Carriages for the first train were authorised for the period ending January 1905,[6] along with an extra Brake Third, presumably as a spare. They were charged to the renewals programme. Given the

BELOW: Figure 9.4
This drawing is the proposal for the new Aberdeen trains, dated 23rd March 1904. It features a Diagram 9 West Coast Joint Stock Dining car of similar length to the Caledonian carriages. The original drawing included a Class '140' 4-4-0 at its head. Note that the corridor side alternated down the train. The company was rightly concerned about the train's weight; an equivalent formation of 48-foot stock, excluding the Restaurant car, would have weighed about 90 tons less, and accommodated about sixty more passengers.

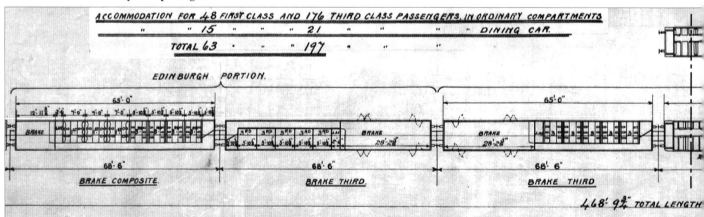

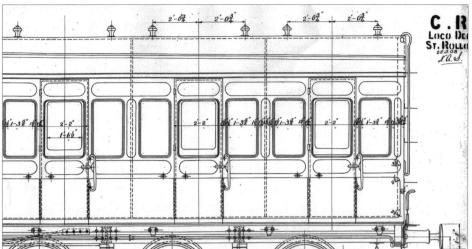

Figures 9.2 and 9.3
These two sections from the St. Rollox drawing of the compartment side of the Diagram 94 Composite give the body and panelling dimensions of the First class (*below*) and Third class (*right*) accommodation. Note the 'automatic draught excluder' on the body panelling below the waistline. This can be seen in the inset to Plate 9.1.

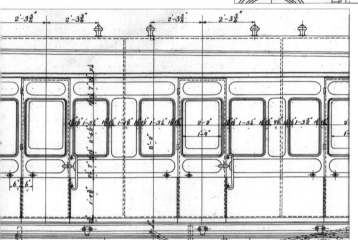

heavy capital expenditure on carriages described in Chapter 8, this is hardly surprising.

The decision to charge the carriages to revenue prompted *The Railway Magazine*[7] to praise the Caley on its prudence and good practice, saying that any other company would have charged them to capital. The message (perhaps suggested by the CR itself) was that the Caledonian was a wealthy company, which could pay a decent shareholder's dividend while also investing in the future. Each complete train cost £6,580, according to the renewal minute quoted above.

The Brake Composite to Diagram 95 (Figure 9.8 and Plate 9.2) was the lead carriage in the Edinburgh portion, marshalled behind the engine. It was built to drawing 12762[8] and order number H227. It had three First and four Third class compartments, seating eighteen

and thirty-two respectively, leaving room for a short guard's and luggage compartment at just over 12 feet. Its number was 146.

Three Diagram 97 5-compartment Brake Thirds (Figure 9.9 and Plate 9.3) were needed for the train, one for the Edinburgh portion and two for Glasgow. The guard's and luggage section was over 27 feet long. Four were built to order H228. The drawing number was 12761.[9] They were allocated a block of numbers from 617 to 620.

The final carriage in the Glasgow portion apart from the Dining car was a Composite with five First and three Third class compartments (Diagram 94, Figure 9.10 and Plate 9.4). Both classes of compartment were 4 inches wider than those in the Brake Composite. The drawing number was 12763[10] and the order number was H226. It was numbered 69.

A second train was authorised in the next half year,[11] again with a spare Brake Third. The order numbers were H230 (Composite 217), H231 (Brake Composite 148) and H232 (Brake Thirds 6, 304, 511 and 523).

Three Third class carriages to order H233 were also authorised in the period ending July 1905. This design was Diagram 96, built to drawing 12922[12] – see Figure 9.11 and Plate 9.5. Nine compartments seated seventy-two passengers. The carriages were numbered 549, 786 and 1000. One appears in a St. Rollox photograph[13] marshalled inside the Edinburgh portion of the Aberdeen train, which suggests that the carriages were intended to strengthen the train if necessary.

LAUNCH OF THE SERVICE

On 6th April 1905, one of the sets, '*strengthened by the addition of a WCJS dining car, the vehicle selected being the coach that obtained the "Grand Prize" at the Paris Exhibition of 1900,*' formed a publicity train from Glasgow to Aberdeen, hauled by

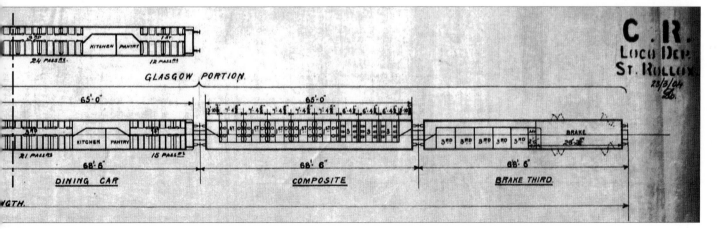

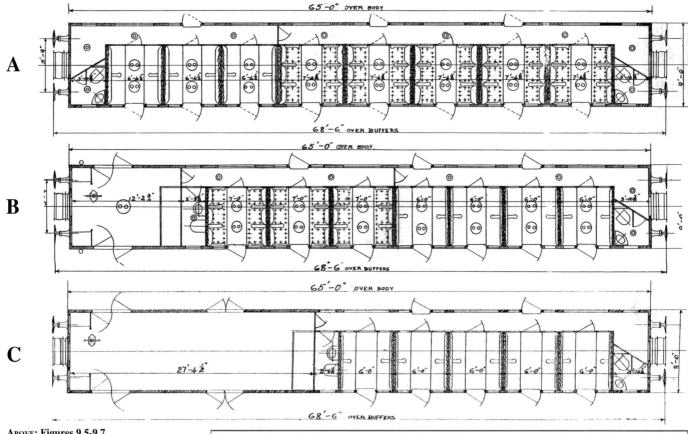

ABOVE: Figures 9.5-9.7
These drawings, taken from the Large Diagram Book, show the internal layout and the actual compartment dimensions for the three types of carriage that formed the Aberdeen trains illustrated in Figure 9.4. Figure 9.5 (*A*) is the Diagram 94 Composite, 9.6 (*B*) the Diagram 95 Brake Composite and 9.7 (*C*) the Diagram 97 Brake Third.

Figure 9.8 (*right*) and Plate 9.2 (*below*)
The Diagram 95 Brake Composite, eight of which were built. The photograph shows the corridor side of LM&SR 7394, which was originally CR263, built in late 1906 to order H255. By this time the higher semi-elliptical roof profile had been adopted. According to the Coaching Plant Stock Book transcription it was broken up at St. Rollox in December 1952.

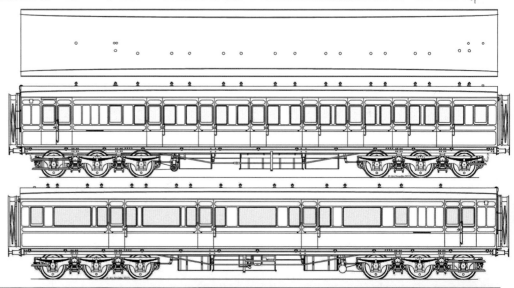

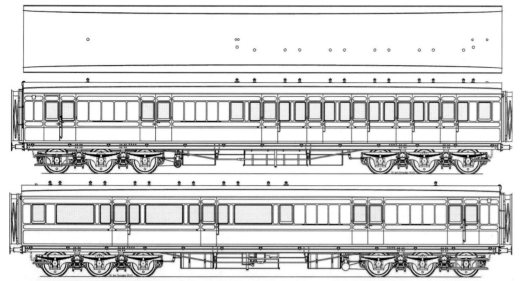

Figure 9.9 and Plate 9.3
Three Diagram 97 Brake Thirds were used in the original 'Grampian Express' formation. Fourteen were built in all. The photograph shows one of the original low-roof carriages at the end of the Glasgow portion at Buchanan Street. The postcard is part of the John Alsop collection in the Caledonian Railway Association archive. Note that the carriage is fitted with Mansell wheels. This may have only applied to the first two Aberdeen service sets and the pioneer Glasgow–Edinburgh vehicles.

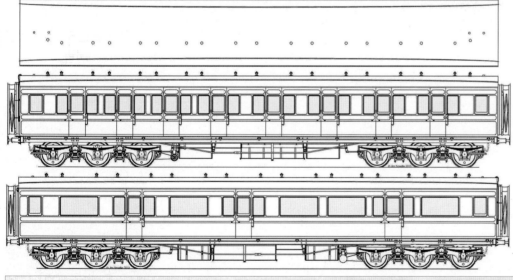

Figure 9.10 and Plate 9.4
The Diagram 94 Composite had five First and three Third class compartments. A total of eleven of these carriages were built, two of which had the original low roofs. The photograph shows the corridor side of Composite number 217, which was built in the first half of 1906 to order H230. It has disc, rather than Mansell, wheels.

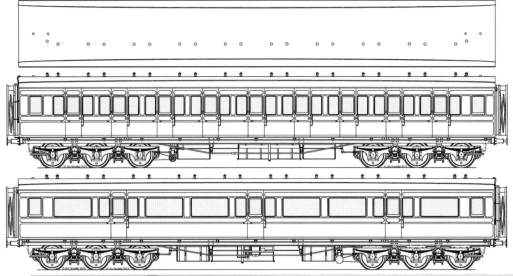

Figure 9.11 and Plate 9.5
The Diagram 96 Thirds were built as strengthening vehicles for the Aberdeen service. Number 1342 was one of ten dual-brake fitted carriages built to order H244 in 1907. The plate provides a good view of the semi-elliptical roof profile.

the Caledonian's pioneer 4-6-0 number 49.[14] The editor of *The Railway Magazine* travelled on the footplate on the southbound journey.

The Dining car was the unique 65-foot 6-inch First class Saloon number 200, which was transferred to the Royal Train in 1914.[15] According to *The Railway Magazine* article, it was after lunch on the northbound trip that '*Mr J F McIntosh, in the course of a few remarks, suggested "The Grampian Express" as a suitable title for the new train.*'

The service of two trains each way began on 10th April. The morning departure from Glasgow was at 10.00 and from Edinburgh at 9.30am. The portions were combined at Perth. The corresponding departure from Aberdeen was at 10.35am. In the evening the southbound train left Aberdeen at 5.30pm. The southbound trains were divided at Perth. Going north, the Glasgow portion of the train left at 5.00pm. The Edinburgh portion left 35 minutes earlier.

PUBLICITY MATERIAL

The Caledonian commissioned a poster to publicise the new corridor train with its new-style carriages; it is shown in Plate 9.6. A variety of posed photographs of the new stock, both singly and in rakes, is contained in the St. Rollox collection at the NRM,[16] but none portray the formation of actual trains in service, except the Glasgow–Edinburgh train described in the non-corridor stock section below. Plate 9.7 shows the evening departure from Glasgow (the 'Granite City') leaving Stirling.

THE 'GRAMPIAN EFFECT'

While the launch of the Aberdeen service gained the Caledonian a great deal of publicity, it did not seem to have a lasting effect on ticket sales. It is only possible to identify aggregate numbers of

ABOVE: Plate 9.6
The original formation of the 'Grampian Express' is correct as seen here, with one of the Wolverton-built Dining Saloons recently acquired by the Caledonian. Pioneer 4-6-0 No. 49 hauled the inaugural train, but in normal service a 4-4-0 was used. The photograph is in the NRM collection, ref: SRX 516.

RIGHT: Plate 9.7
The class leader of the largest McIntosh 4-4-0 design heads the 'Granite City' out of Stirling. The visible portion of the train is composed of low-roofed carriages, headed by a Diagram 97 Brake Third.

RIGHT: Plate 9.8
The weight of the new carriages and the speed of the Aberdeen expresses prompted the CR Board to authorise construction of the '903' class. This extract from the Board minutes bears a date six months after the service was launched, which suggests that the company felt that the existing 4-4-0s were not quite up to the job. The minute authorised the Locomotive Department to build ten Class '908' 4-6-0s for goods traffic and the Class '903's. The 'Atlantics' were the subject of St. Rollox drawings, but the design was abandoned in favour of more 4-4-0s.

people travelling from a particular station, but about 11,000 more passengers were booked from Aberdeen in 1906 compared with the average of the previous years, which may in part be attributable to the new trains. Numbers fell back to the pre-1906 average in subsequent years.

The new stock did, however, have a profound effect on Caledonian locomotive policy. As can be seen in Plate 9.8, the high speed and heavy weight of the new trains were the justification for building five 4-6-0 locomotives, to be charged to the capital account. In the event, the '903' Class was not used regularly on the services and the four trains that ran between Glasgow and Aberdeen were usually entrusted to 4-4-0s, as envisaged in the original marshalling diagram and illustrated in Plate 9.7.

EARLY SERVICE REVISIONS

The original service did not last long. In July 1905 the evening departure from Glasgow did not combine with an Edinburgh portion, but was divided at Perth ticket platform, with the rear

---

Caledonian Railway Company.
14th Nov. 1905.

COPY.   SECRETARY'S OFFICE,
                          GLASGOW, 14th November, 1905. 48

Sir,

I beg leave to append an extract from the Minutes of a Meeting of the Board of Directors of this Company, of date the 14th instant.

Your most obedient Servant,

Secretary.

EXTRACT:

New Engines to Capital Account.

Submitted the General Manager's memo. of 6th instant, recommending that the Directors should authorise the construction of 20 additional engines at a cost of £55,000, viz:

10 six-coupled bogie express goods engines intended for express goods trains between Glasgow and Carlisle and between Glasgow and Aberdeen.

5 six-coupled bogie passenger engines to be used for the Aberdeen and Glasgow Corridor express trains, which are now heavy and booked to run at high speeds.

5 bogie "Atlantic" type of engines to work the Edinburgh and Carlisle express trains and the down tourist and postal trains between Carlisle, Perth and Aberdeen.

10 engines to be built during the half-year ending 31st July 1906, and the remainder during the half-year ending 31st January, 1907.

Ap proved.

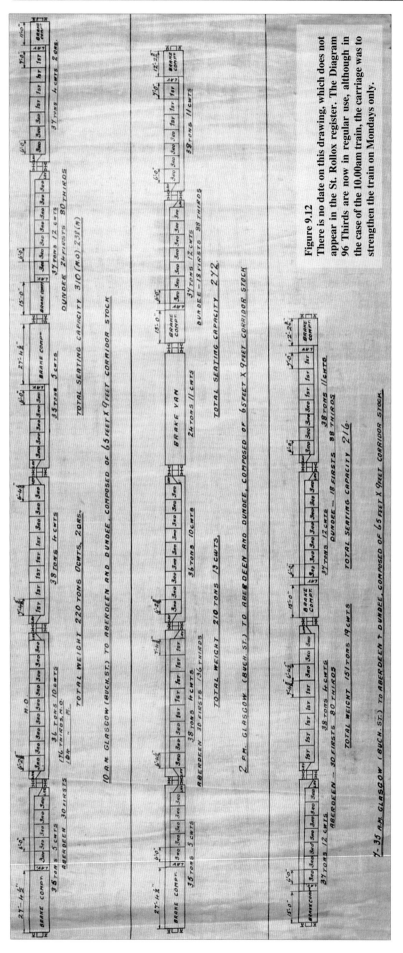

Figure 9.12
There is no date on this drawing, which does not appear in the St. Rollox register. The Diagram 96 Thirds are now in regular use, although in the case of the 10.00am train, the carriage was to strengthen the train on Mondays only.

portion running to Dundee. The morning departure southbound was now divided at Larbert. The Glasgow portion was combined with a train from Oban which had arrived five minutes earlier at the same location. The division and combination process was completed in twelve minutes. These trains certainly needed to run *'True to Time.'* The evening departure from Aberdeen also divided at Larbert. The likely explanation for the change to Larbert from Perth was to allow more time for passengers using the Dining car.

In May/June 1906 the carriages were again employed on services between Glasgow and Dundee/Aberdeen. The trains were divided at Perth ticket platform, according to the Working Timetable. The marshalling of these trains was the subject of an undated and unnumbered drawing that does not appear in the St. Rollox register.[17] It is reproduced here as Figure 9.12. The Edinburgh portion of the morning train now ran straight through to Aberdeen. There was no corresponding Edinburgh departure in the evening.

In October 1906 the 10.00am from Glasgow included one of the new 65-foot 6-inch slip carriages for Crieff. This design is described in a later section. In July 1907 there was a partial reversion to the original service, as the 10.00am from Glasgow combined with an Edinburgh portion at Perth and ran through to Aberdeen. The other two trains continued to serve Aberdeen and Dundee. In October the original 1905 timetable was restored. The May/June and October 1908 Working Timetables reverted to the Aberdeen/Dundee service of 1906.

As more corridor carriages were built, services were extended and the stock was quite widely distributed around the system, sometimes as a single coach in a train of shorter, less luxurious vehicles.

NON-CORRIDOR 65-FOOT STOCK

After building the two sets of carriages for the Aberdeen service, attention turned to non-corridor carriages. The next routes to receive the new-style stock were the Glasgow to Edinburgh and Gourock/Wemyss Bay lines. The short duration of journeys (about an hour or less) did not justify the provision of corridors. Maximum seating capacity was more important on these busy local lines.

The July 1906 Local Working of Carriages Circular for the Edinburgh route shows two sets of *'6-Wheeled Bogie Trains'* in the customary formation of one First and two Brake Thirds, each strengthened by an additional Third on Saturdays. Another set started from Gourock and worked to Glasgow. After a return trip to Edinburgh it went back to Gourock for the following day. More publicity photographs of the new *'bogie trains'* were commissioned. An example appears in Plate 9.9.

In the period ending January 1906, the Traffic Committee authorised the six Brake Thirds and three Firsts to make up the weekday sets.[18] This coincided with an alteration to the end profile. The original roof had a flat centre section. The new profile was semi-elliptic and increased the overall height by 2 inches – see Figure 9.13, which compares the two profiles. With the projection of the Havock ventilators, the carriages were now to the maximum dimensions allowed by the CR loading gauge.

The Diagram 101 Brake Thirds were first to appear – see Figure 9.14 and Plate 9.10. Eight compartments without centre armrests seated ninety-six, and there was a small guard's compartment, as befitted a service which did not carry much luggage. The internal layout is shown in

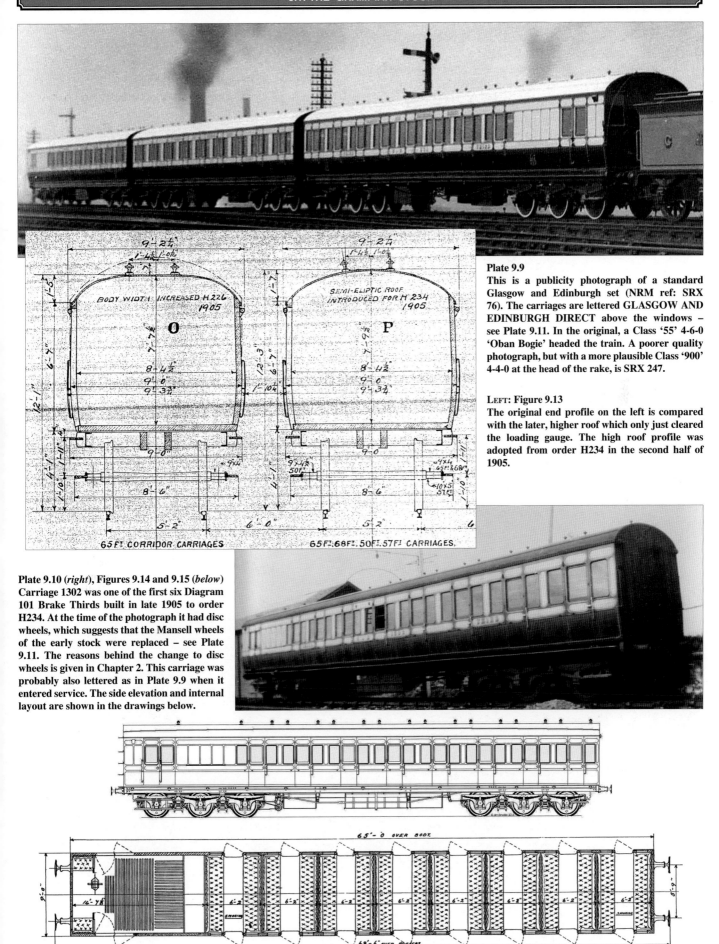

Plate 9.9
This is a publicity photograph of a standard Glasgow and Edinburgh set (NRM ref: SRX 76). The carriages are lettered GLASGOW AND EDINBURGH DIRECT above the windows – see Plate 9.11. In the original, a Class '55' 4-6-0 'Oban Bogie' headed the train. A poorer quality photograph, but with a more plausible Class '900' 4-4-0 at the head of the rake, is SRX 247.

LEFT: **Figure 9.13**
The original end profile on the left is compared with the later, higher roof which only just cleared the loading gauge. The high roof profile was adopted from order H234 in the second half of 1905.

Plate 9.10 (*right*), Figures 9.14 and 9.15 (*below*)
Carriage 1302 was one of the first six Diagram 101 Brake Thirds built in late 1905 to order H234. At the time of the photograph it had disc wheels, which suggests that the Mansell wheels of the early stock were replaced – see Plate 9.11. The reasons behind the change to disc wheels is given in Chapter 2. This carriage was probably also lettered as in Plate 9.9 when it entered service. The side elevation and internal layout are shown in the drawings below.

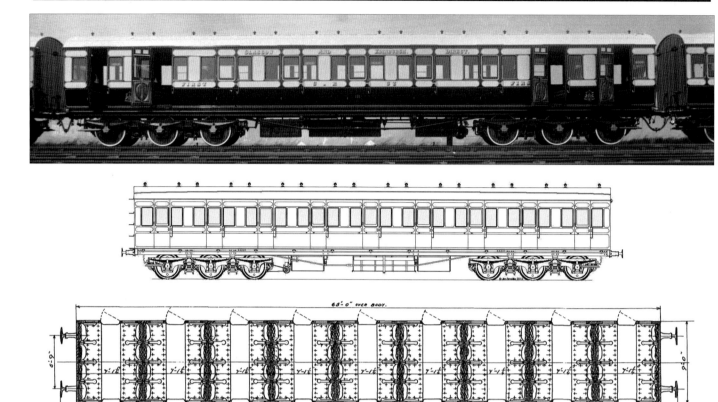

ABOVE: Plate 9.11, Figure 9.16 and 9.17
Like the Aberdeen service, the carriages for the Edinburgh route were originally specially lettered. Diagram 102 First number 67 was one of these pioneer vehicles, built to order H235 in late 1905. In contrast with its companion Brake Third in Plate 9.10, it has Mansell wheels. The original photograph is NRM ref: SRX 517. The side elevation and internal layout are shown in the accompanying drawings.

Plate 9.12
Sir James King, with a magnificent smokebox door embellishment, heads a train of 12-wheel stock at Gourock. The carriages are not the usual non-corridor formation used on the coast services: the front carriage is either a Diagram 95 Brake Composite or a Diagram 97A Brake Third; behind it is a Diagram 96 Third, with the compartment side in view. A heavily retouched version of the photograph was used by the Westinghouse Brake Company as an advertisement – see Plate 2.3.

Figure 9.15. The drawing was 13017 dated 14th April 1905.[19] Three of the carriages to order H234 were numbered 1300, 1302, 1303. A further two, numbered 792 and 1281, were built in the second half of 1908 to order H279.

Three Diagram 102 Firsts were built to order H235. The drawing was 13018,[20] dated 3rd May 1905 – see Figure 9.16 and Plate 9.11. They were treated as replacements in the period ending January 1906[21] and numbered 67, 125 and 130. The Coaching Plant Stock Book records them with seventy-two seats in nine compartments. The Diagram Book (Figure 9.17) and the drawing show them with two armrests each side, limiting the capacity to fifty-four. At some point the armrests must have been removed.

A further six were authorised as part of the capital expenditure for thirty carriages in the period ending July 1906.[22] In fact, it was decided later that eight carriages could be charged to capital. Six carriages to H237 and a further one to H259 were charged to capital in July 1906.[23] They were numbered 306-312. A final carriage was authorised as a replacement for the period ending July 1907[24] and built to order H259, but also charged to capital. It was given number 42.

As well as the third Glasgow–Edinburgh set mentioned above that ran part of the time between Glasgow and Gourock, the July 1906 Marshalling Circular records three *'Six-wheeled Bogie Trains'* on the line to the coast. Trains 1 and 2 comprised one each of the following carriages: First, Composite, Third, 7-compartment Brake Third and 9-compartment Brake Third. These two trains had an extra First in the late afternoon. The third train (number 6) was to the same formation but the Brake Thirds were not differentiated. A photograph of a boat train at Gourock is shown in Plate 9.12.

These carriages all appear on the capital account for the period ending July 1906.[25] The Firsts were among those mentioned above to order H237. Five Diagram 104 Composites, numbered 360-364, were built to order H238. There were four First class compartments in the centre, flanked by three Thirds on either side, seating thirty-two and seventy-two respectively. They were built to drawing 14594.[26] A further example appeared as a replacement in the period ending July 1907 to order H260.[27] A side elevation appears as Figure 9.18.

Five each of the two new types of Brake Third were built to order H240 (Diagram 101B, 7-compartment, numbered 1319-1323) and H241 (Diagram 101A, 9-compartment, numbered 1324-1328). The drawings were 14722[28] (Diagram 101B) and 14710 (Diagram 101A).[29] These drawings were produced for subsequent orders in the period ending January 1909. Side elevations are shown here as Figures 9.19 and 9.20.

NON-CORRIDOR 68-FOOT THIRD

As part of the thirty-six carriages authorised in August 1905 for construction to the capital account, fourteen non-corridor 68-foot Third class carriages were built to order H239. The GA drawing 13237 dated September 1905 has not survived. The surviving underframe drawing is number 13239.[30] The GA that has survived is number 14200,[31] issued in 1907 for the last two carriages of the order, plus a final example built to H261.

The carriages were assigned to Diagram 105. They were a logical development of the Diagram 47 48-foot non-corridor Thirds, which had eight compartments 5 feet 10½ inches between partitions, seating eighty. The compartments in the 12-wheeled carriages were just over

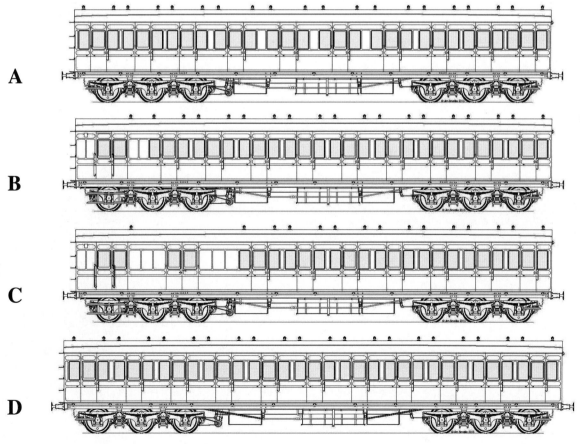

Figures 9.18, 9.19, 9.20 and 9.21
These four side elevations depict the remaining non-corridor designs. Figure 9.18 (*A*) is the Diagram 104 Composite with three Third class compartments on each side of four central First class. Figure 9.19 (*B*) is the Diagram 101A Brake Third. It had narrower compartments than Diagram 101 – coupled with a smaller luggage section, an extra compartment was gained. Diagram 101B (Figure 9.20) (*C*) used the same narrower compartments, but with increased luggage space. Finally, Figure 9.21 (*D*) shows the 11-compartment Third, which was built on a special 68-foot underframe.

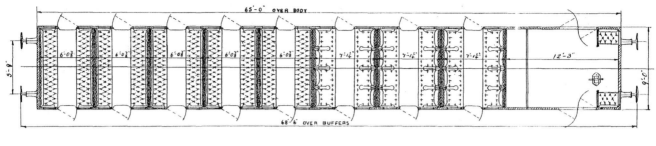

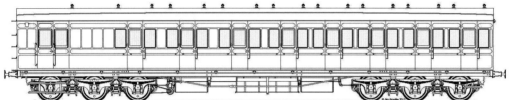

Figures 9.22 and 9.23
The floor plan and side elevation of the Diagram 103 Brake Composite slip carriage.

two inches wider between partitions. As a 10-compartment carriage would have been too short for a 65-foot underframe, it made sense to provide eleven compartments on a slightly extended underframe. The increased width compared with the widest 48-foot stock allowed six passengers per seat, giving a capacity of 132.

Eleven were charged to capital in the period ending July 1906 at a cost of £1,579 each.[32] They were numbered 1305-1315. Number 125 was added a year later. The final three, numbered 1316-1318 appeared in the period ending January 1908.[33] The last carriage in the series, to order H261, was actually authorised as a replacement for the previous period,[34] so should have received the low random number. A drawing of this design is shown in Figure 9.21.

BRAKE COMPOSITE SLIP CARRIAGES

Four slip carriages, described as *'end compartment Brake Composites,'* were authorised against the capital account at the same time as the thirty-six carriages mentioned earlier.[35] They were given Diagram 103, built to order H242 and numbered 365-368. They had five Third class and three First class compartments, with a small guard's and luggage section 12 feet 3 inches long. They were charged to capital in July 1906 at £1,581 each.[36] The internal layout is shown as Figure 9.22 and a side elevation as Figure 9.23.

The original drawing, St. Rollox 13238, has not survived, but Drawing number 14425 for the last two carriages is available.[37] They were authorised as renewals in the period ending January 1909,[38] when they were described as *'Non-Corridor Slip Brake Composites.'* Built to order H282, they were numbered 348 and 373. The workings of these carriages are described in Chapter 2.5.

NUMBER OF NON-CORRIDOR CARRIAGES

The breakdown of 'Grampian' style non-corridor carriages is summarised in the following table. All were 65 feet long, except for Diagram 105.

DIAGRAM	TYPE	TOTAL
101	8-compartment Brake Third	8
101A	9-compartment Brake Third	8
101B	7-compartment Brake Third	8
102	9-compartment First	11
103	Brake Composite 3 First, 5 Third	6
104	Composite 4 First, 6 Third	6
105	68-foot 11-compartment Third	15

LATER CORRIDOR CARRIAGE DESIGNS

Construction of corridor carriages as renewals resumed in the period ending July 1906[39] and continued to the period ending in July 1909.[40] Three new designs of Brake vehicle were introduced during this period.

The Diagram 97A Brake Third (Figure 9.24 and Plate 9.13) was a 7-compartment version of the 5-compartment Diagram 97, with fifty-six seats instead of forty. As a consequence the guard's and luggage section was reduced to 15 feet. Two drawings survive: St. Rollox 13946[41] was for the Brake end only and 14221[42] was a general arrangement of the body. Fourteen were built to orders H247, H252, H266 and H286. Five (numbers 496, 1005 and 1346-1348) had dual brakes.

The Diagram 95A Brake Composite had four First and three Third class compartments, the reverse of Diagram 95 – see Figure 9.25. The resulting guard's and luggage compartment was only 11 feet long. Drawing 13949[43] was issued for the Brake end only. Eight were built with Westinghouse brake only – four to H251, three to H255 and one to H268.

The last new Brake Composite was to Diagram 95B (Plate 9.14 and Figure 9.26). They had five Third class and two First class compartments separated by a lavatory. Drawing 14374 has not survived. Four were built to orders H277 and H285, numbered 371, 372, 374 and 375. All were dual-brake fitted. These carriages were used on the through service between Glasgow and the GWR.

NUMBER OF CORRIDOR CARRIAGES

The breakdown of the various types of 'Grampian' 12-wheeled corridor carriage is summarised in the following table. A figure in brackets denotes those with the original low roof.

DIAGRAM	TYPE	TOTAL
94	Composite 5 First, 3 Third	11 (2)
95	Brake Composite 3 First, 4 Third	11 (2)
95A	Brake Composite 4 First, 3 Third	8
95B	Brake Composite 2 First, 5 Third	4
96	9-compartment Third	16 (3)
97	5-compartment Brake Third	14 (8)
97A	7-compartment Brake Third	14

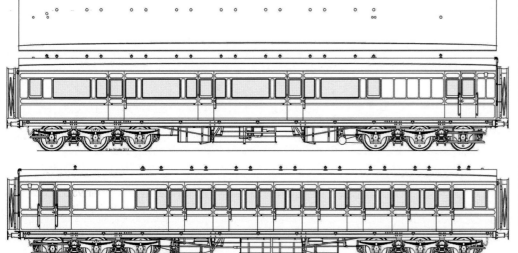

ABOVE: Plate 9.13
The compartment side of 7-compartment Brake Third 1347 at the rear of the train shown in the frontispiece, where the corridor side of the same carriage is shown at the front. Five of the fourteen carriages were fitted with dual brakes. The original photograph is SRX309 in the NRM collection.

LEFT: Figure 9.24
Diagram 97A, corridor and compartment side elevations. This variation of Diagram 97 had seven compartments rather than five.

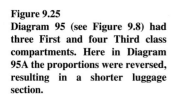

Figure 9.25
Diagram 95 (see Figure 9.8) had three First and four Third class compartments. Here in Diagram 95A the proportions were reversed, resulting in a shorter luggage section.

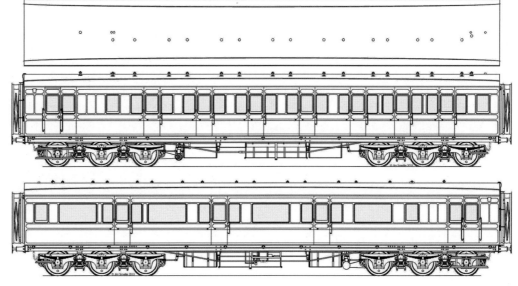

Plate 9.14 and Figure 9.26
One of the four Diagram 95B Brake Composites at Edinburgh Princes Street. The easiest way to identify the subtle variations of the basic Diagram 95 design is to count the number of panels in the luggage section. The two First/five Third class configuration of this diagram, shown in Figure 9.26, resulted in a luggage section midway between those of 95 and 95A. This carriage is CR 375, built in the first half of 1909. It was broken up at Cowlairs in 1951.

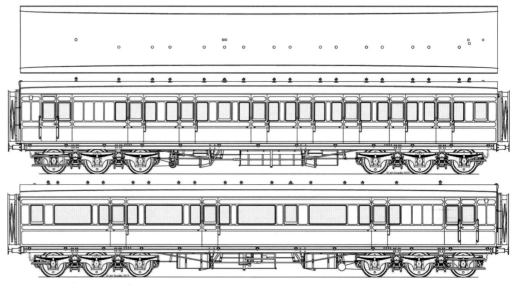

REFERENCES

1. *Caledonian Railway Wagons*, pp. 33-34
2. NRS BR/CAL/1/51 entry 1014
3. *North British Coaches*, pp. 47-48, drawing 39
4. *The Railway Engineer*, August 1905, p. 248
5. RHP to be assigned
6. NRS BR/CAL/1/49 entry 769
7. *The Railway Magazine*, January to June 1905, p. 405
8. NRM 7497/C RHP to be assigned
9. NRM 11397/C RHP to be assigned
10. NRM 7485/C RHP to be assigned
11. NRS BR/CAL/1/50 entry 217
12. NRM 11396/C RHP to be assigned
13. NRM Ref: SRX 172
14. Photographed and described in *The Railway Magazine*, January to June 1905, pp. 404-8
15. *West Coast Joint Stock*, pp. 195-96
16. NRM Ref: SRX 50, 53, 76, 172, 242-44, 247, 308-9, 312, 512, 517-18
17. NRS BR/CAL/5/83
18. *Local Working of Carriages, Southern, Eastern and Western Sections*, July 1906, p. 16
19. NRM 7491/C RHP to be assigned
20. NRM 7493/C RHP to be assigned
21. NRS BR/CAL/1/51 entry 102
22. NRS BR/CAL/1/51 entry 1007
23. NRS BR/CAL/23/11 (17)
24. NRS BR/CAL/1/53 entry 1151
25. NRS BR/CAL/1/51 entry 1131
26. NRM 7496/C RHP to be assigned
27. NRS BR/CAL/1/53 entry 1151
28. NRM 7495/C RHP to be assigned
29. NRM 7492/C RHP to be assigned
30. NRM 8086/C
31. NRM 7484/C (on two sheets) RHP to be assigned
32. NRS BR/CAL/23/11 (17)
33. NRS BR/CAL/23/12 (16)
34. NRS BR/CAL/1/53 entry 1151
35. NRS BR/CAL/1/51 entry 1007
36. NRS BR/CAL/23/11 (17)
37. NRM 7494/C RHP to be assigned
38. NRS BR/CAL/1/56 entry 425
39. NRS BR/CAL/1/51 entry 1131
40. NRS BR/CAL/1/57 entry 111
41. NRM 7490/C RHP to be assigned
42. NRM 7498/C RHP to be assigned
43. NRM 7487/C RHP to be assigned

9.2: CARRIAGES ASSOCIATED WITH THE 'GRAMPIAN' STOCK

Five 50-foot Diagram 99 Third class Saloons were built to order H245 at the same time as the 'Grampian' stock. They are fully described and illustrated in Chapter 13. They are mentioned here because they were lettered in 'Grampian' style, and were obviously designed to be used with the 12-wheeled carriages.

SEMI-CORRIDOR CARRIAGES FOR THE CALLANDER & OBAN

After construction of the 12-wheeled stock ceased, a small number of 50-foot semi-corridor carriages were built to the same standard. They were authorised as replacements in the period ending January 1910.[1] These carriages were the first on the CR with sliding doors from the corridor to the compartments, a feature that was the standard for the rest of its existence. They were built on a common underframe (St. Rollox drawing 14980[2]). According to the drawings register the original set of drawings numbered 14889-91 was annotated 'C&O' and H289, H290 and H291 respectively.

None of these or the body drawings quoted below have survived. All that is available are the seating arrangements in the Large Diagram Book and the sketches in the Small Book. These are shown in Figures 9.27-9.32.

The Diagram 106 Composites (drawing 15121) built to order H289 were numbered 376-378. Four First class compartments had a side corridor leading to one of a pair of lavatories. The other lavatory was linked by a corridor on the opposite side of the carriage to three Third class compartments. There were twenty-five seats for each class. Four further examples were built after the war. Plate 11.3 shows a post-war example.

The Diagram 107 Brake Thirds (drawing 15154) had one lavatory to serve four compartments, seating thirty-four. Five were built to order H290. They were given random numbers including 685, 987 and 995. Seven more were built in 1919/20. One of the post-war carriages is shown in Plate 9.15.

The Diagram 108 Brake Composite was the Diagram 106 design, with a 14-foot Brake section replacing two of the First class

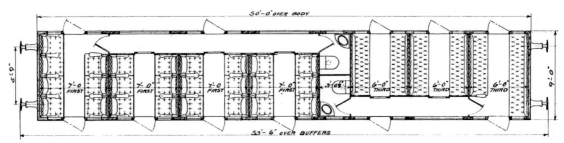

Figures 9.27 and 9.28
The St. Rollox drawings of these semi-corridor designs for the Callander & Oban line have not survived, so the only reliable information is the internal layout and the rough sketches in the Small Diagram Book. These two drawings, from the Large Diagram Book page 106 and Small Book page 78, show the Composite carriage. A photograph of one of the carriages built after the war is shown in Plate 11.3. These carriages also appear in Plates 9.16 and 9.17.

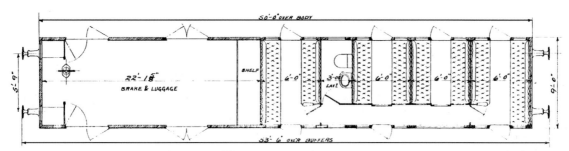

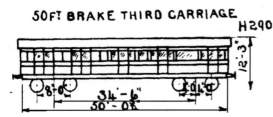

Figures 9.29 and 9.30
Five of these Diagram 107 Semi-corridor Brake Thirds were built during the McIntosh regime. Seven more were built after the war, including the example in Plate 9.15.

Plate 9.15
A Diagram 107 Semi-corridor Brake Third was photographed carrying its second LM&SR number 25681. Its original CR number was 1358. The photograph shows the corridor side. The compartment side of one of these carriages appears in Plate 9.16.

Figures 9.31 and 9.32
Internal layout and side elevation sketch of the Brake Composite design, Large Diagram Book 108 and Small Book 77. An example of this design appears in Plate 9.17.

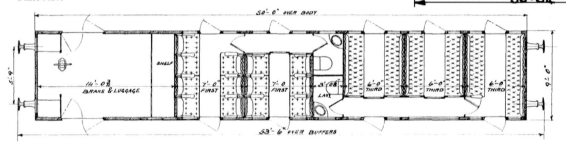

compartments (drawing 15348). This reduced the First class seating to thirteen. Three were built to order H291. The numbers (379-381) followed those of the Diagram 106 carriages.

The *Railway Magazine* described the carriages and their purpose as follows:

> 'New coaches of a special type are now being introduced for use on the Callander and Oban Railway which throughout its entire length of 71 miles presents to the traveller panoramic scenery unsurpassed on any other railway journey.
>
> This circumstance, pleasing enough to the tourist, forced the Caledonian Railway to make the new coaches for use on the Oban line trains of a somewhat different type from the new vehicles on the other sections. The "Grampian" and other modern Caledonian carriages are 65 feet long, and run on two 6-wheeled bogies, but this type of vehicle is not suitable for the Oban line. The new Oban vehicles are 50 feet long and supported on two 4-wheeled bogies. They are semi-corridor; fitted and equipped similarly to the "Grampians," with the exception that the compartment doors slide parallel with the length of the coach, instead of opening outwards into the corridor as in the "Grampian" coaches.
>
> This form of door will be greatly appreciated by passengers who like to pass part of the time in the corridors; they will not be inconvenienced by the opening of compartment doors.'[3]

Two photographs of these carriages on the C&O are shown in Plates 9.16 and 9.17.

PRE-WAR SERVICES ON THE C&O

The *1913 Carriage Marshalling Circular* describes their use on the Callander & Oban. Two sets, comprising a Composite and two Brake Thirds, went north at 8.00am and 12.00 noon from Buchanan Street, returning from Oban at 3.00pm and 6.00pm. A similar set left Buchanan Street at 6.35pm for Stirling; it was combined with the night sleeper from Euston and left Stirling at 5.40am the next day for Oban. The carriages returned direct to Glasgow at 12.35pm.

From Edinburgh, a single Brake Composite travelled as part of a train that terminated at Callander. It was then attached to the 8.00am from Glasgow. It returned south on the 4.15pm from Oban, which was a train comprising portions to Glasgow, Edinburgh Princes Street and Waverley. The latter portion was detached at Larbert.

A similar working left Edinburgh at 9.45pm, balanced on the 12.35pm southbound departure the next day. In the early afternoon a Third and a Brake Composite left Princes Street at 1.25pm. At Stirling they were attached to the 2.07pm departure from Buchanan Street. The Brake Composite returned on the 7.30am and the Third on the 9.45am departures from Oban.

BOGIE PASSENGER BRAKE VANS

Diagram 98 was a 50-foot Brake Van with corridor connections. Drawing number 13470[4] dates from February 1906. The vans had been authorised in the previous year as part of a large capital expenditure programme that was to be spread over two half years.[5]

Plate 9.16
J.B. Sherlock photographed Class '55' 4-6-0 No. 57 on a southbound train at Callander on 26th July 1913. Behind the locomotive is a Diagram 107 Brake Third, this time showing the compartment side – compare with Plate 9.15. The second carriage is a Diagram 106 Composite, with the First class end nearest the camera. The photograph is in the CRA John Alsop collection.

Plate 9.17
Ken Nunn took this photograph of a CR Class '191' 4-6-0 in LM&SR livery hauling the 9.45am departure from Buchanan Street on its approach to Oban in June 1925. A Diagram 108 or its post-war variation 108A Brake Composite, still in CR livery, is directly behind the locomotive, followed by a Diagram 106 Composite with the Third class section leading. In front of the ex-Midland Railway clerestory carriage is a Diagram 107 Brake Third. Pullman Observation car *Maid of Morven* brings up the rear, still in full Pullman livery. The negative is in the NRM LCGB collection, ref: 4448.

Two (numbers 3 and 151) have been traced out of the first order for six (H249), which were charged to the capital account in January 1908.[6] The other four formed part of the CR Ambulance Train described in Chapter 12. Their numbers are not known. Each cost £980. Plate 9.18 is a side view of van number 3.

Their main regular employment was on trains to the north from Glasgow. The *1913 Carriage Marshalling Circular* shows eleven bogie Brake Vans travelling every day between Glasgow and Aberdeen/Oban, with balancing workings either the same day or the next. Another two alternated with HR vans on trains to Inverness. Two more operated on Mondays only to Aberdeen and Dundee.

Six more were built as replacements in the first half of 1914 to order H321,[7] and six in 1917 to order H335. The drawing number was 17272 – see Figure 9.33.[8] It shows 10-foot wheelbase bogies at 32-foot centres (42 feet wheelbase) for H321 and an annotation for 8-foot bogies at 35-foot centres (43 feet wheelbase) subsequently. These twelve vans were assigned to Diagram 98A. The only differences from Diagram 98 were that the wheelbase was given as 43 feet, rather than 42 feet 6 inches, and the length over buffers was 2 inches greater.

SIX-WHEELED PASSENGER BRAKE VANS

Diagram 18 was a 6-inch wider version of the 6-wheeled Diagram 17, but with the guard's door opening inwards rather than outwards. The Small Diagram Book did not recognise them as being significantly different from their predecessors and included them in its Diagram 16.

The drawing number was 14009[9] – see Figure 9.34 and an illustration in Plate 9.19. Like most of their predecessors the vans were dual-brake fitted. Unlike the Diagram 17s, almost all were steam heated rather than fitted with heating pipes, and lit by electricity. For these reasons most of the newer vans survived until after nationalisation, while the original Diagram 17s were withdrawn by 1930.

Sixteen vans were authorised in the period ending July 1907[10] to order H264. Numbers included 6, 8 110, 125 and 152. A further four were built in the period ending January 1909 (order H283),[11] eight to order H288 in the next half year[12] and a further five (order H293) in the next period.[13] Order H283 was an oddity; these four vans were built with gas light and steam heating pipes. Their numbers were 40, 42, 87 and 148.

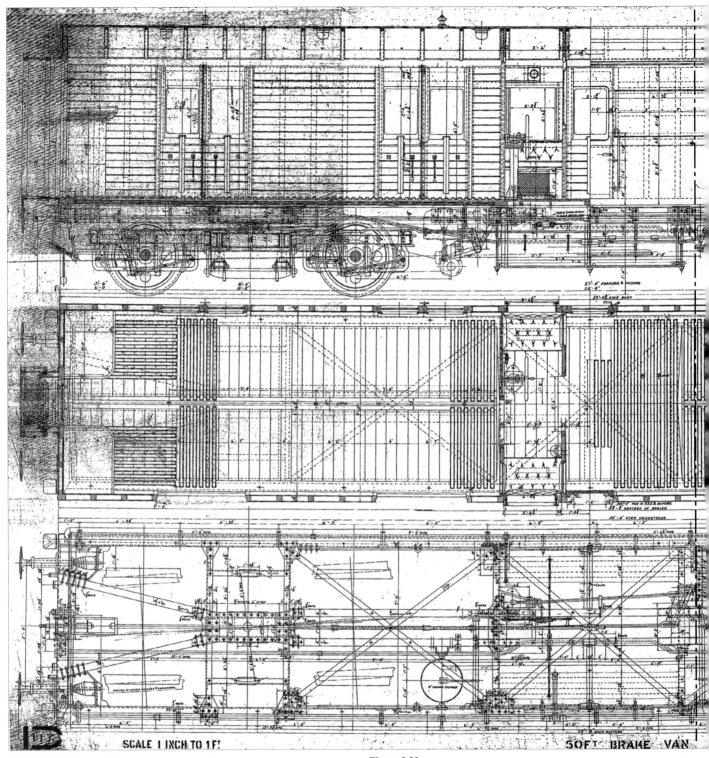

SCALE 1 INCH TO 1 FT   50 FT BRAKE VAN

REFERENCES

 1. NRS BR/CAL/1/57 no entry number
 2. RHP 69152
 3. *The Railway Magazine*, June 1910, p. 198
 4. NRM 7513/C (on two sheets) RHP to be assigned
 5. NRS BR/CAL/1/51/ entry 1007
 6. NRS BR/CAL/23/12 (16)
 7. NRS BR/CAL/1/63 entry 1383
 8. NRM 7512/C (on two sheets)
 9. NRM 7509/C RHP to be assigned
10. NRS BR/CAL/1/53 entry 1151
11. NRS BR/CAL/1/56 entry 425
12. NRS BR/CAL/1/57 entry 111
13. NRS BR/CAL/1/57 no entry number

Figure 9.33
This reproduction of St. Rollox drawing 17272 is the general arrangement of the Diagram 98 Passenger Brake Van.

Facing Page: Plate 9.18
This official photograph (NRM ref: SRX 513) shows one of the first order of two Diagram 98 vans, built in the second half of 1907. No more were built until 1914. Masking out the background has removed the dynamo drive belt. The inclusion of destination board brackets is interesting. They do not appear on the official drawing and there seems to be little justification for them in traffic.

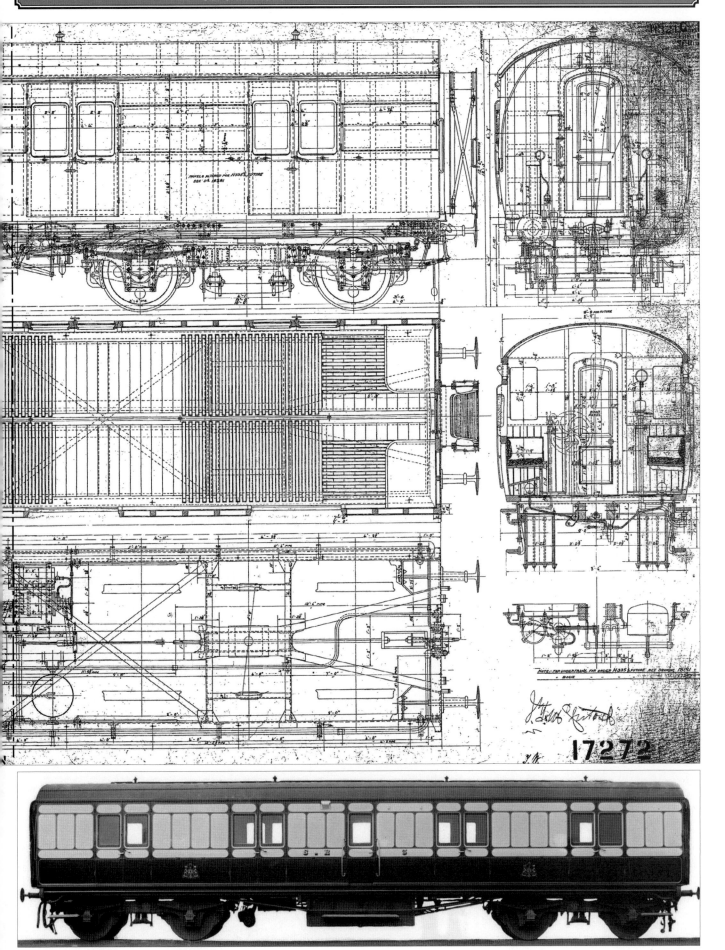

17272

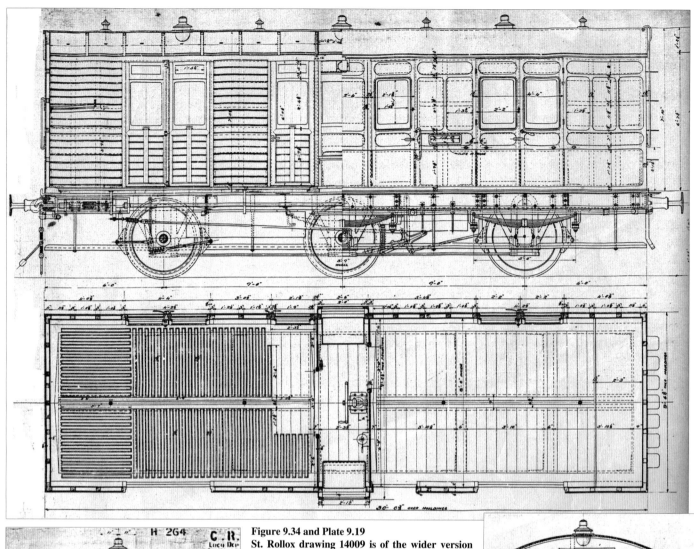

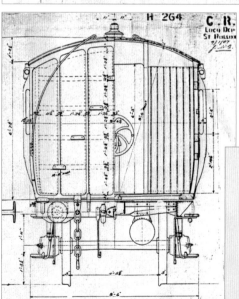

Figure 9.34 and Plate 9.19
St. Rollox drawing 14009 is of the wider version of 6-wheeled Passenger Brake Van to Diagram 18. They were first built in early 1907. The photograph records CR number 145 after receiving its second LM&SR number 34217. By this time the beading at the bottom of the body had been removed, as had the Westinghouse brake gear.

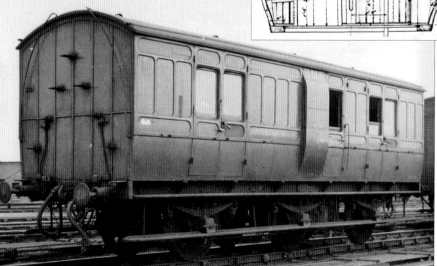

9.3: THE CALEDONIAN RAILWAY DINING CARS

Until the early 1900s the only Dining cars that ran on Caley metals were the West Coast Joint Stock cars on Anglo-Scottish services. Journeys starting and ending in Scotland were deemed too short to justify on-board catering. When the 'Grampian' stock was planned in early 1904, catering was to be introduced on the Glasgow/Edinburgh to Aberdeen run. This was the longest CR inter-city route and therefore the most likely to justify the cost. It was a time of expansion in railway catering provision. For instance, the GWR introduced 70-foot Dining cars for all three classes of passengers in 1904, running fourteen trains daily with catering facilities.[1]

The CR's original intention, shown in the proposed carriage marshalling diagram[2] for the service (Figure 9.4), was to use brand new Diagram 9 West Coast Joint Stock Kitchen Dining cars.

Twelve Dining cars had been built for the WCJS 'Corridor' trains that entered service between London and Scotland in May 1893. Their origins and career as WCJS vehicles are described in Chapter 10 of *West Coast Joint Stock*.[3] They became surplus to requirements when the Diagram 9 Kitchen Dining Saloons were built, and were used by the CR instead.

The Caledonian received their usual one-third proportion of the displaced Saloons in the shape of four cars, which were of two types. The capital cost of the transfer, charged for the period ending January 1906, was £6,738 1s 6d.[4] The cars were used on the Aberdeen service, despite the fact that the seating capacity was only half that of the 1905 WCJS Saloons envisaged in the original carriage marshalling diagram.

THE 45-FOOT DINING SALOONS

Originally intended for the Edinburgh portion of the 'Corridor', three Composite Kitchen Dining Saloons were built in 1893. They appeared on Page 2 of the 1893 L&NWR diagram book. A photograph of the Edinburgh portion of the train appears in Chapter 3, Plate 3.19. Nine First and twelve Third class diners were accommodated in 2+1 formation, separated by a central kitchen.

The carriages originally ran on twelve wheels, but at some time before they were transferred, they were fitted with 4-wheeled bogies. The latter's wheelbase as reported in the CR Coaching Plant Stock Book was 10 feet. This cannot be confirmed from the Large Diagram Book, as no wheelbase dimensions are given. The Small Diagram Book does not include this design. The Stock Book records the transfer date as 1905, which coincides with the launch of the 'Grampian' service.

The two cars taken over by the Caledonian were WCJS 530 and 531, renumbered 38 and 39 in the CR Saloon series, appearing on page 62 of the Large Diagram Book. This is reproduced as Figure

9.35. Their internal layout remained unaltered, but at some time the clerestory roofs were removed. They still had their original roofs when working on the early 'Grampian Express' – see enlargement of the publicity poster reproduced as Plate 9.20.

THE 50-FOOT 6-INCH DINING SALOONS

The two Third class Kitchen Dining Saloons taken over by the Caledonian were originally numbered 483 and 484. They and a third car numbered 485 were coupled to 47-foot 9-inch Dining Saloons 486-488 to make three pairs of dining vehicles for the Glasgow portion of the Scotch expresses. They appeared on page 3 of the 1893 L&NWR diagram book. According to the Coaching Plant Stock Book they were transferred in 1906. A drawing of the original twin Dining set is shown in Figure 9.36. Photographs of the interior and exterior appear in *LNWR Coaches*.[5]

The bodies were 45 feet long, the remainder consisting of a 2-foot 9-inch entrance vestibule at each end. They originally had a 12-seat non-smoking and 6-seat smoking section, with the kitchen at the end of the carriage. They were designated as Third class in the L&NWR Diagram Book and as First class in some of the annual returns.

The CR allocated numbers 40 and 41 in the Saloon series and assigned them to Diagram 63. They were redesignated to seat twelve First class and six Third class diners. Originally the end away from the kitchen had a lavatory and luggage area. This layout is shown in Figure 9.37.

The Caledonian removed the lavatory of both Saloons and used that space and the luggage area opposite to accommodate a further five Third class diners. The new internal layout was shown on the first of two pages numbered 63 in the Large Diagram Book – see the inset to Figure 9.37. This probably happened soon after acquisition,

Plate 9.20 and Figure 9.35
This enlargement from the publicity montage of the 'Grampian Express' (Plate 9.6) shows 45-foot Dining Saloon number 38. The large block lettering seems rather unlikely in a train lettered in the elaborate serif style. In WCJS days, the cars' designation was carried at eaves height. The bogies do not seem to be 10 feet wheelbase as suggested in the Coaching Plant Stock Book. The drawing shows the internal layout as depicted on page 62 of the Large Diagram Book. This was unaltered from WCJS days.

45'-0"
2'-6" | TABLE 10'-0" | BUTLER'S PANTRY | SINK | HEATING APPARATUS | SINK | TABLE 13'-4" | 2'-6"
DINING SALOON FOR 9 FIRST CLASS PASSENGERS.
VESTIBULE
8'-10" KITCHEN | SINK
CUPBOARD FOR PLATES ETC.
HOT CLOSET AND ROASTING GRILL ABOVE
DINING SALOON FOR 12 Third CLASS PASSENGERS
FOLDING DOOR MADE
CORRIDOR
TABLE | TABLE
VESTIBULE

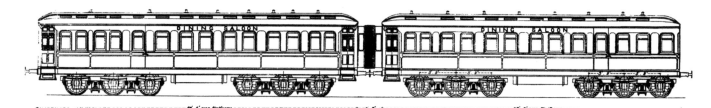

Figure 9.36
This drawing originally appeared in *The Railway Engineer* in 1892, just before the twin Dining carriages entered WCJS service on the Glasgow portion of the 'Corridor'. The two 50-foot 6-inch cars handed over to the Caledonian were of the type on the left.

although no drawings of what were minor structural alterations were made. One Saloon, probably the central Third class, was designated a no-smoking area – see Plate 9.21.

PRE-PULLMAN CAR ERA SERVICES

In the summer of 1908 the Public Timetable advertised *'Breakfast, Luncheon, and Dining Cars between Glasgow, Edinburgh and the North.'* The circuits shown in the following table, which involve three of the four cars, are deduced from the departure times. Northbound Edinburgh passengers joined the Glasgow departures at Perth, where the portions were combined. On the 10.35am from Aberdeen, Edinburgh passengers could use the Dining car as far as Larbert, where the train was divided.

OUTWARD	RETURN
7.40am Glasgow–Perth	
11.37am Perth–Aberdeen	5.30pm Aberdeen–Glasgow
5.00pm Glasgow–Aberdeen	10.35am Aberdeen–Glasgow
7.48pm Perth–Aberdeen	6.45am Aberdeen–Perth

In the year before they were superseded by the Pullman cars, the *July 1913 Marshalling of Main Line Trains* circular shows three Dining Saloons in use on the following circuits:

OUTWARD	RETURN
7.30am Glasgow–Perth	
11.37am Perth–Aberdeen	5.30pm Aberdeen–Glasgow
1.00pm Perth–Glasgow	5.00pm Glasgow–Perth
5.43am Carlisle–Perth	12.25pm Perth–Symington
	3.17pm to Carlisle empty

USE IMMEDIATELY AFTER THE INTRODUCTION OF PULLMANS

The *July 1914 Carriage Marshalling Circular* shows only one Dining car in operation. Its journey was the same as the 1913 circuit from Perth to Carlisle, with minor re-timing. On its southbound journey, it was detached at Carstairs rather than at Symington.

The remaining cars were probably used as spares for the Pullman service, as the fourth Pullman Dining car had not yet been delivered.

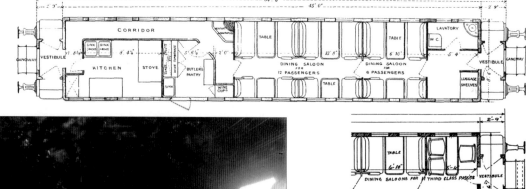

Figure 9.37 and Plate 9.21
The main drawing shows the internal arrangement on acquisition from the WCJS fleet, with two saloons for twelve and six passengers and no class designation. The inset shows the revised arrangement to increase the capacity by installing tables and five armchairs in the original lavatory and luggage area. It appears as the first of two pages 63 in the Large Diagram Book, annotated *'old WCJS 40 & 41.'* The saloons were now designated for the two classes of passenger. The photograph is from the NRM St. Rollox collection (ref. SRX 326) and shows that one saloon was designated as non-smoking.

All CR catering services were terminated on 1st January 1917. The Dining cars, like the Pullmans, were stored until catering was restored on 1st March 1919.

SERVICES AFTER WORLD WAR I

By the time that catering and Pullman car services were reinstated in March 1919, one of the larger diners (number 41) had been converted to an Officers' Saloon. The remaining three cars were deployed on a new service between Carlisle and the north on trains without WCJS catering.

One car ran on a circuit which left Perth at 11.40am for Carstairs, where it was detached. It returned on the 4.17pm from Carstairs and ran to Aberdeen. There is no record of its balancing journey between Aberdeen and Perth. Presumably it was attached to a train as empty stock, which is not recorded in carriage marshalling circulars.

A second car left Glasgow Central for Carlisle at 5.00pm each day. It returned at 6.55am the following morning, attached to the front of the Sleeping Saloons on the overnight train from London.

Finally, a Dining car travelled from Perth to Carlisle at 3.40pm each Sunday, returning to Perth on the 5.25am departure on Monday morning.

In 1920, only one large Dining car remained – number 40. The Pullman car *Duchess of Gordon* had entered service and it was planned to convert the two smaller cars to ordinary Third class carriages, as described below. Number 40 was probably kept as a spare vehicle for the Pullman services.

ALTERATIONS TO 40 AND 41

In December 1919 drawing 20337[6] was issued for a '*steel underframe for saloons No. 40 & 41,*' which included 4-wheeled 8-foot wheelbase bogies. The overall lengths were 50 feet 6 inches for Saloon 40, and 51 feet for Saloon 41. Louvre vents were added to some windows (drawing 19533). In the large Diagram Book they appear on the second page 63 (number 40) and 63A (number 41). Both are described as having 4-wheeled bogies, with total wheelbases of 43 feet and 44 feet respectively.

ALTERATION TO SALOON 40

General arrangement drawing 19300[7] of December 1917 recorded the existing state of Saloon 40 – see Figure 9.38. It differed slightly from the earlier modification to increase the seating capacity – for details, see the caption. A subsequent drawing in May 1918 (St. Rollox 19466, which has not survived) covered the conversion to electric lighting.

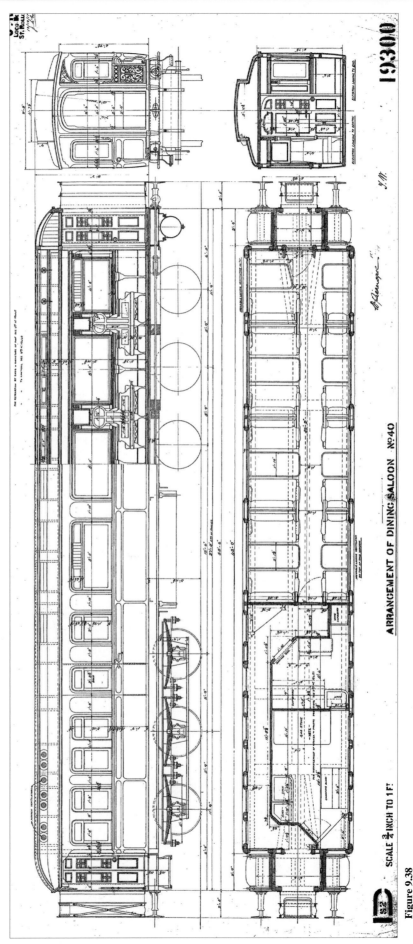

ARRANGEMENT OF DINING SALOON No40

SCALE ¾ INCH TO 1 FT

Figure 9.38
St. Rollox general arrangement drawing 19300 shows the external and internal modifications to Saloon 40, still with its original L&NWR bogies and clerestory roof. Seven Havock ventilators were fitted to the side of the clerestory over the kitchen section, and '*movable louvre ventilators*' to the top of the window at each end of the Dining Saloon. Compared with the inset to Figure 9.37, the two armchairs at the extreme end have been sacrificed to allow wider tables; fixed seats matching the original provision have replaced the other three armchairs. The drawing probably represents the car after the early alteration to increase the number of diners, but before the more extensive modifications that took place in 1921.

The second page 63 in the Large Diagram Book for number 40 is dated 20th October 1921. Figure 9.39 shows the new interior layout. The kitchen was relocated with a larger pantry on the other side of the body, partly to accommodate a lavatory. The drawings recording these alterations were all made in early 1919.

The Large Diagram Book index lists it as a Dining Saloon, as does the Small Book, but in the 1921 Stock List it is described as an Officers' Saloon, along with number 41. It may have served the dual purpose of reserve car for the Pullman services and occasional use for officers.

Number 40 was withdrawn in 1936, having received LM&SR number 15335 at the Grouping and 59 at second renumbering.

CONVERSION OF SALOON 41

Number 41 was earmarked for conversion in 1918 to replace an Officers' Saloon which was *'in unsatisfactory condition and not worth repairing.'*[8] The modifications are described and illustrated in Chapter 13.5. There is a certain amount of confusion, in that the Large Diagram Book index describes the carriage as a *'buffet saloon.'* In the 1921 Stock List it is an Officers' Saloon. It may have been available as a Buffet Saloon for excursion traffic – it would not have been fully utilised as an Officers' Saloon.

CONVERSION OF 38 AND 39

The new roof mentioned previously may have been part of a planned conversion to Third class carriages, which was agreed by the Traffic Committee in December 1919.[9] Diagram 91A (Figure 9.40) shows the altered layout. The interiors were to be gutted and replaced by pairs of seats with *'a centre passage.'* A lavatory was installed at one end. There is no drawing of the modification in the St. Rollox register.

The conversion did not take place immediately, if at all. They were still listed as Dining cars in the January 1921 Stock List and the Diagram Book index. They were not renumbered into the Third class carriage series but were allocated LM&SR numbers in a block with other Saloons. The Coaching Plant Stock Book also records them with 8-foot wheelbase bogies.

The Diagram Book has two unnumbered pages after page 62 which show proposals to alter either or both carriages to dormitories. One drawing is dated 7th January 1931,[10] which suggests that they were not broken up when they were withdrawn from revenue service. The withdrawal dates in the Coaching Plant Stock Book are 1929 (CR 38, LM&SR 15333) and 1930 (CR 39, LM&SR 15334).

REFERENCES
1. *The Railway Engineer*, August 1904, pp. 249-51
2. St. Rollox drawing 12520, RHP to be assigned
3. *West Coast Joint Stock*, pp. 185-91
4. NRS BR/CAL/23/11(18)
5. *LNWR Coaches*, pp. 12-13, 46-49
6. RHP to be assigned
7. NRM 7526/C RHP to be assigned
8. NRS BR/CAL/1/71 entry 222
9. NRS BR/CAL/1/74 entry 22
10. LM&SR drawing 7292, RHP to be assigned

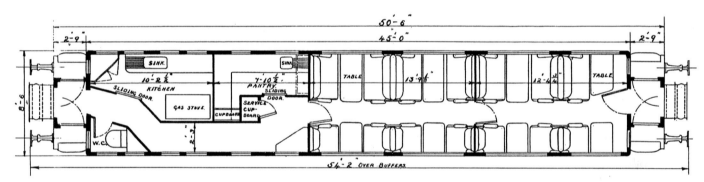

Figure 9.39
This drawing was dated 20th October 1921 in the Large Diagram Book. It shows the kitchen in Saloon 40 relocated to the other side of the carriage and the installation of a lavatory. The dining area remained as in the St. Rollox drawing 19300.

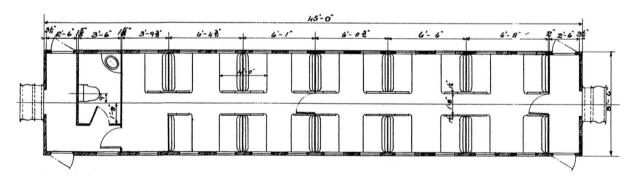

Figure 9.40
The two smaller Saloons 38 and 39 were intended for conversion to Third class carriages in 1919. Diagram 91A shows the new internal layout, but it is doubtful that the conversion took place.

9.4: REBUILDING, CONVERSIONS AND RECLASSIFICATIONS

In March 1905, when the extension to the Crieff & Comrie line to its junction at Balquhidder was near completion, and with the intention of through working *'between Aberdeen and Dundee and Oban via Balquhidder'* the Traffic Committee approved a proposal that the luggage lockers of the six Lambie-designed Diagram 30 Coupé Composites should be equipped with brake apparatus at an estimated cost of £15 each.[1] This explains the inclusion of Diagram 30 among the Brake Composites in the Diagram Book index. These carriages are described in Chapter 7.5. A photograph of one of these carriages on the C&O appears in *Caledonian Railway Livery*.[2]

EX-WEST COAST JOINT STOCK CONVERSIONS

In 1907 the Traffic Committee agreed to the proposal that *'Luggage lockers in 25 old composites and 3rd class carriages be converted into Brake Compartments.'*[3] The carriages involved are described below. Details of their acquisition and renumbering are given in Chapter 8.4.

The Composites were the fourteen WCJS Diagram P16s and the five P17s. All were described as Brake Composites in the 1921 Stock List. The Coaching Plant Stock Book transcription erroneously describes the P17s as Luggage Composites and notes two as having a *'small Bk. Compt.'*

CR Diagram 27A accounted for the nine WCJS P16s that retained their radial bogies. Their numbers were 279-281 and 286-292. Diagram 27B was for the remaining five examples which were mounted on conventional bogies. The P17 carriages 197-301 were allocated LM&SR numbers and were withdrawn after the Grouping but they do not appear in the index or on a page in the Diagram Book. They are, however, in the 1921 Stock List.

The Thirds were the six carriages to WCJS Diagrams P25 and P26. CR Diagram 25 34-foot carriages 959, 960, 1124 and 1125 were assigned to page 16A, which is blank in the Diagram Book. The Coaching Plant Stock Book transcription describes them as luggage Thirds, but in the 1921 Stock List they are Brake Thirds.

The P26 32-foot Third class carriages 1078 and 1079 were assigned to CR Diagram 16B. The diagram shows the addition of a brake stanchion to a floor layout unaltered from WCJS service.[4]

THE NEED FOR MORE COMPOSITE CARRIAGES

In the second half of the 1900s it was decided that not enough carriages catered for both classes of traveller. More Composite carriages were created by downrating some compartments in First class carriages to Third class or, less frequently, vice versa.

The doors were relettered and the compartments were reupholstered in the appropriate style. The converted carriages were assimilated into the nearest relevant Diagram with a suffix letter. Since there were no structural alterations, the more generous dimensions of the former First class compartments remained when downrated to Third. On the other hand, the leg room in 45-foot Brake Thirds was not generous even for Third class passengers, so those who had paid to travel in compartments uprated to First class would have felt particularly hard done by.

In late 1907/early 1908, ten Diagram 21 45-foot Firsts had three compartments converted to Third class and became Diagram 26A. The First class compartments only measured 6 feet 3½ inches between partitions, so they were obvious candidates for conversion. The Traffic Committee authorised the work in October 1907.[5]

The Committee sanctioned a proposal to convert thirty-eight carriages in January 1910.[6] Four ex-WCJS Sleeping Composites with CR numbers 307-310 were converted to Diagram 11A Brake Composites. This was an extensive rebuild, as can be seen by comparing the original WCJS configuration with the CR diagram (Figure 9.41). The thirty-four CR carriages involved are described below.

SIX-WHEELED CARRIAGES

Eight Diagram 9 Composites were created by removing the arm rests from the compartment at either end of Diagram 8 First class carriages built in 1883/84 and retrimming the compartments to Third class standard. This gave spacious Third class accommodation for twenty people. The Firsts were originally numbered 25, 78, 81-83, 96, 101 and 174. They were renumbered 392-399 but not in the same order.

Six Diagram 14 Thirds, originally numbered 69, 129, 405, 488, 821 and 854, were rebuilt in 1910, assigned to a new Diagram 10A and allocated numbers 400-405. The Brake section was formed out of two compartments at one end; the middle two were converted to Firsts. They were fitted with a single central armrest giving sixteen cramped seats. All these carriages were withdrawn between 1925 and 1928. An interior layout and photograph appear as Figure 9.42 and Plate 9.22.

EIGHT-WHEELED CARRIAGES

Ten more Diagram 21 Firsts were converted to Diagram 26A in 1910. They were allocated numbers 406-415. At the same time ten Diagram 34 Brake Thirds had the two compartments nearest the Brake section upgraded to First class, providing sixteen seats with

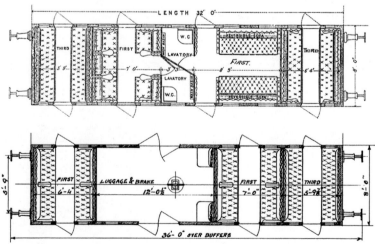

Figure 9.41
These two drawings show how the internal layout of the P20 WCJS Composites (*top*) was converted to make the CR Diagram 11A Brake Composites (*bottom*).

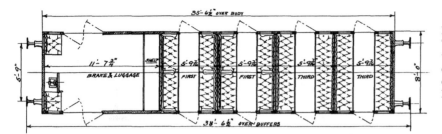

Figure 9.42
This is the internal layout of Diagram 10A, which was created when six Diagram 14 Thirds were converted to Brake Composites in 1910. The First class compartments are over 1 foot narrower than those in Diagram 10.

central arm rests. Their new numbers were 382-391. They were assigned to Diagram 23A.

DOWNRATING TO THIRD CLASS

First class and Composite carriages were frequently downrated to Third class. According to the Coaching Plant Stock Book, this started in 1900 and continued piecemeal for the rest of the Caledonian's existence.

Thirty 31-foot Firsts dating from the 1870s, which originally seated forty, were turned into fifty-seat Thirds. Another, which only sat thirty-two, was turned into a 40-seat carriage. Finally, two 4-wheeled carriages dating from 1865 and a 6-wheeler built five years later had bare wood seats fitted on conversion.

Most of the downrated Composites were 32-foot carriages dating from the late 1870s, but there were also a small number of earlier 31-foot carriages. Twenty-five Composites were downrated, plus nine Brake Composites.

Diagram 13C Lavatory Composite number 30 was rebuilt 'c1923' as a Third and renumbered 400 to Diagram 15A by substituting longitudinal seats for the lavatories and adjacent seats.

INCREASED LUGGAGE SPACE

In February 1914 the Traffic Committee agreed that '15 Composite Carriages should have the brake compartment enlarged by taking in the adjoining passenger compartment.'[7]

Nine were probably the Diagram 27A carriages which the CR had fitted with a brake stanchion in their original, very small, luggage compartment. The diagram shows the modified Brake compartment, with the adjacent Third class compartment annotated 'THIS Compt. Added to Brake.' The addition gave the identical configuration to Diagram 27B.

REBUILT CARRIAGES

Further rebuilding of old carriages seems to have taken place in late 1912 and 1913, although it is not recorded in the minutes. Like the programme initiated in the previous decade, it seems to have been concerned with extending the life of the carriages built in the 1870s. The vehicles concerned may have been those used on workmen's trains. Drawing 16167 was entitled '*Underframe (ordering) for 6-wheeled carriage stock.*' Drawing 16818 was for '*Bridle and tie rod for old carriages.*' Neither drawing survives.

REFERENCES
1. NRS BR/CAL/1/51 entry 504
2. *Caledonian Railway Livery*, Plate 17, p. 160
3. NRS BR/CAL/1/55 entry 14
4. *West Coast Joint Stock*, p. 82
5. NRS BR/CAL/1/55 entry 911
6. NRS BR/CAL/1/58 entry 977
7. NRS BR/CAL/1/64 entry 951

Plate 9.22
This photograph of a Diagram 10A Brake Composite was taken in LM&SR days, probably on the Killin Branch – H.C. Casserley recorded 15103 on the branch in 1931. It shows the windows that were cut in the end with the guard's compartment.

9.5: THE 57-FOOT DESIGNS

In 1911 the first of a series of carriages appeared which would be the principal type built until the end of the company's existence. The 57-foot stock brought the CR to the forefront of early twentieth-century carriage design. McIntosh picked a length which became the standard for British railways for the next fifty years. The early designs were 8 feet 8 inches wide and built on a common underframe to drawing 15982, dated 5th August 1911.[1] They were mounted on 10-foot wheelbase bogies, drawing 15917, dated 27th June.[2]

A New Excursion Set

The first designs to appear were the Diagram 109 Corridor Thirds and the companion Diagram 110 Brake Third. Ten Thirds and two Brake Thirds were built to orders H294 and H295 respectively. All were dual braked. They were authorised as renewals in the period ending January 1912.[3] They were probably intended as a set for excursion traffic. A similar order was authorised for this purpose in 1912,[4] but was not built after being deferred.

The Diagram 109 carriages had eight compartments seating sixty-four passengers, with a lavatory at each end. They were built to drawing 15777, which has not survived. The internal layout is shown in Figure 9.43. They took numbers which were among the 31-foot carriages built in the late 1870s, which were presumably withdrawn when the new carriages entered traffic.

The Diagram 110 Brake Thirds were the Diagram 109 design with two fewer compartments and one reconfigured lavatory, creating a guard's and luggage space 13 feet long – see Figure 9.44. They were numbered 17 and 986. They were built to drawing 15778, which also has not survived. Only the transverse sections and end elevations for the two designs have survived as drawing 16037,[5] dated 1st September 1911. This is shown in Figure 9.45.

The Coaching Plant Stock Book records them as being fitted with '*a pantry*'. Drawings 16323 and 16325 both refer to a '*sink in*

the kitchen compartment' of order H295. The drawings have not survived, but in the Large Diagram Book there is a page numbered 110B, annotated '*16328B*'. This shows the Diagram 110 configuration with one lavatory removed to extend the luggage area, as in the Diagram 110A design described below.

The compartment nearest the Brake end has been converted into a pantry. The page is not included in the index to the Diagram Book and has no equivalent in the Small Book. Presumably an attendant dispensed hot drinks, and perhaps snacks, when the train reached its destination; passengers could not access the pantries when the train was in motion. The altered arrangement is shown in Figure 9.46. A photograph of ex-CR 188 in LM&SR days is seen in Plate 9.23.

General Service Brake Thirds

Two more Diagram 110 Brake Thirds were authorised in the first half of 1912 to order H297.[6] One was number 515, which did not have a pantry; the other number is unknown. It formed part of the CR Ambulance Train, but its prior details are not recorded in the Coaching Plant Stock Book.

Composite Carriages

The next two designs were authorised in the same period as order H297. The Diagram 111 Brake Composite was built to drawing 16093, which has not survived. There were two First and four Third class compartments giving a short guard's and luggage space – see Figure 9.47. There were twelve First class seats and thirty-two Third. Three were built with Westinghouse brake only to order H296. They were numbered 181, 233 and 260. Another two, numbers 180 and 230, were dual-fitted to order H299. Four further examples were built in the second half of 1912 to orders H304 and H305.

A companion Composite, with three First class compartments and four Thirds seating eighteen and thirty-two respectively, was built

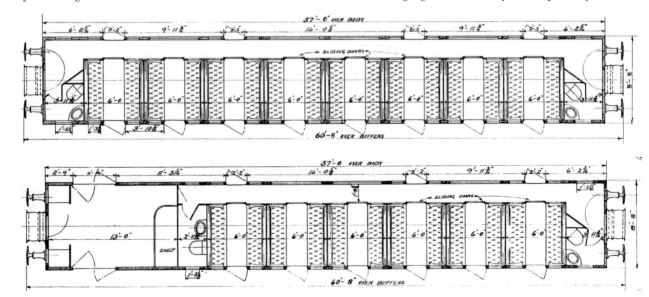

Figures 9.43 and 9.44
These 57-foot Third (A) and Brake Third (B) carriages were probably built as an excursion set.

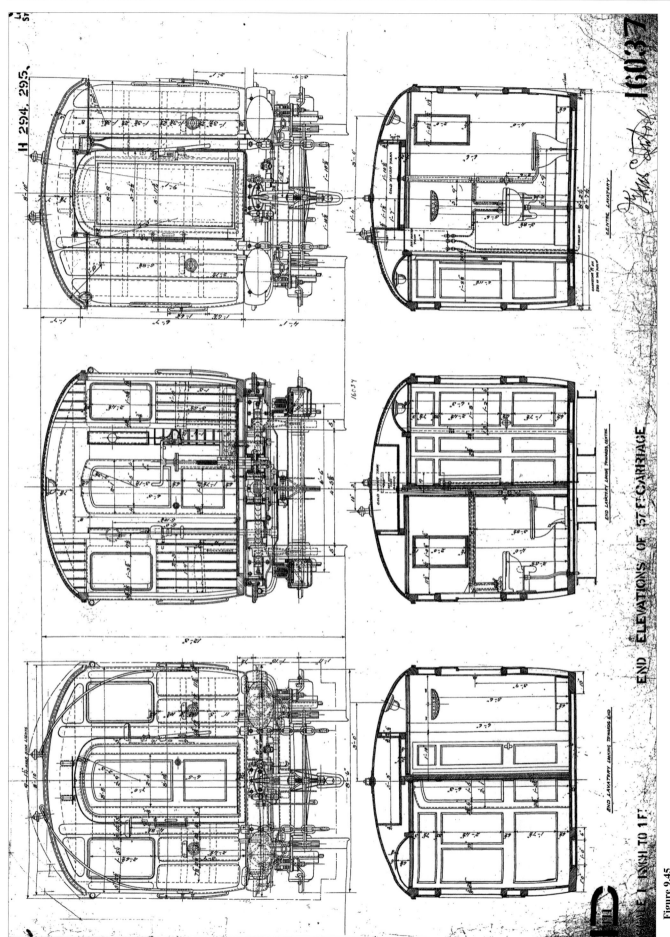

SCALE 1 INCH TO 1 FT   END ELEVATIONS OF 57 FT CARRIAGE

Figure 9.45
St. Rollox drawing 16037 is the only surviving official drawing of these 57-foot vehicles.

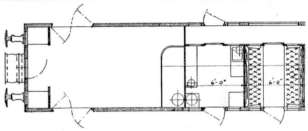

Plate 9.23 (*Above*) **and Figure 9.46** (*Right*)
One of two Diagram 110B Brake Thirds built to order H295. It was originally CR 986, here carrying its first LM&SR number 6565. The odd-shaped window adjacent to the LMS letters may have something to do with the pantry that was fitted in this and another of these vehicles. Unfortunately this cannot be verified as the St. Rollox drawings have not survived. The drawing shows the internal layout of the pantry arrangement in Diagram 110B. Compared with Diagram 110 the lavatory adjacent to the guard's area was removed to create more luggage space and the Third class compartment has been gutted to construct a small kitchen.

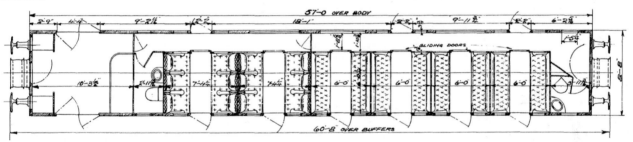

Figure 9.47
The internal layout of Diagram 111.

to drawing 16094 – another that has not survived. The sole example of Diagram 112 to order H298, number 416, had the Westinghouse brake only.

This design was superseded in the next accounting period[7] by a four-First and three-Third class compartment version to drawing 16327, which has not survived. Four carriages were built to order H302, numbered 418-421. They were given Diagram 112A. The Third class compartments were reduced by 3½ inches to accommodate the extra First. There were twenty-four seats in each class. The internal layouts of the two Composite designs are compared in Figure 9.48. Photographs of both sides of 418 in departmental use are shown in Plate 9.24.

Diagram 110A was based on Diagram 110, with the lavatory nearest to the guard's compartment removed to create a 3 feet larger luggage space. A new drawing was not issued for the alteration. Four were built to order H303 in late 1912. As described in Chapter 12, they were converted for use in the CR Ambulance Train.

THE 9 FOOT WIDE CARRIAGES

In the half year ending June 1913, the body profile of the high roof 'Grampian' stock was adopted for 57-foot carriages, increasing the body width by 4 inches to 9 feet. This warranted new diagram numbers. A drawing for a new standard underframe, St. Rollox

16635,[8] was produced on 6th November 1912, annotated for use with orders H306-H320.

None of the new designs had corridor connections, but all had corridor access within the carriage, with the exception of three types which are described separately. The extra width allowed the lavatories to be sited adjacent to each other across the body rather than separately at the ends of the passenger accommodation. This gave about three feet of extra passenger space.

SEMI-CORRIDOR COMPOSITES

The Diagram 113 design had three First and five Third class compartments, separated by a pair of lavatories. Seating capacity was nineteen First and forty-two Third. The internal layout is shown in Figure 9.49 and a side elevation is Figure 9.50. Three carriages, numbered 424-426 were built to order H309 as renewals. The drawing number was 17376.[9] A photograph appears in Plate 9.25.

During the same period, two carriages with four each First and Third class compartments with twenty-five and thirty-four seats respectively were built to order H307. The internal layout is Figure 9.51. They were assigned to Diagram 113A. The drawing number was 17360.[10] Two more were built in the next period to order H313 and a final three to H320 in the period ending June 1914. Numbers were 422, 423, 437, 438 and 442-444. Both these designs had the

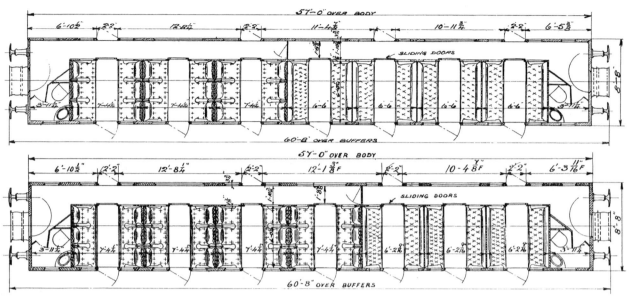

Figure 9.48
The Diagram 112 (*top*) and 112A Corridor Composites compared. In 112A the Third class compartments are narrower to create space for the extra First class accommodation.

ABOVE: Plates 9.24a and 9.24b
These two images show both sides of Diagram 112A Corridor Composite number 418 in departmental use as a mess van, carrying the number 395313. It was based at Perth and broken up in 1977.

Plate 9.25
One of the three Diagram 113 Composites, with the First class end nearest the camera.

Westinghouse brake only. A side elevation is shown in Figure 9.52 and a photograph of 437 in Plate 9.26.

The companion Diagram 115 Brake Composite had two First and four Third class compartments, seating thirteen and thirty-three respectively – see Figure 9.53. They were built to drawings 16955, which has not survived, and 17316.[11] The first six and the last three, to orders H310, H311 and H318, had Westinghouse brakes. They were numbered 427-433 and 439-441. The H312 order was dual-fitted and numbered 433-436. The side elevation is shown in Figure 9.54 and a photograph of number 431 in post-Grouping livery is shown in Plate 9.27.

SEMI-CORRIDOR THIRDS

Orders H308 and H314 in 1913 were for a pair each of Diagram 114 Thirds. Eight compartments, plus a half compartment next to the lavatories in the centre of the carriage, gave seventy-two seats – see Figure 9.55. They were built to drawings 16854, which has not survived, and 17390,[12] which was produced for the later order. Numbers were 347, 395, 962 and 963. The side elevation is Figure 9.56.

The most numerous of the pre-war 57-foot designs was the Brake Third to Diagram 116. This had five compartments, allowing for a large guard's and luggage section just over 23 feet long – see Figure 9.57. The first drawing, 16663 for order H306 built in early 1913, has not survived, but 17338, produced for order H319 which was built in early 1914, is available.[13] The side elevation is Figure 9.58 and a photograph is Plate 9.28. Eleven carriages were allocated random numbers, including 468, 508, 1164, 1165 and 1304.

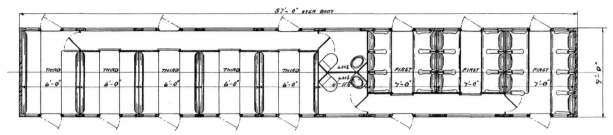

Figures 9.49 (*Above*) and 9.50 (*Right*) The internal layout and side elevation of Diagram 113.

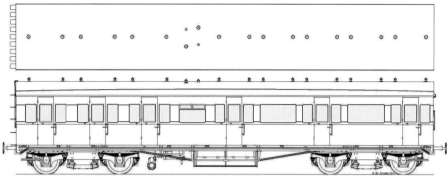

Non-Corridor Carriages

A small number of non-corridor carriages were also built, probably as a set. They were authorised in the renewal programme for the period ending June 1914.[14] More of the first two types were built later by Pickersgill. A single Diagram 117 8-compartment First, number 43, was built to order H315. It had sixty-four seats. The drawing number was 17301.

It was followed by order H316, for one Diagram 118 Third, seating 108 passengers in twelve compartments. The drawing number was 17117. Its running number was 997.

The only two examples of the Diagram 119 Brake Third design, numbered 458 and 683, were built to order H317. Six compartments seated seventy-two. The drawing number was 17135. None of the drawings quoted has survived. Side elevations of the three designs are shown in Figures 9.59-9.61.

Plate 9.26
This shows LM&SR 19960, which was originally CR 437. It was built in the latter half of 1913, and eventually became a Camping coach.

References

1. NRM 8088/C (on two sheets)
2. NRM 11206/C
3. NRS BR/CAL/1/60 entry 442
4. NRS BR/CAL/1/61 entry 988
5. NRM 7499/C RHP to be assigned
6. NRS BR/CAL/1/61 entry 66
7. NRS BR/CAL/1/61 entry 988
8. NRM 8078/C (on two sheets)
9. NRM 7503/C RHP to be assigned
10. NRM 7501/C RHP to be assigned
11. NRM 7505/C RHP to be assigned
12. NRM 7500/C RHP to be assigned
13. NRM 7504/C RHP to be assigned
14. NRS BR/CAL/1/63 entry 1383

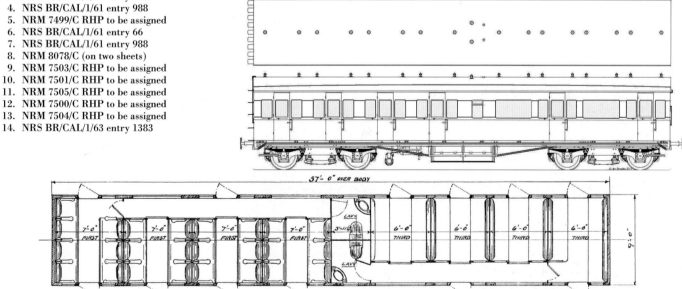

Figures 9.51 and 9.52
The internal layout and side elevation of Diagram 113A, which had an equal number of First and Third class compartments.

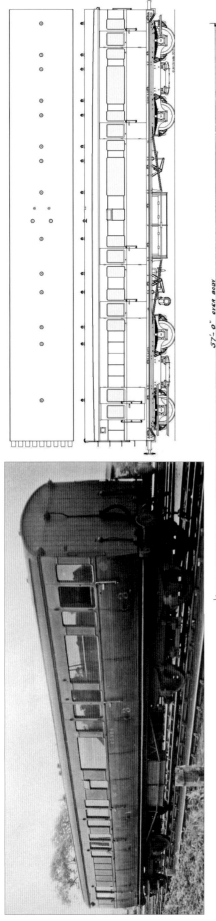

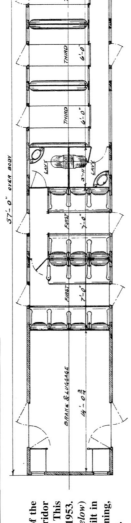

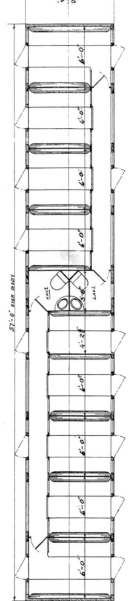

ABOVE AND LEFT: Figures 9.55 and 9.56
Internal layout and side elevation of the Diagram 114 Thirds.

Figures 9.53 and 9.54, Plates 9.27a and 9.27b
Internal layout (*right*) and side elevation (*above right*) of the Diagram 115 Composites. The photograph of the corridor side of LM&SR 25986 (*above*) is NRM ref: LGRP6084. This was originally CR 440, built in 1914 and withdrawn in 1953. A.B. McLeod took the picture of LM&SR 16017 (*below*) (NRM Ref: C124). It was originally Composite 431, built in the second half of 1912 to order H311. The painted lining, which was the convention at the time, looks very strange.

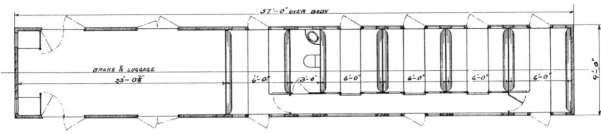

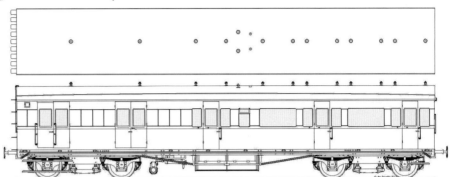

Figures 9.57 and 9.58
The internal layout and side elevation of Diagram 116.

Plate 9.28
This is Semi-corridor Brake Third number 508, built in early 1913, at the end of its life. It became a Signal & Telegraph Department mess van 395071 based at Inverness. It was sold for scrap in 1970.

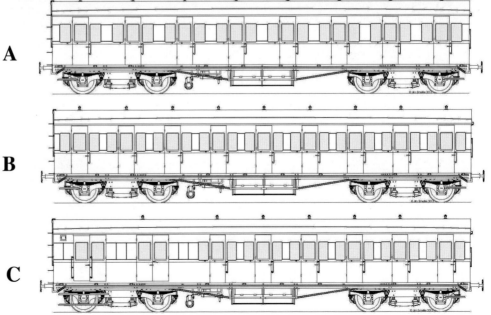

Figures 9.59, 9.60 and 9.61
These three designs were probably built as a set of four carriages in early 1914. The figures show the Diagram 117 First (*A*) and the Diagram 118 Third (*B*); one each of these carriages was built. Two examples of the Diagram 119 Brake Third (*C*) were constructed. More of the first two designs were produced after the war – see Chapter 11.

LEFT: Plate 10.1
The 30 inch by 40 inch poster announcing the Gourock service was issued in July 1914.

ABOVE RIGHT: Plate 10.2
An invitation to day trippers from Glasgow and Edinburgh, which launched the 'Maid of Morven' Observation car service to Oban.

Plate 10.3
The poster advertising the commencement of Pullman car services on the Caledonian. The only variation from the timetable and the carriage marshalling circular is the 6.25am departure from Edinburgh, which was given as 7.45am.

Plate 10.4
The Caley was never shy in blowing its own trumpet. A proud statement announcing the advent of the Pullman car service on the system.

CHAPTER 10
PULLMAN CARS

10.1: PULLMAN SERVICES 1914-1916

While the cars that ran on Caledonian Railway metals were built and owned by the Pullman Car Company and not the CR, they were so intimately associated with the operation of the Caledonian's trains that they have a proper place in this book.

The Pullman Palace Car Company was formed in America in 1863 and services began in the United Kingdom in 1874. The first move to run Pullman cars in Scotland came from the North British who gave notice of their intention to run 'a Pullman car to Perth and Composite Carriages to Aberdeen and Inverness' in 1877.[1] The Caledonian referred the matter to the Railway Commissioners and was 'to be guided by Counsel as to running or not running the Car, pending decision.'[2] Nothing more was heard about the project.

The Caledonian only included Pullman cars in services within Scotland. They ran on some Anglo-Scottish trains in the latter half of 1916 when the WCJS Dining cars were withdrawn, and were attached to others after the war, but they did not travel south of Carlisle.

The cars and their services have been the subject of chapters in books and magazine articles. Conflicting stories have emerged, with statements based on secondary information or supposition and the repetition of supposition as fact.

This chapter attempts to disentangle the facts from the rest and provides new information. It highlights some of the errors made by previous commentators, not to belittle them, but to set the so-called established record straight.

PULLMANS ON THE CALEDONIAN

By 1912, the ex-WCJS Dining cars on the Aberdeen route were becoming outdated, although they were not at the end of their design life. Their seating capacity was also low compared with more modern Dining cars. Two options were open to the Caledonian – build a small number of replacement Dining cars, or use a larger fleet of Pullmans to meet the increased demand for catering facilities on express trains.

The former option had been considered in 1906, when St. Rollox drawing 13820 was issued for a 68-foot Composite Dining car. This was in line with current WCJS developments. The drawing, which has not survived, was presumably of a carriage in the 'Grampian' style on the extended Diagram 105 underframe. Nothing came of the proposal, probably because the Caledonian was heavily committed financially to building 65-foot carriages, as described in Chapter 9.1.

An LM&SR memorandum in 1927,[3] in response to a proposal from the Pullman Car Co. to operate the equivalent of the Queen of Scots service on the West Coast route, stated:

'The prime reasons which influenced [the CR] in agreeing to the [Pullman] cars working were
(a) the old Caledonian dining cars had become obsolete and unremunerative
(b) expenditure on new cars, and cost of maintenance would be avoided
(c) the loss in working the old dining cars would be cut
(d) the facilities would induce passengers to travel via "Caledonian" with consequent benefit to be derived from this form of publicity.'

According to James McEwan, the Board of Directors first considered the possibility of running Pullman cars on internal daytime Caledonian Railway traffic on 29th April 1912.[4] Initially it was proposed to operate twenty-three cars, but by the time an agreement was made between the railway and the Pullman Car Company the number had been reduced to seventeen, with an option to increase the fleet should the venture prove successful. There is no record of this transaction in the CR Board minutes.

One reason for the reduction may have been that an attempt had been made in September 1913 to interest the L&NWR in running Pullman cars from Euston in connection with the planned construction of the Gleneagles Hotel.[5] The proposal was rejected by the L&NWR.

McEwan suggested[6] that a further reason for the reduction in the number of cars may have been that the Pullman Company had cash flow problems at the time. As it was making the capital investment in the venture, the suggestion may well have some validity.

THE FIRST AGREEMENT WITH THE PULLMAN CAR COMPANY

A contract between the two companies was formalised in two 'Minutes of Agreement' dated the 25th and 27th November 1913.[7] The Pullman Car Company was to provide, at its own expense, the seventeen cars. Initially to consist of twelve Buffet cars, four Composite Dining cars and a Buffet Observation car, an amendment on the day of signature substituted a 'drawing room car' for one of the Buffet cars.

Donald Matheson, the CR General Manager, wrote to his Pullman Company co-signatory Davison Dalziel on the 25th November 'one of the spare buffet cars will be made a drawing room car.' This was obviously verbally agreed, because Matheson wrote on the 27th November 'I note that you have already placed an order for the drawing room car.'

This type of vehicle is also mentioned in the May 1915 Working Timetable Appendix, where holders of First class railway passes were required to pay the Pullman supplementary fare 'if they travel in the Observation, Buffet or Parlour Cars.'[8]

As far as can be ascertained, a Parlour car never appeared on the Caledonian. The car referred to in the agreement may have been 'Glencoe'. This car was one of four, three of which bore Scottish names, which formed the 'Eastbourne Pullman' on the LB&SCR in 1914. Pullman Profile No. 1 states that the cars were 'believed to have been ordered for the Caledonian Railway.'[9]

The cars were ideally to be delivered by 1st May 1914, and no later than 1st March 1915 – a year later than envisaged. The Caledonian was to be responsible for hauling the cars while the Pullman Car Company would receive the income from supplementary fares on some services, plus profits from catering.

The agreement was to last for twelve years from 1st March 1915. If additional cars were provided, the termination date of the agreement would be extended to twelve years from the date of the new cars' delivery.

SERVICES AND TIMETABLES AS SET OUT IN THE AGREEMENT

Circuits requiring fourteen cars were described in detail. Two Buffets and one Dining car were designated as 'reserve cars' to allow for maintenance without interrupting services. Most of the trains were composed of the CR's prestige 'Grampian' stock, or in the case of the Callander & Oban circuit carriages, built to 'Grampian' standards, as described in Chapter 9.2. The cars were to be deployed as follows:

Vehicles	Route
3 Buffet cars	Glasgow–Edinburgh
4 Buffet cars	Glasgow–Gourock and Wemyss Bay
1 Buffet car	Glasgow–Moffat
3 Dining cars	Glasgow–Aberdeen
1 Buffet car	Perth–Edinburgh and Aberdeen
1 Buffet car	St. Fillans–Glasgow–Crieff
Buffet Observation car	Glasgow–Oban

On Saturdays only, one of the Edinburgh–Glasgow cars was scheduled to complete a round trip in the early afternoon from Glasgow to Gourock. One of the four Gourock cars was to fill in on the service between Glasgow and Edinburgh.

The CR was confident that the full complement of cars would be delivered on time, as the circuits in the contract were set out in the May and June 1914 Working Timetable, 'Commencing in June – on dates to be announced.' A note at the bottom of the notice which set out the supplementary fares conditions stated: 'The dates on which the Pullman Cars will be introduced on the various Sections of the Line will be announced through the Weekly Notice.'

SUPPLEMENTARY FARES

The Buffet cars were for the use of First class passengers only. They generally operated on short runs during which passengers would expect to stay in the car for the whole journey. Indeed, on the proposed Glasgow–Edinburgh and Glasgow–Gourock/Wemyss Bay circuits the train was composed of non-corridor carriages, which prevented passengers from leaving the car. Maid of Morven's passengers had a much longer journey, but they too travelled in a train without corridor connections.

The Dining cars were available to First and Third class passengers without supplement on longer journeys, but only for the duration of the meal service. The May/June 1914 Public Timetable, which announced the impending commencement of the Pullman service, indicated that passengers could travel the whole journey in the Dining cars on payment of a supplement. The full list of supplementary fares, corresponding to all the services in the agreement, is shown in the table below.

Supp. Fare	Routes
1s 0d	Glasgow to Edinburgh, Gourock, Wemyss Bay, Symington and Stirling. Edinburgh to Stirling
1s 6d	Glasgow or Edinburgh to Callander, Perth, also Gleneagles, Crieff and St. Fillans. Stations between Lamington and Moffat and Coulter and Peebles
2s 6d	Glasgow to Oban
3s 0d	Glasgow or Edinburgh to Aberdeen, including stations north of Perth

PRE-WAR SERVICES

By the outbreak of the World War I only ten cars had been supplied, all built by Cravens. The duties of the eight cars that were said to be in service at any one time were set out in the action for compensation brought by the Pullman Car Co. for loss of earnings

after the Caledonian withdrew services in 1916. They were quoted by Niall Ferguson[10] to be as shown in the table.

Vehicles	Route	Started
3 Buffet cars	Glasgow–Edinburgh	8th June
3 Dining cars	Glasgow–Aberdeen	8th June
1 Buffet car	Glasgow–Gourock	6th July
Buffet Observation car	Glasgow–Oban	3rd August

The contemporary press went into more detail about the timetables. In particular, the description of the services in The Railway Magazine article published in August 1914[11] has been repeated by commentators and become accepted as correct. This is hardly surprising, as the information was said to be given by 'Mr T. Powell, Secretary and Manager of the Pullman Car Co.' As well as the Aberdeen, Edinburgh and Oban routes, it had Buffet cars running to Crieff and Moffat, but not to Gourock. In fact, Powell was summarising the services in the agreement, not what was actually happening with the cars that were available.

A Railway Gazette article published in September[12] was more accurate. As well as mentioning the Dining cars and the Observation car, the article said that:

'an excellent service of buffet cars is already in operation between Glasgow and Edinburgh, and with the completion of a few more cars shortly, services to the Strathearn, Lanark and Clyde coast districts will be similarly provided for.'

The services as laid out in the official timetables and carriage marshalling circulars are described below.

THE GLASGOW–EDINBURGH SERVICE

The Railway Magazine[13] named the designated Buffet cars as Mary Beaton, Mary Hamilton and Annie Laurie. Mary Carmichael and Helen MacGregor were the spares, although the cars would have been regularly rotated into and out of service.

The actual Monday to Friday timetable as described in the Carriage Marshalling Circular[14] and the Public Timetable differed significantly from that set out in the agreement. It started earlier, finished later, and involved sixteen trains, not fourteen. The trains ran either non-stop between the two cities or called at Holytown and Merchiston only. The circuits for the three cars are shown below.

Circuit	Edinburgh Depart	Glasgow Depart
Set 125	9.00am	11.00am
	12.55pm	4.05pm
	7.05pm	10.20pm
	Glasgow Depart	**Edinburgh Depart**
Set 126	8.45am	10.55am
	1.30pm	4.55pm
	6.45pm	9.50pm
	Edinburgh Depart	**Glasgow Depart**
Set 128	7.45am	9.50am
	3.55pm	5.10pm

On Saturdays, an extra train ran each way, departing at 2.20pm. Set 125's 12.55pm departure from Edinburgh was replaced by the 2.20pm. The 4.55pm departure of set 126 from Edinburgh ran one hour earlier, returning at 5.10pm, taking over the Monday to Friday working of set 128. This freed set 128 to take over set 125's 12.55pm and 4.55pm weekday departures from Edinburgh and the return workings.

The stock in sets 125 and 126 interchanged daily. These sets were composed of 'Grampian' style non-corridor stock. In comparison with the previous year, an additional Third class carriage was added, as well as the Pullman. Set 128 was described in the 1913 Local Working of Carriages as a 'bogie train,' presumably of 48-foot stock. This was upgraded on the arrival of the Pullman service to 57-foot stock, the first examples of which had been built in 1912.

THE GLASGOW–ABERDEEN SERVICE

This was the only route in the agreement that already enjoyed catering facilities. In 1913 the Caledonian was running three ex-WCJS Dining cars on services to the north. The circuits, which included a trip from Perth to the south and back to Glasgow, are shown in Chapter 9.3. A fourth ex-WCJS Dining car made a return trip to Perth, with an early morning departure from Buchanan Street, returning at tea time.

The Dining cars *Flora MacDonald*, *Fair Maid of Perth* and *Lass o' Gowrie* replaced the ex-WCJS Dining cars, extended the existing Perth service through to Aberdeen and added an extra service in the middle of the day. The Pullmans were attached to the following departures, from Monday to Saturday:

CIRCUIT	GLASGOW DEPART	ABERDEEN DEPART
1	7.30am	12.50pm
2	10.00am	5.30pm
3	5.00pm	10.35am next day

The 5.30pm from Aberdeen arrived at Glasgow Central rather than Buchanan Street. The ex-WCJS Dining cars continued on services between Carlisle and Perth and as spare vehicles, prior to delivery of the full complement of Pullmans.

THE GLASGOW–GOUROCK SERVICE

There was no mention of a Pullman service to the Clyde coast in the July–September 1914 Public Timetable, the Working Timetable, the service alterations for July, or the Local Working of Carriages document. At the foot of the advertisement for the services to Aberdeen, Edinburgh and Oban on page 2 of the 1914 Public Timetable, was a note saying that there would be a further announcement concerning services 'on other sections.'

In fact, a CR poster (see Plate 10.1) confirms that a limited service did start to Gourock at the date given in the compensation statement cited previously. Although the poster implied that more than one Buffet car was involved, a single car – possibly *Mary Seaton* as mentioned in the press, but perhaps more appropriately *Annie Laurie* given her West of Scotland connections – sufficed for the following circuit:

GLASGOW DEPART	GOUROCK DEPART
8.35am	10.35am
12.45pm	3.55pm
5.20pm	6.45pm

On Saturdays the early afternoon departure from Glasgow was slightly earlier and the last departure from Gourock was twenty minutes later. This circuit was part of the 1913 circuit 127, which did not appear in the July 1914 Local Working of Carriages Circular. It would have meant the restructuring of Clyde Coast circuits 111-113 as published.

The service did not last long. A September supplement to the Public Timetable makes no mention of a Pullman car service, nor does the October Local Working of Carriages Circular.

THE GLASGOW–OBAN SERVICE

Buffet Observation car *Maid of Morven* left Buchanan Street at 8.00am each day. It started its return trip from Oban at 3.00pm between July and September, and at 5.00pm during the rest of the year. Despite the recorded start date of 3rd August as stated in the compensation document, *Bradshaw* does not mention it in the August edition.

One potential market was wealthy day trippers. The 1914 poster advertising the service 'to Oban and back' (see Plate 10.2) promised 'a day in the Western Highlands – historic, romantic, picturesque.' It was the first, and for many years the only, Observation car to be built for a British railway.

PUBLICITY

A concerted effort was made to market the Pullman services. Posters were produced for the various services with the strap line 'Luxury in Travel' – see Plate 10.3. The poster announcing the Aberdeen and Edinburgh services added 'Nothing finer in the world of transit' (Plate 10.4). Public Timetables advertised the services in a special section towards the front of the publication. The 1915 Working Timetable Appendix gave instructions about supplementary fares and ticketing arrangements on the Pullman services.[15] It concluded with the instruction, repeated in the 1921 Appendix, that all CR staff:

'must courteously draw the attention of Passengers about to travel by these Trains to the fact that Pullman Cars are supplied, in order that this Service may be thoroughly known, and every endeavour must be made by the Staff to make the Service a success.'

The marketing effort extended to the uniform cleanliness of the stock. Carriage marshalling circulars give details about the frequency of cleaning. The Pullman cars and accompanying CR carriages were cleaned externally before every journey, and swept and dusted at the termination of each run. Pullman staff cleaned the interior, with the Caledonian responsible for the exterior. This was reinforced in the 1921 Working Timetable, by which time frequency of cleaning had been reduced from the pre-war standard. The General Instructions specified:

'Carriages running in conjunction with the Pullman cars must also be well cleaned, so that the Trains will present an attractive appearance.'[16]

Facilities were initially insufficient at Aberdeen. In late 1915 or early 1916 an 'arrangement for cleaning Pullman car at Aberdeen' was made. This was the subject of St. Rollox drawing 18278 dated 3rd November 1915.[17] The drawing is for a series of brackets attached to sockets at the bottom of the car underframes to support planks which enabled cleaners to reach the whole of the cars' bodies. Part of the drawing is shown in Figure 10.1. By implication, the modification was limited to the Dining cars that ran on the Aberdeen service.

The cars were not to be loose shunted and, in the same General Instruction quoted above,

'the staff are directed to see that these Vehicles are moved cautiously during shunting operations, in order that damage may be prevented.'

EARLY SERVICE ALTERATIONS DURING WORLD WAR I

Shortly after the outbreak of war in August 1914, Pullman services seem to have been temporarily suspended. The September 1914

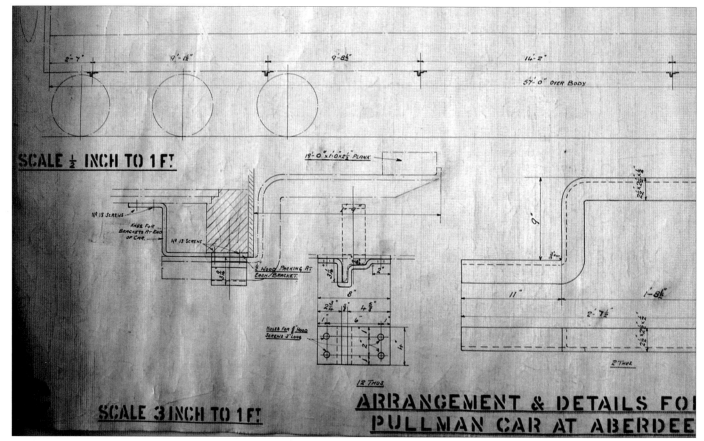

SCALE ½ INCH TO 1 FT

SCALE 3 INCH TO 1 FT

ARRANGEMENT & DETAILS FOR
PULLMAN CAR AT ABERDEE

Figure 10.1
The additional fittings to the restaurant cars on the Aberdeen service to allow cleaning to proper standards. Scaffolding planks rested on the brackets which were fitted into the sockets on the bottom rail of the body.

Public Timetable, which set out the *European War Crisis Restricted Train Service*, does not mention any Pullman cars. A poster dated October 1914 advised that the Glasgow and Edinburgh service had been restored and the refreshment *'tariff reduced.'* The October 1914 Local Working of Carriages Circular number 161 has the cars back on the pre-war circuits with altered timings. The cars on the Glasgow to Edinburgh and Aberdeen routes continued to run during 1915 and 1916.

The service between Glasgow and Oban had been withdrawn by the publication of the October 1914 Carriage Marshalling Circular. It was reinstated in June 1915, when a new poster was issued. Departure from Glasgow was still 8.00am, but the return trip was later, leaving Oban at 4.15pm. From 1st October 1915, the service was suspended again. It is not known whether the service continued in the winter or into 1916.

In June 1915 the Pullman Car Co. was obviously concerned about maximising revenue and making best use of its new assets. It proposed that two ex-Highland Railway clerestory-roofed Sleeping cars should be remodelled and used as spare cars, which would potentially allow the full deployment of the new cars.[18]

According to Tatlow,[19] these vehicles arrived second-hand on the HR in 1885, after use on the Great Northern Railway. They were 36 feet long and mounted on bogies. The Highland had returned them to the Pullman Car Co. in 1911, since when they had been in store. Not surprisingly in view of the cars' age and their sub-standard capacity compared with the new cars, the Caledonian declined the offer.

SERVICE ALTERATIONS IN 1916

In 1916 the war of attrition started on the Western Front with the Battle of Verdun, which opened on 21st February. It was followed

by the Battle of the Somme, which started on 1st July. The strategy was not to wage a war of movement to win territory, but to destroy the enemy's forces by constant bombardment. Both sides in the conflict were aware that any hope of success relied on the availability of a constant stream of men to replace the appalling number of casualties.

The Railway Executive Committee suggested, but did not insist, that train services should be modified to release personnel for active service. Duplication of routes should be abandoned and dining services curtailed. An article in *The Railway Magazine* claimed that by removing all the Restaurant cars in the UK *'at a low estimate over 1,000 men could be released for war service.'*[20]

On the West Coast, the L&NWR took the initiative, informing the CR in a letter dated 17th April that it intended to withdraw all catering services on L&NWR and Anglo-Scottish trains on 1st May and to provide cold luncheon baskets instead. The CR Board's reaction, recorded in the minute noting the L&NWR's unilateral decision,[21] was to:

'regret very much that it is proposed that the Dining Cars should be taken off the West Coast system whilst they are to be continued on the Midland and East Coast routes and urge that the cars should not be taken off the West Coast until there is agreement between all the Companies.'

The formal decision to withdraw services was reported at a West Coast Conference Meeting on 27th April.[22] WCJS Dining cars ceased to run with effect from 1st May. In fact, all Anglo-Scottish catering services ceased at the same time. The East Coast Conference did not seek to take commercial advantage and suspended its services, but catering on trains confined to NER and NBR metals continued.[23] The Caledonian made arrangements as best it could for its internal services. The *Railway Magazine* reported the West Coast Committee's withdrawal,[24] and added:

'Pending further arrangements a Pullman Dining Car is being run on the following services:-
  6.40 a.m. Aberdeen to Perth
  12.20 p.m. Perth to Symington (London train)
  5.36 p.m. Symington, Perth and Aberdeen
    (10.00 a.m. from London, 3.55 p.m. Carlisle)'

The magazine statement is corroborated by the CR Working Timetable for June 1916[25] which refers to the same services, plus the continuation of Pullman Buffet cars on the Glasgow and Edinburgh route. It raises a difficulty, however, because only three Pullman Dining cars had been delivered and, according to the agreement, they were in use between Glasgow and Aberdeen. The most likely explanation is that an ex-WCJS Dining car, or perhaps two, replaced a Pullman on one of the Aberdeen circuits, releasing it for the Anglo-Scottish duty.

SERVICE WITHDRAWAL

The Caledonian finally withdrew all catering services on 31st December 1916. The contract required the railway company to haul its cars, but there is no evidence of consultation with the Pullman Company before services were withdrawn. That said, it could hardly have come as a surprise.

In February 1918 the CR Traffic Committee noted a claim from the Pullman Car Co. for £5,248 as compensation for the lost revenue in 1917.[26] The company also asked that the contract with the Caledonian should be extended by the period during which the service was withdrawn, and asked that *'an assurance should be given them in this respect.'* The Caledonian's General Manager recommended that an assurance be given.

REFERENCES
1. NRS BR/CAL/1/23 entry 1465
2. NRS BR/CAL/1/23 entry 1475
3. TNA RAIL 1007/28
4. *The Caledonian Journal No. 3*, p. 17
5. NRS BR/CAL/1/63 entries 1301-2
6. *The Caledonian Journal No. 3*, p. 17
7. NRS BR/CAL/3/86
8. *Working Timetable Appendix 1915*, p. 97
9. *Pullman Profile No. 1*, p.41
10. *The True Line*, issue 28, p. 6
11. *The Railway Magazine*, July-December 1914, pp. 123-24
12. *The Railway Gazette*, 11th September 1914, pp. 312-18
13. *The Railway Magazine*, July-December 1914, p. 123
14. *Local Working of Carriages, Southern & Eastern Sections*
15. *1915 Working Timetable Appendix*, p. 97
16. *1921 Working Timetables, Supplement to General Instructions 39*, p. 21
17. RHP 68604
18. NRS BR/CAL/1/66 entry 1115
19. *Highland Railway Carriages and Wagons*, pp. 51-52
20. *The Railway Magazine 1916*, part 1, p. 442
21. NRS BR/CAL/1/68 entry 206
22. NRS WCC/1/5 minute 3384
23. *British Railways and the Great War*, volume 1, p. 133
24. *The Railway Magazine 1916*, part 1, p. 441
25. In the CRA Archive, ref: 3/1/2/20, p. 156
26. NRS BR/CAL./1/70 entry 1307

PULLMAN

TARIFF.

BREAKFAST, LUNCHEON or SUPPER - *per person* - **3/-**
TEA or COFFEE, with BREAD and BUTTER per person, 9d.
BUTTERED TOAST, TEA CAKE, CAKE,
  JAM, etc. - - - - - - 3d.
TEA - - - - - *per cup*, 6d.
CAFÉ NOIR (small) - - - - ,, 6d.
CHOCOLATES - - - boxes, 8d. to 2/-
TABLE WATERS - - - per bottle, 6d. and 9d.
SODA - - - - ,, 3d. ,, 6d.
SELTZER or LEMONADE - - per bottle, 4d.
GINGER ALE or GINGER BEER - - ,, 6d.
LEMON SQUASH - - small, 6d.; large, 9d.
LIME JUICE and SODA - - 6d.; ,, 9d.
BOTTLED ALE, STOUT or LAGER - per bottle, 9d.
CIDER - - - - ,, 6d.
BRANDY, COGNAC - - per portion, 9d.
  ,, LIQUEUR, 20 yrs. old - - ,, 1/-
  ,, GAUTIER FRERES or COURVOISIER, 40 yrs. old ,, 1/6
  ,,   ,,   ,, 1865 ,, 2/-
WHISKY—
  "The Antiquary," Dewar's "White Label" - ,, 9d.
DRY GIN - - - - - ,, 9d.
COCKTAILS - - - - ,, 1/-
GIN & BITTERS or VERMOUTH - - ,, 9d.
PORT or SHERRY - - - ,, 9d.
LIQUEURS (various) - per portion, 1/-, 1/3 & 1/6
BOVRIL with BISCUITS - - - per cup, 6d.

SANDWICHES IN VARIETY TO ORDER.

WINES as per List on other side.

CIGARS, CIGARETTES, etc., etc.

Passengers are requested to obtain an Official Receipt at time of payment.

Any complaints should be addressed to—
THOMAS POWELL, *Secretary and Manager*,
The Drawing Room Cars Company Limited, Victoria Station (S.E. & C.Rly.),
Pimlico, S.W.

THE PULLMAN COMPANY LIMITED.

WINE LIST.

No.	HOCKS AND MOSELLE.	Per Bot.	Per ½-Bot.
19.	BODENHEIM	4/-	2/-
21.	RÜDESHEIM	6/6	3/6
22.	BERNCASTELER EXCELSIOR, SPARKLING	8/6	4/6
	CHAMPAGNES.		
36.	MUMM'S "CORDON ROUGE" (1906)	16/-	9/-
37.	MOËT'S IMPERIAL CROWN, BRUT, CUVÉE A.A.	16'-	9/-
38.	MOËT'S DRY IMPERIAL (1906)	16/-	9/-
39.	GEORGE GOULET, EXTRA QUALITY, EXTRA DRY (1906)	14/-	7/6
40.	DUC DE MONTEBELLO CUVÉE EXTRA MAXIMUM SEC (1906)	14/-	7/6
46.	BOLLINGER'S "SPECIAL CUVÉE, VERY DRY"	14/-	7.6
47.	"CHARLES HEIDSIECK" FINEST EXTRA QUALITY, EXTRA DRY (1904)	13/-	7/-
48.	"CHARLES HEIDSIECK" FINEST EXTRA QUALITY, EXTRA DRY (1906)	12/6	6/6
	CLARETS.		
49.	MÉDOC	2/6	1/6
51.	ST. JULIEN	5/-	2/9
	SAUTERNES.		
61.	SAUTERNE	3/6	1/9
65.	GRAVES, White	3/6	2/-
	BURGUNDIES.		
91.	BEAUNE	6/6	3/6
92.	POMMARD	7/6	4/-
	CHABLIS.		
97.	CHABLIS	3/6	1/9

SPIRITS, LIQUEURS, Etc.

LIQUEURS, various - - - from 9d.
BRANDY, COGNAC - - per portion, 6d.
  ,, LIQUEUR, 20 years old - ,, 1/-
  ,, GAUTIER FRERES or COURVOISIER, 1865 - ,, 1/6
WHISKY—
  "The Antiquary," Dewar's "White Label" }
  "Johnnie Walker" (Red Label), Watson's No. 10 } Per glass, 6d.
BOOTH'S (old matured) DRY GIN - per glass, 6d.
GIN & BITTERS or VERMOUTH - ,, 6d.
PORT or SHERRY - - ,, 9d.
GINGER ALE or GINGER BEER - per bot., 4d.
LEMON SQUASH - - Small, 6d. Large, 9d.
MINERAL WATERS—
  Perrier - - per bot., 6d. and 9d.
  Soda, Seltzer or Lemonade - ,, 3d. ,, 6d.

CIGARS, CIGARETTES, Etc., Etc.

Plate 10.5
Two Buffet car menus kindly supplied by Anthony Ford of the Pullman Society. They probably date from 1920. The price of a meal equates to something between £5 and £5.50 today, which does seem like the 'reasonable tariff' quoted in many of the advertisements.

10.2: THE PRE-WAR PULLMAN CARS

Pullman cars differed radically in construction from other UK railway carriages. Instead of a separate underframe that was united to the body, early British Pullman cars followed American practice with underframe and body as an integral unit. Coupled with thick carpeting and heavy furnishings, a journey in a Pullman car was different from any other carriage. J.N. Maskelyne, writing about the cars on the 1908 'Southern Belle',[1] stated:

> 'nothing has EVER equalled their steadiness and quietness, even at 80 m.p.h. Quietness, however, was a striking feature of all Pullman cars in those days, and was noticeable not only from within, but from without as well.'

The section below the waist line was built up around heavy oak truss frames, which were covered by the trademark match-boarding. The longitudinal member at the bottom of each side was 7-inch by 5-inch oak. This stopped short of the entrance vestibules, which were of lighter construction to serve as 'crumple zones' in the event of an accident. An example of construction details is shown in Figure 10.2.

The 6-wheeled bogies were attached direct to the floor. They were both equalised and sprung. The weight of the car was taken on the equalising beams. This contributed to what Maskelyne, in the article quoted above, called 'the most delightful, floating sensation, at any speed.'

The main bogie members were of oak, covered with thin steel plates. The wheelbase was 12 feet, set at 41-foot centres. A drawing of one of these bogies, built by Clayton for the Great Eastern Railway cars of 1921, is in the CRA archive.[2] It is too fragile to allow reproduction. There is, however, a drawing and description in *Pullman Profile No. 1* and a close-up is shown in Plate 10.6.

The bogies of the pre-war cars were originally fitted with Iracier patent axle boxes, but all CR carriages and wagons fitted with these axle boxes had them replaced with RCH standard oil boxes in the latter half of 1920.[3] The Pullman Company followed suit. *Maid of Morven* was carried on American-style equalised bogies.

Pullman cars on other railways were usually marshalled as complete trains. Those on the Caledonian were used singly with CR carriages making up the rest of the train. For this reason the cars were fitted with British Standard gangways, rather than the Pullman pattern. *Maid of Morven*, of course, only had a corridor connection at one end.

The bodies of the buffers, which had oval heads, were fitted with extensions to compensate for the bowed ends to the carriages. Example drawings are St. Rollox 19857[4] dating from 1919 and 21777,[5] which applied to the 1922 cars. Part of the drawing for the extensions on *Duchess of Gordon*, which entered CR service in 1919, is shown in Figure 10.3.

LIVERY OF THE PRE-WAR CARS

Differences of opinion about the livery of the cars in CR service filled several pages of *The Caledonian Journal* and early issues of *The True Line*. Two possibilities for the darker component of the livery were put forward – the well known umber, and a shade known in America as 'Pullman Green.' Both opinions were backed by recognised authorities on Caledonian Railway practice.

The first, non-controversial, point to make is that the early Pullmans on British railways were painted to customer requirements – a 'standard Pullman livery' did not exist in the UK at the time. South Eastern Railway cars were painted crimson lake to match the existing carriage livery. Great Eastern cars were painted green and ivory in 1921.[6] The London Brighton & South Coast painted its cars umber and cream to match the rest of its carriage stock after 1915; before that they were dark red-brown,[7] although that livery is not mentioned in *Pullman Profile*.

The Caledonian could have asked for the cars to be painted in its standard carriage livery, but chose not to, presumably because it wanted Pullman travel to be seen as a special experience. There were two obvious alternative dark colours used by the Pullman Company: 'Pullman Green,' which was part of the Pullman brand in the USA, or L&SWR umber, which was the most common Pullman car colour in England and was evolving into the standard which would be adopted after the war.

THE CASE FOR GREEN

The late Charles Underhill was quite clear that the livery was 'Bronze Green and White.' He cited two eyewitnesses – the paint shop foreman at Cravens (the firm which built the pre-war CR cars and painted Pullmans green after the war for the Great Eastern Railway) and 'an employee of the Caley.'[8] He revealed in a later letter[9] that the CR employee was Graeme Miller, who started work as a premium apprentice in 1911, left on military service in 1916 and returned to eventually become Chief Draughtsman at St. Rollox. When asked by Underhill what colour the Pullmans were, Miller replied 'they were green to start with, though they got repainted brown about 1924.'[10]

Underhill also made reference to an article in *Models, Railways & Locomotives* which specifically mentioned the green colour for CR cars, and the green livery of the first Hornby Pullmans, 'including those sold with a CR loco.'

Brian Haresnape was another protagonist of the green livery, but only as a probability. In his book on the Pullmans, he wrote about the first cars delivered to the CR: 'there is some evidence that the CR Pullmans carried a green and cream livery to begin with, although this has not been positively authenticated.'[11] He reiterated this in correspondence with Charles Underhill, and then qualified the statement, adding,

> 'a printed sample that I have of USA Standard Pullman green is virtually the same as umber brown in some lighting conditions – this could have created confusion in some people's minds!'

THE CASE FOR BROWN

James McEwan was the most prominent advocate of the livery which he described[12] as 'the usual cream and golden brown of the Pullman Car Co.' In another article,[13] he quoted from two newspapers which described the lower body colour as 'very dark ochre' and 'dark umber' respectively. He did not mention the sources or the dates that they were written. Finally he quoted Alan Dunbar, who saw the cars while they were in store during the war in

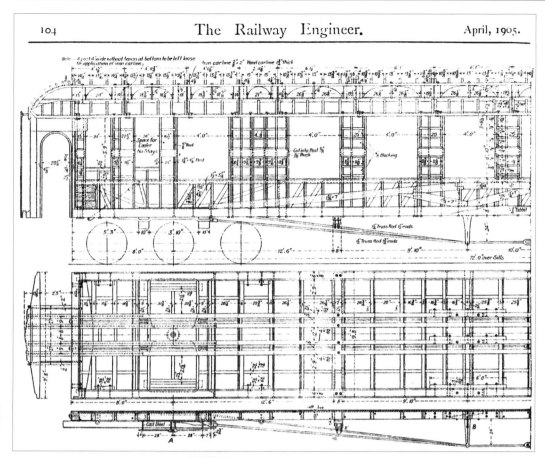

104   The Railway Engineer.   April, 1905.

Figure 10.2
This drawing in *The Railway Engineer* shows the massive construction of a typical Pullman car – in this case an American example. By contrast, the entrance vestibules are very lightly constructed to act as a 'crumple zone' in the event of an accident.

Plate 10.6
A.B. McLeod took this close-up of a Pullman 6-wheeled bogie. The NRM collection reference number is C134. The axle boxes are RCH standard, fitted to early Pullman bogies after it was decided to remove Iracier patent oil boxes from all CR rolling stock in 1920 – see the photograph of *Mary Beaton* (Plate 10.8).

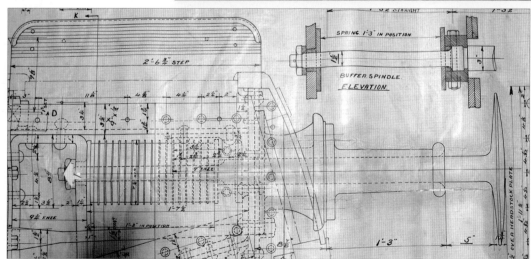

Figure 10.3
Buffer extensions were fitted to all the cars to compensate for the bowed ends of the bodies. This shows the extension fitted to *Duchess of Gordon* – from St. Rollox drawing 19857.

the St. Rollox carriage paint shop. Dunbar said that they had brown lower sides.

McEwan then went on to offer the argument that green would have meant that the cars would look like carriages coming off the Highland Railway, which the Caley would surely never countenance. He seemed to think that the fact that brown had been adopted for CR non-passenger coaching stock and the 'somewhat ancient carriages used on the Cathcart Ry.' reinforced his argument.

As further evidence of this livery, The Railway Magazine, immediately after the introduction of the first cars on the Caledonian,[14] described it as 'standard Pullman colours, dark amber [sic] below and cream or ivory tint above.'

McEwan did, however, make some concession towards green. In the second article quoted he speculated that the varnish made 'the golden brown appear to have a green tinge in certain lights.' This idea was supported by Hamilton Ellis and A.B. MacLeod, who stated that the LB&SCR's 'burnt umber' livery 'had a distinct greenish tinge.'[15]

CONCLUSION

The arguments for one colour or the other are not necessarily mutually exclusive. Neither side seems to have considered the effect of varnish, which would have tended to tint green paint brown. Tom Barbour[16] cited the official history of the Clayton Wagon Co. which built the four cars that were delivered just before the Caledonian ceased to exist in 1923. They were described as 'finished externally in umber with panelling and fascia boards in ivory white with gold lining.' The cars that had been built three years previously for the Great Eastern Railway were originally green, but in 1924 were:

'completely renovated and the exteriors were painted in the now standard Pullman colours of umber and cream, with scroll lines and gold decoration.'

This suggests that the pre-war CR cars could indeed, as Miller said, have been green, but that they were repainted brown just after the Grouping, when the Pullman Car Co. finally adopted a standard livery. This interpretation is, however, contradicted by the 1914 Railway Magazine article mentioned above. Some cars may have been repainted earlier when they were refurbished by Cravens.

THE NAMES OF THE CARS

All the CR Pullman cars were given names of famous Scottish women in history or literature. The most likely origins of the names of the first ten cars are shown below.

Car Name	Origin
Flora MacDonald	While living on Benbecula, she accompanied Bonnie Prince Charlie on his flight to Skye after Culloden
Fair Maid of Perth	Catharine Glover, heroine of the Waverley novel of the same name
Lass o' Gowrie	Heroine of a poem by Lady Nairne. The Carse of Gowrie is on the north bank of the Tay, between Perth and Dundee
Mary Hamilton	The un-named narrator of the sixteenth-century ballad 'The Fower Marys' who are traditionally believed to be ladies-in-waiting to a Queen of Scotland. She was condemned to death for killing her infant child, fathered by the King of Scotland
Mary Beaton	One of the 'Fower Marys'
Mary Seaton	One of the 'Fower Marys'
Mary Carmichael	The last of the 'Fower Marys'
Annie Laurie	Heroine of a song based on a poem by William Douglas. In real life she married Alexander Fergusson, the 14th Laird of Craigdarroch, near Moniaive
Helen MacGregor	Wife of Rob Roy MacGregor, the famous Jacobite outlaw, whose lands were in the Trossachs. She, her husband and two sons are buried in Balquhidder Kirk
Maid of Morven	The subject of a lament by Sir Harold Boulton, who wrote the Skye Boat Song. The maiden was lost in a storm off the Point of Ardnamurchan

As well as celebrating Scottish women, most of the names had a geographical resonance with the routes on which they originally

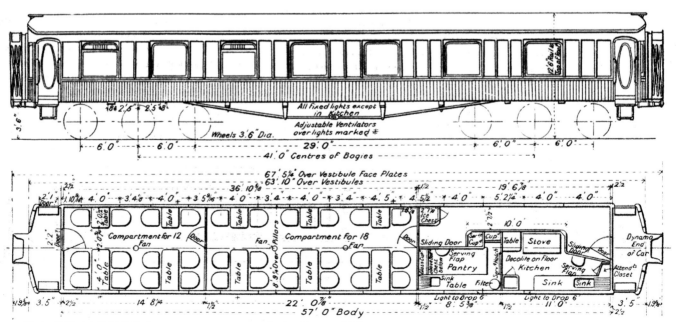

ran. The 'Fower Marys' with their Holyrood House connection ran on the Glasgow to Edinburgh route. The Dining cars all ran through Perthshire on the way to Aberdeen. Oban was as near as the Caledonian Railway got to Ardnamurchan.

Décor and Internal Arrangements – An Introduction

Extravagant and exotic internal decoration was an integral part of the Pullman brand. It reflected the moneyed class's taste for luxury and conspicuous consumption that prevailed before and immediately after World War I. Each car was decorated in a different style, made up of a combination of different woods and to several decorative 'schools.' The interior details of each car were described in Pullman leaflets and published in the contemporary railway press. The reports were summarised in *Pullman Profiles*, from which the descriptions below were taken.

Seating in open saloons was unusual at this stage of carriage development in the UK. Apart from the Family and Invalid Saloons which were essentially for private hire, passengers were used to travelling in compartments. The only CR general service Saloons were the five Third class corridor carriages built by McIntosh in 1907. Details of the internal layout of the various types of Pullman car are taken from the drawings contained in the Large Carriage Diagram Book.

The 12-Wheeled Dining Cars

The three Dining cars accommodated twelve First and eighteen Third class passengers. They were assigned to page 55 of the Caledonian Railway's Large Diagram Book. They were built by Cravens and retained the classic American style of assembly. The entrance vestibule at each end meant that the length of the passenger saloon and kitchen was 57 feet. A kitchen and pantry with a combined length of 19 feet 6 inches was accessed by sliding doors. There was no lavatory, because these were available in adjacent 'Grampian Stock' vehicles. The doors were recessed in the body sides – see Figure 10.4 and the photograph of *Lass o' Gowrie* in Plate 10.7.

The 12-Wheeled Buffet Cars

The six Buffet cars delivered prior to World War I were placed on page 54 of the Large Diagram Book. The overall dimensions were the same as the Dining cars. Immediately after the entrance vestibule was a short side-corridor giving access both to a lavatory

and a small compartment seven feet between partitions. According to *The Railway Magazine*,[17] this was 'a private compartment for four, which can be reserved as desired.' A lavatory was necessary, because the rest of the train was composed of non-corridor stock.

There were two further saloons but, for no apparent reason, only one seat was provided at each side, rather than 2+1 configuration. Accommodation was therefore eight and nine passengers respectively. The kitchen and pantry area was 6 feet 9 inches smaller than in the Dining cars. Drawings of the side elevation and interior layout form Figure 10.5 and the photograph of *Mary Beaton* is Plate 10.8.

The ceilings were simpler than in the Dining cars, in an ivory hue, whilst the floor had a rich crimson velvet pile carpet which matched the crimson morocco upholstery of the chairs.

Mary Seaton was decorated in Italian walnut inlaid with shaded holly in what was described as 'Italian renaissance' style with panels of burr walnut. *Mary Carmichael* was similar but furnished in pear tree veneer, also inlaid with shaded holly wood, the main panels being decorated with oak leaves and acorns. Its carpet was blue velvet pile, matching the velvet-upholstered chairs.

Mary Beaton had similar internal decorations to the Dining car *Fair Maid of Perth*, with mahogany veneer, but this time in Louis XIV style. *Mary Hamilton* was decorated in 'plum' mahogany with a shaded inlay in Pergolesi style, the main panels being decorated with drapery, corn husks and a beaded oval, whilst its carpet was rich green, matching the silk blinds and morocco-upholstered chairs.

Helen MacGregor's mahogany panels were inlaid with chestnut in a Sheraton style with green morocco chairs and a matching carpet, whilst *Annie Laurie* had 'curl mahogany' panels in Adam style and matching green carpet, blinds and morocco chairs. In addition, the cars had a bow-fronted cabinet at the end of the compartment, surmounted by an ormolu clock, containing cigarettes, alcoholic spirits, cruet sets and silverware.

The Buffet Observation Car

As originally conceived, the 'Pullman Observatory Car' was a 12-wheeled vehicle with similar overall dimensions to the other pre-war cars. The drawing is shown in Figure 10.6. It was to seat twelve passengers in the observation section, ten in the dining section and a further four in a 'family compartment.' There were no catering facilities.

The design was impractical because the turntable at Oban was only 50 feet in diameter. In any case, apart from the WCJS 65-foot Sleeping car on the through service to and from Euston, 12-wheeled carriages

FACING PAGE: Figure 10.4
The side elevation and interior layout of the 1914 Dining cars. The two compartments were furnished with green morocco leather dining seats in a 2+1 configuration, plain green carpets and various styles of mahogany-veneered panelling. *Fair Maid of Perth* was described as Louis XVI style, *Flora MacDonald* as Robert Adam and *Lass o' Gowrie* as Michelangelo Pergolesi.

RIGHT: Plate 10.7
Dining car *Lass o' Gowrie* with attendants waiting to welcome passengers. Judging by the roof line in the background and the wooden platform, the photograph was taken at Buchanan Street. The car's immaculate condition suggests that it may have been the inaugural trip, which took place on 8th June 1914.

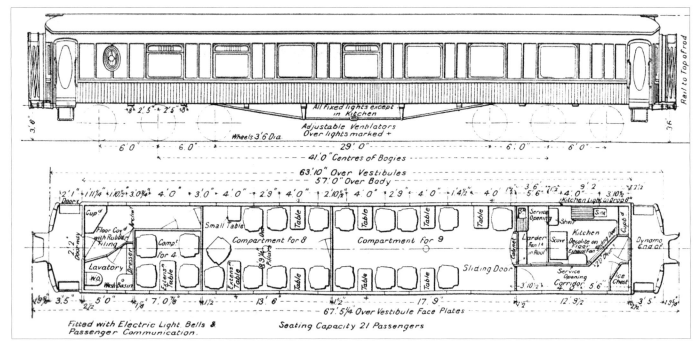

Figure 10.5 and Plate 10.8
Side elevation and interior layout of the 1914 Buffet cars. The small compartment at the left could be hired for private parties. There seems to be no good reason why more seats could not have been provided in the main saloons. The publicity photograph of *Mary Beaton* was taken outside Cravens Works at Sheffield. Note the Iracier axle boxes, which were fitted to all the pre-war cars; they were removed in 1920.

were banned from the Callander & Oban.[18] The design also had little commercial merit for the Pullman Car Co., unless it was coupled to a Pullman catering vehicle. This was not envisaged in the agreement.

In the design that appeared on the C&O in 1914, a kitchen was included and the carriage seated twenty-two people. At the end away from the buffet area of *Maid of Morven*, a curved window with three panels extended from floor to cantrail height which provided occupants with panoramic views of the surrounding countryside. A curved waist-high hand rail was fitted inside.

In contrast to the small compartment in the centre of the car, the large side windows of the observation saloon were separated by thin frames, giving an 'open air' effect. It was assigned to Diagram 55A in the Large Diagram Book. The car was two feet shorter overall than the other pre-war cars. A drawing and side elevation are shown in Figure 10.7. A photograph of the car in service is shown in Plate 10.9 and an interior view in Plate 10.10. A photograph of the car in early LM&SR days is shown in Plate 17 of Chapter 9.

Despite being 4¾ inches thick, the glass panels at the observation end were considered to be vulnerable on two counts. The first was a possible danger to the public, despite the waist-level hand rail

mentioned above. According to James McEwan, test runs were made with the car on the Callander & Oban before it entered revenue service on 3rd August 1914.[19]

'A locomotive and a traffic inspector travelled with the car … to keep an eye on general handling. Drivers were ordered to brake cautiously at all stoppages so that no passenger would be propelled through the glass window at the rear.'

Secondly, the glass was regularly at risk from shunting shocks. As the last vehicle in the train it was turned at the end of each journey. It was drawn off the train to be positioned on, and then removed from, the turntable, and finally propelled into the platform for the rest of the train to be attached in front of it. Quoting from the McEwan article again:

'The station pilot drivers were given orders to buffer-up, as the late John Barr [The Caley's Locomotive Running Superintendent] put it to them, as giving your mother-in-law a kiss.'

As already stated, the turntable at Oban was only 50 feet in diameter in Caledonian days. The car's extreme wheelbase was 47 feet 9 inches and the body was over 57½ feet long, with buffers protruding a further 1 foot 9 inches at each end. This 'tight fit' is said to have frequently resulted in broken panes of glass in the observation section, although the actual cause has never been explained in detail. There was apparently no problem on the 60-foot turntable at Buchanan Street, where the shunting procedures were exactly the same as at Oban. Plate 10.16 shows the car on the extended Oban turntable.

The internal fittings were provided by the high quality furniture makers Waring & Gillow, consisting of six moveable armchairs with matching foot stools in the observation area. The rest of the car seated sixteen. Eight moveable chairs were disposed around four tables in the observation saloon towards the centre of the carriage. The remainder were seated around tables in a compartment partitioned off from the observation saloon and the kitchen area. The arrangement echoed the one chair each side configuration of the Buffet cars.

Heavy floor to ceiling curtains, colour unknown but probably matching the carpet described in the caption to Plate 10.10, were fitted to the bow windows of the observation section. Drawing them might seem to defeat the purpose of the car, but at least part of the trip from Oban during the winter timetable would have taken place in darkness. As in any house or grand hotel, the curtains would have been drawn. The curtains were removed at an unknown date after the Grouping, possibly when the car was repainted in overall crimson in the mid 1930s.

The kitchen was 7 feet 6 inches long. Beyond it, towards the end of the coach, was a lavatory. This was necessary because the rest of the train was composed of semi-corridor stock which, although furnished with lavatories, did not have corridor connections. Just before the entrance vestibule there was a small luggage area and a folding seat for a guard, who was provided with a handbrake. This was needed to secure the carriage while it was being turned at the end of each journey.

REFERENCES

1. *The Model Railway News*, January 1959, p. 11
2. CRA Ref: 6/1/1/6/8
3. NRS BR/CAL/1/75 entry 528
4. RHP 68606
5. RHP 68603
6. *Pullman Profile No. 1*, p. 171
7. *The Model Railway News*, January 1959, p. 11
8. *The Caledonian Journal*, issue 5, p. 21
9. *The True Line*, issue 36, p. 28
10. Correspondence between Underhill and Long, 1994.
11. *Pullman – Travelling in Style*, p. 88
12. *The Caledonian Journal*, issue 3, p. 17
13. *The True Line*, issue 25, p. 9
14. *The Railway Magazine*, August 1914, p. 123
15. Correspondence between Underhill and Long, 1994
16. *The True Line*, issue 38, p. 28
17. *The Railway Magazine*, July-December 1914, p. 123
18. *1915 Working Timetable Appendix (Northern Section)*, p. 46
19. *The Caledonian Journal*, issue 3, p. 18

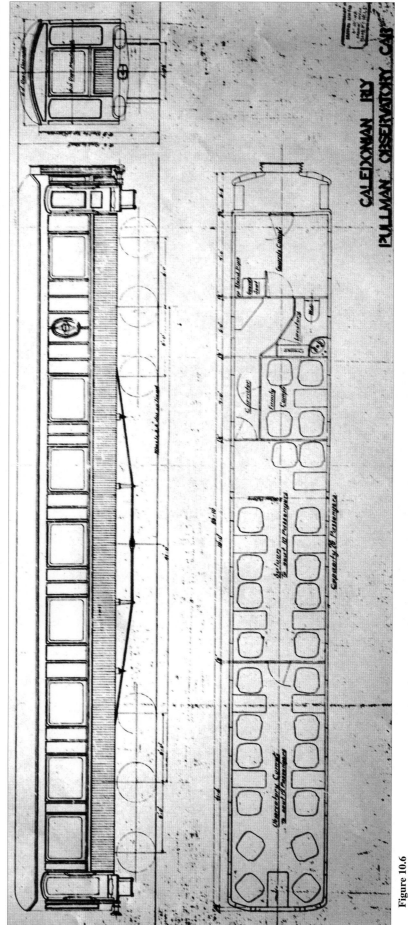

CALEDONIAN RLY
PULLMAN OBSERVATORY CARS

Figure 10.6
This was Cravens' original conception of the Pullman Observation car. It was a minimal modification to the end of a standard Pullman body shell. The 4-seat 'family compartment' echoes the arrangement on the Buffet cars. Nobody seems to have told the manufacturer that such a car would not fit on the Oban turntable until later.

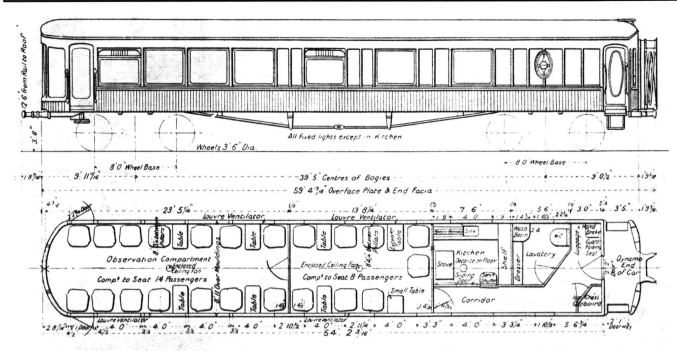

Figure 10.7, Plates 10.9 and 10.10

Interior and side elevation of *Maid of Morven* as built (*top*). In comparison with Figure 10.6, catering facilities have been included at the sacrifice of the small 'family compartment'; the guard's accommodation has been replaced by a folding seat in the entrance vestibule, allowing the length to be reduced to fit the Oban turntable. The other gain is in the observation area, where the end is more curved and the glass extends from top to bottom of the body.

Plate 10.9 (*above*) is a photograph taken in early LM&SR days – the carriage behind is painted crimson. The Pullman insignia has not yet been painted over. Compared with early pictures, the seats have antimacassars. The buffer extensions fitted to all the Pullman cars on the Caley are very prominent.

Plate 10.10 (*right*) is a view from the observation section back down the car. According to John Thomas in the *Callander and Oban Railway*, the chairs were upholstered in brown tapestry with a floral trellis design. The internal decoration was in the Sheraton style. The walls were panelled in pear wood, with marquetry pilasters, detailed after Pergolesi. The light brackets were chased metal and the table lamps had hand-painted silk shades. A heavy brown carpet covered the floor.

10.3: POST-WAR PULLMAN CARS AND SERVICES

Services restarted on 1st March 1919. The Caledonian had applied for permission to do this just as the war was about to end, when it was told by the Board of Trade that *'no Pullman cars be run on the Caledonian Railway until further notice.'*[1] After a new approach to the Board of Trade, restoration was agreed in November.[2] The CR Board minute recording the restoration of services is shown in Plate 10.11.

The compensation issue with the Pullman Company had also been settled, although it does not seem to have been paid until 1922. In November 1918 the Board had approved a memorandum from the General Manager that:

'under the agreement with the Government Auditor, the Pullman Company have agreed to accept compensation to the amount of £4,500 per annum. The compensation is a working expense within the meaning of the control arrangement with the Government.'[3]

New contracts between the Caledonian and the Pullman Car Company were signed on 28th July and 19th August 1919.[4] They extended the original agreement until 1st March 1930 in recognition of the interruption to the service. The extension was for three years, despite the fact that the majority of services were only interrupted for two years and three months.

McEWAN'S DESCRIPTION OF THE RESTORED SERVICE

James McEwan,[5] quoting from a publicity handout dated May 1919 (source not mentioned and not found in the McEwan archive), suggested that the pre-war Gourock and Wemyss Bay service did not reappear. *Mary Seaton* joined the other three Marys on the Glasgow–Edinburgh route. Probably one of the four cars was kept as a reserve, to release *Helen MacGregor* for a service to Aberdeen.

Maid of Morven resumed its service from Glasgow to Oban. Edinburgh was included as an additional starting point for Aberdeen services. New Buffet car *Duchess of Gordon* and the pre-war designated spare car *Helen MacGregor* were part of this circuit, making five cars in all.

The Buffet car *Annie Laurie* from the pre-war Glasgow–Edinburgh circuit was included in the 'Tinto Express', which ran each way between Glasgow and Moffat.

Hardly any of these statements are substantiated by the CR posters[6] advertising the restoration of Pullman services, which are the basis of the following description.

SERVICES IN MARCH 1919

The Glasgow to Edinburgh service was reduced to ten trains, but still employed three Buffet cars. A copy of the 1919 Local Working of Carriages Circular has not survived in the public domain, which precludes a description of the circuits. The departures as set out in the Public Timetable were as follows:

GLASGOW DEPART	EDINBURGH DEPART
8.40am	8.50am
11.00am	11.00am
1.30pm	1.30pm
4.00pm	3.45pm
5.05pm	5.00pm

All the trains stopped at Holytown. On Saturdays, the last departure ran at 6.45pm from Glasgow and 7.05pm from Edinburgh.

The Aberdeen services were reconfigured to make the maximum use of two cars by serving two meals on each full round trip. A car serving breakfast left Buchanan Street at 7.00am. It was detached at Perth and coupled onto the following train from Glasgow which had left at 9.45am. Luncheon was then served to Aberdeen. In the evening, tea was served as far as Perth on the 5.00pm departure from Buchanan Street. The car was then attached to the 6.15pm from Glasgow, when dinner was served to Aberdeen.

In the reverse direction, breakfast was served as far as Perth on the 6.10am from Aberdeen. The car was then attached to the 9.00am from Aberdeen, serving an early luncheon from Perth to Glasgow. The car on the 5.30pm departure from Aberdeen ran straight through to Glasgow, serving tea and dinner.

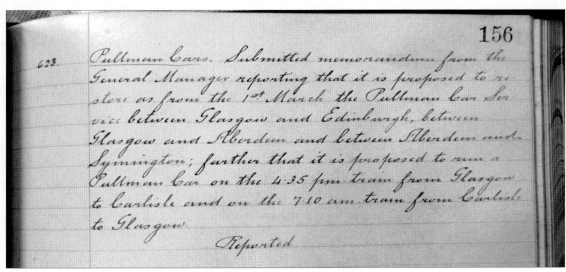

Plate 10.11
The Board minute (NRS BR/CAL/1/72 entry 623) recording the restoration of Pullman services in March 1919.

Another car was engaged in a circuit between Aberdeen and the south. The 6.10am departure from Aberdeen served breakfast as far as Perth, where it was detached. It was coupled to the 11.40am from Perth and served luncheon as far as Carstairs. It returned at 4.17pm from Carstairs – as part of the train which had left Euston at 9.15am – serving tea and dinner through to Aberdeen.

Finally, there was a return trip between Carlisle and Glasgow. A car was attached to the 11.30pm overnight train from Euston, which left Carlisle at 6.55am. It returned on the 4.35pm from Glasgow, serving tea and dinner.

The Glasgow to Oban service with *Maid of Morven* was not mentioned on the March restoration poster. It ran from July 1919 to its pre-war timetable. The rest of the Pullman services, with the exception of the Glasgow to Carlisle round trip, were altered and are described in the next subsection.

July 1919 Services

The poster advertising the July services highlighted a number of changes. It is reproduced as Plate 10.12. During the week, there were now six trains each way between Glasgow and Edinburgh, with the late Saturday only departures forming the extra services. The 5.00 and 5.05pm departures from each city did not run on Saturdays.

On the Aberdeen route, the early morning departure from Buchanan Street ran as before, being detached at Perth and running to Aberdeen on the next train. The evening departure ran straight through to Aberdeen. Two through workings to Glasgow ran from Aberdeen, leaving at 10.30am and 5.30pm. Passengers on the 6.10am departure were still served by a Pullman car to Perth, which returned to Aberdeen attached to the 1.30pm departure from Buchanan Street. Similarly, the passengers on the 6.15pm from Buchanan Street could still dine north of Perth, on the return working of a car that left Aberdeen at noon, attached to a train of West Coast Joint Stock.

The 'Temporary Additional Car'

In June 1919, the Pullman Company offered a car *'presently working on the South Eastern & Chatham Railway'* on temporary transfer to the Caledonian. The type of car was not specified. The Traffic Committee agreed to the offer, provided that the *'Work of painting and necessary alterations ... be carried out by the Company at the expense of Pullman Car Coy.'*[7]

McEwan suggested that the car was named *Baroness Nairne*, and that it was quickly returned to the SE&CR following *'trouble with its bogies.'* It was mentioned in the publicity handout cited by him as rostered on the Glasgow–Crieff circuit. He thought that the car

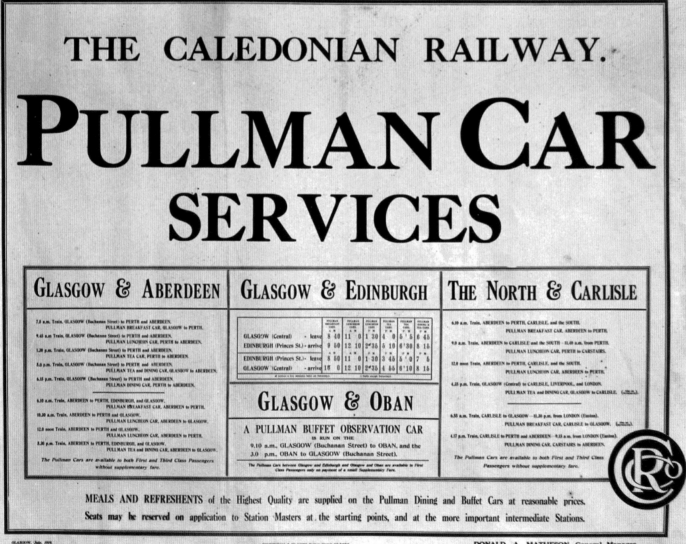

Plate 10.12
This poster shows the July 1919 services. The Oban circuit has been added for the summer season. The services are described in detail in the text.

was originally *'either Saxony or Sorrento or a composite mixture of both. Records are too vague to allow for a satisfactory statement.'*[8]

There is no mention of *Baroness Nairne* in any other contemporary publication. In real life, Baroness Nairne was the alternative title of Lady Nairne, and this may have been the original name that was intended for the car that was introduced two years later. It was certainly quoted in a *Railway Magazine* article in 1914.[9]

Geoffrey Cox found it hard to credit McEwan's speculations about the car's origins.[10] He pointed out that a car called *Saxony* never ran on the SE&CR. *Sorrento* was a Parlour car without kitchen facilities, which would have required major interior remodelling to suit CR requirements.

The 'temporary car' was in fact *Duchess of Gordon*, which was delivered in August 1919, and the temporary arrangement became permanent. The dimensions, internal layout and external appearance of *Duchess of Gordon* match the photograph and description of *Shamrock* in *The Railway Gazette*.[11]

The Dining car *Shamrock* was built in 1911 by the Birmingham Railway Carriage & Wagon Co. for the South Eastern & Chatham Railway's 'Continental Express' from London Victoria to Queenborough Pier. This service ceased in 1914 and did not resume after the Armistice, making the car redundant. It obviously suited the Pullman Company financially to augment its CR fleet with an existing car which was not earning money rather than build new.

There are numerous St. Rollox drawings, starting in June 1919, which detail alterations to this car when it became *Duchess of Gordon*. For instance, 20117 and 20133 dealt with modifications to the buffers. Drawings 20130 and 20134 covered the brakes and 20167 was the general arrangement.

SERVICES IN 1920

In July 1920 the services changed again, according to the Main Line Carriage Workings.[12] *Maid of Morven* ran to its pre-war timetable. There were now four dining car circuits to Aberdeen. *Duchess of Gordon* was no doubt the extra vehicle.

CIRCUIT	GLASGOW DEPART	ABERDEEN DEPART
1	7.15am	12.30pm
2	10.10am	5.30pm
3	1.30pm	6.10am next day
4	5.00pm	10.30am next day

The car on the 12.30pm from Aberdeen was detached at Perth and went forward to Glasgow on a later train so that two meals could

be served. The 5.30pm departure's destination was Glasgow Central, and the stock went empty to Buchanan Street for next day's morning departure.

Two other services ran south to Carlisle. One Buffet car left Glasgow Central at 5.00pm, the return journey was at 6.55am. A second car left Perth at 11.20am, returning from Carlisle at 4.20pm. There was also a Sunday only departure from Perth at 3.40pm. The return journey on Monday left Carlisle at 5.25am.

Between Glasgow and Edinburgh the Local Carriage Working Circular had Pullman Buffet cars marshalled in sets 140-142, which were made up of 57-foot corridor carriages, rather than the pre-war non-corridor 12-wheeled stock. This of course meant that there was now free movement throughout the train. The service used three Buffet cars and reverted to the fourteen trains of the original agreement, as shown below:

CIRCUIT	GLASGOW DEPART	EDINBURGH DEPART
Set 140	9.50am	1.35pm
	4.00pm	7.05pm

CIRCUIT	EDINBURGH DEPART	GLASGOW DEPART
Set 141	6.20am	8.40am
	11.00am	1.35pm
	3.45pm (SO)	6.45pm
	4.55pm (SX)	
Set 142	8.50am	11.00am
	3.45pm (SX)	5.05pm (SX)

SERVICES IN 1921

Pullmans were restricted to the Glasgow–Aberdeen and Glasgow–Edinburgh routes. *Maid of Morven* did not run. The Main Line Carriage Marshalling Circular showed the same four circuits to Aberdeen as in 1920. With minor differences in times, the Glasgow–Edinburgh circuits were the same as the previous year. A photograph of a Pullman car on a Glasgow–Edinburgh train in 1921 is shown in Plate 10.13.

NEW PULLMAN CARS IN 1922

In February 1921 the Pullman Car Co. informed the CR that two Dining cars were under construction by the Midland Railway Carriage & Wagon Co. in accordance with the 1913 agreement. The CR refused to accept the cars on the grounds that it had already received the four Dining cars in the original agreement and it had not ordered any more. Neither party was correct, as four Dining cars

Plate 10.13
Ken Nunn photographed Class '140' 4-4-0 No. 923 leaving Glasgow Central at 1.35pm for Edinburgh on 31st August 1921. The photograph is in the NRM LCGB collection, ref: 3202. The train is set 141 in the July 1921 Local Working of Carriages Circular, which comprised a Brake Third, Third, First, Pullman car, Third and Brake Third. This set's first trip was from Edinburgh at 6.20am, so the formation should be read in reverse order for a train leaving Glasgow. The leading carriage is to Diagram 122 (the only Brake Third design with just two passenger doors on the corridor side), followed by a Diagram 109 8-compartment Third. A Diagram 123 First is behind the Pullman Buffet car.

Plate 10.14
A 1922 view of a Glasgow–Aberdeen express near Luncarty, taken by Henry Salmon. It shows superheated 'Dunalastair IV' No. 117. The bank of lubricators on the running plate does nothing for its appearance. Behind 117 is a Diagram 95 Brake Composite, then a Diagram 97 Brake Third, followed by a Diagram 96 Third, all with the corridor side facing the camera. One of the pre-war 12-wheeled Pullman cars is followed by another two carriages, probably a Third and a Brake Composite. The photograph is from the John Alsop collection, CRA ref: CR0117 – 94837.

were specified in the original agreement, only three of which had been delivered.

With fundamentally flawed cases on both sides, a separate contract was eventually drawn up in May 1922,[13] by which time government control of the railways had ceased. Under the new agreement the Caley accepted the two cars *'without prejudice to their contention foresaid that they were not obliged to do so.'* It also persisted with its story that it already had all the Dining cars in the agreement; the new cars were to be *'used and run in like manner as the four dining cars'*.

The agreements were extended to 28th February 1934, even though the clause in the original agreement stated that any extension depended on cars being supplied over and above the original seventeen.

As part of the agreement to accept the two Dining cars the Caledonian paid £8,500 *'without prejudice'* as partial compensation for Pullman's loss of earnings between 31st December 1916 and 1st March 1919. This sum was recovered from the government through the Defence of the Realm War Losses Commission.

This brought the number of cars to thirteen, four short of the planned complement. The four missing cars were those intended for the Clyde coast service, which had only ever employed one car and had not been reinstated after the war. The new cars were named *Lady Nairne* and *Bonnie Jean*.[14]

SERVICES IN 1922

In the February Public Timetable the four journeys to Aberdeen were the same as in the two previous years.[15] There was an extra evening departure from Aberdeen at 7.30pm (7.45pm on Saturdays) which arrived at Glasgow Central shortly after midnight. A photograph of an Aberdeen express taken in this year is shown in Plate 10.14.

The Glasgow to Edinburgh services continued to the same pattern as 1920/21, with sometimes a few minutes variation in timing. The 4.50pm from Edinburgh and the 5.05pm from Glasgow did not run on Saturdays.

In a new development, Dundee was served by a car which was attached to the 11.00pm departure from Euston on arrival at Carlisle in the early morning. There was no balancing working for the car except on Sundays.

In the summer service timetable a Pullman Dining car was introduced to and from Aviemore,[16] presumably from the Dundee service, which did not appear. The 10.00am departure to Inverness from Buchanan Street arrived there at 2.43pm. On the return journey the car was attached to a train which left Inverness at 3.30pm and arrived at Aviemore at 4.40pm. The train reached Buchanan Street at 9.30pm. According to the *Railway Magazine*,[17] the newly delivered car *Lady Nairne* was put on this service.

Apparently the Aviemore service proved so popular that a second car was added. The *Railway Magazine* reported that this was laid on from 21st August until 14th October. It also stated that twelve cars on the CR in July carried 16,814 passengers and in August thirteen cars carried 18,090 passengers.[18] It appears from this statement that all the cars were operational, with no spares in reserve.

Maid of Morven now left for Oban at 10.00am as part of the train to Inverness. The train divided at Stirling and the Oban portion was combined with a set of carriages from Edinburgh. Its return departure remained the same as before, at 3.50pm.

POST-WAR USE OF STEEL UNDERFRAMES

One disadvantage of the integral wooden type of construction was that it required regular maintenance, which explains the need for spare cars. It deteriorated if the carriages were stored out of service for any length of time, which is what happened during the war. According to McEwan, some of the first CR cars were so affected and were reconditioned with steel solebars at Cravens in 1919 (*Fair Maid of Perth*, *Flora MacDonald* and *Annie Laurie*) and 1921 (*Lass o' Gowrie*).[19] *Maid of Morven's* solebars were said to have been replaced with new oak members after the Grouping. A Dining car showing the effect of seriously deteriorated framing in early post-Grouping days is shown in Plate 10.15, which undermines the credibility of McEwan's statement that the cars were repaired earlier.

Plate 10.15
Taken early in LM&SR era, the deterioration in the framing of the Pullman Dining car on an express leaving Aberdeen is very pronounced. The photograph is in the H.G. Tidey collection at the NRM, ref: 9292.

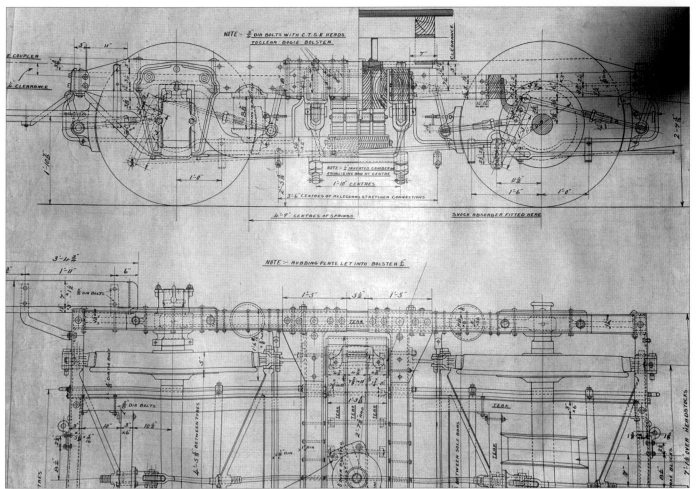

Figure 10.9
The American-style equalised 4-wheel bogie was fitted to *Maid of Morven* and *Duchess of Gordon*. This is from St. Rollox drawing number 20158 (NRS RHP 67557) of the bogie fitted to *Duchess of Gordon*.

Plate 10.16
Maid of Morven on the turntable at Oban sometime shortly after 1934, when the LM&SR terminated the Pullman Car Co. contract and bought the cars for a knock-down price. The curtains have been removed from the observation windows; the Pullman insignia has been painted over and the number in the restaurant car series added above the name. Later the cars would be painted all-over crimson. By this time the turntable was 60 feet in diameter, so there was no problem with the tight fit that was allegedly the cause of broken windows.

Steel framing was used for the post-war cars, as wood of sufficient quality and length was virtually unobtainable and in any case prohibitively expensive. The steel underframes were married to the integral body and underframe concept. A further benefit of steel components was the dramatically reduced tare weight. *The Railway Gazette* quoted the two CR cars delivered in 1921 as weighing 31 tons, which compared with 42 tons for a slightly longer pre-war wooden car.[20]

THE EIGHT-WHEELED DINING CARS

The first 8-wheeled Dining car to be delivered after the war was *Duchess of Gordon*, which entered service in August 1919. The car measured 57 feet 6 inches over vestibules. Like *Maid of Morven* it ran on American style equalised bogies. *Duchess of Gordon*'s bogie is shown in Figure 10.9. The kitchen area was approximately 18 feet 6 inches long. It seated twenty-four passengers in one large saloon just under 27 feet 6 inches long in the usual 2+1 configuration. A lavatory and space for luggage was provided at the opposite end to the kitchen. It appeared on page 55B of the Diagram Book. This is reproduced in Figure 10.10.

The Caledonian named the car after Jane Gordon, who lived in the latter half of the eighteenth century. Her claims to fame were the establishment of the Strathspey as a dance form, patronage of Robert Burns, acting as a prominent political hostess after she and her husband moved to London and, with her husband, the raising of the Gordon Highlanders regiment.

When it was originally built as *Shamrock* in 1911, *The Railway Gazette*[21] published an interior view which is shown in Plate 10.17. The décor and furnishings probably remained the same after its transfer to the Caledonian. There is an exterior view of the car in Plate 10.18.

The other two Dining cars were named *Lady Nairne* and *Bonnie Jean*. According to the Coaching Plant Stock Book they entered service in March 1922. The cars had new bodies built by Metropolitan on the underframes of Great Western Railway 57-foot 'Toplight' carriages which had been intended for use in Continental ambulance trains for the American Forces in France. *Lady Nairne* and *Bonnie Jean* retained the GWR 9-foot wheelbase bogies from their previous existence as 'Toplight' style carriages.

The former car celebrated Carolina Nairne, who was born an Oliphant, a prominent Jacobite family who owned extensive lands in

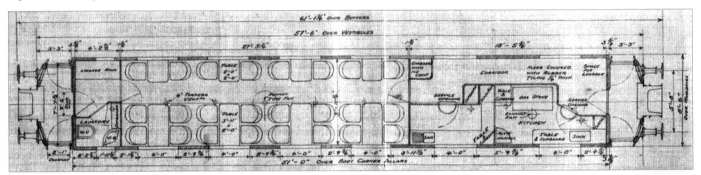

Figure 10.10 and Plate 10.17
The internal layout (*above*) is taken from page 55B of the CR Large Carriage Diagram Book. Plate 10.15, the interior view of *Shamrock* as first built, was published in *The Railway Gazette*. The décor was described as follows *'The wall panelling is in mahogany richly inlaid with shaded satinwood. The design of the enrichments of the panels, doors, friezes etc. are Chippendale in character. The panels have for their centres a rich fiddle veneer. The dining tables are of mahogany, the tops of which are protected with plate glass. The chairs have been designed so as to give a maximum of comfort as a lounge or dining chair. These are upholstered in deep green morocco finished with gilt nails. A rich red pile carpet harmonises with the mahogany, and forms a good setting for the green morocco of the chairs. The blinds are of a green figured silk.'*

Plate 10.18
The photograph of *Duchess of Gordon* in service shows the LM&SR number 210 above the name. The Pullman insignia have been painted over. Compared with the interior view of the car as built, the table lamps seem to have changed. According to *The Railway Gazette* they were originally *'fitted in dainty green silk shades lined with rose colour.'*

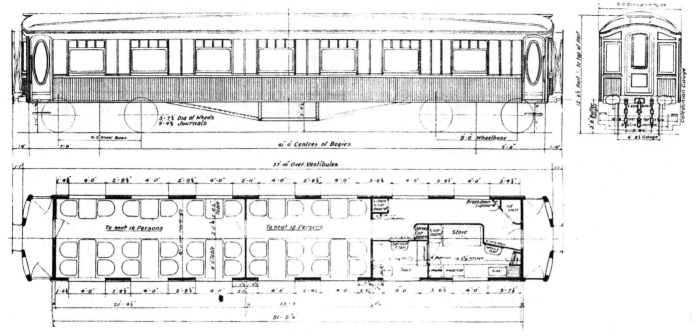

Figure 10.11
These drawings were published in *The Railway Gazette* when *Lady Nairne* and *Bonnie Jean* were built.

Perthshire. There was a previous railway connection, as a Laurence Oliphant was involved with the building of the Scottish Central Railway. Under the pseudonym Mrs Bogan of Bogan, Carolina published a collection of poems entitled *The Scottish Minstrel*, many of which she had composed herself. One was *Lass o' Gowrie*, which gave its name to a pre-war Pullman car. Another was the famous *Charlie is my Darling*.

Bonnie Jean was Jean Armour, the wife of Robert Burns and the subject of his poem of the same name. She was also known as the 'Mauchline Belle,' the name given to another Pullman Dining car delivered at the end of the Caley's existence.

Although of standard Pullman appearance, they were built with steel underframes and ran on GWR-pattern 4-wheeled bogies. Both cars accommodated twelve First and eighteen Third class passengers. They appeared on page 55C of the Diagram Book. Two drawings exist, both dated 31st January 1921.[22]

Internally their appearance differed. According to *The Railway Gazette*,[23] *Lady Nairne*'s decoration was inlaid mahogany in the Adam style in the First class areas, featuring oval panels of curl mahogany veneer. It was furnished with mahogany chairs upholstered in green leather finished with gilt nails and a green velvet pile carpet. The drawing from *The Railway Gazette* is shown in Figure 10.11.

The corresponding areas of *Bonnie Jean* were carpeted in crimson velvet pile, with crimson leather upholstery to the chairs, and mahogany quartered panelling with inlaid floral decoration in green with rose-coloured flowers.

The Third class bays in both vehicles had similar decoration. Two compartments had green-upholstered chairs with a matching carpet strip, whilst the third compartment was upholstered in crimson with matching carpet strip. The floor in all three bays was covered in green linoleum. All tables were of '*the removable type*' made of mahogany with glass tops. Ceilings were domed with covered sides and panelled centres.

LIVERY OF THE IMMEDIATE POST-WAR CARS

When *Duchess of Gordon* was running on the SE&CR, it would have been painted crimson lake. As stated in the previous section, it was repainted on its arrival at St. Rollox in 1919. It would

have been painted the same colour as the rest of the CR fleet at that time.

Lady Nairne and *Bonnie Jean* were built at the same time as three cars for the LB&SCR – indeed, *The Railway Gazette* published a photograph of the five cars as a complete train.[24] It seems most likely that all the cars were painted the same colour, in other words the LB&SCR carriage livery, which not long afterwards was adopted as the standard Pullman livery in the UK. This is confirmed in a *Railway Magazine* paragraph, which states that all the cars were identically '*finished in the standard Pullman colours – umber and cream.*'[25]

THE RENAMING OF *LADY NAIRNE*

Press photographs[26] of the car on delivery show that its name was *Lady Nairne* with a terminal 'e'. This was the correct spelling of the name from the creation of the baronetcy in 1681 and at its restoration in 1824, following forfeiture after the 1715 uprising. There is to this day a Lady Nairne. The name has no connection with the town of Nairn; as mentioned previously it comes from a family in Strathord.

According to McEwan, the car was renamed (in his view correctly) as *Lady Nairn* by the spring of 1922, the work being done at St. Rollox.[27] The register entries for two drawings dated April 1922 (St. Rollox 21770 and 21777) both refer to *Lady Nairne* and *Bonnie Jean*. The entry for St. Rollox drawing 22481 also has *Lady Nairne*. This is dated December 1923. None of these drawings has survived. LM&SR drawing C1166,[28] signed by Irvine Kempt Junior and dated 5th September 1929, was for the vacuum brake arrangement on *Bonnie Jean* and *Lady Nairne*. The Coaching Plant Stock Book also records the car with a terminal 'e', but this record may have been written when it entered traffic, and not subsequently altered.

There is no firm evidence to support McEwan's statement. He may have been trying to reconcile the name with the use of the car on the service to Aviemore. It seems highly unlikely that the Caledonian, with its strong sense of public relations, would perpetrate such an error and the residence of the real Lady Nairne was firmly located in Caley territory.

REFERENCES

1. Quoted in NRS BR/CAL/1/72 entry 309
2. NRS BR/CAL/1/72 entry 309
3. NRS BR/CAL/1/72 entry 643
4. NRS BR/CAL/3/87
5. *The Caledonian Journal*, issue 3, p. 18
6. NRS BR/CAL/4/160
7. NRS BR/CAL/1/73 entry 205
8. *The Caledonian Journal*, issue 3, p. 18
9. *The Railway Magazine*, July-December 1914, p. 123
10. *The Caledonian Journal*, issue 5, p. 23
11. *The Railway Gazette*, 31st March 1911, pp. 318-19
12. CRA Archive ref: 3/3/2/9
13. NRS BR/CAL/3/88 CRA Archive ref: 2/2/1/4/2
14. *The Railway Gazette*, 13th October 1922, pp. 447-48
15. NRM ALS4/132/G7
16. NRS BR/TT/S/54/63
17. *The Railway Magazine*, July-December, p. 244
18. *The Railway Magazine*, January 1923, p. 75
19. *The Caledonian Journal*, issue 3, p. 18
20. *The Railway Gazette*, 13th October 1922, p. 417
21. *The Railway Gazette*, 31st March 1911, p. 319
22. Birmingham City Archive refs: MS99 9046 (body) and 9080A (bogie)
23. *The Railway Gazette*, 13th October 1922, p. 417
24. *The Railway Gazette*, 13th October 1922, p. 417
25. *The Railway Magazine*, March 1923, pp. 249-50
26. *The Railway Gazette*, 13th October 1922, pp. 447-48
27. *The Caledonian Journal*, issue 3, p. 18
28. RHP 67553

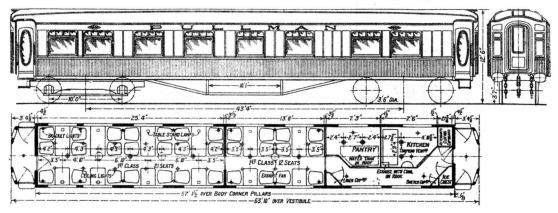

Figures 10.12 and 10.13
The drawings depict the cars that were delivered in May 1923, a month before the Caledonian ceased to exist. Figure 10.12 (*above*) shows the First class Dining cars, Figure 10.13 (*right*) the Third class Buffet car number 80.

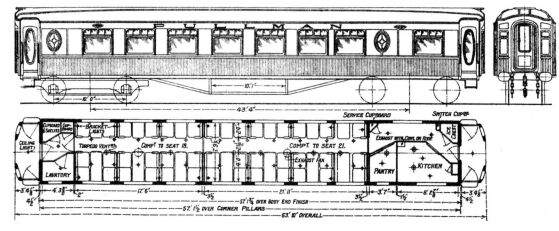

Plate 10.19
This photograph shows Third class car 80 on a short train. This was probably the additional service mentioned in *The Railway Magazine*. The two carriages behind the locomotive are a Diagram 122 Brake Third and a Diagram 112 Composite. The rear Brake vehicle may be a Composite to Diagram 111 or one of the three Brake Third variations of Diagram 110.

10.4: THE LM&SR TAKES OVER

Anew agreement was signed with the Pullman Car Co. for three additional cars in January 1923.[1] Legally the CR still existed, because it did not agree terms for its absorption into the LM&SR until June, but it was participating as far as traffic was concerned in the new company, which had been operational from January. The new agreement did not extend the duration of that made in July 1922. It stipulated:

'the last mentioned cars are not to be held to be allocated to any particular route or trains … but are to be used … on such of their routes and trains as they (the CR) deem suitable – the arrangements … will allow to the reasonable advantage of the Pullman Car Co.'

This condition was obviously imposed by the LM&SR, which planned to run Pullman Dining cars on the Glasgow & South Western and Highland sections as well as on the Caledonian.

CARS DELIVERED UNDER THE 1923 AGREEMENT

Four cars were actually delivered in May 1923, which finally brought the fleet up to the seventeen vehicles agreed in the original contract. The new arrivals were three First class Dining cars and a Third class Buffet car. *The Railway Gazette* reported that:

'the structural and decorative design throughout strikes a new and original note in Pullman car construction. The main objects have been to produce a car with steel underframe and four-wheeled bogies, whilst fully preserving the qualities of steady and quiet running so characteristic of the Pullman cars in service … which have wooden underframes and six-wheeled equalising bar type bogies.'[2]

The cars were of the now standard wooden Pullman K type. The all Third car was not named, being given the number 80. This was the custom on lines south of the border. As will be seen from the quotation below, it ran on the Oban line alongside *Maid of Morven*. The 1925 Pullman service guide, quoted in *Pullman Profile No. 2*, stated that the car was available,

'for 3rd Class passengers only on payment of a supplementary fare of 2s 6d [the normal supplement from Glasgow to Oban]. 1st Class passengers are provided with meals in the carriage adjoining the buffet car.'

According to a *Railway Magazine* article about the Callander & Oban Railway,[3] it operated on the 5.10pm departure from Glasgow and returned on the additional train leaving Oban at 11.15am. This service was put on during June, July and August. It last appeared in the LM&SR timetable of 1926.

The Coaching Plant Stock Book does not mention the car, which suggests that it was always considered as a temporary addition and not part of the 1923 agreement. According to *Pullman Profile No. 2* it was transferred to the L&NER in summer 1927, where it was renumbered 27.[4]

Compared with the original agreement, the final CR Pullman fleet consisted of nine Dining cars instead of four, with a consequent reduction in the number of Buffet cars from twelve to seven, plus the Observation car. Three Dining cars were First class rather than Composite, and one Buffet car was Third class rather than First.

THE DINING CARS

Dining cars *Lass o' Ballochmyle*, *Mauchline Belle* and *Meg Dods* had two separate compartments for First class passengers, one seating twelve and the other twenty-one. Although their length over vestibules was the same as the pre-war Dining cars, they ran on 4-wheeled bogies, with a wheelbase of 10 feet. The bogie centres were almost identical to those on the 12-wheeled cars. They appeared on Page 55D of the Diagram Book. Interior plan and side elevations are reproduced in Figure 10.12.

Lass o' Ballochmyle and *Mauchline Belle* were named after women in poems by Robert Burns. The latter was Jean Arthur, Burns' wife, who was also commemorated by Pullman car *Bonnie Jean*. Appropriately, they were put into service on the former Glasgow & South Western Railway's lines. *Meg Dods* was the landlady of the Cleikum Inn in Peebles, in the novel *St. Ronan's Well* by Walter Scott. The name suggests that the car may have been destined for what was called in Caley days the 'Tinto' express.

Meg Dods was decorated in mahogany and pear tree veneer with holly inlays, a deep red carpet and matching leather upholstered chairs. *Lass o' Ballochmyle* was decorated in the empire style with pear tree veneer inlaid with diamond-shaped areas of green-toned satinwood. The carpets and upholstery were in matching green. *Mauchline Belle* was also decorated in pear tree and mahogany, but with coloured sycamore inlays, the chairs being upholstered in red leather with a matching Wilton carpet.

According to a near-contemporary modeller's drawing by Stewart Reidpath Ltd,[5] the corridors and vestibules were also finished in mahogany and their floors were covered in *'interlocking rubber tiling in alternative tints of black and white.'*

THE THIRD CLASS BUFFET CAR

Car No. 80 sat thirty-nine passengers in fixed high-back 2+1 seating. A kitchen 8 feet 3 inches long and a smaller pantry were provided. It did not appear in the Diagram Book, but an elevation and seating plan were reproduced in *The Railway Gazette* (these are shown in Figure 10.13),[6] which also provided the information about the interior quoted below. The car was photographed on the additional train mentioned earlier – see Plate 10.19.

It was panelled throughout in figured mahogany with centre panels of Pommele mahogany. The panels were outlined in inlaid boxwood, this decoration being repeated in friezes and pilasters. The floor covering was red Duratex, a form of hard-wearing rubber-backed carpeting.

THE LM&SR REGIME

When the Caledonian was finally absorbed by the LM&SR, the new company took over the contract with the Pullman Car Co. Numbers in the catering carriage series were allocated immediately. The number appeared above the name of the car, as seen in the photograph of *Duchess of Gordon* (Plate 10.18). The cars remained in Pullman livery for over a decade, but with the Pullman lettering and other identification painted over.

CARS DELIVERED IN 1927

Although outside the scope of this book, six more K-type cars were delivered to the LM&SR in 1927, three of which were included in the Coaching Plant Stock Book. They are mentioned here because McEwan wrote that the three cars in question, *Jeanie Deans, Jenny Geddes* and *Diana Vernon*, were delivered in September 1922.[7]

He was possibly misled by the LM&SR numbers assigned to the cars. The numbers, as can be seen in the table below, were applied in broad chronological order of delivery against the agreement, except for these three cars, which were inserted after *Duchess of Gordon* (delivered in 1919). *Queen Margaret, Kate Dalrymple* and *Helen of Mar*, the other cars delivered in 1927, appeared at the end of the LM&SR number series. These cars are not mentioned in the Coaching Plant Stock Book, presumably because they, like *Lass o' Ballochmyle, Mauchline Belle* and *Meg Dods*, did not operate on the old CR system.

These six cars brought the total number up to one short of that envisaged at the beginning of discussions between the Caledonian and the Pullman Car Co. in 1912. They were, however, dispersed across the LM&SR's Scottish territory, rather than running exclusively on Caledonian metals.

REPAINTING AND WITHDRAWAL

The final agreement with the Pullman Car Co. was due to expire at the end of February 1934 and the LM&SR purchased the cars in the previous December. According to *The Railway Gazette*, the book value of the twenty-two cars was £152,000, but, because they could not be redeployed elsewhere, the company was forced to accept £21,000. This was the LM&SR's estimate of the cost of replacing the cars with standard catering vehicles.[8]

Eventually all the cars were painted crimson and lost their names. This happened piecemeal over a period between 1934 and 1936. An example of the new livery is shown in Plate 10.20. As can be seen in the following table, the eleven cars built prior to World War I were withdrawn before the outbreak of World War II. The remainder survived into the nationalisation era.

LM&SR No.	OLD CAR NAME	DELIVERY DATE	WITHDRAWN
200	*Mary Hamilton*	1914	November 1937
201	*Mary Beaton*	1914	October 1936
202	*Mary Seaton*	1914	February 1936
203	*Mary Carmichael*	1914	October 1936
204	*Annie Laurie*	1914	November 1937
205	*Helen MacGregor*	1914	February 1936
206	*Flora McDonald*	1914	October 1937
207	*Fair Maid of Perth*	1914	December 1937
208	*Lass o' Gowrie*	1914	October 1937
209	*Maid of Morven*	1914	December 1937
210	*Duchess of Gordon*	1919	December 1937
211	*Jeanie Deans*	1927	August 1948
212	*Jenny Geddes*	1927	May 1955
213	*Diana Vernon*	1927	March 1955
214	*Lady Nairne*	1922	December 1960
215	*Bonnie Jean*	1922	May 1955
216	*Lass o' Ballochmyle*	1923	January 1961
217	*Meg Dods*	1923	May 1961
218	*Mauchline Belle*	1923	April 1961
219	*Queen Margaret*	1927	May 1961
220	*Kate Dalrymple*	1927	July 1961
221	*Helen of Mar*	1927	May 1958

REFERENCES
1. NRS BR/CAL/3/89 CRA Archive ref: 2/2/1/4/4
2. *The Railway Gazette*, 29th June 1923, pp. 961-64
3. *The Railway Magazine*, July 1923, pp. 10-18
4. *Pullman Profile No. 2*, p. 48
5. CRA Archive ref: 6/1/1/6/6
6. *The Railway Gazette*, 29th June 1923, pp. 961-62
7. *The Caledonian Journal*, issue 3, p. 29
8. *The Railway Gazette*, 1934 p. 224

Plate 10.20
Jeanie Deans was delivered in 1927. It is shown here as an example of the LM&SR livery that was applied to all the Pullman cars in the mid-1930s after the takeover from the Pullman Car Co. Modellers need never worry about wonky oval buffers again.

CHAPTER 11
GENERAL SERVICE STOCK 1914-1923

11.1: CONSTRUCTION AUTHORISED UP TO 1917

William Pickersgill succeeded McIntosh as Locomotive Superintendent in May 1914, having worked in tandem with his predecessor from February. His term of office was characterised by financial stringency. Also, he was prevented from taking major initiatives because the Railway Executive Committee assumed control of the UK's railways on behalf of the government when war against Germany was declared on 4th August 1914. Donald Matheson of the Caledonian was the only Scottish railway general manager representative among the ten REC members.[1]

MODIFICATION TO 'GRAMPIAN' BRAKE THIRDS

In November 1915 the Traffic Committee received and approved a proposal from Pickersgill:

'to enlarge the brake Compartments in eight 65ft Third Class. Carriages so as to provide more accommodation for luggage and parcels traffic.'

Blueprints 101 and 101A, which corresponded to the pages in the Large Diagram Book, were submitted and it was agreed to get the work done, charged to revenue.[2] The estimated cost was £11 per carriage. The 1921 Stock List, which shows sixteen 8-compartment Brake Thirds, confirms the modification.

Non-corridor Diagram 101A carriages 227, 454, 518, 1324-1328 were modified to conform to Diagram 101 by removing the compartment next to the guard's section. This would have resulted in an alteration to the panelling following the suppression of windows and the removal of the compartment doors – compare the two part elevations in Figure 11.1.

Although Diagram 101A ceased to exist as a result, the two sets of running numbers were still shown to the old diagrams in the index to the Large Diagram Book. The transcription of the Coaching Plant Stock Book also still makes the distinction.

DIAGRAM 117 NON-CORRIDOR FIRSTS

One carriage to this design had been built under the McIntosh regime. Its details are in Chapter 9 (Figure 9.59). Eight more were built in the early years of the war to orders H324, H328 and H332. The last of these orders was authorised for the period ending December 1915,[3] but the Coaching Plant Stock Book records the building date as September 1916. Numbers were 9, 10, 18, 41, 43, 55, 59, 136 and 160. They probably replaced 31-foot carriages with the same numbers. A photograph of number 18 in BR livery is shown as Plate 11.1.

DIAGRAM 118 NON-CORRIDOR THIRDS

The first carriages to this design were built to order H326 in the period ending December 1914. Nine compartments accommodated 108 passengers – see Figure 9.60. Eight carriages comprised the first order.[4] A further fourteen were built in 1915/16 to orders H330 and H334. More were built post-war, making a total of forty-four. Although the post-war carriages were given St. Rollox order numbers, they were actually built by Metropolitan and Hurst, Nelson. They are described and illustrated in Chapter 11.3.

DIAGRAM 119B BRAKE THIRDS

This was the most numerous type of Pickersgill carriage. It was a variation of the 6-compartment Diagram 119, which is described in Chapter 9.5. It had five compartments seating sixty, and a very large guard's and luggage compartment, just over 25 feet long. Another variation, Diagram 119A with seven compartments, was not built, although drawings for both versions were issued in 1913. St. Rollox drawing 16953 was for Diagram 119A and 16954 for Diagram 119B. Neither has survived.

The first carriages to order H323 had 10-foot wheelbase bogies – see Figure 11.2. Six were authorised at the same time as the Diagram 118 Thirds. The drawing number for the Brake compartment was 17466.[5]

Before carriage construction ceased, a further ten were built to orders H327, H331 and H337. All these and future carriages of this type had 8-foot wheelbase bogies. The new underframe was the subject of drawing 17572.[6] More were built after the war, making forty-seven in all. A post-war example is shown in Plate 11.11 and a post-war St. Rollox drawing of the Brake end side elevation and transverse sections is Figure 11.14.

DIAGRAM 121 NON-CORRIDOR COMPOSITES

Four carriages were built to order H325. They were authorised as renewals in the period ending December 1914.[7] They were built to drawing 17420, which has not survived. Four First and five Third class compartments seated thirty-two and sixty respectively. The First class compartments were about 6 inches narrower between partitions than usual to accommodate the fifth Third class compartment. They had 10-foot wheelbase bogies. Their numbers were 4, 23, 85 and 232. A side elevation and internal layout is shown in Figure 11.3.

DIAGRAM 121A NON-CORRIDOR COMPOSITES

This variation of Diagram 121 had four compartments for each class. The reduction of one Third class compartment gave very spacious accommodation, compared with the cramped First class

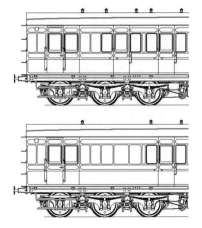

Figure 11.1
These two part elevations show the modification to the carriages of Diagram 101A to turn them into Diagram 101, with a larger Brake compartment. It is possible that the new panels in the guard's compartment were equally spaced; as shown here, the wider panel reveals the old door drop light.

compartments of Diagram 121. The central First class compartments were 7 feet 6 inches between partitions. The Third class, situated at the ends, were only one foot less. The bogie wheelbase was 8 feet. The side elevation and internal layout are shown in Figure 11.4. The Diagram 121A page is annotated 18106. This drawing number is described as a *'Diagram for Composite Carriage'* in the Register. It has not survived.

The first carriages to this design were built in 1915/16, four to H329 and two to H333. The minute recording the renewals programme for the period ending December 1916 only records five carriages to this configuration.[8] St. Rollox built six more after the war.

CESSATION OF THE BUILDING PROGRAMME

In April 1916, orders for the thirty-three carriages that had been placed with three outside contractors two months previously were cancelled by order of the Ministry of Munitions.[9] These carriages were the sixteen replacement vehicles for those requisitioned for Ambulance Train 23, plus the whole of the carriage replacement programme for the half year ending June 1916. The Birmingham Carriage & Wagon Co. rendered an account to the Caledonian for materials they had acquired for its part of the order. The CR Board agreed to purchase them at a cost of £2,363 10s 7d.[10]

With the exception of the last two Diagram 119B Brake Thirds to order H337 mentioned above and the Brake Vans described below, which were probably constructed from these materials, rolling stock construction ceased until 1919. The Traffic Committee continued to meet every six months, however, and approved the replacement

programme as usual. The backlog of construction and the steps taken to overcome it are discussed in the next section.

50-FOOT BRAKE VANS

The six Diagram 98A vans to order H335 were authorised as 6-wheeled vehicles to Diagram 17, but the whole of the renewal programme for the half year ending December 1917 was remitted to the Board, who referred it back to the Traffic Committee *'for further consideration.'*[11] It seems that the process resulted in an alteration to this part of the programme. Drawing 19244 was issued in November 1917 for the underframe of *'50 foot passenger brake van and carriage.'*[12] The original St. Rollox drawing of these vans, but with 10-foot wheelbase bogies, is shown in Chapter 9 (Figure 9.33). Figure 11.5 is a modeller's drawing of the design.

LACK OF CARRIAGE HEATING

In December 1917, the Traffic Committee had reported, under the heading *'Scarcity of Carriages fitted with Steam Heating,'* that difficulty was being experienced in making up main line trains for *'want of Third Class carriages.'* It was agreed that thirty 8-compartment bogie Thirds and ten 6-compartment bogie Brake Thirds should be fitted at a total cost of £2,890. The work was authorised *'but only on condition that Government agrees to this being treated as special war expenditure.'*[13] It is not possible to ascertain whether government approval was received or that the fitting was carried out.

Plate 11.1
Diagram 107 Corridor First in BR days as SC10633M, showing the compartment side. It was originally CR 18, one of six built in the early years of the World War I. It was broken up at St. Rollox in 1956.

REFERENCES
1. *British Railways and the Great War*, volume 1, p. 44
2. NRS BR/CAL/1/67 entry 621
3. NRS BR/CAL/1/66 entry 568
4. NRS BR/CAL/1/64 entry 1149
5. NRM 8008/C
6. NRM 8077/C (on two sheets)
7. NRS BR/CAL/1/64 entry 1149
8. NRS BR/CAL/1/68 entry 98
9. NRS BR/CAL/1/68 entry 100
10. NRS BR/CAL/5/4, extract from a meeting of the Loco & Stores Committee, 11th July 1916
11. NRS BR/CAL/1/69 entry 605
12. RHP 69144
13. NRS BR/CAL/1/70 entry 979

RIGHT: Figure 11.2
This shows the side elevation of the Diagram 119B Brake Third. A post-war works drawing of the brake end is shown in Figure 11.14.

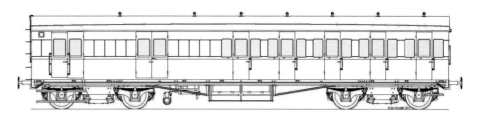

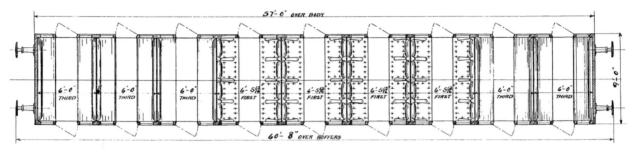

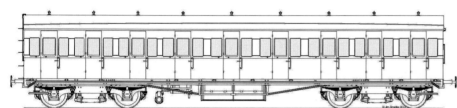

ABOVE AND LEFT: Figure 11.3
The Diagram 121 Composite is shown here with 10-foot wheelbase bogies, plus the internal layout. Four were built to order H325 in the second half of 1914.

ABOVE AND RIGHT: Figure 11.4
A side elevation and internal layout of Diagram 121A. Comparing the internal layouts of Diagram 121 (four First and five Third class compartments) and 121A (four compartments for each class) shows that the leg room in Diagram 121A was much more generous for both classes of traveller.

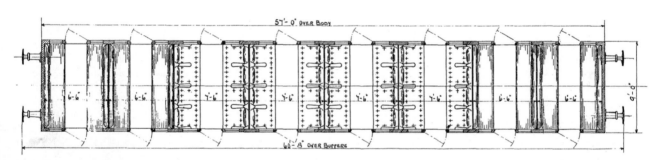

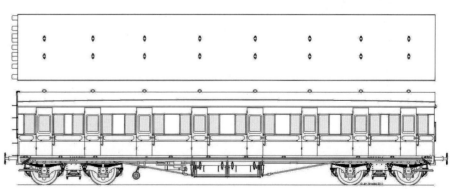

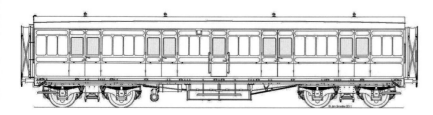

LEFT: Figure 11.5
A side elevation drawing of the Diagram 98A 50-foot Passenger Brake Van. There is a St. Rollox works drawing in Chapter 9, Figure 9.33.

11.2: The 1919 Coaching Stock Crisis

With the end of the war the backlog in locomotive, carriage and wagon construction had to be made up. Matters were made worse by the poor economic state of the railway companies and the country in general, plus serious inflation in the cost of materials and labour.

It was some months before the day-to-day running of the Caledonian was sufficiently under control to permit a review of the state of its stock and the work that it should undertake, although preliminary work was under way in the drawing office. Drawing 19869, dated 13th March 1919, was a general arrangement for a 50-foot Corridor Composite carriage. Number 19883 was the lavatory arrangement for a 9-foot wide carriage 57 feet long, and in April the body framing for a carriage of these dimensions was issued to drawing 19899. None of these drawings has survived.

The information in this section is contained in a book of extracts from Board and Committee minutes and internal correspondence at senior management level.[1]

On 4th June 1919 the General Manager, Donald Matheson, met 'as the result of pressure in the working in respect of rolling stock' with William Pickersgill, the Locomotive Superintendent, Robert Killin, Superintendent of the Line, John Ballantyne, Chief Goods Manager, Alex Black, the Coaching Plant Superintendent, and James Ramsay, the Goods and Mineral Plant Superintendent.

Locomotive construction was not a problem. Pickersgill was confident that he could fulfil his commitment to build thirty-one and keep abreast of future needs. The carriage renewal programme from January 1916 comprised 161 vehicles, none of which had been built. This included six Covered Carriage Trucks, which were discussed in *Caledonian Railway Wagons*,[2] and are not included in this survey.

Carriage Type	Number
57-foot Corridor Brake Van	8
50-foot Corridor Brake Van	2
57-foot Corridor Brake Third	2
57-foot Corridor Third	11
57-foot Corridor Brake Third	7
57-foot Corridor First	4
57-foot Corridor Third	10
57-foot Semi-corridor Brake Composite	7
50-foot Corridor Composite	4
50-foot Semi-corridor Brake Third	7
50-foot Semi-corridor Brake Composite	5
57-foot non-corridor Composite	5
57-foot non-corridor Composite	13
57-foot non-corridor Brake Third	29
57-foot non-corridor Third	12
30-foot 4-wheeled First	7
30-foot 4-wheeled Third	22
30-foot 4-wheeled Brake Third	10
30-foot 6-wheeled Brake Van	6

With the sixteen vehicles which had been sent for use in the Ambulance Train, the shortfall was the 171 vehicles, plus the Carriage

Trucks, listed in the above table – differences in compartment numbers caused the apparent duplication of certain types of carriage.

When the Caledonian commissioned an inventory of carriages in 1874, the estimated life expectancy of a passenger vehicle was twenty-eight years. The use of steel underframes instead of wood had increased the expected lifespan of a carriage in 1919 to thirty-two years. The L&NWR expected its WCJS carriages to last one year longer, according to its calculation of the residual value of the carriages destroyed at Quintinshill in 1915.[3]

Of the 2,087 carriages owned by the CR on 4th June, more than a third were over thirty years old and therefore technically life-expired or very nearly so. The analysis in the memorandum is shown below. The percentages have been added by the author.

Number of Carriages	Age	% of Total
505	Under 20 years old	24%
767	Over 20 and under 30 years old	37%
580	Over 30 and under 40 years old	28%
235	Over 40 years old	11%

The memorandum went on to say that the average age of the carriage fleet was twenty-five years and, given the large number of life-expired vehicles still in service, it was obviously vital that the company increased its rate of construction of new carriages. St. Rollox was actually building sixteen at the time of the meeting, but that was less than one tenth of the backlog.

Pickersgill considered that it would be impossible to meet the required rate of construction at St. Rollox and '[he] suggests the necessity of orders for carriages being placed with outside builders.'

It was considered unreasonable to place an immediate order for 161 new carriages, but the meeting recommended that orders for sixty should be placed as soon as possible. These carriages, all 57 feet long, were considered by the Superintendent of the line 'to be the most urgently required.' It was accepted that it might be advisable to place three orders separately, or even to delay placing part of the total to secure the best price.

Carriage Heating

Just over one quarter of CR carriages had steam heating apparatus at the time of the review. Matheson noted that:

'During the war there were numerous complaints as to the temperature of carriages, particularly in the conveyance of soldiers.

The general public have also complained and it is desirable that an additional number of carriages should be steam heated.'

The detailed recommendation is included in the section on heating in Chapter 3.4.

Appointment of a Sub-Committee

On 10th June the Board of Directors remitted consideration of Matheson's memorandum to a sub-committee of Directors consisting of Messrs Allan (the Chairman of the Board), Chrystal, Gordon, Stewart and Colonel Denny.[4]

THE DELIBERATIONS OF THE SUB-COMMITTEE

A memorandum from Matheson, setting out the task of the sub-committee at its meeting on 7th July, changed the terms of reference by reducing the number of carriages from the original sixty:

'The Directors may consider the expediency of renewing about 20 to 40 additional carriages ... and of placing the orders for these with outside firms.'

The briefing paper went on to say that the number of carriages had fallen over a five year period, but seating capacity had risen to compensate. The larger vehicles envisaged for the future would increase capacity by just under 10%.

'If the 177 carriages falling to be "renewed" are renewed the stock would be increased by 160 carriages and the seating capacity by about 11,091.'

Matheson gave further evidence of the deterioration that had resulted during the war. His figures differed slightly, but not significantly, from those in his previous memorandum.

CARRIAGE STOCK	DEC. 1913	DEC. 1918
Under 20 years old	930 (44%)	571 (27%)
Over 20 and under 30 years old	622 (29%)	738 (35%)
Over 30 and under 40 years old	505 (24%)	622 (30%)
Over 40 years old	52 (3%)	161 (8%)
Total carriage stock	2,109	2,092
Total seating capacity	114,282	116,145

Matheson's reports reveal that Pickersgill expected 'the most he could accomplish by the end of this year will be 36 carriages and thereby reduce the deficit in renewal from 177 to 141 vehicles.'

Matheson went on to the crux of the problem:

'replacement in the meantime is impractical if not impossible having regard to
(1) the difficulty in getting labour and materials
(2) the cost
That is to say, even if the vehicles were ordered [from outside firms] now they could not be delivered for a considerable time and the cost is practically prohibitive. The difference in cost between the 1913 and 1919 prices can be described as being very great.'

FINANCING THE WORK

With work at a standstill during the latter half of the war, an unspent renewal fund had accrued, amounting to £461,727 for carriages and wagons. This was calculated at 2½% per annum on the capital cost of the carriage stock. For 1919 this was £30,452. CR management recognised that this calculation, which assumed a carriage life of forty years, was unrealistic given the actual life of eight years less. The wagon stock allowance was calculated at 1.757%.

Matheson noted that, providing certain criteria were met, the government would pay the difference in the cost of constructing carriages in 1919 compared with 1913, 'but that does not lessen the necessity of there being careful consideration of the economics.'

It was this consideration that had resulted in the reduction in the recommended building programme from sixty carriages to '20 or even 40 vehicles.'

THE OPTIONS PRESENTED TO THE SUB-COMMITTEE

Two groups of carriages, each of twenty vehicles, were offered for consideration.

GROUP A

'7 57-feet Corridor Brake Third Class Carriages with four compartments in each
4 57-feet Corridor First Class Carriages with seven compartments in each
9 57-feet Corridor Third Class Carriages with eight compartments in each'

GROUP B

'1 57-feet Corridor Third Class Carriage with eight compartments
7 57-feet Lavatory Brake Composite Carriages with two First Class and 4 Third Class compartments in each
5 57-feet non-lavatory Composite Carriages with four First and 4 Third Class compartments in each
7 57-feet non-lavatory Brake Third Class Carriages with five compartments in each'

The estimated cost if purchased from outside contractors was £128,000 for Group A, and £125,000 for Group B, compared with estimates of £25,648 and £24,569 respectively at 1913 prices. Had St. Rollox the capacity to build the carriages the cost would have been £52,575 for Group A and £58,349 for Group B. The amounts provided under the renewals programme were £25,068 and £24,780 respectively.

THE SUB-COMMITTEE'S DECISIONS

Apart from the thirty-six carriages which were to be built by the Caledonian, the sub-committee decided that only the twenty carriages in Group A should be put out to tender. Metropolitan won the contract, but did not complete it until the first half of 1921.

After the war, quotations from outside contractors routinely included a clause stating that the material and labour costs included were those current at the time of the quote and that increases would be passed on. In November 1921 the Finance Committee authorised payment of a:

'Claim for increased cost by Metropolitan Carriage & Wagon & Finance Coy. in connection with the construction of 20 Carriages ordered by the Company on 10th July 1919.'[5]

The sub-committee endorsed the recommendation that two hundred carriages per year should be fitted with steam heating and agreed that the expenditure should be charged to revenue. It pointed out that the estimated cost of £18,200 was almost double the pre-war figure of £9,600.

REFERENCES
1. NRS BR/CAL/5/6
2. *Caledonian Railway Wagons*, p. 205
3. NRS BR/WCC/1/5 minute 3368
4. NRS BR/CAL/1/73 entry 110
5. NRS BR/CAL/1/78 entry 308

11.3: POST-WAR BOGIE CARRIAGES AND BRAKE VANS

Carriage building resumed in mid-1919 after the sub-committee had made its recommendations. The first vehicles to come out of St. Rollox were eight 57-foot Passenger Brake Vans, which were already under construction, because they were to have formed part of the American Ambulance Train, as described in Chapter 12. The order numbers were H338-H340.

They were given Diagram 98B. St. Rollox drawing 19759 dated 16th December 1918 refers.[1] It is annotated 'converted from Ward Car MD25.' Numbers were 25, 79, 117, 149, 160, 163, 194 and 223. A side elevation is shown in Figure 11.6. They remained in service until after nationalisation – a photograph of the last van to be constructed is shown in BR livery in Plate 11.2.

Two Diagram 98A 50-foot Brake Vans numbered 107 and 192 were also built in the period ending December 1919 to order H341, which completed the bogie Brake Van backlog.

THE PROGRAMME TO REMOVE THE BACKLOG

The basic programme from the period ending June 1920 to December 1921 was for St. Rollox to build sixteen carriages in each half year, amounting to sixty-four vehicles. A further fifty carriages were commissioned from outside contractors.

50-FOOT SEMI-CORRIDOR STOCK

The next priority after building the Brake Vans in 1919 was to build 50-foot carriages, some of which replaced the six that had been converted for Ambulance Train 23. A total of sixteen were built in 1919 and 1920, in line with the summary of unbuilt stock. They were all McIntosh designs dating from 1910. A full description of these carriages appears in Chapter 9.2. A new underframe drawing was issued – St. Rollox 19244.[2] None of the new carriage drawings quoted below has survived.

Four Diagram 106 Composites were built to orders H342 and H345. Their numbers were 14, 44, 192 and 197. The drawing number was 19809. There is a photograph of number 44 at Plate 11.3. Seven Brake Thirds were built to orders H343 and H347. They were Diagram 107. A new drawing was issued – number 19994B. The two built in 1919 were numbered 256, 286, and the last five were 1356-1360.

Five Brake Composites formed orders H344 and H346. In the original McIntosh Diagram 108, First class compartments were 7 feet wide. Pickersgill increased the leg room by 2 inches. The lavatories were also enlarged by 8 inches giving a 1-foot reduction in the Brake compartment. These alterations and the use of 8-foot wheelbase

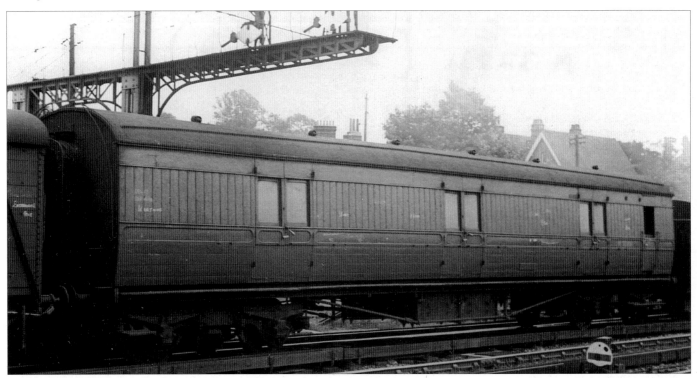

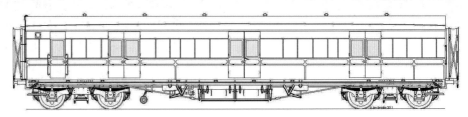

Plate 11.2 and Figure 11.6,
The 57-foot Passenger Brake Vans were converted from stock intended for the US Army ambulance train. The photograph was taken at Redhill in July 1950 and shows one of the vans in BR livery.

Plate 11.3
This H.R. Norman photograph, taken at Inverness on 16th June 1934, shows one of the four post-war Diagram 106 Semi-corridor Composites. Vacuum brakes had been fitted the year previously. LM&SR 19952 was originally CR44, built to order H342. It was withdrawn in June 1954. The photograph is in the LGRP collection at the NRM, ref: 6081.

bogies merited a new diagram – number 108A – see Figure 11.7. The drawing number was 19801, which has not survived. The running numbers were 21, 47, 118, 127 and 184. A photograph of 127 in BR days is shown in Plate 11.4.

THE SITUATION IN MID-1920

In July 1920 a Traffic Committee minute recorded the General Manager's report on progress towards clearing the backlog of replacements and recommendations for future construction.[3]

'the total number of Carriages which the Directors have authorised since 1916 and which have not yet been put into traffic is 177, of that number 53 are under construction by outside firms and 42 in the Company's workshop.

It is recommended that when the 42 are put into traffic the Locomotive Superintendent should be authorised to proceed with the construction of the following 16 vehicles:

10, 57ft non Lavatory Brake Thirds 5 compartment
5, 57ft non Lavatory Composites 4 First 4 Third
1, 57ft Corridor Third 8 compartment'

This recommendation formed the sixteen carriages in the renewal programme for the period ending December 1920. A grand total of 168 carriages were built from the beginning of 1920 to the Grouping. The bogie vehicles and 6-wheeled Brake Vans are described below by size and type. The 4-wheeled carriages for the Balerno Branch are described in Chapter 11.4.

THE PROGRAMME FOR 1922

In the period ending June 1922, thirty-seven carriages were authorised, sixteen of which were to be built by Pickering.[4] In the final half year before the CR's planned absorption into the LM&SR, twenty-one more carriages were authorised.

57-FOOT CARRIAGES

After construction of the 50-foot stock was underway, attention turned to a mixture of corridor, semi-corridor and non-corridor 57-foot stock. Five of the designs were new – the Diagram 121B non-corridor Composite, the two Brake Third designs to Diagrams 122 and 122A, the Diagram 123 Corridor First and the Diagram 124 Corridor Third.

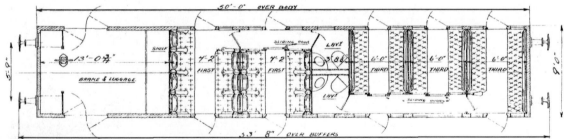

Figure 11.7, Plate 11.4
The drawing shows the internal layout of the Diagram 108A Brake Composite. The original Diagram 108 carriages were designed for the Callander and Oban service. Diagram 108A was the same design but with 8-foot wheelbase bogies and slightly altered internal dimensions. The photograph was taken at Killin Junction, probably about 1950, judging by the BRITISH RAILWAYS on the tank side of the CR Class '439' 0-4-4T. Carriage M25973 was originally CR 127, built in the second half of 1922 to order H346. It was withdrawn in December 1955.

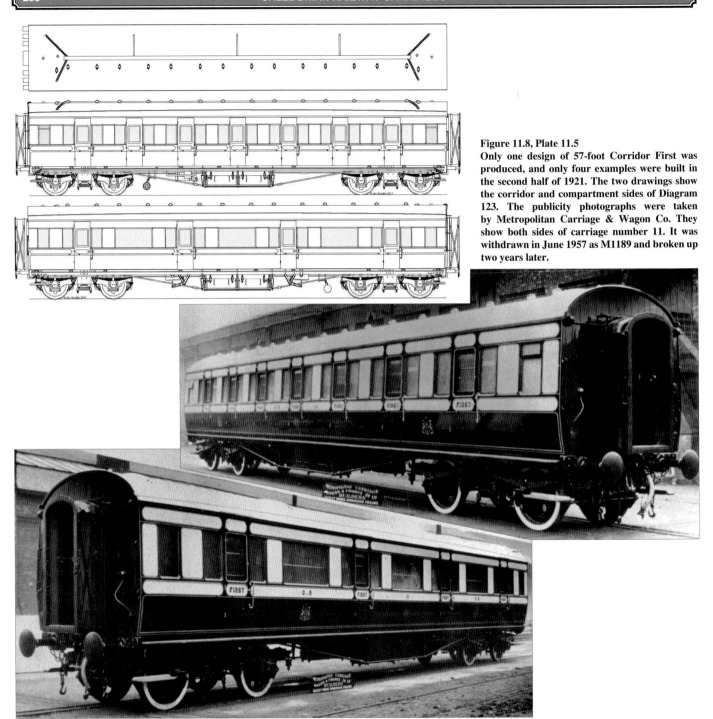

Figure 11.8, Plate 11.5
Only one design of 57-foot Corridor First was produced, and only four examples were built in the second half of 1921. The two drawings show the corridor and compartment sides of Diagram 123. The publicity photographs were taken by Metropolitan Carriage & Wagon Co. They show both sides of carriage number 11. It was withdrawn in June 1957 as M1189 and broken up two years later.

CORRIDOR FIRSTS

Four carriages to Diagram 123 were built by Metropolitan. They had been authorised by the sub-committee in 1919 but only entered service during the period ending June 1921, according to the Coaching Plant Stock Book. It was the only 57-foot Corridor First design, seating forty-two passengers in seven compartments. Their numbers were 11, 36, 127 and 141. A drawing has not been traced in the St. Rollox register. The side elevations are shown in Figure 11.8. Both sides of the carriage are illustrated in Plate 11.5.

CORRIDOR COMPOSITES

Pickering built four carriages, numbered 460-463, to Diagram 112B in the first half of 1923 to card order 39202. This variation

on Diagram 112A had 8-foot wheelbase bogies rather than 10-foot. While the diagram appears in the Large Book, there is no record of these carriages in the index. A photograph of the first of the order is shown in Plate 11.6. Number 464 is in the care of the Scottish Railway Preservation Society.

CORRIDOR BRAKE COMPOSITES

Diagram 111A was a 9 foot wide version of the pre-war Diagram 111 which was four inches narrower. The internal layout of the original design is shown in Figure 9.47. It was fitted with 8-foot wheelbase bogies rather than 10-foot. Four were built by Pickering in 1923. They were part of the tender for sixteen carriages which was accepted in May 1922. They were numbered 464-467. St. Rollox drawing 22004, issued in November 1921, has not survived.

CORRIDOR THIRDS

Diagram 124 was another new design, with eight compartments 6 feet between partitions and a lavatory at each end. In the period ending June 1921 Metropolitan delivered nine carriages numbered 1368-1376. They had been authorised by the sub-committee in 1919. In the second half of 1921 St. Rollox built one example to order H359, followed by four from Pickering in 1922 built to card order 39206. The breakdown of costs for one of these carriages is shown in Plate 11.7. These last five carriages were numbered 1430, 1444-1447.

A drawing for this design has not been traced in the St. Rollox register. A Pickering version of drawing 20489 for the lettering layout is in the HMRS collection.[5] A Metropolitan general arrangement drawing is also available.[6] The two side elevations are shown in Figure 11.9.

CORRIDOR BRAKE THIRDS

The first design of Brake Third had four compartments seating thirty-two and was assigned to Diagram 122. Metropolitan built seven, numbered 1361-1367. They were the last part of the 1919 contract with Metropolitan that entered service during the first half of 1921. The original drawing 19901 has not survived. The two side elevations are Figure 11.10. One of these carriages is seen behind the locomotive in Plate 10.13.

Diagram 122A was the five compartment version, seating forty. Pickering built four of these carriages in 1923 to card order 39204. They were numbered 1448-1451. The lettering layout for the Pickering order is in the HMRS collection.[7] The equivalent St. Rollox drawing was number 21780, which has not survived. The elevations are Figure 11.11. The photograph is Plate 11.8.

SEMI-CORRIDOR BRAKE COMPOSITES

Diagram 115A was the same configuration as the pre-war Diagram 115. There was 2 inches extra width between partitions in the First class compartments, with a consequent reduction of 4 inches in the guard's and luggage compartment. A shelf was fitted in the luggage section, which was lacking in Diagram 115. Bogies were 8-foot wheelbase rather than 10 feet.

St. Rollox built seven to order H348 in the period ending December 1920 as part of the sixteen carriages authorised as renewals.[8] This was another part of the programme that had been halted by the war – drawing 18806, which is annotated for H348, is dated October 1916.[9] Pickering built a further five in 1922 to card order number 39200. Both sides of the carriage were photographed – see Plate 11.9. Drawing 21983[10] was issued for the contract. They were allocated numbers 468-472. The Pickering drawing of the lettering layout is in the HMRS collection.[11]

Plate 11.6
CR 460 was one of four Diagram 112B Corridor Composites built by Pickering in the first half of 1923. A companion carriage has been preserved by the Scottish Railway Preservation Society.

Plate 11.7
The Pickering cost breakdown of one of the Diagram 124 Corridor Thirds, built to card order 39206. Note the underlining of the word 'Actual.' In an era of high inflation, price rises during the period between quotation and construction were passed on to the customer. In this case the order was placed in May 1922, but the carriages were delivered in December. It is also interesting to see that the price received was over £100 less than that as calculated.

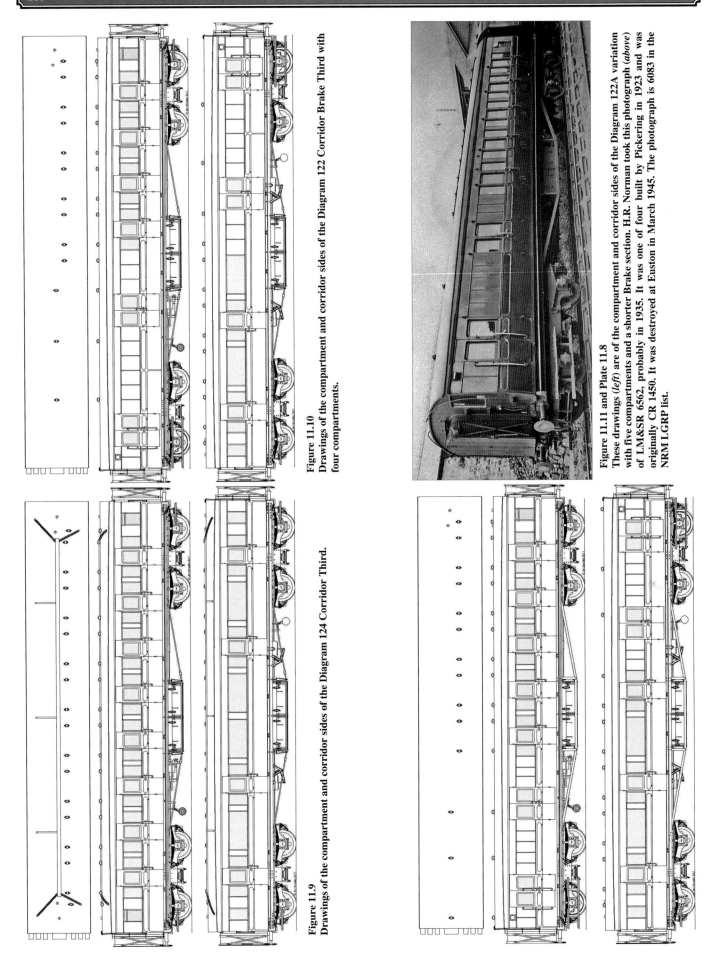

Figure 11.10
Drawings of the compartment and corridor sides of the Diagram 122 Corridor Brake Third with four compartments.

Figure 11.9
Drawings of the compartment and corridor sides of the Diagram 124 Corridor Third.

Figure 11.11 and Plate 11.8
These drawings (*left*) are of the compartment and corridor sides of the Diagram 122A variation with five compartments and a shorter Brake section. H.R. Norman took this photograph (*above*) of LM&SR 6562, probably in 1935. It was one of four built by Pickering in 1923 and was originally CR 1450. It was destroyed at Euston in March 1945. The photograph is 6083 in the NRM LGRP list.

NON-CORRIDOR COMPOSITES

Six Composites to Diagram 121A were built at St. Rollox in 1921 to order H358. The design was first built in 1915. Two were allocated random numbers; there was also a block of numbers from 447-451.

The Diagram 121B Composites were a new design with three First and five Third class compartments, rather than the four compartments of each class of Diagram 121A. The drawing number was 21772,[12] which is reproduced as Figure 11.12. The lettering layout was the subject of drawing 21782, which has not survived.

The new configuration resulted in even more spacious Third class compartments – over 6 feet 8 inches between partitions, as shown in the internal layout (Figure 11.13). The Clayton Wagon Company, which was also engaged in building CR 20-ton Goods Brake Vans at the time, built eight carriages in 1922. They were numbered 452-459. St. Rollox built five more to orders H366-H368 in 1923, numbered 473-477.

NON-CORRIDOR THIRDS AND BRAKE THIRDS

The largest number of carriages to be built were Thirds and Brake Thirds. The twenty-one Thirds to Diagram 118 were to a design that first appeared in 1914. A side elevation is shown in Chapter 9, Figure 9.60. The original intention was to build them at St. Rollox to order numbers H351 in the period ending December 1921 and H360-H362 during the next year. In the event, construction of the first ten was sub-contracted to Hurst, Nelson,[13] and Metropolitan for the rest. The Hurst, Nelson carriages were numbered 1410-1419 and the Metropolitan 1432-1437 and 1455-1459. One of the Metropolitan-built carriages is shown in Plate 11.10.

St. Rollox built twenty-three Diagram 119B Brake Thirds to orders H349, H356, H357, H363-H365 between 1920 and 1922. Metropolitan built six more in 1922. Drawing 21779 was issued for the contract (Figure 11.14).[14] Some received random numbers, but there were also three blocks of numbers: 1420-1429, 1438-1443 and 1452-1455. A photograph of a Metropolitan-built example appears in Plate 11.11.

BRAKE VANS

The other Brake Vans to be built after the war were a new 6-wheeled design, built to order H355, authorised in the period ending December 1921. As discussed in Chapter 11.1, they had been authorised in 1917, but bogie vans had been built instead. Six were built to general arrangement drawing 20957 (Figure 11.15).[15] They had a pressed steel underframe to drawing 20708.[16] Although they were 6 inches wider than the other 6-wheeled Brake Vans, they were included in Diagram 17 and allocated random numbers including 13 and 67. They lasted until the 1950s.

THE ADDITION OF HEATING

In accordance with the sub-committee's recommendation, a series of drawings was issued in late September/early October 1919 showing the heating pipe arrangements to be applied to a variety of 45- and 48-foot carriages. The first set of drawings was numbered 20171-20174 and the second set 20193-20205. None has survived. Drummond's 49-foot Firsts were modified in 1920 to drawing 20866 – another drawing that has not survived.

CONVERSIONS

In December 1919 the Traffic Committee agreed to convert seven Saloons into ordinary Third class carriages.[17] The vehicles concerned were the ex-WCJS Dining cars 38 and 39, First class Saloons 32 and 36 and Family Saloons 2, 11 and 31. The conversions had not taken place when the January 1921 Stock List was published.

At an unknown date, the Coaching Plant Stock Book records that seven Diagram 14 6-wheeled Thirds were converted to Diagram 16 Brake Thirds. The seats from one end compartment were removed to create guard's accommodation but no luggage space. This reduced the seating capacity from sixty to fifty. The seven carriages retained their original numbers, which were 24, 42, 106, 461, 805, 807 and 853. They were still described as Third class in the 1921 Stock List.

ABOVE AND RIGHT: Plate 11.9
These are Pickering publicity photographs of the two sides of Diagram 115A Semi-corridor Brake Composite number 468, the first of an order for five carriages built in the second half of 1922. It eventually became Camping Coach number 39, having been successively LM&SR 16054 and 25995.

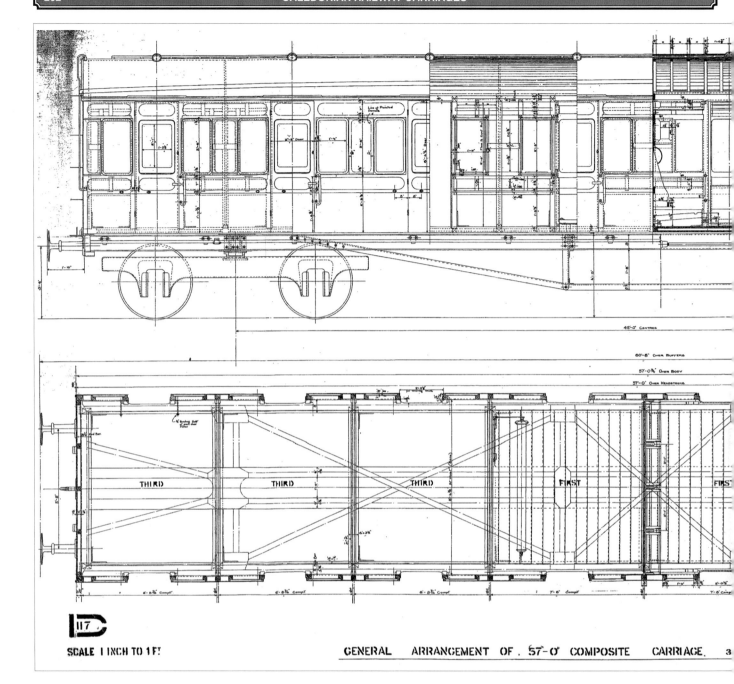

SCALE 1 INCH TO 1 FT.

GENERAL ARRANGEMENT OF 57'-0" COMPOSITE CARRIAGE. 3

REFERENCES
1. NRM 7511/C RHP to be assigned
2. NRM 8079/C
3. NRS BR/CAL/1/75 entry 491
4. NRS BR/CAL/1/79 entries 259 and 425 respectively
5. HMRS drawing ref: 0147
6. Birmingham City Archive ref: MS99 704/49-50
7. HMRS drawing ref: 0146
8. NRS BR/CAL/1/75 entry 566
9. NRM 7502/C RHP to be assigned
10. RHP to be assigned
11. HMRS drawing ref: 0148
12. NRM 7507/C (on two sheets) RHP to be assigned
13. NRS BR/CAL/1/74 entry 1109
14. NRM 7506/C (on two sheets) RHP to be assigned
15. NRM 7517/C
16. NRM 8070/C RHP 69135
17. NRS BR/CAL/1/74 entry 22

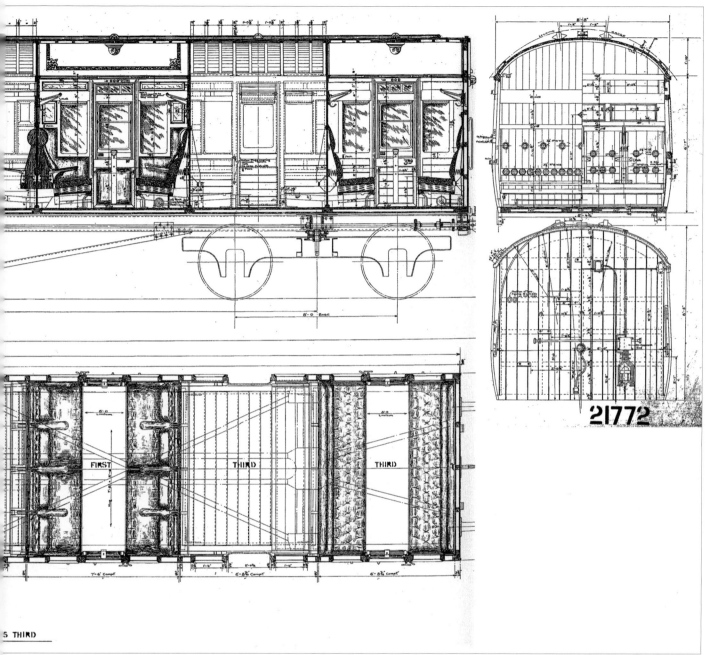

Figures 11.12 and 11.13
St. Rollox drawing 21772 (*above*) is the general arrangement of the Diagram 121B non-corridor Composite. The internal layout (*below*) from the Large Diagram Book shows the generous dimensions of the compartments.

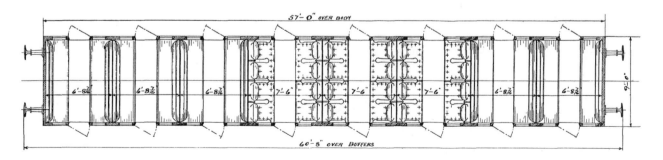

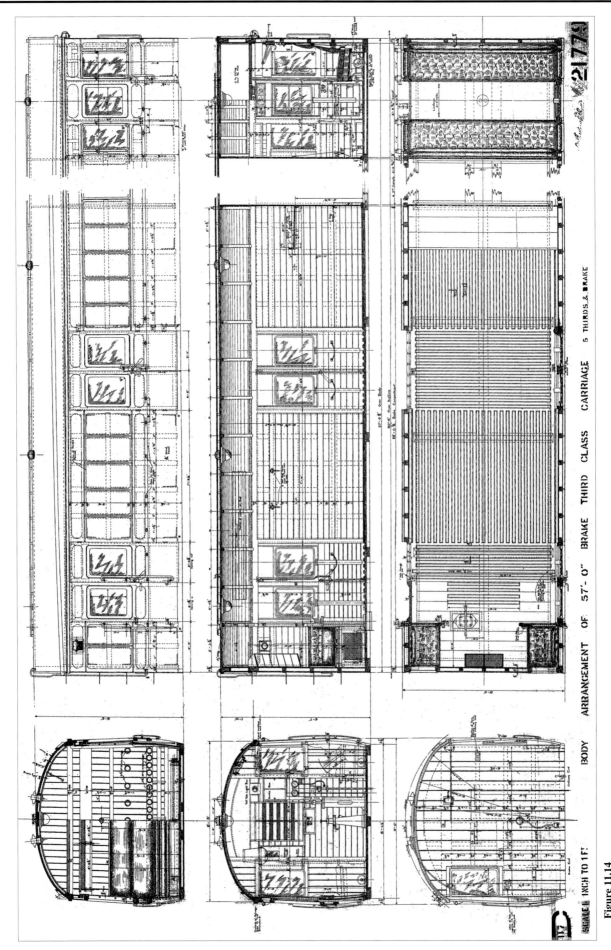

BODY ARRANGEMENT OF 57'-0" BRAKE THIRD CLASS CARRIAGE 5 THIRDS & BRAKE

SCALE ½ INCH TO 1 FT.

Figure 11.14
St. Rollox drawing 21779 was for the Diagram 119B Brake Third with five compartments.

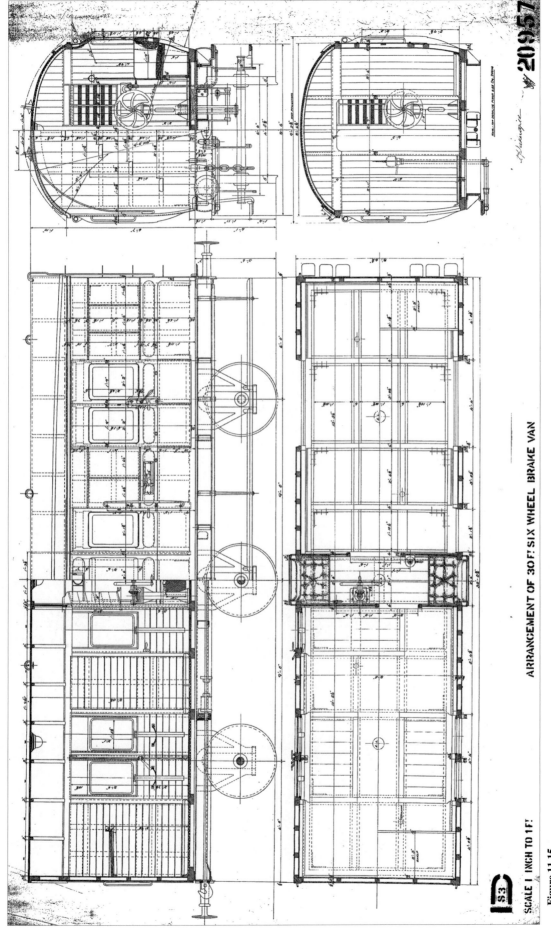

Figure 11.15
This was the final design of 6-wheeled Passenger Brake Van to St. Rollox drawing 20957.

LEFT: Plate 11.10
This is Diagram 118 Third number 1458 in a publicity photograph from Metropolitan. It was withdrawn in May 1955, having carried LM&SR numbers 19122 and 15539.

LEFT: Plate 11.11
Diagram 119B Brake Third CR 1442 was built by Metroplitan in 1922. It was broken up at St. Rollox in December 1954. Its LM&SR numbers were 19110, then 24284.

BELOW: Plate 11.12
Pickering took this publicity photograph of a rake of Balerno Branch carriages standing at Wishaw awaiting delivery. In order from the rear it consists of Brake Third number 1405, two Thirds numbered 1390 and 1391, First number 133, two Thirds 1392 and 1393, and Brake Third 1404. While nicely symmetrical, this was not the formation of the branch trains.

11.4: NEW STOCK FOR THE BALERNO BRANCH

In 1920/21, when most companies were withdrawing 4-wheeled stock and had ceased building 6-wheeled vehicles some years previously, the Balerno Branch in Edinburgh could still only be operated by 4-wheeled carriages. Curves were so sharp and clearances so tight that 6-wheeled wagons, which had an average wheelbase of 18 feet, were prohibited from running on the branch.[1]

New carriages were built suitable for a residential clientele. They displaced life-expired Drummond-designed stock dating from the mid-1880s. One of the old First class carriages carrying a Balerno Branch destination board appears in *Caledonian Cavalcade*.[2]

BUILDING HISTORY

As we have seen in the Chapter 11.2, the new carriages were first submitted for approval as replacements for the periods ending 30th June and 31st December 1917, when the original stock described in Chapter 7 was at the end of its design life. In the first period eight Thirds and four each Firsts and Brake Thirds were sanctioned.[3] Six months later three more Firsts, fourteen Thirds and six Brake Thirds were approved.[4]

A composite drawing of the bodies of the three types of carriage was produced in October 1916.[5] This is shown in Figure 11.16. Two weeks later drawing 18836 showed the make-up of a 'Train for Balerno Branch.' It has not survived. Drawings 18996-98 produced in March 1917 recorded the brake and heating pipes and the heater arrangement. The 30-foot all-steel underframe had been drawn slightly earlier to drawing 18985.[6] The wheelbase was 16 feet 9 inches. That of the Firsts was 16 feet.

St. Rollox did not have the capacity to build the carriages, and the Ministry of Munitions had objected to the use of outside contractors earlier in 1916.[7] Construction finally began in 1920. St. Rollox was responsible for the carriages which were authorised first, but only four Thirds were built, not eight. The original underframe drawing was reissued and annotated with St. Rollox order numbers H353 and H354.

A tender valued at £66,793 was accepted in May from R.Y. Pickering for the twenty-three carriages authorised for December 1917.[8] New drawings were issued as part of the contract. Drawing 20540,[9] dated 6th April 1920, was the repeat of 18815, but with the torpedo roof ventilators offset from the centre line. A further difference concerned the ends. The 1916 drawing showed two types of end, one with mahogany and steel panels, the other wood-cased. The new drawing only showed the mahogany and steel type. To confuse matters further, drawing 20915 dated 12th October 1920 showed both types of end.

Drawings 20541 and 20547, which have not survived, were for the interiors and the bearing springs. Drawing 20677,[10] dated 6th May 1920, was for the First class carriage underframe.

The four Firsts put in service in December 1920 were built at St. Rollox to order H352. The remaining three built by Pickering entered service in December 1921.[11] Four Thirds to St. Rollox order H353 went into service by December 1920. Fourteen more were built by Pickering and put in service December 1921.[12] Four Brake Thirds were built at St. Rollox to order H354 and put in service by June 1921. The six built by Pickering were in service by December 1921.[13]

Although the carriages were replacements, only the seven Firsts took existing stock numbers. The numbers allocated to the Firsts were already vacant when the Coaching Plant Stock Book was compiled, except for 133, which was a 31-foot carriage built in 1873 and withdrawn in 1918.

The displaced Third class carriages were not withdrawn until after the Grouping, so new running numbers were allocated in blocks. The H353 Thirds were numbered 1378-1385 and H354 Brake Thirds 1386-1389. The Pickering-built Thirds followed, from 1390-1403, and the Brake Thirds from 1404-1409.

DESIGN FEATURES

Close coupling to reduce end throw and avoid buffer locking was achieved through buffers with short sockets. The buffer projection was 1 foot 5½ inches rather than the conventional 1 foot 10 inches. The screw couplings were also correspondingly shorter. There was no room on the underframe for conventional leaf springing, so the buffer rams bore on india-rubber springs.

The carriages were steam heated and fitted with the Stone's electric light. As the Pickering publicity photograph (Plate 11.12) shows, only the Brake Thirds had dynamos and accumulators – they supplied power to the rest of the train. The accumulator boxes filled the space between the wheels, causing the dynamo to be sited outside the wheelbase.

The Firsts were 28 feet 10 inches long and sat thirty-two in four compartments each just over 7 feet wide. The Thirds had five compartments 6 feet wide seating sixty, so were 30 feet 10 inches long. The Brake Thirds were the same length as the Thirds with three compartments, giving thirty-six seats. A detailed drawing of the Brake Third body is shown in Figure 11.17.

As built, only the Brake Thirds had lower footboards immediately below the guard's compartment. Pickering drawing 10435[14] was for additional footboards, but is annotated 'Not used 18/5/21.' They were not fitted in the Pickering publicity photograph. Photographs of the carriages in service show that continuous footboards were fitted to all classes of carriage. The date of this addition is not known.

Pickering drawing 10192[15] (Figure 11.18) also showed the two types of end, but is marked 'cancelled.' Other Pickering drawings for the First and Brake Third carriages[16] show only the wood-cased ends. It is reasonable therefore to infer that only wood-cased ends were used. There is no contradictory photographic evidence.

The body profile and leg room in the compartments were identical to the contemporary 9 foot wide 57-foot carriages so passenger comfort was not compromised, at least in First class. The extra width compared with the carriages they replaced allowed the Firsts to have armrests between each seat. In the Third class compartments the extra width was deemed sufficient to accommodate six passengers per seat rather than five, as was the case in the 57-foot carriages.

The carriages were renumbered three times by the LM&SR. The stock was withdrawn in May 1952 at the end of its design life, which proves its fitness for purpose. Photographs of all three diagrams were taken on the branch at Juniper Green, just before the carriages were broken up. These are Plates 11.13-11.15.

EXTRA BRAKE THIRDS

Two drawings in the Diagram Book, numbered C1529 and C1530, show a Diagram 2A Third converted to Brake Third

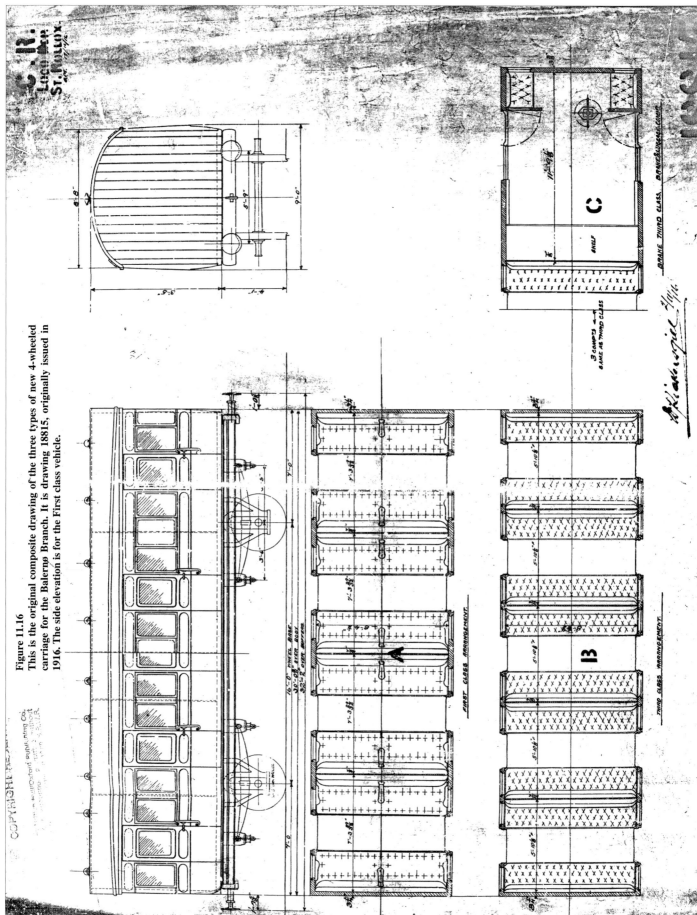

Figure 11.16
This is the original composite drawing of the three types of new 4-wheeled carriage for the Balerno Branch. It is drawing 18815, originally issued in 1916. The side elevation is for the First class vehicle.

by removing two compartments at one end. C1530 had the doors to the guard's compartment as the original Brake Third. C1529 had double doors opening outwards adjacent to the passenger section and a single inward-opening door towards the end. Another drawing, C1533, shows conversion of the end compartment to a smaller Brake compartment with double doors.

This conversion would only have been necessary if the number of set trains on the service had been increased. There is no trace in the Coaching Plant Stock Book of the vehicles concerned, so it is reasonable to assume that the proposals were not implemented.

SERVICE ON THE BRANCH

Just before the new sets were introduced the basic service on the branch required three sets of vehicles comprising three Firsts, five Thirds and two Brake Thirds.[17] Seating capacity was 406, of which 96 were First class. On Saturdays the sets were made up to thirteen vehicles. This was a great improvement on the pre-war service, which had only offered 324 seats, 64 of which were First class. The 1913 marshalling circular insisted that *'All the Ordinary trains ... are worked by three sets of four-wheeled carriages ... consisting of 2 Firsts, 4 Thirds, and 2 Brake Thirds. On Saturdays the Trains to be made up to 18 Vehicles.'*[18]

The Third class carriages that were replaced had fewer seats than their replacements, which enabled the new sets to be marshalled as four Thirds, and two each Firsts and Brake Thirds – the same configuration as in 1913. The sets were strengthened by three Thirds and one Brake Third at peak times; which left only one coach spare of each type.

The standard set's seating capacity was 376, of which 64 were in First class. This was only just short of an equivalent-length train made up of 57-foot stock, which, if marshalled one First, two Thirds and two Brake Thirds, had 400 seats, including 64 Firsts.

REFERENCES
1. *Working Timetable Appendix 1915*, pp. 67-68
2. *Caledonian Cavalcade*, p. 55
3. NRS BR/CAL/1/68 entry 1016
4. NRS BR/CAL/1/69 entry 605
5. St. Rollox 18815, RHP 11200
6. NRM 7529/C RHP to be assigned
7. NRS BR/CAL/1/68 entry 100
8. NRS BR/CAL/1/74 entry 1109
9. NRM 11201/C
10. NRM 7528/C RHP to be assigned
11. Pickering card order 37159
12. Pickering card order 37161
13. Pickering card order 37163
14. HMRS drawing ref: 0158
15. HMRS drawing ref: 0157
16. RYP 10340 (HMRS drawing ref: 0153) and 10346 (HMRS drawing ref: 0159) respectively
17. *Local Working of Carriages July 1921*, p. 17
18. *Local Working of Carriages July 1913*, p. 18

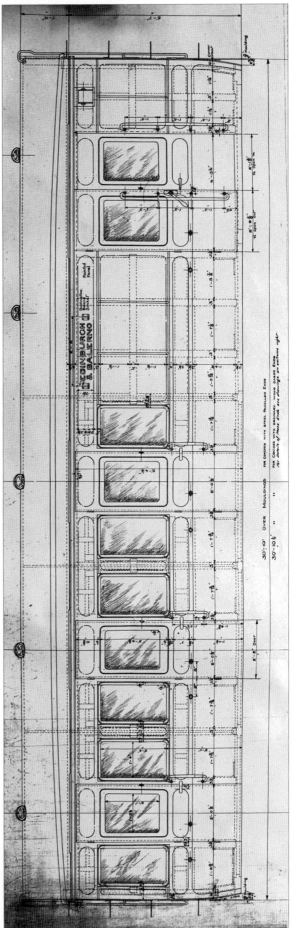

Figure 11.17
Part of St. Rollox drawing 20915 for the Balerno stock Brake Third body. It mentions the two types of end construction. Note also the specification for the painted panelling at the top of the body.

Figure 11.18
This is Pickering working drawing 10192, with details of the application of numbers and Crests. The steel end variation is marked *'cancelled'*.

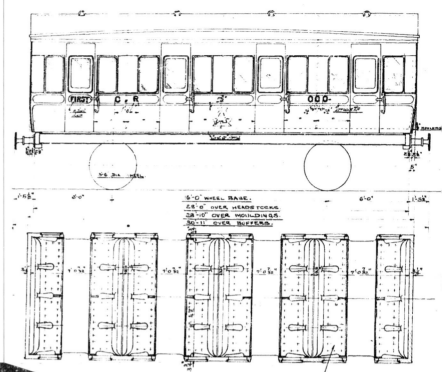

— FIRST CLASS CARRIAGE. —

SEE DRG. Nº 10427 FOR SEATS

Plates 11.13-11.15
All three types of Balerno carriage were photographed at Juniper Green in 1952. First 26056 (*below left*) was originally CR 133, 5-compartment Third 26717 (*below right*) was CR 1392 and Brake Third 27809 (*facing page*) was CR 1409. All were built by Pickering.

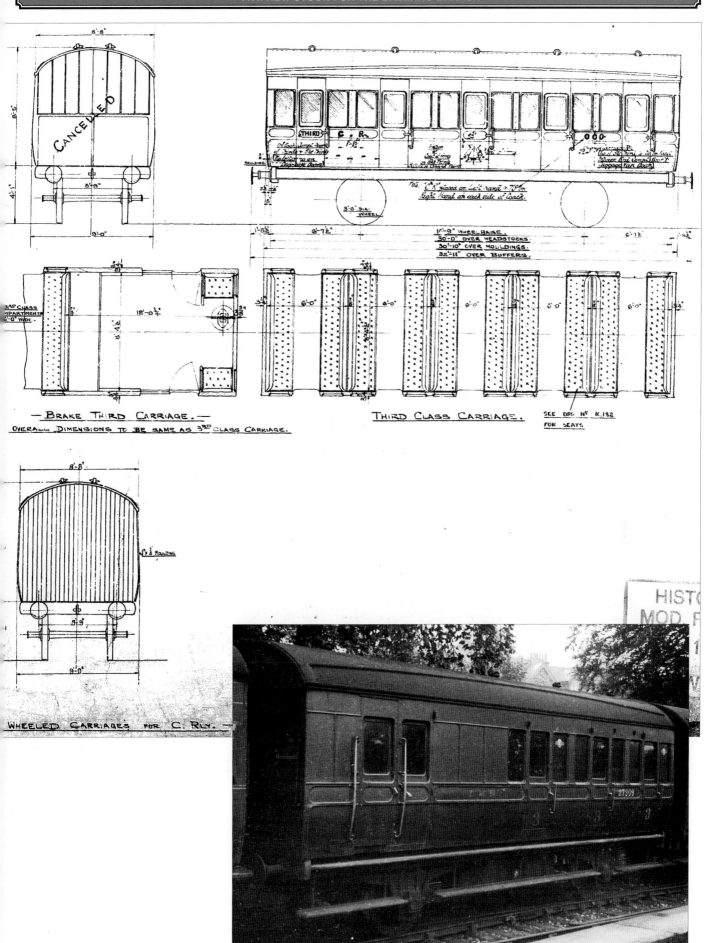

— BRAKE THIRD CARRIAGE.—

OVERALL DIMENSIONS TO BE SAME AS 3RD CLASS CARRIAGE.

THIRD CLASS CARRIAGE.

SEE DRG. Nº IC.182 FOR SEATS

WHEELED CARRIAGES FOR C. RLY.

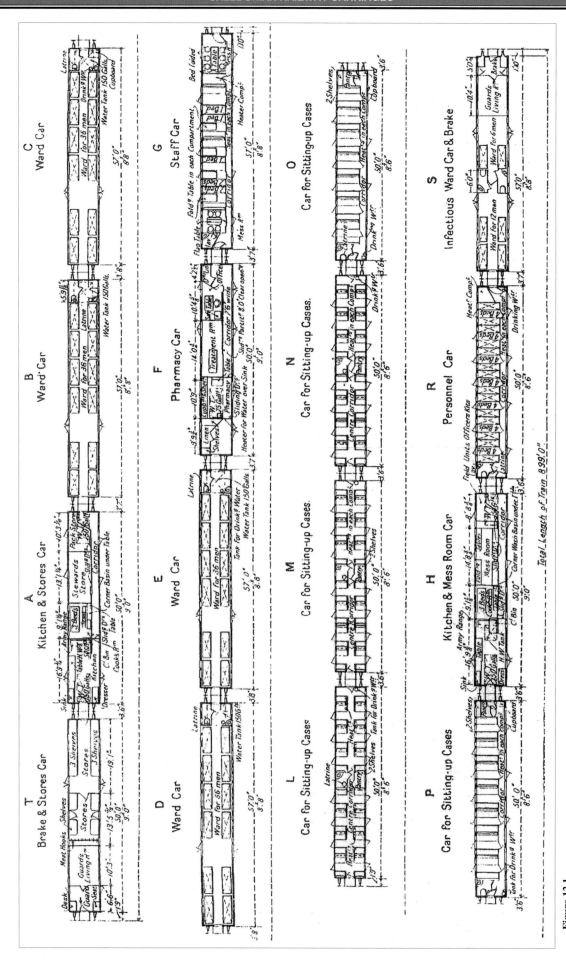

Figure 12.1
St. Rollox drawing 17981 shows the formation of the Caledonian Ambulance Train number 23 and the modifications made to the carriages.

CHAPTER 12
AMBULANCE AND OTHER WAR SERVICE TRAINS

The provision of dedicated ambulance trains developed during various conflicts in the nineteenth century. The first vehicles in the UK carried troops wounded in the Boer War from Southampton Docks to the military hospital at Netley.[1]

The outbreak of World War I resulted in a pressing need for ambulance trains for service on the Continent. This had been foreseen, and the 'Organization of an Expeditionary Force of Six Divisions for Overseas' of 1907 made provision for constructing six ambulance trains.

The very high casualties in the trenches coupled with the inadequacy of French rolling stock created an urgent need for increased provision. The first ambulance train from the United Kingdom arrived in France in November 1914, adapted from existing L&NWR rolling stock.

An 'Ambulance Trains for the Continent Sub-committee' of the Railway Executive Committee was set up, which included William Pickersgill among its members. The sub-committee produced a design for a standard 16-vehicle ambulance train. In April 1915 the War Office requested a further eight trains from United Kingdom railway companies. One was produced by the CR, which had not previously contributed an ambulance train.[2]

CONTINENTAL AMBULANCE TRAIN No. 23

The CR Ambulance Train used existing 57-foot and 50-foot carriages which, apart from the four Passenger Brake Vans and the five cars for sitting-up cases, were subject to considerable

internal alteration, as Figure 12.1 shows. This is a reproduction of St. Rollox drawing 17981, a copy of which is in the CRA archive.[3] The carriages were chosen because they had corridor connections, electric light, steam heating and dual brake systems. The cost of conversion was estimated at £12,000-£13,000.[4]

The drawings for the various modifications were made over a period from May to November, the bulk of them issued between May and August. The drawings have not survived. A full description of the internal fittings in the carriages can be found in an article by L. Tolley in *The True Line*, issue 54, pp. 35-37.

The train's formation from front to rear was as follows:

NUMBER	TYPE LETTER	DESCRIPTION
1 off	T	Brake and Stores Car
1 off	A	Kitchen and Stores Car
4 off	B, C, D, E	Wards for Lying-down Cases
1 off	F	Pharmacy Car
1 off	G	Staff Car
5 off	L, M, N, O, P	Cars for Sitting-up Cases
1 off	H	Kitchen and Mess Room Car
1 off	R	Personnel Car
1 off	S	Infectious Ward Car and Brake

The types of carriage making up the train are shown in the table below. The basic information was contained in some notes made by Graeme Miller, who became the Chief Draughtsman at St. Rollox.

TYPE LETTER	DESCRIPTION	CR NUMBERS	CR DIAGRAM	ORDER
T	50 feet by 9 feet Bogie Brake Van	Not traced	98	H249
A	50 feet by 9 feet Bogie Brake Van	Not traced	98	H249
B, C, D, E	57 feet by 8 feet 8 inches Corridor Brake Third	656, 663, 958, 964	110A	H303
F	50 feet by 9 feet Bogie Brake Van	Not traced	98	H249
G	57 feet by 8 feet 8 inches side Corridor Third	Not traced	110	H297
L, M, N	50 feet by 8 feet 6 inches Corridor Open Third	976, 977, 978	91	H198
O, P	50 feet by 8 feet 6 inches Side Corridor Third	983, 984	90	H202
H	50 feet by 9 feet Bogie Brake Van	Not traced	98	H249
R	50 feet by 8 feet Side Corridor Third	985	90	H202
S	57 feet by 8 feet 8 inches Corridor Brake Composite	Not traced	111	H304

Plate 12.1
Ambulance Train 23 posed behind Class '908' 4-6-0 No. 910. The carriages are painted all-over khaki. The light patches on the sides are red cross symbols on a white background.

These were amplified by Charles Underhill and Niall Ferguson in letters to *The True Line*.[5] Niall submitted further information with corrections and amplifications in a later issue.[6] The carriage numbers, where known, have been cross-checked with the Coaching Plant Stock Book. A posed picture of the train is shown in Plate 12.1.

According to a contemporary report which showed eight interior views and a reproduction of the St. Rollox drawing,[7] the train was 300 yards long, weighed 442 tons and accommodated 454 patients – 162 lying down and 292 sitting up. There were also forty-four officials, made up of two guards, six cooks, four medical officers, four nurses and twenty-eight orderlies.

Inside, the carriages were painted white. The exteriors,

'are painted khaki colour with a prominent Red Cross in the centre of each coach. Each car bears the train number on its sides and ends together with a distinctive letter for identification.'

A preliminary inspection of the completed train was arranged on 26th August 1915 at St. Rollox Works, followed by public exhibitions at centres around the Caledonian system between 2nd September and 2nd October. The first port of call was Glasgow, where the train was open to the public for three days. The poster advertising the event is shown in Plate 12.2.

A full list of the venues is included in Tolley's article. There is also a complete set of the posters advertising the events in the National Records of Scotland archive.[8] An official opening ceremony was performed at each location. A charge of at least one shilling was made for each person inspecting the vehicles, the money going to the Scottish branch of the Red Cross Society. At the Aberdeen exhibition the beneficiary was the Aberdeen Fund for the Transport of Wounded – see Plate 12.3. About 260,000 people inspected the train, and £13,255 was collected.

The train was commissioned at Etaples. It entered service on 3rd March 1916 and conveyed wounded soldiers from railheads at the front to the Channel ports for evacuation to hospitals in the UK. Some details of its exploits during hostilities were recorded by Niall Ferguson in *The True Line*, issue 62, pp. 8-10, where he states that it was demobilised on 14th April 1919.

REPLACEMENT CARRIAGES

When the General Manager sought approval to provide the Ambulance Train on 1st June 1915, he also asked for authority *'to substitute new carriages.'*[9] This was important because the carriages were among the most modern on the system, with electric lighting and steam heat. The Traffic Committee agreed work on the Ambulance Train, but delayed the replacements, remitting the General Manager,

'to obtain definitive arrangement with the Executive Committee as to the replacement (when such work can be undertaken) without loss to this company.'

A recommendation for the calculation of compensation had already been made by the Ambulance trains sub-Committee and accepted by the Railway Executive Committee. It was to be *'the cost of replacing existing vehicles, together with that of fitting and of transport to destination.'*[10] The CR Traffic Committee reported in October[11] concerning the replacement of coaching stock that *'16 vehicles were used in providing the Ambulance Train which were dating back from 1901, that is about 14 years.'*

The new vehicles were not like-for-like replacements, but *'of improved character.'* The four Passenger Brake Vans were not to be replaced. According to the same minute the new carriages were to be:

'2, 57ft Corridor Brake Thirds, 5 compartments
11, 57ft Corridor Thirds, 8 compartments
1, 50ft Semi Corridor Brake Composite, 6 compartment
2, 50ft Semi Corridor Thirds, 5 compartment
All fitted with electric light, steam heating.'

The carriage replacement programme for the period ending June 1916, which was only agreed in the January, included the Brake Vans among seventeen vehicles.[12] They were:

'4, 50ft Corridor Brake Vans, dual brakes
3, 50ft Semi Corridor Composite, 4 First, 3 Third
4, 50ft Semi Corridor Brake Third, 4 compt.
3, 50ft Semi Corridor Brake Composite, 2 First, 3 Third
3, 57ft Semi Corridor Brake Composite, 2 First, 4 Third'

In early February 1916 the Loco & Stores Committee split the contract to build the sixteen Ambulance Train replacements plus the seventeen carriages equally between Hurst, Nelson, the Birmingham Carriage & Wagon Co., and the Metropolitan Carriage & Wagon Co.[13] The agreement to replace the Ambulance Train was countermanded by higher authority, along with the other carriages in the renewals programme. In early April the Traffic Committee reported that:

Plate 12.2
The poster advertising the first exhibition of the train at Glasgow on the first Thursday to Saturday in September. Thousand did respond to the invitation – over a quarter of a million people visited the train in the course of its exhibition tour.

'as the Ministry of Munitions have objected to the work of building the Carriages, orders placed with Metropolitan, Birmingham and Hurst Nelson have been cancelled.'[14]

RETURN OF AMBULANCE TRAIN STOCK AFTER THE WAR

In February 1920 the CR was asked 'if they would be prepared to take back the Ambulance Train consisting of 16 passenger vehicles which they provided in 1915.'[15] The delay after the Armistice may have been due to the fact that, according to a Railway Magazine article written some years later by a soldier who served in World War I,[16] it became the leave train code-named 'Gertrude'. This was one of fourteen trains plying between Calais and Cologne. The Traffic Committee recorded that:

'The Locomotive Superintendent considers it would not be economical to reconvert the vehicles into passenger carrying vehicles. The General Manager recommends that the Company should take back only the underframes and bogies.'

The carriages which were built on the recovered underframes cannot be identified with certainty, but ten each of 50-foot and 57-foot stock were built by St. Rollox in the period ending December 1920 to orders H345-H349.

AMBULANCE TRAIN FOR THE US GOVERNMENT

In April 1917 the USA entered the war and naturally required ambulance trains with their own medical staff. In August 1918, the CR Board authorised the construction of a train for the US government 'subject to suitable conditions of payment.'[17]

Agreement about payment seems to have been reached, as St. Rollox made a large number of drawings against order MD25 between late August and November, numbered in the range 19579 to 19715. None have survived.

There is no record of the train being offered back to the Caledonian. It is reasonable to assume that growing confidence that Germany would be defeated and the imminent signing of the Armistice caused the project to be cancelled. Construction of the train was certainly started, as St. Rollox drawing 19759[18] was for the body of a 57-foot Brake Van and annotated 'converted from ward cars' with the reference MD25. The use of these vans in general service is described in Chapter 11.3.

ROYAL NAVY AMBULANCE TRAIN No. 2

Although this train was not composed of Caledonian stock, it was stabled at Dawsholm and hauled by CR engines. It made a weekly return trip from the south of England to Larbert Hospital which had

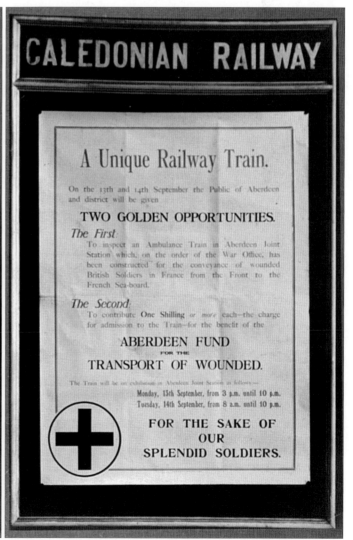

Plates 12.3A and 12.3B
After visiting Glasgow, the train visited Dundee the following Friday and Saturday, and Aberdeen on the next Monday and Tuesday. All the contributions went to the British Red Cross Society, except at Aberdeen.

Plate 12.4
Royal Navy Ambulance Train number 2, posed at Dawsholm. The third, fourth and fifth carriages are West Coast Joint Stock Diagram 13 Family Saloons.

been commandeered as a naval hospital; it also transferred patients to the hospital at Stobhill on the outskirts of Glasgow. It avoided the centre of Glasgow by running via Rutherglen.

The L&NWR had produced the first Naval Ambulance Train and the powers-that-be were so impressed that four more were ordered.[19] Train number 2 entered service in June 1915. It was composed of twelve L&NWR and WCJS vehicles. Livery was 'navy grey.' A full description of the L&NWR-built ambulance trains has been published by the LNWR Society.[20]

The train normally ran at night so that it could not be seen. It was felt that morale would be badly affected if it was seen to run frequently. A posed photograph of the train is shown as Plate 12.4.

The train may also have travelled to the far North. In the spring and early summer of 1918 there was a severe influenza epidemic in the Grand Fleet, which was anchored in Scapa Flow. Over 10,000 people were affected. All the naval hospitals were filled with patients and '500 more, for whom accommodation could not otherwise be provided, were sent to the military hospitals at Glasgow.'[21]

SPECIAL MILITARY TRANSPORT TRAINS

In November 1916, a Traffic Committee minute[22] approved the upgrade of thirty carriages to form two 'special military trains to the South.' The first required the fitting of steam heating to fourteen 6-wheeled Lavatory Thirds, which already had dual brakes. St. Rollox drawing 18878 recorded the modification. Drawing 18891 dated 5th December gave further details. Neither has survived. Both had the order number MD22 included in the drawing register entry.

These Diagram 15 carriages had been built to orders H62 and H66 in 1891. According to the Coaching Plant Stock Book their running numbers were 95, 178, 209, 211, 212, 224, 497, 870-876. The Stock Book gives the date of September 1917 for the fitting of steam heating for seven of the carriages, and no date for the rest.

The second train comprised sixteen bogie Lavatory Thirds, which already had steam heating. In this case vacuum brake gear was required. Drawing 18860 was for the dual brake on 48-foot Lavatory Thirds. Drawing 18881 was for 'vacuum and steam heating on 45-foot and 48-foot carriages.' 18895, annotated order MD23, showed the pipe clip arrangement. None of the drawings has survived.

The carriages were probably the eight 45-foot Diagram 32s built to order H165 in the half year ending July 1898 and the 48-foot Diagram 43s built in the next period to order H169. The running numbers for the 45-foot carriages were 3, 192, 253, 466, 547, 598, 635 and 647. The 48-foot numbers were 68, 75, 436, 499, 502, 525, 538 and 602.

The Coaching Plant Stock Book records all the carriages as dual brake fitted, and implies that they were so fitted when built. The register entry for drawing 18892 produced in December 1916 stated that the arrangement of the dual brake was specifically for 48-foot Lavatory Third carriages, which suggests otherwise.

THE LEAVE AND DEMOBILISATION TRAIN

Two minutes refer to this train. In June 1919 it had been returned from overseas, but the Board reported that:

'The Train requires considerable repair and the Locomotive Superintendent has been instructed to have the work carried out.'[23]

In September the Board received a report on its condition.[24] There are no drawings concerning this train in the St. Rollox register, which leads to the supposition that it was a rake of carriages requisitioned for the purpose. A reference made to the train in the 1933 Railway Magazine article previously quoted said that a rake of CR 6-wheeled coaches formed the demobilisation train.[25] Nothing further is known about the vehicles in question, or how many were involved.

REFERENCES
1. British Railways and the Great War, volume 1, p. 196
2. British Railways and the Great War, volume 1, pp. 203, 208
3. CRA Ref: 3/4/1/6
4. NRS BR/CAL/1/67 entry 464
5. The True Line, issue 56, p. 28
6. The True Line, issue 62, p. 22
7. The Railway Gazette, 24th September 1915, pp. 300-3
8. NRS BR/CAL/4/160
9. NRS BR/CAL/1/66 entry 1029
10. British Railways and the Great War, volume 1, p. 204
11. NRS BR/CAL/1/67 entry 464
12. NRS BR/CAL/1/67 entry 1010
13. NRS BR/CAL/1/67 entry 1136
14. NRS BR/CAL/1/68 entry 100
15. NRS BR/CAL/1/74 entry 468
16. The Railway Magazine, February 1933 issue, p. 127
17. NRS BR/CAL/1/71 entry 1038
18. NRM 7511/C RHP to be assigned
19. British Railways and the Great War, volume 2, p. 567
20. LNWR Great War Ambulance Trains, Premier Portfolio Series No. 11
21. British Railways and the Great War, volume 2, p. 580
22. NRS BR/CAL/1/68 entry 1454
23. NRS BR/CAL/1/73 entry 107
24. NRS BR/CAL/1/73 entry 867
25. The Railway Magazine, February 1933 issue, p. 130

CHAPTER 13
SALOONS, FAMILY AND INVALID CARRIAGES
13.1: EARLY SALOONS AND FAMILY CARRIAGES

Saloons of various types were specialised vehicles which did not regularly run in ordinary service trains. Apart from Officers' and Inspection Saloons, they were usually hired for a particular occasion – often for tourism and leisure. In Scotland, this reached a peak in August, just before the 'Glorious Twelfth,' when households complete with luggage and servants decamped to the grouse moors. Many of the moors were in Highland Railway territory, which necessitated the vacuum brake as well as the Westinghouse system, when continuous brakes were adopted in the 1880s. Another regular use was for football excursions. Supporters travelled in ordinary carriages, while the club committee went in a Saloon.

Because they were 'special occasion' carriages, they did not accumulate a large mileage. As a result, they lasted far longer than their general service contemporaries. In addition they were some of the first vehicles to be fitted with lavatories, and many were luxuriously appointed. As such, they were still acceptable to travellers even when they were life-expired in accountancy terms.

The Coaching Plant Stock Book lists fifty-eight Saloons. Two had been built in 1868 and nineteen dated from the 1870s. Almost all had been renumbered to make way for more modern Saloons, but were still deemed fit for service up to the mid-1920s.

Another valuable source of information is the Saloon Diagram Book. This is dated June 1896 and shows a number of Saloons that were withdrawn prior to the compilation of the Coaching Plant Stock Book. Information on the early Saloons is not complete and in some cases contradictory. It has not been possible to identify positively all the Saloons and assign them to numbers. The four Dining Saloons are discussed in Chapter 9.3.

SALOONS 1 AND 2

Even before the opening of the line throughout from Carlisle to Glasgow, CR Directors reckoned that money might be made by catering for wealthy people wishing to hire an entire carriage for the use of themselves and their family. In May 1847 *The North British Railway & Shipping Journal* reported:

'A novel First Class carriage is to be constructed expressly for through trains between Scotland and England designed by Mr. Sinclair. The body of the carriage will be the usual size divided into two compartments, the one larger than the other. Both divisions will be fitted with cushions, pillows and everything suitable for comfortable lying down full-length. The larger division will accommodate six persons, the smaller one, communicating with the other, is principally intended for ladies and will afford room for two. In this latter division there will be all those conveniences which ladies and invalids appreciate.'[1]

The CR Board, which included a significant Grand Junction contingent, seem to have set out to capture the market in luxury Anglo-Scottish traffic:

'This counterpoise to the "berths" of the Glasgow and Liverpool steamers will draw to the railway numerous families, invalids and others who, without it, would prefer the boat.'

The Saloon was probably the subject of drawing 120. It may have been the first railway carriage to offer sleeping accommodation. Travel by night implies that it would have been oil, or perhaps candle, lit.

The concept of a luxurious private conveyance was obviously successful, as in December of the following year, when the main line had been open throughout for nine months, a second Saloon was constructed at Greenock to a different internal layout, probably to drawing 169. It was designed for day travel, as there is no mention of sleeping accommodation in the description from the same newspaper:

'The contrivance and workmanship reflect the utmost credit on all engaged in its erection … The interior is divided into two parts by a sliding panel, on which are placed two large mirrors. Each apartment is furnished with two roomy and easy armchairs and two convenient sofas, all covered with morocco; in the centre is a folding table, and abundant room is left for passing round it. Altogether each division forms a comfortable and elegant little parlour. The hangings are dark blue edged with white, and the windows are ornamentally stained. Outside the carriage at each end a short platform is fixed on which travellers may get out to enjoy the scenery through which the train passes. While in motion the saloon was extremely steady and altogether we had not previously seen any carriage which combines so entirely every requisite for securing comfort, and in fact luxury, in travelling. We believe such carriages may be at any time specially engaged by parties on the Caledonian line at very little above ordinary fares.'[2]

In fact, hiring a Saloon did not require a supplementary fare. The June 1853 timetable states that *'Parties of not less than Eight (on giving due notice) can have the Use of a Saloon Carriage by paying First Class fares.'*[3]

One Saloon appears to have had a very short life. In January 1849 a fire at Lothian Road station destroyed five carriages, *'including one of the new saloons built at Greenock.'*[4] Apparently the Caledonian immediately rebuilt at least the Saloon, as the half-yearly return to the Board of Trade for June 1849 shows the company as owning two Saloons.

From the almost identical internal layouts in the Saloon Diagram Book[5] (Figures 13.1 and 13.2) and the previously quoted descriptions of the two Saloons, the first built was probably the fire victim and its replacement was built to match the second Saloon, with the interior space equally divided and two end platforms as mentioned in the press report.

Although the original drawings have not survived, one of the Saloons, renumbered 2A, appears in two photographs in the St. Rollox collection at the NRM.[6] Scaling from the photographs, the body was about 6 feet 9 inches to the eaves, much more generous than a Second class carriage[7] built at Greenock at around the same time, which had an eaves height of 5 feet 3 inches.

The 1850 valuation described them as *'2 saloons, Greenock made'* and worth together £1,250. This was half as much again as a First class carriage (valued at just over £389), which gives a clear indication of the high specification and level of furnishing to which these Saloons were built.

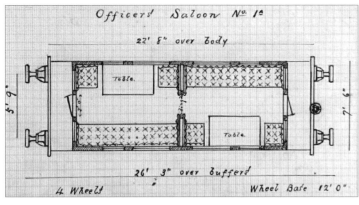

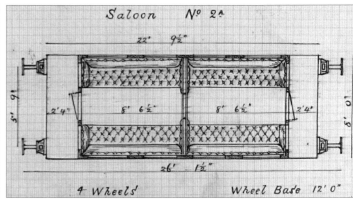

Figures 13.1 and 13.2, Plates 13.1 and 13.2
The first drawing from the Saloon Diagram Book shows Saloon 1A, furnished as an Officers' Saloon. The close resemblance between the dimensions

and internal layout of this Saloon and number 2A in the next drawing suggests that 1A was the replacement vehicle for the original Saloon that was destroyed in the Lothian Road fire. In the second drawing, Saloon 2A is shown as a public service vehicle, but with different furnishings to those originally fitted. The two official St. Rollox photographs show Saloon 2A. The letter A looks newly painted compared with the number. In the first photograph, it is out of use with the windows boarded up. It still has 4-foot diameter wheels with twelve spokes. There is no brake gear. The scroll irons are elaborately shaped, as befits a luxury vehicle. The ornate guard rail offered the only protection around the *'short platform … on which travellers may get out to enjoy the scenery through which the train passes.'* One wonders how many passengers were brave enough to make use of this facility when travelling at a speed previously unknown to man. The second photograph shows 2A back in service as another Officers' Saloon, fitted with clasp brakes and a handbrake stanchion on one verandah. Eyelets for the Harrison cord alarm system have been fitted and curved handrails aid ascent onto the verandahs from ground level. There appear to be curtains to the windows on one side only. The Saloon now has steam heating. The scroll irons have been tied together and are braced to the end of the underframe.

The 1874 Inventory valued the Saloons at £310 each. Using Yarrow's valuation formula, they should have been worth virtually nothing, being twenty-five and twenty-seven years old respectively. They may have seen so little service that the formula, which must have been based on the life expectancy of rolling stock in normal traffic, was considered inappropriate.

In 1884 two West Coast Joint Stock Sleeping carriages were acquired. One of these carriages is known from the Coaching Plant Stock Book to have received number 2 in the Saloon series. It is reasonable to assume that the other carriage was allocated the

number 1. It certainly did not receive the number 3, which went to a Saloon built in 1876. These carriages are described in the next section. It is reasonable to assume that the original Saloons were then duplicated by the addition of an A suffix.

The Saloon Diagram Book shows the two Saloons still in service in 1896, which must have been after the time that one of the St. Rollox photographs of number 2A was taken, as the clearer of the two photographs (Plate 13.1) shows it out of service with the windows boarded up.

In the second (Plate 13.2) it is restored to service with the addition of clasp brakes, Westinghouse brake equipment, a handbrake worked from one verandah and steam heating pipes. The brakes were fitted after 1896, as a handbrake is not shown in the Saloon Diagram Book. Saloon 1A was already fitted with a brake when the Saloon Book was published. It had probably been fitted with continuous brakes and a handbrake in 1882, to drawings 3080 and 3082 which have not survived.

After restoration to service the original CR Saloon number 1 became Officers' Saloon 1A – in this guise it is described in Section 13.5. Number 2, also suffixed A, was still in public service when the Saloon Diagram Book was published in 1896. Its internal layout is shown in Figure 13.2, as it appears on page 2 in the Saloon Diagram Book. The fact that it was later fitted with a handbrake suggests that it followed 1A into departmental use as an Inspection Saloon. Its withdrawal date is unknown. It may have been replaced by either Saloon 1430 or 1431 when they entered departmental service in 1904. Neither of the Greenock-built Saloons is recorded in the Coaching Plant Stock Book.

THE GREENOCK SUGAR BROKERS' SALOON

In July 1859 a *'large Second Class carriage was converted to a First Class smoking carriage.'* This was for the use of the Greenock sugar brokers. McEwan describes it as having two compartments seating nineteen around the sides and the ends.[8] The seats were covered in oilcloth and spittoons were provided. Its livery was said to be *'dull blue externally and white.'* It probably lasted until 1872, when it was replaced by Saloon number 9. This replacement carriage is discussed in Chapter 13.2.

FAMILY CARRIAGE BUILT IN 1862

Saloons 1 and 2 sufficed for the Caledonian's wealthier clientele for some years, as a third Saloon carriage only appeared in the half-yearly return for July 1862. It had been discussed from the start of the previous year, when drawings were submitted and resubmitted in January and February.[9] There is no record of either of these drawings in the St. Rollox register. The minute noting the second submission said that the design was to be *'remitted to the Chairman.'*

The carriage obviously differed significantly from the two earlier Saloons, because it was described as a *'family carriage,'* a new category in the rolling stock returns. It was described as a renewal in the half yearly report to shareholders for January 1863. It was probably numbered 78, as a Loco & Stores Committee minute ten years later refers to a Saloon bearing this number which was deemed to be *'too antiquated for the present fashion.'*[10] The minute recorded the decision to convert it *'into an ordinary Carriage, as proposed, and a new Family Carriage to be built at St Rollox'*.

The 1874 Inventory, which began in February and took just over six months to complete, probably lists the original vehicle as a Saloon, as yet unconverted, among the Composite carriages. Its valuation of £230 was the same as 3-compartment 4-wheeled Composites in the same numbering block, which suggests that the two Second class compartments of a conventional carriage may have been opened up as one and the seating rearranged longitudinally. The body would have been modified by the removal of the redundant compartment door. Conversion back to the original arrangement in 1874 would have been relatively easy.

SALOONS ACQUIRED BY AMALGAMATION

The 1874 Inventory includes four First class carriages with one compartment in each numbered 139, 144, 145 and 197. All were described as Saloons; they were also included in the separate Saloon inventory, but not as such in the half-yearly rolling stock return. The first three of these carriages were probably converted

from Composite to First class in 1857. The process is described in Chapter 5.4, p. 111.

Number 197 was the last in a block of twenty-one 4-wheeled First class carriages which were valued at £260. Sixty First class carriages were absorbed into CR stock from the Scottish Central Railway. The rolling stock return records the acquisition of one Family carriage from the SCR, although the configuration described in the inventory was a simple Open Saloon.

The rolling stock return also shows the addition of a Scottish North Eastern Railway Family carriage in January 1867, although there is no such vehicle in any SNER Board of Trade return. This was probably Saloon number 3.

The 1874 Inventory describes it as having one First class, two Second class and a half Third class compartments. The last named would be for servants, which fits the concept of a Family carriage. It ran on six wheels and was valued at £400. What it looked like is unknown.

Saloon number 3 was replaced during the half year ending January 1877 by another 6-wheeled Saloon, which is described later in this section. Some of the SNER carriages were withdrawn quite soon after acquisition by the CR, so the apparently short life of this Saloon is not surprising.

FAMILY CARRIAGES BUILT IN 1867

On 1st May 1867, Conner was asked to prepare drawings for *'two Family Carriages'*[11] They were to be of different types, because the minute continued *'Approved and authority to build one of each pattern.'* The designs were obviously of special interest. On 28th May the Board of Directors reported that:

> The elevations of the Family Carriages about to be built were submitted and Mr Conner, who was present, received instructions.'[12]

The drawings in question were St. Rollox 793 and 794. The register which records drawings 1 to 5627 (the rewritten version of the original first register and part of the second) lists drawing 793 as *'Family Carriage WC at one end Servants Compt at other end'* and 794 erroneously as *'ditto.'* The entries in the original register listing drawings 1 to 3508 are very faint but read as follows:

> *'793 Family Carraige [sic] w/c at one end, servants compt at other 25 ft. 5ins. long*
> *794 Family Carriage w/c in Centre, servants compt at end 23 ft. long 10/9/67'*

A report from Conner which included a tracing of the preferred design was finally approved at a Board Meeting on 11th June. The minute implies that two options had been reduced to one, which was to be capable of conversion into an Invalid carriage.[13]

The capital expenditure return for the half year ending July 1868 records a charge to St. Rollox for *'two Family Carriages,'*[14] but does not specify the amount, thus making it impossible to relate them with absolute certainty to the list of Saloons in the 1874 Inventory. Their addition does not appear in the rolling stock return.

Their original numbers were probably 4 and 5. The 1874 Inventory records these 4-wheeled Saloons as having one each First and Second class sections, plus a half Third class. They were valued at £440 each.

The CRA's transcription of the Coaching Plant Stock Book suggests that numbers 4 and 5 had identical dimensions and that they were renumbered 1430 and 1431 in 1894 to make way for two Lambie-designed Picnic Saloons. This is contradicted by the Saloon Diagram Book which shows 1430 and 1431 as two different designs on pages 16 and 17 respectively – see Figures 13.3 and 13.4. In fact no dimensions are given against 1430 in the Coaching Plant Stock Book. Both are quoted with a building date of 1868.

The Saloon Diagram Book's two diagrams correspond to the lengths given in the descriptions of drawings 793 and 794. Diagram 16 refers to the 25-foot 5-inch carriage, which by 1896 carried the number 1430. It was 8 feet wide and the wheelbase was 15 feet. Access was through doors wide enough to take a wheelchair into a 2-foot 4-inch wide vestibule towards one end of the carriage with the lavatory at the extreme end. The rest of the Saloon was passenger accommodation with seats along the sides and across the end. There were five large windows to the saloon section.

A partition created a larger and smaller space with a small table in the larger area. This would have been a later addition, as it would have been an obstacle for a wheelchair user.

Diagram 17 was for the short Saloon, although it was 3 inches wider than Diagram 16. It did not conform to the description for drawing 794. It was to the same configuration as the larger Saloon, without the entrance vestibule. This confirms that one design was finally adopted, as the Board minute implies. Access was directly into the saloon area at the centre of the carriage through wide doors. The saloon area had two large windows on each side of the door. Its wheelbase was 13 feet 7 inches. Its number in 1896 was 1431.

Clearly, removal of the interior partitions and alterations to the seats in both carriages had taken place before 1896. The vehicles' role as Invalid carriages was made redundant by the construction of Invalid Saloon 19 in 1889. They may have been remodelled then or when they were replaced by Picnic Saloons in 1893/94 and renumbered. Ten years later they became Officers' Saloons. In this guise they are described in Section 13.5.

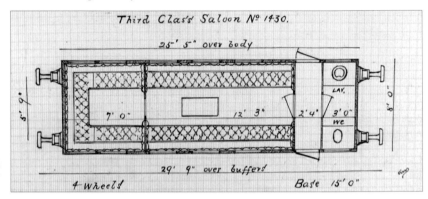

Figures 13.3 and 13.4
Saloon Diagram book pages 16 and 17 show two Third class Saloons which were probably originally Family Saloons 4 and 5, built in the first half of 1868.

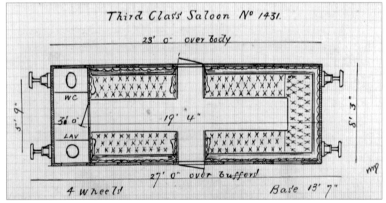

REFERENCES
1. *The North British Railway & Shipping Journal*, 29th May 1847
2. *The North British Railway & Shipping Journal*, 12th December 1848
3. *Time Table No. 70*, CRA Archive ref: 3/1/2/1
4. *The Greenock Advertiser*, 25th January 1849
5. *Saloon Diagram Book*, pp. 1-2
6. NRM St. Rollox collection, SRX 323, 324
7. See Plate 5.1
8. McEwan Archive ref: T25/1/30
9. NRS BR/CAL/1/12 entries 1356 and 1396
10. NRS BR/CAL/1/21 entry 403
11. NRS BR/CAL/1/15 entry 1480
12. NRS BR/CAL/1/15 entry 1578
13. NRS BR/CAL/1/15 entry 1612
14. NRS BR/CAL/23/18

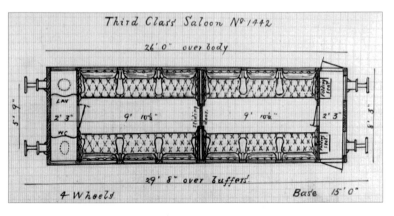

Figure 13.5
Page 19 of the Saloon Diagram Book probably shows the internal layout of Saloon number 7, built by Ashbury in 1872 for service on the Callander & Oban. It now carries number 1442 and is designated Third class, despite the luxurious upholstery.

13.2: SALOONS BUILT IN THE 1870S

In May 1870 the Traffic Committee was asked to consider a *'Family Carriage for the Scottish Central Line.'* The Loco & Stores Committee approved the recommendation on the same day, authorising *'Mr Conner to build a First Class Family Carriage in place of No. 146.'*[1]

It was probably built to drawing 974. Drawing 989 detailed the scroll irons. Subsequent drawings which may have applied to this carriage depicted two versions of a *'Rose, Thistle and Shamrock design for Window of Family Carriage.'*[2] None of the drawings have survived.

There is no mention of a replacement or additional Family Carriage or Saloon in the rolling stock returns for 1870 or 1871. Twenty First class carriages were withdrawn in the period ending January 1871 and two in the subsequent period, but no replacements were recorded. There is no First class carriage carrying number 146 in the 1874 Inventory.

Three Family carriages cannot be positively accounted for in the Saloon inventory. They had four wheels, were First class only and numbered 139, 144, 145. It is possible that the replacement for carriage 146 was one of these three.

SALOONS 6 AND 7 FOR THE CALLANDER & OBAN RAILWAY

The next mention of Saloons was for the Callander & Oban Railway, which in January 1871 had only been opened as far as Glen Ogle summit. It was possible that it would terminate at Tyndrum, as the Callander & Oban Abandonment Act had been passed in May 1870. In March 1871 Conner reported to the Board[3] that *'tenders for a plain Saloon had been ordered to be taken.'* Some time earlier, proposals for a Saloon for the C&O had been produced to drawing 954, which has not survived.

Two months later *'plans were submitted'* to the Loco & Stores Committee which agreed to *'Take tenders for one according to plan and instruct Mr Conner to convert another.'*[4] St. Rollox drawings 1127 and 1141 refer. Drawing 1190 was for a *'safety handrail for Callander & Oban Saloon Carriage,'* which suggests some sort of observation area for one of the vehicles. None of the drawings have survived.

The conversion probably became Saloon number 6. The 1874 Inventory described it as a 6-wheeled Family Saloon with one Second class compartment, a half Third class and a luggage compartment. The valuation was £500.

It was probably scrapped when a 40-foot Invalid Saloon bearing the same number was put into service in 1894. This meant that its dimensions and internal layout were not recorded in the Saloon Diagram Book.

It may have been converted from a Tri-Composite carriage, a number of which were being built at the same time. These usually had two First, one Second and two Third class compartments. It would have been a simple matter to combine the First class and Second class compartments into a saloon, with access through the original Second class compartment to one of the Third class compartments, the remainder being converted into luggage space.

The capital expenditure return for the half year ending January 1872 records an Ashbury Saloon charged at £430.[5] This would probably have been Saloon number 7. According to the 1874 Inventory, where it was valued at £430, it was an all First class

carriage divided into two compartments, which fits the description of a *'plain saloon.'*

It was renumbered 1442 in 1895 to make way for a Lambie First class Day Saloon. It is shown on page 19 of the Saloon Diagram Book, where it is described as Third class, despite the fact that the seats had armrests, and were generously proportioned, as befits a vehicle that was originally First class. It was 26 feet long by 8 feet 3 inches wide. It had four wheels. The wheelbase was 15 feet. The Saloon Book page is shown in Figure 13.5.

Access was by doors at one end to a lobby with two folding seats. At the far end of the carriage, beyond two equal sized saloons separated by a sliding door with longitudinal seating for six passengers in each, was a compartment containing a commode and a washbasin. There were two windows in the end with the entrance.

The Coaching Plant Stock Book records it as oil-lit, fitted with dual brakes and painted with white upper panels. It was withdrawn in June 1919. At some point after the publication of the Saloon Diagram Book the armrests must have been removed, as the Coaching Plant Stock Book records it as having twenty-four seats.

FAMILY CARRIAGE NUMBER 8

In August 1871 a Family carriage was requested *'to be stationed at Aberdeen.'*[6] The Loco & Stores Committee authorised tenders to be taken. In November Metropolitan's tender was accepted. The drawing,[7] dated 1st November, is shown in Figure 13.6. The price was £509 10s and it was stipulated that the vehicle was to be delivered within two months.[8] An additional Saloon appeared in the half yearly return for the period ending January 1872, but it was not charged to the capital account until the next period.[9] It was valued at £510 in the 1874 Inventory.

The Saloon was 28 feet 4 inches long and 7 feet 8½ inches wide on a 6-wheel underframe with a wheelbase of 18 feet. It was divided into two compartments, one 9 feet long, and the other 19 feet 4 inches. The smaller one was for servants. At the end there was an area 4 feet deep for luggage, then a door and a bench seat, backing onto the other compartment, upholstered to Second class standard.

The main compartment was subdivided into three areas. The largest was 13 feet 6 inches long and in it, backing onto the servants' compartment, was another bench seat, with two armrests. A bench seat ran along each side of the compartment and continuous with the transverse seat.

In the middle of the central space was a drop-leaf table, and at the opposite end was a transverse door which gave access to an entrance vestibule 2 feet 4½ inches wide where the carriage doors were located. Beyond that area was another transverse door to a compartment 3 feet long, containing on one side a washbasin in a vanity unit and on the other a commode.

Externally the Saloon differed in style from the contemporary compartment carriages. There were only two doors per side and they were not quite symmetrically placed. Between each door and the carriage end was a single large window, approximately 3 feet across, one illuminating the lavatory and the other the luggage space. Between the external doors there were five more such windows, identical in size, one in the servants' compartment and the others in the principal saloon.

Above all the windows were individual working ventilators and in

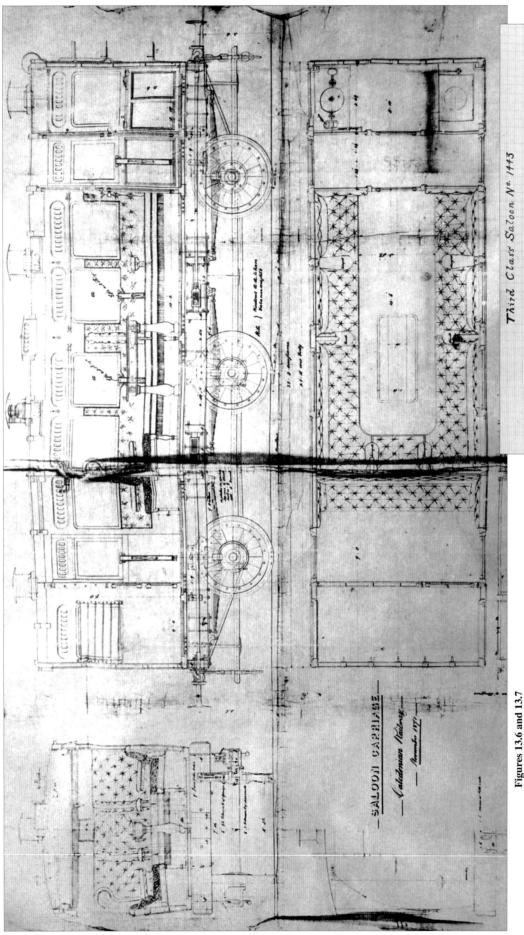

SALOON CARRIAGE

Caledonian Railway

Third Class Saloon Nº 1443

28' 4" over body

31' 4" over buffers

Wheel Base 18' 0"

6 Wheels

Figures 13.6 and 13.7
The Metropolitan works drawing (*above*) is in very poor condition but is included here to show the original interior furnishing of Family carriage number 8 'to be stationed at Aberdeen.' It has been redrawn by John Boyle (*facing page*). The internal layout (Figure 13.7, *right*) is from page 20 of the 1896 Saloon Diagram Book after the Saloon had been renumbered to 1443 one year earlier. It was downrated to all Third class and an additional bench seat was fitted in the original luggage compartment after the partition was removed.

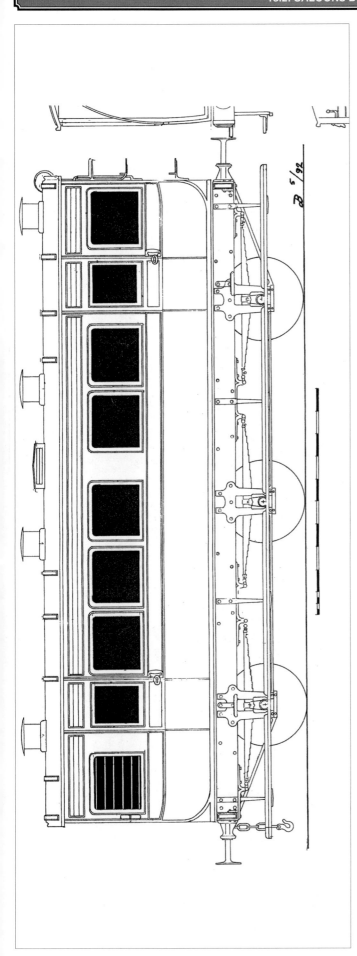

the middle of the principal saloon there was a rotating roof ventilator, operated by the motion of the train. The main saloon had two roof lamps, and there were two others, one for the servants' compartment and the other for the lavatory.

The Saloon was originally number 8. It was renumbered 1443 in 1895 to make way for a Diagram 58 First class Day Saloon. As recorded on page 20 of the Saloon Diagram Book one year later, it had been derated to Third class by the removal of the arm rests from the large saloon – see Figure 13.7. Capacity was increased by an additional transverse seat in what had been the luggage area. According to the Coaching Plant Stock Book it was gas-lit and dual braked. It was withdrawn in June 1921, in all-over brown livery.

SALOON CARRIAGE 9 FOR GREENOCK

In May 1872 it was decided that a Saloon carriage was needed for use on the Greenock line but, instead of asking for tenders from outside contractors, the vehicle was to be built at St. Rollox.[10] It may have been the response to a complaint by Greenock sugar brokers, whose business with the Caledonian merited the dedicated carriage discussed in Chapter 13.1. In February 1872[11] the Traffic Committee had recorded the need for a replacement, estimated cost £300. *'The present carriage is a low one and the Brokers complain that it oscillates considerably.'* The half-yearly return for January 1873 shows one Saloon worn out and replaced, which supports the theory.

The St. Rollox drawing was number 1273, which has not survived. The Saloon was probably allocated number 9. In the 1874 Inventory, where it was valued at £430, this Saloon was recorded as having six wheels and two First class compartments. According to the Coaching Plant Stock Book it was renumbered 1444 and was downrated to Third class. It had been superseded by one of the four Diagram 58 Lambie Day Saloons built to order H120, which were added to the fleet in July 1895.

Page 9 of the Saloon Diagram Book still has it as a First class Saloon so the change of class must have happened after 1896. It was 30 feet long by 8 feet 3 inches wide, with a total wheelbase of 18 feet 6 inches. Access to the compartments was by two doors each side, towards the centre of the carriage. It was dual brake fitted. The Coaching Plant Stock Book records its eventual withdrawal as November 1919. It was oil-lit to the end and was painted with white upper panels.

FIRST CLASS SALOON 10

This Saloon was built by Metropolitan and entered on the capital return during the half year ending January 1875,[12] but after the inventory was completed in November 1874. It was entered as an addition in the rolling stock return. The Loco & Stores Committee authorised it in May 1874 as a replacement, at a cost of £662.[13] The entry in the Capital expenditure return does not record the cost, which suggests that it was, rightly, not charged to capital.

Renumbered 1445 according to the Coaching Plant Stock Book, it appeared on page 9 of the Saloon Diagram Book, which also includes Saloon number 9. The Coaching Plant Stock Book gives carriages 9 and 10 identical seating patterns. These two facts suggest that they were the same design. A Metropolitan drawing[14] for a Caledonian Saloon is dated 2nd June 1874 – see Figure 13.8. It shows a carriage with the internal layout to page 9 of the Diagram Book. The furnishings mark it as First class. The drawing is annotated *'No. 294.'* This may be a works order number – the highest numbered First class carriage in the 1874 Inventory was 241.

Like number 9, it was recorded as oil-lit, dual brake fitted and painted with white upper panels. It was withdrawn in 1923. It did not appear in the January 1921 Stock List, which suggests that it was already stored out of use. The twin compartments with no internal communication between the two were not very convenient, which probably accounts for its removal from traffic.

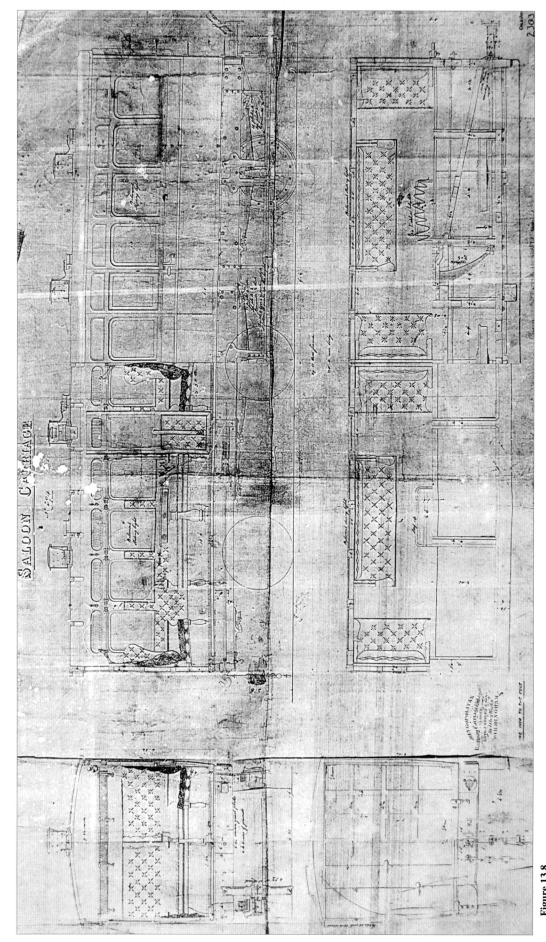

Figure 13.8
This is Metropolitan drawing 2303 for the Saloon which became CR number 10 and subsequently 1445. It was probably identical to the Saloon that was built for the Greenock sugar brokers three years earlier in 1872.

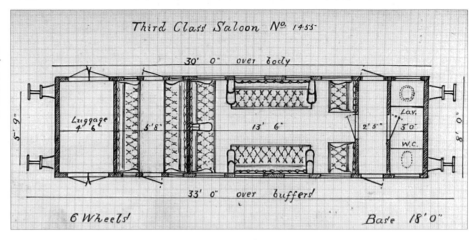

Figure 13.9
The internal layout of Saloon 1455, originally Family Saloon number 11. It is on page 21 of the Saloon Diagram Book. The configuration is typical of a Family Saloon with First class accommodation (and access to the only lavatory) at one end, a servants' compartment and a luggage section.

FAMILY SALOON 11, REPLACEMENT FOR SALOON 78

Saloon 78 was deemed unfit for purpose in December 1873, when its replacement with a new Family Saloon was approved.[15] Drawing 1658, which dates to the middle of May 1874, probably refers to this vehicle, as a Loco & Stores Committee minute in late April 'sanctions the building of a saloon carriage.'[16] As the original Saloon was converted to an ordinary carriage it would have retained its number. The new carriage would have been allocated the next number in the Saloon series. The drawing has not survived, but the register entry refers to it as 'Saloon Carriage No. 10.'

It seems that the Metropolitan-built Saloon, although authorised slightly later, was completed first and thus 'jumped the queue' in the numbering sequence. Instead of number 10, the St. Rollox Saloon would have received number 11. This is substantiated by the Coaching Plant Stock Book, which records this Saloon as entering service in the half year ending July 1875. Although there is no corresponding entry in the half yearly return, a Family carriage is recorded as a replacement in the half year ending January 1876.

It was superseded in the Saloon number series by a Diagram 57 Family carriage which entered service in the half year ending January 1895. It was renumbered 1455 and appeared in this guise on page 21 of the Saloon Diagram Book – see Figure 13.9.

The diagram shows a 30-foot by 8-foot carriage with a wheelbase of 18 feet. Its layout is for a Family Saloon, with a luggage and servants' compartment at one end. The main saloon was entered through a vestibule which also gave access to a lavatory and washbasin at the end of the carriage.

The Coaching Plant Stock Book transcription records its withdrawal date as 1924. It was oil-lit, dual brake fitted and painted with white upper panels.

COUPÉ-LIT SLEEPING SALOON 12

In February 1875 the CR began, with L&NWR approval, to investigate an alternative form of Sleeping carriage 'somewhat on the model of those used by the Eastern Railway in France.'[17] It was probably intended from the outset to run in connection with the steamer from Larne to Stranraer which was first established in 1872. The CR had been operating the line since 1864 with the L&NWR's blessing.

Plans of a Coupé-Lit carriage were submitted to the Board within a fortnight[18] and it was agreed that one carriage should be built as soon as possible. The plans had been obtained direct from France. The Traffic Committee 'Read a letter from Messrs G. Devaux & Co. London asking for a payment of 5 or 10 guineas on behalf of Mr Saunce for his trouble in obtaining the plans of the Coupé-Lits on the French Lines' and decided to 'remit 5 guineas.'[19]

St. Rollox started work to drawings 1834-1836 and 1846, which have not survived. In August, Conner reported that the carriage would take another two months to complete.[20] It was charged to the capital account in the half year ending January 1876 at £776 6s 1d.[21]

The carriage seems to have had a short life in its original state. In August 1877, St. Rollox drawing 2229 was for a 'Composite carriage of two Sleeping, one First and one Third Class compts.' This carriage was certainly built, as it is referred to in other drawings[22] as 'Number 12 Sleeping Carriage.' It may have been treated as a rebuild of the 1875 carriage, as there is no mention of it in the rolling stock returns.

As built, there was no lavatory. West Coast Joint Stock quotes a Joint Committee minute of May 1878[23] which noted that:

'It was agreed to make the usual extra charge for sleeping in Caledonian coupé-lit carriage No. 12, now running between Stranraer and Euston although not provided with a lavatory.'

This was rectified in March 1879 when drawing 2513 was issued for 'Lavatory and w/c for Number 12 Sleeping Carriage.' A drawing[24] issued in September the previous year, for a lavatory only, seems not to have been implemented.

The 1880 Working Timetable[25] states that the carriage ran on the through service to Euston which left Stranraer at 8.30pm. It was 'provided with Pillows, Rugs and Lavatory Accommodation.' The carriage must have worked turn and turn-about with a similar WCJS Sleeping Saloon. The use of more than one 'sleeping carriage' is mentioned in West Coast Conference minutes.[26]

The L&NWR Public Timetables for November 1881, 1882, 1884 and April 1885 confirm the working, with minor variations in timings.[27] The train from Stranraer was added at Carlisle to the 4.40pm departure from Aberdeen. It left Carlisle 12.15am, arriving Euston at 8.00am. Northbound, the service left Euston at 9.00pm, arriving Stranraer at 8.55am.

Number 12 was probably used on the Stranraer service until 1885, when the Caledonian's 21-year agreement to run the Portpatrick line expired, to be replaced by a service run under joint ownership by the CR, G&SWR, L&NWR and the Midland Railway.

Carriage number 12 on page 12 of the Saloon Diagram Book (Figure 13.10) had a lavatory compartment at one end and a luggage box at the other, with a completely open saloon in between. Access was via one door on each side into a lobby at the lavatory end. Presumably the inside of the Sleeping carriage had been gutted, and the space originally occupied by beds was furnished with a long bench seat on either side. The Saloon's number was taken by a 48-foot Third class Saloon built in the half year ending January 1899. The Coaching Plant Stock Book does not record the ex-Sleeping Saloon, so it was probably withdrawn when the new number 12 entered service.

REPLACEMENT FOR SALOON 3

The Third class Saloon recorded in the Coaching Plant Stock Book as originally numbered 3 was built in 1876. There are no minutes concerning this carriage. The rolling stock return for July records the withdrawal of one Family carriage and its renewal in the next six-monthly period. As discussed in Chapter 13.1, the first number 3 was probably acquired from the Scottish North Eastern Railway.

Its replacement was built to St. Rollox drawing 1944, dated 24th January 1876, which has not survived. On page 10 of the Saloon Diagram Book (Figure 13.11) it is shown as a 30 foot long vehicle running on six wheels with an 18-foot wheelbase. Its main dimensions and internal configuration were identical to those of Family Saloon 13, which is described below.

Saloon number 3 became 1414 in April 1899, when the last of the three 48-foot Third class Saloons entered service. It was withdrawn in 1921, painted with white upper panels and gas-lit.

FAMILY SALOONS 13 AND 14

In March 1878, Cravens tendered successfully to supply 'two Family Carriages and Two Invalid Carriages' at £520 each,[28] which duly appeared in the capital expenditure return for the half year ending January 1879. The tender had been authorised in the previous November,[29] when the carriages were described as 'of the LNWR pattern.' The Family Saloons received numbers 13 and 14. The Invalid Saloons, which are described in the next sub-section, were numbered 15 and 16.

It is probable that at least three of these carriages was built to St. Rollox drawings 2323 and 2324 (for an Invalid carriage, 6 wheels) and 2325 and 2326 (for a Family carriage). The pairs of drawings, for the interior and exterior in each case, were dated 26th and 29th January 1878 respectively.

Figures 13.12 and 13.13 (pages 5 and 6 of the Saloon Diagram Book) show different internal layouts and door arrangements for the two Family Saloons, although they shared a common length and wheelbase (30 feet and 18 feet on six wheels respectively).

The close resemblance between the layouts of Saloons number 3 and 14 might suggest that number 14 was built to a slightly modified version of the drawing for Saloon number 3, and that the pair of drawings referred to above were for Saloon 14.

They were renumbered 1420 and 1421 in 1899 to make way for a bogie Third class Saloon and Family Saloon respectively. The Coaching Plant Stock Book records their withdrawal date as June 1921, by which time 1420 had been fitted with electric light. 1421 remained oil-lit to the end. Both had white upper panels.

INVALID SALOONS 15 AND 16

The Invalid Saloons' body and wheelbase were shorter than the Family Saloons, although still mounted on six wheels. In common with other Invalid Saloons, the doors giving access to the bed area were wide enough to accommodate wheelchairs. The internal layout is shown on page 8 of the Saloon Diagram Book (Figure 13.14).

The transcription of the Coaching Plant Stock Book follows the order list by stating that they were converted to Third class Saloons in 1892 to order H77, describing them as 'old Family Carriage.' This cannot be correct, as the Saloon Diagram Book, which is dated June 1896, still describes them as Invalid Saloons and shows them fitted with a bed.

The Stock Book records that number 15 was renumbered 1422 to make way for the second of the McIntosh clerestory roof Family Saloons, which entered service during the half year ending January 1900. Number 16 retained its original number until withdrawal.

Both were oil-lit and had white upper panels. They were withdrawn in June 1919.

SALOONS 20-27

As part of the tender for the Family and Invalid carriages, the minute records that Cravens also secured an order for 'eight First Class and Saloon Carriages' at £391 each. Comparison of the unit prices of these vehicles and the Family and Invalid Saloons identifies them as shorter vehicles, having four wheels. The capital expenditure return for July 1878 records the acquisition from Cravens of four Saloons at a unit price of £771. By this time, Saloons were included with Composites in the half yearly returns, so it is difficult to identify either type positively. There is, however, an entry for January 1879 for the addition of four carriages in this category. There is no record anywhere of four Saloons large enough to cost £771, so one can only assume that a clerical error occurred, and in reality twice the stated number of Saloons were acquired at half the unit price.

Six of the original numbers are recorded as 69, 72, 73, 75-77. The eight carriages were renumbered 20-27 into the next vacant numbers in the saloon series in January 1895 and recorded as such in the index of the Saloon Diagram Book (Plate 1.6) one year later. The page of the Saloon Book is shown in Figure 13.15.

A single door on each side was located towards one end of the body. The Coaching Plant Stock Book and the Saloon Diagram Book describe them as 'Third Class saloons.' They may have had the armrests removed at the time of renumbering. Number 26, old number 72, was converted into an Inspection Saloon in 1911. It is described and illustrated in Chapter 13.5.

Saloons 24 and 27 were not traced in the Coaching Plant Stock Book transcription. Two Composites or Saloons were deducted from stock in the July 1904 return, which may refer to these carriages – perhaps they were accident victims. Numbers 20, 21, 23, 25 were still in traffic in the January 1921 Stock List. The final two (numbers 20 and 21) were withdrawn in January 1924. The Saloons were oil-lit, unheated and painted brown.

REFERENCES
1. NRS BR/CAL/1/18 entries 682 and 696
2. St. Rollox 1044/8
3. NRS BR/CAL/1/19 entry 288
4. NRS BR/CAL/1/19 entry 378
5. NRS BR/CAL/23/1 (30)
6. NRS BR/CAL/1/19 entry 960
7. Birmingham City Archive ref: MS99 2283. CRA Archive ref: 6/1/1/2/6
8. NRS BR/CAL/1/19 entry 1310
9. NRS BR/CAL/23/1 (29)
10. NRS BR/CAL/1/20 entry 8
11. NRS BR/CAL/1/19 entry 1591
12. NRS BR/CAL/23/2 (52)
13. NRS BR/CAL/1/21 entry 1288
14. Birmingham City Archive ref: MS99 2303. CRA Archive ref: 6/1/1/2/13
15. NRS BR/CAL/1/21 entry 403
16. NRS BR/CAL/1/21 entry 1217
17. NRS BR/WCC/1/7 minute 1358
18. NRS BR/CAL/1/22 entry 429
19. NRS BR/CAL/1/22 entry 626
20. NRS BR/CAL/1/2 entry 1104
21. NRS BR/CAL/23/2 (53)
22. St. Rollox 2422, 2443 and 2513
23. NRS BR/WCC/1/7 minute 1614 (3)
24. St. Rollox 2422
25. NRS BR/TT/S/54/7
26. NRS BR/WCC/1/7 minute 1635
27. NRM ALS4/132/D8
28. NRS BR/CAL/1/24 entry 456
29. NRS BR/CAL/1/24 entry 8

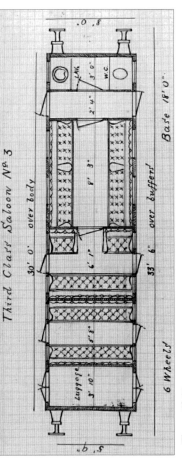

Third Class Saloon Nº 3

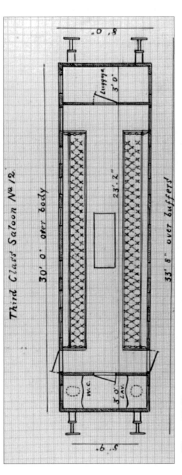

Third Class Saloon Nº 12.

Figure 13.10
This is carriage 12, also page 12 of the Saloon Diagram Book, by which time it was a Third class Saloon. It was originally the CR's only Sleeping carriage, and ran from Stranraer to London during the period when the Caledonian operated the Port Patrick Railway. It was probably withdrawn in late 1898, when it was replaced by a 48-foot Saloon.

Figure 13.11
Page 10 of the Saloon Diagram Book refers to Saloon number 3, built in 1876. It became 1414 in April 1899.

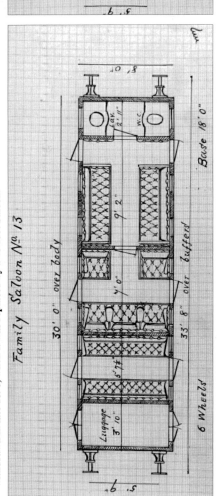

Third Class Saloon Nº 14.

Family Saloon Nº 13

Figures 13.12 and 13.13
These two drawings are pages 5 and 6 of the Saloon Diagram Book. They refer to Family carriages 13 and 14, built by Cravens in the latter half of 1878. Saloon 13's internal layout is similar to that of Saloon number 3, shown in Figure 13.11. Saloon 14's internal layout may have been altered at some point before the publication of the Saloon Diagram Book, as it does not conform to the accepted configuration for a Family Saloon.

This is page 8 of the Saloon Diagram Book, depicting the two Invalid Saloons built by Cravens at the same time as Family carriages 13 and 14. The doors to the main saloon are wider than normal to allow wheelchair access.
RIGHT: Figure 13.15
This drawing from page 13 of the Saloon Diagram Book shows the very simple internal layout of the eight Saloons built by Cravens at the same time as the Family and Invalid carriages. By the time the Diagram Book was published they were down-rated to Third class, probably by the simple removal of the armrests.

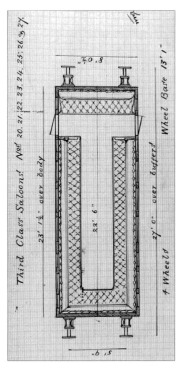

Third Class Saloons Nº 20, 21, 22, 23, 24, 25, 26, & 27.

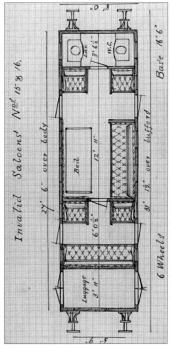

Invalid Saloons Nº 15 & 16.

13.3: DRUMMOND AND LAMBIE SALOONS AND FAMILY CARRIAGES

Drummond's two Third class Saloons must have been authorised during the second half of 1885, as drawings 4702 (for panelling and framing)[1] and 4717 (the general arrangement)[2] were dated mid- and late November respectively. There is no minute authorising their construction, which was executed to order H11.

The carriages were assigned to page 50 of the Large Diagram Book – see Figure 13.16. The underframe and general body style were consistent with the standard Drummond 35-foot 6½-inch by 8 feet wide 6-wheeled carriages, but the small number of doors allowed larger windows. A photograph is shown as Plate 13.3.

They were numbered next in sequence as 17 and 18, so they did not replace two carriages in the Saloon number series. They were not charged to the capital expenditure account. The July 1886 rolling stock return records two carriages replacing two *'worn out'* Saloons or Composites. The old vehicles may have been 144 and 145, which were described as Saloons in the 1874 Inventory, but are otherwise unaccounted for.

There was a luggage compartment at one end, then two large saloons with longitudinal seating separated by a partition and door with external doors at one end only. A lavatory and washbasin separated by a central passage and a compartment on the end completed the interior. Seating capacity was twenty-five. Steam heating was added in 1905, to drawing 13101. The two vehicles survived until 1928 and 1929, having been renumbered 15316 and 15317 by the LM&SR.

EX-WEST COAST JOINT STOCK CARRIAGES 101 AND 104

In 1884 the Caledonian acquired two of the four pioneer 6-wheeled Sleeping carriages, which had apparently not been a great success during their ten years on Anglo-Scottish services.[3] One was recorded in the Coaching Plant Stock Book as number 2. The other probably received the number 1, replacing the two pioneer Saloons described in the section 13.1, which were not withdrawn but received duplicate numbers 1A and 2A.

Plate 13.3 and Figure 13.16
Drummond's Diagram 50 Third class Saloons were built to the same general style as his 6-wheeled carriages for general service, as can be seen in Plate 13.3. The torpedo ventilators are unusual for CR carriages of this era. The gas recipients (CR terminology) were located transversely.

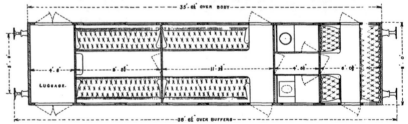

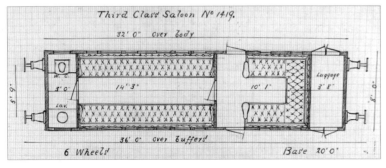

LEFT: Figure 13.17
Two of the pioneer WCJS Sleeping Saloons were acquired by the Caledonian in 1884 and converted into Third class Saloons. One survived to appear on page 15 of the Saloon Diagram Book as number 1419.

The carriages acquired by the CR were converted to Third class Saloons. The toilet and lavatory compartments were removed from one end and replaced by an enlarged luggage compartment. A pair of doors replaced the original windows. The rest of the interior was remodelled as two saloons. This layout appeared on page 15 of the Saloon Diagram Book (see Figure 13.17).

It is not known how long the Saloon assumed to be number 1 survived, but, as its companion, renumbered 1419, is the only 32 foot long vehicle in the Saloon Diagram Book, it must have been withdrawn before 1896. The vacant number 1 was taken by ex-WCJS Composite 293 when it was converted to the Inspection Saloon known as the 'Blue Saloon' in 1902. This Saloon is described in section 13.5.

Number 2 was renumbered following the construction of the two Diagram 57 Family carriages in 1893 which are described below. The Coaching Plant Stock Book gives a withdrawal date of 1921. That was the date it ceased revenue service, but it was not broken up. St. Rollox drawing 21249, dated 30th July 1921,[4] shows its conversion to a 'travelling dormitory for tradesmen.' Its eventual scrapping date is not known.

INVALID SALOON 19 AND HORSE-DRAWN CARRIAGE

A 40-foot Invalid Saloon to order H50 was authorised in December 1889.[5] St. Rollox drawing number 6182[6] is dated 25th December. A minute noting that gas lights were to be fitted in April 1890[7] suggests that construction was well advanced before Drummond's resignation. Pintsch's offer for five lights and two reservoirs at £25 was accepted. It was charged to the capital account during Smellie's tenure in the half year ending January 1891, at a cost of £885.[8]

Two versions of the furnishings in an identical internal layout are included on page 56 of the Diagram Book, where it was described as a 'bogie saloon.' It is assumed that the lower diagram (reproduced

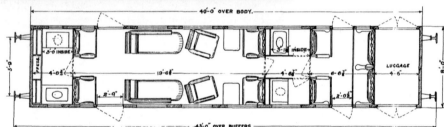

Plate 13.4 and Figure 13.18
The figure shows the internal layout of Diagram 56 Invalid Saloon number 19. Plate 13.4 is an exterior view of the Saloon, taken at Dundee West. The wide door which allowed wheelchair access is at the far end.

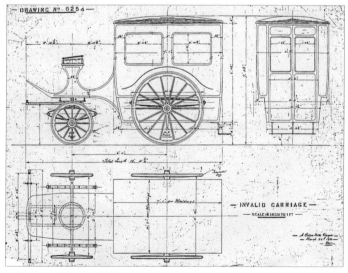
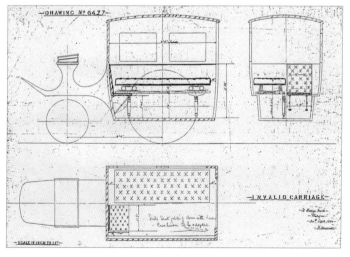

Figures 13.19 and 13.20
The 'street invalid carriage' associated with Saloon number 19 is shown here. It would have fitted easily on a short Open Carriage Truck, twelve of which had been built in 1889. The interior view was drawn six months later. The hand-written annotation reads 'side seat folding down with loose cushion to be adopted.'

DRAWING N⁰ 6899

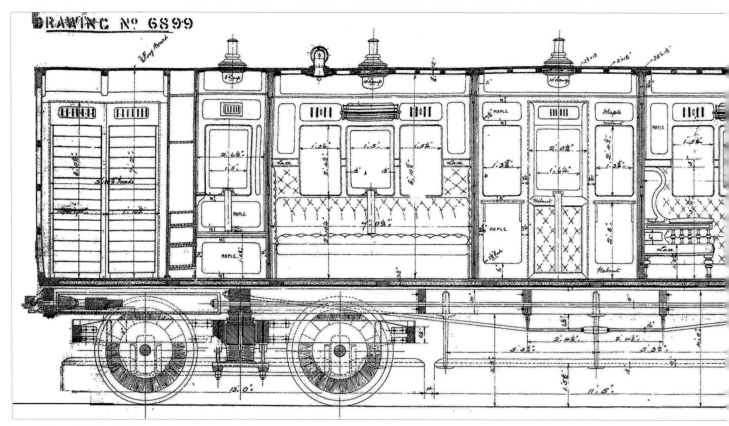

Figures 13.21 and 13.22
A pair of St. Rollox drawings showing the interior and exterior elevations of the Diagram 57 Family Saloon, two of which were built in 1892.

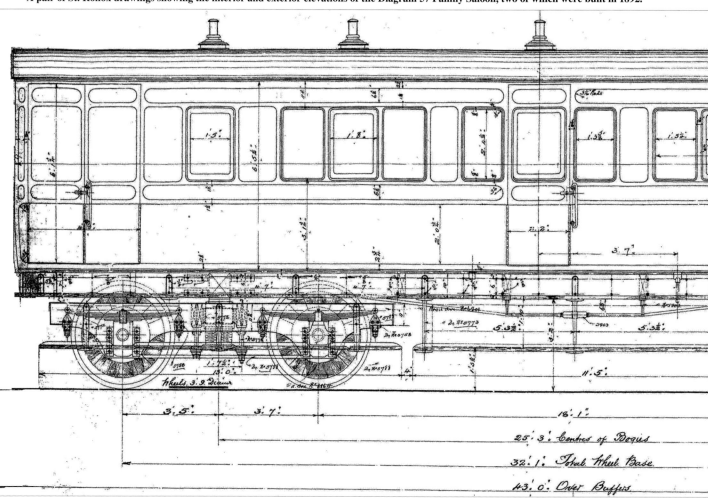

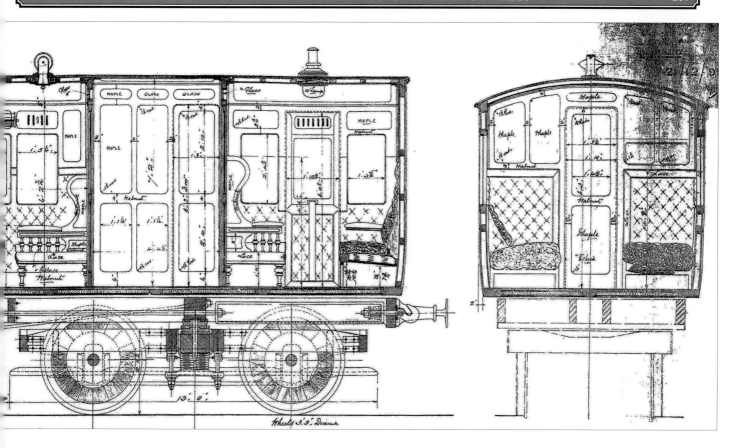

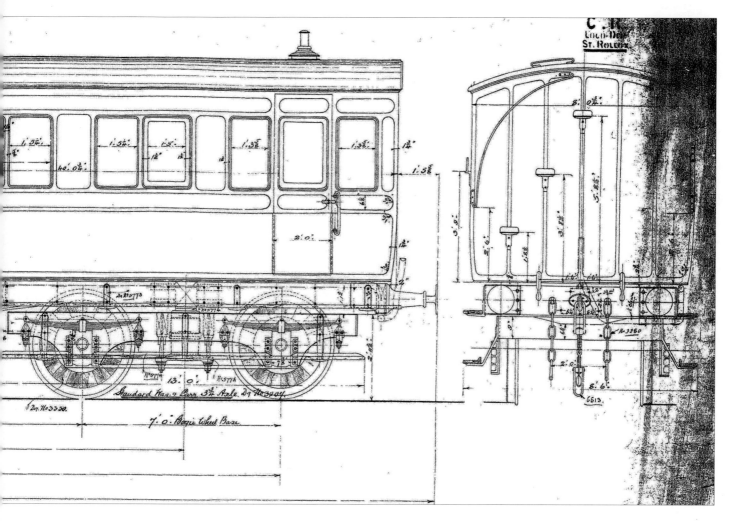

Figures 13.23 and 13.24
The Diagram 57 Family Saloons were numbered 1 and 2. Another example, numbered 11, was built in 1894. Figure 13.24 (*below*) is an enlargement to show the elaborate veneering which was a feature of these carriages. This example is in the ladies' lavatory. It and the equivalent gentlemen's facility merited separate detailed drawings. The plan of the interior layout (*right*) is taken from the Large Diagram Book.

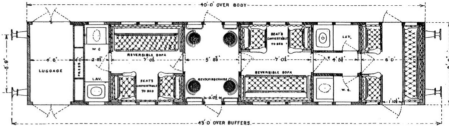

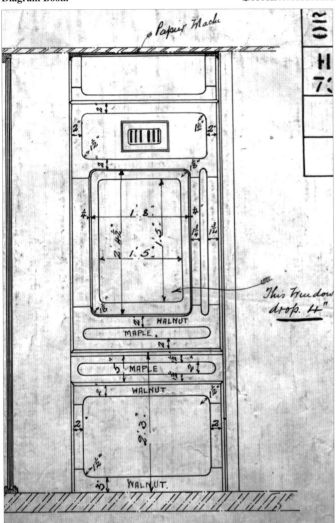

as Figure 13.18), which is annotated with the running number and order number, was the version that was actually adopted.

There was a lavatory and washbasin at one end, a large saloon, a further lavatory and washbasin, a servants' compartment seating six and a separate luggage compartment. The large saloon was accessed through 2-foot 9-inch doors to accommodate a wheelchair. The furniture included chaises longues but the series of official photographs show a single bed on one side.[9] The Coaching Plant Stock Book says '*4 Rocking Chairs, 2 couches and 2 end seats.*' It received the number 19. An exterior view is shown in Plate 13.4. After the Grouping it was renumbered 15318 and was withdrawn in 1929.

A horse-drawn vehicle was built to order H53, described in the Coaching Plant Stock Book transcription and on St. Rollox drawing 6240 as a '*street invalid carriage.*' This drawing has not survived, but two other drawings (6254 external details and 6477 internal (Figures 13.19 and 13.20 respectively) have survived.[10] It was charged to the capital account in the same period as the Invalid Saloon at £135.

This is the only example of a non-rail vehicle built to a rolling stock order number and charged to capital expenditure. This suggests that the two vehicles were conceived as a package to transport an invalid from home to, for example, a sanatorium or hydropathic establishment. It raises the intriguing possibility that the road carriage might have travelled on a Carriage Truck to transport the patient when the destination was reached.

FAMILY CARRIAGES 1, 2 AND 11

Two Diagram 57 40-foot Family Saloons were authorised in the rolling stock replacement programme for the half year ending January 1892,[11] but only entered service in the period ending January 1893, according to the rolling stock return. They were built to St. Rollox drawings 6899 (sectional elevation and plan, Figure 13.21)[12] and 6901 (outside elevation and underframe, Figure 13.22).[13] The drawings, which date from December 1891, are entitled '*Family Carriage with Sleeping Accommodation.*' A further sectional drawing, number 6912, has not survived. The order number was H73.

They seated sixteen First class passengers plus six Third in the servants' compartment at one end. Two First class saloons were each furnished with a pair of seats which could be pulled out to form a bed on one side and a longitudinal reversible sofa on the other. The Coaching Plant Stock Book's annotation was '*Four sleeping berths can be made up in this carriage.*'

There was a central compartment with exterior doors. On drawing 6899 this space was empty, but in the Diagram Book, four revolving chairs are shown – see Figure 13.23.

There were two lavatories and associated washbasins. One, near the end luggage compartment, was for the exclusive use of First class passengers. The other was off a short central corridor that connected the First class saloon to the servants' compartment. The two drawings detailing the panelling for the facilities were designated as '*ladies*' and '*gents*' (St. Rollox 6976 and 6979 respectively).[14] The larger of the two, between the First class saloon and the servant's accommodation, was the ladies. This is shown in Figure 13.24.

They were numbered 1 and 2, replacing the ex-West Coast Joint Stock Third class Saloons which had been acquired in 1884. Number 1 was renumbered 31 in 1902 to make way for the 'Blue Saloon,' as described in Chapter 13.5.

Saloon number 11 was built to the same drawings, and was authorised for construction in the half year ending January 1895.[15] It replaced a 30-foot Third class Saloon built in 1875, which was renumbered 1455. Annotations on the interior plan view on drawing 6899 specify that 2½ inch torpedo ventilators were to be fitted to order H115, which refers to this Saloon. Page 3 of the Saloon Diagram Book also shows numbers 1, 2 and 11 as the same design. This corrects an error in the transcription of the Coaching Plant Stock Book which suggests that it was built to the same design as Saloons 7-10 described below.

All three Saloons were approved for conversion to '*ordinary Third Class carriages*' in a minute of December 1919, which also authorised conversion of Dining cars 38 and 39, plus Saloons 32 and 36.[16] The Coaching Plant Stock Book records number 2's conversion date as March 1922. A second Diagram 57 in the Large

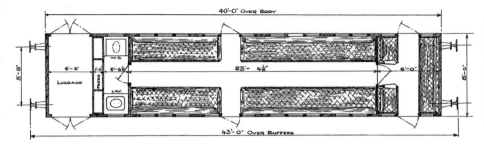

Figure 13.25
This shows the alterations to the interior of the Diagram 57 Saloons. The large lavatory compartment was removed and fixed bench seating was fitted. Although the conversion was authorised in 1919, number 2 was only converted in 1922 and the conversion of the other two Saloons had not been carried out at the beginning of 1921.

Book annotated *'Alteration to 40' 0" Family Saloon No. 2'* records this event – see Figure 13.25.

The conversion dates of numbers 11 and 31 were not recorded, but had not happened by January 1921, according to that year's Stock List. The Stock Book records the conversion of number 11 with no date. There are two diagrams in the Large Diagram Book – a separate page marked *'Page 57'* and Diagram 57A. The only difference is that in Diagram 57A the lavatory is increased in length with a corresponding reduction in the saloon area.

Both diagrams show the same configuration – the luggage compartment and the servants' compartment at the other end were retained but the rest consisted of longitudinal seating. This involved the removal of the large lavatory and washbasin compartments. The lavatory compartment at the luggage end retained. A flush toilet and washbasin fed by a tank were fitted rather than a commode and washbasin.

The two Saloons were renumbered 15302 and 15311 respectively at the Grouping. Number 1, as 31, was withdrawn in 1925 without receiving an LM&SR number. Number 11 lasted until 1929; number 2 survived for four years longer.

PICNIC SALOONS 4 AND 5

Two Third class Picnic Saloons were built to order H102 and St. Rollox drawing 7344.[17] They replaced First class Open Saloons 4 and 5, which were built in 1868. They were probably among the 28 *'coaching vehicles'* authorised as replacements for the half year ending January 1894.[18] The old Saloons were renumbered 1430 and 1431, and used as Officers' Saloons at Perth and Carlisle. In this role they are described in Chapter 13.5.

The new Picnic Saloons were on page 51 of the Diagram Book. Dimensions were a throwback to the Drummond regime. The body was 35 feet 6½ inches by 8 feet wide with a 6-wheel underframe. The wheelbase was 23 feet. The simplified Lambie panelling style was used – see Figure 13.26. A poor quality photograph of one of the Saloons is shown in Plate 13.5.

Internally the layout was symmetrical with lavatory at the end, transverse seating with a gap to give access to the lavatory, external

doors, then longitudinal seats to a centre partition. Seating capacity was thirty-two. They were withdrawn in 1928 and 1931, carrying numbers 15304 and 15305.

INVALID SALOON 6

At the same time as the Picnic Saloons were under construction, Lambie built a Saloon to the same design as Drummond Saloon 19 that had appeared three years earlier. It had two-layer panelling compared with three layers of the Drummond original. Plate 13.6 is an official photograph of the interior and 13.7 of the exterior.

Presumably it too was among the *'28 coaching vehicles'* mentioned above that were authorised for the half year ending January 1894. It was built to order H103. The original drawing seems to have been re-used – the only drawings in the register pertaining to H103 are for the altered external panelling (St. Rollox 7331) and 7392 for *'photos parcel rack etc.'* Neither has survived.

It was assigned to page 56A of the Diagram Book (Figure 13.27). Compared with Figure 13.18 a sink and heater replaced the lavatory accommodation at the end of the carriage. The only other difference to the internal layout was access to the luggage box from the servants' compartment, resulting in one less Third class seat.

This Saloon replaced a 6-wheeled Saloon dating from the early 1870s which was presumably withdrawn as it did not receive a duplicate number. The new number 6 was withdrawn in 1929, carrying the number 15306.

DAY SALOONS 7-10

Four Day Saloons were authorised for construction as renewals in the half year ending July 1895.[19] The minute described them as *'First Class Bogie Day Saloon, 2 compartment & Lavatory at each end, dual brake.'* They replaced Third class Saloons dating from the early 1870s, which were renumbered 1442-1445.

The St. Rollox general arrangement drawing for these Saloons was number 7719[20] and the order number was H120. The drawing only shows the inside of the carriage body and its framing. The interior drawing, number 7725, has not survived. They appeared on page 58

Plate 13.5
The photograph is cropped from a postcard view of Larbert. One of the Diagram 51 Third class Picnic Saloons is immediately behind the locomotive. Even in this poor quality view the torpedo ventilators are very apparent.

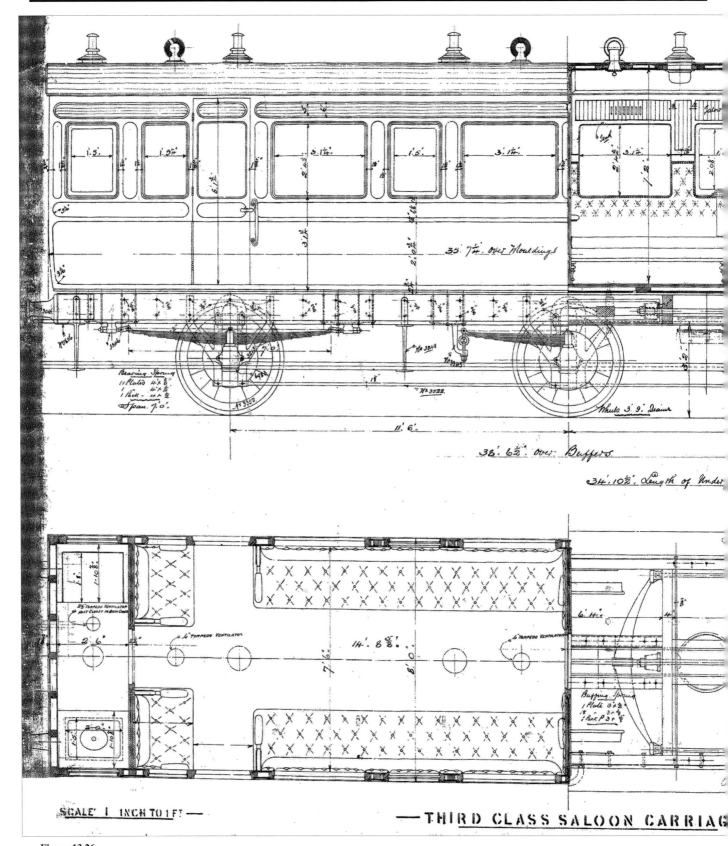

Figure 13.26
St. Rollox drawing 7344 was for a pair of Diagram 51 Third class Picnic Saloons built in the second half of 1893. The dimensions were to the standard introduced by Drummond, but the panelling was simplified in Lambie style. Torpedo ventilators were unusual at this stage in CR carriage history.

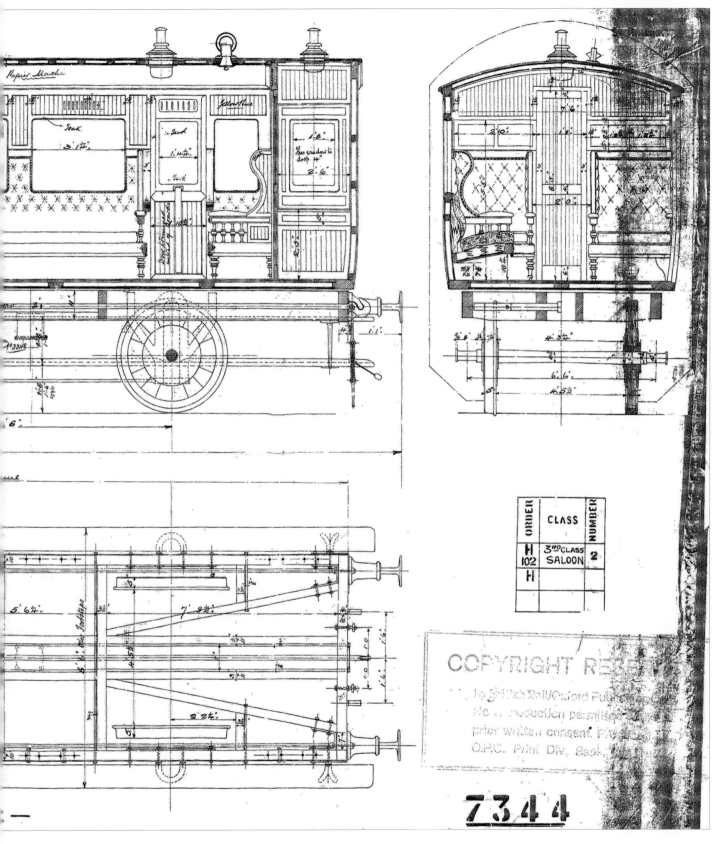

ORDER	CLASS	NUMBER
H 102	3RD CLASS SALOON	2
H		

7344

of the Large Diagram Book. This is reproduced as Figure 13.28. Although they were entered on the index page of the Saloon Diagram Book, no drawing was produced for them.

According to the Coaching Plant Stock Book, two were trimmed (that is, upholstered) in blue cloth, one in crimson velvet and the fourth in old gold crisp cloth. The Register states that numbers 8-10 were reclassified at an unknown date as Thirds, still with twenty-four seats. The 1921 Stock List records them all as *'First Class.'* Numbers 7 and 8 were fitted with heating in 1905.[21]

The Saloons were renumbered 15307-15310 by the LM&SR. Number 15308 was withdrawn in 1927, followed a year later by 15307 and 15310. Number 15309 lasted until 1929.

REFERENCES
1. NRM 7523/C (on two sheets) RHP 70024
2. NRM 7521/C (on two sheets)
3. *West Coast Joint Stock*, p. 66
4. NRM 11227/C
5. NRS BR/CAL/1/33 entry 852
6. RHP 68430
7. NRS BR/CAL/1/33 entry 1388
8. NRS BR/CAL/23/7 (34)
9. NRM St. Rollox collection SRX 310-11
10. NRM 11391/R RHP 70054 and NRM 11388/R RHP 70057 respectively
11. NRS BR/CAL/1/34 entry 1217
12. NRM 7462/C RHP 70070
13. NRM 7464/C RHP 70072
14. RHP 67698 and 67699
15. NRS BR/CAL/1/38 entry 77
16. NRS BR/CAL/1/74 entry 22
17. NRM 7522/C RHP 70082
18. NRS BR/CAL/1/36 entry 616
19. NRS BR/CAL/1/38 entry 77
20. NRM 7524/C RHP 70092
21. NRS BR/CAL/1/51 entry 595

RIGHT: Plate 13.6
One of several views in the NRM St. Rollox collection of the interior of Diagram 56A Invalid Saloon number 6. It is distinguishable from Diagram 56 by the split seating in the furthest compartment which allowed internal access to the luggage section. This photograph is SRX 311. The wheelchair is parked where a small table extends into the interior. Presumably it was arranged to drop down. The opposite table is in the horizontal position. A bed has replaced one of the chaises longues and the armchair moved to the other end of the bed. The blanket has 'Caledonian Rly' and 'Glasgow' woven in script lettering. The elaborate decoration is noteworthy.

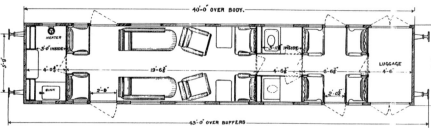

LEFT: Figure 13.27
This shows the differences between Diagrams 56 and 56A. The later layout gave internal access to the luggage compartment, and a sink and heater replaced the end lavatory.

BELOW: Plate 13.7
The exterior view of a Diagram 56A carriage, with the simplified panelling introduced by Lambie – compare this with the three-layer panelling on the Drummond-built Saloon in Plate 13.4.

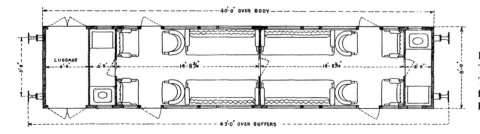

Figure 13.28
The interior layout of the Diagram 58 Day Saloon. The surviving drawing only shows the interior framing of the carriage body and there is no known photograph.

13.4: McIntosh Period Saloons

Prior to 1900, McIntosh built a small number of Saloons as replacements for carriages built in the late 1870s which were approaching the end of their design lives. The new Saloons were all bogie vehicles. Except where stated they benefitted from heating. All were dual brake-fitted. Nine carriages acquired from the West Coast Joint Stock in the early 1900s are also described in this section.

THIRD CLASS SALOONS 3, 12 AND 13

Three 48 foot long Saloons were authorised in the half year ending January 1899[1] to order H170 and St. Rollox drawing 8991.[2] They appeared on page 59 of the Diagram Book (Figure 13.29). Numbered 3, 12 and 13, they replaced 30-foot Third class Saloon 3 (renumbered 1414) and Family Saloon 13 (renumbered 1420). The old Third class Saloon number 12 which was originally built as a Sleeping carriage was scrapped.

Two minutes in 1899 suggest that Stones & Co. fitted two with electric light.[3] There is no reference to the third carriage. The drawing shows that they were intended to be lit by gas. The Stock Book and the 1921 list record them all as gas-lit.

Two saloons were entered by doors towards the end of the body. The internal layout was symmetrical with two centre lavatories separating the saloons and a luggage compartment at each end. According to the Diagram Book each carriage seated thirty-six. The Coaching Plant Stock Book and the 1921 Stock List give the capacity as forty-two seats. This was probably achieved by removing the large armrests seen in the Diagram Book.

They lasted until the early 1930s, receiving LM&SR numbers 15303, 15312 and 15313.

FAMILY SALOONS 14 AND 15

McIntosh's two Family Saloons were grand affairs – the only carriages built at St. Rollox with clerestory roofs. They were authorised for construction in the half years ending July 1899[4] and January 1900[5] to order H175 at a cost of £1,400 each. The only design of Family Saloon in the WCJS fleet was under construction at the same time, and there is more than a passing resemblance between the CR- and Wolverton-built carriages.[6] An example of the WCJS Diagram 13 design on CR metals is shown in Plate 13.8.

As originally authorised they were to be 48 feet long, but the minute extract for the second carriage has 50 feet added in pencil.[7] The St. Rollox GA drawing was 9631, which has not survived, but a modeller's drawing is shown as Figure 13.30. They replaced a Third class Open Saloon and an Invalid Saloon, which were renumbered 1421 and 1422 respectively.

The Saloons appeared on page 60 of the Diagram Book – see Figure 13.31. According to the Coaching Plant Stock Book, number 14 was upholstered in green cloth, and 15 in old gold. In June 1899, John A. Wood Ltd. made an offer to supply moquette for the upholstery. The offer was accepted 'to the pattern selected 8s 6d per yard 52 inches wide.'[8] This represents over £40 at today's prices.

The 1906 Working Timetable Appendix reported that the Saloons 'have been fitted with curtains round the Sleeping Berths' and that boxes to store them when the Saloons were used for day services had been placed under the seat in the servant's quarters.[9] The berths in question were the reversible sofas and the 'seats convertible to bed' on one side of the carriage.

Number 15 was based at Edinburgh on photographic evidence; it is believed that number 14 was based at Glasgow. The Saloons were sometimes commandeered for inspection purposes. They had windows in one end and are described in the Coaching Plant Stock Book as fitted with a 'gas ring' which made them suitable for the duty. Two St. Rollox official photographs, one of which is shown here as Plate 13.9, record one of the Saloons on an inspection of the westward extension of the line from Comrie round to Balquhidder in 1905. They did, however, lack steps for access at track level, as will be seen in Plate 13.10.

It is possible that Saloon 14 was fitted with a corridor connection at one end. In October 1917, drawing 19252 was issued, entitled 'gangway for saloon 14.' It has not survived. Diagram 60 in the Large Diagram Book does not show a gangway.

The Saloons were allocated, but did not carry, LM&SR numbers. The Coaching Plant Stock Book gives their withdrawal date as 1926. This may have been when they left revenue service and became travelling dormitories, each for fourteen people. The furnishings and

ABOVE: Plate 13.8
This shows a partial view of the WCJS diagram 13 Family Saloons which were built at the same time as the two McIntosh Saloons, 14 and 15. The photograph was taken at Ballachulish.

LEFT: Figure 13.29
Three Third class Saloons were built to Diagram 59.

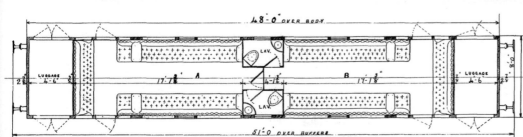

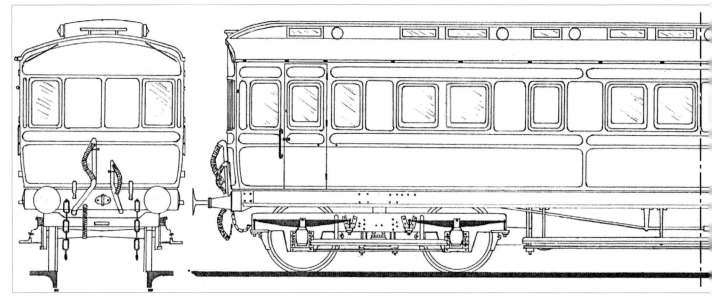

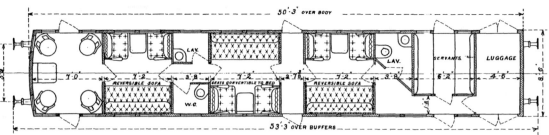

Figures 13.30 and 13.31
Peter Bunce drew the side and end elevations of the Diagram 60 Saloon. He also drew an interior layout, but this has been sacrificed to include the official version (*left*), which describes the furnishing.

lavatories were replaced by pairs of bunks one above the other. This arrangement also appears on page 60 in the Large Diagram Book, reproduced as Figure 13.32.

THIRD CLASS SALOONS 28-30

Two 6-wheeled Day Saloons and one Sleeping Saloon were taken over by the Caledonian from the West Coast Joint Stock in 1899. The first, renumbered CR 28 (WCJS Diagram P11) had been built in 1875. The carriages that received CR numbers 29 and 30 were built a year later to diagram P12. They were 32 feet long with a total wheelbase of 20 feet.[10]

The CR converted the carriages into Third class Open Saloons. The new internal layout of number 28 is not recorded, but numbers 29 and 30 appeared on page 53 of the Large Diagram Book – see Figure 13.33. The lavatory and toilet compartments had been removed from one end. All the seats were removed, including the transverse seats that formed the division into two saloons. The resulting open space was filled with benches along the sides and at one end, providing thirty seats. One pair of doors was also removed.

By the time that the Diagram Book was compiled, number 28 was not included, although the Coaching Plant Stock Book records it as being in service until 1925. The 1921 Stock List records all three carriages, with number 28 steam heated. The remaining two Saloons also lasted until just after the Grouping according to the Coaching Plant Stock Book, but were not assigned LM&SR numbers.

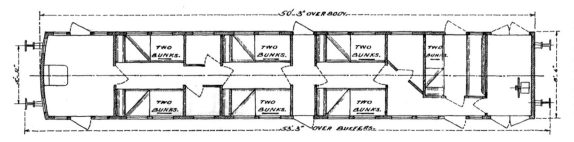

LEFT: Figure 13.32
Although strictly outside the time-frame of this book, page 60 of the Large Diagram Book shows the eventual conversion of the McIntosh Family Saloons to travelling dormitories.

RIGHT: Figure 13.33
These are ex-WCJS Saloons acquired by the CR, renumbered 29 and 30, and extensively modified to become Diagram 53 Third class Saloons.

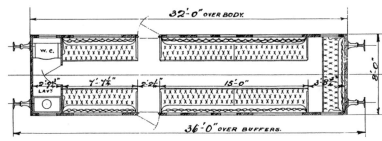

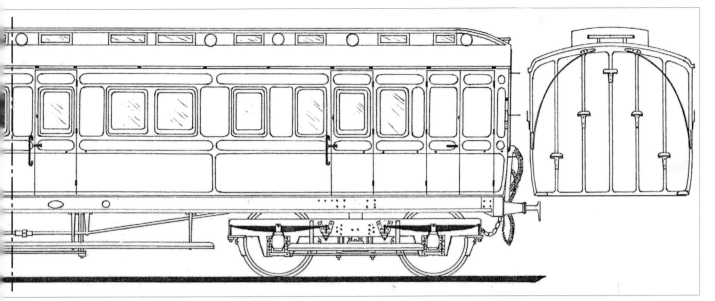

Plate 13.9
This photograph is SRX 182 in the NRM collection. It shows 4-2-2 No. 123 on an inspection trip over the newly-built extension of the Crieff and Comrie line round to Balquhidder. It is posed on the bridge at Dundurn, just east of St. Fillans. The second carriage is as interesting as the Family Saloon. It is a Diagram 22 Brake Composite, four of which were built in 1890 and a further four in early 1897. This carriage has a three-figure number, so it is either 103 or 155 of the latter order.

Plate 13.10
A group of high heid yins posing in front of Saloon 14. Its lack of low level footboards, compared with those on Saloon number 1, is an obvious drawback to its use as an Inspection Saloon. Number 14 differed from number 15 in having a full stop after the word 'SALOON' – see the illustration in *Caledonian Railway Livery*, p. 249.

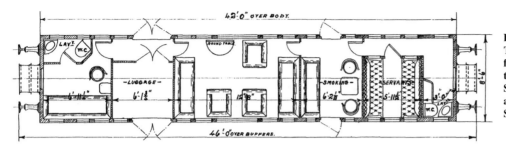

Figure 13.34
The Saloons to Diagram 61 were converted from WCJS Sleeping Saloons. Although the diagram describes them as First class Saloons, the accommodation for servants and luggage clearly marks them as Family Saloons.

42-FOOT SALOONS

Fifteen 42-foot Sleeping Saloons became surplus to WCJS requirements in 1904. The six assigned to the Caledonian were built to three different Wolverton diagrams, but were converted by the Caledonian into two types of Saloon. The first type involved CR numbers 32, 36 and 37; the second type comprised carriage that became CR 33-35.

SALOONS 32–37

Caledonian numbers 32, 36 and 37 were originally WCJS diagram P10 Sleeping Saloons that were marshalled in pairs with a corridor connection at one end only. Four were built in 1883-85 with radial trucks, but 8-foot L&NWR bogies were fitted at some time during the following decade.[11]

The Caledonian gutted the interior to provide three First class Saloons, a luggage compartment and accommodation for servants. The blank end was fitted with a corridor connection, which entailed the remodelling of the lavatory and washbasin compartment at that end of the carriage. The modifications were to drawing 12549, which has not survived. The drawing register says that they were converted to Day Saloons.

They were assigned to page 61 of the Diagram Book (Figure 13.34) where they were described as 'First Class Saloon.' The Coaching Plant Stock Book describes them as 'Corridor Family Saloon' and gives their withdrawal dates as 1925/26.

By then, numbers 32 and 36 were supposed to have been converted into Third class carriages to St. Rollox order MD34. This was authorised in December 1919,[12] but the 1921 Stock Register still records all three as 'Family Carriages.' There was no drawing of the modification, and the new layout was not recorded in the Diagram Book. They were all given LM&SR numbers in the Saloon series. These facts suggest that the conversion was not in fact carried out.

SALOONS 33-35

The three cars renumbered by the CR 33-35 were originally converted to Picnic Saloons with two slightly different internal layouts, although the Diagram Book merely describes them as 'Third Class.' A drawing of one of these Saloons as altered to run on bogies is in *West Coast Joint Stock*, pp. 204-5.

The CR's alterations to the body were detailed in drawing 12479, which has not survived. Externally the single doors to the attendant's area were replaced by double doors, giving direct access to a luggage locker on one side and to a small lobby on the other, which was all that remained of the original side corridor which ran between the two entrance doors

Saloon 33 had only one private section by the luggage locker, which was marked 'smoking or ladies' on Diagram 65 – see Figure 13.35. The other end of the carriage had a longitudinal seat on one side and movable chairs on the other.

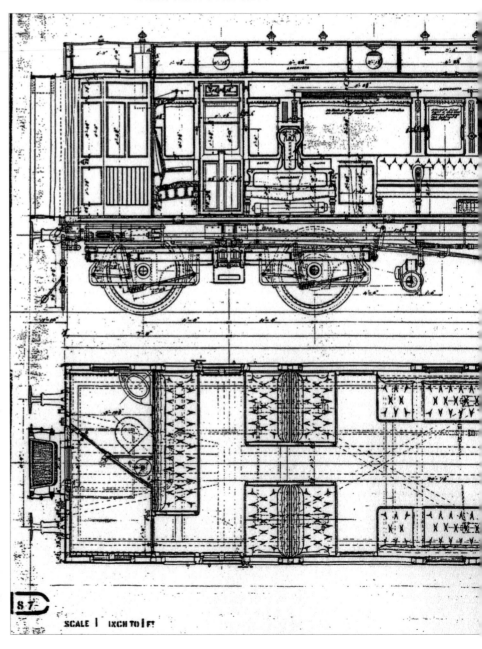

SCALE 1 INCH TO 1 FT

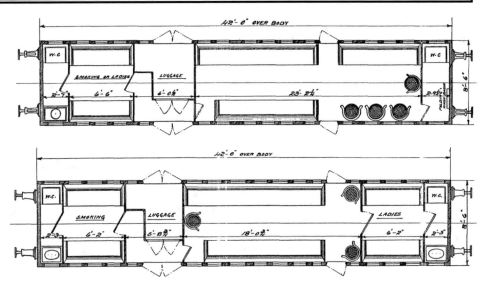

Figures 13.35 and 13.36
Diagrams 64 and 65 had the same alterations to the body on acquisition by the Caledonian, but the internal layouts differed. Diagram 65 shows the alterations to WCJS Sleeping Saloon 264, which became CR Third class Saloon 33. A small compartment was provided for smokers or ladies. Diagram 64 refers to WCJS 101 and 102, which became CR 34 and 35. In this variation, ladies could be private and smoking could take place elsewhere.

BELOW: Figure 13.37
The Diagram 99 Corridor Third class Saloons were one of the designs that was built to 'Grampian' stock standards and style. The drawing is a reproduction of St. Rollox 14104.

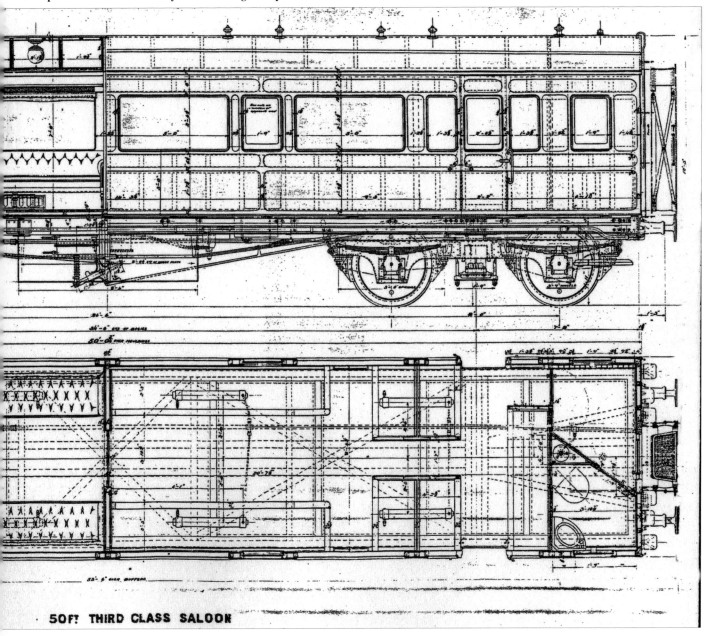

50FT THIRD CLASS SALOON

Saloons 34 and 35 had a smoking compartment at the luggage locker end and a private ladies compartment at the other. They were on page 64 of the Diagram Book (Figure 13.36).

CORRIDOR THIRD CLASS SALOONS 42-46

Five 50-foot Corridor Saloons were built to order H245 and charged to the capital account for the period ending January 1908.[13] They cost £1,280 each. They were probably authorised in August 1905[14] among sixty-six passenger vehicles that were to be built 'on Capital Account, divided between two half years.' This would explain why the order number was out of sequence for 1907.

The St. Rollox drawing number was 14104, dated 5th April 1907.[15] This is reproduced as Figure 13.37.

The 'Grampian' stock was being built at the time, and the Saloons were lettered in the same ornate style. They were assigned to page 99 in the Diagram Book. They were considered sufficiently important to have official photographs of exterior and interior. The photographs are shown in Plates 13.11 and 13.12.

They were given consecutive numbers from 42 to 46, renumbered 15337-15341 by the LM&SR at the Grouping and 933-937 in 1931. Only two withdrawal dates are known. Number 42 lasted until 1941 and 46 was withdrawn four years earlier.

ABOVE: Plate 13.11
This is the exterior view of the Diagram 99 Corridor Third class Saloons – NRM ref: SRX 332. The lettering is the same style as the 'Grampian' stock.

LEFT: Plate 13.12
The interior view of the Saloon illustrated above (NRM ref: SRX 329) is taken from the centre of the carriage, with the entrance to the lavatory in the left background. The electroliers are the same style as those fitted in the 'Grampian' carriages. The other protrusions from the Lincrusta lined ceiling are the Havock ventilators. The floor is covered in black and white 'Decolite,' which was used in some Pullman cars. Even with the blinds pulled down on one side, the Saloon has a very light and airy atmosphere.

REFERENCES
1. NRS BR/CAL/5/11 entry 321
2. NRM 11252/C RHP 70121
3. NRS BR/CAL/1/42 entries 649 and 1501
4. NRS BR/CAL/1/42 entry 537
5. NRS BR/CAL/1/42 entry 1033
6. *West Coast Joint Stock*, pp. 217-21
7. NRS BR/CAL/5/11 p. 387
8. NRS BR/CAL/1/42 entry 1290
9. *West Coast Joint Stock*, pp. 70-71
10. *General Instructions*, p. 67
11. *West Coast Joint Stock*, pp. 206-7
12. NRS BR/CAL/1/74 entry 22
13. NRS BR/CAL/23/12 (16)
14. NRS BR/CAL/1/51 entry 1007
15. NRM 7527/C on two sheets RHP to be assigned

13.5: OFFICERS' AND INSPECTION SALOONS

Railway officials made frequent trips around the system in private conveyances to inspect their empires. The general configuration of these carriages was that of an Open Saloon, with tables for consultation of drawings and writing notes. Furnishing was to First class standard. Windows were provided in one or both ends to allow observation of the track. Catering and lavatory accommodation was usually provided, and double foot boards were fitted beneath doors to allow access to and from track level.

PROPOSED SELF-PROPELLED SALOON

The CR contemplated building a steam railcar in October 1877, when a drawing was made for a *'proposed officer's steam carriage.'*[1] There is no reference to this design in company minutes and the drawing has not survived. The concept of a locomotive linked to a carriage had been developed in the 1840s and '50s.[2] The proposal may have been similar to the L&SWR's 'Bug' which Drummond built for his personal use in 1899.

OFFICERS' SALOON 1A

This was one of the two original Saloons built at Greenock in 1848, which were described in Section 13.1. It became an Officers' Saloon in 1894 and was associated with Officers' Tank Engine 1A, later 1200. The Saloon was fitted with a handbrake operated from one of the verandahs. Part of the seating was removed in each Saloon to be replaced by a table. The revised internal layout is shown in Figure 13.1. Footsteps were added to St. Rollox drawing 7533, dated May 1894. It was replaced by the 'Blue Saloon' (described below) in 1902, when it was presumably scrapped.

The photograph of Saloon 2A (Plate 13.2) shows a handbrake fitted in the same place as on Saloon 1A. This fitting was not needed for ordinary revenue service, which suggests that it, too, was restored as an inspection vehicle. If so, this happened after 1896, because the Saloon Diagram Book shows it with its original internal layout. It may have been the Officers' Saloon that was replaced by the converted ex-WCJS Dining Saloon number 41, which is described later in this section.

OFFICERS' SALOONS 1430 AND 1431

These two 4-wheeled carriages of differing lengths were originally built as First class Open Saloons in 1868, when they probably carried numbers 4 and 5. Their numbers were taken by the two Diagram 51 Lambie Third class Picnic Saloons built to order H102 in 1894.

The 1896 Saloon Diagram Book records them as Third class Saloons on pages 16 and 17. However, the later Coaching Plant Stock Book records them as First class. They did not appear in the Diagram Book. According to the Stock Book they became Officers' Saloons in 1904, allocated to Perth (1430) and Carlisle (1431). Although the Stock Book states that the Saloons were oil-lit, three St. Rollox drawings[3] show that electric lighting was to be fitted in February 1920. This had not taken place at the time that the 1921 Stock List was compiled. Number 1431 is recorded in the Stock Book as steam heated.

Number 1430 was withdrawn in 1925 without being allocated an LM&SR number. The withdrawal date of 1431 is not recorded, but it carried LM&SR number 15343, which suggests that it survived at least for a few years after Grouping. Both were painted brown.

THE 'BLUE SALOON'

West Coast Joint Stock 6-wheeled Lavatory Tri-Composite number 199 was built in 1880. It was one of the four carriages to L&NWR diagram P18 which came into CR hands in 1898.[4] They are discussed in Chapter 8.4. The design was unique in the WCJS fleet as it had *coupé* ends with two windows, to accommodate half compartments.

It was renumbered 293 in the Caledonian Composite carriage series and ran in general passenger service for a few years. It was converted to Officers' Saloon number 1 on 21st March 1902, to St. Rollox drawing 11107. The drawing for the conversion has not survived. The renumbering caused 40-foot Family carriage number 1 to become 31 in April of that year. The old Officers' Saloon 1A was probably scrapped at the same time.

It was assigned to page 52 of the Diagram Book, where it was described as an *'Officers' Saloon.'* The Caledonian added a centre window at one end, and completely gutted and reappointed the interior. The two interior layouts can be compared in Figures 13.38 and 13.39. A handbrake was sited in the attendant's compartment, which was fitted with a gas stove and sink. It was fitted with electric light and steam heating.

It carried three liveries during its time as an Officers' Saloon. A photograph not long after its conversion (Plate 13.13) shows it in all-over dark blue livery to match 4-2-2 No. 123, which by then had been withdrawn from general service and was the designated Royal Train Pilot and Inspection Saloon engine. The carriage is lined, perhaps in white to match the locomotive.

Two later photographs, taken at the same time and believed to date from 1913, show No. 123 repainted in light blue. The Saloon now appears to be painted in two shades of blue, with the darker colour applied to the beading on the upper half of the sides and the ends. The lining looks more subdued and was probably gold. The photograph (Plate 13.14) also shows the elaborate lettering style. The Coaching Plant Stock Book states that it was repainted in passenger livery with white upper panels on 10th November 1919. The carriage was withdrawn in 1924.

SALOON 26

This 4-wheeled carriage had been built by Cravens in 1878 as part of an order for eight Saloons, as described in Chapter 13.2. Originally numbered 72, it was renumbered into the Saloon series with its companion vehicles in the half year ending January 1895.

In 1911, it was converted into an Inspection Saloon, retaining its second number. The work involved was the subject of drawing 15621 dated 24th December 1910, which has not survived. It appeared on page 52A of the Diagram Book – see Figure 13.40.

Three windows were cut in both ends. The interior was remodelled into two equal sized compartments with a lavatory between them. The lavatory was the subject of drawing 15633.[5] A handbrake was fitted in the access space between the compartments to drawing 15638. The

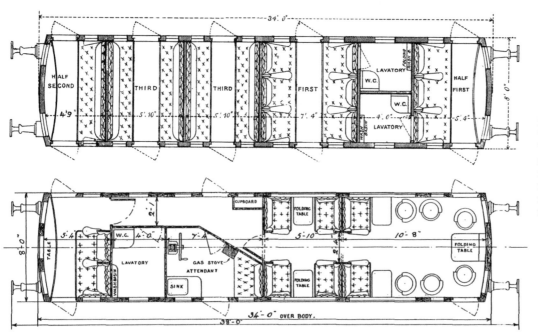

Figures 13.38 and 13.39
The first view shows the layout of WCJS Lavatory Composite 199 on acquisition by the Caledonian in 1898. It ran unaltered as CR 293 until 1902, when it was converted to the Diagram 52 Officers' Saloon number 1 (*lower left*).

Plates 13.13 and 13.14
The first illustration (NRM ref: SRX 186) shows the Diagram 52 Officers' Saloon in its first one-colour livery, matching 4-2-2 No. 123. The second illustration dates from 1913 and shows the other side of the vehicle. The Saloon now appears to have been painted in two shades of blue, and the number to be newly applied in gold compared with the company letters, which remain in the same colour as the first photograph.

Plate 13.15
Both of the known photographs of this Saloon are poor quality. In this example, Saloon 26 is halted on a bridge. Given the activity below, it may have been carrying out a deflection test. The Class '782' 0-6-0T only has a steam brake, so the Saloon's brakes are inoperative. One of these saloons appears as the second carriage in Plate 5.7.

Figure 13.40
Diagram 52A was assigned to one of the Cravens-built Saloons of 1878 when it was converted to an Officers' Saloon in 1911, retaining the number it received in 1895. The original Saloon layout is shown in Figure 13.15.

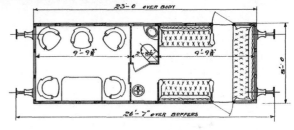

end seat and part of the longitudinal seating at the door end was retained. At the other end, a table was fitted, and this compartment was furnished with five loose armchairs.

Although the photographs of this Saloon are poor quality (see Plate 13.15) it is clear that Havock ventilators were fitted, as were dual brakes, steam heating equipment and electric lighting. Steps were added below the original footboard to allow access from track level. The Coaching Plant Stock Book states that it was broken up in 1926, painted brown overall.

Dining Saloon 40

The 1921 Stock List describes this Saloon, along with number 41, as an *'officers' saloon.'* There is no record of an alteration to the carriage, but a second Diagram 63, dated 20th October 1921, shows extensive alterations to the catering facilities. As illustrated and discussed in Chapter 9.3 (Figure 9.39 shows the new layout), the Saloon may have served the dual purpose of spare Dining car for Pullman services and occasional use as an Officers' Saloon.

Converted Dining Saloon 41

In April 1918 the conversion of CR Dining Saloon 41 was authorised to replace an Officers' Saloon which was stated to be *'in unsatisfactory condition and not worth repairing.'*[6] The running number of the Saloon to be replaced was not recorded in the minute and there is no obvious candidate in the Coaching Plant Stock Book. It is possible that it replaced Saloon 2A, which was discussed earlier in this section.

The conversion was detailed in various drawings between 19438 and 19525, dated from April to August. The general arrangement drawing of the body is 19501.[7] The conversion was not completed until 1920, after drawing 20337[8] was issued in December 1919 for *'steel underframe for saloons No. 40 & 41,'* which included 4-wheeled bogies.

Wider vestibules were fitted which increased the length to 51 feet 0¾ inches over mouldings. The interior was completely remodelled.

The saloon area in the middle of the carriage was fitted with a false roof with coved ends. There was a corridor connection at one end only. A handbrake stanchion was added in the vestibule area. The other end was fitted with three windows. A high elliptical roof was fitted, as shown in Figure 13.41, which is taken from the GA drawing.

The kitchen area and lavatory were relocated. The main dining area was gutted and refitted with tables and individual chairs. Page 63A of the Large Diagram Book, also dated 20th October 1921 and reproduced as Figure 13.42, shows the details and is compared with the original layout shown in Figure 13.43.

The Saloon had an extraordinarily long life. Allocated number 15555 at the Grouping, it became Engineer's Saloon 45018 in 1933. It was probably at this point that a corridor connection was added at the other end.[9] A photograph appears as Plate 13.16. Gresley bogies were fitted in 1955, and following damage in a collision, a new observation end was fitted in 1960. It remained in service in Scotland until 1972, when it was purchased for preservation.[10]

References
1. St. Rollox drawing 2265
2. http://en.wikipedia.org/wiki/British_steam_railcars
3. Numbers 20472/3/4
4. *West Coast Joint Stock*, pp. 79-81
5. RHP 67717
6. NRS BR/CAL/1/71 entry 222
7. NRM 7518/C RHP
8. RHP
9. LM&SR drawing GC262S RHP to be assigned
10. *West Coast Joint Stock*, pp. 191-92

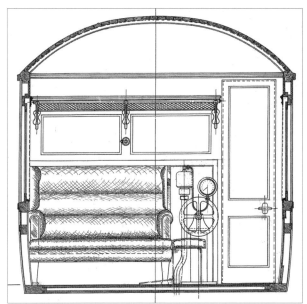

LEFT: Figure 13.41
This shows the new high elliptical roof profile applied to Dining Saloon 41 when it became an Officers' Saloon. The view is taken from the left-hand entrance vestibule in the Diagram 63A drawing below, with the handbrake stanchion between the seat and the door to the corridor.

BELOW: Figures 13.42 and 13.43
Diagram 63A (*below, upper*) represents the Officers' Saloon internal layout. Compared with the original Diagram 63 (*below, lower* – also in Chapter 9 as Figure 9.37), the catering facilities have been relocated and the rest of the interior has been gutted and refurnished. A lavatory has been added.

BOTTOM: Plate 13.16
A.B. McLeod took this photograph at Tain (NRM ref: C131). It shows Dining Saloon 41 after 1933 when it became Engineer's Department number 45018. The panelling betrays its WCJS origins, but the underframe dates from 1920. The bogies are later still, being LM&SR standard 9-foot wheelbase.

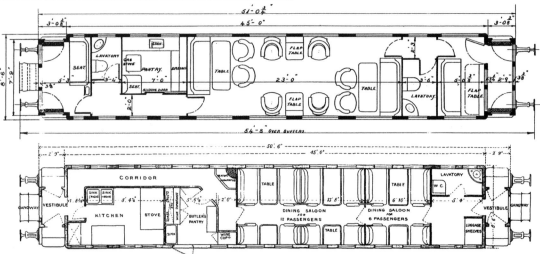

CHAPTER 14
ROYAL MAIL VEHICLES

14.1: LEGISLATION AND INFRASTRUCTURE

On 14th August 1838 the Act to provide for the conveyance of mail by railways at a standardised fee became law.[1] Railway transport of mail started as soon as the Liverpool & Manchester Railway opened and followed the expansion of the system. The Act was an attempt to address complaints to the Postmaster General about late arrivals due to breakdown or the slowness of services.

The Act empowered the Postmaster General to require railway companies to transport mails by ordinary or special trains as he might direct. Companies were also to provide carriages fitted for the sorting of letters if so instructed. These carriages were staffed by Royal Mail employees. The Royal Arms were to be painted on the side of carriages dedicated to mail service, *'in lieu of the name of the owner and of the number of the carriage.'*

Parcels post was separate from mail and subject to separate agreements, which were not enforced by Act of Parliament. There is one reference in CR minutes. In 1882 the Board noted:

'the Railway companies have come to an arrangement with the Post Office (Conditionally on approval), the Railway Companies to receive 55% of receipts and the Post Office 45%.'[2]

The Caledonian, like other railways, developed a system for transporting parcels. The Brake Vans in passenger trains were used for conveying items rapidly. For less urgent items 'road vans' were used. These were usually covered goods vans which were marshalled on goods trains. The Callander & Oban line was allocated a special design of van for this traffic.[3] In 1903 a fleet of open bogie wagons was established to convey parcels by express goods train between Scotland's cities.[4]

On arrival at their destination, parcels were transported to the addressee by carriers. The CR used a mixture of its own vehicles and those of William Wordie & Co.

DEVELOPMENT OF AUTOMATIC LINESIDE APPARATUS

Automatic mailbag exchange apparatus had been used experimentally since 1838. The first patent was gained by Nathaniel Worsdell, who was employed by the Grand Junction Railway. He proposed a licence arrangement with the Post Office, which was refused.

A similar system was designed by John Ramsay, a senior clerk in the GPO, while the protracted negotiations between Worsdell and the Post Office were taking place. It consisted of a system of nets and arms for receiving and despatching mail bags or pouches.[5] The lineside equipment was first installed *'at all the necessary stations between London and Liverpool.'*

The apparatus was prone to numerous failures. John Dicker, an Inspector of Mail Coaches, was appointed to look after and repair the apparatus as he saw fit. He could not cope with the workload of keeping the ten sets of apparatus in order over a distance of about 150 miles, so three were removed.

In 1848 Dicker used his experience to completely modify the system. Nets were provided at the lineside apparatus, leather pouches protected the mailbags and a new type of net was provided for the carriages which gripped and detached the pouch from the lineside standard.

At this point the Post Office took advice from an expert in patent law. His opinion was that Ramsay's and Dicker's systems both infringed Worsdell's patent. In 1852 the patent expired and the Post Office was free to finalise Dicker's design and agree its adoption with railway companies. A contemporary CR Board minute records:

'the Post Office desire to erect at several stations an improved apparatus for the receipt and delivery of Mail bags and to fit up the vans with corresponding machinery.'[6]

Apparatus was installed on the Caledonian at Abington, Beattock, Ecclefechan, Gretna, Lockerbie, Motherwell, and Symington, and on the Scottish Central at Auchterarder, Bridge of Allan, Dunblane and Greenloaning. A photograph of the apparatus forms Plate 14.1. A drawing (numbered 4783 and undated, but not in the St. Rollox register)[7] shows the arrangement. It is reproduced as Figure 14.1.

Equipment for picking up and setting down mailbags was fitted to carriages. Arms which were swung out from the carriage body carried the mailbags to be set down. A retractable net, which was recessed into the body, picked up mailbags from the lineside.

The apparatus was fitted on one side of the carriage only. This entailed turning the carriage before starting each journey. According to *West Coast Joint Stock*, Glasgow arrivals were worked round the Cathcart Circle. At Aberdeen the Ferryhill turntable was used.[8]

After installing the apparatus, the service to Scotland was accelerated. From 1st March 1853 mail from London reached Edinburgh in 11 hours 45 minutes instead of 18 hours 55 minutes, and Perth in 15 hours exactly instead of 17 hours 43 minutes.[9] On 1st June 1855 additional exchange equipment was brought into use between Carlisle and Perth which enabled a further acceleration.

FATALITY AT BEATTOCK

In 1889 the first fatal accident caused by lineside apparatus occurred on the Caledonian, which led to a modification to the net arrangement on the side of the carriages. Miss Pirie, a passenger from Aberdeen on the mail train, became sick and,

'just as the train was approaching Beattock leaned so far out of the carriage window in order to vomit that her head came into violent collision with the pouch suspended from the standard and was driven back against the side of the window and carriage. She died a few hours afterwards from concussion of the brain.'[10]

The train was travelling at about 60 mph at the time, and Miss Pirie's head knocked the mailbag pouch off the apparatus, which was situated about 500 yards north of Beattock station. Her mother brought an action against the Caledonian. The Board of Trade enquiry,[11] conducted by Major-General Hutchinson, attached no blame to the company. The BoT granted Miss Pirie's mother a compassionate allowance of £50.

The enquiry found that the apparatus was inherently dangerous. As will be seen from Figure 14.1, when loaded and swung into position it infringed a BoT regulation that *'nothing shall be erected on any railway less than 2 feet 4 inches from the side of the widest carriage in use on that railway.'* Quite why this state of affairs had

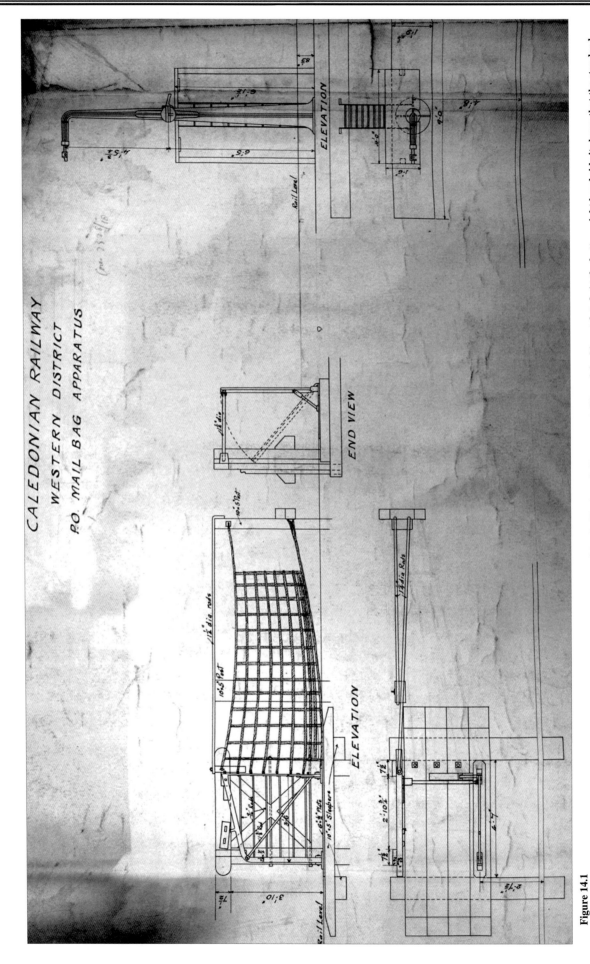

Figure 14.1
This drawing is not in the St. Rollox drawings register. It may have been produced by the Engineer's Department. The original is not dated. At the bottom right hand side it shows that the standard on which the mailbag pouch was hung was only 4 feet 8 inches away from the nearside rail. When swung out through 90 degrees, it placed the pouch foul of the Board of Trade requirement that nothing should be closer to the side of the widest carriage than 2 feet 4 inches. This caused the fatal accident to Miss Pirie in 1889.

Plate 14.1
One of the sets of lineside apparatus on the main line between Carlisle and Glasgow.

been allowed in the first place, and then to continue for about fifty years, is a mystery. The BoT had perhaps turned a blind eye to the situation, because the likelihood of an accident occurring was so remote. Hutchinson did, however, state:

'it is wonderful that, seeing the number of these obstructions in existence, this, so far as I am aware, is the first passenger accident which has been caused by them.'

Of course, the potential for an accident had grown as the width of carriages increased. By 1889, WCJS and CR carriages were eight feet wide, which placed anyone leaning out of a window in greater jeopardy.

The enquiry report prefaced its strictures about the apparatus by saying that its usefulness and convenience were unquestioned. Hutchinson continued:

'The existence of a heavy obstruction weighing, if full, about half a hundredweight, and hanging, if motionless, from 8 to 13 inches (and closer if oscillating) from the side of the carriage, just above the level of the head of a passenger leaning out of a carriage window, is certainly most dangerous ...'

Once the fatality had occurred, the BoT had to take action to enforce its regulation. Hutchinson offered his opinion:

'The Board of Trade ought not be satisfied that the safety of the public has been properly secured short of any arrangement which will allow of the tops of the pouches being kept below the level of the sills of the carriage windows, and of the straps which support them being 28 inches from the sides of the widest carriages.'

RESPONSE TO THE ENQUIRY FINDINGS

Hutchinson summarised the difficulties faced by the Post Office authorities in making the apparatus safe as follows:

'if the pouch were suspended at such a height as to be well above the level of the sills of the carriage windows, it would involve a net too high to pass under many of the older bridges; if the pouch were suspended below the sill of the carriage

windows it would interfere with the delivery apparatus; if the pouch were kept far enough from the side of the carriage to afford reasonable clearance it would so largely increase the force of the blow on the attachments of the net when the pouch was received into it, as to render impracticable to increase the clearance to any great extent.'

The Post Office immediately tested the only immediately possible solution of those suggested by Hutchinson. A new carriage net and frame was developed which allowed the apparatus to be moved further away from the rails. In a footnote to the report Hutchinson remarked that although the experiment was a success, it

'cannot be made general on account of narrow bridges and other standing obstructions, and that the original clearance of 8 to 13 inches is all that can be obtained.'

As a temporary compromise, the Postmaster General was informed that if lineside apparatus could not be re-sited, the Board of Trade could require the mail vehicles to be marshalled at the front of trains. The Post Office was not happy with this suggestion. It claimed that it would lead to difficulties in train marshalling and expose their employees to risk in the event of a head-on collision. The BoT then increased the pressure by intimating that unless something was done, it might be moved to forbid the use of the lineside apparatus altogether.

After considerable experimentation, which included a prize competition with a main award of £200 (about £130,000 in today's terms), an extended net arrangement was eventually fitted to TPOs, allowing the apparatus to be moved away from the track.

REFERENCES
1. Railways (Conveyance of Mails) Act 1838 (1 & 2 Vict. c. 98)
2. NRS BR/CAL/1/27 entry 882
3. *Caledonian Railway Wagons*, pp. 164-65
4. *Caledonian Railway Wagons*, pp. 150-51
5. POST 18/110 p. 3
6. NRS BR/CAL/1/10 entry 796
7. RHP to be assigned
8. *West Coast Joint Stock*, p. 264
9. POST 18/110 p. 15
10. POST 18/110 pp. 75-76
11. RAIL 1053/78/2

14.2: Early Mail Services on the Caledonian

Immediately after the Caledonian's line from Carlisle to Beattock opened on 10th September 1847, the Post Office approached the company for facilities for the carriage of mails. A CR Board minute records 'arrangements with the Post Office for carrying mail after 11 October.'[1] On 26th October, the company was asked to:

'provide the whole or as much as is necessary of the inside of a Second Class carriage in each of the trains which daily (Sundays included) leave Carlisle at 9.16 a.m. and 9.16 p.m. (London time) respectively for the railway station at Beattock Bridge, and also in each of the trains which daily (Sundays included) leave Beattock Bridge at 1.48 p.m. and 11.29 p.m. (London time) for Carlisle.'[2]

With the imminent opening of the entire line, the Caledonian was asked on 28th January 1848 to provide a sorting carriage, but it did not enter service until October. That was about the same time as the railway mail service was extended to Perth, following the opening of the Scottish Central Railway.

From October 1849 the Post Office agreement required the Caledonian to make available:

'a sufficient number of separate or Post Office carriages for sorting letters on the 8.11 a.m. departure from Carlisle to Castle Cary Railway Junction, also carriages for the 12.00 noon departure from Castle Cary Railway Junction to Carlisle'

And to:

'appropriate exclusively one compartment of a Second Class carriage on the 11.34 a.m. Carstairs Junction – Edinburgh and 12.30 p.m. return also the 12.20 p.m. Glasgow – Motherwell and 12.15 p.m. return.'[3]

By this time the service had been extended to Aberdeen. One might expect the mails to have travelled over the Scottish Midland Junction's main line through Strathmore to Forfar, and thence via the Aberdeen Railway, but that was not the case. From Perth the mails were taken to Dundee by the Dundee & Perth Railway. They were off-loaded at Dundee (West) station, transferred through the city to Dundee (East) and loaded into a Dundee & Arbroath Railway train to Arbroath, where they were finally transferred into an Aberdeen Railway train.

There was a bitter controversy, fuelled by the Managers of the Dundee & Perth and the Scottish Midland Junction Railways and mostly carried out in the public press, but it was not until July 1850 that mails were carried by the more direct route via Forfar. An agreement was made concerning the train called the 'London Night Mail' that the SMJR, effective from 30th September, would provide 'a box or imperial in a First Class carriage' on the 3.08pm departure from Perth for Forfar, and on the 8.25am return. The timing was a creditable 40 minutes for the 32 miles.[4]

The change of route meant that, instead of arriving in Aberdeen at 7.46am, the mail arrived at 6.28am in time for the first delivery of the day. Even so, the Post Office was still not prepared to require

a sorting carriage beyond Perth, and traffic for Aberdeen was transferred from Perth in a Bag Tender.

In 1851 the Superintendent of Mails enquired whether it would be possible for the CR to convey mailbags 'in the charge of their own guards' to Edinburgh and Glasgow by the Night express, that is, without incurring the expense of a dedicated vehicle. The CR Board's reply was:

'that this train is put on as an experiment and that at present is so unremunerative that we cannot undertake to continue it for any time, but if the Post Office wish to send bags by it the Directors will be ready to convey them.'[5]

The minute went on to say that any price would be agreed by arbitration. CR minutes do not record the outcome, but there is no mention of this service in the 1855 schedule as laid out below.

Services Exclusively on Caledonian Metals in 1855

Mail services starting and terminating on the Caledonian increased considerably over the same period. By 1855 the following trains were used by the Post Office to carry mails, although often in a dedicated compartment of an ordinary carriage rather than in a Travelling Post Office.[6]

Service	Time
Coatbridge–Glasgow (Buchanan St.)	9.15am
Glasgow (Buchanan St.)–Coatbridge	3.00pm
Edinburgh–Motherwell	3.00pm
Motherwell–Edinburgh	11.13am
Glasgow (South Side)–Hamilton	8.00am
Hamilton–Glasgow (South Side)	12.00 noon 5.00pm
Glasgow (South Side)–Crofthead	12.00 noon
Crofthead–Glasgow (South Side)	11.00am
Greenock–Paisley	11.30am
Paisley–Greenock	11.36am 3.16pm 6.16pm

The apparent imbalance in the services between Paisley and Greenock was due to the volume of Irish Mail traffic.

Services in 1857

By 1857 the number of postal services over purely Caledonian metals had increased. A new agreement consolidated the 1855 agreement and added a list of services in central Scotland.[7] The annual value of the contract was £243 18s. Two schedules listed the company's trains on which mail would be carried; these are reproduced opposite. The first listed the trains on which mail was to be carried and the facilities which the CR would provide for Post Office staff.

SERVICE	FACILITIES PROVIDED
Carlisle–Greenhill Night Mail Carlisle–Greenhill Day Mail	A Travelling Post Office
Carstairs–Edinburgh Night Mail Carstairs–Edinburgh Day Mail Motherwell–Glasgow Night Mail Coatbridge–Glasgow Day Mail Glasgow–Motherwell Day Mail	A compartment of a Second class carriage fitted as the Postmaster General requires
Shiels Junction–Glasgow Day Mail Glasgow–Shiels Junction Night Mail Paisley–Greenock Night Mail Greenock–Paisley Day Mail	Company's guards to take charge of the bags
Paisley–Greenock Irish Mail	Mail guard to be provided with a seat in a Second class carriage

The Shiels Junction services probably describe a section of a longer working, as the schedule states that the train was not required to stop there in either direction. Later Working Timetables (for example, April 1878)[8] show mail trains from Wemyss Bay and Gourock to Glasgow Bridge Street, which were probably the later equivalents of these trains.

Analysis of the timings for the Carlisle and Greenhill Day and Night Mails provides additional information as to the number of vehicles involved. To carry out the roster of both Night and Day Mails, three TPOs were in service at any time with one, and probably two, spare vehicles.

The Night Mail left Carlisle for Greenhill daily at 5.54am, arriving at 9.00am, and started the return journey at 4.07pm, regaining Carlisle at 7.34pm.

The Day Mail ran between the same two stations. It did not run on Sundays but on other days it left Carlisle at 7.00pm, arriving at Greenhill at 10.30pm. The corresponding return journey left Greenhill at 8.11pm, arriving at Carlisle at 12.03am. The return working left Greenhill before the northbound train had arrived, so the Day Mail needed two TPOs to maintain the service.

Schedule No. 2 listed the local services in central Scotland on which the Caledonian's own guards took charge of the mail bags. The services between Paisley and Greenock were virtually identical to those in 1855.

SERVICE	DEPART	ARRIVE
Coatbridge–Glasgow	9.15am	9.55am
Glasgow–Coatbridge	3.00pm	3.34pm
Edinburgh–Motherwell	3.00pm	5.12pm
Motherwell–Edinburgh	11.13am	1.30pm
Glasgow–Hamilton	8.00am	8.30am
Hamilton–Glasgow	12.00 noon	12.28pm
Hamilton–Glasgow	5.00pm	5.30pm
Glasgow–Neilston	12.00 noon	12.35pm
Neilston–Edinburgh	11.07am	11.30am
Paisley–Greenock	11.16am	12.25pm
Paisley–Greenock	3.16pm	4.00pm
Paisley–Greenock	6.16pm	6.50pm
Greenock–Paisley	11.30am	12.11pm

SERVICES IN 1867

The schedules remained unaltered for at least ten years, as the next agreement dates from 1867. This agreement recognised that the CR had taken over the Scottish Central and Scottish North Eastern railways. It included services from Carlisle to Perth and Aberdeen, as well as services between the latter two cities.[9]

SERVICE	FACILITIES PROVIDED
Carlisle–Perth Night Mail Carlisle–Glasgow Day Mail Coatbridge–Perth Day Mail Perth–Carlisle Day Mail Perth–Aberdeen Night Mail and return Perth–Aberdeen Day Mail and return Carlisle–Aberdeen Night Mail Glasgow–Coatbridge Night Mail and return Greenock–Paisley Day Mail	A Travelling Post Office
Glasgow–Coatbridge Night Mail Edinburgh–Carstairs Night Mail and return Edinburgh–Carstairs Day Mail and return Glasgow–Carlisle Day Mail Glasgow–Motherwell Day Mail	A compartment of a carriage or a van at the convenience of the railway company

In addition, guards were responsible for conveying mail between Shiels Junction and Motherwell, Paisley and Greenock, and Dundee, Perth and Guthrie.

THE 1873 AGREEMENT

This new agreement added extra trains and new destinations, all requiring Travelling Post Offices, as set out in the table below.[10] The schedule also included mail to be conveyed under the charge of the guard to an extended number of places, such as Crieff.

SERVICE
Carlisle–Aberdeen Special Night Mail and return
Carlisle–Aberdeen Night Mail and return
Aberdeen–Carlisle Limited Night Mail
Holytown–Glasgow Special Night Mail and return
Motherwell–Glasgow Night Mail and return
Glasgow–Law Junction Night Mail
Strawfrank Junction–Edinburgh and Granton Down Special Night Mail. The guard was in charge of the mail from Edinburgh to Granton
Edinburgh–Carstairs Up Special Night Mail
Edinburgh–Carstairs Up Limited Night Mail

REFERENCES
1. NRS BR/CAL/1/8 18th September 1847
2. CRA Archive ref: 2/2/1/1/1
3. CRA Archive ref: 2/2/1/1/2
4. CRA Archive ref: 2/2/1/1/3
5. NRS BR/CAL/1/10 entry 292
6. Referred to in POST 11/2 agreement 5
7. POST 11/2 agreement 5
8. NRS BR/TT/S/54/5
9. POST 11/8 agreement 34
10. POST 11/8 agreement 36

14.3: EARLY CR POST OFFICE VEHICLES

The Post Office carriage requested in early 1848 did not enter service until October. In a Return of New Plant made for the Caledonian Board in June 1849[1] two TPOs were mentioned, built at a cost of £800 for the pair. The two vehicles also featured in the return to the Board of Trade for the half year ended 31st July 1849.

They were built to drawings 171 and 181, which have not survived. Drawing 171 specifies a 6-wheeled vehicle, which makes it one of the first to be owned by the Caledonian. Drawings 176 and 177 were for the 6-wheeled underframe.

A Board Minute of February 1849 mentioned a letter from Robert Sinclair stating that *'he had commenced construction of the two additional Travelling Post Offices.'*[2] This is confirmed by the rolling stock valuation of March 1850, when the company had four TPOs valued at a total of £1,448 7s 4d.[3] Post Office vehicle number 4 in the 1874 Inventory was a 6-wheeler. It may have been built to the same drawing as number 2.

In a further report to the Board made in 1855, Sinclair stated that the Caledonian owned five TPOs in 1851 and that none had been built between then and the beginning of 1855.[4] This directly contradicts the half-yearly returns for the period from January 1852 until January 1854, which reported that the company owned six. There is no evidence to explain the discrepancy, but the Caledonian's allocation of numbers 6 and 7 to the Scottish Central TPOs when the SCR amalgamated with the Caledonian in 1865 suggests that Sinclair's report of five vehicles was correct.

THE MODIFIED SECOND CLASS CARRIAGES

The 1849 Post Office requirement to *'appropriate exclusively one compartment of a Second Class carriage'* for the Carstairs–Edinburgh and Glasgow–Motherwell services seems to have resulted in considerable internal modification. The 1850 Valuation lists a separate charge of £200 for *'additional fittings to two carriages to turn them into Post Offices,'* although it is not clear which services required them. At the time, a Second class carriage was valued at just under £300.

By 1857 five duties in Schedule No. 1 specifically required modified carriages – see the previous section. The Edinburgh and Motherwell Day and Night Mails could be covered by one each, with a third on the Coatbridge service. In the 1874 Inventory Second class carriages 73-76 are described as having two passenger compartments and one called *'Mail Bag'*. This suggests that two more carriages were modified after 1850, with one of the resulting stock of four presumably kept as a spare.

ADDITIONS AND WITHDRAWALS IN THE 1860s

In the rolling stock return for the period ending June 1863 one TPO was added. In the next period two were recorded as *'worn out'* and in January 1864 there was a renewal, bringing the total back to five vehicles. It seems that the intention was to replace two worn out vehicles, but one of the replacements was built before the withdrawals took place, making it technically an addition for a short period. There is no matching entry in the capital expenditure return, which supports the argument that the two new carriages were genuine replacements.

One of the withdrawn carriages can be positively identified. The 1894 Post Office roster quoted in Chapter 14.5 gives the building date of number 2 as 1863, which must have made it one of the renewals. The Inventory's high valuation of £380 is further evidence. The other was probably number 4, another 6-wheeled vehicle in the Inventory. This would leave 4-wheeled TPOs 1 and 3 as survivors of the original fleet, along with 6-wheeler number 5.

Plate 14.2
Niall Ferguson provided this photograph, which was taken at Crewe in 1881. It shows two short Post Office vehicles dating from the 1860s. They are probably L&NWR vehicles, but the nearer example bears a resemblance to the CR design in St. Rollox drawing 531, reproduced in Figure 14.2.

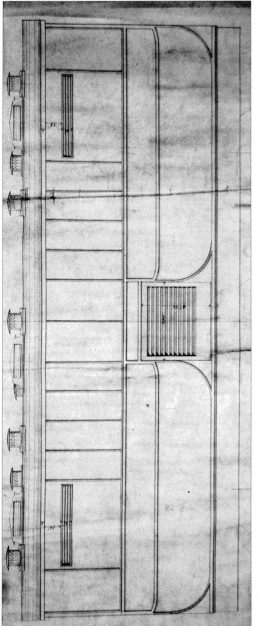

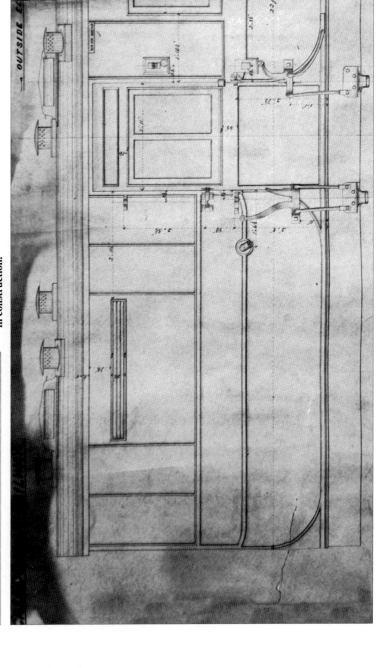

Figure 14.2

St. Rollox drawing 531 dates from the 1860s. It probably depicts the two TPOs built as replacements in 1863. One was certainly CR number 2, the other may have been number 4. The vehicle is fitted with apparatus for setting down mailbags, but no pick-up net. On the original drawing, faint lines indicate that the underframe had six wheels with a wheelbase of 13 feet. The carriage in Plate 14.2 is similar in construction.

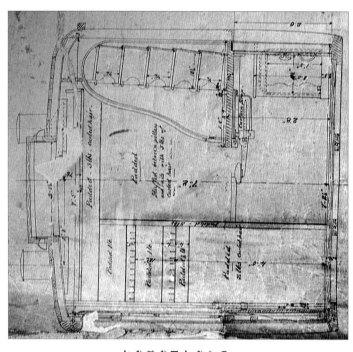

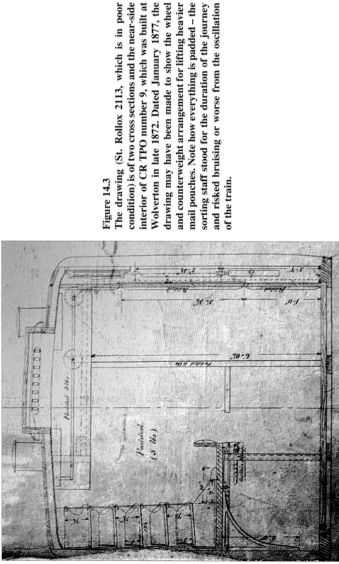

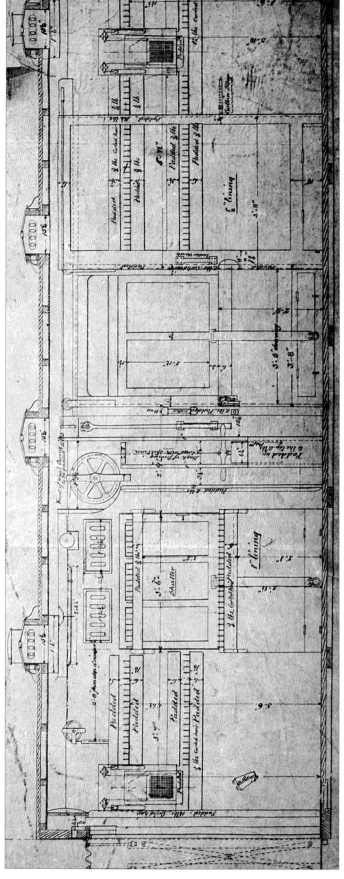

Figure 14.3
The drawing (St. Rollox 2113, which is in poor condition) is of two cross sections and the near-side interior of CR TPO number 9, which was built at Wolverton in late 1872. Dated January 1877, the drawing may have been made to show the wheel and counterweight arrangement for lifting heavier mail pouches. Note how everything is padded – the sorting staff stood for the duration of the journey and risked bruising or worse from the oscillation of the train.

One or both of the renewals was built to drawing 531.[5] Although the original does not bear a date, it must have been post 1860 when drawing 476 for a horsebox was issued. The drawing is reproduced as Figure 14.2. It shows a 22-foot vehicle with the still-current stagecoach detailing. The drawing shows the wheelbase centres at 13 feet equally divided – it ran on six wheels. Drawing 530 was for the internal arrangement and the 'undercarriage' was the subject of drawing 532. Neither of these two drawings has survived. A similar carriage is illustrated in Plate 14.2.

According to the rolling stock return, the CR added a further TPO in the period ending January 1867. It had been charged to the capital account against 'St. Rollox wages and stores' in July 1866.[6] This was CR 8, the next available number after the two Scottish Central TPOs described below, which were added to the CR fleet in the same period. It was 22 feet 6 inches long according to the description at its transfer to the WCJS fleet. It had six wheels and was valued at £390 in the 1874 Inventory.

Scottish Central Railway Vehicles

The Scottish Central Railway first invited a tender for the construction of a TPO in September 1857, when an offer to build two for £370 was put before the Board for approval.[7] Nothing seems to have come of this initiative, as a minute recorded: 'urge Mr. Allan to proceed with the Post Office carriages,' in February 1860.[8] The vehicles first appeared in the half year return for the period ending 31st January 1861.

By January 1864 the company claimed to own a further two. According to the half yearly return, only two postal vehicles were taken over by the Caledonian Railway when they assumed control of the SCR in 1865. A note in the L&NWR minutes says that these had been built in 1860 and so must have been the original two.

What became of the two supposedly built in 1864 is uncertain. They may have been converted to some other type of vehicle, but towards the end of the Scottish Central Railway's independent existence almost all decisions were referred to the Caledonian for ratification and it may well be that, with the imminent unification of the two companies, construction was cancelled.

The use of the two SCR TPOs between 1866 and 1873 is not known, but they may have continued with their original duties. As shown in the list that was started in 1873 which is set out later in this section, the two vehicles, now numbered 6 and 7 in the Caledonian's Post Office vehicle series, were still based in SCR/SNER territory. In 1875 they stood spare at Perth on alternate weeks 'for through postal purposes.'[9] On 15th April 1875, Conner issued instructions that one of the two book racks in each carriage was to be removed and fitted into Post Office Carriages 9 and 10 when they happened to pass through Perth.[10]

Construction in the 1870s

In 1871 St. Rollox produced drawing 1145 for 'Third Class altered to Post Office for Portpatrick line.' The drawing has not survived and there is no mention of the alteration in the CR minutes. The carriage involved does not seem to have been part of the Port Patrick line fleet, which was separately identified in the 1874 Inventory. A Caledonian Third must have been altered for the purpose. The 1874 Inventory does not mention such a carriage.

Post Office minutes concerning rolling stock are fragmentary. They first specifically mention Caledonian vehicles in 1872, when an estimate was obtained from Richard Bore, the L&NWR Carriage Superintendent, for alterations to an unspecified

number of Caledonian postal vehicles. This involved widening the doors, the addition of an apparatus window, and the provision of lifting apparatus.[11] The latter was a system based on a counterweight which was introduced to cope with the increased weight of mailbags.

In 1872 the Caledonian acquired a new vehicle, number 9, and with it adopted a new length of 26 feet for postal vehicles. The L&NWR seems to have been adopted the length at the same time.[12] The half-yearly return for the period ending 31st January 1873 gives a total of nine Caledonian postal vehicles in service, as do those for the following two six-monthly periods.

The Traffic Committee had authorised number 9 in February at an estimated cost of £413. It was required to 'run through between Euston and Perth.'[13] The carriage was built at Wolverton. The capital expenditure return for January 1873 records one Post Office Van built by 'LNWR Co.' at a cost of £428 3s 6d.[14] This cost was repeated in the handover Appendix. This vehicle is the subject of St. Rollox drawing 2113, which is dated January 1877.[15] The drawing depicts the interior only of the carriage – see Figure 14.3.

In June 1872 the Loco & Stores Committee sought tenders for six additional Passenger Brake Vans and one Post Office carriage.[16] There is no further record of the tender process, but there seems to have been a change of plan. The capital expenditure return for the period ending July 1873 records seven Passenger Brake Vans from Ashbury.[17] The rolling stock return confirms the addition of seven Luggage Vans.

In October 1873 a Post Office carriage was required,[18] probably that mentioned in the previous year. A Loco & Stores Committee minute a fortnight later states 'the LNW Company to build.'[19] It was charged to the capital account in July 1874, built by 'LNWR Co' for £460.[20] This was CR number 10. It was to the same design as number 9. Both carriages and number 5 built in 1887 were put on the same page in the WCJS diagram book when they formed part of the new joint mail fleet – see Figure 14.4. Details of the handover are described in the next section.

In May 1874 the Traffic Committee authorised a 'new Post Office Sorting Tender' at an estimated cost of £485.[21] This was recorded in the accounting period ending July, also from the 'LNWR Co.' at an unspecified price.[22] It received number 11. The WCJS handover Appendix, giving number 10's building cost correctly at £460, quotes number 11 at £505 10s.

Like TPO number 9, this was the subject of St. Rollox drawings of a later date. Drawing 2062 dated 6th October 1876 was for 'Post Office Carriage No. 11.' A fortnight later drawing 2071 was issued for a 'Post Office carriage underframe.' Neither drawing has survived.

The next Post Office Minute to mention Caledonian vehicles dates from July 1875.[23] It instructs Conner to get the L&NWR to add gangway doors and green baize curtains to Caledonian Post Offices 9 and 10 'while the carriages are at Euston.'

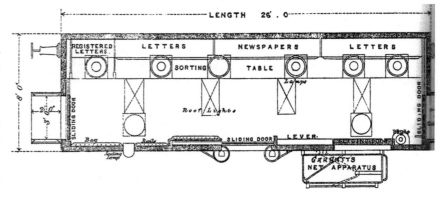

Figure 14.4
A plan view of the same design of vehicle as that illustrated in Figure 14.3. The near side is at the bottom of the drawing. This was page 41 of the L&NWR diagram book.

TPO number 5 was replaced in 1877, according to the WCJS handover list, which recorded the replacement vehicle. One TPO was recorded as 'worn-out' in the rolling stock return for the period ending January 1877 and its renewal in the next period. This vehicle seems to have been built at St. Rollox. It was probably the subject of drawings 2115 of January 1877 ('*Body Frame for Post Office Carriage No. 5*') and 2196 of June 1877 ('*Bearing springs for Post Office Carriage No. 5*'). Neither has survived.

DEPLOYMENT IN 1875

Among the Post Office minutes,[24] a barely legible pencil-written list of Caledonian Postal Vehicles and their duties, dated 26th March 1873, lists 11 carriages. As TPO 11 was not built until the second half of 1874, the list must have been updated to include later construction. The list does not correlate with the schedule in the 1873 Post Office agreement described in the previous section. It represents the situation in the years before the two company's fleets were broken up to contribute to the West Coast Joint Stock fleet, which is described in the next section.

CR No.	Duty	Notes
1	Spare at Perth	Old L&NWR
2	Glasgow Tender	Spare at Carlisle
3	Post Office Day Mail	Spare at Carlisle
4	Greenock Branch	
5	Post Office Limited Mail	London to Aberdeen
6	Post Office	Spare at Aberdeen
7	Post Office	Spare at Perth
8	Post Office Day Mail	Originally Glasgow & London
9	Post Office Limited Mail	
10	Post Office Limited Mail	
11	Glasgow and London	

The table suggests that three CR carriages were rostered on the 'Limited Mail,' and ran between London and Scotland. In the opening to the chapter on TPOs in *West Coast Joint Stock*, the authors state that until November 1877 the two companies' Post Office carriages did not cross the Anglo-Scottish border. This assertion is based on the West Coast Committee minute recording the reason for establishing a joint fleet, which said that mails had to be transferred at Carlisle.[25] The reason for the transhipment of mail was to avoid a build up of mileage charges. The West Coast Conference had formally recognised this in 1861, at which time passengers and luggage were also transferred from the vehicles of one company to another at Carlisle.[26]

ADDITIONS IN 1878

In October 1877 the Traffic Committee agreed to take tenders for '*two new Travelling Post Office Sorting Tenders.*'[27] In the following March, Cravens' offer to build one of these carriages was accepted as part of a tender for Invalid and Family carriages and 4-wheeled Saloons.[28] St. Rollox drawings 2281 and 2305 were

for the outside elevation and interior respectively. The first was signed off in November 1877, the second in December. Neither has survived.

The capital return for January 1879 records one Post Office at £550.[29] This was number 12 which was intended to run between London and Glasgow. This and the details of number 13 described below were added in ink to the pencil list quoted above from the Post Office minutes. Number 12 was a '*new TPO for Mr Hobson*' and was '*built 1878 and fitted at St. Rollox.*'

The other new vehicle was given number 13. It was built by the L&NWR and was intended '*to run thro between London and Aberdeen.*' There is no capital expenditure record, and the January 1879 rolling stock return records one carriage each worn out, renewal, and additional. The WCJS handover appendix gives its original cost as £550, the same as number 12.

DEPLOYMENT IN 1878

On 2nd October 1878, about six months before the West Coast Joint Stock fleet was established, a list in the Post Office minutes sets out the duties of the L&NWR and CR fleets. As far as the latter was concerned, it was:

'*proposed that Nos. 5-9, 10 and 13 shall be Night Mail TPO carriages and one of these kept spare at Perth and that No. 8 shall be kept spare for the Day Mail.*'

TPO number 12 was originally included in the list, but was crossed out. It was described as a '*new carriage built by the Cal. along with No. 13 in 1878. This No. 12 is Mr. Hobson's carriage.*'

REFERENCES
1. NRS BR/CAL/1/1
2. NRS BR/CAL/1/8 14th February 1849
3. NRS BR/CAL/1/1 pp. 414-16
4. NRS BR/CAL/4/14/62 Letter to Mr Johnstone Esq. 15th January 1855
5. RHP to be assigned
6. NRS BR/CAL/23/16
7. NRS BR/SCC/1/26 p. 6
8. NRS BR/SCC/1/26 p. 74
9. NRS BR/WCC/1/7 minute 1814
10. In POST 18/18
11. In POST 18/18
12. *West Coast Joint Stock*, p. 230
13. NRS BR/CAL/1/19 entry 1592
14. NRS BR/CAL/23/1 (29)
15. RHP to be assigned
16. NRS BR/CAL/1/20 entry 104
17. NRS BR/CAL/23/1 (29)
18. NRS BR/CAL/1/21 entry 78
19. NRS BR/CAL/1/21 entry 191
20. NRS BR/CAL/23/2 (42)
21. NRS BR/CAL/1/21 entry 1330
22. NRS BR/CAL/23/2 (52)
23. In POST 18/18
24. In POST 18/18
25. NRS BR/WCC/1/7 minute 1566
26. NRS BR/WCC/1/6 minute 156
27. NRS BR/CAL/1/23 entry 1868
28. NRS BR/CAL/1/24 entry 456
29. NRS BR/CAL/23/3 (43)

14.4: THE GROWTH IN ANGLO-SCOTTISH TRAFFIC

By 1859 Anglo-Scottish traffic had increased to the extent that it could no longer be accommodated in vehicles attached to ordinary service trains. A dedicated train known as the 'Limited Mail' started on 1st February 1859 between London and Perth. Although intended as a special mail service, some passengers and general parcel traffic were conveyed.

The train reduced the journey time between Euston and both Edinburgh and Glasgow by a further two hours. Night mail posted in London now arrived in time for the morning delivery in those cities. After its first month in operation the composition of the train was modified so that it left Euston as:

Glasgow P.O. Tender; Perth TPO; Perth carriage; Edinburgh Brake; P.O. District Sorting carriage; Liverpool P.O. Tender; Dublin P.O. Tender; Midland P.O. Tender.

The Edinburgh portion was detached at Carstairs and the Glasgow section at Gartsherrie.

ESTABLISHMENT OF THE WCJS MAIL FLEET

In June 1877 the West Coast Committee, recognising '*the inconvenience experienced at Carlisle in dealing with the Limited Mail, owing to the exchange of Caledonian and London and North Western Post Office Carriages,*' authorised the two general managers to:

'*confer with the Post Office Authorities with a view to arrangements being made for the vehicles to go through, in which case it may be desirable for the Post Office Vehicles to become Joint Stock.*'[1]

The Post Office agreed to the proposal in October and said that through traffic could commence '*as soon as the alterations to the sorting vehicles are completed.*'[2]

This took some time, as it was February 1879 when the CR and the L&NWR included postal vehicles in the West Coast Joint Stock fleet.[3] The Caledonian's share involved their seven most modern vehicles. The L&NWR contributed nine carriages, which tended to be older and shorter. The West Coast Conference minute which led to the establishment of the joint fleet and the full list of carriages involved is shown in Plates 14.3 and 14.4.

The transfer took place on 1st November 1879.[4] The half yearly return records the transfer of the CR carriages and the capital expenditure record shows that they were credited to the accounts at £2,945.[5] The CR carriages are shown in the table below, which is taken from the West Coast Conference minutes.[6]

L. & N. W. Co.
Mr. FINDLAY. (in the Chair).
,, KAY.
,, NEELE.
,, CATTLE.

Caledonian Co.
Mr. SMITHELLS
,, KEMPT.
,, WARD.
,, CURRER.

Mr. SMALL, *Principal Traffic Agent.*
,, ENTWISTLE, *Secretary.*

Mr. BORE (L. & N. W. Co.) also attended the Meeting during the consideration of the several questions affecting West Coast Stock.

Read—Minutes of last Meeting (26th September, 1879).

Post Office Vehicles to be converted into West Coast Joint Stock— (Minute 1689).

(1.) The Superintendents reported that, in carrying out Minute 1714 of last Meeting, nine Post Office vehicles belonging to the London and North Western Company and seven of the Caledonian Company's had been converted into West Coast Joint Stock, and that, according to the estimated present values of these vehicles, as agreed between Mr. Bore (London and North Western Co.) and Mr. Brittain (Caledonian Co.), and to the proportions contributed by the two Companies towards the original cost of West Coast stock, there was a money balance of £758 10s. 7d. due from the London and North Western Co. to the Caledonian Co.

It was agreed to treat these vehicles as West Coast Joint stock as from 1st November, 1879.

(*Vide Appendix A for statement of details.*)

ABOVE: Plate 14.3
West Coast Conference minute 1734 records the handover of TPOs by the two companies to form the WCJS fleet, and the financial reconciliation in favour of the Caledonian. The CR contributed fewer vehicles but they were newer than those from the L&NWR. The minute refers to Appendix A, which is shown in the next Plate.

RIGHT: Plate 14.4
Appendix A is the list of vehicles that made up the original WCJS fleet, and the value attached to them at handover. Only one CR carriage dates from the 1860s, compared with six of the L&NWR's.

APPENDIX.

A.

Transfer of London and North Western and Caledonian Post Office Vehicles to West Coast Stock, *vide* West Coast Conference Minutes, 1689, 1714, and 1734.

		Original No. of Post Office.	Present West Coast No.	Date when Built.	Cost.	Present Value.	TOTAL.
					£ s. d.	£ s. d.	£ s. d.
London and North Western Post Office		1	183	1872	436 2 1	361 19 5	
,,	,,	2	184	1872	436 2 1	361 19 5	
,,	,,	6	186	1860	397 10 8	298 3 0	
,,	,,	7	187	1860	397 10 8	298 3 0	
,,	,,	8	188	1860	397 10 8	298 3 0	
,,	,,	9	189	1860	397 10 8	298 3 0	
,,	,,	10	190	1861	397 10 8	298 3 0	
,,	,,	11	191	1861	397 10 8	298 3 0	
,,	,,	21	185	1879	525 18 8	525 18 8	
							3,038 15 6
Caledonian Post Office	... ...	5	192	1877	484 14 0	420 0 0	
,,	,, ...	8	193	1866	420 0 0	275 0 0	
,,	,, ...	9	194	1872	428 3 6	350 0 0	
,,	,, ...	10	195	1874	460 0 0	400 0 0	
,,	,, ...	11	196	1874	505 10 0	450 0 0	
,,	,, ...	12	197	1878	550 0 0	525 0 0	
,,	,, ...	13	198	1878	550 0 0	525 0 0	
							2,945 0 0
							5,983 15 6

		£ s. d.	£ s. d.
London and North Western proportion of West Coast Stock ...	63·46 ÷ 5,983 15 6 =	3,797 6 1
Caledonian proportion of West Coast Stock	36·54 ÷ 5,983 15 6 =	2,186 9 5
			5,983 15 6

	£ s. d.
London and North Western proportion as above	3,797 6 1
Present Value of London and North Western Offices as above	3,038 15 6
Balance due to Caledonian Company on the transaction	758 10 7

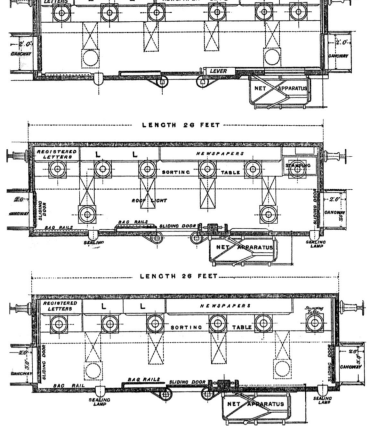

CR No.	Length	Built	WCJS No.
5	26 feet	1877	192
8	22 feet 6 inches	1866	193
9	26 feet	1872	194
10	26 feet	1874	195
11	26 feet	1874	196
12	26 feet	1878	197
13	26 feet	1878	198

The dates of construction given in the West Coast Conference Appendix vary slightly from those given in Chapter 14.2. The WCJS dates refer to the calendar year in which they were constructed, rather than the CR accounting period in which the vehicles were recorded as assets.

According to *West Coast Joint Stock*,[7] the 1893 WCJS Diagram Book placed Caledonian vehicles 5, 9 and 10 on Page 41, presumably because they were identical. The diagram is shown in Figure 14.4. Numbers 11, 12, and 13 were placed on pages, 39, 39A and 38 respectively – see Figure 14.5. WCJS 193, previously CR 8, did not feature in the 1893 Book because in December 1885 it was handed over to the L&NWR instead of being returned to the Caledonian.

WEST COAST JOINT STOCK SERVICES

Some of the services are described in *West Coast Joint Stock*, as are the subsequent designs of TPO.[8] The Post Office Archive records that on 6th January 1883 the ex-Caledonian TPOs were deployed as follows. Numbers 192, 194-198 were rostered on the 'Night Mail', with the last named standing spare at Carlisle. Number 195 could '*only run in rear*' for some reason. The other carriage was rostered as spare at Perth on the 'Day Mail'. A photograph of the Up mail train leaving Aberdeen in 1896 is shown in Plate 14.5.

Figure 14.5
From top to bottom, these L&NWR diagrams show the interiors of CR 13 (later WCJS 198), CR 11 (later WCJS 196) and CR 12, which became WCJS 197 and returned to the Caledonian as number 2 in 1900. CR 11 also returned to its parent company in 1900 and was '*destroyed by fire*' in 1906.

REFERENCES
1. NRS BR/WCC/1/7 minute 1566
2. NRS BR/WCC/1/7 minute 1589
3. NRS BR/WCC/1/7 minute 1668
4. NRS BR/WCC/1/7 minute 1734
5. NRS BR/CAL/23/4 (37)
6. NRS BR/WCC/1/7 Appendix A to minute 1734
7. *West Coast Joint Stock*, pp. 230-32
8. *West Coast Joint Stock*, Chapter 13

Plate 14.5
Caledonian Railway 2-4-0 No. 119 leaves Aberdeen with the Up Mail in 1896. The photograph was taken by Dr Tice Budden. The original is in the NRM collection (LGRP 21576).

14.5: LATER CR VEHICLES AND SERVICES

The handover of seven vehicles left the Caledonian with six relatively old postal carriages for internal traffic, although there was a considerable reduction in the number of duties to be covered as a result of the formation of the WCJS fleet. In the two years after the establishment of the WCJS fleet the rolling stock returns record that three carriages were disposed of. The first was withdrawn in the half year ending January 1881. The obvious candidates were either CR 1 or 3, the last survivors of the original fleet, built before 1850. Number 1 is the most likely, as the Caledonian acquired a WCJS vehicle in 1886 and allocated the number to it.

The CR suggested that the ex-SCR vehicles could be transferred to the WCJS fleet. The L&NWR thought them too small to be used on the through postal service.[1] It was suggested in the same minute that they should be converted into WCJS Fish Vans *'if practicable.'* They were deemed unsuitable as they were *'at least 4ft 6ins shorter than the present WCJS Fish Vans.'*[2] These first WCJS Fish Vans were 25 feet long,[3] so the old SCR vehicles must have been about 20 feet or 20 feet 6 inches long. That said, the 1874 Inventory shows that they ran on six wheels, so the wheelbase was probably about 13 feet, like the early CR and L&NWR vehicles.

The CR Board did not give up hope of finding someone willing to pay money for them, and in August 1881 the Highland Railway bought the pair for £100.[4] There is no record of this transaction in the capital expenditure return. The corresponding rolling stock return records two Post Office Vans as *'worn out.'*

The HR probably allocated numbers 5 and 6 in its postal vehicle series. Their subsequent history is uncertain, but they had almost certainly disappeared by the early 1890s, when HR Travelling Post Offices 5 and 6 were described as having bogies.[5]

At the beginning of 1882, the Caledonian Railway owned three TPOs for its internal services. It is impossible to be certain as to their identity, as they may have been renumbered after the formation of the WCJS fleet, but they were probably the original CR numbers 2, 3 and 4.

1886 ADDITION TO THE CR FLEET

In 1886 the Caledonian acquired an additional TPO from the WCJS, at the same time as the L&NWR received the CR's old number 8. Number 183, which had been transferred to the WCJS in 1878, was replaced with a new vehicle and handed over to the Caledonian.[6]

The capital return for the end of January 1886 recorded a charge of £374.[7]

The L&NWR had built this TPO in 1872. It was 26 feet long, and was allocated number 1 by the Caledonian, replacing the previous number 1 which had been disposed of in the half year ending 31st January 1881.

AN UNIMPLEMENTED DESIGN

St. Rollox drawing 6518 was dated 15th October 1890. It has not survived. It was an *'arrangement for a 35-foot 6½ inch Travelling Post Office.'* Hugh Smellie evidently entertained the idea of modernising the Caledonian TPO fleet. He had already built a modern 6-wheeled TPO for the G&SWR – see Plate 14.6. The length of the proposed carriage suggests a 6-wheeled vehicle to Drummond design conventions.

By this time the WCJS fleet included 42-foot radial TPOs, although construction of 32-foot vehicles continued.[8] The CR design may have been the van to order H59 for a *'post office carriage'* that has not been traced in the transcription of the Coaching Plant Stock Book. The project was probably still-born because of Smellie's death – his successor John Lambie obviously did not think it worth pursuing.

SERVICES IN 1894

The Caledonian now had four TPOs, but numbers 3 and 4 seem not to have been in service, as the Post Office Carriage Roster for 1894,[9] the next one that survives, features only two carriages. The roster was updated to 1902.

No.	LENGTH	NETS	DELIVERY ARMS	BUILT
1	25 feet 6 inches	1 near side	2 near side	1872
2	22 feet	1 near side	2 near side	1863

Neither vehicle had gangways; both were oil-lit. Although the length of number 1 is given by the Post Office as 25 feet 6 inches instead of 26 feet it must logically be the carriage acquired in 1885. The duty of the two vehicles was described as *'Edinburgh and Carstairs Sorting Tender.'* One left Edinburgh at 6.00pm daily for Carstairs, and returned on the Down Special Mail. The other was kept as a spare at Perth.

Plate 14.6
Hugh Smellie designed this TPO for the G&SWR in 1887. He planned to modernise the CR fleet, but his plan was not implemented due to his death. Thanks to Stuart Rankin for the photograph.

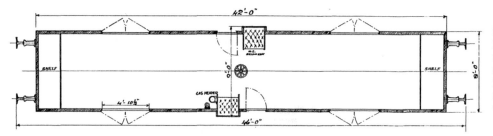

Figure 14.6
Page 35A of the Large Diagram Book depicts the WCJS Postal Brake Vans 341 and 342 after their acquisition by the Caledonian in 1910. They became CR 270 and 271, and at some point lost the corridor connections that were originally fitted.

ADDITIONS IN 1900

In October 1900 the Caledonian acquired two postal carriages as a result of disposals from the WCJS, on this occasion getting back two of their own vehicles. WCJS 196 and 197 were previously Caledonian 26-foot TPOs 11 and 12 respectively. They were fitted with gangways at each end, and given numbers 1 and 2 respectively in the Caledonian Railway series. The acquisition was recorded in the capital expenditure return, but the cost was not shown.[10]

According to the half-yearly returns, the TPOs previously numbered 1 and 2 that were built in 1872 and 1863 respectively were not disposed of but, presumably renumbered, remained on the books until at least 1913, when detailed returns ceased.

By the time of their return to the Caledonian, WCJS 196 and 197 had been converted from oil to gas lighting, and had one net and two delivery arms each, on the near side.[11]

SERVICES IN THE EARLY 1900S

A year later the Roster shows three carriages in use on the same duty, the additional vehicle being CR number 3. According to the Coaching Plant Stock Book it was built in 1868. It had been renumbered in October 1900 but its previous number is not known. Either 1 or 2 was running at any one time whilst the other was kept as a spare at Perth. Number 3 was also kept as a spare, but at Stepps Road, Glasgow.

A return was also made to a previous era. One compartment of a passenger carriage was reserved for letters on the Sunday 9.05pm Glasgow–Carlisle train, described by the Post Office as the 'Glasgow and Carlisle Bag Duty.'

SERVICE CHANGES IN 1902

By October 1902 the roster was known as the 'Edinburgh and Carstairs Night Mail.' The change was probably of recent origin as the Post Office used the same printed forms as in 1894, crossing through the earlier description and writing the new in longhand.[12]

Other alterations were made in addition to the change of title. The duty still left Edinburgh for Carstairs at 6.00pm daily but it was no longer returned by the Down Special Mail. Instead it was attached to the first passenger train of the following day. The most important change was that the duty was the responsibility of two entirely different vehicles.

SERVICES IN 1907

By 1907 the Post Office Roster showed the Edinburgh and Carstairs Night Mail as once again operated by carriages 1 and 2.[13] One was running and one stood spare at Perth. This contradicts *West Coast Joint Stock*, which states that number 1 was '*destroyed by fire*' in June 1906. Presumably number 2 worked the roster without a spare.

TPO 3 was not mentioned because it had been assimilated into the Luggage and Brake Van series in December 1905. It was initially given the number 31 and was renumbered 126 in June 1918. It was withdrawn in 1924 according to the Coaching Plant Stock Book. It was painted all-over brown.

ADDITIONS TO STOCK IN 1910

The Caledonian received two other postal vehicles from the WCJS, 42-foot Postal Brake Vans 341 and 342, built to diagram P30 in 1885. Originally they had radial underframes, but bogies were fitted in 1892/93.[14] In this guise they were identical to the general service WCJS vans to diagram 81, but with droplights in the doors. A photograph of the diagram 81 design appears in West Coast Joint Stock.[15] They were originally fitted with side gangways, modified to a central position in 1905.

They were transferred in March 1910, renumbered CR 270 and 271. There is no record of a capital expenditure transaction. According to *West Coast Joint Stock*, their underframes were worn out, which suggests that the CR mounted them on new underframes with Fox 8-foot bogies. The relevant West Coast minute describes them as '*in bad condition.*'[16]

In the Coaching Plant Stock Book they are described as '*postal brake vans*' with gangways. In the Large Diagram Book they appeared on page 35A without gangways, described as '*brake vans*' – see Figure 14.6. The 1921 Stock List confirms that they did not have corridor connections. There is no record of their removal. They were withdrawn in 1923.

SERVICES IN 1915

This roster[17] is the last pre-Grouping issue available in the Post Office Archive. Number 2 was still responsible for the same duty as in 1907, but letters were no longer sorted en route. Its duty was now known as the 'Edinburgh and Carstairs Bag Tender Night Mail.' It was returned by the first passenger train on the following day. WCJS 32-foot sorting carriage number 349 was kept as spare at Carlisle.

REFERENCES
1. NRS BR/WCC/1/7 minute 1877
2. NRS BR/WCC/1/7 minute 1903
3. *West Coast Joint Stock*, p. 275
4. NRS BR/CAL/1/26 entry 1240
5. *Highland Railway Carriages and Wagons*, p. 116
6. NRS BR/WCC/1/8 minute 2201
7. NRS BR/CAL/23/6 (33)
8. *West Coast Joint Stock*, pp. 245-48
9. POST 18/20
10. NRS BR/CAL/23/10 (41)
11. POST 18/20
12. POST 18/21
13. POST 18/22
14. *West Coast Joint Stock*, p. 244
15. *West Coast Joint Stock*, p. 224
16. NRS BR/WCC/1/4 minute 3192
17. POST 18/23

CHAPTER 15
SPECIAL PURPOSE VEHICLES

15.1: DUMMY VANS, THE CORPSE BOX AND THE PRISON CAR

The first known mention of 'Dummy Vans' was in the rolling stock return for the half year ending July 1872, when two *'dummy luggage vans'* were added to the fleet *'converted at expense of Revenue from Greenock Stand Up Carriages.'* The stand-up carriages were 24 feet long, according to the St. Rollox register entry for drawing 290. There was no drawing for the modification, which suggests that the work was of a minor nature.

According to the 1874 Inventory, the vans were numbered 142 and 143, valued at £130 each. They may have lasted until 1897 and 1894 respectively, when new Passenger Brake Vans bearing these numbers entered service as part of the renewal programme.

In 1877, the Loco & Stores Committee ordered six more vans from Metropolitan at a cost of £116 10s each.[1] They were built to Metropolitan drawing 2307.[2] The original drawing is not suitable for reproduction. A modeller's drawing based on the original is available from the CRA,[3] and an article by Jim Summers describing his model of the van was published in *The True Line.*[4] Dimensions and construction were similar to the same company's 1871 Covered Fish and Game Truck design[5] with differences in the door and body bracing. Presumably, the modified Greenock vans resembled this.

The running numbers of the six extra vans are not known, although they would have been in the Luggage and Brake Van series. Their withdrawal date is not known. If they survived long enough, they were probably among a number of vehicles in the Coaching Plant Stock Book whose origin cannot be traced.

THE CORPSE BOX

Very little is known about this design, examples of which were used to transport bodies of clan chiefs and the like to ancestral burial plots. An 1871 Traffic Committee minute approved the conveyance of the corpses of company servants and members of their families at the rate of 3d per mile for adults, 1½d for children and free of charge *'if killed on company service,'*[6] but it is unlikely that the Corpse Box was used, as it is not mentioned in the 1874 inventory. The only mention of the Corpse Box in the minutes concerns the fitting of dual brakes in March 1887, presumably to the only one of its type.[7]

There is no drawing listed in the St. Rollox registers or any record in the rolling stock returns. It was not charged to capital, which, combined with the lack of a drawing, suggests that it was an adaptation of an existing vehicle. Like the Dummy Vans, it may have been among the untraced numbers in the Luggage Van series. It does not figure in the 1921 Stock List. The Coaching Plant Stock Book

does not record it, which suggests that it was withdrawn prior to 1914. It was probably painted brown.

In default of any information, the design may have resembled the North British Railway version. According to Hutchison,[8] the North British owned six *'corpse vans;'* Sewell's description[9] says that three were built in 1892, which of course post-dates the CR vehicle. There is no known photograph of either design.

THE PRISON CAR

A single Prison Car was authorised in September 1884. Although not mentioned in CR minutes, its purpose was explained in a West Coast Conference minute.[10]

'Allusion was made to the disadvantage to the West Coast Route in not having a vehicle for the conveyance of prisoners from Stirling to London, similar to that supplied by the North British Company.'

A later West Coast Committee minute[11] recorded that instructions had been given for a vehicle to be built. The car was built to H1, the second order in the newly established coaching stock series. It was charged to the capital account for the period ending July 1885 at £259 13s 1d.[12] The original St. Rollox drawing number was 4172.[13] It had a 28-foot 6-inch body, 8 feet wide. These were the dimensions for Drummond's 4-wheeled carriages, which were built at the same time. It was based on the body of a 5-compartment Third to Diagram 2 – see Chapter 7.1, pp. 143-5.

Originally, there were no windows. The internal layout comprised four compartments, each with a bench seat for six prisoners. Entrance was by a door towards the centre of the carriage. A wide centre aisle ran the whole length of the carriage with a urinal at each end. In the middle next to the doors there was an upholstered seat for warders on each side. There were two large ventilators on the centre line of the roof towards each end.

According to a press article about St. Rollox Works,

'in keeping with the philanthropic and humanising tendencies of the age, [it] is fitted with gas and provided with heating apparatus for providing hot coffee for the notorious voyagers.'[14]

The NBR van referred to in the West Coast Conference minute was not the one drawn by Hutchison and described in *NBR Coaches.*[15] This vehicle was built in 1890 in connection with the opening of Peterhead hard labour prison. Sewell speculates that the new Prison Car *'would seem to have been a replacement for an old four wheeled carriage of dubious origin.'* The fact that there was only one NBR Prison Car suggests that the CR car probably ceased transporting prisoners to London in 1890 and changed its destination to Peterhead.

In 1895 the interior was altered to drawing 7787,[16] perhaps influenced by the layout of the 1890 North British van. The modified layout is shown in Figure 15.1, which is a reproduction from page 5 of the Large Diagram Book. The equivalent page in the Small Book is 18, which shows the same layout.

The new layout was a symmetrical arrangement of four cells towards each end fitted with wooden bench seats. The cell doors were described on the drawing as *'collapsible.'* A wide corridor changed

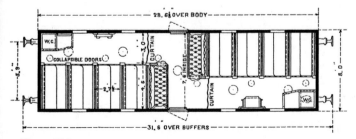

Figure 15.1
This drawing shows the revised Prison Car layout, adopted in 1895 and recorded on Page 5 of the Large Diagram Book.

sides on the centre line of the coach. WCs which offered a degree of privacy replaced the urinals. Windows were now fitted, covered with metal slats. The prisoners' accommodation was separated by curtains from the two upholstered seats for warders. Havock ventilators were fitted.

The van was painted all-over brown according to the Coaching Plant Stock Book, where it is recorded among the Luggage Vans. It was recorded as dual brake fitted and heated. It bore the number 1 and lasted until 1923. The 1921 Stock list states that it was gas-lit.

James McEwan suggested that it became a travelling van for the Permanent Way department after it was withdrawn from service.[17] This information was provided by St. Rollox carriage shop employees, and McEwan acknowledged that the information was purely anecdotal. He was also told that an 8- to 10-inch royal crown was part of the original livery, in place of the CR coat of arms.

REFERENCES
1. NRS BR/CAL/1/23 entry 1197
2. Birmingham City Archive ref: MS99 2307
3. CRA Archive ref: 3/4/1/23/7
4. *The True Line*, issue 62, pp. 20-22, photograph p. 13
5. Birmingham City Archive ref: MS99 2265
6. NRS BR/CAL/1/19 entry 593
7. NRS BR/CAL/5/11 page 35
8. *The Model Railway News*, February 1945, p. 35
9. *North British Coaches*, pp. 54-55
10. NRS BR/WCC/8 minute 2077
11. NRS BR/WCC/8 minute 2098
12. NRS BR/CAL/23/5 (32)
13. NRM 7467/C (on two sheets) RHP 70022
14. *The Glasgow Herald*, 31st May 1886
15. Article and drawing by Hutchison, *The Model Railway News*, June 1945, pp. 106-8. Described and drawn in *North British Coaches*, pp. 55-56
16. NRM 7466/C RHP 70094
17. Correspondence with John Boyle in 1987

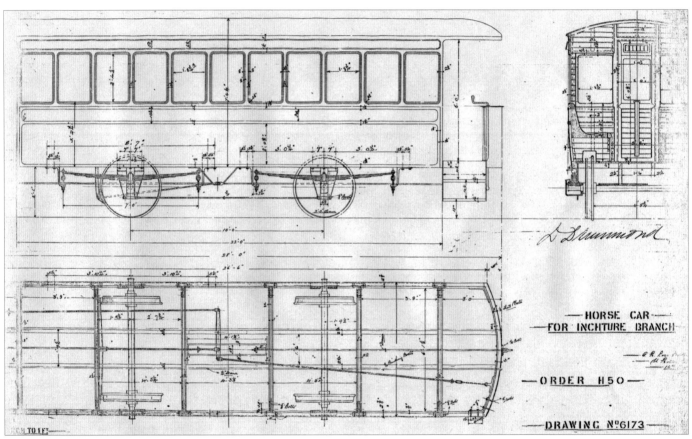

Figure 15.2
St. Rollox drawing 6173 of the *'Inchture Horse Car'* as originally conceived. The left-hand end of the drawing is unsuitable for reproduction, but was similar to the right-hand end.

15.2: THE INCHTURE HORSE BUS

The Dundee & Perth Railway opened its line between Dundee (West) station and Perth in 1847. The line was laid close to the Tay, in part to avoid passing too close to the seat of Lord Kinnaird, who was the first Chairman of the railway.[1] After constructing the main line the company intended to build three branches under the Dundee and Perth Railway (Alteration and Extension) Act[2] to two villages and a small harbour which were some distance from the main line.

Land for one branch, from Errol station to the scattered community of Inchmichael, was purchased and a line was laid. The branch *'was opened in 1849, but closed in 1852, the traffic never paying expenses, and the rails were taken up in 1854.'*[3]

Another branch was to diverge from Inchture station and go south to Polgavie harbour on the north bank of the Tay. The land to be purchased for this line was set out in the schedule to the Act,[4] but it was not built.

The last of the three branches was opened in 1848. It ran almost due north alongside a lane from Inchture station to cross what became the A90 road at a place known as Crossgates, on the south-west edge of Inchture village. From Crossgates the line continued to a tile works. The section beyond Crossgates was in use until about 1900, when the track was lifted just beyond the A90, leaving two sidings for wagon loads of manure for use as agricultural fertiliser.

Goods traffic over the line was usually locomotive hauled, as was passenger traffic in the early years, but, for most of its existence, passengers who were not prepared to walk about a mile and a half from Inchture village to the station could travel in a horse-drawn railway carriage which made the return journey between Crossgates and Inchture station to connect with the trains which ran along the Dundee to Perth line.

THE ORIGINAL VEHICLE

No drawings or photographs of the original carriage are known to exist. It was not separately identified in the 1874 inventory. It may have been one of the two *'mixed class closed carriages'* which were recorded in the inspection report prior to opening the line.[5] These carriages had a central First class compartment flanked by two Thirds.

THE CALEDONIAN VEHICLE

In December 1889 and January 1890, general arrangement drawings (St. Rollox 6173 for the exterior[6] and 6216 for the interior[7]) were produced for the original carriage's replacement with a purpose-built 4-wheel vehicle designed by Dugald Drummond and built at St. Rollox to order H50. The drawing of the exterior is reproduced as Figure 15.2.

The minute authorising its construction described it as *'a new Horse carriage with accommodation for 6 First and 22 Third class passengers and Driver's platform.'*[8] The interior was divided into two compartments by a partition located between the third and fourth windows at the braked axle end. Although it was technically a replacement, the car was charged to the capital account at a cost of £157.[9] This may have been because the original vehicle did not appear in the 1874 inventory, so it could not be replaced.

The car was of very light construction – the body's outer skin was only ⅜ inch thick. It had a simple handbrake that acted on both wheels on one axle. The brake could be applied from either end of the car by turning a handle which actuated a rod that ran the length of the underframe, along the centre line. The means of turning the movement of the brake handle through 90 degrees was shown on drawing 6227, which has not survived.

Comparing the GA to the photographs shows a considerable difference between the design on paper and its execution. The car was much shorter than planned, with seven windows rather than eleven, giving a likely overall length of 14 feet. It is not known whether the planned amount of First class accommodation was maintained at the expense of the Third class. The latter compartment's capacity must have been less than originally intended, but the amount of the reduction is unknown. The vehicle does not figure in either diagram book.

Scaling off the almost broadside photograph reproduced as Plate 15.1, the wheelbase was nine feet, not ten. The springs were underslung rather than in the conventional position that was shown on the drawing and were at 6 feet 6 inches centres, not 7 feet. The change in springing was the subject of drawing 6581, issued in late November 1890.

The driver's platforms were originally open, protected by an awning formed by the projecting roof, as in the official drawing. A Valentine photograph shows it in this condition.[10] The photographs reproduced here as Plates 15.1 and 15.2 show different modifications to each end.

At the First class end, the passenger compartment was extended to occupy half the platform. Passengers could therefore only mount the entrance platform on the left-hand side looking forwards. Perhaps this served to maintain the planned number of First class seats in the shortened body. At the Third class end, the left hand of the platform was similarly blocked off by extending the body panelling below waist height. There is no record of a drawing for these modifications.

LIVERY AND INTERIOR FITTINGS

The vehicle was painted and lettered in standard Caledonian carriage livery with white upper panels. It bore a CR Crest and was identified as 'C R 1'. The First class section was fitted with longitudinal seats in saloon style upholstered in blue of an unspecified shade. Third class passengers made do with plain wooden seats, also arranged longitudinally. The windows in both compartments had curtains, colour unknown, but perhaps blue to match the First class upholstery. There was no evidence of artificial lighting, despite the fact that in winter the last two return journeys would have been in twilight or full night.

WORKING THE BRANCH

An awning supported by cast iron columns at the side of Inchture station building gave shelter at the main line end of its route (see Plate 15.1). The carriage's home was at Crossgates, where one building served as carriage shed, stable, parcels and booking office, as shown in Plate 15.2.

From the opening of the service until 1907 the driver was Bob Speed, whose duties were taken over by his son. By 1916 he was succeeded in turn by a George Imlay who presumably served until the closure of the service.

The morning and afternoon timetables for 1907 are shown below. It offered one less trip than in 1878, when there was a return journey to meet a train arriving at tea time. On four of the six round trips, the bus connected with trains travelling in both directions. On the last departure of the morning this required a stay for 1½ hours at Inchture station. In 1878 and 1907 the First class single fare was 4d and the Third class 2d. There was no significant change in the 1915 timetable, and the fares remained the same.

Depart village	8.10am	8.55am	11.15am
Perth–Dundee train	8.30am	9.16am	11.36am
Dundee–Perth train		9.40am	1.06pm
Depart station	8.35am	9.45am	1.10pm

Depart village	2.50pm	4.05pm	6.15pm
Perth–Dundee train	3.11pm	4.43pm	6.30pm
Dundee–Perth train		4.25pm	6.40pm
Depart station	3.15pm	4.45pm	6.45pm

CLOSURE

This occurred on 1st January 1917, when the rails between Inchture station and Crossgates were lifted for use on the Western Front. They were part of a consignment of rolling stock and permanent way materials whose transfer was authorised in December 1916.[11] The permanent way amounted to 12 miles of track.[12] The branch was never re-opened to passenger traffic; the growth in motor transport after the war would have made it redundant.

REFERENCES
1. *The Locomotive*, 15th August 1907
2. 10 & 11 Vict. Cap. Lxxxix
3. *The Locomotive*, 15th August 1907
4. RHP 47707, dated 1846, contains details of the parcels of land to be purchased for all three branches
5. TNA MT6/4/28 Dundee & Perth Ry. Inspecting Officer's report, 11th May 1847
6. NRM 11389/C RHP 70049
7. NRM 11390/C RHP 70051
8. NRS BR/CAL/1/33 entry 1395
9. NRS BR/CAL/23/7(32)
10. Reproduced in the Angus Railway Group's *Steam Album Volume 3*, p. 39, *Through Scotland with the Caledonian Railway*, p. 127 and *Caledonian Railway Livery*, p. 260
11. NRS NR/CAL/1/69 entry 201
12. *Railways and the Great War*, Volume 2, p. 656

Plate 15.1
The Horse Car is parked under the awning at Inchture station, with the Perth starting signal reflected in a window. Compared with the drawing in Figure 15.2, the overall length and the wheelbase are both shorter than originally envisaged. The springing arrangement is also different. The livery and insignia are standard coaching stock style, although the purist might expect a dot between the C and R and not after the number.

Plate 15.2
The other end of the line at Crossgates, which was the base for the Horse Car, its motive power and its driver. In this and the previous photograph, the modifications to the entrance at each end can be seen.

15.3: THE CONNEL FERRY RAIL MOTOR

In 1903 the Ballachulish Branch of the Callander & Oban Railway was opened. It involved two major bridges. One, adjacent to the junction station at Connel Ferry, crossed the mouth of Loch Etive. Although the railway line was single track, the bridge was built wide enough to accommodate a footway alongside the rails. The C&O made no arrangements for its use prior to opening of the branch, presumably because a bargain would be easier to drive when the bridge actually existed.

The C&O always led a hand-to-mouth existence and constantly strived to squeeze every penny of revenue from those who lived in its hinterland. After the line opened it offered free pedestrian access across the bridge, provided the Lorn District Committee which administered the area paid a rent of £800 per annum. The Committee declined to pay. The C&O retaliated by building North Connel halt on the far side of the bridge, which opened on 7th March 1904. The bridge remained closed to pedestrians, and people who wished to cross the bridge had to travel by train and, of course, buy a ticket.

The North Connel station traffic record[1] indicates that, while a considerable number of people used the bridge and were issued tickets, receipts did not make a great contribution to the extra initial cost of providing the pedestrian walk way. Over the first five years, an annual average of just over 2,800 passengers was booked, 6,400 tickets were issued and about 340 parcels were collected. Total receipts for the five years were £396 – almost exactly half of what had been demanded for one year's access.

From the opening of the branch, passenger trains included Open Carriage Trucks to carry motor vehicles. With only five trains each way per day, this did not satisfy the increasing number of wealthy touring motorists, who otherwise had to travel about ninety miles via Tyndrum and Glencoe if they wished to reach Ballachulish from the Oban area or vice versa. Requests were made to permit cars to cross the bridge between trains. The C&O deemed the walkway to be unsuitable for motor vehicles. The stalemate over non-railway access continued until 1909.

On 11th May the Caledonian Board ordered that a Durham-Churchill petrol-driven charabanc be altered to run on railway tracks so that it could operate a shuttle service between Connel Ferry and Benderloch. The charabanc had been purchased in 1906 to connect Newton Mearns and Eaglesham with the railway system at Clarkston. A photograph of the charabanc in its road traffic guise appears in Caledonian Railway Livery.[2]

The Caledonian's involvement in this road service had ceased at the end of January, and the charabanc was not required by the person who took over operations.[3] The continuing refusal to negotiate over access across the bridge may have been connected with the impending availability of a vehicle which could be a new source of revenue for the C&O.

ALTERATIONS TO THE BUS FOR RAIL USE

Drawings within the number series 15002 and 15048 recorded the alterations required. Various components, such as mudguards and access steps from road level, were removed. The road wheels were replaced by 3-foot 9-inch disc wheels pierced with four large holes. The steering mechanism was locked straight ahead, and there is no sign of the steering wheel or steering column in photographs. A steel plate was fixed at the rear of the vehicle, together with a rubber sprung drawhook and side chains.[4] Sanding gear was provided for the rear driven axle.[5] A pair of brake blocks acted on the rear of the back wheels.

The gearbox from the Argyll Motor Co. was altered to enable the bus to travel at the same speed in both directions – on the road, it was limited to 4 m.p.h. in reverse. At £12, the modification was much cheaper than providing a turntable at Benderloch.[6] The total cost of the conversion was £797 10s.[7] For that sort of money, the CR could build ten cattle wagons.

LIVERY

As far as can be ascertained, the livery of the vehicle has never been recorded. It did not appear to change when it was converted to rail use. It was mainly a light colour with a darker surround to the panels – see Plate 15.3.

Two possible colour schemes are based on the locomotive and coaching stock liveries respectively. CR horse-drawn road vehicles tended to be the painted as if they were coaching stock, but they were not fitted with a prime mover.[8] The rail motor was certainly not the same colour as its companion purple-brown Carriage Truck. In 'locomotive' guise, it would have been light blue with maroon edges. If treated as a railway carriage, the main colour would have been white with purple lake edges. Presumably in both cases the underframe and running gear were black. Light blue seems the more likely livery.

The plain block lettering is another unknown quantity. It is clearly a dark colour, as it was when advertising the Eaglesham bus service, but does not seem to be black. The lettering is shown in Plate 15.4.

SERVICE AND TIMETABLE

Motor cars were carried on an Open Carriage Truck attached to the rear of the bus. Although operating instructions ruled that a maximum of two could be used, all the photographs of the vehicle in service show it coupled to just one such truck, usually No. 1541. A similar truck, No. 1591, was also photographed,[9] which suggests that two trucks were indeed available if needs be.

The service commenced on 1st July 1909. The bus ran in reverse from Connel Ferry, pushing the Carriage Truck before it. At Benderloch the truck was propelled directly into the loading dock. On return to Connel Ferry the bus ran forward through the station before reversing to propel the Carriage Truck into the dock platform at the east end of the station. Presumably, this was where the bus was serviced, with petrol being brought either up from Oban or delivered by rail in two-gallon cans.

The bus had twenty wooden slatted seats set in five tiers, plus three more on the upholstered bench seat beside the driver. Transparent side curtains could be lowered as protection against the elements. The single fare was 2d from Connel Ferry to North Connel and 3d to Benderloch. '*The charge for the conveyance of a MOTOR CAR will be 15/-.*'

The 1909 timetable[10] advertised ten scheduled return journeys, starting from Connel Ferry at 7.45am and finishing with a return journey from North Connel at 7.30pm. Services to North Connel only carried passengers because access was a footpath; those that ran through to Benderloch conveyed the Open Carriage Truck if required.

Plate 15.3
The rail motor posed for an official photograph (NRM St. Rollox collection, ref: SRX361A) at the end of Connel Bridge. The narrow space between the rails and the side of the bridge is very clear. A standard CR trespass sign is mounted on the telegraph pole.

Plate 15.4
This well-known view is included to show the lettering on the side panel of the rail motor and the seating arrangement. It was taken at the same time as the previous photograph and is NRM reference SRX361B. The brake gear and its cross linkage can just be seen, acting on the rear pair of wheels. The rail motor is coupled to Open Carriage Truck 1541.

The Benderloch trips left Connel Ferry at 8.25am, 1.00pm, 2.30pm and 6.20pm. Unusually, a comparable service was worked on Sundays, but starting later and with five services running through to Benderloch. The journey to Benderloch took 15 minutes.

In 1910 an extra return trip was incorporated, and the times of departure altered slightly. The 1910 timetable[11] acknowledged the growth in motor car use. It stated:

'special runs will be made, when required, with Passengers on payment of the minimum charge; also with Motor Cars in either direction at any hour clear of the booked runs on application to the Station Master at Connel Ferry or Benderloch.'

Service Usage

The service was a reasonable success, according to the annual traffic statistics.[12] Before and after the service, Benderloch and Connel Ferry reported carriage traffic in single figures. For the five years that the service ran, the figures are shown below. The part year of 1914 recorded 109 carriages in each direction. Interestingly, southbound traffic was heavier than northbound in four out of the five full years of operation.

	1909	1910	1911	1912	1913
Benderloch	241	312	434	248	594
Connel Ferry	212	107	236	24	774

Total earnings for the carriage of motor cars over the five and a half years were £2,532. There was also extra revenue from the rail motor's passengers which cannot be identified.

The End of the Service

As can be seen from the statistics, there was severe pressure on the service in 1912, when the drop in carriages conveyed suggests that it was not operational for significant periods. This must have created considerable dissatisfaction. The Caledonian reported in response to requests for motor car access that *'it is impossible to form a roadway for vehicles on the bridge.'* In September, the *Oban Times*[13] reported that the Lorn District Committee had received a petition with 146 signatures of residents from the parishes on the south side of the bridge asking for a footpath over the bridge to be opened.

In April 1913 the newspaper reported that a private individual had approached the Board of Trade about the possibility of operating a chain ferry across the mouth of the loch all the year round, and that it had received the general approval of the District Committee.

In July the *Oban Times* reported that the Caledonian had offered access to pedestrians and bicycles only, for £200 per annum plus half the cost of providing access tracks and fencing between the footway and the track at an estimated cost to the District Committee of a further £100. The Committee thought that the price was reasonable *'considering the expenditure already made by the Company'* but that it was excessive when considering the small geographical area of benefit compared with the whole of the district it served. The same article recorded that the Committee supported the application for the chain ferry *'especially in view of the inadequate railway service.'*

Faced with the threatened loss of revenue to the chain ferry, the C&O abandoned its stance that the bridge was unsuitable for vehicular traffic. It erected gates at each end of the bridge so that road and foot traffic could cross when it was not in use by trains, on payment of a toll. The new arrangement entailed complex electrical interlocking to prevent the possibility of road and rail traffic entering the bridge at the same time. At the north end, the space between the rails was filled in to allow cars and pedestrians to cross the track and access the roadway.

Inspection of the New Arrangements

The work was complete and ready for inspection on 1st June 1914. Major Pringle of the Board of Trade reported on the alterations on 20th July. He described the new works as follows:

'The roadway approach on each side of the bridge has been fenced and the track (on the west side of the bridgeway) has been asphalted and provided with suitable wheel guards. There is a gateman's hut and two gates at each end, one for vehicles and one for pedestrian traffic. These gates are controlled by a special occupation key which when not in use is kept locked in an instrument in either of the gateway huts.

The width of track available for pedestrian and vehicular traffic is 6ft. 8in. only. There is room therefore neither for wheeled vehicles to pass on the bridge, nor for a train and vehicle to pass each other, with safety.'[14]

He went on to report that he had tried every way possible to override the electric locking system and had failed in his attempts to create an unsafe situation. He therefore concluded that the bridge could be opened for road and rail traffic.

New Tolls

The newspaper reported that, *'in anticipation of a large increase in the number of cars crossing the bridge'* the C&O had fixed lower rates than those for rail-borne traffic. Charges as reported in the press ranged from 2d for foot passengers and dogs to 10s for motor cars. Commercial vehicles were not allowed; herds of sheep and cattle were also effectively prohibited. Livestock were only allowed one at a time at the exorbitant price of 5s per animal. The press cutting announcing the tolls is shown in Plate 15.5.

This was an interim arrangement, because an enquiry was to be held by the Board of Trade. Access commenced on 22nd June 1914 and the last time that the motorbus conveyed cars across the bridge was two days earlier, on 20th June. The bus service continued for foot passengers until October.

The Fate of the Rail Motor

The rail motor was brought to St. Rollox where it was converted back to a standard road vehicle at an unknown cost. The Caledonian had no use for it and it was put up for sale in March the following year *'at the best price available.'*[15] It only realised £21, and the £776 10s loss on the original conversion cost was written off.[16]

Board of Trade Enquiry

This was not the end of the story as far as people crossing the bridge was concerned. The Lorn District Committee lodged objections about the charges, the requirement that sheep and cattle could only be driven across one by one and the hours of opening (one hour before sunrise, one after sunset). They also asked that the bridge should be open at all hours to doctors. The Committee would have no objection to *'the old ferry rates which were 10d a score for sheep, 8d a score for lambs up to a year old and 4d each for cattle.'* Proceedings of the Enquiry were reported in the *Oban Times* on 8th August.[17]

The process and outcome of the Enquiry is in Board of Trade records.[18] The Enquiry was conducted by Sherriff McKenzie, the Sherriff Principal of Argyllshire, who charged 10 guineas per day for his services. Twenty-three objections had been received, from private individuals to the Lorn District Committee, touring organisations including the Automobile Association and the Highlands & Islands

Medical Service Board, which supported the request for the bridge to be opened for medical professionals at night.

The railway's case was that the bridge was originally designed to allow a footway alongside the tracks at an extra cost of £11,700, but a formal agreement was not negotiated prior to construction and had never been agreed since. Driving herds of livestock across the bridge would be dangerous to the animals. More importantly from the railway's perspective, animals should be carried by rail and not be driven on foot.

The C&O was also firmly against allowing commercial vehicles over the bridge as it would reduce the traffic carried by the railway. Finally, it would incur considerable extra cost to open the railway in the hours of darkness on the off-chance that someone wished to cross, as extra staff and electric lighting would be needed. The possibility of allowing free access to the bridge during the night at the risk of the user was not considered as an option.

The District Committee argued that opening the bridge to road traffic had destroyed the possibility of a ferry, and that the monopoly thus created would cause hardship in the Benderloch area, which

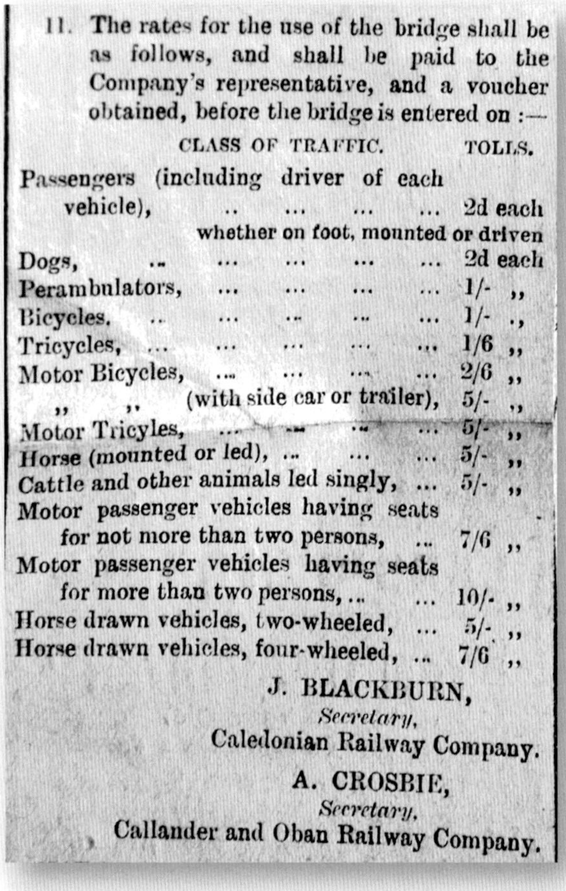

11. The rates for the use of the bridge shall be as follows, and shall be paid to the Company's representative, and a voucher obtained, before the bridge is entered on :—

CLASS OF TRAFFIC.	TOLLS.
Passengers (including driver of each vehicle), whether on foot, mounted or driven	2d each
Dogs,	2d each
Perambulators,	1/- ,,
Bicycles,	1/- ,,
Tricycles,	1/6 ,,
Motor Bicycles,	2/6 ,,
,, ,, (with side car or trailer),	5/- ,,
Motor Tricyles,	5/- ,,
Horse (mounted or led),	5/- ,,
Cattle and other animals led singly,	5/- ,,
Motor passenger vehicles having seats for not more than two persons,	7/6 ,,
Motor passenger vehicles having seats for more than two persons,	10/- ,,
Horse drawn vehicles, two-wheeled,	5/- ,,
Horse drawn vehicles, four-wheeled,	7/6 ,,

J. BLACKBURN,
Secretary,
Caledonian Railway Company.

A. CROSBIE,
Secretary,
Callander and Oban Railway Company.

Plate 15.5
The press cutting from the *Oban Times* which shows the list of tolls that were introduced as a temporary measure pending the Board of Trade enquiry.

amounted to about 800 people. There should be preferential rates for local people and locally registered motor vehicles. *'It was not right of the Railway Company to thwart the ferry scheme and prevent the needs of the people being served as a whole by shutting the bridge after dark.'*

The press report ended with the statement that on conclusion of the evidence Sherriff McKenzie heard counsel and that he would report to the Board of Trade.

Outcome of the Enquiry

McKenzie's judgement on 10th September was purely on the amount of tolls to be levied. There was no ruling about opening times, which remained restricted to the hours of daylight. The railway's proposals for the pedestrian tolls were approved. He upheld the principle of individual charges for livestock, thus protecting the railway's cattle truck business, but introduced differential rates of 5s for a bull, 3s for a cow and 2s for a pig or sheep. He favoured the leisured classes by reducing the tolls for vehicles. They were now to be 7s 6d for a 2-seater car (later reduced to 6s 6d) and 10s (reduced to 8s 6d) for a car with more than two seats. Finally, against the Caledonian's interests, he allowed access to commercial vehicles at 10s.

Toll Earnings

Regular reports to the Traffic Committee were made on the money earned from travellers crossing the bridge. As an example, the income for 1916 was £376 8s 3d.[19] This was 13% lower than the £430 average annual earnings of the rail motor. As might be expected, the lowest earning month was January, when £9 17s 8d was received. The peak months were July and August, when over £96 – almost one quarter of the annual income – was collected. In August 1922, it was reported that the bridge was used *'by 6,009 foot passengers, by 852 motor cars and by 290 cycles.'*[20] A reasonable estimate based on the 1914 tolls suggests that takings were about £900.

REFERENCES
1. NRS BR/CAL/4/89
2. *Caledonian Railway Livery*, p. 261
3. NRS BR/CAL/5/12
4. St. Rollox drawing 15021
5. St. Rollox drawing 15034
6. NRS BR/CAL/5/12/31/565
7. NRS BR/CAL/23/12(10)
8. See for instance *Caledonian Railway Livery*, p. 261
9. *The True Line*, issue 106, p. 32
10. Poster reproduced in *The True Line*, issue 10, p. 2
11. NRS BR/TT(S) 54/43
12. NRS BR/CAL/4/90
13. Press cuttings collected in NRS BR/CAL/4/151
14. TNA MT6/2325
15. NRS BR/CAL/5/13
16. NRS BR/CAL/23/14
17. Press cuttings in NRS BR/CAL/4/151
18. TNA MT6/2325
19. NRS BR/CAL/1/69 entry 507
20. *The Railway Magazine*, January 1923, p. 77

CHAPTER 16
SOME UNIMPLEMENTED DESIGN PROPOSALS

16.1: THE STEAM MOTOR CARRIAGE

At the start of the twentieth century a number of railway companies built steam railcars. There were two basic designs – a powered bogie enclosed in a rigid body, or an articulated engine unit and carriage, pivoting on a pin. The concept was introduced to compete with electric tramways that were capturing traffic in suburban areas or to provide a lower cost service on lightly used country branch lines.

Electric tramcars had demonstrated superior acceleration and hill climbing ability compared to steam traction. It was this power of acceleration that prompted the GER to build the 'Decapod,' which proved in theory that there was no reason to justify the expense of electrifying the 'Jazz Service' out of Liverpool Street.

Before the Caledonian actively considered a steam-powered vehicle, the Traffic Committee recorded the following minute in June 1903:

'80 HP engine and gear for Railway Cars, proposal to fit up one of the Company's carriages for experimental purposes.'[1]

A month previously, the North Eastern Railway had built two 'Autocars', numbered 3170 and 3171. At the time, the NER was electrifying its Tyneside suburban network. Raven, who was then Assistant Chief Mechanical Engineer, went a stage further by designing a vehicle that generated its own energy for routes that could not justify full-scale electrification. The Autocars had an 85 hp Napier petrol engine which drove a dynamo to power electric motors. The design was the world's first use of an internal combustion engine in a passenger carrying rail vehicle.

Nothing more is known about the CR proposal for a petrol-electric car – there is no record of a drawing in the St. Rollox register. One must assume that no action was taken beyond considering it as a possibility.

In February 1906 St. Rollox considered building a steam-powered rail motor. By this time, five railways had built articulated designs, and about thirty vehicles were in service. The biggest user was the

Taff Vale Railway. In Scotland, the G&SWR and GNSR had built three and two respectively.

St. Rollox produced three drawings, presumably of different designs, over the space of a week. Perhaps the power unit was the same in each proposal and the differences related to the passenger carriage. Two have not survived – drawing 13509 for a *'Proposed Steam Motor Train'* and 13516 for a *'Proposed Steam Motor Carriage.'* Drawing 13507 (see Figure 16.1), also for a *'Proposed Steam Motor Carriage,'* has survived.[2] It was for an articulated vehicle.

The drawing, which is an outline only, shows an open Saloon carriage with the locomotive portion enclosed in matching body work. This was unusual, as in most articulated designs the locomotive component was left open; it was the rigid design that had the power unit enclosed. The double footsteps under the doors suggest that it was intended for use on branch lines with low-level halt platforms rather than to counter tramcar competition in urban areas.

The power unit was an outside cylindered 0-4-0T with 3-foot 9-inch diameter wheels to match the carriage bogie. The main differences from the contemporary Class '611' 0-4-0ST were the size of the cylinders and the heating area, as the following table shows. The rail motor's higher boiler pressure partially compensated for these reductions. The low tractive effort of the rail motor's power unit was not very important, given that it only had to move one loaded carriage, plus perhaps a short tail load.

	CLASS '611'	RAIL MOTOR
Wheel diameter	3 feet 8 inches	3 feet 9 inches
Cylinders	14 by 20 inches	12 by 16 inches
Boiler pressure	140 p.s.i.	160 p.s.i.
Tubes	632 square feet	434.5 square feet
Firebox	52 square feet	58.5 square feet
Grate area	10.25 square feet	10.25 square feet
Tractive force	10,601 lb.	6,144 lb.

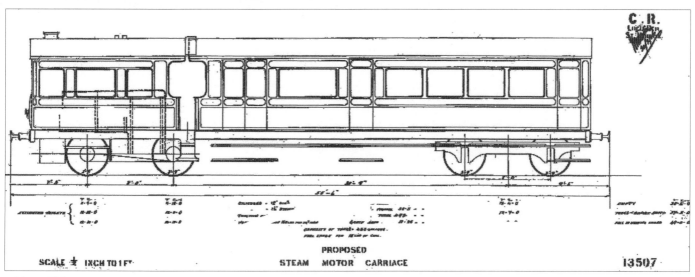

Figure 16.1.
St. Rollox drawing 13507 shows the proposed *'steam motor carriage'* of 1906.

The passenger saloon was similar in style to Lambie's Picnic Saloons 4 and 5. Passengers entered at the centre of the body with a driver's compartment at one end and the guard's van nearest the power unit. There is no plan view of the passenger section, but the seats must have been disposed along the sides of the compartment, as in other saloons.

The small area next to the guard's van door may have been intended for First class passengers. At about 7 feet 6 inches long it would have seated three people per side. The larger part of the passenger section was about 17 feet 6 inches long, perhaps offering twelve Third class seats per side – a total of around thirty seats. This was slightly less than a Diagram 10 Drummond 6-wheeled Brake Composite, which seated thirty-six.

POSSIBLE USES FOR THE RAIL MOTOR

A number of CR branches provided their basic service with just one carriage. In the 1913 Carriage Marshalling Circular the Dolphinton, Irvine and Kilbirnie services in the Southern section were possibilities for a rail motor. On the Northern section, the Bonnybridge, Kilsyth and Methven services were operated with one carriage. The Killin Branch was also a one carriage line, but the gradient up to Killin Junction might have been too severe.

The strongest candidate was the Bankfoot Railway, which opened in May 1906, just after the rail motor drawing was produced. The railway was built with a capital of £17,000 under the Light Railway Act of 1896, and was operated from the start by the Caledonian. The CR absorbed the railway in 1913, after subscribing £4,500 in additional capital in 1910. A copy of the share certificate is on the Rail Archive website.[3]

UNLIKELY ECONOMIC BENEFIT

The CR did not proceed with the rail motor concept, probably for a combination of economic and operational reasons. The cost savings of a railcar were said to be more apparent than actual. *The Railway Engineer*,[4] in response to a claim made by the Chairman of the Taff Vale Railway that the operational cost was about one third that of working an engine and four carriages, pointed out that it was fallacious to compare the cost of running a single-carriage railcar with that of a four-carriage train, and went on to comment:

'Assuming the wage to be the same, we very much doubt whether there would be very much difference in the cost of operating a steam-carriage and that of one carriage with a separate engine of suitable power, and the repairs would probably be lighter in the long run with the latter.'

There was also an inherent problem of inflexibility. If either the power unit or the carriage needed maintenance or repair, both units were put out of action, unless a fleet of rail cars was put in place to justify a spare power unit and carriage portion.

REFERENCES
1. NRS BR/CAL/1/47 entry 1267
2. NRM 7419/E RHP
3. www.railarchive.org.uk/images/pages/Bankfoot%20Light%20Railway.htm
4. *The Railway Engineer*, March 1904, pp. 72-73

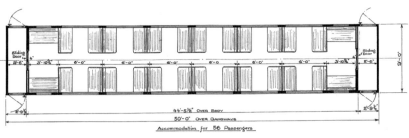

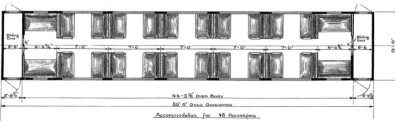

RIGHT: **Figures 16.2 and 16.3**
Proposed open Third class carriages for the Cathcart Circle. There is more leg room in the Figure 16.3 design, which reduced the seating capacity.

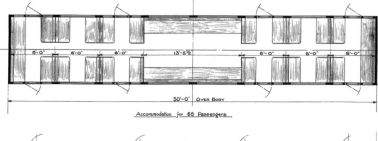

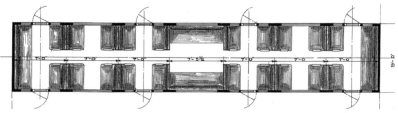

LEFT: **Figures 16.4 and 16.5**
In these two designs, the open space provided by the longitudinal seats at the centre of the carriage would have provided standing room for a number of passengers. This area was reduced by the increased leg room provided in the Figure 16.5 design.

16.2: Spacious Suburban Carriages and Corridor Stock

Designs that were not implemented abounded on all railways. On the Caledonian, these ranged from the spectacular, such as the McIntosh 'Pacific'[1] and Pickersgill's 2-10-2 freight locomotive,[2] to the potentially revolutionary, for example the proposed standard ranges of metal mineral and goods wagons.[3]

There are a number of tantalising references to radical carriage designs in the drawings registers. What did the *'proposed bogie carriage'*[4] of February 1876 look like? The date coincides with Brittain's succession to Conner. Could it have taken CR carriage development off in a completely different direction? In mid-1893 Lambie signed off a drawing of *'Proposed Twin carriages to run between Edinburgh, Perth and Aberdeen via Stirling.'*[5] Were they articulated, or pairs of carriages joined by vestibules? In 1911, two years after the modifications that created the Connel rail motor, a *'Petrol Motor Rail Car'* was drawn.[6] Would it have been a more viable proposition than the steam motor carriage?

This section deals with some proposals which could have changed the face of CR suburban traffic. The drawings are taken from a set of tracings used as artwork for printing a version of the Large Carriage Diagram Book, which at the time of writing were at The Ballast Trust.[7] Although undated, they were preceded and succeeded by drawings of designs that existed prior to the Grouping. The designs cannot be related to any drawings in the St. Rollox register, which suggests that they were outlines of ideas that were quickly abandoned.

Some of the carriages were arranged in saloon style. This may have been designed to allow a large number of standing passengers, which would have increased the carriage's capacity – a similar arrangement to that used on the London Underground. The compartment designs only offered slightly improved comfort, with more leg room than existing carriages.

Upgraded Stock for the Cathcart Circle

Late in 1913, the original Drummond-built 4-wheeled carriages on the Cathcart Circle service were at the end of their design life. Two drawings about possible replacements in the St. Rollox register have not survived. The first, St. Rollox 17221, was entitled *'Proposed Trains for Cathcart Circle.'* The second, issued in January 1914 under the title *'Proposed 50-foot carriage for Cathcart Circle'* was number 17249.

One set of diagrams may refer to this proposal. Alternatively, the designs may have been considered at the end of the Caledonian's existence, only to have been abandoned in favour of the LM&SR 54-foot designs that were introduced on the service in 1925.

The designs consisted of four versions of Saloon Third and two compartment Thirds. Two of the Saloons had end doors only leading to vestibules (Figures 16.2 and 16.3). The other two had four doors on each side – Figures 16.4 and 16.5. The conventional designs had eight and seven compartments (Figures 16.6 and 16.7 respectively). In each pair of drawings, one had increased leg room, reducing the seating capacity.

Six-Wheeled Stock

This set of proposals was for First class and Brake Third carriages 37 feet long by 9 feet wide on a 24-foot wheelbase. Three of the designs, a First, a Third and a Brake Third, had conventional compartments. Two variations of the First class carriage were drawn – see Figures 16.8 and 16.9. The latter had armrests, which reduced each compartment's seating capacity by two. The Third and Brake Third are shown in Figures 16.10 and 16.11. The other two designs, for a Third and a Brake Third, had seats in a saloon configuration, with access through vestibules at the end of the body (Figures 16.12 and 16.13).

High Capacity Saloon Carriage

The final design in the set was for a Third class Saloon with four doors on each side. Eighty seats were arranged in two compartments. This drawing had a sketched side elevation which showed light-weight seats and large windows. One assumes that the body was to have been of all-metal construction. It is shown in Figure 16.14.

Figures 16.6 and 16.7
The Figure 16.6 design offered no advance in seating capacity over the 45-foot and 48-foot Thirds and Brake Thirds of the 1890s/1900s. The extra length merely allowed three inches extra leg room in each compartment, compared with the Diagram 47 8 feet 6 inches wide 48-foot carriages. The Figure 16.7 design increased the leg room by 1 foot to the old standard for First class, but still sat five passengers on each side.

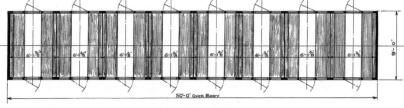

Accommodation for 80 Passengers

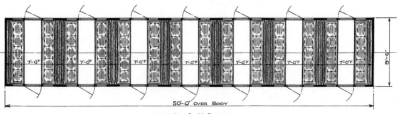

Accommodation for 70 Passengers

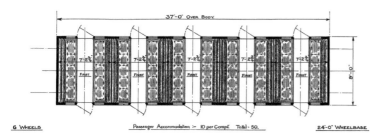

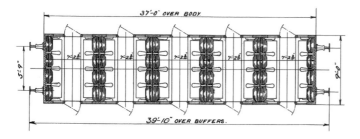

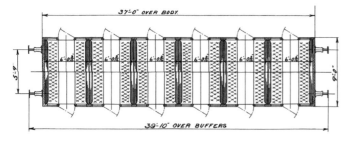

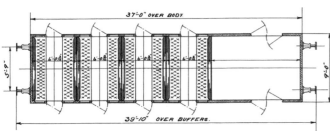

ABOVE: Figures 16.8, 16.9, 16.10 and 16.11
As in the 50-foot compartment carriage proposals, these 37-foot carriages were lengthened versions of the Drummond 6-wheeled designs of the 1880s, with the total wheelbase increased by 1 foot. Seating capacity in the Figure 16.9 First is reduced by the introduction of arm rests.

PICKERSGILL 58-FOOT 6-INCH CARRIAGES

Two side-corridor gangwayed vehicles are shown at the end of the Large Diagram Book, but not in the index or the Coaching Plant Stock Book. The wheelbase in each case was 51 feet 6 inches. Diagram 125 was an 8-compartment Third seating sixty-four, with lavatories at each end. It was essentially a Diagram 124 vehicle with two inches extra legroom in each compartment.

Diagram 126 was a Brake Composite with two First class and four Third class compartments and two lavatories, seating twelve and thirty-two. Again, the Third class compartments were two inches wider. It had the same capacity as Diagram 111, although the arrangement of the lavatories was different.

REFERENCES
1. St. Rollox 17161 NRM 7397/E RHP to be assigned
2. St. Rollox 19696 NRM7362/E
3. St. Rollox 11161, NRM GER15771 and St. Rollox 19700, RHP to be assigned
4. St. Rollox 1952
5. St. Rollox 7306
6. St. Rollox 15997
7. RHP numbers to be assigned

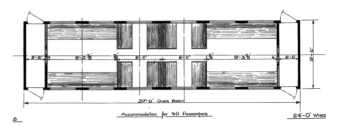

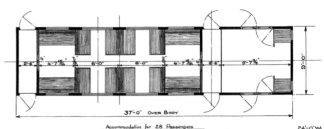

ABOVE: Figures 16.12 and 16.13
These Saloon designs offered fewer seats than the compartment stock, but would have allowed a fair number of standing passengers.

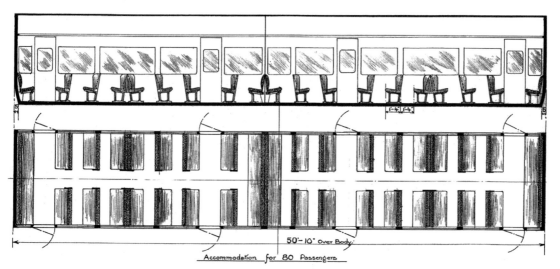

Figure 16.14
The seating capacity was no better than a 45-foot Third, but the open Saloons offered a considerable amount of standing room in the centre aisle. The seat frames look as if they were to be made of metal, which would have offered a saving in tare weight.

APPENDIX I: NUMBERS OF CARRIAGES IN TRAFFIC

This appendix uses information from valuations and censuses of rolling stock that were commissioned from time to time by the Caledonian. In some cases it will be seen that the exercise was carried out because of financial difficulties; the Board of Directors wished to value their assets as security against existing debt or to raise further capital.

THE 1849 ROLLING STOCK VALUATION

Less than three years after the opening of the line between Carlisle and Glasgow, the Caledonian faced financial ruin. In February 1850 matters came to a head, following a shareholders' committee of enquiry which had been set up in September 1849. The original Board of Directors resigned and a new Board was appointed. Mortgages were taken out to pay bank debts. Details are given in David Ross' history of the Caledonian.[1]

Part of the contingency plan was to value the rolling stock. This was tabled at the General Meeting in March 1850 and recorded in CR minutes.[2] It enumerated and put a value on 'new stock' (that built by the Caledonian), and 'old stock' from the Wishaw & Coltness and the Garnkirk & Glasgow railways. The CR stock is shown in the table below. It was valued at purchase price because,

'taking the cost price merely as a symbolic expression for the intrinsic usefulness of the value of the plant when new, it is found that the same sum represents its present condition; in other words the plant is at present at least as effective as when placed on the line and is of the same intrinsic value.'

CARRIAGE TYPE	NUMBER	VALUE
First class	35	£13,630
Second class	45	£12,840
Third class	48	£11,750
Composite	15	£4,065
Saloons, Greenock made	2	£1,250
Post Office	4	£1,448 7s 4d
Luggage Van	9	£1,800
TOTALS	158	£46,783 7s 4d

In addition there were fittings costing £200 to two Second class carriages 'to make them into Post Offices.' Presumably these carriages remained within the Second class numbers.

THE 1855 ROLLING STOCK REVIEW

Locomotive Superintendent Robert Sinclair conducted this review for the benefit of CR Board members. One of its purposes was to report on the state of the carriages taken over from the railways around Glasgow. It took the form of a letter to the Board[3] which gave the information set out in the following table.

Its starting point was the number of CR carriages in 1851. The 'added' row comprised the remnants of the stock that had been taken

over from the Wishaw & Coltness, the Garnkirk & Glasgow and the Greenock railways. The 'built' row showed the carriages constructed by the CR between 1851 and the time of the review.

	FIRST	SECOND	THIRD	COMP	LUGG
CR 1851	32	43	48	18	11
Added	7	38	19	1	5
Built	10	12	8	0	0
1855	49	93	75	19	16

THE 1867 ROLLING STOCK CENSUS

In October 1867 the Caledonian Board decided to make a list of all its plant. This was an appropriate time as a large amount of rolling stock, including over 400 carriages, had been absorbed from the Scottish Central and Scottish North Eastern railways in 1866 and 1867, and its precise condition was probably an unknown quantity. The Board:

'ordered that a return be obtained of all the Rolling Stock, Engines, Carriages, Wagons etc. belonging to the Company by taking stock at all the stations as on one day and by statements from the Clearing House'

The 'statements from the Clearing House' were necessary to identify plant that was off the CR system.

The matter was remitted to the General Manager 'to have this carried out as expeditiously as possible.'[4] On 3rd November an inventory of the entire carriage stock that could be found anywhere on the company's system and elsewhere on that day was duly taken. The result was recorded as an extra rolling stock return. The following table compares the census findings with the Board of Trade return for the previous July.

CARRIAGE TYPE	JULY 1867	CENSUS
First class	203	200
Second/Third class	547	546
Composite	91	95
Saloon	2	3
Family carriage	2	2
Post Office	8	
Luggage Van	103	110

Half-yearly returns to the Board of Trade were not always accurate, as they were the product of cumulative additions and subtractions, so a list such as that obtained on the 3rd November 1867 is of interest as a measure of how accurate the half-yearly returns could be. The figures for the carriage stock in existence on census day, whilst not identical with those in July, actually correlate well. Presumably the Post Office vehicles were not included because they were not part of general service stock.

The Rolling Stock Valuation of 1874

Another crisis in the Caledonian Railway's finances resulted in a further inventory being taken. The valuation of locomotives and carriages was undertaken by Thomas Richardson Yarrow, who stated in the declaration which accompanied his valuation to have been employed in the construction and valuation of railway plant from 1839 until his retirement. He was well known to the Caledonian, as he was the Engineer of the Scottish Central Railway up to its absorption into the CR in 1865. The Caledonian paid him three guineas per day.[5] Yarrow also made a separate valuation of Portpatrick Railway stock. The number of CR vehicles is shown in the following table, with the 1867 census figures for comparison.

Carriage Type	1867 Census	1874
First class	200	212
Second/Third class	546	703
Composite	95	168
Saloon	3	4
Family carriage	2	5
Post Office (from July 1867 return)	8	10
Luggage Van	110	154

Most of the large increases in the Second/Third class and Composite carriage stock took place in 1869/70, as described in Chapter 6.

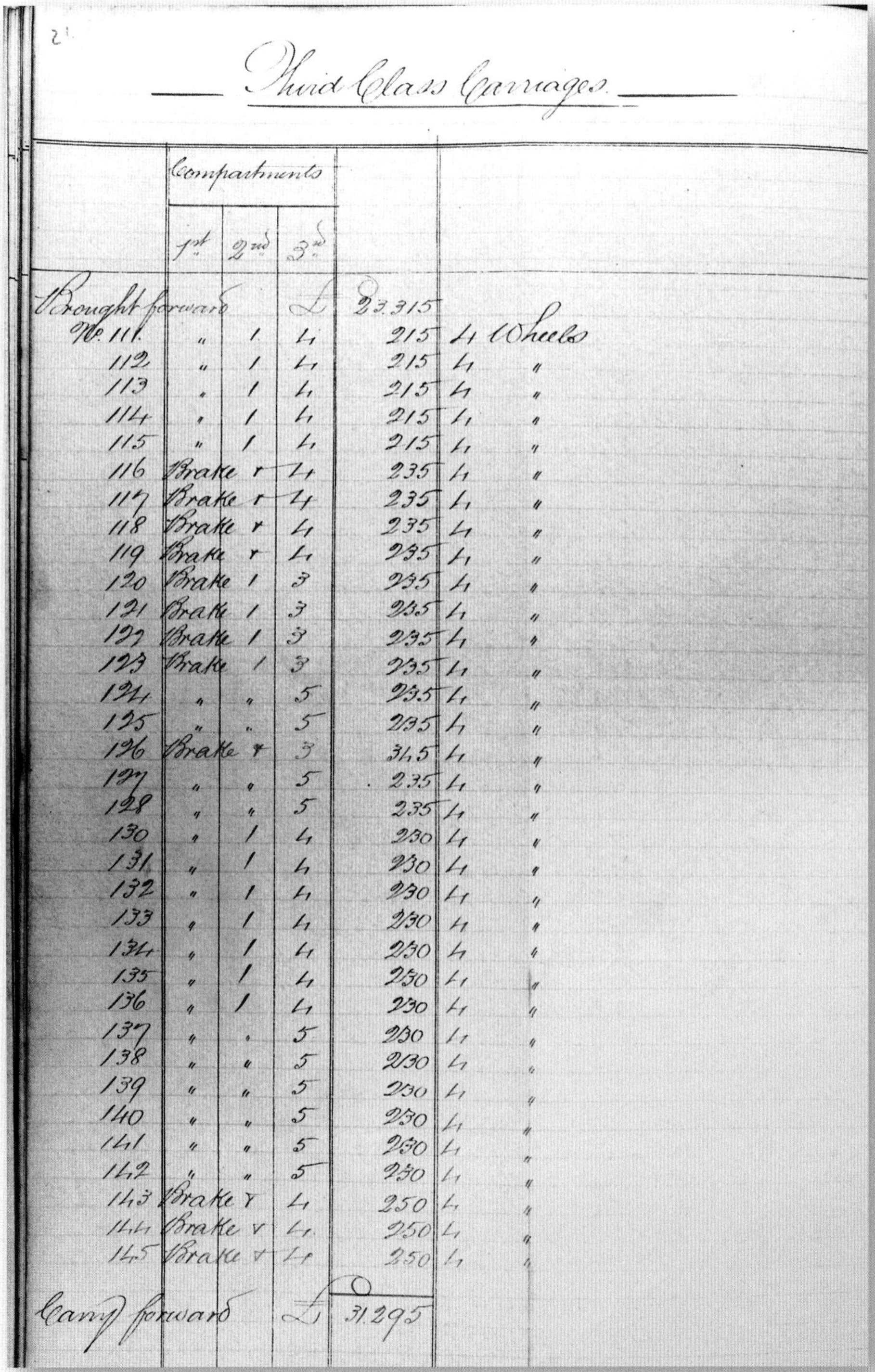

Third Class Carriages

	Compartments 1st	2nd	3rd	£	
Brought forward				23,315	
No. 111	"	1	4	215	4 Wheels
112	"	1	4	215	4 "
113	"	1	4	215	4 "
114	"	1	4	215	4 "
115	"	1	4	215	4 "
116	Brake	r	4	235	4 "
117	Brake	r	4	235	4 "
118	Brake	r	4	235	4 "
119	Brake	r	4	235	4 "
120	Brake	1	3	235	4 "
121	Brake	1	3	235	4 "
122	Brake	1	3	235	4 "
123	Brake	1	3	235	4 "
124	"	"	5	235	4 "
125	"	"	5	235	4 "
126	Brake	r	3	345	4 "
127	"	"	5	235	4 "
128	"	"	5	235	4 "
130	"	1	4	230	4 "
131	"	1	4	230	4 "
132	"	1	4	230	4 "
133	"	1	4	230	4 "
134	"	1	4	230	4 "
135	"	1	4	230	4 "
136	"	1	4	230	4 "
137	"	"	5	230	4 "
138	"	"	5	230	4 "
139	"	"	5	230	4 "
140	"	"	5	230	4 "
141	"	"	5	230	4 "
142	"	"	5	230	4 "
143	Brake	r	4	250	4 "
144	Brake	r	4	250	4 "
145	Brake	r	4	250	4 "
Carry forward			£	31,295	

Plate A.1

Oddities and Inconsistencies

Some of the Third class carriages as described by Yarrow were very odd. Numbers 570, 577, 578, 583 and 584 had seven compartments, as did 576, which also had a Brake compartment. Number 582 was a 6-compartment Brake. No other carriages had more than six compartments. Their valuation was very low compared with other 6-wheeled carriages, which would suggest that they were old, which only increases their curiosity value.

There were also inconsistencies in the entries. Seventy-one of the carriages in the Third class section were actually Second/Third Composites. Some examples can be seen in Plate A.1. This had the effect of over-stating the number of Second/Third class carriages in the table above with a corresponding understatement of the Composite numbers.

The Valuation Process

Yarrow's instructions were to value the plant at what he considered it would be worth to the company itself or to a third party who might wish to purchase it. His valuation for the entire carriage plant, including non-passenger coaching stock, came to £384,237.

In his hand-written report,[6] Yarrow claimed that he had personally inspected every locomotive and item of passenger stock belonging to the company, starting on 10th February 1874 and finishing on 24th August. The Caledonian provided him with the construction date and original cost of each vehicle. He stated that he:

> *'struck a basis of value by getting at (1) the age of the Engine (or Carriage) (2) condition and (3) I allowed so much for depreciation.'*

Yarrow assumed, from his railway experience, that the working life of a carriage was twenty-eight years and he therefore divided the initial cost of the vehicle by thirty – the additional two years being added to allow for scrap value. He went on to say:

> *'My rule in arriving at the present value of an Engine or Carriage is – to divide the estimated original cost by 30, multiply the amount by the number of years the Engine*

or Carriage had been on the line, the product will be the present value I put on such Engine or Carriage.'

The formula as stated produces a valuation which is the reverse of straight line depreciation, where an asset reduces in value by a set amount each year over its useful life, until it is worth nothing or a nominal sum as scrap. Using the formula, a carriage costing £300 is worth £100 after ten years, £150 at the mid-point in its life and £200 after twenty years' service. Straight line depreciation gives the same figure as Yarrow's at the mid-point, but £200 after ten years and £100 after twenty years.

It seems much more likely that what Yarrow actually did was to subtract one thirtieth of the initial cost of the carriage for each year since its construction.

INTERPRETING THE INVENTORY INFORMATION

The inventory grouped the passenger carriages by class and by running number within each class. Yarrow gave four items of information for each carriage – its number, the number of wheels, the number of compartments of each class, and his valuation.

This is not enough information to be certain of the identity of each vehicle, particularly when it comes to Third class carriages. Yarrow was supplied with more information by the Caledonian, such as the original cost and the building date of each vehicle. Both would have been of great use when analysing his inventory, but unfortunately they are not set down in his report.

Carriages charged to capital expenditure were allocated new consecutive numbers which extended the number series, while those that were replacements took the numbers of the carriages that they replaced. Niall Ferguson tabulated the entries for each type of vehicle by the values placed on them. This shows up blocks of carriages that can be matched with a degree of confidence to orders as described in Board minutes and capital expenditure returns.

STOCK NUMBERS 1880-1910

The following information is tabulated from the Board of Trade returns for January in each year. By this time Saloons and Family carriages were not counted separately but amalgamated with Composites.

CARRIAGE TYPE	1880	1890	1900	1910
First class	213	228	277	265
Second/Third class	770	750	1,149	1,306
Composite and Saloon	195	256	303	353
Post Office	5	3	3	5
Luggage Van	176	186	201	221

The large increases during the last decade of the nineteenth century and the first decade of the twentieth are described in Chapters 8 and 9. The Luggage Van numbers included sixty-three vans designed to carry luggage, fish and fruit as well as the Passenger Brake Vans. Records in this format ceased in 1912.

THE 1921 COACHING STOCK LIST

As recounted in Chapter 1, the CR apparently published an annual list of carriages and non-passenger coaching stock in service, correct as at the first of January. The 1921 list has survived, bound in with the copy of the Working Timetable that is in the NRS archive.[7] It is reproduced in full overleaf. A summary is shown in the following table. It did not include the carriages that were reserved for workmen's trains.

CARRIAGE TYPE	NUMBER
First class	242
Composite	229
Brake Composite	216
Third	861
Brake Third	508
Saloon	51
Passenger Brake Van	160

STOCK AFTER THE 1923 GROUPING

A detailed breakdown for the carriages handed over to the LM&SR in June 1923 is not available, because the carriage types were changed to *'uniform class'* or *'composite.'*

The copy of the Large Diagram Book in The National Archive[8] contains notes giving the number of carriages extant to each diagram. It probably dates from 1924. The number of each type of carriage is shown below. When compared with the 1921 Stock List, the figures reflect the withdrawal of a large number of carriages immediately after the Caley was absorbed into the LM&SR in June 1923.

CARRIAGE TYPE	NUMBER
First class	215
Composite	221
Brake Composite	218
Third	715
Brake Third	437
Saloon	38
Passenger Brake Van	160

REFERENCES
1. *The Caledonian Railway*, pp. 49-56
2. NRS BR/CAL/1/1 pp. 414-16
3. NRS BR/CAL/1/11 entry 199
4. NRS BR/CAL/1/16 entry 165
5. NRS BR/CAL/1/22 entry 277
6. NRS BR/CAL/5/15
7. NRS BR/TT/S/54/61
8. TNA RAIL 422/104

No. 3. As at 1st January, 1921.

CALEDONIAN RAILWAY.

LIST OF COACHING VEHICLES.

Explanation of References.

Brake, - - - - W—Westinghouse. D—Dual.
Steam-Heating, - - - H—Steam-heated.
Lighting, - - - - E—Electric. G—Gas. O—Oil Lamps.
Lavatory, - - - - - L—Lavatory in 1st Class. L L—Lavatory in both Classes.

Total Number of Vehicles.	Class of Vehicle.	Number of Wheels.	Compartments. 1st.	Compartments. 3rd.	Seating Capacity. 1st.	Seating Capacity. 3rd.	Lettered Numbers of Vehicles.	Weight. Tons.	Length. Feet.	Brake.	Lavatory Accommodation.	Steam-heating.	Light.
3	Officers' Saloons -	4	...	...	...	...	26 - - - - -	...	23	W	...	H	E
							1430 - - - - -	...	25½	W	...	...	O
							1431 - - - - -	...	23	W	...	H	O
1	do. -	6	...	...	...	...	1 - - - - -	15	34	W	...	H	E
2	Officers' Saloons -	8	...	...	...	...	40, 41 - - - -	36	50½	D	...	H	E
2	Dining Cars (Corridor) - -	8	1	1	9	12	38, 39 - - - -	29	45	D	...	H	E
3	Family Carriages (Corridor) -	8	3	1	20	8	32, 36, 37 - - -	26	42	D	L L	H	G
2	Family Carriages -	8	3	1	22	6	14, 15 - - - -	26	50	D	L L	H	E
3	do.	8	2	1	16	6	2, 11, 31 - - - -	21	40	D	L L	...	G
2	do.	8	1	1	11	6	6, 19 - - - - -	20	40	D	L L	H	G
4	1st Class Saloons -	8	2	...	24	...	7, 8 - - - - -	20	40	D	L	H	G
							9, 10 - - - - -	20	40	D	L	...	G
3	3rd Class Saloons -	8	...	2	...	42	3, 12, 13 - - - -	21½	48	D	L	H	G
3	do. -	8	...	3	...	32	33, 34, 35 - - -	23½	42	D	L	H	G
5	do. (Corridor)	8	...	2	...	48	42, 43, 44, 45, 46 -	28	50	D	L	H	E
2	do. -	6	...	2	...	32	4, 5 - - - - -	16	35½	D	L	H	G
2	do. -	6	...	3	...	25	17, 18 - - - -	14½	35½	D	L	H	G
3	do. -	6	...	2	...	30	28 - - - - -	13½	32	D	L	H	G
							29, 30 - - - -	13	32	D	L	...	G
6	do. -	6	...	1	...	25	1414, 1443 - - - -	...	30	D	L	...	G
							1419, 1420 - - - -	...	30	D	L	...	E
							1421, 1455 - - - -	...	30	D	L	...	O
1	do. -	6	...	2	...	32	1445 - - - - -	...	30	W	...	...	O
4	do. -	4	...	1	...	25	20, 21, 23, 25 - -	9	23	W	...	...	O
51	Saloons,												
2	1st Class Carriages	6	4	...	32	...	14, 16 - - - -	...	...	W	...	...	O
4	do.	4	4	...	32	...	13, 132, 196, 227, -	...	29	W	...	H	E
36	do.	4	4	...	32	...	20, 40, 45, 47, 63, 64, 98, 100, 102, 104 to 113, 115 to 121, 150, 151, 153, 168, 179, 181, 182	10½	28½	W	...	...	G
							6, 92, 189 - - - -	12½	30	W	...	...	G
53	do.	6	5	...	40	...	19, 22, 24, 26, 28, 30, 31, 32, 33, 34, 48, 49, 51 to 54, 57, 58, 60, 65, 66, 71, 79, 80, 84 to 91, 93 to 95, 97, 114, 123, 139, 140, 142, 145, 148, 175, 176, 177, 178, 183, 190, 191, 194, 197	14	35½	W	...	...	G
							180 - - - - -	14	35½	W	...	H	G

2

Total Number of Vehicles.	Class of Vehicle.	Number of Wheels.	Compartments. 1st.	Compartments. 3rd.	Seating Capacity. 1st.	Seating Capacity. 3rd.	Lettered Numbers of Vehicles.	Weight. Tons.	Length. Feet.	Brake.	Lavatory Accommodation.	Steam-heating.	Light.
1	1st Class Carriages	8	6	...	26	...	4 - - - - -	22	45½	W	L	H	G
18	do.	8	6	...	32	...	156, 157, 248 - -	22	45½	W	L	...	G
							158, 159, 161, 203, 204, 205, 239 to 247 - -	22	45½	W	L	H	G
27	do.	8	7	...	42	...	1, 103, 122 - - - -	24	48	W	...	...	E
							44, 70, 249, 251, 252, 253, 254, 256, 257, 258, 259, 263, 269, 271, 272, 279, 283, 284, 285, 288, 290, 293 - - -	24	48	W	...	...	G
							277, 304 - - - -	24	48	W	...	H	E
81	do.	8	7	...	56	...	2, 3, 5, 68, 124, 226, 228, 305 - - -	24	48	W	...	H	E
							7, 8, 38, 129 - -	24	48	W	...	...	E
							69, 73, 74, 75, 154, 155, 162 to 166, 169, 171, 173, 200, 206 to 211, 214 to 218, 220 to 223, 229, 230, 231, 235 to 238, 250, 255, 260, 262, 264, 265, 266, 268, 270, 273, 274, 280, 281, 282, 286, 287, 289, 292, 294, 298, 299, 301 - -	24	48	W	...	...	G
							219, 232, 276, 278 - -	21½	45	W	...	H	G
							295, 296, 297, 300, 302, 303 - - - -	24	48	W	...	H	G
9	do.	8	8	...	64	...	9, 10, 18, 41, 43, 55, 59, 136, 160 - - -	29	57	W	...	H	E
11	do. -	12	9	...	72	...	42, 67, 125, 130, 306, 307, 308, 309, 310, 311, 312 - - - -	37	65	W	...	H	E
242	1st Class Carriages.												
40	Composites - -	6	2	3	16	30	5, 36, 55, 60, 79, 83, 84, 87, 88, 156, 158, 177, 178, 179, 186, 187, 190, 193, 195, 196, 198, 199, 200, 202, 203, 206, 209, 211, 212, 213 -	...	...	W	...	...	G
							201, 204, 205, 207, 208, 210 - - - -	14	32	D	...	...	G
							62, 78, 185, 189, -	...	32	W	...	...	O
8	do. - -	6	3	2	18	20	392 to 399 - - -	13½	35½	W	...	...	G
6	do. - -	6	2	2	12	20	16, 17, 18, 20, 22, 24 -	...	30½	D	L	...	G
6	do - -	6	2	2	16	20	218, 219, 220, 221, 222, 223 - - - -	14	30	D	L	...	G
3	do. - -	6	2	2	10	20	275, 277, 278 - -	13	32½	D	L	...	G
14	do. - -	6	2	3	12	30	8, 9, 10, 11, 13, 42 -	14½	35½	W	L	...	G
							25, 26, 27, 28, 29, 30 -	14½	35½	D	L	...	G
							40, 41 - - -	14½	35½	W	L	H	G
3	do. - -	6	1½	2½	9	25	294, 295, 296 - -	13	34	D	L	...	G
5	do - -	6	1½	3	9	30	302, 303, 304, 305, 306	13	34	D	L	...	G
17	do. - -	8	1½	3	7	28	321 to 330, 334, 335, 336, 337, 339, 340, 341	22½	42	D	L L	H	G
10	do. - -	8	3½	2	21	20	19, 39, 54, 71, 82, 102, 106, 107, 225, 226 -	22½	45¼	W	L	H	G
3	do. - -	8	3½	2	24	18	129, 141, 152 - -	24	48	D	L L	H	G

4

Brake Composites—Continued. / Brake Composites. / 3rd Class Carriages.

Total Number of Vehicles	Class of Vehicle	Number of Wheels	Compartments 1st	Compartments 3rd	Seating Capacity 1st	Seating Capacity 3rd	Lettered Numbers of Vehicles	Weight (Tons)	Length (Feet)	Brake	Lavatory Acc.	Steam-heating	Light
8	Brake Composites—Continued.	8	2	3	16	30	37, 38, 155 -	20½	45	W		H	G
		8	2	3	12	3	53, 59 -	20½	45	W		H	G
							64, 68, 103 -	20½	45	W			G
33	do.	8	2	4	16	40	43, 45, 63, 89, 90, 108, 109, 164, 229, 250, 253, 382 to 391	20½	45	W			G
6	do.	12		5		50	162, 166, 167, 176, 251, 252, 254, 270, 271, 272, 273, 274	35½	65	W		H	E
4	do.	8	3	3	24	24	348, 365, 366, 367, 368, 373	25	50	D	L	H	E
11	do. (Corridor)	12	3	4	12	32	81, 133, 144, 147	38½	65	W	L	H	E
8	do. (do.)	12	4	3	24	24	57, 76, 132, 146, 148, 238, 293, 369, 370	38½	65	D	L	H	E
4	do. (do.)	12	4	5	12	40	120, 138	37	65	W	L	H	E
9	do. (do.)	12	4	4	12	32	58, 117, 151, 154, 173, 228, 262, 263	33½	65	D	L	H	E
							371, 372, 374, 375	33½	57	W	L	H	G
8	do. (Corridor inside)	8	2	3	13	25	128, 157, 180, 230, 417	33½	57	D	L	H	E
	do. (do.)	8	2	4	13	33	181, 233, 260, 276		57	D	L	H	E
20	do. (do.)						21, 47, 118, 127, 184, 379 to 381	28½	50	W			O
							61, 131, 159, 188, 191, 427 to 432, 439, 440, 441	30	57	W		H	E
							433 to 436, 445, 446	30½	57	D			
216	**Brake Composites.**												
8	3rd Class Carriages	4		4		40	783, 785, 787, 788, 789, 3039, 3061, 3119	9½		W			O
4	do.	4		5		60	1378 to 1381		31	W		H	E
44	do.	4		5		50	31, 60, 62, 71, 177, 208, 223, 268, 270, 283, 452, 456, 470, 472, 474, 476, 481, 482, 484, 493, 522, 531, 539, 540, 543, 585, 588, 591, 593, 597, 601, 631, 634, 636, 651	10	28¼	W			G
54	do.	6		5		50	681, 682, 688, 689, 690, 692, 693, 694, 696, 2, 52, 67, 112, 129, 463, 488, 506, 533, 565, 594, 632, 646, 665, 673, 740, 957, 970, 971, 975, 977, 978, 983, 1043, 1169, 1286, 1294 -	10	28¼				O
42	do.	6		5		42	84, 104, 290, 399, 528, 628, 630, 699, 700, 777, 778, 779, 974, 984, 985, 1285, 1297, 1299, 1332, 1333, 1355, 1377, 11, 99, 139, 143, 154, 166, 180, 181, 183, 187, 323, 326, 877 to 892, 95, 178, 209, 211, 212, 224, 497, 870 to 876	14	35½	W	L	G	G
3	do.	8		5		46	1278, 1279, 1280	22	42	D	L	H	G

3

Composites—Continued. / Composites. / Brake Composites.

Total Number of Vehicles	Class of Vehicle	Number of Wheels	Compartments 1st	Compartments 3rd	Seating Capacity 1st	Seating Capacity 3rd	Lettered Numbers of Vehicles	Weight (Tons)	Length (Feet)	Brake	Lavatory Acc.	Steam-heating	Light
35	Composites—Continued.	8	3	4	24	40	72, 73, 92, 93, 94, 95, 96, 97, 112, 119, 122, 126, 160, 170, 243, 255, 257, 258, 266	21	45	W			G
		8		4		40	259, 265, 267, 268, 269	21	45	W		H	G
		8					104	21½	45	W		H	E
6	do.	8	4	3	18	40	311, 314, 315, 316, 317, 318, 319, 320	21½	48	D		H	G
15	do.	8	4	4	32	30	312, 313	21	48	W			G
5	do.	8	4	3	24	30	163, 168, 227, 239, 245, 247	21	45	W		H	G
7	do.	8	4	4	25	25	12, 125, 139, 142, 143, 145, 153, 332, 333, 355, 407, 410, 413, 414, 415	21	45	W		H	G
6	do. (Corridor inside)	8	4	4	32	48	406, 408, 409, 411, 412	28	50	W	L	H	E
4	do.	8	4	4	32	60	14, 44, 192, 197, 376, 377, 378	29	57	W	L	H	E
7	do. (Corridor inside)	8	4	5	25	34	116, 123, 124, 182, 183, 214	30	57	W	L	H	E
3	do. (do.) (Corridor)	8	3	5	19	42	4, 23, 85, 232	31	57	W	L	H	E
4	do.	8	3	3	24	32	422, 423, 437, 438, 442, 443, 444	33½	57	W	L	H	E
	do.	8	3	4	24	24	424, 425, 426	33½	57	D	L	H	E
	do.	8	2	4	12	32	416	25	50	W	L	H	E
11	do.	12	5	3	30	24	418, 419, 420, 421	38	65	W	L	H	E
							86, 110, 171, 175	38	65	D	L	H	E
6	do.	12	4	6	32	72	15, 69, 121, 135, 136, 137, 140, 174, 217, 256	37	65	W	L	H	E
							130						
							134, 360, 361, 362, 363, 364						
229	**Composites.**												
5	Brake Composites-	6	1	3	8	30	49, 52, 235, 236, 237		30½	W			G
1	do.	4	2	2	16	20	149	13½	32	W			O
4	do.	6	2	1	8	10	307 to 310 -	14½	35½	W		H	G
							1, 2 -						
21	do.	6	2	2	16	20	3, 6, 7, 46, 48, 51, 75, 77, 80, 194, 215, 216, 231, 400 to 405 -	14	35½	W			G
1	do.	6	1	3	8	30	50	14½	35½	W			O
7	do.	6	2	2	12	20	31, 32, 33, 34, 35, 261, 264	14	34	W			G
3	do.	6	1½	2½	9	20	297, 298, 299, 300, 301	19	42	D	L		G
14	do.	6	1½	3	7	25	279, 280, 281, 282, 283, 284, 285, 286, 287, 288, 289, 290, 291, 292 -	22	45	D	L	H	G
5	do.	6	1½	3	9	28	65, 98, 99, 100, 101	22	45	W	L	H	G
13	do.	6	1	3½	9	28	70, 74, 91, 111, 150, 101, 165, 240, 241, 242, 244, 246, 248	18½	42	D	L	H	G
4	do.	6	1½	3½	5	35	66, 67, 105, 224	23	45	D	L	H	E
3	do.	6		3	5	24	331, 349, 350	24	48	D	L	H	G
7	do.	6	1½	3	10	26	172, 249						
15	do.	8	2		10	16	338, 342, 343, 344, 345, 346, 347, 351, 352, 353, 354, 356, 357, 358, 359	23	45	D	L	H	G

6

Light	Steam-heating	Lavatory Accommodation	Brake	Length (Feet)	Weight (Tons)	Lettered Numbers of Vehicles	Seating Capacity 1st	Seating Capacity 3rd	Compartments 1st	Compartments 3rd	No. of Wheels	Class of Vehicle	Total No. of Vehicles
E			W	48	22½	19, 22							
E	H		W	48	22½	126, 438, 650, 657, 1074, 1123, 1291							
G			W	45 and 48	22½	37, 66, 127, 168, 169, 174, 175, 179, 195, 202, 207, 216, 217, 230, 244, 250, 252, 293, 319, 327, 328, 329, 330, 332, 334, 336, 349, 359, 362, 363, 366, 368, 369, 371, 372, 375, 376, 378, 381, 382, 386, 387, 389, 390, 392, 414, 471, 495, 509, 537, 552, 555, 559, 569, 589, 595, 849, 893, 896, 898 to 907, 913 to 926, 938 to 952, 989 to 993, 1072, to 1031, 1057 to 1071, 1080 to 1098, 1099, 1100 to 1101, 1104, 1105, 1113, 1137, 1139, 1140, 1138, 1141, 1144, 1148, 1149, 1150, 1154, 1156, 1147, 1151, 1152, 1153, 1155, 1209, 1211, 1214, 1185 to 1208, 1210, 1212, 1213, 1215 to 1223, 1225, 1226, 1227, 1224, 1228, 1231, 1233, 1229, 1230, 1232, 1234, 1236, 1238 to 1242, 1244, 1245, 1247, 1248, 1235, 1237, 1243, 1246, 1251, 1253, 1249, 1250, 1252, 1254		80		8	8	3rd Class Carriages —Continued.	297
G	H		W	45 and 48	22½	367, 894, 895, 897, 927, 426, 494, 527, 656, 663, 695, 698, 958, 964, 968, 969, 973, 976, 997, 998, 1102, 1103, 1106 to 1136, 1112, 1126 to 1136, 1138, 1141, 1144, 1148, 1149, 1150, 1154, 1156, 1072, 1181, 1183, 1295, 1301, 1351, 1353, 1354		108		9	8	do.	23
H E	H		W	57	28½	125, 1306 to 1318		132		9	8	do. (Corridor)	15
E	H	L	W	68	37½	979, 980, 982		56		11	12	do. (Corridor)	3
E	H	L	D	50	25	784, 786, 1000		72		7	8	do. (do.)	16
E	H	L	W	65	36½	549, 1298, 1335 to 1344		64		9	12	do. (do.)	10
E	H	L	D	65	36½	1001, 503, 535, 542, 553, 467							
H	L		D	57	33½	684, 697, 1284, 1288, 1289		72		8½	8	do. (Corridor inside)	4
H	L		W	57	30½	347, 395, 962, 963						3rd Class Carriages.	861

5

Light	Steam-heating	Lavatory Accommodation	Brake	Length (Feet)	Weight (Tons)	Lettered Numbers of Vehicles	Seating Capacity 1st	Seating Capacity 3rd	Compartments 1st	Compartments 3rd	No. of Wheels	Class of Vehicle	Total No. of Vehicles
G			W	35½	13	12, 13, 15, 23, 24, 26, 30, 38, 39, 42, 43, 44, 45, 47, 48, 49, 50, 53, 55, 56, 57, 61, 69, 70, 72, 74, 76, 79, 81, 82, 83, 86, 87, 88, 90, 91, 92, 93, 94, 96, 98, 100, 101, 102, 103, 106, 109, 111, 114, 115, 116, 118, 119, 120, 121, 123, 130, 131, 132, 133, 136, 137, 138, 141, 142, 144 to 147, 149, 151, 153, 160, 161, 167, 173, 176, 182, 184, 185, 186, 188, 189, 190, 193, 194, 198, 206, 213, 215, 221, 222, 238, 241, 245, 246, 249, 254, 269, 280, 285, 287, 300, 301, 302, 305, 306, 308, 310, 315, 318, 320, 321, 331, 338, 339, 340, 344, 345, 352, 355, 361, 364, 365, 373, 374, 377, 379, 380, 384, 401, 405, 412, 419, 420, 422, 424, 432, 445, 447, 461, 465, 501, 504, 505, 556, 560, 561, 564, 566, 570, 573, 574, 578, 579, 580, 596, 621, 622, 625, 626, 627, 659, 661, 702, 705, 708 to 712, 714 to 720, 723 to 730, 732 to 735, 751 to 756, 762, 763, 775, 800 to 815, 817 to 820, 823, 824, 825, 827 to 831, 833 to 848, 850, 851, 852, 853, 3073, 3166		60		6	6	3rd Class Carriages —Continued.	304
H G	H		W	35½	13	36, 59, 108, 124, 135, 150, 214, 346, 358, 396, 434, 473, 558, 703, 822, 826, 832							
G			D	35½	13	28, 128, 148, 155 to 158, 242, 282, 360, 532, 554							
O			W	35½	13	14, 97, 110, 233, 247, 263, 557, 562, 572, 577, 583, 623, 713, 721, 722, 731, 757, 758, 759, 760, 761, 764, 765, 766, 776						do.	
O			D	35½	13							do.	
G H	H	L	D	45 and 48	22	3, 68, 75, 192, 253, 436, 466, 475, 479, 499, 502, 507, 514, 519, 525, 530, 536, 538, 541, 544, 547, 548, 551, 586, 598, 602, 635, 637, 639, 641, 643, 647, 648, 652		54		6	8	do.	34

8

Class of Vehicle	Total No. of Vehicles	No. of Wheels	Comp. 1st	Comp. 3rd	Seating 1st	Seating 3rd	Lettered Numbers of Vehicles	Weight (Tons)	Length (Feet)	Brake	Lavatory Accom.	Steam-heating	Light
Brake 3rd Class—*Continued.*	4	8		6		60	600, 633, 640, 644, 649, 662, 664, 666, 669, 670, 671, 672, 674, 675, 676, 908, 909, 910, 928 to 937, 994, 1032 to 1036, 1039 to 1042, 1044 to 1047, 1049, 1051, 1116, 1117, 1119, 1120, 1157, 1158, 1159, 1162, 1163, 1167, 1171, 1174, 1175, 1177, 1178, 1179, 1184	20 and 21	45 and 48	W			G
do.	21	8		7		70	816, 911, 912, 1048, 1050, 1052, 1054, 1114, 1115, 1118, 1121, 1122, 1166, 1168, 1172, 1173, 1176, 1180, 1182, 1255, 1256, 1258 to 1266, 1268 to 1274	20	45	W		H	G
do.	2	8		5		60	1257, 1267 - 1037, 1038	21	48	D / W		H / H	G / E
do.	8	8 / 12		6 / 7		72 / 84	638, 642, 645, 667 - 54, 65, 240, 257, 294, 325, 398, 439, 462, 563, 599, 624, 653, 655, 687, 691, 967, 1077, 1283, 1287, 1292	21 / 21	45 / 49	W		H	E
do. (Corridor)	16	12		8		96	458, 683 - 343, 686, 972, 1319 to 1323 - 107, 227, 454, 518, 571, 792, 966, 1281, 1300, 1302, 1303, 1324 to 1328	28 / 35½	57 / 65	W		H / H	E / E
do. (do.)	3	8		6		48	17, 986 - 515	35	65	W	L	H	E
do. (do.)	14	12		5		40	6, 281, 304, 511, 523, 617, 618, 619, 620, 965, 996, 1076, 1349, 1350 - 117, 197, 409, 981, 1329, 1330, 1331, 1334, 1345	33½ / 33	57 / 57	D / W	L / L	H / H	E / E
do. (do.)	14	12		7		56	496, 1055, 1346, 1347, 1348	35	65	W	L	H	E
do. (Corridor inside)	12	8		4		34	256, 286, 529, 685, 987, 995, 1056, 1356 to 1360	37½ / 33	57 / 57	W / D	L	H	E
do. (do.)	11	8		5		44	460, 477, 508, 999, 1160, 1161, 1164, 1165, 1170, 1290, 1304	26½	50	W	L	H	E
Brakes, 3rd Class.	508							29	57	W	L	H	E
Total Carriages.	2107												

7

Class of Vehicle	Total No. of Vehicles	No. of Wheels	Comp. 1st	Comp. 3rd	Seating 1st	Seating 3rd	Lettered Numbers of Vehicles	Weight (Tons)	Length (Feet)	Brake	Lavatory Accom.	Steam-heating	Light
Brake 3rd Class	2	4		2		20	790, 791	10	...	W			O
do.	74	4		3		30	1, 9, 32, 58, 73, 77, 78, 80, 89, 105, 113, 122, 134, 140, 152, 159, 162, 163, 164, 165, 170, 171, 172, 191, 196, 220, 226, 231, 232, 234, 251, 255, 258, 259, 260, 261, 262, 264, 265, 272, 273, 274, 276, 288, 295, 299, 313, 317, 333, 337, 341, 348, 361, 353, 357, 391, 397, 403, 406, 408, 416, 437, 451, 513, 575, 587, 603, 660, 677, 701, 706, 707, 961, 3085	9½	28½	W			G
do.	115	6		4		40	10, 20, 864, 867, 51, 64, 199, 200, 201, 203, 204, 205, 219, 239, 243, 248, 271, 277, 279, 284, 289, 291, 402, 404, 407, 413, 415, 417, 418, 428, 430, 440, 442, 444, 490, 658, 668, 704, 739, 744, 745, 773, 774, 793, 799, 855 to 863, 865, 866, 868, 869, 1078, 1079, 3103, 237	9½ / 14	28½ / 35½	W / W		H	O / G
do.	4	6		5		50	25, 225, 229, 235, 278, 350, 370, 394, 400, 411, 423, 433, 441, 443, 448, 450, 498, 567, 568, 576, 582, 584, 592, 629, 678, 679, 680, 738, 741, 742, 743, 748, 749, 767 to 772, 794 to 798, 1053, 1296, 1352, 3045, 3047, 3069, 3142, 3144, 3147	14	35½	W			G
do.	6	6		4		32	959, 960, 1124, 1125, 41, 85, 435, 1275, 1276, 1277	14	35½	D			G
do.	26	6 / 8		4		40	297, 610, 654, 459, 605, 607, 608, 609, 606, 953, 954, 955, 956, 29, 63, 335, 510, 604, 611 to 616, 988, 1075	14 / 22 / 22 / 21 / 18	34 / 45 / 48 / 42	W / D / W / D	L	H / H / H	G / G / E / G / G / E
do.	176	8		6		60	4, 5, 7, 8, 16, 18, 21, 27, 33, 34, 35, 40, 46, 210, 218, 228, 236, 266, 267, 275, 292, 296, 298, 303, 307, 309, 311, 312, 314, 316, 322, 324, 342, 354, 356, 383, 385, 388, 393, 410, 425, 427, 429, 431, 446, 449, 453, 455, 457, 464, 468, 469, 478, 480, 483, 485, 486, 487, 489, 491, 492, 512, 516, 517, 520, 521, 524, 526, 534, 545, 546, 550, 581, 590	20 and 21	45 and 48	W			G

10

Total Number of Vehicles	Class of Vehicle	Number of Wheels	Carrying Capacity (Tons)	Lettered Numbers of Vehicles	Weight (Tons)	Length (Feet)	Brake	Steam-heating	Light
42	Covered Carriage Trucks	6	6	11, 14, 89, 123, 125, 132 to 144, 152, 157 to 160, 170, 175 to 187, 191 to 195	...	29	D	...	...
2	do.	8	10	164, 165	...	46¾	D	H	...
				1520, 1540, 1544, 1547, 1554, 1557, 1589, 1594, 1595		15½	D	H	
19	Open Carriage Trucks	4	3	1586		15½	W		
				1531, 1541, 1543, 1591		15½	D		
				32, 33, 42, 43, 44		23½	D		
26	do.	6	10	31, 34, 35, 36, 72 to 76, 92, 93, 95, 96, 97, 153 to 156, 171 to 174		27⅓	D	H	
5	do.	8	8	166 to 169		29½	D	H	
26	Open Milk Trucks	4	3	103, 112, 161, 162, 163, 116, 118, 124, 1505, 1507, 1509, 1513, 1516, 1521, 1524, 1528, 1529, 1550, 1551, 1575, 1578, 1579, 1583, 1596, 1598, 1614, 1623, 1648, 1649, 1661, 1663,		45	D		
2	do.	6	3	1592, 1632,		23 to 27	D		
1	do.	6	3	1663		28	D		
1	do.	4	3	117		24	D		
	do.	4	3	1581		24	W		
14	Milk Wagons (Goods Stock)	4	3	1055, 1152, 1798, 1831, 1849, 2038, 3272, 4106, 4159, 4247, 4281, 5340, 5822, 9465		15			
214	Fish Trucks (Goods Stock)	4	8 and 10	530, 1186, 1205, 1209, 1225, 1309, 1480, 1492, 1571, 1607, 1610, 1663, 1691, 1713, 1749, 1839, 1846, 1949, 1971, 2045, 2054, 2285, 2360, 2564, 2568, 2596, 2601, 2714, 2717, 2730, 2733, 2740, 2746, 3051, 3101, 3122, 3126, 3202, 3229, 3243, 3271, 3662, 3739, 4142, 4453, 4738, 5338, 5544, 5383, 5391, 5394, 5460, 5464, 5682, 5737, 6793, 6845, 7127, 7261, 7432, 675, 786, 855, 892, 902, 961, 1035, 1160, 1255, 1264, 1268, 1810, 1342, 1490, 1715, 1718, 1855, 1880, 1892, 1917, 2291, 2711, 2829, 2837, 2874, 2892, 2904, 2958, 2974, 3009, 3022, 3024, 3027, 3060, 3131, 3139, 3293, 3500, 3602, 3615, 3663, 3704, 3706, 3760, 3773, 3780, 3839, 3886, 3896, 3927, 4000, 4010, 4021, 4024, 4032, 4036, 4071, 4133, 4176, 4216, 4373, 4382, 4385, 4427, 4436, 4465, 4507, 4513, 4515, 4516, 4533, 4537, 4648, 4563, 4569, 4580, 4715, 4720, 4775, 4776, 4787, 4812, 4817, 4849, 4852, 5600, 5610, 5612, 5615, 5626, 5822, 5894, 5932, 6127, 6130, 6132, 6152, 6154, 6157, 6158, 6179, 6213, 6220, 6222, 6223, 6226, 6230, 6238, 6264, 6294, 6322, 6328, 6329, 6335, 6341, 6350, 6357, 6366, 6391, 6395, 6409, 6412, 6418, 6430, 6443, 6461, 6480, 6484, 6500, 6504, 6507, 6510, 6522, 6524, 6531, 6534, 6535, 6536, 6543, 6366, 6569, 6573, 6584, 6585, 6596, 6617, 6618, 6621, 6628, 6638, 6647, 6829, 6834, 9223		15	D		
16	Motor Car Vans (Goods Stock)	6	6	73283 to 73392, 73537 to 73542		29	D	H	
4	Refrigerator Fish Vans (Goods Stock)	6	6	73585 to 73588, 73588			D	H	

R. KILLIN,
Superintendent of the Line.

M'CORQUODALE & CO. LTD. GLASGOW & LONDON

9

Total Number of Vehicles	Class of Vehicle	Number of Wheels	Carrying Capacity (Tons)	Lettered Numbers of Vehicles	Weight (Tons)	Length (Feet)	Brake	Steam-heating	Light
17	Brake Vans (Single end)	4	3	21, 48, 55, 60, 61	9	23½	W		G
				24, 33, 49, 54, 69, 70, 73, 78, 85, 86					O
				93, 153		23½	W		G
9	Brake Vans	6	4	35, 47, 56, 65, 66	9	30	W		O
				39, 68, 99, 158		30	W		
70	do.	6	4	15, 16, 17, 18, 19, 20, 27, 37, 45, 51, 53, 57, 59, 62, 71, 75, 76, 87, 89, 113, 121, 133, 138, 143, 160, 177, 181, 182, 183	12	30	D		G
			6	6, 8, 40, 42, 81, 88, 105, 110, 111, 134, 146, 148, 152	13½	30	D	H	G
			4	172, 174, 175, 176, 178, 179, 180, 184	12	30	D	H	E
			6	11, 22, 23, 26, 36, 82, 102, 120, 123, 126, 145, 164, 187	14½	30	D	H	G
40	do. (Corridor)		5	38, 46, 77, 90	20	45	D	H	G
			5	41, 80, 83, 233	21	48	D		G
			5	92, 98, 108, 115, 135, 136, 147, 155, 224 to 232	20	45	D	H	E
			6	270, 271	21	48	D	H	E
16	do. (do.)	8	5	5, 34, 140, 141, 144, 154	18	42	D		G
8		8	6	3, 4, 44, 58, 72, 84, 96, 104, 107, 112, 128, 151, 161, 162, 195, 242	21½	48	D	H	E
160		8	6	25, 79, 117, 149, 160, 163, 194, 223	25½ / 27¼	50 / 57	D	H	E
2	Dust Extractor Vans	6	...	1, 2,	...	28¾	W		O
1	Prison Van	4	...		...	18½	D	H	G
142	Horse Boxes	4		1 to 4, 6 to 48, 50 to 52, 54 to 58, 60 to 64, 67 to 69, 72, 73, 75 to 87, 115, 116, 117, 1811		18½	D	H	O
				88 to 114, 1800, 1801, 1803, 1804, 1806, 1808, 1809, 1810, 1812, 1816, 1818 to 1824, 1828 to 1834, 1836, 1837, 1839, 1849, 1852 to 1856					
				1813					
24	do. (double)	6		118 to 141		28¾	D	H	O
6	Cattle Vans	4		53, 59, 65, 66, 70, 71		28¾	D	H	O
7	Meat Vans	6	6	145 to 148, 188 to 190		28¾	W	H	O
84	Fish Vans	6	6	1, 2, 46 to 50, 210, 211, 212, 214, 217, 222, 234, 236, 237, 51, 52, 53, 55, 56, 57, 59, 61, 62, 64 to 71, 77 to 80, 88, 90, 91, 104 to 111, 113, 114, 115, 131, 149, 150, 151, 197 to 200, 202, 203, 54, 60, 63, 86, 87, 101, 130, 201, 213, 215, 216, 218, 219, 220, 221, 235, 238, 239		28¾	D	H	O
33	do.			248 to 266, 268, 269, 1636, 122, 128, 129		28¾	D	H	O
7	Milk Vans	4	3	1510, 1630, 1635, 1640, 1641, 1652, 1653, 1654	9½	21	W	H	
3	do.	6	4	3, 4, 5, 12, 13, 15, 126, 19, 20, 127	9½	21	D	H	O
36	Covered Carriage Trucks	4	3	7, 16, 17, 18, 21, 22, 23, 27, 28, 29, 30, 37 to 41, 45, 58, 94, 98, 99, 100, 102, 121-	9½	21	D	H	O
				119, 120					
				6, 8, 9, 10, 24, 25, 26, 122, 128, 129					

APPENDIX II: DIAGRAM BOOK NUMBERS

This appendix cross-references the large and small diagram books which served as references for Caledonian Railway Company servants. The Small Diagram Book was compiled in the last years of the nineteenth century; the Large Book was started towards the end of the CR's independent existence. The Large Book has been used throughout this work, because it records the additional diagrams of West Coast Joint Stock carriages which were absorbed into the CR fleet. The transcription of the Coaching Plant Stock Book, however, uses the Small Book, and references in the enthusiasts' press tend to use this convention. This appendix is offered to remove the confusion. Non-passenger coaching stock has not been included. Diagram 51A does not appear as a drawing. Diagrams 120, 125 and 126 appear in the Large Book but were not built. Carriages are non-corridor unless otherwise stated.

DIAGRAM BOOK			DIAGRAM BOOK		
LARGE	SMALL	DESCRIPTION	LARGE	SMALL	DESCRIPTION
1	13	First 28ft 6in	22	23	Composite 45ft (2 First, 3 Third) with Brake and luggage compartment
1A	101	First 28ft 10in (Balerno Branch stock)	22A		Radial underframe Lavatory Brake Composite 42ft (1 First, 3½ Third) ex-WCJS 1896
2	14	Third 28ft 6in	23	28	Composite 45ft (2 First, 4 Third) with Brake and luggage compartment
2A	102	Third 30ft 10in (Balerno Branch stock)	23A		Brake Composite 45ft (2 First, 4 Third) converted 1910 from Diagram 34 Brake Third
3	15	Brake Third 28ft 6in	24	2	Coupé Lavatory First 45ft 6in
3A	103	Brake Third 30ft 10in (Balerno Branch stock)	24A		Coupé Lavatory First 45ft 6in with altered lavatory accommodation post 1923
4	17	Passenger Brake Van	25		Coupé Lavatory First 45ft 6in
5	18	Prison Car	25A		Third 45ft 6in converted post 1923 from Coupé Lavatory First
6	51	First 30ft	26	36	Composite 45ft (3 First, 4 Third)
7	52	Third 30ft	26A		Composite 45ft (4 First, 3 Third) converted 1907/8 and 1910 from Diagram 21 First
8	7	First 35ft 6½in	26B		Coupé Composite 45ft 6in (2 First, 4 Third) conversion from Diagram 24/5 probably did not take place
9		Composite 35ft 6½in (3 First, 2 Third) converted 1910 from Diagram 8 First	27		Coupé Lavatory Composite 45ft 3in
10	11	Composite 35ft 6½in (2 First, 2 Third) with Brake and luggage compartment	27A		Coupé Lavatory Brake Composite 42ft (1½ First, 3½ Third) ex-WCJS 1897/98
10A		Brake Composite 35ft 6½in (2 First, 2 Third) converted 1910 from Diagram 14 Third	27B		Coupé Lavatory Brake Composite 42ft (1½ First, 2½ Third) ex-WCJS 1897/98
11	22	Composite 35ft 6½in (1 First, 3 Third) with Brake and luggage compartment	28		Coupé Composite 45ft 3in (3½ First, 2 Third)
11A		Brake Composite 32ft (2 First, 1 Third) converted 1898 from ex-WCJS stock	29	29	Coupé Lavatory Composite 45ft 3in (3½ First, 2 Third)
12		Composite 30ft (1 First, 3 Third) with luggage compartment converted from ex-WCJS Tri-Composite 1887	29A		Lavatory Composite 42ft (1½ First, 3 Third) with luggage compartment ex-WCJS 1902/3
13	12	Lavatory Composite 30ft (2 First, 2 Third) ex-WCJS 1889	29B		Lavatory Brake Composite 45ft (2 First, 2 Third) ex-WCJS 1903. Four used as slip carriages.
13A		Lavatory Composite 32ft (2 First, 2 Third) ex-WCJS 1896	30	30	Coupé Lavatory Luggage Composite 45ft 3in (1½ First, 3 Third)
13B		Coupé Lavatory Composite 34ft (1½ First, 3 Third) ex-WCJS 1898	31	35	Coupé Lavatory Brake Composite 45ft 3in (1½ First, 3 Third)
13C	8	Lavatory Composite 35ft 6½in (2 First, 3 Third)	31A		Coupé Brake Third 45ft 3in, converted 1925 from Diagram 31
14	10	Third 35ft 6½in	32	34	Lavatory Third 45ft
15	20	Lavatory Third 35ft 6½in	32A		Lavatory Third 42ft with luggage compartment ex-WCJS 1903
15A		Third 35ft 6½in converted 'circa 1923' from Diagram 13C Lavatory Composite No. 30	33	4	Third 45ft
16	21	Third 35ft 6½in with Brake and luggage compartment	34	6	Brake Third 45ft
16A		Brake Third 31ft converted 1897 from WCJS Luggage Third	34A		Brake Third 42ft radial wheels ex-WCJS 1896
16B		Brake Third 32ft converted 1896 from WCJS Luggage Third	34B		Lavatory Brake Third 42ft ex-WCJS 1903
17	16	Passenger Brake Van	34C		Lavatory Brake Third 45ft ex-WCJS 1902
17A		Passenger Brake Van ex-WCJS 1901	34D		Brake Third 42ft converted 1921/23 from Diagram 22A Lavatory Brake Composite
17B		Passenger Brake Van ex-WCJS 1901			
18		Passenger Brake Van			
19	1	First 49ft			
20	5	Brake Third 49ft			
21	3	First 45ft			

DIAGRAM BOOK		
LARGE	SMALL	DESCRIPTION
35	31	Passenger Brake Van 45ft
35A		Passenger Brake Van 42ft ex-WCJS Postal Brake Van 1910
36	38	Coupé Lavatory Brake Composite 48ft 3in
36A		Lavatory Brake Composite 42ft ex-WCJS 1903
36B		Lavatory Brake Composite 45ft ex-WCJS 1903
37	41	Lavatory 3rd 48ft
37A		Third 48ft converted from Diagram 37
38	44	First 48ft
39	40	Third 48ft
40	43	Brake Third 48ft
41	39	Passenger Brake Van 48ft
42	47	Passenger Brake Van 48ft x 8ft 6in wide
42A		Kitchen car for breakdown train, converted 1917 from Diagram 42
43	48	Lavatory Third 48ft x 8ft 6in wide
44	45	Lavatory Composite 48ft x 8ft 6in wide
45	49	Brake Third 48ft x 8ft 6in – 5 compartments
45A		Brake Third 48ft x 8ft 6in – 6 compartments
46	50	First 48ft x 8ft 6in
47	46	Third 48ft x 8ft 6in
48	86	Coupé Lavatory Composite 48ft 3in x 8ft 6in
49	57	Coupé Lavatory Brake Composite 48ft 3in x 8ft 6in Brake compartment at centre
49A		Coupé Lavatory Brake Composite 48ft 3in x 8ft 6in Brake compartment at end
50	9	6-wheeled Third class Saloon 35ft 6½in
51	33	6-wheeled Third class Picnic Saloon 35ft 6½in
52		6-wheeled Officers' Saloon 34ft. Converted 1902 from ex-WCJS Coupé Composite (CR Diagram 13B)
52A		4-wheeled Officers' Saloon No. 26 converted 1911 from CR Diagram 51A
53		6-wheeled Third class Saloon 32ft
54		12-wheeled Pullman Buffet car pre-World War I
55		12-wheeled Pullman Dining car pre-World War I
55A		Pullman Observation car Maid of Morven
55B		8-wheeled Pullman Dining car Duchess of Gordon
55C		8-wheeled Pullman Dining cars Lady Nairne and Bonnie Jean
56	19	Invalid Saloon 40ft
56A		Invalid Saloon 40ft
57	24	Family Saloon 40ft
57A		Third class Saloon converted post 1921 from Diagram 57
58	32	Day Saloon 40ft
59	37	Third class Saloon 48ft
60	42	Family Saloon 50ft 3in converted probably 1926 to travelling dormitory with same diagram number
61		First class Saloon 42ft
62		Composite Dining Saloon 45ft ex-WCJS 1905
63	105	Composite Dining Saloon 50ft 6in ex-WCJS 1906
63A	106	Composite Dining Saloon 50ft 6in altered internal layout 1921
64		Third class Saloon 42ft
65		Third class Saloon 42ft converted from WCJS Sleeping Saloon
90	55	Corridor Lavatory Third 50ft
91	54	Corridor Lavatory Third 50ft with centre passage
91A		Corridor Lavatory Third 45ft with centre passage converted from Diagram 62 Dining Saloon
92	56	Corridor Lavatory Composite 50ft

DIAGRAM BOOK		
LARGE	SMALL	DESCRIPTION
93	59	Semi-corridor Lavatory Brake Composite 50ft
94	61	Corridor Composite (5 First, 3 Third) 65ft
95	62	Corridor Brake Composite (3 First, 4 Third) 65ft
95A	74	Corridor Brake Composite (4 First, 3 Third) 65ft
95B	76	Corridor Brake Composite (2 First, 5 Third) 65ft
96	64	Corridor Third 65ft
97	63	Corridor Brake Third 65ft – 5 compartments
97A		Corridor Brake Third 65ft – 7 compartments
98	73	Corridor Passenger Brake Van 50ft – 10ft wheelbase bogies
98A		Corridor Passenger Brake Van 50ft – 8ft wheelbase bogies
98B	104	Corridor Passenger Brake Van 57ft
99	75	Corridor Third class Saloon 50ft
101	65	Brake Third 65ft – 8 compartments
101A	70	Brake Third 65ft – 9 compartments
101B	69	Brake Third 65ft – 7 compartments
102	66	First 65ft
103	71	Brake Composite (3 First, 5 Third) 65ft
104	67	Composite (4 First, 6 Third) 65ft
105	68	Third 68ft
106	78	Semi-corridor Composite (4 First, 3 Third) 50ft
107	79	Semi-corridor Brake Third 50ft
108	77	Semi-corridor Brake Composite (2 First, 3 Third) 50ft – 10ft wheelbase bogies
108A		Semi-corridor Brake Composite (2 First, 3 Third) 50ft – 8ft wheelbase bogies
109	80	Corridor Third 57ft
110	81	Corridor Brake Third 57ft – 6 compartments, 2 lavatories
110A	85	Corridor Brake Third 57ft – 6 compartments, 1 lavatory
110B		Corridor Brake Third 57ft – 5 compartments, 1 attendant's compartment, 1 lavatory
111	82	Corridor Brake Composite (2 First, 4 Third) 57ft x 8ft 8in
111A		Corridor Brake Composite (2 First, 4 Third) 57ft x 9ft
112	83	Corridor Composite (3 First, 4 Third) 57ft
112A	84	Corridor Composite (3 First, 4 Third) 57ft
112B		Corridor Composite (4 First, 3 Third) 57ft
112C		Corridor Composite (3 First, 4 Third) 57ft
113	87	Semi-corridor Composite (3 First, 5 Third) 57ft
113A	88	Semi-corridor Composite (4 First, 4 Third) 57ft
114	89	Semi-corridor Third 57ft
115	90	Semi-corridor Brake Composite (2 First, 4 Third) 57ft
115A		Semi-corridor Brake Composite (2 First, 4 Third) 57ft. Smaller Brake compartment
116	91	Semi-corridor Brake Third 57ft – 5 compartments
117	92	First 57ft
118	93	Third 57ft
119	94	Brake Third 57ft – 6 compartments
119A		Brake Third 57ft – 7 compartments
119B	95	Brake Third 57ft – 5 compartments
121	96	Composite (4 First, 5 Third) 57ft
121A	97	Composite (4 First, 4 Third) 57ft
121B	108	Composite (3 First, 5 Third) 57ft
122	98	Corridor Brake Third 57ft – 4 compartments
122A	107	Corridor Brake Third 57ft – 5 compartments
123	99	Corridor First 57ft
124	100	Corridor Third 57ft

APPENDIX III: ST. ROLLOX CARRIAGE ORDER NUMBERS

Non-passenger coaching stock orders are not included. These were tabulated in *Caledonian Railway Wagons and Non-Passenger Coaching Stock*. Dates expressed in months and years are the accountancy periods during which the vehicles were built. Dates and descriptions are taken from the transcription of the Coaching Plant Stock Book. In some cases the transcription entry has been altered. Carriages are non-corridor unless otherwise stated. Early 48-foot carriages were 8 feet wide. The wider carriages started with order H182, which included carriages of both widths.

ORDER	DATE	No. BUILT	DESCRIPTION	ADDITIONAL NOTES	DIAGRAM BOOK LARGE	DIAGRAM BOOK SMALL
H0	1885	30	Third 35ft 6½in		14	10
H1	1885	1	Prison Car 28ft 6in		5	18
H2	1885	30	Third 35ft 6½in		14	10
H3	1885	6	First 28ft 6in	5 traced	1	13
H3	1885	4	Third 28ft 6in		2	14
H3	1885	4	Brake Third 28ft 6in	Records show a total of 12 built 1885	3	15
H4	1885	6	Tri-Composite 30ft 6in	Ex-WCJS. None traced		
H5	1885	10	Passenger Brake Van 30ft	9 vans traced	17	16
H6	1885	10	Brake Third 28ft 6in	Records show a total of 12 built 1885	3	15
H7	01/1888	10	Passenger Brake Van 30ft	4 vans traced	17	16
H9	1886	10	Third 28ft 6in		2	14
H10	1886	10	Brake Third 28ft 6in	29 built in 1886 – see also H15	3	15
H11	1886	2	Third Saloon 35ft 6½in		50	9
H12	1886	20	Third 35ft 6½in		14	10
H13	1886	10	Third 35ft 6½in		14	10
H15	1886	10	Brake Third 28ft 6in	Records show 29 built 1886	3	15
H16	1886	3	First 28ft 6in	9 extra traced	1	13
H16	1887	2	Third 28ft 6in	2 extra traced	2	14
H16	1887	3	Brake Third 28ft 6in	8 carriages built 1887 – see also H17	3	15
H17	1887	3	First 28ft 6in	5 extra traced	1	13
H17	1887	3	Third 28ft 6in		2	14
H17	1887	2	Brake Third 28ft 6in	8 carriages built 1887	3	15
H19	1887	2	First 49ft		19	1
H20	1887	4	Brake Third 49ft		20	5
H21	1887	10	Third 35ft 6½in	8 traced	14	10
H23	01/1888	20	Third 35ft 6½in	19 traced	14	10
H26	07/1888	10	Third 35ft 6½in	9 traced	14	10
H28	07/1888	5	Composite 35ft 6½in		13C	8
H29	07/1888	5	Brake Composite 35ft 6½in		10	11
H30	07/1889	6	Coupé First 45ft 6in	5 traced	24	2
H31	01/1889	5	Brake Third 45ft		34	6
H31	07/1889	7	Brake Third 45ft		34	6
H32	07/1889	30	Third 35ft 6½in	None traced	14	10
H33	07/1889	2	Brake Third 45ft		34	6
H37	1889	7	Composite 30ft 6in	Converted from ex-WCJS Composite	13	
H39	07/1889	6	Third 45ft		33	4
H42	1889	6	Composite 35ft 6½in		13C	8
H43	1889	6	Composite 30ft	Converted from ex-WCJS Tri-Composite	13	12
ORDERS 1890-1894						
H34	01/1890	9	First 45ft		21	3
H40	01/1890	2	Brake Third 45ft		34	6
H44		8		Cathcart carriages converted into bogies		
H46	1890	1	Horse Drawn Carriage	For Inchture Branch		

ORDER	DATE	No. BUILT	DESCRIPTION	ADDITIONAL NOTES	DIAGRAM BOOK LARGE	SMALL
H47	07/1890	4	First 45ft		21	3
H48	07/1890	8	Third 45ft		33	4
H49	07/1890	4	Brake Third 45ft		34	6
H52	07/1890	4	Brake Composite 35ft 6½in		10	11
H50	01/1891	1	Invalid Saloon 40ft		56	19
H54	02/1891	4	First 45ft		21	3
H55	01/1891	8	Third 45ft		33	4
H56	01/1891	6	Third 28ft 6in		2	14
H57	01/1891	3	Brake Composite 45ft		22	23
H58	01/1891	6	Passenger Brake Van 30ft	5 traced, 1 built for C&O. See also H67	17	16
H59		1	Post Office	Not traced		
H62	07/1891	35	Third 35ft 6½in		15	20
H63	01/1891	14	Brake Third 35ft 6½in	13 traced – one built for Killin Branch	16	21
H63	01/1891	1	Brake Composite 35ft 6½in	For Killin Branch	11	22
H64	08/1891	3	Composite 35ft 6½in		13C	8
H65	07/1891	15	Brake Third 35ft 6½in		16	21
H66	07/1891	7	Third 35ft 6½in		15	20
H67	07/1891	5	Passenger Brake Van 30ft	1 extra van traced – balancing H58	17	16
H71	01/1892	15	Third 35ft 6½in	14 traced	14	10
H72	02/1892	4	Coupé First 45ft 6in		24	2
H73	01/1892	2	Family Saloon 40ft		57	24
H77	1892	2	Third Saloon 27ft 6in	Converted Family Carriages 16 and 1422		
H78	07/1892	20	Third 45ft		33	4
H79	07/1892	5	Passenger Brake Van 30ft		17	16
H80	07/1892	7	Brake Third 45ft	6 traced	34	6
H81	07/1892	3	Brake Composite 45ft	2 traced	23	28
H82	07/1892	5	First 45ft		21	3
H83	01/1893	15	Third 45ft		33	4
H84	01/1893	5	Brake Third 45ft		34	6
H85	01/1893	8	Third 45ft		33	4
H86	01/1893	5	Brake Third 45ft		34	6
H87	01/1893	5	Passenger Brake Van 30ft		17	16
H90	07/1893	5	First 45ft		21	3
H91	07/1893	5	Brake Composite 45ft		23	28
H92	07/1893	5	Passenger Brake Van 30ft		17	16
H96	07/1893	10	First 45ft		21	3
H97	07/1893	5	Composite 45ft		26	36
H98	07/1893	5	Brake Composite 45ft		23	28
H100	01/1894	5	Third 45ft		33	4
H101	01/1894	5	Brake Third 45ft		34	6
H102	01/1894	2	Third Picnic Saloon 35ft 7¼in		51	33
H103	01/1894	1	Invalid Saloon 40ft		56	19
H107	07/1894	15	Third 45ft		33	4
H108	07/1894	5	Composite 45ft		26	36
H109	07/1894	6	Coupé Composite 45ft 3in		30	30
H110	07/1894	6	Coupé Composite 45ft 3in		29	29
H111	07/1894	5	Passenger Brake Van 30ft	4 traced	17	16
ORDERS 1895-1899						
H114	01/1895	20	Brake Third 45ft		34	6
H115	01/1895	1	First – Day Saloon 40ft		58	32
H118	01/1895	5	Brake Composite 45ft		23	28
H119	07/1895	5	Coupé First 45ft 6in		24	2
H120	07/1895	4	First – Day Saloon 40ft		58	32
H121	07/1895	10	Composite 45ft		26	36

Order	Date	No. Built	Description	Additional Notes	Diagram Book Large	Diagram Book Small
H124	07/1895	5	Brake Third 45ft		34	6
H125	07/1895	5	Coupé First 45ft 6in		24	2
H126	01/1896	12	First 45ft		21	3
H129	01/1896	15	Third 45ft		33	4
H130	07/1896	6	Brake Composite 45ft		23	28
H131	07/1896	2	Coupé Composite 45ft 3in		28	29
H132	07/1896	2	Coupé Composite 45ft 3in		27	30
H133	07/1896	10	Brake Third 45ft	1 extra traced – see also H139	34	6
H136	07/1896	5	First 45ft		21	3
H137	07/1896	15	Third 45ft		33	4
H138	01/1897	6	First 45ft	3 with 42 seats and 3 with 56 seats	21	3
H139	01/1897	12	Brake Third 45ft	11 traced, balancing extra to H133	34	6
H142	01/1897	15	Third 45ft		33	4
H143	01/1897	5	First 45ft		21	3
H144	01/1897	9	Brake Third 45ft		34	6
H147	06/1897	6	Brake Van 45ft		35	31
H148	07/1897	5	Brake Composite 45ft		22	23
H149	07/1897	5	Brake Third 45ft		34	6
H151	01/1897	19	Third 45ft		33	4
H152	07/1897	15	First 45ft		21	3
H153	07/1897	36	Third 45ft		33	4
H154	07/1897	23	Brake Third 45ft		34	6
H155	01/1898	20	First 45ft	1 with electric lighting	21	3
H156	01/1898	30	Third 45ft	With Wood's Patent spring seat	33	4
H157	01/1898	28	Brake Third 45ft	With Wood's Patent spring seat. 27 traced	34	6
H158	01/1898	2	Coupé Composite 45ft 3in		28	29
H159	01/1898	6	Composite 45ft	1 with electric lighting	26	36
H160	01/1898	5	Brake Van 45ft		35	31
H161	07/1898	5	Third 45ft		33	4
H165	07/1898	8	Third 45ft		32	34
H166	07/1898	6	Composite 45ft		26	36
H167	1898	5	Coupé Brake Composite 45ft 3in	None traced	31	35
H169	01/1899	9	Lavatory Third 48ft	8 traced	37	41
H170	01/1899	3	Third Saloon 48ft		59	37
H171	07/1898	5	Coupé Brake Composite 48ft 3in		36	38
H174	07/1899	5	Brake Third 48ft	4 traced	40	43
H175	07/1899	2	Family Saloon 50ft 3in	Steam heating	60	42
H176	07/1899	8	First 48ft		38	44
H177	07/1899	5	Brake Van 48ft		41	39
Orders 1900-1904						
H179	07/1900	10	Brake Third 48ft		40	43
H180	01/1900	5	Brake Van 48ft		41	39
H182	01/1900	26	Third 48ft x 8ft wide		39	40
H182	07/1900	4	Third 48ft x 8ft wide		39	40
H182	07/1900	32	Third 48ft x 8ft 6in wide		47	46
H182	01/1901	6	Third 48ft x 8ft 6in wide		47	46
H182	07/1901	2	Third 48ft x 8ft 6in wide		47	46
H183	07/1900	10	First 48ft		46	50
H184	01/1901	10	Brake Van 48ft		42	47
H185	07/1900	20	Brake Third 48ft		45	49
H186	01/1900	10	Composite 48ft		44	45
H187	07/1900	12	Lavatory Third 48ft		43	48
H192	07/1901	6	Lavatory Third 48ft		43	48
H193	07/1901	4	Coupé Composite 48ft 3in	3 traced	48	86

Order	Date	No. Built	Description	Additional Notes	Diagram Book Large	Small
H194	07/1901	4	Brake Van 48ft	1 traced – remainder possibly converted to kitchen cars for breakdown trains	42	47
H196	07/1901	5	Brake Third 48ft		45	49
H197	07/1901	5	Brake Van 48ft	None traced	42	47
H198	01/1899	5	Brake Composite 48ft 3in	Steam heating	49	57
H199	07/1901	3	First 30ft		6	51
H200	07/1901	4	Third 30ft		7	52
H201	07/1901	2	Brake Third 30ft		7B	53
H202	01/1902	3	Corridor Third 50ft	Centre passage and lavatory	91	54
H202	01/1902	3	Corridor Third 50ft	Side corridor	90	55
H203	01/1902	4	Corridor Composite 50ft	Steam heating	92	56
H206	07/1902	6	First 48ft		46	50
H207	01/1903	3	Third 50ft	Steam heating. To Ambulance Train 1915	90	55
H209	01/1903	4	Semi-corridor Brake Composite 48ft	Steam heating	49	57
H211	01/1903	6	Third 48ft		47	46
H214	07/1903	4	Coupé Brake Composite 48ft 3in	Steam heating	49A	58
H215	07/1903	6	Brake Third 48ft	5 traced	45A	60
H219	01/1904	4	Corridor Brake Composite 50ft	Steam heating	93	59
H220	01/1904	8	Brake Third 48ft	6 with electric light	45A	60
H222	07/1904	5	Brake Third 48ft		45A	60
H223	07/1904	6	Brake Van 48ft		42	47
			ORDERS 1905-1909			
H226	01/1905	1	Corridor Composite 65ft	Steam heating	94	61
H227	01/1905	1	Corridor Brake Composite 65ft	Steam heating	95	62
H228	01/1905	4	Corridor Brake Third 65ft	Steam heating	97	63
H229	01/1905	4	Brake Third 48ft x 8ft 6in wide		45A	60
H230	07/1905	1	Corridor Composite 65ft	Steam heating	94	61
H231	07/1905	1	Corridor Brake Composite 65ft	Steam heating	95	62
H232	07/1905	4	Corridor Brake Third 65ft	Steam heating	97	63
H233	07/1905	3	Corridor Third 65ft	Steam heating	96	64
H234	01/1906	6	Brake Third 65ft	Steam heating	101	65
H235	01/1906	3	First 65ft	Steam heating	102	66
H237	07/1906	6	First 65ft	Steam heating	102	66
H238	07/1906	5	Composite 65ft	Steam heating	104	67
H239	07/1906	11	Third 68ft	Steam heating	105	68
H239	07/1907	1	Third 68ft	Steam heating	105	68
H239	01/1908	2	Third 68ft	Steam heating	105	68
H240	02/1906	2	Brake Third 65ft	Steam heating	101B	69
H240	07/1906	3	Brake Third 65ft	Steam heating	101B	69
H241	02/1906	2	Brake Third 65ft	Steam heating	101A	70
H241	07/1906	3	Brake Third 65ft	Steam heating	101A	70
H242	07/1906	4	Brake Composite 65ft	Steam heating. Slip carriages	103	71
H243	01/1907	2	Corridor Composite 65ft	Steam heating	94	61
H243	07/1907	4	Corridor Composite 65ft	Steam heating	94	61
H244	07/1907	10	Corridor Third 65ft	Steam heating	96	64
H245	12/1907	5	Corridor Third Saloon 50ft	Steam heating	99	75
H246	01/1907	2	Corridor Brake Third 65ft	Steam heating	97	63
H247	07/1906	3	Corridor Brake Third 65ft	Steam heating	97A	72
H247	01/1907	1	Corridor Brake Third 65ft	Steam heating	97A	72
H248	01/1907	3	Corridor Brake Composite 65ft	Steam heating	95	62
H248	07/1907	1	Corridor Brake Composite 65ft	Steam heating	95	62
H249	01/1908	6	Corridor Brake Van 50ft	2 vans traced. 4 to Ambulance Train 1915	98	73
H251	07/1906	4	Corridor Brake Composite 65ft	Steam heating	95A	74
H252	01/1907	1	Corridor Brake Third 65ft	Steam heating	97A	72

Order	Date	No. Built	Description	Additional Notes	Diagram Book Large	Diagram Book Small
H252	07/1907	2	Corridor Brake Third 65ft	Steam heating	97A	72
H253	01/1908	1	Corridor Composite 65ft	Steam heating	94	61
H255	01/1907	3	Corridor Brake Composite 65ft	Steam heating	95A	74
H256	07/1907	4	Corridor Brake Third 65ft	Steam heating	97	63
H257	07/1907	2	Corridor Brake Third 65ft	Steam heating	97A	72
H259	07/1907	2	First 65ft	Steam heating	102	66
H260	07/1907	1	Composite 65ft	Steam heating	104	67
H261	01/1908	1	Third 68ft	Steam heating	105	68
H262	07/1907	1	Brake Third 65ft	Steam heating	101A	70
H263	07/1907	1	Brake Third 65ft	Steam heating	101B	69
H264	07/1907	16	Brake Van 30ft	Steam heating	17	16
H266	01/1908	3	Corridor Brake Third 65ft	Steam heating	97A	72
H267	01/1908	1	Corridor Brake Composite 65ft	Steam heating	95	62
H268	01/1908	1	Brake Composite 65ft	Steam heating	95A	74
H269	07/1908	1	Corridor Composite 65ft	Steam heating	94	61
H274	07/1908	4	Corridor Brake Composite 65ft	Steam heating	95	62
H275	07/1908	1	Corridor Composite 65ft	Steam heating	94	61
H276	07/1908	1	Corridor Third 65ft	Steam heating	96	64
H277	07/1908	2	Corridor Brake Composite 65ft	Steam heating	95B	76
H279	01/1909	2	Brake Third 65ft	Steam heating	101	65
H280	01/1909	2	Brake Third 65ft	Steam heating	101A	70
H281	01/1909	2	Brake Third 65ft	Steam heating	101B	69
H282	01/1909	2	Brake Composite 65ft	Steam heating. Slip carriages	103	71
H283	01/1909	4	Brake Van 30ft		17	16
H285	07/1909	2	Corridor Brake Composite 65ft	Steam heating	95B	76
H286	07/1909	2	Corridor Brake Third 65ft	Steam heating	97A	72
H287	07/1909	2	Corridor Third 65ft	Steam heating	96	64
H288	07/1909	4	Brake Van 30ft	4 extra vans traced	17	16
Orders 1910-1914						
H289	01/1910	3	Semi-corridor Composite 50ft		106	78
H290	01/1910	5	Semi-corridor Brake Third 50ft		107	79
H291	01/1910	3	Semi-corridor Brake Composite 50ft		108	77
H293	01/1910	4	Brake Van 30ft	1 extra van traced	17	16
H294	01/1912	10	Corridor Third 57ft		109	80
H295	01/1912	2	Corridor Brake Third 57ft		110	81
H296	07/1912	3	Corridor Brake Composite 57ft		111	82
H297	07/1912	2	Corridor Brake Third 57ft	1 converted to Ambulance train 1915	110	81
H298	07/1912	1	Corridor Composite 57ft		112	83
H299	07/1912	2	Corridor Brake Composite 57ft		111	82
H302	01/1913	4	Corridor Composite 57ft		112A	84
H303	01/1913	4	Corridor Brake Third 57ft	All converted to Ambulance Train 1915	110A	85
H304	01/1913	2	Corridor Brake Composite 57ft	1 converted to Ambulance Train 1915	111	82
H305	01/1913	3	Corridor Brake Composite 57ft		111	82
H306	06/1913	6	Corridor Brake Third 57ft		116	91
H307	06/1913	2	Semi-corridor Composite 57ft		113A	88
H308	06/1913	2	Semi-corridor Third 57ft		114	89
H309	06/1913	3	Semi-corridor Composite 57ft		113	87
H310	06/1913	2	Semi-corridor Brake Composite 57ft		115	90
H311	12/1913	4	Semi-corridor Brake Composite 57ft		115	90
H312	12/1913	4	Semi-corridor Brake Composite 57ft		115	90
H313	12/1913	2	Semi-corridor Composite 57ft		113A	88
H314	12/1913	2	Semi-corridor Third 57ft		114	89
H315	1913	1	First 57ft	Steam heating	117	92
H316	12/1913	1	Third 57ft		118	93

Order	Date	No. Built	Description	Additional Notes	Diagram Book Large	Diagram Book Small
H317	12/1913	2	Brake Third 57ft		119	94
H318	06/1914	3	Semi-corridor Brake Composite 57ft		115	90
H319	07/1914	5	Semi-corridor Brake Third 57ft		116	91
H320	06/1914	3	Semi-corridor Composite 57ft		113A	88
H321	06/1914	6	Corridor Brake Van 50ft		98	73
H323	12/1914	6	Brake Third 57ft		119B	95
H324	1914	1	First 57ft	Steam heating. 1 extra traced	117	92
H325	12/1914	4	Composite 57ft		121	96
H326	12/1914	8	Third 57ft		118	93
H328	1914	2	First 57ft	Steam heating	117	92
Orders 1915-1922						
H327	01/1916	6	Brake Third 57ft		119B	95
H329	01/1916	4	Composite 57ft		121A	97
H330	01/1916	8	Third 57ft		118	93
H331	01/1916	2	Brake Third 57ft		119B	95
H331	08/1916	2	Brake Third 57ft		119B	95
H332	1915	1	First 57ft	Steam heating. 4 extra traced	117	92
H333	12/1916	4	Composite 57ft	2 traced	121A	97
H334	12/1916	6	Third 57ft		118	93
H335	06/1917	6	Brake Van 50ft		98	73
H337	12/1917	2	Brake Third 57ft		119B	95
H338	06/1919	4	Corridor Brake Van 57ft	Ex-1918 US Forces Ambulance Train	98B	104
H339	06/1919	1	Corridor Brake Van 57ft	Ex-1918 US Forces Ambulance Train	98B	104
H340	06/1919	3	Corridor Brake Van 57ft	Ex-1918 US Forces Ambulance Train	98B	104
H341	12/1919	2	Corridor Brake Van 50ft		98	73
H342	12/1919	2	Semi-corridor Composite 50ft	Ex-Ambulance Train 1918	106	78
H343	12/1919	2	Semi-corridor Brake Third 50ft		107	79
H344	12/1919	2	Semi-corridor Brake Composite 50ft	Ex-Ambulance Train 1918	108	77
H345	12/1920	2	Semi-corridor Composite 50ft	Ex-Ambulance Train 1918	106	78
H346	12/1920	3	Semi-corridor Brake Composite 50ft	Ex-Ambulance Train 1918	108	77
H347	12/1920	5	Semi-corridor Brake Third 50ft		107	79
H348	12/1920	7	Brake Composite 57ft		115A	109
H349	12/1920	3	Brake Third 57ft		119B	95
H351	12/1921	10	Third 57ft	Sub-contracted to Hurst, Nelson	118	93
H351	12/1922	6	Third 57ft	Sub-contracted to Metropolitan C&W	118	93
H352	12/1920	4	First 28ft 10in	Steam heating	1A	101
H353	12/1920	4	Third 30ft 10in		2A	102
H353	06/1921	4	Third 30ft 10in		2A	102
H354	06/1921	4	Brake Third 30ft 10in		3A	103
H355	12/1921	6	Brake Van 30ft	Steam heating pipes	17	16
H356	12/1921	4	Brake Third 57ft		119B	95
H357	12/1921	6	Brake Third 57ft		119B	95
H358	12/1921	5	Composite 57ft	1 extra traced	121A	97
H359	12/1921	1	Corridor Third 57ft		124	100
H360	12/1922	1	Third 57ft	Sub-contracted to Metropolitan C&W	118	93
H361	12/1922	1	Third 57ft	Sub-contracted to Metropolitan C&W	118	93
H362	12/1922	3	Third 57ft	Sub-contracted to Metropolitan C&W	118	93
H363	12/1922	2	Brake Third 57ft		119B	95
H364	12/1922	4	Brake Third 57ft		119B	95
H365	12/1922	4	Brake Third 57ft		119B	95
H366	12/1922	2	Composite 57ft		121B	108
H367	12/1922	1	Composite 57ft		121B	108
H368	12/1922	2	Composite 57ft		121B	108

Appendix IV: Known Orders Placed with Contractors

Date is when the tender was accepted. This is taken from Company minutes in the series NRS BR/CAL/1/. Where possible the orders have been cross-checked against the capital expenditure records and the half-yearly rolling stock returns. The spelling 'break' or 'brake' is as written in the minute.

Date	Description		Contractor
	Orders Pre-1850		
14/07/1846	5	First class	Wallace of Perth
	5	Composite	
	10	Second class	Croall of Edinburgh
	10	Third class	
	5	Composite	Dunn of Lancaster
	Orders 1855-1859		
21/01/1857	10	First class	Joseph Wright & Sons
	14	Third class	Brown, Marshall & Co.
	14	Third class with Second class compartment	
		Breaks to be attached to 4 each of the Third class and Composites	
11/08/1858	6	Passenger Brake Van	Brown, Marshall & Co.
	Orders 1860-1869		
14/02/1860	10	Double Composite	Brown, Marshall & Co.
11/03/1862	2	Passenger Break Van	Ashbury CW&I Co. for Lockerbie line
	4	Third class	
	4	Composite	
25/03/1862	4	Third class Coupé	Ashbury CW&I Co.
	2	Third class with Break	
	2	Passenger Break Van	
15/03/1864	6	Passenger Break Van	Ashbury CW&I Co.
	5	First class	
	22	Third class	
	2	Third class with Break	
	7	Composite	
10/10/1865	20	Third class	Oldbury C&W Co.
	6	Third class with Break	
	8	First and Second class Composite	
	4	Passenger Break Van	
	29	Third class	Brown, Marshall & Co.
11/06/1867	14	First class	Metropolitan C&W Co. for Cleland & Midcalder Railway
	13	Composite	
	15	Second class	
	13	Third class	
	5	Third class with Break end	
	12	Passenger Brake Van	
24/11/1868	2	Composite	Metropolitan C&W Co.
	14	Third class	
	4	Passenger Break Van	
27/04/1869	4	Composite	Ashbury CW&I Co. 'to run between Carlisle and Aberdeen.'
07/12/1869	5	Composite 5-compartments, 6 wheels	Metropolitan C&W Co.
	18	Third class 5-compartments, 4 wheels	
	Orders 1870-1879		
18/01/1870	30	First class	Metropolitan C&W Co. for Greenock line
24/05/1870	13	Third class with Break	Brown, Marshall & Co.
10/01/1871	20	First/Second class Composite	Metropolitan C&W Co.
	10	Second/Third class Composite	
03/08/1871	3	First class	Metropolitan C&W Co.
	7	Passenger Brake Van	Ashbury CW&I Co.
14/02/1872	6	Composite	Metropolitan C&W Co.
	2	Passenger Break Van	
07/01/1873	8	Third class	Ashbury CW&I Co.
	7	Composite	Metropolitan C&W Co.

Date		Description	Contractor
16/12/1873	20	Third class	Metropolitan C&W Co.
	10	Third class with Break	
	10	Third class	Brown, Marshall & Co.
	10	Third class	
	7	Third class	
	3	Tri-Composite	
	2	Bi-Composite	
12/05/1874		Saloon	Metropolitan C&W Co.
18/01/1876	6	Third class 6-compartments	Ashbury CW&I Co.
	6	Third class 4-compartments with Brake and luggage	
27/06/1877	12	First class	Brown, Marshall & Co.
	13	Tri-Composite	Metropolitan C&W Co.
	2	Composite with Brake	Craven Bros
	6	Second class	Lancaster Co.
23/10/1877	10	First class	Brown, Marshall & Co.
	10	Second class	
	8	Third class with Brake	
	8	Third class	
06/03/1878	2	Family Carriage	Craven Bros
	2	Invalid Carriage	
	2	Post Office Van	
	8	First class and Saloon	
	7	Second and Third class Composite	Lancaster Wagon Co.
	3	Third class with Brake	
	2	Passenger Brake Van	
21/01/1879	8	Composite	Brown, Marshall & Co.
	16	Third class with Brake	
30/09/1879	10	Third class	Ashbury CW&I Co.
	10	Third class with Brake	
ORDERS 1880-1889			
16/11/1880	15	Third class	Craven Bros
	15	Third with Brake	
	7	Passenger Brake Van	Oldbury
	20	First class	Brown, Marshall & Co.
	3	Composite	
07/12/1881	20	Composite	Midland RC&W Co.
	10	First class	Birmingham Railway C&W Co.
	10	Third class 6-compartment	
	10	Third 4-compartment with luggage and Brake	
	10	Passenger Brake Van	Oldbury
09/01/1883	40	Third class	Brown, Marshall & Co.
	15	First class	Birmingham Railway C&W Co.
	5	Passenger Brake Van	
08/1883	20	Third class	Ashbury CW&I Co.
	20	Third class with Brake	
	15	First class	Midland C&W Co
	5	First class	
25/01/1899	1	First class with electric light (CR Diagram 38)	Hurst, Nelson
ORDERS 1900-1922			
07/1904	1	Third class with electric light (CR Diagram 47)	R.Y. Pickering
1905	1	First class with electric light (CR Diagram 46)	R.Y. Pickering
10/07/1919	7	Corridor Brake Third (CR Diagram 122)	Metropolitan C&W Co.
	4	Corridor First class (CR Diagram 123)	
	9	Corridor Third class (CR Diagram 124)	
04/05/1920	3	First class, 4-wheels (CR Diagram 1A)	R.Y. Pickering
	14	Third class, 4-wheels (CR Diagram 2A)	
	6	Brake Third, 4-wheels (CR Diagram 3A)	
12/1921	10	Third class (CR Diagram 118)	Hurst, Nelson
	11	Third class (CR Diagram 118)	Metropolitan C&W Co.
16/05/1922	4	Corridor Composite (CR Diagram 112B)	R.Y. Pickering
	4	Corridor Third class (CR Diagram 124)	
	4	Corridor Brake Third (CR Diagram 122A)	
	4	Corridor Brake Composite (CR Diagram 111A)	
22/12/1922	5	Semi-corridor Brake Composite (CR Diagram 115A)	R.Y. Pickering
	8	Composite (CR Diagram 121B)	Clayton Wagon Co.
	6	Brake Third (CR Diagram 119B)	Metropolitan C&W Co.

APPENDIX V: ST. ROLLOX AND CONTRACTORS' DRAWINGS

Non-passenger coaching stock drawings are not included. These were tabulated in *Caledonian Railway Wagons and Non-Passenger Coaching Stock*. Dates and descriptions are taken from the St. Rollox drawings registers and in some cases from the drawings themselves. The diagram numbers refer to the Large Diagram Book. A blank entry in both archive reference columns indicates a drawing that is awaiting cataloguing and the allocation of an RHP number by The Ballast Trust.

SRX No.	DATE	DESCRIPTION	DIAG No.	NRM	RHP
531		Post Office van, outside elevation			
2113	1876	Post Office van No. 9, interior. Number/date deduced from SRX register			
2813	1880	Arrangement of gearing of chain brake L&NWR carriages			68374
3060	1881	Carriage coupling			68482
3268		5-compartment First, 6-wheel. Traced from drawing dated 23/10/82, shows lettering & CR on buffers. NRM on two sheets	8	7465/C	70007
3285	1882	6-compartment Third, 6-wheel, GA. NRM on two sheets	14	7480/C	70011
3329	10/1882	Passenger Brake Van, 4-wheel, GA	4	7474/C	70005
3428	11/1882	Arrangement of Westinghouse brake, First and Third class carriages			68566
3434	1883	Cord communication to engine, details			67881
3454	06/1883	Cord communication apparatus			69656 69659
3614	07/1883	Third class carriage 4-wheel with luggage compartment, no. 406. NRM on two sheets	3	7479/C	70002
3657	08/1883	Carriage axle box, oil			68493 68563
3702	10/1883	Tri-Composite, 6-wheel, GA. NRM drawing on two sheets. Not built.		7481/C	70014
3849	01/1884	5-compartment Third centre buffers, 4-wheel, GA. NRM on two sheets.	2	7483/C	70018
3879	01/1884	4-compartment First centre buffers, 4-wheel, GA. NRM on two sheets.	1	7482/C	70019
3893	02/1884	Centre buffer and draw gear. Arrangement for close coupled trains			70020
3987	02/1884	Bearing spring for close coupled carriages			68376
3997	05/1884	Arrangement of vacuum and pressure brake, WCJS carriages			68570
4014	06/1884	Builders plate for carriages			70021
4172	11/1884	Prison Van GA. Interior altered to drawing 7787. NRM on two sheets	5	7467/C	70022
4225	11/1884	Exhaust steam pipe arrangement for heating carriages			67501
4370	04/1885	30ft Passenger Brake Van, 6-wheel, GA. NRM on two sheets	17	7510/C	70043
4428	05/1885	Spring arrangement for Tri-Composite carriage			68572
4486	07/1885	Pressure and vacuum brake arrangement, 6-wheel Passenger Brake Van	17		68619
4683	10/1885	Arrangement of Westinghouse and vacuum brake, 6-wheel Saloon	50		68567 68620
4702	11/1885	6-wheel Saloon, GA of panelling and framing. NRM on two sheets	50	7523/C	70024
4717	11/1885	Arrangement of Saloon. NRM on two sheets.	50	7521/C	
4779	01/1886	Arrangement of water closet for Saloon	50		67724
4783	1891	Lineside Mail Apparatus – this CR drawing is not in the St. Rollox register			
4785	02/1886	Arrangement of lavatory for Saloon	50		67689
4854	03/1886	Arrangement of supporting Saloon body	50		69658
5074	11/1886	49ft First, GA. NRM on two sheets.	19	7476/C	70028
5104	12/1886	49ft Brake Third, GA. NRM on two sheets	20	7460/C	70029
5234	03/1887	3-way cock for exhaust steam heating. Class '125' 4-4-0			70030
5484	10/1887	Standard carriage axle box			68508
5597	02/1888	Standard axle box for carriages			68506
5621	02/1888	6-wheel Lavatory Composite, GA. NRM on two sheets	13	7468/C	70035
5645	03/1888	Arrangement of lavatory: 6-wheel Composite	13		67708
5755	07/1888	45ft Brake Third, GA	34	7472/C	70039
5759	08/1888	45ft carriage, brake rigging			
5762	08/1888	45ft 6in Lavatory First, *coupé* end, GA	24	7470/C	70040
5783	08/1888	Axlebox for 45ft carriage			68510
5799	09/1888	Arrangement of Westinghouse brake on 45ft carriage			67559
5805	09/1888	45ft carriage body truss rods			
5808	09/1888	45ft carriage underframe and brake arrangement			68419

SRX No.	Date	Description	Diag No.	NRM	RHP
5827	10/1888	Arrangement of lavatory: 45ft carriage			67709
5905	12/1888	45ft 7-compartment First, GA	21	11230/C	70041
6000	04/1889	45ft 8-compartment Third, GA	33	7471/C	70042
6041	05/1889	Radial bogie for 4-wheel carriages			68464
6173	12/1889	Horse Drawn Car for Inchture Branch, GA		11389/C	70049
6175	12/1889	Invalid bogie carriage (section of interior)	57		68431
6182	12/1889	Invalid bogie carriage (Saloon) H73	57		68430
6199	02/1890	Axle box for Inchture horse car			68059
6201	02/1890	Bogie arrangement for Invalid carriage	57		68058
6216	02/1890	Horse drawn car for Inchture Branch, GA. More detailed than 6173		11390/C	70051
6254	03/1890	Horse drawn Invalid carriage, external details		11391/R	70054
6476	09/1890	Brake Composite, GA. Shows details of lettering, 3 off to H57	22	7459/C	70056
6477	09/1890	Horse drawn Invalid carriage, internal details		11388/R	70057
6486	09/1890	6-wheel Brake Third, GA. Shows lettering, H63 15 off, H65 15 off	16	7458/C	70058
6494	10/1890	Compound brake work for Post Office van			68621
6501	10/1890	Passenger Brake Van, 6-wheel, GA. Details of lettering	17	7478/C	70059
6536	10/1890	6-wheel Lavatory Third, GA	15	7475/C	70062
6552	11/1890	Arrangement of brakes, bogie Brake Composite carriage	22		68568
6564	11/1890	6-wheel Tri-Composite, GA. Not built		7473/C	70063
6602	12/1890	Arrangement of water pipes, Third Class Lavatory compartment	15		67710
6609	12/1890	6-wheel Brake Composite, GA. For Killin Branch.	11	7469/C	70064
6749	05/1891	Arrangement of Westinghouse brake, old 4-wheel carriages and Brake Van			68569
6799	07/1891	Alteration to axle box cover, 45ft carriage			68507
6835	09/1891	Alteration to lubricating arrangement: carriage axle box No. 10			68542
6864	10/1891	Axlebox for 45ft carriages			67526 68502
6899	11/1891	40ft Family carriage, GA. H73 for 2 off	57	7462/C	70070
6899	11/1891	40ft Family carriage, arrangement of interior (end section). Modification H115	57	7463/C	70071
6901	12/1891	40ft Family carriage, GA of sleeping accommodation. H73	57	7464/C	70072
6935	02/1892	General arrangement of bogie for 45ft carriage			67556
6941	02/1892	Brake arrangement for 4-wheel carriage			67302
6976	031892	Panelling in interior of ladies lavatory, 40ft Family carriage	57		67698
6979	03/1892	Panelling in interior of gents lavatory, 40ft Family carriage	57		67699
6983	04/1892	Axlebox for 6-wheel carriages			68499 68500
7026	06/1892	Brake Composite, GA. H81	23	8001/C	69133
7107	10/1892	Arrangement of Westinghouse and handbrake 30ft Passenger Brake Van	17		67298
7344	09/1893	6-wheel Third class Picnic Saloon, GA. H102, 2 off	51	7522/C	70082
7546	06/1894	Lavatories and luggage Coupé Composite, GA. H109	30	7453/C	70087
7650	06/1894	Lavatory for First class Coupé carriage	24		67711
7665	12/1894	Test of 'Consolidated' heated train between Glasgow & Edinburgh			70091
7719	04/1895	40ft Day Saloon, GA of body. H120	58	7524/C	70092
7723	04/1895	45ft Coupé First, alteration of woodwork in lavatory	24		67700
7764	06/1895	Interior of lavatory: First class 40ft Day Saloon	58		67703
7777	07/1895	Arrangement of dual brake, 40ft carriages	58		67297
7783	07/1895	Carriage foot warmer			70093
7787	07/1895	Prison Van, alteration to interior, GA	5	7466/C	70094
7928	12/1895	First class lavatory arrangement for 45ft Coupé Composite carriage	31		67702
7929	12/1895	Third class lavatory arrangement for 45ft Coupé Composite carriage	31		67707
8067	06/1896	45ft 3in Coupé Composite, GA. H131. For H158 lavatory details drawing 8587, drawing 8464 for underframe	28	7452/C	70097
8274	02/1897	Arrangement of 45ft underframe for bogie carriage			68761
8333	03/1897	45ft Brake Van, GA. To Dimensions 'A' for 48ft van H147, H177	35 41	7515/C	70099
8464	05/1897	Standard underframe for bogie carriage			68757
8518	06/1897	Proposed position of dynamo bogie underframe			69625
8587	08/1897	First class lavatory arrangement	28		67704
8792	01/1898	Third class lavatory arrangement			67693
8821	02/1898	Underframe for 49ft bogie carriage	19, 20		68811
8825	02/1898	45ft Third with lavatories, GA. To Dimensions 'A' for 48ft H165	32, 37	7454/C	70114
8854	03/1898	Carriage lamp fittings			68449

SRX No.	Date	Description	Diag No.	Archive Ref. NRM	RHP
8861	03/1898	45ft Coupé Brake Composite, GA body only. 45ft & 48ft H167, H171	31, 36	8004/C	69154
8914	04/1898	48ft carriage underframe			68756
8991	06/1898	48ft Third Saloon, GA. H170	59	11252/C	70121
9007	06/1898	End elevation and lavatory arrangement, Third class Saloon	59		68574
9021	06/1898	48ft 8-compartment Third, GA. H182, Nos. 1185 to 1214, No. 650	47	7451/C	70122
9021	06/1898	48ft Third, end views	47	8005/C	69169
9224	10/1898	8ft carriage bogie, GA. Coloured drawing mounted on backing			68447
9606	04/1899	48ft Brake Third, 8ft broad, GA of Brake compartment H174. 'Hair cushions to be used in place of wooden seats for order H179'	40	7447/C	70129
9822	08/1899	Arrangement of brake on 48ft bogie carriages			
9840	09/1899	Number board for excursion trains			67862
9870	09/1899	48ft First, GA	38	7456/C	70133
9888	09/1899	48ft Brake Composite underframe. H186	44		68810
9892	10/1899	Fox's patent pressed steel carriage bogie			69629
10014	12/1899	Brake Third, Brake compartment. H185	45	7488/C	70134
10052	01/1900	Third Class lavatory arrangement			67692
10150	03/1900	48ft First, GA	46	7445/C	70138
10150	03/1900	48ft First, end elevations. H183	46	8007/C	69167
10175	03/1900	30ft 10in Third & Brake Third	7, 7B		
10226	05/1900	48ft Brake Van, GA, 3 cross sections	42	7486/C	70141
10226	05/1900	48ft Brake Van, GA. H184	42	7514/C	70140
10344	08/1900	48ft Third, GA. H182	47	7457/C	70142
10344	08/1900	48ft Third, end elevations	47	8006/C	69166
10366	08/1900	Coupé First, lavatory arrangement			67694
10371	08/1900	Coup Composite, First class lavatory arrangement	44		67705
10372	08/1900	Arrangement of Third class lavatory in Coupé Composite	44		67691
10432	09/1900	Handles for inside doors of carriages			68609
10511	11/1900	48ft Lavatory Third, GA. H187	43	7448/C	70143
10511	11/1900	Lavatory Third, 3 cross sections	43	7489/C	70144
10562	12/1900	48ft Composite. H186	44	8002/C	69165
10589	01/1901	GA of 4-wheeled underframes. H199, 200, 201	6, 7, 7B		70145
10654	02/1901	First & Third carriages, 4 wheels, GA of bodies. H199, 200, 201	6, 7	7531/C	70146
10694	02/1901	48ft 3in Coupé Lavatory Composite, GA. H193	48	7455/C	70147
10906	07/1901	8in lamp. Showing lamp in corridor and lavatory. H202	90		
10987	09/1901	End elevations of First, Third and lavatory compartments, 50ft carriages			67715
11262	02/1902	50ft corridor carriage underframe. H202, H203, H207, H209		8084/C	69150
11272	02/1902	General arrangement for Fox's patent pressed steel bogie			68448
11302	03/1902	Coupé Semi-corridor Brake Composite, GA of Body	49	7449/C	
11314	03/1902	Arrangement of electric light switch on end of carriage			69607
11780	12/1902	Brake Third. GA of Brake compartment showing cycle rack. H215	45A	7450/C	
11978	04/1903	48ft 3in Coupé Composite, GA of body. H214	49A	7444/C	
12131	07/1903	Bogie carriage underframe. Arrangement of steel headstock. H220	45A	8071/C	69134
12176	08/1903	50ft Corridor Brake Composite, GA body only. H219	93	8003/C	69155
12268	10/1903	Slip coupling for carriages			68809
12342	11/1903	Arrangement of slip coupling			68805
12345	11/1903	Details of stopcock for slip coupling			68807
12352	11/1903	Details of slip coupling			68808
12392	12/1903	Brake Third. GA of Brake compartment. Shows cycle rack. H222	45A	7446/C	
12520	03/1904	Proposed corridor train, for Glasgow, Edinburgh and Aberdeen service.			
12557	04/1904	Underframe for 48ft bogie carriage			68812
12666	07/1904	65ft carriage underframe, GA. H226	94	11394/C	
12761	09/1904	5-compartment Corridor Brake Third, GA. H228	97	11397/C	
12762	09/1904	65ft Brake Composite, GA. H227	95	7497/C	
12763	09/1904	65ft Composite, GA. H226	94	7485/C	
12775	09/1904	6¼ gallon hot water tank for lavatories			
12777	09/1904	Mouldings for interiors of 65ft carriages			69613
12787	10/1904	Fox's patent pressed steel carriage bogie – 6-wheeled			67558
12799	10/1904	65ft carriage stock, 6 cross sections		11250/C	
12812	10/1904	6-wheel carriage bogie, GA. With alterations			67555
12922	01/1905	65ft Corridor Third, GA. H233	96	11396/C	
12942	02/1905	100 paper holder lavatory fitting			

SRX No.	Date	Description	Diag No.	Archive Ref. NRM	RHP
13017	04/1905	65ft 8-compartment Brake Third, GA of body. H234, H279	101	7491/C	
13018	04/1905	65ft First, GA of body. H235	102	7493/C	
13188	09/1905	Net rod bracket			69611
13215	09/1905	Lavatory tap for carriages			69660
13239	09/1905	68ft Third, GA of underframe. H239	105	8086/C	69153
13413	12/1905	Arrangement of slip coupling for 65ft carriages			68803
13469	02/1906	Net rod bracket			69662
13470	02/1906	50ft Passenger Brake Van, GA. H249. NRM on two sheets.	98	7513/C	
13507	02/1906	Proposed steam rail car, outline diagram		7419/E	
13606	04/1906	Gas tank for carriages			67453
13933	10/1906	30ft steel underframe for 6-wheel carriage		8067/C	
13946	11/1906	65ft Brake Third, plan of Brake end. H247, H252, H257	97A	7490/C	
13949	11/1906	65ft Brake Composite, plan of Brake end. H251, H255	95A	7487/C	
14009	01/1907	30ft Passenger Brake Van, GA. H264	18	7509/C	
14053	01/1907	Oil lamp			
14063	02/1907	Standard gas lamp fitted with inverted incandescent burner			68491
14087	03/1907	Arrangement of 30ft underframe for 6-wheel Brake Van	18		68760
14104	04/1907	50ft Third Saloon. H245. NRM on two sheets.	99	7527/C	
14109	04/1907	Alarm bell and details for slip carriage			68797
14145	05/1907	Fox's pressed steel underframe for 6-wheel vehicles			69136
14200	06/1907	68ft Third, GA. H239. NRM on two sheets.	105	7484/C	
14221	09/1907	65ft Brake Third, GA. H247	97A	7498/C	
14363	10/1907	Dynamo driving pulleys on axle			69666
14366	10/1907	50ft Saloon, GA of underframe. H245	99	7525/C	
14374	10/1907	65ft Brake Composite	95B		
14425	12/1907	65ft Brake Composite slip carriage, GA. H242	103	7494/C	
14594	05/1908	65ft Composite, GA. H238	104	7496/C	
14598	05/1908	3ft 6in Mansell wheel, bonded with iron bar			69615
14601	05/1908	65ft Brake Composite, GA. H277	95B	11393/C	
14691	09/1908	Electric light connections			69626
14704	09/1908	Slip drawhook and details			68804
14705	09/1908	Slip arrangement for 65ft carriages			68801 69648
14708	09/1908	General arrangement of 6-wheel carriage bogie			68439
14709	09/1908	Slip drawhook and details			68798
14710	09/1908	65ft 9-compartment Brake Third, GA of body. H241	101A	7492/C	
14722	09/1908	65ft 7-compartment Brake Third, GA of body. H240	101B	7495/C	
14823	01/1909	65ft carriage, GA of underframe. H285		8087/C	69157
14980	05/1909	50ft carriage underframe. H289, H290, H291. NRM on two sheets	106, 107, 108	8065/C	69152
15011	05/1909	Lavatory arrangement for Composite and Brake Composite carriages			67719
15102	09/1909	Vacuum hose pipe arrangement, Third No. 532 and Composite No. 30			68459
15460	07/1910	30ft steel underframe for 6-wheel vehicles, GA		8073/C	
15622	12/1910	Arrangement and details of slip hook for 48ft carriages			68800
15625	12/1910	Arrangement and details of slip hook for old WCJS carriages			68806
15633	12/1910	Lavatory arrangement for Officers' Saloon			67717
15713	02/1911	Steel disc carriage wheel (2 hole)			69663
15833	05/1911	10in x 5in carriage axle box			68733
15917	06/1911	4-wheel carriage bogie, GA. 3ft 6in wheels, 10ft wheel base. H294	109	11206/C	
15982	07/1911	57ft carriage, GA of underframe. H294, H295-H299, H302-H305. NRM on two sheets		8088/C	69186
16037	08/1911	57ft Carriage, 6 end sections. H294-H295	109, 110	7499/C	
16283	02/1912	Gas by-pass on end of carriage			69618
16549	09/1912	Lavatory arrangements for 57ft carriages			67706 67712 67713
16635	11/1912	57ft underframe, GA. H306-H320. NRM on two sheets		8078/C	69187
16643	11/1912	Net rod bracket			69661
16693	12/1912	Lavatory arrangement, semi-corridor carriages			67721
16958	05/1913	Lavatory arrangement, semi-corridor carriages			67690
17272	11/1913	50ft Passenger Brake Van, GA. H321. NRM on two sheets.	98	7512/C	
17316	03/1914	57ft x 9ft Semi-corridor Brake Composite, GA of body. H318	115	7505/C	

SRX No.	Date	Description	Diag No.	Archive Ref. NRM	RHP
17338	03/1914	57ft x 9ft Semi-corridor Brake Third, GA of body. H319	116	7504/C	
17360	04/1914	57ft x 9ft Semi-corridor Composite, GA of body. H320	113A	7501/C	
17376	05/1914	57ft x 9ft Semi-corridor Composite, GA of body. H309	113	7503/C	
17390	06/1914	57ft x 9ft Semi-corridor Third, GA of body. H314	114	7500/C	
17466	08/1914	Brake and luggage compartment end for Brake Third. H323	119B	8008/C	69168
17572	10/1914	57ft carriage underframe, GA. H327-H334, H337. NRM on two sheets.		8077/C	69161
18191	09/1915	50ft Brake Van underframe, GA	98A	8080/C	69159
18278	11/1915	Cleaning arrangements – Pullman cars at Aberdeen Station			68604
18404	01/1916	Lavatory arrangement for 57ft x 8ft 8in carriages			67723
18430	02/1916	Lavatory arrangement for 50ft x 9ft carriages			67718
18806	10/1916	Semi-corridor Brake Composite, 57ft x 9ft, GA of body. H348	115A	7502/C	
18815	10/1916	30ft suburban carriages, GA. First, Third, Brake Third on one drawing.	1A, 2A, 3A	11200/C	
18959	02/1917	Screw coupling for close coupled carriages	1A, 2A, 3A		67451 69642
18985	02/1917	4-wheel Third, GA of underframe, close coupled. H353, H354	2A	7529/C	
19028	03/1917	Standard axle guard for 4-wheel carriages			69643
19201	08/1917	Torpedo ventilator and inside attachment			68490
19220	09/1917	Arrangement of carriage bogie, 3ft 6in wheels			68446
19244	10/1917	50ft carriage and van underframe, GA. H341-H344		8079/C	69184
19287	11/1917	57ft carriage underframe GA. NRM on two sheets.		8089/C	69158
19300	12/1917	Dining Saloon No. 40, GA	63	7526/C	
19321	01/1918	Dining Saloon No. 40, louvre ventilators	63		69604
19501	06/1918	Saloon No. 41, GA of body	63	7518/C	
19523	06/1918	Lavatory arrangement, Saloon No.41	63		67722
19759	12/1918	57ft Passenger Brake Van, GA. Converted from Ward Car MD25	98B	7511/C	
19857	03/1919	Buffer socket – Pullman cars			68606
19883	03/1919	Lavatory arrangement for 57ft x 9ft carriages			67696 67714
19888	03/1919	57ft x 9ft carriages, lavatory arrangement			67697 67701
19922	04/1919	Gas tank and hangers for Pullman car			68584
20109	08/1919	Platform arrangement for Pullman cars			68583
20158	09/1919	Bogie, Pullman car 'Duchess of Gordon'			67557
20223	10/1919	Glass for window of smoking compartment			68417
20337	12/1919	Steel underframe for Saloons Nos. 40 and 41	63		
20414	01/1920	Lavatory arrangement for semi-corridor carriages			67716
20435	01/1920	Carriage bogie arrangement 3ft 6in wheel, 8ft wheel base			
20540	04/1920	Balerno Branch carriages, GA. 9ft broad	1A, 2A, 3A	11201/C	
20668	04/1920	Body framing for 4-wheel carriages (Balerno Branch)			68416
20677	04/1920	28ft carriage underframe GA. Was drawing 18985, Balerno First	1A	7528/C	
20900	09/1920	Arrangement of 30ft underframe for 6-wheel Passenger Brake Van			68755
20915	10/1920	30ft Brake Third, 4-wheel, GA of body	3A	7533/C	
20942	10/1920	4-compartment First, 4-wheel, GA of body	1A	7532/C	
20957	11/1920	30ft Passenger Brake Van, 6-wheel, GA. H355	17	7517/C	
21080	02/1921	57ft Brake Third, GA of Body and 2 end sections. NRM on two sheets.		7508/C	
21142	04/1921	Additional footboards for 4-wheel carriages	1A, 2A, 3A		69639
21153	04/1921	Soiled towel receptacle for carriage lavatories			68415
21157	04/1921	Towel rack for carriage lavatories			68414
21249	07/1921	Ex-WCJS Saloon 1419. Conversion to travelling dormitory for tradesmen		11227/C	
21470	02/1922	57ft bogie carriage underframe, GA. H360. NRM on two sheets.		8076/C	69160
21772	04/1922	57ft Brake Composite, GA of body with 3 end sections. NRM on two sheets	121B	7507/C	
21777	04/1922	Buffer socket Pullman cars			68603
21779	04/1922	57ft Brake Third, GA of body with 3 end sections	119B	7506/C	
21930	08/1922	Interior of First class compartment			
21954	09/1922	Arrangement of panels in First class lavatory, semi-corridor carriage			67695
21980	10/1922	Finishing, First class lavatory, Corridor Composite carriage			67720
21983	10/1922	Lettering etc. on 57ft Semi-corridor Brake Composite Nos. 468-472	115A		
22027	12/1922	Carriage bogie, 4-wheel, 3ft 6in diameter, 8ft wheelbase, GA		11205/C	

Pullman Car Co.

No.	Date	Description	Archive Ref. NRM	RHP
48	1916	Buffer head and spindle for Pullman cars		68589
52	1916	Drawhook for Pullman cars		68591

Brown, Marshall & Co.

SRX No.	Date	Description	Archive Ref. NRM	RHP
7871	07/1895	6-wheel Third, GA. Shows lettering and CR on buffers. On two sheets	7461/C	
7873	01/1884	Carriage axle box, oil		

Joseph Wright and Metropolitan Carriage & Wagon Co. for Scottish Central Railway

Date	Description	Ref: MS99
1862	First class carriage, *coupé* ends GA	4184
1864	First class carriage GA	4185
1862	Second class carriage GA	4198
1862	Second class carriage GA	4209
1862	Second class carriage – transverse section	4210
1862	Passenger Luggage and Break Van GA	4297

Metropolitan Carriage & Wagon Co. for Caledonian Railway

Date	Description	Ref: MS99
09/1867	5-compartment Third, 14ft 6in wheelbase, 24ft long	2311
09/1867	5-compartment Second, 14ft 6in wheelbase	2300
10/1867	Passenger Break Van, 20ft 10in long. Alterations in red refer to order of October 1868	2254
10/1867	3 x First, 1 x Third Bi-Composite, 14ft 6in wheelbase, 24ft 9¼in long	2256
10/1867	4-compartment First, 14ft 6in wheelbase, 26ft 3¾in long	2257
10/1867	Break compartment, 'break compartment seat for 505'	2258
01/1869	3 x First, 1 x Second Bi-Composite, 14ft 6in wheelbase, 24ft 9¾in long	2294
01/1869	5-compartment Third, 4-wheel, 24ft long	2310
09/1869	4-compartment Composite, 7ft 6in x 7ft 6in wheelbase, 23ft 2¾in long	2301
10/1869	2 x First, 1 x Second, 2 x Third Tri-Composite, 9ft 3in x 9ft 3in wheelbase, 'four to this'	2288
01/1870	5-compartment Third, 14ft 6in wheelbase, 24ft long	2284
01/1870	4-compartment First, 8ft 3in x 8ft 3in wheelbase. Alterations 07/08/1871	2314
03/1871	4-compartment Luggage Composite carriage, 9ft 3in x 9ft 3in wheelbase, 29ft 11in long	2262
03/1871	2 x Second, 4 x Third Bi-Composite carriage, 15ft wheelbase, 27ft 5in long	2299
11/1871	Saloon carriage, 9ft x 9ft wheelbase, 28ft 3in long	2283
03/1872	Passenger Break Van, 12ft wheelbase, 20ft 10in long	2267
03/1872	Carriage (body only), 5-compartment	2270
02/1874	5-compartment Third, 4-wheel, 26ft 5in long, lettering details shown	2305
03/1874	5-compartment First, 9ft x 9ft wheelbase	2277
06/1874	Saloon carriage, 9ft 3in x 9ft 3in wheelbase, 29ft 11in long	2303
05/1877	Dummy van, 4-wheel, 16ft 6in long	2307
08/1877	2 x First, 1 x 2nd, 2 x Third Tri-Composite, 10ft x 10ft wheelbase, 31ft 11in long	2285
09/1922	57ft by 8ft 8in Corridor Third (CR Diagram 124) on two sheets	704 747
1922	Pullman Car Ltd/CR First class Dining Car converted from Ambulance Train	9046
1922	Arrangement of bogie for above	9080A
09/1922	57ft Third (CR Diagram 118) on two sheets	704 749
09/1922	57ft Brake Third (CR Diagram 119B) on two sheets	704 751
09/1922	57ft First (CR Diagram 123) on two sheets	704 753

INDEX

alarm systems, *see* communication
ambulance trains,
 CR No. 23,
  carriages converted for, 273
  carriages, planned replacements, 274
  formation, 272-3
  publicity, 274-5
  return after war, 275
 Royal Navy No. 2, 275-6
 US government, 275

Balerno Branch,
 services, 269
 stock 1920, 266-71
  building history, 267
  design features, 267
bicycle racks in Brake Thirds, 60, 180-1
bogies,
 Drummond, 42, 153
 Fox, 4-wheeled 8ft, 43-4
 Fox, 4-wheeled 10ft, 42, 43, 212-3
 Fox, 6-wheeled, 42, 44, 195
 pivot centres, offset, 42, 153-4
brakes,
 automatic vacuum,
  adopted by L&NWR 1886, 30-1
  description, 31
 Clark-Webb patent,
  abandoned by L&NWR 1883, 30
  description, 24-5
  drawbacks, 26, 30
  fitted to CR Saloons 1874, 25
  fitted to WCJS carriages 1874, 25, 27
  Lockerbie accident 1883, 30
  performance at Newark trials, 26
  Perth accident 1883, 30
 continuous,
  Board of Trade recommendation 1862, 22
  CR decision to adopt 1880, 28
  CR early involvement with, 22
  comparison of failure rates, 26
  Railway Returns (Continuous Brakes) Act 1878, 27-8
  Regulation of Railways Act 1889, 32
 dual system,
  carriages fitted with, 2-3, 30, 150, 177, 179-81, 185, 206-7, 211, 221, 224
  description, 31
  fitted retrospectively 1916, 276
 early non-continuous on CR, 21
 simple vacuum,
  accident at Carlisle 1886, 30
  adopted by L&NWR 1883/84, 30
  description and drawbacks, 30
  excluded under Regulation of Railways Act 1889, 31
  fitted to CR carriages 1884, 30
  fitted to WCJS carriages 1884, 30
  performance at NBR trial, 26

Steel-McInnes,
 abandoned by CR 1880, 29
 description, 23, 25
 drawbacks, 29
 Newark brake trials, 25
 passenger alarm, 39
 trial on CR 1875/77, 25, 27
 trial on Callander & Oban Railway 1879, 27
Westinghouse automatic,
 adopted by CR 1880, 29
 arrangement on carriages, 28, 32, 162
 capital expenditure, 29, 31
 description, 23
 early misgivings about, 27
 fitting to old carriages 1891-93, 31-2
 maintenance costs on NBR, 28
 performance at NBR trial, 26
 performance at Newark trials, 26
 piped only vehicles, 29, 31
 progress in fitting 1882, 29
 trials on CR 1877, 27
Westinghouse non-automatic,
 description, 22, 23
 passenger alarm, 39
 trial on CR 1872, 22
brake trials,
 Newark 1875,
  CR use of Steel-McInnes brake, 25
  shortcomings of the trials, 26
  types tested, 25
 NBR 1876, 26-7
breaksmen, classes of, 21-2
Brittain, George 1876-82,
 contractor-built carriages,
  in 1877-79, 54, 137-41
  in 1881-82, 141-2
 Dummy Vans 1878, 137, 321
 Greenock Railway Third class 1876, 137
 St. Rollox-built carriages 1876, 137
 Saloons, 286-7
builders plate, St. Rollox, 91, 92

Callander & Oban Railway,
 45ft carriages 1890, 157
 carriage requirements 1879, 139-40
 Connel Ferry rail motor 1909, 325-8
 Pullman cars and services, 237-41, 243, 244, 245, 248, 249
 Saloons 1871, 280-1
 Semi-corridor carriages 1909, 209-10
 Steel-McInnes brake trial 1879, 27
carriage body construction, 47
carriage cleaning, 53-4
carriage footboards, continuous, 33
carriage sheds and sidings, 51-3
carriage wheels, *see* wheels
Cathcart Circle,
 4-wheeled carriages, 145-6
 up-graded stock proposals 1913, 330-1

classes of travel,
 CR statistics, 58, 59
 Fourth class on Greenock line, 58, 137
 'Parliamentary' trains, 57
 Second class,
  end of on CR 1892, 59
  end of on MR 1872/8, 58-9
  end of on WCJS 1893, 59
  varying standards, 57-8
 Third class,
  CR's encouragement of, 57
  prevalence in Scotland, 57
Cleland & Midcalder Railway, stock for, 1868, 118-23
coaching stock crisis 1919, 254-5
combined alarm,
 adopted by CR 1900, 39
 carriages with combined alarm and cord systems, 40
 combination of passenger and crew alarms 1898, 39
 description, 39
 retrospective fitting on CR 1900-6, 39-40
communication,
 between guard and driver,
  CR adopts Harrison cord 1860, 34
  circular urging progress 1858, 33
  first experiments on CR 1858, 34
  Tyler Report 1865, 33-5
  see also combined alarm, cord alarm
 between passengers and train crew,
  experiments on CR 1866, 36
  extended to all trains 1899, 39
  investigation and report on good practice 1864, 36
  limited to trains travelling more than 20 miles between stations 1868, 37
  public demands for adoption, 35-6
  railway companies' opposition to, 35, 36
  railway managers sub-committee findings 1898, 38-9
  required under Regulation of Railways Act 1868, 37
  systems approved 1868, 37
  see also combined alarm, cord alarm, electrical passenger alarm
Connel Bridge,
 access after closure of rail motor service, 327
 Board of Trade enquiry re tolls, 327-8
 early pedestrian access dispute, 325
Connel Ferry rail motor,
 modifications and livery, 325-6
 service closure and disposal, 327
 service details, 325, 327
 traffic statistics, 327
Conner, Benjamin 1857-76,
 additional and replacement carriages 1868/69, 122-4
 carriages built 1865-7, 110

Cleland & Midcalder Railway stock 1868, 118-23
contractor-built carriages,
    in 1857, 106-7
    in 1871-73, 129-133
    in 1874, 132-5
Dummy Vans, 321
Greenock Railway First class, 1870, 127-8
Lanarkshire lines and Solway Junction Railway stock 1870, 125-7
Lockerbie line stock 1863, 108
'new branch lines' stock 1864, 108
Passenger Brake Vans 1858, 107
Port Patrick Railway stock 1864, 109-10
Robbins patent carriage 1870, 126-7
St. Rollox designs 1867/70, 121-2, 128-9
Saloons, 279-86
Third class carriages 1856, 101, 106-7
cord alarm,
    adopted as passenger alarm by West Coast Conference and probably by CR 1869, 37
    adopted by CR and L&NWR 1860, 34
    approved as passenger alarm 1868, 37
    condemned by railway managers sub-committee 1898, 38-9
    deficiencies of system, 38
    description, 34, 37
    means of alerting the driver, 34-5
    withdrawal of BoT approval 1873, 38
    see also communication
Corpse Box, 321
corridor carriages,
    control of passengers' movements, 86
    early CR 1901, 86
    first WCJS train 1893, 84-6
    see also semi-corridor carriages
Coupé-Lit Sleeping Saloon 1875, 66, 285, 287

Day Saloons No's 7-10 1895, 293, 295-6
    see also Picnic Saloons No's 4-5 1894
destination boards, 91, 92
Dining cars,
    alterations to No's 40/41 in 1906, 215-7
    alterations to No's 40/41 in 1919, 217
    conversion of No's 38/39 in 1919, 218
    conversion of No. 40 to Officers' Saloon in 1921, 218, 305
    conversion of No. 41 to Officers' Saloon in 1918, 217, 305, 306
    post-war services, 217
    pre-war services, 216
    types of, 84-5, 215-6
dogs, 60
Drummond, Dugald 1882-90,
    brake trial on NBR, 26-7
    carriage heating by exhaust steam, 98-100
    carriages,
        4-wheeled,
            1884-85, 1891, 143-6
            radial axles and semi-permanent coupling, 145-6
        6-wheeled,
            1883-91, 148-52
            contractor-built 1883, 148-50
            with lavatories 1888-89, 150-1
        45ft 1888, 156-8

45ft for C&O and Gourock lines 1889, 157
49ft 1887, 153-5
Corpse Box, 321
Inchture horse bus 1890 322-4
Passenger Brake Vans,
    4-wheeled 1883-84, 147-8
    6-wheeled 1885-94, 152
Prison Car, 321-2
report on Westinghouse brake maintenance costs on NBR, 28
Saloons, 288-92
Dummy Vans 1872,
    converted from 'stand-ups' 1872, 321
    Metropolitan C&W 1878, 137, 321

electrical passenger alarm
    approved 1868, 37
    mentioned as potentially the most effective method 1864, 36
    no system recommended 1898, 38-9
    on CR 1889, 38
empty carriage stock working, 53

Family carriages,
    acquired from SNER 1867, 279
    built 1862, 279
    built 1867, 279-80
    for Scottish Central line 1870, 281
    No's 1, 2 and 11 1893/95, 290-3
    No. 11 1874, 285
    No's 13 and 14 1878, 286-7
    No's 14 and 15 1899, 297-9
    stationed at Aberdeen 1871, 281-3
    Third class No. 3 1876, 286-7
flexible wheelbase systems,
    descriptions of, 41
    trials on CR 1882, 41-2

Garnkirk and Wishaw railways, condition of stock on acquisition by CR 1850, 105
'Grampian Express,'
    Aberdeen and Dundee formations, 202
    launch and publicity 1905, 197, 200-1
    original formation, 196-7
Greenock Railway,
    carriage livery, 87
    condition of stock on acquisition by CR 1850, 105
    Fourth class on, 58, 137
    iron carriage underframes, 46
    new stock 1851-5, 105-6
    new stock 1870, 128
    passenger complaints and Board of Trade report 1868, 127
    poor standards of comfort on, 58, 127
    Saloon No. 9 1872, 283
    'stand-ups,' 58, 137
    sugar brokers' Saloon 1859, 87, 279
    Third class carriages 1876, 137

heating,
    by exhaust steam,
        description, 68-9
        experiments on CR 1883-87, 69-70
        locomotives fitted with apparatus, 68-9
    by stove, 67
    carriage hoses, trouble with, 70

Consolidated Heating Co. system,
    cost of fitting 1905/1919, 72, 73
    description, 70, 71
    early applications on CR, 71, 72
    fitted as standard on CR 1905, 72
    fitted on West Coast Joint Stock 1900, 71
    heating before train departure, 72
    tested on CR 1894, 70-1
Dr Bell's system 1893, 70, 71
foot warmers, 67
lack of carriages with, 73, 252, 254
pipes fitted to NPCS, 73
retrospective fitting 1919, 73, 255, 261
services with heated carriages 1909, 73
horse bus, Inchture
    closure of service, 324
    description of the route, 322
    modifications to vehicle, 323
    original design, 322
    timetable and fares, 324
horse-drawn Invalid carriage, for Saloon No. 19, 289, 292

Inchture horse bus, see horse bus, Inchture
internal décor and furnishing,
    Balerno Branch stock 1920, 100
    carriages built 1860s and 1870s, 95
    Drummond period, 95,
    early carriages, 95, 101-2
    'Grampian' stock, 56, 97-9
    Greenock-built saloons, 1847/48, 277
    immediately pre-Drummond, 95
    Lambie and McIntosh period, 72, 96-7
    Lincrusta Walton, 99-100
    Pickersgill period, 99-100, 263
    Saloons, 100, 277, 302
Invalid carriages,
    No. 6 1894, 293, 296
    No's 15 and 16 1878, 286-7
    No. 19 and horse-drawn carriage 1890, 289, 292
inventories and censuses, 10, 333-5

Killin Branch Brake Composite 1891, 160-1

Lambie, John 1891-95,
    Brake Composite, Killin Branch 1891, 160-1
    Composite carriages, 45ft 1891, 163-5
    Coupé carriages,
        45ft 1894, 165-8
        post-grouping modifications, 165-6, 168
    Saloons, 292-6
    simplified panelling style, 162-3
Lanarkshire lines stock 1870, 125-7
lavatories,
    access via tip-up seats, 83-4, 165-8
    corridor access, 48ft stock, 84, 177/9
    early West Coast Joint Stock, 83
    for guards, 84-5
    in Drummond and immediate successors' carriages, 83, 159-60
    initially fitted to carriages on long-distance services only, 84
    problems and precautions, 84-5
leave and demobilisation train, 276

letters and numbers,
  'Blue Saloon', 304
  'Grampian' style, 92-93, 302
  numbers inside carriages, 93, 97-9, 168
  Saloon letters, 1899 93, 299
  standard block style, 92-3
lighting,
  electric,
    adopted for new construction 1905, 81
    carriages fitted in the early 1900s, 80-1,
      180, 182
    experiments on CR 1896, 80
  gas,
    experiments on CR 1881, 78-9
    first use on SCR 1862, 77
    gas-lit survivals, 82
    Laidlaw system, 79
    lamp lighting and cleaning, 79-80
    Pintsch flat burner system, 78-9
    Pintsch incandescent burner system,
      adopted by CR 1908, 79
      description, 79, 80
      installation programme and cost, 79
      test on Maryhill–Airdrie train 1905,
        79
    Pope system, 78
    supply, control and charging, 53, 79
  oil,
    lamp drawing, 77
    survivals in 20th century, 80
livery,
  all-over brown 1873, 88
  all-over brown post-1892, 89
  CR and L&NWR compared, 88-9
  carriage lakes, 88-9
  colour of Brake Van ends, 89, 163
  contemporary descriptions 1890/97, 88
  crests, 90-1
  early CR, 87
  lining, 89
  mixed liveries in same train, 89
  monograms, 91, 92
  Pickersgill, 89-90, 91
  reinstatement of white upper panels 1892,
    88
  roofs and underframes, 89
  uniform liveries 1869, 87-8
  white, 88
  see also internal décor and furnishing,
    letters and numbers
Lockerbie line carriages 1863, 108
luggage,
  conveyance and allowances, 59-60
  racks in compartments, 59-60, 97-8
  transfer and delivery, 60
  workmen's tools allowance, 61

McIntosh, John 1895-1914,
  bicycle racks in Brake Thirds, 180-1
  carriage conversions 1897/1901, 185
  carriage conversions, ex-WCJS 1907, 219
  carriage conversions to Composite, 219-20
  carriage rebuilding 1903/12, 185, 220
  carriages,
    4-wheeled 1901, 185-6
    45ft high roof 1896, 171-4
    45ft low roof, 171
    45ft new designs 1898, 174-6

45ft variations to existing designs 1896,
  174
48ft 8 feet wide 1899, 177
48ft 8 feet 6 inches wide 1900, 177-82
50ft 1901-4, 185-90
50ft semi-corridor for C&O 1909,
  209-11
57ft corridor, 8 feet 8 inches wide 1911,
  221-4
57ft non-corridor, 9 feet wide 1914,
  225, 227
57ft semi-corridor, 9 feet wide 1913,
  223-7
65ft corridor 1904-9, 195-202, 206-8
65ft non-corridor 1905-9, 202-5
68ft non-corridor 1905-7, 205-6
Cathcart Circle, up-graded stock proposal
  1913, 330-1
Connel Ferry rail motor 1909, 325-8
Coupé Composite conversion 1905, 219
Dining cars, 215-8
excursion set, 57ft 1911, 221, 223
Passenger Brake Vans,
  6-wheeled 1907, 211, 214
  45ft 1897, 181, 183, 184
  48ft 1899, 183-4
  50ft 1907, 210-3
Saloons, 209, 297-302
slip carriages,
  48ft 1903, 49, 180, 182-3
  65ft 1906, 1909, 49, 206
steam motor carriage proposal 1906,
  329-30
military transport trains, 276
murder, first on UK railway train, 36

numbering,
  at January 1921, 336-40
  at the Grouping, 94
  by LM&SR, 94
  conventions, CR, 93
  down-rating and reclassification, 93
  duplicate numbers, 93
  within class, 93

Officers' Saloons,
  'Blue Saloon' 1902, 303-4
  converted from,
    1847 Saloons, 303
    1868 First class Saloons, 303
    1878 Third class Saloon, 303, 305
    Dining Saloon No. 40 1921, 218, 305
    Dining Saloon No. 41 1918, 217, 305-6
  proposed self-propelled 1877, 303

'Parliamentary' trains, 57
Pickersgill, William 1914-23,
  ambulance and war service trains, 272-6
  Balerno Branch stock 1920, 266-71
  carriage conversions, post-war, 261
  carriage heating, additional, 1919, 261
  carriages,
    50ft semi-corridor 1919-20, 256-7
    57ft corridor 1921-23, 258-60
    57ft non-corridor 1920-22, 261-4, 266
    57ft semi-corridor 1920-22, 259, 261
  carriages built to 1917, 251-3
  cessation of construction 1917, 252

coaching stock crisis 1919 and post-war
  construction programme, 254-6
modification to 'Grampian' Brake Thirds
  1915, 251
Passenger Brake Vans,
  6-wheeled 1921, 261, 265
  50ft 1919, 252-3
  57ft 1919, 256
proposed 58ft 6-in carriages, 332
Picnic Saloons No's 4-5 1894, 293-5
  see also Day Saloons No's 7-10 1895
Port Patrick Railway stock 1864, 109-10
Post Office vehicles, CR,
  built 1848/49, 312
  built 1860s, 312-3, 315
  built 1870s, 314-6
  deployment 1875 and 1878, 316
  deployment 1894 and 1900s, 319-20
  ex-Scottish Central Railway, 315, 319
  modified Second class carriages 1848/49,
    312
  transfer from WCJS 1886, 319
  transfers from WCJS 1900/10, 320
  transfers to WCJS 1879, 317-8
  unimplemented TPO design 1890, 319
  see also Royal Mail services
Prison Car 1885, 321-2
Pullman Car Co. and CR,
  advertisements and publicity, 228, 231,
    233, 242
  agreement pre-war, 229-30
  agreements post-war, 241, 249
  compensation for lost revenue, 241-2
  service reinstatement 1919, 241-2
  service withdrawal 1916, 233
  services,
    early war years, 231-3
    post-war commissioned by CR, 241-4
    pre-war, 230-1
  supplementary fares, 230
Pullman Car Co. and LM&SR,
  Buffet car, Third class 1923, 248-9
  cars delivered in 1927, 250
  Dining cars 1923, 248-9
  numbering and withdrawal dates, 250
  repainting, 249, 250
Pullman cars,
  post-war CR,
    Dining cars, 8-wheeled, 242, 246-7
    Lady Nairne, renaming, 247
    steel underframes, 244, 246
  pre-war,
    Buffet cars, 237-8
    construction details, 234, 235
    Dining cars, 236-7
    livery, 234, 236
    names, 236-7
    Observation car, 238-40, 245

repair and maintenance,
  damage and refurbishment, 55-6, 196
  examination in traffic, 55
  numbers requiring repair, 8, 55
  running-in, 2-3, 55
residential expresses 1911,
  advertising and named trains, 64-5
  destinations served, 63
  stock used, 64

Royal Mail services,
    Beattock fatality 1889, 307, 309
    early Anglo-Scottish, 317
    establishment of WCJS fleet 1879, 317-8
    exclusively on CR 1855-73, 310-1
    exclusively on CR 1900-15, 320
    legislation, 307
    lineside apparatus, 307-9
    see also Post Office vehicles

Saloon carriages,
    4-wheeled No's 20-27 1878/79, 286-7
    acquired from SCR 1865, 279
    converted from WCJS Sleeping Saloons
        1884, 169, 288-9
    Corridor Third class 1907, 300-3
    Coupé-Lit Sleeping 1875, 66, 285, 287
    First class No. 10 1874, 283-4
    First class, ex-WCJS 1904, 300
    for Callander & Oban 1871, 280-1
    for Greenock line 1872, 283
    Greenock built 1847/48, 277-9
    Greenock sugar brokers' 1859, 87, 279
    Third class,
        48ft 1898, 297
        ex-WCJS 1899, 298, 300
        ex-WCJS 1904, 300, 302
        No's 17 and 18 1886, 288
    see also Family carriages, Invalid
        carriages, Officers' Saloons, Picnic
        Saloons, Day Saloons
Scottish Central Railway,
    Composites and Thirds, 113, 115, 121
    Coupé First 1862, 111-2
    First class 1864, 111, 113
    first gas-lit train 1862, 77
    number of carriages acquired, 111
    Passenger Brake Vans 1862, 113, 116
    Post Office vehicles, 315, 319
    Saloons, 111, 279
    Second class 1862, 111-2, 114
Scottish North Eastern Railway,
    Composites 1860/62, 117-8
    condition of stock at acquisition, 113-4
    Family carriage, 279
    First class, 114
    number of carriages acquired, 111
    Passenger Brake Vans, 117-8
    Second and Third class, 114, 116-7
    stock later used on excursion traffic, 117
semi-corridor carriages, 86, 182, 209-11,
    223-7, 256-7, 259
Sinclair, Robert 1847-56,
    Garnkirk and Wishaw railways stock
        1850, 105
    Greenock Railway stock 1850, 105

Greenock Railway stock, new 1851-5, 106
    northern section carriages 1847, 102-3
    southern section carriages 1847, 101
Sleeping Saloons,
    CR Coupé-Lit No. 12, 66, 285, 287
    CR proposal to use Pullmans 1880, 66
    CR proposals 1876/86, 66
    early WCJS 1872-4, 66
    WCJS acquired by CR, 169, 192-3, 288-9
slip carriages,
    CR 48ft 1903, 49, 180, 182-3
    CR 65ft 1906 and 1909, 49, 206
    converted from WCJS 1903, 49, 194
    destinations and slipping stations, 48
    lamp codes, 49
    post-war working, 50
    safety aspects, 50
    services on CR 1906-14, 48
    slipping procedure, 49
    specialised equipment, 49-50
    working home, 50, 183
Smellie, Hugh 1890-1,
    Brake Third, 8, 159, 161
    Lavatory Third, 8, 159-60
    Passenger Brake Vans, 159
    unimplemented TPO design, 319
smoking,
    ash trays, 76
    compartments and signs, 75-6
    early prohibition on CR, 74
    permitted under Regulation of Railways
        Act, 1868, 74-5
Solway Junction Railway stock 1870, 125-7
sources of information,
    books and the press, 19-20
    Caledonian Railway, 8-14
    constituent and associated railway
        companies, 15-16
    contractors' records, 13, 17-18
steam motor carriage 1906, 329-30

Travelling Gas Tanks, 53

underframes,
    6-wheeled, centre axle side play, 42
    all-steel, 46, 177-8
    construction principles, 46
    integral with body, 153-4, 234-5
    iron, adopted by WCJS 1882, 46
    iron, on Greenock line, 46
    steel and wood, 46
    steel, for non-bogie stock, 46
    wood, 46
unimplemented proposals,
    58ft 6-in carriages, 332
    high capacity carriage, 331-2

steam motor carriage 1906, 329-30
TPO design 1890, 319
up-graded 6-wheeled carriages, 331-2
up-graded Cathcart Circle stock 1913,
    330-1

ventilation,
    Anderson patent, 73-4, 159, 160
    CR standard above doors, 73, 141
    early, above doors, 73
    Havock, 73-4
    Laycock torpedo, 74

West Coast Joint Stock,
    apportionment of capital cost, 131-2
    Consolidated Heating Co. system adopted
        1900, 71
    first all-corridor train 1893, 84-6
    iron underframes adopted 1882, 46
    lavatories in early carriages, 83
    passenger cord alarm adopted 1869, 37
    Post Office fleet establishment 1879,
        317-8
    Sleeping Saloons, first experiment 1872,
        66
West Coast Joint Stock, surplus to CR,
    acquired 1871, 131-2
    acquired 1882/93, 169-70
    acquired 1895-98, 191-2
    acquired 1901-3, 192-4
    conversion to 'Blue Saloon' 1902, 303-4
    conversion to slip carriage 1903, 49, 194
    conversions 1907, 219
    Day and Sleeping saloons converted
        1899/1904, 298, 300, 302
    Dining cars 1905, 215-8
    Luggage vans 1874, 135
    Post Office vehicles 1900/10, 320
    Sleeping carriages converted to Saloons,
        in 1884, 169, 288-9
        in 1904, 192-3, 298
wheels,
    early carriage, 43, 44
    Mansell patent, 43-5
        modification for track circuiting, 46
        removal from 'Grampian' stock, 44
    steel disc, 45, 46
workmen's trains,
    Beattock service, 63
    Cheap Trains Act 1883, 61
    Clydebank services 1906, 1913 and 1921,
        62-3
    South West Scotland services, 63
    stations approved by BoT, 61
    volume of traffic, 63

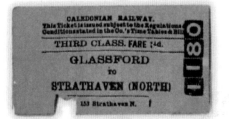